When Will We Talk about Hitler?

Worlds of Memory

Editors:
Jeffrey Olick, University of Virginia
Aline Sierp, Maastricht University
Jenny Wüstenberg, York University

Published in collaboration with the Memory Studies Association

This book series publishes innovative and rigorous scholarship in the interdisciplinary and global field of memory studies. Memory studies includes all inquiries into the ways we—both individually and collectively—are shaped by the past. How do we represent the past to ourselves and to others? How do those representations shape our actions and understandings, whether explicitly or unconsciously? The "memory" we study encompasses the near-infinitude of practices and processes humans use to engage with the past, the incredible variety of representations they produce, and the range of individuals and institutions involved in doing so.

Guided by the mandate of the Memory Studies Association to provide a forum for conversations among subfields, regions, and research traditions, Worlds of Memory focuses on cutting-edge research that pushes the boundaries of the field and can provide insights for memory scholars outside of a particular specialization. In the process, it seeks to make memory studies more accessible, diverse, and open to novel approaches.

Volume 1
When Will We Talk about Hitler?
German Students and the Nazi Past
Alexandra Oeser

WHEN WILL WE TALK ABOUT HITLER?

German Students and the Nazi Past

Alexandra Oeser

Translated from the French by Katharine Throssell

berghahn
NEW YORK • OXFORD
www.berghahnbooks.com

Published in 2019 by
Berghahn Books
www.berghahnbooks.com

English-language edition
© 2019, 2023 Berghahn Books
First paperback edition published in 2023

French-language edition
© 2010 CIERA and Éditions de la Maison des sciences de l'homme, Paris, France

Originally published in French as
Enseigner Hitler: Les adolescents face au passé nazi en Allemagne in 2010

All rights reserved. Except for the quotation of short passages
for the purposes of criticism and review, no part of this book
may be reproduced in any form or by any means, electronic or
mechanical, including photocopying, recording, or any information
storage and retrieval system now known or to be invented,
without written permission of the publisher.

Library of Congress Cataloging-in-Publication Data
Names: Oeser, Alexandra, author. | Throssell, Katharine, translator.
Title: When will we talk about Hitler? : German students and the Nazi past /
  Alexandra Oeser ; translated from French by Katharine Throssell.
Other titles: Enseigner Hitler. English
Description: English-language edition. | New York : Berghahn Books, 2019. |
  "Originally published by Maison des Sciences de l'Homme as Enseigner
  Hitler: Les adolescents face au passe nazi en Allemagne in 2010"-- Title
  verso. | Includes bibliographical references and index.
Identifiers: LCCN 2019015069 (print) | LCCN 2019981166 (ebook) | ISBN
  9781789202861 (hardback) | ISBN 9781789202878 (ebook)
Subjects: LCSH: National socialism--Study and teaching
  (Secondary)--Germany. | High school students--Germany--Attitudes. |
  Teenagers--Germany--Attitudes. | Germany--History--1933-1945--Study and
  teaching (Secondary)
Classification: LCC DD256.49 .O4713 2019 (print) | LCC DD256.49 (ebook) |
  DDC 943.086091/143--dc23
LC record available at https://lccn.loc.gov/2019015069
LC ebook record available at https://lccn.loc.gov/2019981166

British Library Cataloguing in Publication Data
A catalogue record for this book is available from the British Library

ISBN 978-1-78920-286-1 hardback
ISBN 978-1-80073-644-3 paperback
ISBN 978-1-78920-287-8 ebook

https://doi.org/10.3167/9781789202861

To my mother, Veronika Oeser, née Grawitz
(20 September 1944–21 August 2017)

CONTENTS

List of Figures and Tables	ix
Preface to the English Edition (2019)	xi
Acknowledgments	xix
List of Abbreviations	xxi
Introduction	1
Chapter 1 Education in the Service of Democracy	39
Chapter 2 Talking about the Nazi Past in Class and Succeeding at School	81
Chapter 3 Gender, Family, and the Nazi Past(s)	124
Chapter 4 The Nazi Past as an Everyday Resource for Adolescents	176
Chapter 5 The Social and Cultural Limits to Appropriations of the Nazi Past	223
Chapter 6 Peer-Group Dynamics and Playful Uses of the Past	278
Conclusion From Memory to Appropriation(s)	309

Appendix 1
The German School System   322

Appendix 2
Structure of Interviews with Students   326

Appendix 3
Summary Table of Teachers   335

Appendix 4
List of Teachers Interviewed   337

Appendix 5
List of Students Interviewed   349

References   367

Index   383

FIGURES AND TABLES

Figures

Figure 0.1 Articles on the Nazi past in the weekly newspaper *Der Spiegel*, 1969–2000. Total articles covering the period 1933–1945. 2

Figure 0.2 Number of publications on National Socialism in Germany between 1972 and 2002, by theme and by five-year period. 3

Figure 0.3 Number of television programs on the ARD mentioning the Nazi past between 1994 and 2002. 4

Figure 2.1 Student's drawing of the Neuengamme concentration camp. 86

Figure 2.2 Text and image by Kevin and Martin on life in the concentration camps. 88

Figure 3.1 The *Gaudiplom* belonging to Ms Neumeier's father. 161

Figure 5.1 Extract from Moher's homework: "European Judaism in the Nineteenth Century." 235

Figure 5.2 Presence of a subject mentioning the Nazi past on the first German television channel (ARD) according to the program type (1994–2001). 252

Tables

Table 0.1 Socio-professional categories (SPC) of the parents of students interviewed at Weinberg. 16

Table 0.2 Educational qualifications of parents of the students interviewed at Weinberg. 17

Table 0.3 Socio-professional categories of the parents of students interviewed at Wiesi. 19

Table 0.4 Educational qualifications of the parents of students interviewed at Wiesi. 20

Table 0.5	Nationality of the parents of students interviewed at Wiesi.	20
Table 0.6	Socio-professional categories of the parents of students interviewed at Monnet.	21
Table 0.7	Educational qualifications of the parents of students interviewed at Monnet.	22
Table 0.8	Socio-professional categories of the parents of students interviewed at the 100th.	23
Table 0.9	Educational qualifications of parents of students interviewed at the 100th.	23
Table 3.1	Students' academic progress in history by sex for Mr Schulze's class (end of eighth grade, beginning of ninth grade).	138
Table A.1	Summary table of the school systems in the FRG and the GDR.	324
Table A.2	Comparison of the four schools participating in the study.	325
Table A.3	Summary table of teachers (social origins, age, place of study, sex).	335

Preface to the English Edition (2019)

As a German historian and sociologist who has worked in France since 2001, living and working in another academic context has provided a more distanced perspective on the politics of history in Germany and particularly on the question of the continuing presence of the German Nazi past in adolescent lives. Initially published in France, this book is positioned within French sociology for a French publishing market. This explains the many French references and examples in the book. The exchange between French and German literature on history, memory, political sociology, and sociology of family and education is part of the initial work of translation and importation of a German subject into a French publishing market.

This book has its origins in the debate between the German writer Martin Walser and the then chairman of the Central Council of Jews in Germany Ignatz Bubis in 1998. In the speech in the Frankfurter *Paulskirche* after he received the Peace Prize of the German Book Trade for his literary work, Walser stated that he no longer wanted to see the "Auschwitz club" on television; Bubis reacted by accusing Walser of anti-Semitism. A year-long debate followed, published extensively in the *Frankfurter Allgemeine Zeitung* (*FAZ*) (one of the two main daily newspapers in Germany, situated politically at the center-right) involving many German political and intellectual figures. The debate quickly centered on the question of a "generational divide": the "third generation" being accused by those taking Ignatz Bubis's side of no longer giving priority to the Nazi past, and thus not honoring the "second generation's" accomplishments. Both Martin Walser and Ignatz Bubis received more than a thousand letters from Germans who expressed their support for one or the other. The letters and newspaper interventions were collected into a volume by Frank Schirrmacher a year later (Schirrmacher 1999). Analyzing these letters, I noticed that the few adolescents who joined the debate strongly supported Martin Walser, whereas Ignatz Bubis got support from adults who were, for the most part, from either the war or postwar generations. I also noticed that all the letters came from educated, middle-class families. Wanting to know more about this apparent "generational divide," but also about the adolescents from working-class families who did not read the *FAZ* and had not participated in the debate, I decided to study the transmission of history in schools, in order to see what adolescents did or did not do with the Nazi past in their everyday lives and to produce my own material on this question. To see if the intuitive impression I had upon reading the letters held true, I chose two schools from a privileged neighborhood and two from a working-class area. Adding the East-West political divide of Germany into the picture, I chose to structure the research design around the cities of Hamburg and Leipzig.

Based on first-hand interviews (n=137), observation of history classes (200 hours), and private archives of students and teachers in these two cities, this book explores how German high school students reacted to the teaching of their country's Nazi history, and how they have appropriated and used this past. It takes adolescents' engagements with these topics seriously. The fundamental question the book asks is: "What does the education system do to its students, and what do the students do with what school has to offer them?" I get at this crucial question through the example of a subject that is hugely important for the institution. The book shows to what extent transmission of knowledge is far from being a passive process of reception by students. The latter actively give meaning to what they learn in school in and through their everyday life activities, with friends, with and against teachers, and within their families. The book thus provides an in-depth, empirically based analysis of the forms of transmission and reception of this complex past, addressing the question of how history is appropriated by students inside and outside the classroom, depending on gender, social class, and academic success. It also demonstrates that the analysis of group dynamics inside the classroom and in the schoolyard is essential to understanding how these adolescents use the past in their own ways, which are not foreseen (nor desired) by their teachers, nor by the institution itself. The East-West comparison allows me to demonstrate that the different teaching practices of the FRG (Federal Republic of Germany or West Germany) and the GDR (German Democratic Republic or East Germany) still affect the teachers twenty years after reunification. One would have thought that the political divide would also influence students' representations on Nazi history, but the comparison proves that this is not generally the case. Instead, it is social and gender differences that influence the ways in which students use the Nazi past.

Changes in German Politics

Many things have changed in Germany over the last fifteen years, particularly in the political field. When this research was conducted, neither Die

Linke (The Left)[1] nor the AfD (Alternative für Deutschland, the extreme right-wing party) existed yet. Their creation in 2007 (Die Linke) and 2013 (AfD) is evidence of a significant evolution in the configuration of German politics as well as a recent normalization of extreme right-wing discourses and practices. These changes have played out in very different ways in the two cities where this research was conducted, Hamburg and Leipzig. Both cities occupy particular positions within Germany. Hamburg, second largest city in Germany, is home to one of the main commercial ports in Europe, it has a large working class and a rich commercial bourgeoisie, as well as a very diverse political left. It is also one of the central destinations for immigrants, notably from Iran, Iraq, Afghanistan, and Turkey. Leipzig, on the other hand, is among the ten largest cities in Germany and the largest in the territory of the former GDR. At the end of the 1980s, still as part of the GDR, a large portion of the population participated in the *Bürgerbewegung*: demonstrations for the opening of the frontiers and a change of regime took place every Monday in the city.

The turn of the twenty-first century brought significant changes for both cities, particularly concerning the extreme right. The AfD doubled its votes in Hamburg between 2013 and 2018, from an insignificant 3 percent to a little over 7 percent. In Leipzig, its support base skyrocketed in certain districts, expanding from a low of 6 percent in 2013 to reach 28 percent in 2018. In Hamburg, Die Linke also gained voters' support, but less spectacularly, passing from a little over 7 percent to almost 11 percent. It now constitutes the fourth largest political party in Hamburg, after the CDU (Christian Democratic Union), the SPD (Social Democratic Party) and the Greens. However, in Leipzig they have lost up to 5 percentage points, although they nevertheless constitute the second largest political force in that city, after the CDU, obtaining between 15 percent and 22 percent of the vote, depending on the district. The *Land*, Saxony, is the center of extreme-right activity in Germany; it is where the AfD is most successful,[2] where the NSU (National Socialist Underground) crimes were committed in the early years of the 2000s (and where the perpetrators have been tried since 2011), and more recently it has been the site of anti-immigration riots in Chemnitz. Alongside this, like in many European countries, the traditional left represented by the SPD has lost its status as the second major party in all the East German *Länder*, where the more left-wing Die Linke has taken second place after the CDU.

Looking at the way adolescents appropriated and mobilized the history of Nazism through interviews from the 2000s may help us understand some of the origins of these political changes and what might be a serious challenge to the consensus on dominant interpretations of German history. Indeed, the "Never Again" formula—the interpretation of "never again" being in fact fluid and changing—or what German historians have called the politics of history (*Geschichtspolitik*) (Wolfrum 1999) is rooted in a consensus concerning the evils of Nazism, dictatorship, and the Holocaust. Political priority given to preserve democracy has been well established in the FRG since the 1980s. It was even paradoxically reinforced by reunification, as I explain in this book. The overwhelming strength of the consensus left little space for debate and questioning of German politics of history, which might have contributed to creating forms of opposition that were neither predicted nor desired by the politics of culture and education. This book helps us to understand these forms of opposition.

The subjects of this study were born in Germany in the late 1980s and their relation to German history and politics was forged during their adolescence, in the wake of reunification. Today they are in their late twenties and early thirties, and they are helping to drive Germany's recent political changes. It is members of this generation who have given their support to the AfD (men between the ages of twenty-five and sixty constitute the main electoral body of the AfD),[3] but also to Die Linke, along with the traditional parties, the CDU, the SPD, and the Greens.

An understanding of what happened during the political socialization of this generation fifteen years ago can help us analyze the political landscape in Germany today. The conclusions of this research are unexpectedly relevant in today's environment. Chapters 4, 5, and 6, for example, specifically address the minority of students who explicitly opposed their teachers' interpretations of the Nazi past. They developed different forms of historical interpretations; some even saw national-socialist history in a positive light. In the chapter on playful uses of the past, we observe how young people pushed the boundaries of acceptable discourse among their peers, using the Nazi past to shock, provoke, and impress. Their play constitutes a lens that shows appropriations of politics in activities that are normally considered "a-political" (playing games, decorating rooms, shopping, etc.). Opening up the very definition of what belongs to the realm of politics allows us to consider the very real challenges posed by the far-right today in their imbrication with everyday worries of ordinary people. Although I do not know what has become of these students, the book provides some insight into the everyday strategies and practices young people developed to forge a political position for themselves. It also questions the argument, common among teachers, that the teaching of the Nazi past will somehow render students "immune" to extreme right-wing positions. Finally, by following students from school into their families, it questions the school's real influence over students' democratic positions. The complex interaction between school, family, and peer groups involved in the way students appropriate history lessons shows that the school cannot work miracles and is by no means solely responsible for adolescents' practices.

This study also helps us to understand the teachers' positions as generational ones; in Hamburg, it was the 1968 generation, and in Leipzig, the first FDJ (Freie Deutsche Jugend) generation, that experienced 1989 as a major break in their professional and private lives. It establishes a connection between teachers' political, educational, and family experiences and the way they taught history in the classroom. This generational position also shaped students' positions toward the past, in their encounters with their parents' and grandparents' experience. The comparative microanalysis reveals the complexity of this articulation at a specific moment in time, and during a key phase of their education: adolescence. This complexity is due to the intersections and meanderings (*Gemengelage*; Lüdtke 2017: 117) of class and gender, but also of family, school, politics, and territory.

From Memory to Appropriations of History

In this book I focus on the uses and appropriations of history, rather than mobilizing concepts related to memory. In the years since its initial publication, this choice has been a subject of query among French readers and commentators of the book. As a result, I want to remind the reader of the theoretical framework this book is based upon. This will help explain the choices I made and elucidate my use of the concept "appropriations of history," in opposition to, but also in dialogue with, contemporary uses of the concept "memory." Readers who are less interested in the theoretical debates may turn directly to the next section.

In the early 2000s, the field of memory studies was growing rapidly, but it was already clear to me that the concept was often used in contradictory and political ways. I therefore chose to move away from the notion of collective memory, linked to the notion of a group, in order to focus on the intersection of different groups. Indeed, the adolescents I studied move between families, school, and peer groups, and it is the way they situate themselves within these different groups of belonging as they appropriate the past that becomes the focus of this study. Using the notion of "appropriations of history" allows me to refer to an active process of permanent construction and reconstruction of the past, the adolescents giving it meaning within these social frameworks.

Many uses of the notion of memory have a tendency to blind us to the very subject (transmission of history) we want to study. They refer to concepts that are just as criticized and problematic (identity, nation); they underline a rigid separation between historians and other institutions; they have a tendency to essentialize groups and render invisible important parts of the processes of production of history (such as finance, economics, kin-relations, historical practices) and the very functioning of their power relations. Finding alternatives for the notion of memory (in the plural, varying with their specific use and context), such as the notion of "appropriations of history" when I talk about the students, allowed me to better take into account pre-existing and highly productive debates on identity, nation, history, and everyday life.

Indeed, this book builds on the accomplishments of the German history of everyday life (*Alltagsgeschichte*). In Germany, the first study of popular fascist "memories" in the Ruhr, by Lutz Niethammer, Alexander von Plato, and their research group (1983–85), was conducted by a group of historians of the everyday. For a long time, they were the only ones exploring the shift from "official" to "popular" memories. It seems remarkable that this study, conducted at the same time as Pierre Nora's *Lieux de mémoire* (Nora [1984–93] 1997),[4] has had comparatively little lasting resonance among French or international historians. It is true that the two studies follow opposite logics. German historians are interested in popular narrative representations of the Nazi past among working families of the Ruhr, mainly relying on interviews. They also do not excessively use the term "memory," but mobilize the concept of the history of everyday lives and that of social culture. They thus situate their study within the larger project of the history of everyday life (Lüdtke 1995).

Gerald Sider and Gavin Smith have proposed using "histories" in plural to describe the multiple processes of appropriations of the past (Sider and Smith 1997: 12). In order to understand them, historians have to know "what is locally known" (histories) and integrate it into—and consider it part of—the "production of history." What Sider and Smith say about the relationship between "history" and multiple "histories" is just as true for what others have called "history" and "memory." It is their interplay in the process of producing history and what is considered to be part of history that should interest us. The theoretical distinction between the two, which occurs automatically when we use the term memory, can thus obstruct the comprehension of the process of production of history.

The definition of history therefore depends on who formulates it. It differs between professionals and non professionals. But the notion of "memory" homogenizes forms of appropriation by defining them solely by opposition to (professional) "history." On the contrary, studying forms of appropriation of history, as I have done in this book by analyzing adolescents' appropriations of the Nazi past can provide a micro-level reconstruction of the complexity of meanings that history and histories can represent in the everyday lives of ordinary people. Conversely, as though by mirror image, it can also reveal the force by which a narrow definition of history (as Western, written, and discovered through the mediation of traces of the past) is imposed and its consequences for those whose practices do not correspond to this definition. The study of forms of appropriation that are neither foreseen nor intended (by historians or by institutions) can thus mirror professional rules and norms involved in the production of history, which constitutes an important (if not the most important) pillar of legitimate culture. The use of histories (plural) allows us to reconstruct the link between professional historians and other social spheres, such as politics, school, work, and family, while taking into account the power relations at work in these spaces.

Working in Schools: From Transmission to Everyday Uses of the Past

This book is based not only on interviews with students and teachers but also on very time-consuming participant observation in history classes and school-yards. This method, common in educational studies and pedagogy, remains unusual in European sociology, even though sociologists have increased their presence in the classroom over the last fifteen years (Ahlrichs et al. 2015; Francis 2000; Jouvenceau 2018; Throssell 2015). The empirical and comparative approach (social and geographical, between Hamburg and Leipzig, in a bourgeois and a disadvantaged neighborhood in each town) allowed an in-depth analysis of social and political/territorial factors influencing appropriations of history. It was precisely the systematic research design in four different schools that led to the results discussed here. If I had to redo the study, I would probably include two schools from a rural environment, as well as introduce more systematically the question of religion (Catholicism, Protestantism, and Islam), notably in the context of the recent rise of the extreme right in rural Europe. As it is, the differences between rural and urban Germany remain in the shadows of the book and would provide an interesting avenue for future research.

The choice of school as an experimental terrain to analyze appropriations of history is still relevant today. Nowhere else do we have the encounter of different social classes and backgrounds on such an everyday basis, even though the segregation of neighborhoods still limits these encounters. Schools are also heuristic fieldsites because they are very effective in creating group dynamics, which have a major influence on appropriations of the past. There is a strong argument to be made in favor of combining research on schools with research on families and exploring the interaction of the two in their reciprocal role in the creation of modern citizens. Unfortunately, this still seems to be somewhat of a black box in political sociology, few attempt the time-consuming enterprise of bridging the theoretical and practical divide between sociology of education and sociology of the family. However, by observing the school environment and then by following the actors into their families and peer-groups, this book has investigated some xviii • Preface

of the major spaces of the production of democratic practices. We have seen that adolescents forge an opinion on history, politics, and the state by living their everyday lives: at school, in peer-groups, in the classroom, in the family and between siblings, as well as in interacting with teachers and the curriculum. It is these practices of everyday life that are at the center of this book.

Alexandra Oeser, 11 November 2018

Notes

1. Die Linke is a fusion of the WASG and the PDS in 2007. WASG (Alternative Vote for Social Justice) was founded in 2004 from left-wing members of the SPD (Social Democratic Party) and Union members. The PDS (Party of Democratic Socialism) was the successor of the SED (Socialist Unity Party of East Germany) in 1990.
2. Der Bundeswahlleiter, "Bundestagwahl 2017," retrieved 2 February 2019 from https://www.bundeswahlleiter.de/bundestagswahlen/2017/ergebnisse/bund-99.html.
3. Statistisches Bundesamt: Destatits, "Genesis-Online Datenbank," retrieved 2 February 2019 from https://www-genesis.destatis.de.
4. Part of this monumental work was translated into English in 1996 by Arthur Goldhammer under the title *Realms of Memory: Rethinking the French Past*. It gives English speakers access to 46 of the 132 articles that made up the French edition, which brought together a large portion of the French historical community. The original contains seven volumes and more than five thousand pages, published in the very prestigious *Bibliothèque illustrée des histoires*, written by 130 historians, which might explain its broad consensus and international success. The rapid internationalization of Nora's approach can be seen in the following texts, which all reproduce the same "realms of memory" model for various countries: François and Schulze (2001) for Germany, Sabrow (2009) for the GDR; Kmec, et al. (2008) for Luxemburg; Isnenghi (2006) for Italy, etc.

ACKNOWLEDGMENTS

This translation has been financed by the Institut Universitaire de France (IUF). I would like to thank my translator, Katharine Throssell, for the work she did on the book and for the many stimulating discussions we had on language and content. Her comments changed some of the views I had on the manuscript. I would like to thank Jacques Revel and Alf Lüdtke who have guided my work in France and Germany and have followed it since 2001. Marie-Claire Lavabre has accompanied this work since its beginning, and she has been a dear friend and encouraging head of institute during the time of translation. The critical reading by French editors Jay Rowell and Hervé Joly has significantly influenced the final form of the book, as well as work of Mathilde Lefebvre, who has done the formal rereading and copy editing of the French version of the manuscript. I thank Berghahn Books, notably Chris Chappell for the work on the English manuscript and Ilana Brown and Caroline Kuhtz for their insightful comments and the precise copyediting.

This book has profited from multiple readings of one or several chapters by: Lucie Bargel, Assia Boutaleb, Florent Brayard, Elise Cruzel, Eric Darras, Delphine Espango, Eric Fassin, Sibylle Gollac, Stéphanie Guyon, Patrick Lehingue, Nina Leonhard, Elissa Mailänder Koslov, Julien Morel d'Arleux, Olivier Philippe, Julien Weisbein, and Ariane Zambiras, whom I would like to thank again, ten years later, for their critical remarks and long-term support, which now allows for a publication in English.

Eric Darras has personally and intellectually accompanied this work. I remain in debt to him, his trust, and his support, even years after his departure. Our work together has always been a deep source of inspiration for me.

Without the teachers' and students' willingness to talk to me and let me into their classrooms in Leipzig and Hamburg, this book would not exist. They have not only let me into their professional and family life, many have also developed a deep interest in my work, which has helped me to continue reflecting on the transmission of the Nazi past for over ten years and return to the subject ten years later.

xx • Acknowledgments

I would like to thank scholars from near and far for having come back to me after reading my work and for having engaged in its critical discussion, some of them continually over several years, others in specific circumstances: Valérie Opériol and Charles Heimberg as well as Felicitas Macgilchrist, Julien Fretel, and Michelle Zancarini-Fournel, Christian Baudelot, Laurent Bonelli, Antonin Cohen, Jie-Hyun Lim, Bernard Pudal, Arnault Skornicki, Tamir Sorek, and Dorothee Wierling. Their critical readings have inspired me in my recent work.

The research has profited from the financing of the CIERA and the University of Erfurt. I would like to thank Ms Vogel and Haupt for their interview transcriptions.

Alon Confino and Leora Auslander have closely followed and encouraged the English publication of this book. Leora Auslander has critically read the preface of the 2019 edition. I would like to thank them for their friendship and longstanding encouragement of my work.

I would like to thank my family, and particularly my parents, for their unconditional support for this research in spite of its not always pleasant discoveries, which are also theirs.

ABBREVIATIONS

AfD   Alternative für Deutschland. Alternative for Germany. Extreme right-wing party founded in 2013.

ARD   *Arbeitsgemeinschaft der öffentlich-rechtlichen Rundfunkanstalten der Bundesrepublik Deutschland.* Main public television channel in Germany.

BDM   Bund Deutscher Mädel. Hitler Youth for girls between the ages of ten and eighteen. Included the *Jungmädelbund*, for girls from ten to thirteen. Obligatory for German "non-Jewish" girls from 1936 onward. With 4.5 million members in 1944, it was the largest organization of young women in the world.

CDU   Christlich Demokratische Union. Center right party of the FRG.

DKP   Deutsche Kommunistische Partei. Communist Party in the FRG. After the censorship of the KPD in 1968 was lifted by the FRG government, became the successor of the KPD.

DVU   Deutsche Volks Union. One of the three extreme-right parties of the FRG, with the NPD and the Republikaner, before the AfD existed. It was founded as an association and directed by the editor Gerhard Frey and became a political party in 1987. Until now it has stayed relatively insignificant.

EOS   Erweiterte Oberschule. High school in the GDR that led to the Abitur. Students had to pass the POS (eight or ten years) in order to be able to continue for two (or four) more years at the EOS.

FAP   Freiheitliche Arbeiterpartei. Free German Workers' Party. Extreme-right party founded in 1979 in the FRG. Minor party that experienced some growth after reunification. It was outlawed in 1995.

FAZ   *Frankfurter Allgemeine Zeitung.* National daily newspaper containing political, economic, and cultural news. Along with the *Süddeutsche Zeitung*, it is one of the main daily newspapers. A bit more liberal than the *Süddeutsche*.

FDJ   Freie Deutsche Jugend. Youth organization of the GDR

FDP	Freie Demokratische Partei. Liberal political party in the FRG. Created in 1948. With moderate electoral success, it has been important as a coalition party between 1949 and 1998.
FRG	Federal Republic of Germany (West Germany)
GDR	German Democratic Republic (East Germany)
GEI	Georg Eckert Institut für internationale Schulbuchforschung. Research institute on school books in Braunschweig. Founded in the 1950s as a collaborative institute of different West-German *Länder*, it has a political objective. It oversees the production of school books and intervenes in political guidelines of education, nationally and internationally. The institute collects all existing German (and many international) school books published since the beginning of the twentieth century and also employs a research team, specializing in comparative text book analysis.
HIAG	Hilfgemeinschaft auf Gegenseitigkeit der ehemaligen Angehörigen der Waffen-SS. Self-help groups for former members of the Waffen-SS. The federal organization existed until 1992, but regional groups continue to exist. Extreme-right wing, they try to improve the image of the Waffen-SS among the German population.
HJ	Hitlerjugend. Hitler Youth (1922–1945). Youth organization of the NSDAP, members were boys between the ages of fourteen and eighteen years old. Obligatory from 1936, it had up to 8.7 million members, 98 percent of the male population was part of it.
KPD	Kommunistische Partei Deutschlands. German communist party.
NPD	One of the three extreme-right parties, with the DVU and the Republikaner, before the AfD existed.
NS	National Socialism. The short form is very often used by the interviewees as an adjective as well as a noun to refer to anything that has a link to the Nazi past.
NSDAP	Nationalsozialistische Deutsche Arbeiterpartei. National Socialist party, extreme-right German political party founded in the early 1920s. Rose to power on 30 January 1933, with the nomination of its leader Adolf Hitler as German Chancellor by the marshal and President of the German Reich Paul von Hindenburg. Declared illegal as a criminal organization in the Nuremberg trial of 1946.
NSU	National-Sozialistischer Untergrund. National Socialist Underground. Extreme right-wing organization.
POS	*Polytechnische Oberschule.* Unified junior high school in the GDR, for students under sixteen years old. The courses were technical and meant to prepare for a specific job. Students could either stay

	only eight years at the POS, followed by an apprenticeship afterwards, or they could go for ten years and leave with a diploma, the *Mittlere Reife*, equivalent of the *Realschulabschluss* in the FRG.
PDS	Partei des demokratischen Sozialismus. Party of Democratic Socialism, successor of the SED in 1990. In 2007, it joined with the WASG, from the FRG, to form the new party Die Linke (The left).
PISA	Program for international student assessment. Founded in 2000 by the OECD, this is a triennial international survey that aims to evaluate education systems worldwide by testing the skills and knowledge of fifteen-year-old students.
RTL	Radio Television Luxembourg. Founded in 1986 as RTL plus, a private German television channel. Since 1993, it has had one of the largest audiences of television channels in Germany, although after 2006, the public channels have been more popular.
SA	*Sturmabteilung*. Literally storm detachment. Also called Brownshirts. Functioned as a paramilitary unit that helped the NSDAP to power from the 1920s to the 1930s. The SA became disempowered in 1934, after Hitler ordered the "blood purge," also known as the "night of long knives." The SA continued to exist, but was superseded by the SS (*Schutzstaffel*).
SED	Sozialistische Einheitspartei Deutschlands. Socialist Unity Party of Germany. Principal governing party of the GDR. It was founded in 1946 through the fusion of the German Social Democratic Party (SPD) and the German Communist Party (KPD) in the Soviet occupation zone. On the 3 December 1989, the Central Committee withdrew and the party was renamed PDS in 1990.
SPC	Socio-professional categories.
SPD	Sozialdemokratische Partei Deutschlands. German Social Democratic Party. Founded in 1863, it is the oldest German party.
WASG	Arbeit & Soziale Gerechtigkeit – die Wahlalternative. Alternative Vote for Social Justice. Founded in 2004 from left-wing members of the SPD (Social Democratic Party) and Union members, it fused with the PDS in 2007 to form Die Linke.
ZDF	*Zweites deutsches Fernsehen*. Second public television channel in Germany.

INTRODUCTION

The imminent demise of all those who personally witnessed Nazism raises the urgent question of how the Nazi past should be transmitted to future generations. Indeed, it is often "when actors die that we worry about salvaging their memory" (Noiriel 1989: 1,453). In Germany, therefore, the presence of the Nazi past in the media and in publishing, as well as in school textbooks and teaching practices, has steadily increased in recent decades.

A quantitative analysis of articles from *Der Spiegel* between 1969 and 2000[1] shows an increase in publications on Nazism in the most widely sold weekly newspaper in Germany (see Figure 0.1).

In each edition of *Der Spiegel* since 1969, there have been on average 1.7 articles that cover the period between 1933 and 1945. This number more than doubled in the space of a few years after 1977. The year 1979, in which the US television series *Holocaust* was shown in Germany, marked the beginning of the media interest in this theme (Lüdtke 1993b), which reflects the growing importance of the subject in debates in the political arena. The 1980s, which saw the second peak in interest, were also marked by "memory debates" that led to what was then called the "strange epidemic of memory" or the "fanaticism of history" (Assmann and Frevert 1999). The end of the twentieth century and the first years of the twenty-first confirm the explosion of publications on this subject: more than one book per day was published on the Third Reich and more than one book every three days[2] on the National Socialist extermination policy.[3] Supposing that these publications respond to

2 • When Will We Talk about Hitler?

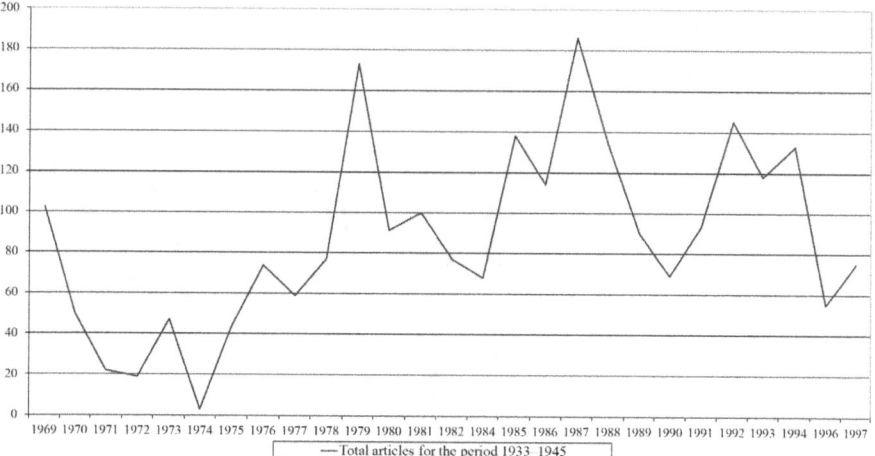

Figure 0.1 Articles on the Nazi past in the weekly newspaper *Der Spiegel*, 1969–2000. Total articles covering the period 1933–1945. Figure created by the author.

a certain demand, and taking into account the structural subordination of the media field to the political field (Benson and Neveu 2005; Darras 1995), we can surmise that there was an increase in the German public's interest in this theme over the last years of the twentieth century. Publications on Nazism have quadrupled between 1972 and 2002; those on the National Socialist policy of extermination were multiplied twelvefold, as we can clearly see in Figure 0.2 opposite.

Television coverage on the subject is still abundant in daily programs like television news or talk shows, as we can see in this example of the ARD,[4] one of the three German public television channels.

On the ARD channel alone, National Socialism was mentioned in various programs 1.6 times per week on average, with fluctuations around the main commemorative dates. The Nazi extermination policy represents nearly half of the themes covered with an average of forty programs per year.

What does this overwhelming presence of the Nazi past in German media and publishing mean? And why has it not managed to appease the fears of forgetting the past? What links can we establish between the controversies arising in the political and media fields and the perspectives of the "younger generations" on this "past in the present"?

The debates about the transmission of the Nazi past are marked by a deep fear of collective amnesia, particularly for "future generations." The media often deliberately describe young people as ignorant or blasé. From youth depicted as under or badly informed to youth described as "saturated" (*übersättigt*), these generalizing accusations dominate any understanding of the

Introduction • 3

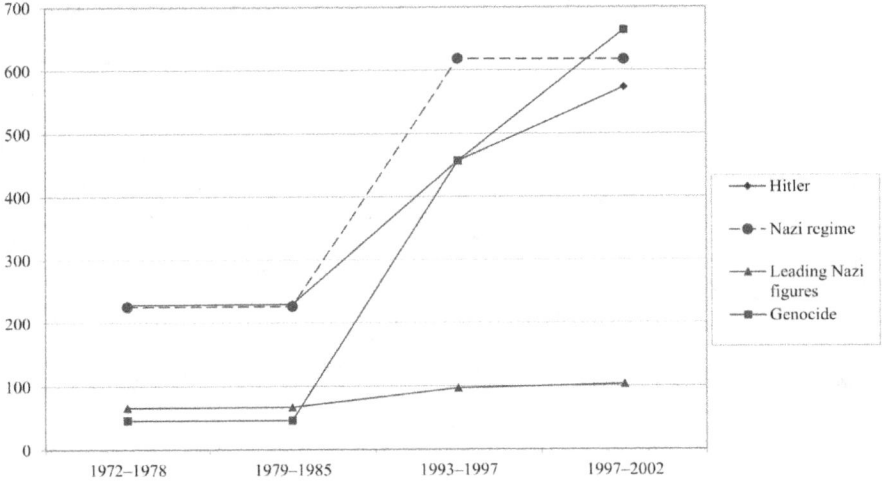

Figure 0.2 Number of publications on National Socialism in Germany between 1972 and 2002, by theme and by five-year period. Figure created by the author.

significations or usages of the past for today's adolescents born just before the fall of the Berlin Wall. Several factors seem to be behind the inability of scientific analysis to see the sociological stakes articulating the transmission of the Nazi past. First, the question that drives these studies is often poorly constructed. Asking how the Nazi past should be transmitted "to the young," leads to a homogenization of "the young" as a uniform category, in opposition to "their parents' generation." We forget that "youth is just a word" (Bourdieu [1980] 1995). Second, this question leads to a confusion between issues to do with knowledge and those to do with politics and morality. We need to untangle these two kinds of issues in order to understand their interaction, while refusing a binary opposition between rationality and emotion, and we need to take seriously the effects of the latter on the course of history (Burke 2005; Prochasson 2008). Third, the lack of empirical research leads to this question being treated on a theoretical level only, as a matter of principle, which prevents differentiated analysis.

Some German researchers, who base their analysis on quantitative studies measuring students' mastery of historical facts, claim that "the young" are incompetent and that they "lack knowledge." (Neumann and Noelle-Neumann 1993; Silberman and Stoffers 2000). Even though their conclusions have in fact been mitigated by comparative studies (Borries, Pandel, and Rüsen 1991), they seem to persist. For others, the responsibility of this "hostile" attitude lies with an "overflow of (suffocating) memory."[5]

To escape from this analytical dead end, this book aims to analyze the "contextualized" uses of the Nazi past by German adolescents between

4 • When Will We Talk about Hitler?

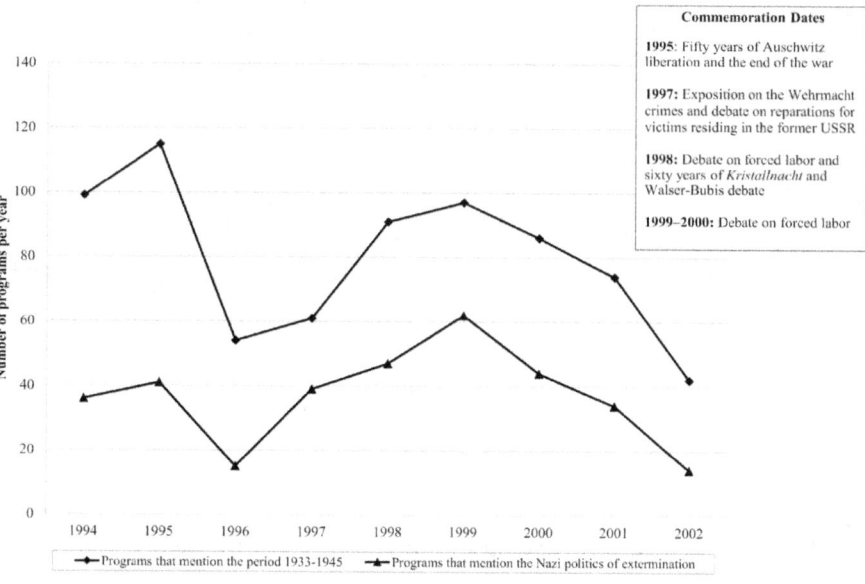

Figure 0.3 Number of television programs on the ARD mentioning the Nazi past between 1994 and 2002. Figure created by the author.

fourteen and eighteen years old. To do this, it takes into account their origins and social trajectories, their gender, age, family and peer groups, as well as their interests and political engagements. It also looks at their daily activities, both inside and outside of school, with their families and friends.

For a Sociology of the Reappropriation of History

In recent years, the historiographic debates about the relationship between history and memory have led to the development of a new subfield within history. In France, this has occurred in particular around the *Realms of Memory Project*, run by Pierre Nora ([1984–1993] 1997). This new field studies "memory" as "second degree history" (Nora 2002) and questions the "political uses of the past" (Hartog and Revel 2001). Gérard Noiriel (1989: 1,425) has emphasized the potential of this historiographic shift, no longer investigating the past itself but rather the ways in which the past is constructed, shaped, institutionalized, and transmitted. This could bring historical studies closer to comprehensive sociology (from Max Weber to the present day Anglo-Saxon interactionists) in analyzing "representations" of the past as well as the role of lived experience (*Erlebnis*), which are at the heart of questions about "memory."

Over the course of the last twenty years, memory has become a field of study in its own right; to the point that American historian Alon Confino declared that "memory" was "perhaps *the* leading term, in cultural history" (Confino 1997: 1,386; 2004, 2005). Yet the concept remains vague, which is why it is used in a plethora of different studies without much theoretical or methodological coherence between them (Lavabre 1994, 2000, 2001). The confusion between what has been called "memory policy," "memory from above," or "official memory" (Lavabre 1994; Confino 1997, 2004, 2006), and collective memories, which are seen as an ersatz "public opinion" for the historian, contributes to the lack of analysis of the concept. Ubiquitous canonical references to Maurice Halbwachs have thus meant that the existence of "collective memories" has been postulated rather than studied.

In the political field, there are complex processes of "memory construction," which are initiated and conducted by "memory entrepreneurs" (Pollak 1993; Strauss [1959] 1997) who compete to produce legitimate definitions of a given past. Marie-Claire Lavabre has analyzed these "politics of memory" (1991, 1994, 2000, and 2001) that take shape in political discourses, institutions, monuments, or "sites of memory," as well as through media and school textbooks. Yet the mere existence of these sites or realms of memory is by no means sufficient for the analysis of the collective nature of memory. As the sociology of reception has shown, professional and intellectual reasoning is not the same as profane reasoning. Readings are social, they depend on the habitus of the readers; they are therefore plural and sometimes contradictory, and they are always complex (Bourdieu, Darbel, and Schnapper [1969] 1991; Chartier [1985] 2003; S. Hall [1973] 1994). In 1939, Halbwachs used a musical analogy to illustrate this fact: "there are two ways to learn to remember sounds, one is highbrow, the other lowbrow, and there is no relationship between the two" (Halbwachs [1939] 1997: 33). A musician who understands music theory will not remember a symphony in the same way as someone who never learned to read music and will remember the rhythm of a melody, rather than the orchestral production as a whole. In the same way, the professional historian who reads a history book (or analyzes a memorial or visits a museum) will not do so in the same way as a non-historian. The former will read the book thinking about the other historians who have written on the subject, observing agreements and disagreements within the discipline. The layman will think about something else completely: the events they learn about in the book, perhaps also the interpretation of the historian, but not necessarily in the terms of historiographic debate. It therefore seems possible to say, with Halbwachs, that there are (at least) three different ways of learning (i.e., giving meaning to) history. One is erudite (by history professionals), another is specific to the political field, and at least one is mainstream or based on common sense.[6] Above all, these three categories of actors do not obey the same social rules, nor belong to the same groups.

However, we still have to take into account the interactions between these different readings of history—given that historians, like musicians, are sometimes not able to completely isolate themselves from general society. It is these logics of interaction that must be understood in order to analyze the mobilization and appropriations of the Nazi past by adolescents today. This is, indeed, what Halbwachs does when he explains how collective memory functions, taking opposition to his doctoral supervisor Henri Bergson ([1896] 1911) in a famous demonstration.

> It's that in reality, we are never alone. . . . because we always carry with us, and inside us a quantity of people who are distinct from ourselves. . . . I arrive in London for the first time . . . Passing in front of Westminster I think about what my historian friend told me (or about what I read in a history book, which comes to the same thing,). Crossing the bridge, I consider the effect of the perspective that my painter friend had pointed out to me (or which had struck me in a painting, or an engraving). I guide myself through my mental map. . . . Impressions [of the town] remind me of Dickens' novels read during my childhood: I therefore walk with Dickens. In all these moments, all these circumstances I cannot say I am alone, that I think alone, because I place myself mentally in such or such a group, with that architect, and beyond him with those whom he merely interpreted for me, or with that painter (and his group) . . ., with a novelist. Other people have shared these memories with me. Moreover, they help me to recall them: to remember I turn toward them, momentarily adopt their point of view, enter into their group, of which I continue to be a member. (Halbwachs [1939] 1997: 52–53)[7]

If we apply it to World War II and the Nazi past, Halbwachs's observation helps to analyze the collective nature of recollection.[8] This is not simply a matter of focusing on the memory itself, to use Halbwachs's example, on stories or history books, written, read, or retold. This is about examining the (collective) experience that actualizes these memories, for example, in a walk around London (or in our case a classroom, playground, conversations with friends or family, visits to historical sites or museums and so forth).

The memory of the Nazi past, like all recollections, is thus constructed collectively. For those who participated in the war, it can evoke these experiences, and the groups with whom they shared them (soldiers, police, colleagues, the administration, neighbors, friends, children, or parents, etc.). Adolescents born just before the fall of the Berlin Wall do not belong to these same groups: they did not live through the Nazi past themselves. They have read books, heard about it in the media and in their families, just like their parents. They learn about this past in the pacified surroundings of the everyday: in the classroom, at the family dinner table, in the street, or in the playground with their friends.

We live in complex societies that obey the principle of organic solidarity in the division of social labor. Each individual thus occupies a specific role in different institutions, which are increasingly numerous and composite, particularly because of the acceleration in changes to social morphology (Durkheim [1893] 2014). In this book we will look at themes covering families, children of immigrants, the redefinition of gender roles, different urban contexts, national reunification, and others. These social frames redirect memories of Nazism—both inside and outside the school context.

However, given the excesses that often accompany the use of the term, I will not refer to "collective memory" in this book, although I continue to construct my approach following Halbwachs. The question of the collective nature and the collective frameworks of reappropriations will be posed throughout this study, which focuses on the uses of history in the school context, and students' daily appropriations and reappropriations of the history of Nazism.

The School as the Social Framework for Adolescents' Reappropriations

Field Notes: June 2003

I walk into the eighth-grade class that I will follow and observe over the next year. During the first weeks I accompany the students every day in all subjects to get to know them, and after that I only attend history classes. They are now in class with Ms Baltig.[9] As she enters, she is a little disturbed by my presence (the teachers were informed of my presence by the principal, Mr Schulze). "Ah," she says, "you should have come to another class. This is the worst time slot of them all."

Ms Baltig explains the Napoleonic wars. Two students, seated in front, participate actively in the class. There is permanent background noise, students talking together. Kai, who is repeating the year, has put himself in the back row. He brought a friend from another school. They talk together and complain about school. Elisabeth exchanges notes with her two neighbors. Alexandra and Maren also write notes, but between themselves. Kai, at the back of the class, is reading the newspaper, ostensibly bored, in spite of the presence of his friend. When he raises his head to ask a question, Ms Baltig ignores him, which provokes an ironic "thanks a lot" from Kai. Isabelle intervenes, "Ms Baltig, Kai asked a question." No longer able to ignore Kai, Ms Baltig asks him to repeat the question. Apparently Kai, in spite of his behavior, is following the class. His question is aimed not only to interrogate but also to destabilize his teacher: "and who was worse, Napoleon or Hitler?" Ms Baltig is evasive, uncertain; she gets upset and mutters incomprehensibly, which makes Maren laugh. Thomas begins to roll little bits of paper to throw at his classmates. Ms Baltig realizes, which makes Kerstin laugh, making fun of Thomas's inability to conceal his naughtiness from the teacher.

This kind of scene reveals the ordinary issues of everyday schooling. We can see the inherent difficulty in wanting to measure the role and effects of the school on the historical knowledge and political conscience of students. Teachers and students are also occupied in practices other than the simple "transmission of knowledge," practices that must also be analyzed in order to understand their relationship to the knowledge that is transmitted. This classroom scene raises several of the key questions that are behind this research.

First, Kai's question is symptomatic of the attitude that the students have toward the Nazi past. "Hitler" is present, in their heads and their discourses, well before he is covered in class. What meaning does the evocation of the Nazi past have for the students? In what respect is it linked, not only to the social and educative path of the student, but also their age, gender, generation, and family? How are practices inscribed in relations between students? The fact that Kai is repeating the year, for example, has a strong impact on his place in the class. His blatant boredom demonstrates a desire to set himself apart from the other younger students (during breaks he meets up with his older friends, who constitute a reference group for him). This is a way of reminding both others and himself that he has already covered this subject last year and affirms a—rather typically masculine—"anti-school" stance (Connell 1989).

This interaction also raises a series of questions about the processes of appropriation. How can we understand what happens at school and in the classroom? What place and what function does the Nazi past occupy here? To what extent can we talk about the transmission of knowledge, or rather, as Pierre Ansart (1981) suggests, of the "inculcation with an affective relationship to history"? How do students appropriate the past? From these questions emerge the theoretical frameworks and interrogations behind this research.

For more than a century, the school system has fed debates and hopes about its effects in terms of "citizenship, equality and wealth" (Baudelot and Leclercq 2005: 10). It has raised questions about the school's contribution to making "good citizens," to reducing social inequalities through education for the most disadvantaged, and increasing the gross domestic product (GDP) by increasing the global level of education. All of these themes remain present, implicitly or explicitly, in the vast majority of research on school as an institution.

On one hand, there is what can be called, for want of a better term, the "production of knowledge," which refers to its legitimate definition by political institutions, such as ministers, or commissions established to define the curriculum and textbooks. This production has been studied in detail since the beginning of the century, but especially closely since the 1950s, by historians of didactics,[10] who analyze the "knowledge" content of school materials. Thus, along with research by American historians such as Eva and Martin Kolinsky (1974, 1992), it was the researchers of the Georg Eckert Institute (GEI) who constantly worked at decrypting the programs, texts, or images in history textbooks, in order to reveal their "weaknesses" or "historical inaccuracies" with the constant goal of improving their quality. Nazism is today, without a doubt, the subject that is the most closely analyzed in the area of school materials. German school texts and the historians of the GEI even serve as an example for experts in other countries, such as Rwanda, to "better deal with the painful past" through school curricula and history texts.

On the other hand, there is what is habitually called the "reception" of this knowledge by the students. Both sociologists and researchers in education sciences, as well as a few historians, have attempted to quantitatively identify the cognitive skills of students. The study that has had the most impact on the political and media fields in recent times, in spite of serious criticism about its research design, and because of its "alarming" conclusions (about lack of knowledge) is PISA, the Program for International Student Assessment (OECD 2005). Researchers working with the historian of didactics Jörn Rüsen (until recently director of the Kulturwissenschaftliches Institut of Essen) or those at the University of Hamburg with Bodo von Borries (1995) have come to very different conclusions, providing a detailed analysis of the historical knowledge of German adolescents since the end of the 1980s. Contrary to popular thought, they have demonstrated that knowledge is much more detailed for the Nazi period than for any other period of history (Borries, Pantel, and Rüsen 1991; Mierow 1991). Finally, the concrete role of teachers and the autonomy of interpretation relative to the history to be transmitted have only been dealt with more recently, particularly from a sociological, generational, and biographic perspective. A number of studies were conducted (especially in education sciences) on teachers in the former German Democratic Republic (GDR) and their adaptation to the new teaching system after reunification, based on analysis of interviews with the teachers (Benrath 2005; Fabel-Lamla 2006).

The concepts of production, reception and transmission (borrowed from theories of culture and communication) treat the cultural as if it were material; suggesting that it is possible to transmit culture or knowledge (cultural capital) in the same way as we hand over an object. Nevertheless, this metaphor rapidly reaches its limits. Conceptualizing knowledge as capital (human

10 • When Will We Talk about Hitler?

or cultural), different from economic capital, as Pierre Bourdieu did—either alone ([1979] 2010, 1989) or with Jean-Claude Passeron ([1964] 1985)—opened the way for quantification and differentiation that allowed considerable progress in studies on education (Baudelot and Leclercq 2005). But the use of the economic metaphor specifically makes it difficult to conceive of the process of appropriation (Lahire 1995). Therefore, adolescents will not simply receive, rather they will interpret what they learn; they will transform it through processes of appropriation. The German historian Alf Lüdtke reminds us that

> In the process of perception and evacuation, articulation and silence (or mutism), people (*Menschen*) do not only follow the codes of discourses and representations that they find in place. More exactly: they rely on these images, words and grammars, even as they recompose them for each new use. In their practices . . . actors transform the realities of things and circumstances that are apparently so stable, . . . at the same time, they vary and rewrite (*überschreiben*) the ways of perceiving the world and history in their heads.[11] (Lüdtke 1994: 146)

In German, these processes of permanent rewriting and transformation are referred to by the term *Aneignung* (Lüdtke 1995b). Here we need to identify several different levels: first, perception, an act of the senses; then interpretation and reinterpretation, which are acts of consciousness; and finally appropriation, which involves a third level (Bourdieu [1979] 2010). *Aneignung*, as defined above, refers to the whole process.[12] We can translate this concept by "reappropriation" in order to emphasize its transformative dimension without forgetting the social dimensions that influence these practices or the dimension that is constitutive of individual personality (which is contained in the term "appropriation" and even more in the term "incorporation").

These processes of reappropriation are neither permanent nor stable; instead we must consider them interactive social processes. A classroom is a specific place that obeys specific rules particular to an institution of which the goal is to transmit knowledge, and perhaps also civic behavior. But the functioning of the class and the pedagogic relationship is also dependent on relations between professors and students and between students. These relationships are not merely functional. Professors have their own personal and family lives, they have their own life histories, their own reappropriations of the past. The students have theirs. Therefore we must identify the factors that are decisive here. Depending on how these factors interact, the (Nazi) past can be a resource, a burden, or have no effect at all. Parallel to this, these reappropriations of the Nazi past confront each other in a specific place, the classroom. Here power relations are played out, between the teacher and the students, but also between students themselves.

Introduction • 11

The use of this concept of reappropriation also allows us to study what the students do with the past transmitted to them at school; how they give meaning to it in their everyday school lives. The students' multiple appropriations of the past are articulated through social frames, such as social origin, trajectory, generational belonging, gender, etc. Classroom observation, such as it is practiced by sociologists of education in the United States, and particularly those who attempt to identify the role of gender in the transmission of knowledge (Canada and Pringle 1995; Smith 1990; Tidball 1980),[13] therefore constitutes a useful approach for studying these reappropriations.

School Experience: Between *Eigensinn*, Social Frames, and Reappropriations

Three concepts, often seen as contradictory, have been helpful to me in understanding how references to the Nazi past are used in the school context. Two have already been mentioned: reappropriation and social frameworks. Before we look at the ways in which they have been useful in my fieldwork and how they work together, it is important to look closely at the third concept, *Eigensinn*, developed by Alf Lüdtke (1993a, 1994, 1995a, 1996), discussed intensively by other researchers such as Thomas Lindenberger (2015) or myself (Oeser 2017a, 2017b).

Lüdtke refers to *Eigensinn* as "denoting willfulness, spontaneous self-will, a kind of self-affirmation, an act of (re)appropriating alienated social relations on and off the shop floor by self-assertive prankishness, demarcating a space of one's own" (Lüdtke 1995d: 313). For a long time it was difficult for me to grasp the plurality, the ambiguity, and the contradictions in the students' uses and reappropriations of the Nazi past; it was even more difficult to describe their own logics and the meaning(s) that they gave to their uses of this past. It was the very principle of the students' *Eigensinn* in their uses and reappropriations of the Nazi past that seemed key, and yet continued to escape me. However, this concept enabled me to escape the "dead end" of only focusing on the "effects" of teaching the Nazi past on the students.

Lüdtke developed this concept in the 1980s in the context of his research on industrial workers in the nineteenth and twentieth centuries. He sought to distance himself from the Marxist reading that consisted—in its more populist versions—in the search for "class consciousness" in the form of a specifically proletarian "desire to resist" or in "revolutionary energy" that would prove the existence of the "working class." Lüdtke therefore proposed an alternative to this binary between populism and pity (see also Grignon and Passeron 1989; Hoggart [1957] 2006; Revel 1986).

Lüdtke described the workers' forms of sociability at work, creating space and time for the self, and for the workers as a group, which allowed for moments of escape from the hierarchical relations with superiors. These forms of sociability are created by workers operating as a group and according to their own rules. *Eigensinn* thus refers to the parallel and paradoxical existence of resistance and distance from resistance, "being oneself" and "being with others," but especially the commitment (*Hingabe*), at once joyful, uncalculating, and self-interested, to regaining one's integrity. *Eigensinn* is thus, for Lüdtke, an example of the *Gleichzeitigkeit des Ungleichzeitigen*, a notion borrowed from the philosopher Ernst Bloch ([1935] 1977), the simultaneity of opposites, or literally the synchrony of asynchrony, translated by Ritter as nonsynchronism. Bloch uses this term to describe the coexistence of "modernity" and "traditions" in the everyday thought of the 1920s. *Eigensinn* thus enables a conceptualization of elements considered antagonistic or contradictory, in particular the "objective" socio-economic conditions and the "subjective" meanings given to them by agents.

The concept of *Eigensinn* has also allowed German historians to describe the plurality, the ambiguities, and contradictions of the representations and practices of people living under dictatorial regimes; under German fascism (Lüdtke1995c), or under the East German Communist Party (Socialistische Einheitspartei Deutschlands, SED) (Lindberger 1999). The term was more generally used to describe individuals' everyday appropriations and uses of the structures of domination (*Herrschaftsstrukturen*). Lüdtke thus emphasizes that "following an order mechanically is impossible. Only permanent reinterpretations ensure the success [and the effectiveness of an order]" (Lüdtke 1991a: 14). Lüdtke evokes Weber's famous definition of *Herrschaft*, by using the German word *Befehl*, in order to better mark his opposition to it. Yet the concept of *Eigensinn* allows us to move beyond the binary opposition between the dominant and the dominated, in order to conceptualize intersections and multiple interpretations. It allows us to perceive the reciprocity of power relations that contribute to the conservation and functioning of the social order (*Ordnung*) by adaptation, reinterpretation, and appropriation of the commands (*Befehl*) that maintain order.[14]

Eigensinn has often been confused with "resistance," a confusion that is perhaps linked to the etymological origin of the term and its literal meaning of "stubbornness." Instead it designates a range of possible appropriations of a specific situation or frame. These forms of appropriation run, for example, from fervent participation in a political ideology (such as Nazism), to apparent loyalty concealing an inner distance or resistant practices, to passive avoidance or openly demonstrated opposition. Conversely, it is not necessary to ideologically adhere to the regime in order to participate in its functioning. Multiple uses of the(se) frame(s) can coexist in the same person, always in relation to a (or several) primary group(s).

Moreover, *Eigensinn* also serves to underline the gap between the objectives of a policy and its social uses. Thus, the desire for (total) mastery over the functioning of society (by a dictatorial regime, for example) is never able to dictate the plural, ambiguous, and contradictory uses (and effects) of these policies.

Applying this concept to the forms of reappropriations of the Nazi past enables us to grasp their plurality and accommodate the students' inventiveness, moving away from the binary alternative between refusal and acceptance in order to describe these reappropriations in all their complexity. What is true for an order is most certainly equally true for less explicit attempts to homogenize representations. The desire(s) to homogenize representations of the Nazi past most certainly exist, such as the one to impose a single (or several) specific affective reaction(s) to this past. But the concept of *Eigensinn*, applied to this context, allows us to shift our interrogation toward an approach in terms of multiple appropriations and uses.

This first shift in our questioning raises the issue of the social frames in which these multiple and contradictory uses become meaningful. Although it is certain that the uses of the past cannot be reduced to an alternative between acceptance or rejection of school and what is transmitted there, I observed certain consistencies and noted that these appropriations were not infinitely variable. Multiple sources in sociology were useful here to analyze the social frames of these appropriations.

The differences between the East and the West for example—which were highly visible for teachers interviewed in Hamburg and Leipzig—disappeared almost completely for the students. But other kinds of differences were visible. Girls and boys talked about the Nazi past in different ways, for example. Do we see these gender differences, which are so clear in the classroom and are extensively analyzed in the sociology of education (see Baudelot and Establet 1992; Belotti [1973] 1975; Duru-Bellat 2002; Thorne 1993), between brothers and sisters, or between mothers and fathers? How do these family frames interact with those of the school in perceptions of the Nazi past?

A second ensemble of differences, more difficult to grasp, can be found between students from different social backgrounds, and particularly among those from migrant backgrounds (Creet and Kitzmann 2011; Georgi 2003). We know that there are complicated links between family migratory histories and success at school (Beaud [2002], 2003; Delcroix 2001; Sayad 1991, 1999) and these studies have been used to ask whether there are links between the uses of the past and success at school. Political sociology has shown that there is also a link between political or militant engagement and cultural capital (Gaxie 1978; Gaxie, Hubé, and Rowell 2013). These analyses have been useful in understanding the students' appropriations and uses of the Nazi past.

Urban sociology and the sociology of social relegation (Foote-Whyte [1943] 1993), but also the studies on the *Eigensinn* of factory workers (Certeau [1980] 1988; Lüdtke 1992b, 1995a, 2016), have allowed us to move beyond an analysis that is overly formatted by the study of school mechanisms. Certain students may demonstrate indifference, or even open opposition to me and my study, but this does not prevent them developing their own uses of this past—from playing with model tanks to daily jokes about Hitler and "the Jews" in the playground. In order to understand what is at stake in these extracurricular usages of Nazism, it was necessary to take into account the importance of peer groups—both inside and outside the classroom, in the playground, in the street, and at home. The multiple and complex operations of entangled appropriations and their social frames thus constitute the heart of this research. A research framework based on interviews, observations, and archival study was set up to explore them.

Corpus and Method

The goal of a twofold comparison—both social and territorial—justified the choice of four very different schools as the key sites for the fieldwork. The tripartite division of the German secondary school system leads to strong social segregation among students from an early age. The *Gymnasium* only accepts students (from age ten) who are considered "capable" of continuing on to the *Abitur* (high school diploma), which advantages children from privileged backgrounds. The *Hauptschule* (nine years of school, until students are fifteen years old) and *Realschule* (ten years of school, until students are sixteen years old), both of which are generally followed by an apprenticeship, provide less academic, more vocational education, accepting all the children who cannot go to the *Gymnasium*. Their student bodies are fairly homogenous in social terms and relatively low in the social hierarchy. The *Gesamtschule* is a hybrid form of school that combines the three other forms in a single institution. It was invented in the 1970s in the Federal Republic of Germany (FRG) in order to address the problem of social segregation. We will see that that this option was not overly successful: the *Gesamtschulen* failed to create either social diversity or equitable regroupings of the other three forms of school. Moreover, social segregation is paralleled by ethnic segregation: students from families who have recently immigrated are most often placed in the *Haupt* and *Realschulen* or in the *Gesamtschule* but only very rarely in the *Gymnasien*.[15]

Introduction • 15

The Choice of the Fieldwork Sites: Four German Schools

Before dealing with the problems raised by a comparative approach or the interview and observation techniques used, a presentation of the schools and student populations will provide an initial perspective on the field-work.[16] Two major towns—one in the east (Leipzig), the other in the west (Hamburg)—were chosen particularly because of their size. Leipzig is one of the few very large cities in the east, given that Berlin was excluded from the outset because of its unique situation. Faced with the complexity of the German education system, which the sixteen federal *Länder* are responsible for, I looked for a local government and educational policies that were stable, in order to simplify the study in terms of public policies of the different *Länder*. The town of Hamburg (which is also a *Land* in its own right) had been governed by the Sozialdemokratische Partei Deutschlands (Social Democrat Party, SPD, later associated with the Greens) for more than forty years, up until the end of the study. The *Land* of Saxe had been governed by the Christlich Demokratische Union (Christian-Democrat Union, CDU) since reunification. Moreover, having lived for sixteen years in Hamburg myself, my familiarity with the town and its institutions enabled me to reduce entry difficulties in two of these four field sites.[17] Two schools were chosen in each of these two towns. Because "young people" are not a homogenous social category, it was necessary to analyze the ways in which the students' uses and appropriations of the Nazi past were inscribed in social practices determined notably by class differences. In each town, the schools were therefore chosen in contrasting urban environments, from two extremes of the social hierarchy (within the public school system), including a bourgeois neighborhood (where the two *Gymnasien* are located) and a disadvantaged neighborhood (where the *Gesamtschule* in Hamburg and the *Mittelschule*[18] in Leipzig are located).

Weinberg in Hamburg

Weinberg is a wealthy neighborhood in Hamburg, far from the center but accessible by subway. It is close to the forests and fields that surround the town. The neighborhood forms a kind of village, with a small center of shops, cafés, a library, a cinema, bars, and a large market. The old brick building of the Weinberg *Gymnasium* is classified as a historic monument. It is a two-story building, built around a courtyard with sunken gardens at the level of the basements. A series of bay windows lets sun and light into the classrooms. The site of the building is situated on a small hillside in the middle of a wood beside a lake: a "perfectly charming" place. The streets of

16 • When Will We Talk about Hitler?

the neighborhood are calm and bordered by large individual houses with gardens and garages, often for expensive cars. The external courtyard of the school is equipped to receive hundreds of bicycles. A gym is attached to the school, a little way down the hill. Ms Heide, a young history teacher who recently arrived in Hamburg considered herself "lucky" to have been appointed to this school.

> Yes, of course, it's a very good school. On all levels: the colleagues, the students, the building, the site. Well, yes, the neighborhood, you can say a lot about it, it's perhaps a little too posh (*gutbürgerlich*), on one hand. But on the other, these are students with whom we can really work. And the parents are so involved. I was afraid, coming to Hamburg, to find myself in a social hotspot (*sozialer Brennpunkt*). But here it's very calm. I was lucky.[19]

Ms Heide was not wrong in her "feeling" of social homogeneity among the students' parents, as we can see in Table 0.1 below, which shows the professions of the parents who participated in the study.

Almost all of the parents of the students interviewed were employed; only three mothers out of thirty-eight were at home, and no one was unemployed. More than half of the parents were managers or in intellectual professions (nineteen were teachers), the others were predominantly doctors and legal practitioners (lawyers or magistrates), and a few were in political positions. Just under a quarter of them were business owners and a few were retail traders. Almost all of the fathers (thirty-three out of thirty-eight) were therefore in the categories of senior management or business owners. One-quarter of the parents were in intermediary professions or were employees, and these were mostly mothers, in particular the wives of business owners who worked in their husbands' companies. Among these women there were also primary school teachers and a few nurses. There were no agricultural professions among the parents, and only one manual worker. This professional distribution is confirmed by the parents' educational qualifications (Table 0.2).

Table 0.1 Socio-professional categories (SPC) of the parents of students interviewed at Weinberg.

SPC	Craftsmen, retail traders, business owners	Senior executives, intellectual professions (including teachers)	Intermediate professions	Employees, service personnel	Workers	Home-makers	Unem-ployed	Total
Mother	1	15(9)	8	11	0	3	0	38
Father	8	25(10)	4	0	1	0	0	38
Total	9	40(19)	12	11	1	3	0	76

Table 0.2 Educational qualifications of parents of the students interviewed at Weinberg.

Parents' education	Primary education	Secondary education/ apprenticeship	High school diploma	University studies	PhD
Mother	0	4	13	21	0
Father	0	3	7	24	4
Total	0	7	20	45	4

Almost two-thirds of the parents had access to higher education (four with PhDs), and nearly all had passed the *Abitur* exams. Although these figures might not be strictly representative (in the statistical sense) of the student body as a whole, they nevertheless give a perspective of the social milieu in which the students are growing up. It is important to bear in mind that I spoke to a whole class of students in this school and there is no reason to think that this class is particularly different from the others from a social perspective.

The Gesamtschule *Wiesi in Hamburg*

Wiesenbergshafen is an outlying suburb of Hamburg with no real center. To get there, one has to cross the motorway that encircles the town and against which the neighborhood is built. It is made up of dilapidated gray concrete high-rise housing estates from the 1970s, some of which are empty. There are no shops, no cafés, and no cinema in the neighborhood. The inhabitants use an affectionate pet name for the area and its school (Wiesi). Across from the Wiesenbergshafen *Gesamtschule* is an abandoned ten-story parking structure. The gray concrete building is open-sided and covered in graffiti, and the wind whistles through it. The school across the road is a metallic orange block with blue waves painted over it. The entry, on the side of the building and a little difficult to find, leads into a large hall, very clean and bright due to the numerous windows and light coming in from above. The space is calm. On one side, in front of the windows, is an oversized map of the world, centered on Africa and South America. To the left of the map is a sign with an inscription, combining fundamental law, human rights, and school rules.

Human dignity is untouchable,
Freedom is always the freedom of our fellow citizens as well
The value of a person does not depend on their origin, their religion,
their gender or their sexuality.
All people must be respected and treated as having equal rights.
Each member of the school community has the right
to freely express their opinions in the form they wish.
In our school, violence is not acceptable,

against neither people nor things,
neither physically, nor verbally.
These rules are compulsory.

To the right of this sign is a notice board with the flags of the following thirty-three countries—the nationalities of the students at the school—aligned vertically in German alphabetical order: Afghanistan, Albania, Algeria, Bosnia, China, Denmark, Germany, Ecuador, Ivory Coast, England, Ghana, Greece, India, Italy, Iran, Japan, Yugoslavia, Cape Verde, Kazakhstan, Croatia, Libya, Macedonia, Niger, Pakistan, Philippines, Poland, Russia, Sierra Leone, Sudan, Turkey, Tunisia, Ukraine, Vietnam.

These details provide a good perspective on what is so particular about Wiesi. Founded in 1972 as one of the first *Gesamtschulen* of the FRG (today there are thirty-eight in Hamburg), it was a "pilot school." The creation of the *Gesamtschulen* was an initiative of the social-democrat governments, who, from 1969, attempted to overcome the educational and social segregation of students set up by the tripartite system. Theoretically, in seventh grade, when students enter secondary school, the *Gesamtschule* was supposed be comprised of 30 percent of students at *Hauptschule* level (ninth grade), 30 percent of students with *Realschule* level (tenth grade), and 30 percent of students considered "capable" of taking the *Abitur* exams (*Gymnasium* students). This was not the case at Wiesi however, and it was not exceptional in this respect. Only 3–7 percent of the students continued school after the *Realschulabschluss* exams at age sixteen, because the parents who wanted their children to pursue longer studies had sent them to *Gymnasium* from the beginning of secondary school. Situated in one of the more difficult areas of Hamburg, Wiesi is one of the few *Ganztagsschulen* (full-time schools) with classes until five o'clock in the afternoon. As such it also offers many activities: the public library is in the same building, there are communal areas such as a billiard room, pinball machines, internet rooms, and a large cafeteria where students pay for meals according to their parents' income (some therefore eat almost for free). As a "pilot school," Wiesi attracts "committed" teachers.

> I absolutely wanted to be able to accompany children from disadvantaged backgrounds to higher education. And so, I applied for one of the two *Ganztags-Gesamtschulen*—at the time there were eight *Gesamtschulen* in Hamburg. And I absolutely wanted to be in one of the two *Ganztags-Gesamtschulen*. And nowhere else. And as a *Gymnasium* teacher![20]

The teachers at Wiesi defend a "left-wing" vision of pedagogy and a large number of them—in fact all those who arrived in the 1970s and who are nearing retirement age—declare themselves "Marxists." Even today they are members of a political party (SPD/Socialist Party or die Grünen/the Greens).[21]

Table 0.3 Socio-professional categories of the parents of students interviewed at Wiesi.

SPC	Craftsmen, retail traders, business owners	Senior executives, intellectual professions (including teachers)	Intermediate professions	Employees, service personnel	Workers	Home-makers	Unem-ployed	Total
Mother	0	0	4	6	3	8	1	22
Father	5	1	2	1	11	0	2	22
Total	5	1	6	7	14	8	3	44

Two had been card-holding members of the Deutsche Kommunistische Partei (Communist Party/DKP) until its dissolution in 1989. By comparison, in Weinberg, only two teachers had been members of a party—the SPD—and only for a few years in the 1970s. The teachers at Wiesi are also sufficiently convinced of the virtues of the *Gesamtschule* system to send their own children there.

The student body at Wiesi is clearly less privileged than that of Weinberg (see Table 0.3).

Nearly a quarter of the students' parents are workers (fourteen of forty-four). A little over a third of mothers are at home (eight of twenty-two), and among the others five are employed as cleaners; but there are also several intermediary professions, often in the areas of health and social work. Among fathers, there are a few who are self-employed and have their own shops. The trade category should not be misinterpreted here: the fathers work in their shops alone (they are sausage merchants [*Würstchenbudenbesitzer*] or kebab sellers) or as craftsmen, quite unlike the major businesses of the parents at the *Gymnasium* in Weinberg. One of the fathers is a doctor but he lives in the United Kingdom and his daughter has never met him. Unemployment is underreported by the students in the interviews. In fact, the vice principal and several teachers affirm that 30 percent of parents at the school do not work at all and live on social assistance.[22]

It is interesting to note that the educational qualifications of the parents only partially correspond to their professional activity (see Table 0.4):

The relatively large number of parents with university degrees, or who have passed the *Abitur* university entrance exams (fifteen of forty-four) can be explained by the German immigration policies of the 1980s and 1990s. These are Afghan or Iranian immigrants who opposed the Taliban or the Islamic revolution, or they are families who fled the war in the former Yugoslavia (see Table 0.5). These populations are from intellectual groups,

Table 0.4 Educational qualifications of the parents of students interviewed at Wiesi.

Parents' education	None	Primary education	Secondary education/ Apprenticeship	Abitur/ High school diploma	University education	PhD	Don't know	Total
Mother	2	3	9	4	3	0	1	22
Father	0	2	11	4	4	0	1	22
Total	2	5	20	8	7	0	2	44

Table 0.5 Nationality of the parents of students interviewed at Wiesi. This is the only school in which the nationality of the parents is relevant. In the other schools, a large majority of students have German parents and grandparents.

Nationality	German born in Germany	German born elsewhere	Afghanistan	Iran	Former Yugoslavia	Russia/ USSR	Turkey	Total
Mother	8	0	5	2	2	3	2	22
Father	6	2	4	3	2	3	2	22
Total	14	2	9	5	4	6	4	44

managers, and elites in their countries of origin, but their degrees and qualifications were not recognized in Germany. They therefore often perform manual work or are employees or shopkeepers, professions that do not match their levels of education.

This table is not representative of the total student body at Wiesi (we have already seen the thirty-three nationalities that are present at the school). However, it does show just how over-qualified the parents are for their current professions. Moreover, it reflects the large proportion of students with either one or both parents who have a nationality other than German. Of the twenty-two students interviewed, only five were born to two German parents. This corresponds to the estimation of Herbert Weise, a teacher at the school: "I only have two students out of twenty-two who are from two generations of German-Germans, with German grandmothers and grandfathers on both sides. More or less all the others have family histories involving migration."[23] This specificity initially seemed to be an inconvenience, to the point where I was ready to begin looking for a less "atypical" school. However, upon investigation, it became clear that in Hamburg, the schools in so-called "difficult" areas also tend to have students with non-German parents. So Wiesi was not that atypical after all for a disadvantaged neighborhood in Hamburg, a town in which the non-German population is high (17 percent).[24] The research at Wiesi also allowed me to take into account the way these young, so-called "foreign," Germans relate to German history, which considerably enriched the analysis.

Table 0.6 Socio-professional categories of the parents of students interviewed at Monnet. One of the students does not know his father.

SPC	Craftsmen, retail traders, business owners	Senior executives, intellectual professions (including teachers)	Intermediate professions	Employees, service personnel	Workers	Home-makers	Unem-ployed	Total
Mother	1	11(3)	5	3	0	0	1	21
Father	4	11(4)	2	2	1	0	0	20
Total	5	22(7)	7	5	1	0	1	41

Gymnasium *Monnet in Leipzig*

The *Gymnasium* Monnet in Leipzig looks like a castle. It is situated within a residential neighborhood, quite close to the center of town, surrounded by carefully restored early twentieth-century buildings. The wrought iron gate leads the visitor into a grand entryway in front of the majestic stairs leading into the Renaissance-era building. Although the inside does not look much like a castle, the high ceilings and large rooms nevertheless make it a comfortable place to work. It is not the most famous *Gymnasium* in Leipzig (that title goes to the *Thomasschule*[25]) but its reputation in the town is well established.

My welcome at the *Gymnasium* Monnet was warm, but the principal Mr Wolff insisted that I obtain prior agreement from the Leipzig school district (*Regionalschulamt*) before I could begin the study in his school. This was the first major difference with Hamburg, where entry into the schools and access to students and parents was characterized by a lack of formal institutional barriers. Three weeks of negotiation (including an interview at the *Regionalschulamt*) and several administrative forms later, I was able to begin my fieldwork.

The students at Monnet come from families that are as well-off as the students in Weinberg (see Table 0.6). More than half of parents are managers or in intellectual professions, are self-employed or own businesses, and there are also a few retail traders. Among the intellectual professions, there are fewer teachers than at Weinberg but there are more artists and cultural workers. Another noteworthy difference is that the mothers have the same levels of qualification as the fathers (with an exception made for the two PhDs). None of them work in their husbands' businesses or are homemakers by choice. Only one had been unemployed for a few months at the time of the interview.

Table 0.7 Educational qualifications of the parents of students interviewed at Monnet.

Parents' education	Secondary education	High school diploma	University studies	PhD	Total
Mother	7	4	10	0	21
Father	6	2	10	2	20
Total	13	6	20	2	41

The level of educational qualifications reflects this professional distribution, as we can see in Table 0.7.

One particularity consists in the fact that many parents took up their studies again after reunification (nearly a third). This was the case for four people who had not been able to pursue their studies for political reasons (their parents were clergymen or businessmen[26]), but also for others who had chosen not to continue their schooling or who lost their jobs because of economic restructuring after reunification. Another interesting characteristic lies in the fact that people who had only obtained the *Polytechnische Oberschule* degree (POS, a vocational qualification),[27] found work as technicians or in self-employment.

The 100th Mittelschule *in Leipzig*

The 100th *Mittelschule* is a little outside of town in a Leipzig suburb. The neighborhood is made up of high-rise housing blocks and the school is in a rundown building, painted pale yellow, and covered in graffiti. A four-lane motorway runs alongside it. The 100th is completely closed to the outside; you have to ring the bell to enter. "Security measures," explained the (female) principal, "you never know . . ." The doors only open onto the courtyard during break times. The neighborhood is known for its "occasional violence" among "extreme-right groups." "But they've left our school," said one teacher, "they were among our students, a few years ago, but they're working now. Among the younger ones, it's finished." The students interviewed from this school come from disadvantaged backgrounds. What sets their parents apart is the high percentage of long-term unemployment, particularly among the mothers, some of whom lost their jobs during reunification (*Wende*) and were never reemployed.

These are mostly children of employees with a few shopkeepers. The general profile of students overall is hardly more favorable. The parents' qualifications correspond to their SPC.

Most of these parents obtained a diploma from the *Polytechnische Oberschule* (POS); very few only have a primary school certificate, which is perhaps

Table 0.8 Socio-professional categories of the parents of students interviewed at the 100th. Three students do not know their father.

SPC	Craftsmen, retail traders, business owners	Senior executives, intellectual professions (including teachers)	Intermediate professions	Employees, service personnel	Workers	Home-makers	Unem-ployed (for more than 4 years)	Total
Mother	1	0	1	2	0	1	6	11
Father	2	0	0	2	2	0	2	8
Total	3	0	1	3	5	0	8	19

Table 0.9 Educational qualifications of parents of students interviewed at the 100th.

Parents' education	Primary school	Polytechnische Oberschule	High school diploma	University studies	PhD	Total
Mother	0	10	1	0	0	11
Father	1	5	2	0	0	8
Total	1	15	3	0	0	19

linked to the fact that they are younger than the parents in Hamburg. Instead of three generations since the war, here there are often four. In the east, there are more generations because parents had their children at a younger age. These parents were of the generation born in the 1960s.

Although there was massive immigration in the FRG after the 1960s, immigration in the GDR was much more limited, with a specific geographical focus on Southeast Asia, in particular Vietnam and Laos, which is absent from this particular suburb.[28]

A "Post-Wall" Generation

Born between 1984 and 1989, the students interviewed in this study are in a shared generational location,[29] even though difference between old and new *Länder* have far from disappeared. One essential difference consists in the smaller generation gaps in the east. Thus, among the students interviewed in Leipzig (and for whom I have this information), twenty belong to the fourth generation since the war (their four grandparents were born between 1935 and 1950). Five students have two grandparents born before 1931, and some have great-grandparents still living.

The students in Hamburg and Leipzig are quite similar in terms of their political concerns. Indeed, the events that they refer to—especially international events—are the same: the war in Iraq, US policy. In terms of domestic policy, unemployment is their primary concern and is still more of a sensitive subject in the east than in the west. Xenophobia is also a recurring theme. They are too young to have experienced the fall of the Berlin Wall and unified Germany constitutes their central political reference point. Their knowledge about the former division of the country remains very vague, although effective divisions continue to exist. We can see this in the phenomenon of *Ostalgie* (nostalgia for East Germany) incarnated by certain products and cultural practices, such as the German films *Sonnenallee* (Sun Alley), directed by Leander Haußmann in 1999,[30] or the 2003 film *Good Bye Lenin!* by Wolfgang Becker.[31] These films mobilize objects considered representative of the former GDR such as Trabant miniature cars, "walking signal" key rings (nicknamed *Ampelmännchen*, little man with a big hat), or indeed the expressions *Ossi/Wessi* themselves, which all became "endangered species" after the reunification.

Like most citizens in pluralist regimes, and particularly the youngest among them (Percheron 1978), most of the respondents, aged between fourteen and eighteen, show little interest in politics. Their opinions are not well reasoned, and they do not consider themselves socially or technically competent in this area. For example, they are not able to identify the main political parties, nor feel themselves socially authorized to express their opinions because of their age (see Bourdieu 1979; Gaxie 1978; Memmi 1985).

A Micro-Comparative Approach

These social differences and specificities constitute the primary material and interest of this study, which applies a comparative monographical approach (Beaud 1996), using four case studies—four school monographs—in order to observe differences and similarities. The micro-level analysis is inspired by Italian micro-history (Ginzburg [1976] 1980, [1979] 1980, 1993), oral history (Perks and Thompson 1998), and *Alltagsgeschichte* or history of the everyday (Lüdtke 1995a, 1998, and 2006). In particular, it follows the founding studies by German historians Lutz Niethammer and Alexander von Plato, who studied the forms of appropriation of the Nazi past in the 1980s in the Ruhr (Niethammer and von Plato 1983–1985). The comparative approach reduces the risk of over or under interpretation of processes that might be explicable only in a local context. The objective of this analysis is to develop a more general argument, beyond the singularity that can be observed in a particular case. Comparison helps us to achieve this, "with the belief that these minuscule lives also participate, in their way, in 'grand' history, which they give a different, discrete, complex vision of" (Passeron and Revel 2005).

Introduction • 25

We therefore seek to document "massive phenomena," in this case the forms of appropriation of the Nazi past, by "perceiving individual strategies, individual or familial biographic trajectories, of the men [women and children], who have been confronted with them" (Revel 1996: 12). These individual strategies provide clues about the importance of political facts that are outside the direct control of individuals, who are living history on a daily basis (Levi [1985] 1989: 14).

The Different Methods of the Study

The observational approach, combined with interviews, allows us to identify the classroom interactions between students and teachers, but also between students. Here we must remember that German classes are run slightly differently than they are elsewhere. For example, the traditional lecture-style class has almost entirely disappeared in Germany, replaced by work on documents, research projects, and group discussions. This process of the disappearance of traditional lecture-style class is in itself a collective moral lesson of the authoritarian regime. This is facilitated by the freedom that teachers have in choosing the way they teach history—the ministerial and *Länder* curriculum is only specified in general terms—and by the importance of classroom assessment in the evaluation of students. It is therefore possible to observe the student interaction in class relatively easily. Conversely, these interactions can only be understood in light of the sociological biography of the protagonists (see Beaud 1996). Interviews open up the possibility of analyzing representations of the past, both with teachers and students, and provide additional information about their trajectories, their social origins, and even the roles of their grandparents during the war. After these interviews I was in a better position to understand their interactions in class—particularly with regard to the students—and to interpret them in light of this information. Between February 2002, when I started my first preliminary interviews, and September 2004, at the end of the fieldwork, 137 interviews were conducted (including thirty-two with teachers), between one and ten hours long and two hours long on average. In addition to this, I performed approximately two hundred hours of observation in history classes.[32]

I began the interviews with a question about German history, asking the students to tell me if there was an event, a moment, or a period in the history of their country that they found particularly interesting. This was an open question, which was intended to gage the importance of Nazism in their lives.[33] Although the older adolescents and those from more privileged backgrounds were able to speak freely at length about this, the interview protocol[34] turned out to be essential (although insufficient) for younger respondents or those from less privileged backgrounds with whom the interviews were also shorter. The specific difficulties encountered during interviews on "history" with students from working-class families were therefore compensated for by the observations carried out in class and during break times.

I concluded the interviews with a questionnaire in order to associate their discourses with key sociological information concerning them individually. This made the analysis easier and provides a summary document.[35] This questionnaire contains a problematic but nevertheless important question. I asked the interviewees to rank their parents and grandparents in four categories, according to their relationship to Nazism: member/supporter, *Mitläufer* (follower),[36] resister, and persecuted. Almost all the teachers, as well as a large number of students asked that I add an extra category: "passive resister-fighter" (*passive Wiederstandskämpfer*), which is an oxymoron that seems devoid of sense. This expression reveals a certain uneasiness among the interviewees to categorize their family members, which is certainly provoked by the simplistic nature of such categorization—obliging them to judge their parents and grandparents before an outsider (the interviewer).[37] This request therefore does not automatically mean that the interviewees see their parents and grandparents as "heroes." However, it does demonstrate the limitations of the questionnaire approach for this kind of research. Indeed, the range of possible responses was specifically designed to oblige the respondents to judge their grandparents without explaining their choice: categorizing them as "collaborators" corresponds to a moral condemnation of one's grandparents before the interviewer; categorizing them as "resister" when it is not entirely justified is akin to "glorification." This therefore provokes them to refuse this conflictual situation. This "exit strategy" (Hirschman 1970) is expressed through the embarrassment of the respondents and their desire to add an additional category that does not oblige them to choose. The focus groups and individual in-depth repeated interviews provide better insight into the ambiguity and complexity of the relations between generations.

The distribution of the interviews is not perfectly balanced. Given that I had the possibility to follow a class at Weinberg for a whole year (once a week for their history class), I interviewed all the students in that ninth grade class. This was the opportunity to access students with low grades, or those who see themselves as struggling, in a "good school." Unfortunately, due to lack of time, this intensive approach was not possible in the other schools. An in-depth case study in Weinberg and a relatively in-depth case study in Wiesi are thus compared with less in-depth studies at the *Gymnasium* Monnet and the *Mittelschule* in Leipzig (Oeser 2007a).

Co-constructing Discourses through Interviews

It is now standard practice to be attentive to the role of the interviewer in both observation and interviews, and to be aware of their possible contribution to the production of the interview material, in particular in the construction of biographical coherence after the fact (Bertaux 1980, 1981; Bourdieu 1986; Peneff 1990; Pudal 1989). The biographical approach, but also all social science analysis more generally, constructs a kind of artificial coherence that otherwise may have remained fragmented and incoherent. Moreover, the relationship between the interviewer and the interviewee involves a certain amount of retrospective reconstruction, because it obliges the interviewer to create a coherent discourse where the interviewee does not necessarily see any. Attempting to reconstruct the meaning that social actors give to their own actions can only ever be a provisional result, and the analysis must take into account the situation in which this construction of meaning was collectively created. However, it is important to try to identify the social logics at work in these temporary reconstitutions, as much as in the social trajectories of the interviewees.

The theme of the Nazi past presents specific interview challenges. Although it is relatively easy to get respondents talking about the school, family history is another matter entirely. The emotional weight of this subject is sometimes so strong that three of my interviewees broke down and cried, others became verbally aggressive toward me—and one left the room mid-interview and never came back. I encountered difficulties similar to those described by Olivier Schwartz during his research into the private lives of workers. However, they were exacerbated here by the fact that this research concerns not only the intimate private lives of respondents, but investigation of a past that is taboo, even shameful. The "breech of intimacy" is thus even more invasive. Through the relationship of trust I was able to establish with the interviewees, I created conditions that enabled me to "steal": their trust, their intimacy, and their family pride. Revealing my own family history[38] in the interview context might have facilitated their openness, but engaging in what Schwartz calls "the [excessive] gift of the self, often grueling, is also perverse because it is essentially manipulative: we open ourselves up to theft so that we may steal in our turn" (Schwartz 1990: 53).

"Why Are You Spying on Us?"

Conducting observation in the classroom is not always easy because of the dual relationship established: with the teachers on one hand and with the students on the other. Just as with any fieldwork, it is first necessary to "find one's place." The presence of an observer in a classroom breaks a kind of taboo—classes are always held behind closed doors. For German teachers the situation evokes the *Referendariat*, the two-year inspection period during which trainee teachers have to teach in front of a more experienced teacher. This is generally what my presence reminded some of the Hamburg teachers of. Mr Schulze, for example, always took the time after class to explain what he was doing during the class, as though I was a trainee teacher. This relationship was easier for the older teachers, because unlike the inspection, it put them in a position of prestige, as transmitting their knowledge and expertise. Ms Heide, a young teacher, who had just passed the exam, was more hesitant to allow me to attend her classes—seeing me more as a judge than as an apprentice (she had never had to train another teacher). Mr Schulze by comparison had trained several dozen young teachers and participated in many examination committees over the course of his thirty-year career.

In Leipzig, the situation was different. As I was born in Hamburg, I was first considered a *Wessi* in the former GDR. The image of the (Western) inspection is very present here. In this context it was the older professors who categorically refused to allow me to attend their classes, except when they were "obliged" to accept by the hierarchy, which was the case of Ms Seidengleich. The younger teachers, however, accepted me more readily. Ms Meersteiner, although she remained hesitant, saw herself as having had no teaching experience under the GDR (she started work in 1988), so she considered herself less likely to be stigmatized. Mr Wolff, who also allowed me to observe his class, had a particular legitimacy—as the new school principal he had been "certified" by the administration and was therefore "on the right side." To convince the teachers who remained reluctant I learned to openly talk about my West German origins from the very beginning of the interview. At this point I sometimes criticized the FRG to show—if not my neutrality—at least my openness to critical opinions and arguments. Because the interviews were long and repeated several times, I was able to overcome this suspicion by progressively establishing a relationship of trust.

When I began to follow Mr Schulze's class in Hamburg, the students found my presence strange. On the first day, my note-taking was a particular source of attention, even though I had already introduced myself to present my research. During a sports class at the end of the day, Karsten came to see me and asked: "Why are you spying on us?" (*Warum belauschen Sie uns?*) I did not have an answer. "I would like to get to know you," I replied. He remained skeptical, "So who am I then?" These adolescents felt observed and rightly so. My presence was disturbing to them. On that particular day, Lisa and Maren did not want to participate in sports and hid behind a nut tree near the field to collect some nuts. They realized that I had noticed them, and

Introduction • 29

with some irony, called out to me "We are collecting nuts. You can write that down in the log: Lisa and Maren collect nuts."

However, given I was there, they thought they might as well make the most of it. Later in the day, Elisabeth pulled me aside and said, "Can you convince the teacher that we can use a calculator on the exam?" She was disappointed when I explained that the math teacher is unlikely to listen to me. Not only was I constantly watching them, but I was also useless! This put me in a difficult position. It was when I decided to only attend the history classes that the relationship became easier and the students got used to my presence.

In addition to my fieldwork, I also studied the archives in Weinberg, where all the *Abitur* exams are preserved, dating back to 1983.[39] I also photocopied papers from exams held in the classes I observed (and corrections made by the teachers), and included them in the analysis. I also incorporated the films shown in the classes I attended and the documents distributed in class.

Describe, Record, Translate

I used a particular protocol in order to transcribe the interviews. The goal of an exact transcription, recording silences, laughs, and noises, was considered important in order to provide a reading that was the closest possible to what was actually said—even though moving from oral to written language is already an initial "translation." This is why I always re-listened to the recording when reading the interviews transcribed for the analysis. Interpretative comments were added (in brackets) in order to make the discussions easier to understand. As this book was originally published in French, a second translation came after the analysis—translating the interviews originally made in German into French. The temporality is important here. I was able to integrate my analysis of the German interviews into the French translation. A third translation came with the publication of the book in English. Throughout the book, I have worked closely with the translator to navigate between the French translation and the original German of the interviews. All translation (like all description) is already an interpretation (Geertz 1973), it is always open to critique and questions. This is why I have sometimes added the original German wording, and I have added explanations of the translations and choices made when it seemed particularly important.

Moreover, in order to reflect the casual language of the German remarks, I have sometimes chosen linguistically "incorrect" language, or informal or colloquial terms. What is important here is not so much the words themselves; the syntax, the intonation, and all the para-verbal clues contribute significantly to the meaning. A word-for-word translation would be unable to capture that. For example, in German, the end-of-phrase expressions (such as *und irgendwie sowas, nech*, "or something like that") add nothing semantically but make the phrase informal and casual. This playing with syntax exists in different forms in English (for example, the expressions "like" or "you know," which give an oral character to the phrase). It was therefore sometimes more important to me to convey the tone, the level of language, rather than to look for exact expressions that would be meaningless in different translations. There is therefore a significant distance between the French and the English translations of original German testimonies, due to the attention to colloquial language and the importance given to intonation and underlying tones. This also leads to a choice of expressions in French and English that seem more familiar than the German. This is not "dumbing down" the language but trying (wherever possible) to be faithful to expressions for which there is not always a direct equivalent in English. I therefore opted for a more liberal translation, with greater subjectivity in the hope of making it more rigorous. Indeed, given that it is difficult to transcribe intonations and effects of syntax (Beaud and Weber 1997) and even more difficult to translate them, I had to play with the language. This choice is linked to the belief that discourses have a range of meanings and we must attempt to translate them as a whole.

Indeed, language does not only convey thought, it also structures it. Translation, although sometimes complex, is also a means of making explicit that which is implicit in the "self-evidence" of communication; there are specific difficulties with translation because it always involves a transformation of thought. However, this approach has the advantage of being an explicit study of the implications and associations imposed by language as the primary frame of speech and therefore thought.

Personal Involvement

Richard Hoggart ([1957] 2006), in his "social self-analysis" of working-class culture, warned against the dangers of an author becoming psychologically involved in his or her object. From a working-class background himself, he was referring to his own tendency to be nostalgic about the old working-class culture and refuse recent changes—nostalgia against which he struggled during the whole process of writing of his book. Moreover, he noted

> a tendency in myself, because the subject is so much part of my origins and growth, to be unwarrantedly sharp toward those features in working-class life of which I disapprove. Related to this is the urge to lay one's ghosts; at the worst, it can be a temptation to "do down" one's class, out of a pressing ambiguity in one's attitudes to it. (Hoggart [1957] 2006: 4–5)

Like Hoggart (and perhaps like all researchers in social sciences), I chose to study a subject that resonated with me on a personal level. In my own analytic work, I found a similar tendency in the "tone, the unconscious emphasis and the rest" that reveal "the [woman] saying it" (Hoggart [1957] 2006: 5). As a university professor,[40] I undoubtedly had an ambiguous relationship with the teachers I interviewed, and perhaps a desire to set myself apart from them even more because they were close to me both in profession and origins (I am the daughter of a secondary school teacher). Hoggart pursued his analysis in emphasizing the fact that he was also likely to "overvalue the features of working-class life of which I approve . . . as though I was subconsciously saying to my present acquaintance—see, in spite of it all, such a childhood is richer than yours" (Hoggart [1957] 2006: 5). In my fieldwork, this tendency to idealize my origins appears through a more or less strong identification—or perhaps idealization?—with the students (particularly the students of the *Gymnasium*) who were receiving the same education I received. It is through comparison with other institutions and through my own self-reflexivity that I have tried to address this bias, as much as possible.

The risks associated with the researcher's involvement can also be found at another level. I am from a family in which both sides, maternal and paternal, were involved in Nazism. On my mother's side, my great uncle was a doctor in the SS (*Reichzarzt SS*) under Himmler, responsible for the coordination of medical experiments in the concentration camps. On my father's side, my grandfather was a member of the NSDAP (the National Socialist Party for German Workers) and director of a coal mine in Upper Silesia. The forced labor in the mines and the shootings at the end of the war caused the death of around two thousand prisoners of war and civilian workers. My family is trapped in a deep, three-generation silence about the crimes committed by family members. This omnipresent past had daily repercussions on my research and my writing that I had to constantly force myself to control. First, the family silence provoked in me a kind of "inquisitorial" attitude toward Nazism. This personal stance was most certainly the impetus of this research—although it was initially unconscious. In this sense, the researcher's involvement can be a resource, as well as a risk. But in universalizing my personal attitude, for a long time I was unable to refrain from morally condemning the interviewees who had not questioned their own family past. This was also a part of my need to "lay my ghosts to rest" combined with a kind of class-based ethnocentrism demanding a more or less intellectualized relationship to the Nazi past. Similarly, I have had to master a tendency to react positively to the ways of treating the Nazi past that I approved of, particularly when it involved a critical stance toward the family past—and therefore corresponded to my own approach.

In Leipzig, my position in relation to the fieldwork was not exactly the same. Here I dealt with the problems of being an outsider (a *Wessi*) rather than an insider. Moreover, my position was not so removed from that which Hoggart condemned as a "middle-class Marxist," observing the working class, rather open to populist interpretation, either by glorification or compassion for his or her object of study (see also Grignon and Passeron 1989; Revel 1986). My relationship toward the respondents in Leipzig was doubly influenced by my own position as a researcher with critical left-wing pretentions of the FRG. I was stuck between a tendency to idealize the socialist convictions of the teachers on the one hand, and on the other, to pity these "people of the East" recovering from dictatorship.

At this stage, I cannot improve upon Hoggart's conclusion that "a writer has to meet these struggles as [s]he can, and in the very process of writing" ([1957] 2006: 5).

The Chapters

The organization of this book follows an analytic structure, moving from the teachers and teaching framework to the students. Chapter by chapter it deals with different relations to Nazism—initially legitimate, and later illegitimate—and the practices of students' appropriations of the Nazi past, which follow different social logics: gendered, class, "anti-system," refusal, and last but not least, amusement or play. The first chapter will attempt to explain the conditions of emergence and the stages of a specific pedagogy used to transmit an "affective relation" to history and politics through the teaching of the Nazi past. It is known as the pedagogy of emotional upheaval (*Betroffenheitspädagogik*[41]). It consists in provoking the students' emotions, particularly through the use of audiovisual material in order to incite them to identify with the victims of history (Gudehus 2006). This identification should lead them to reject this past and adopt the more "suitable" political alternative: the pluralist regime. Pedagogical use of emotion works together with more "critical" uses however: the two are not exclusive and exist in parallel. The political "wager" underlying this approach, which contributes to the "burning" importance of the subject, is the (unverified) hypothesis that we only need to find the "right" relationship to the memory of Nazism in order to educate all the inhabitants of the Federal Republic as "good democratic citizens." This would avoid, among other things, citizens becoming racist and/or extremist, raising questions about civic education. This is the "wager" that is at the heart of the politico-pedagogical framework of the teaching of Nazism in Germany, even though or despite the fact that "ultimately we know very little about the true effects of education on the level of racism and other ethnocentric behavior" (Baudelot and Leclercq 2005: 95)[42]. The first chapter of the book aims to elucidate this "wager."

The second chapter deals with the "good students" and the social and school conditions that contribute to the adoption of the discourses on Nazism that are legitimate in the school context. What words should be used, what language, which images, how should one's responsibilities be described in order to succeed in class? However, beyond the simple relation between the students and teachers, other issues bring adolescents to develop particular relations to the Nazi past: some students even make this appropriation of the past the first step in a life-long path, drawing on their social and family trajectories, their involvement in a group (political militants, for example). We will use three case studies to look at the conditions that are favorable to such a transformation. It is from these questions that we leave the problems of pedagogy to focus on our central concern: the social frames of different forms of appropriation.

The first one of these frames will be covered in the third chapter. The forms of appropriation of the Nazi past obey gendered logics; whether in the classrooms, in the playground or around the family table, "gender" roles influence the way students position themselves, and how they give meaning to this past. This is because appropriating history is a social process, linked to the dispositions and situations of the students. Here, gender also serves to make connections between different universes (family, parents, brothers and sisters, peers, school) in which the continuity of gender relations will contribute to the strength of the influence of this factor on the way history is appropriated by the students.

The fourth chapter studies the way in which the students who are particularly interested in the Nazi past use their knowledge, often acquired outside school, to criticize the FRG. It shows that the students who combine several disadvantages at school (families in economic difficulties, low levels of cultural capital) will not make the same use of the Nazi past as those who have inherited more cultural capital. The form that their "anti-system" criticisms take depends on the context, social belonging, and the resources the students have at their disposal. From criticisms of public policies, to criticisms of the government system, these students use the Nazi past outside institutional rules and frameworks and/or teachers' expectations and sometimes directly against them.

The fifth chapter, however, analyzes the students who are not (or no longer) interested in the Nazi past in order to see the limits of these appropriations. The objective of this chapter is to understand the social conditions that lead to an impossibility to give meaning to the Nazi past, or to a certain tiredness about the subject.

A sixth and final chapter, more based on the sociology of interactions, sets out to identify the logics that are specific to the groups (of boys) who use the Nazi past in the playground to affirm their masculinity. Through jokes, insults, and teasing, the Nazi past is caricatured, used as a weapon, or used to make friends laugh. The teachers do not see these extracurricular uses of the past in a positive light, and most of the time they are performed out of their spheres of vision and influence. Although some students' comments might be "politically" shocking for the reader, the objective here is not to judge them, but to understand the social logics behind them.

Notes

1. Although quantitative analysis may not be sufficient in itself, it can provide an initial impression as to the media presence on the subject. This analysis is based on the study of the *Der Spiegel* index between 1969 and 2000. This index is organized by year and, in addition to the title, it contains a short description of the contents and keywords of each article.
2. Figures based on a frequency analysis using the index of the German National Bibliography (*Deutsche Nationalbibliographie* 1997-April 2002).
3. The term "extermination policy" refers to the genocide of Jews, Gypsies, and handicapped people, as well as the extermination of other targeted groups. The latter include political opponents and resistance members, particularly communists, Slavs, homosexuals, Freemasons, Jehovah's Witnesses, etc. Talking about an extermination policy emphasizes the fact that this was a rational policy that was planned by actors and implied conscious will. These criminals often remain absent, not only from the content of discourses on the past but also from the terms that are used in these discourses. It is therefore important to use a different terminology from that used by the interviewees. By using the adjective "National Socialist" or "Nazi," I am referring to the crimes planned by the National Socialist regime but put into place with the active support and passive tolerance of the immense majority of the German people, whether they explicitly adhered to the Nazi doctrine or not. On this particular problem, see, among others, Hilberg (1992).
4. The ARD (*Arbeitgemeinschaft der öffentlich-rechtlichen Rundfunkanstalten der Bundesrepublik Deutschland*) is the leading public television channel in Germany based on a consortium of regional channels: MDR (*Mitteldeutscher Rundfunk*), SWR (*Südwestrundfunk*), WDR (*Westdeutscher Rundfunk*), NDR (*Norddeutscher Rundfunk*), HR (*Hessischer Rundfunk*), SR (*Saarländischer Rundfunk*), RB (*Radio Bremen*), BR (*Bayerischer Rundfunk*), and RBB (*Rundfunk Berlin-Brandenburg*). The ARD is the only channel that agreed to send me documents including the index of the eight previous years of programs dealing with Nazi Germany, accompanied by a small description of each program, varying from one line to several paragraphs long. These documents provide the basis for this analysis.
5. The German expression "we must remember" (*wir müssen uns erinnern*) or "we must not forget" (*wir dürfen nicht vergessen*), which is closer to the English-language adage "lest we forget" evokes the moral duty to remember.
6. This is a distinction between three visions, but this clearly does not imply that there would be only one erudite way of learning history, only one political or one non-

specialist way. On the contrary, these categories each regroup thousands of ways of learning history.

7. The text of Halbwachs is based on the English translation by F. Dritter (1980) but has been amended when necessary.

8. Here we use the term "recollection" to emphasize the active dimension of memory, the act of recalling what Halbwachs illustrates above.

9. All the surnames and first names have been modified, as have the names of schools and sites, in order to ensure the anonymity of the respondents. The modified names have been chosen to reflect the way the interviewees presented themselves: with just their surname, their first and second names, or just their first name. This presentation seems to reflect the relationship I established with them, expressing more or less proximity and familiarity between interviewer and interviewee (using informal language and calling a teacher by their first name is not the same as remaining formal and using their surname). Because of this, I chose to preserve these differences, which reflect different relationships with respondents, even though it meant giving up a harmony that might have been easier for the reader. In order to better situate the respondents socially, a summary table presents the teachers' origins, ages, and places of training in Appendix 3 along with short biographies, including teachers' social characteristics in Appendix 4. Summaries for the students can be found in Appendix 5.

10. The didactics of history is a discipline in its own right in Germany.

11. Translated from the French, original translation from German by Alexandra Oeser.

12. It is important to recall that the initial interpretations and appropriations are in a constant state of flux, subject to permanent evolutions and reinterpretations. The term "reappropriation" is therefore used to cover all these processes and their evolutions.

13. These approaches consist, for example, in counting the turns and speaking time for boys and girls respectively in different classroom configurations, depending notably on the sex of the teacher, classroom diversity, etc.

14. On the question of the way Max Weber has been interpreted in France and the debates around the functioning of domination, the political order, and questions of obedience, see Darras (2008).

15. For an overall vision of the German school system, see Appendix 1.

16. The neighborhoods have been given (invented) pseudonyms to preserve their anonymity.

17. In view of the size of the fieldwork and the costs associated with it, and in light of the lack of funding available in human and social sciences, having access to accommodation at no cost for two years greatly facilitated this research.

18. This is an establishment created in the new (Eastern) *Länder* after reunification, inspired by the *Haupt* and *Realschule* of the old *Länder* (of the West). See Appendix 1.

19. Interview 18 February 2003.

20. Interview with Herbert Weise, 22 April 2003. All names are pseudonyms to preserve the anonymity of respondents. A list of participants cited in the text can be found in the appendices.

21. The left-wing party *Die Linke* did not yet exist at the time of the study. It was founded in 2007.

22. They have access to this information when organizing class trips, for example. Children whose parents receive social payments have access to financial assistance if they provide an attestation from the administration.

23. Informal conversation, 24 April 2003.

24. Hamburg is second only to Berlin in terms of the population of foreign nationals living there. The official figures only indicate a person's own nationality, so it is impossible to

have figures at the town level as to the percentage of people with foreign parents, or those who immigrated to Germany as children and acquired nationality since. There are no ethnic statistics in Germany.

25. The *Thomasschule* is the only school in Leipzig that has more than 50 percent of its teaching staff from the former *Länder* of the FRG, which is why it was eliminated from the study.

26. The GDR of the 1950s had a policy of massively increasing the overall level of education, which was particularly advantageous for workers and peasants, and especially for women. Only one quarter of the first generation of the GDR (the generation of the parents) left school after eight years, 10 percent went all the way to the final high school exams in the mid-1960s, and the rest ended their school career after ten years of schooling. In 1961, access to university was set at 6 percent of the total student population each year. In fact, this percentage put an end to a period of increasing access to higher education in the GDR and had consequences for the state regulation of this access (see Wierling 2002: 267–88).

27. Between 1959 and 1964, the law on the socialist construction of the school system in the GDR progressively replaced the eight years of primary school with a single school that lasted ten years, known as the *Polytechnische Oberschule* (POS). This school prepared students for the position that they would fulfill in socialist society. To pass the *Abitur* exams (for the high school diploma), one had to attend the *Erweiterte Oberschule* (EOS), which lasted twelve years. The move to the EOS happened after the eighth year of POS, by attending preparatory classes (Wierling 2002: 119–20). See also Table A.2 in Appendix 1.

28. In Leipzig, the foreign population remained under 3 percent for a long time, only rising to barely 5 percent since the 2000s.

29. Karl Mannheim distinguished "generational location" from "generational whole" and "generational unit," a distinction that allows a definition of connections that are more or less close between individuals within a cohort. Mannheim defined "generational location" (*Generationslagerung*) as belonging to a specific historico-social unit, which contains potential possibilities of providing structuring principles (Mannheim [1928] 1970). He talks about a generational whole "when real, social and intellectual, content . . . make real connections between the individuals who are in the same generational location." Even though they are in the same generational location, the students, unlike the teachers, do not (yet) belong to a generational whole. On the importance of Mannheim's generational theory for British sociology, see Pilcher (1994).

30. The film exists with English subtitles. It was adapted from the novel by Thomas Brussig, *Am kürzeren Ende der Sonnenallee* (Frankfurt/Main: Fischer Taschenbuch Verlag, 1999).

31. The film, screenplay by Bernd Lichtenberg and winner of many cinematographic awards, also exists with English subtitles.

32. One hundred of these interviews were fully transcribed, which corresponds to 2,500 pages of text. In addition, there are seven hundred pages of field notes written during the class observations and informal discussions in corridors or during meals. The fact that certain interviews were exceptionally long can be explained by the fact that I returned to see the interviewees several times, particularly the teachers. One non-directive biographic interview at the beginning was generally followed with a more directive interview, in which I asked specific questions about the events I had not understood as I re-transcribed the first interview. Then, during a third encounter I applied the interview protocol that can be found in Appendix 2.

33. The biographical approach is less relevant for adolescents because of their young age.
34. See Appendix 2.
35. See Appendix 2 for the model questionnaire distributed in Hamburg. It was slightly adapted for Leipzig.
36. The term *Mitläufer* (one who runs alongside), sometimes inappropriately translated as bystander in English, is often used in the context of a dictatorship, and in particular for Nazism, to refer to people who are not part of the resistance but who were not active members of the NSDAP or the authoritarian or dictatorial regime. This term refers to those who "went along," the German word implying a much more active perspective of contribution to the crimes. Created during the occupation after the war to distinguish the "real culprits" from those who did not deserve punishment, the term has changed in connotation. Instead of enabling a "positive" distinction, it became pejorative. We used the English term "follower" here to translate it, which has probably a slightly less pejorative connotation than the German.
37. The demand also expresses a desire to protect the reputation, and thus the symbolic capital, of the group.
38. See below, section "Personal Involvement."
39. The *Abitur* exam is held within the school, with normal classroom teachers.
40. At the time of writing, I was an assistant lecturer at the Institute of Political Studies in Toulouse, where I taught first and second year students who were scarcely three or four years older than the youngest students in the classes I was observing here.
41. This expression is difficult to translate because of its ambiguity. *Betroffenheit* means "emotion," but in German it may also refer to the fact of "being touched" by an event or even "being involved." In the theory of *Betroffenheitspädagogik* both of these meanings are present. They refer to the emotion felt by the students and their implication in the learning process. The expression "pedagogy of emotion" seems weak, and "emotional upheaval" seems to more adequately reflect the dual signification of this expression.
42. This observation is also true for Germany on the effects of politicization of memory policy specifically relating to Nazism.

Chapter 1

EDUCATION IN THE SERVICE OF DEMOCRACY

> History classes are always also civic education and poli-
> tics classes. Of course, I don't teach history for history's
> sake, but because *I hope*[1] that I can help the students to
> find their direction in today's world, and to teach them
> to develop specific attention, a sharp mind. You might
> ask, "What's a sharp mind?" It's, it's being informed,
> following current affairs, and possibly participating in
> them, as a responsible citizen, belonging to a society.
> —Ms Simone, interview of 9 April 2003

The connection between civic education and teaching history, mentioned
by the teacher in the quote above, is fundamental to democratic education. In Germany, civic education, *politische Bildung*, is not a discipline in
itself at school as it often is in other countries. Those who teach history,
ethics, religion, and social studies (*Gemeinschaftskunde*), or those who teach
Politik (a subject that combines history, geography, and social studies), in the
Gesamtschulen, are therefore also responsible for civic education.[2] The interpenetration between the teaching of history and civic education is therefore
at the very heart of the educational project that was progressively developed
in Germany in the wake of World War II, and this chapter will seek to understand its consequences.

In order to do this, it is important to begin by analyzing the development of a specific pedagogy that emerged in the 1970s–1980s and was

particularly "fashionable" in teaching National Socialism in the FRG: the *Betroffenheitspädagogik*, or the pedagogy of emotional upheaval.[3] We will then move on to look at the pedagogical objectives of the teaching of Nazi history, which aim to make a connection with the students' civic education. In order to try and understand the central place of the Nazi extermination policy in German history classes in this period, we will study the ways in which history teachers implement this pedagogy of emotional upheaval as part of their classes. We will conclude the chapter by looking at the limits of the use of this specific pedagogy in the way the students learn about Nazi history.

A Short History of *Betroffenheitspädagogik* in the FRG

This pedagogy has its roots in a debate about the role of emotions in politics, which dates back to the early twentieth century. It was an issue both during the Nazi period and at the beginning of the FRG and the GDR.

In the West Germany of the 1970s, in the wake of the 1968 student protests, a new movement in the didactics of history was launched. This movement emphasized the need to take into account the role of "feelings" in teaching this discipline and in teaching the history of Nazism in particular. After reunification, it encountered renewed interest among specialists, as we can see in two major conferences, one held in 1990 on the didactics of politics, and the other in 1991 on history (Mütter and Uffelmann 1992; Schiele and Schneider 1991). These conferences focused specifically on the problem of the role of emotion in learning about history, drawing on Gestalt pedagogy (*Gestaltspädagogik*) and pedagogy of action (*Erlebnispädagogik*), both of which were widely discussed during the 1970s and 1980s (Brown 1978; Gies 1995; Petzold and Brown 1977; Schulz-Hageleit 1987).

Betroffenheitspädagogik is the product of a broader political and social movement that distanced itself from the cognitive perception of the past. Analyzed by Alf Lüdtke (1993b), it reintegrated "emotion" into the analysis and practice of didactics. In other words, the pedagogy of emotional upheaval emphasized the usefulness of being able to "persuade" students on an emotional level. The American television series *Holocaust*, which aired in Germany in 1979, clearly illustrates this change in approach. Indeed, its phenomenal success could lead us to think that it played a role in creating an emotional breakthrough in the population's consciousness on the theme of the national socialist past (Lüdtke 1993b). As far as the Nazi past is concerned, this call for emotion can be explained by the political criticism regarding the lack of empathy for the suffering of the victims among the population and political actors in post-war Germany.

As early as 1945, the Allied Forces attempted to address this lack of empathy by organizing (forced) visits to the concentration camps just after their liberation, for the inhabitants of the neighboring towns and often for people in administrative positions within the town. They were therefore obliged to witness the reality of the camps and sometimes to bury the dead prisoners. There are photographs of these visits showing German people next to mountains of bodies, sometimes stone-faced but most often shocked. The German historian Habbo Knoch (2001: 127) provides a highly relevant explanation as to why these photos were displayed. Because they were considered a proof of the atrocities of this war, the bodies were arranged in such a way as to shock the viewer as much as possible. At Buchenwald, for example, piles of bodies were actually reconstructed several times in the week following the liberation of the camps, in order to show them to German visitors and to photograph them (Knigge 1996: 201–3). These photographs were used by the occupying forces to raise awareness, first through international newspapers, and then, from April 1945, through the Allied press in Germany. From mid-May 1945, the photographs of the bodies in the camps were displayed on posters in shop windows with slogans such as "These atrocities: your fault!" (H. Knoch 2001: 143–44, Brink 1998: 23–99). The use of emotion in the "reeducation" of the German people was therefore present in the Allies' news campaign policies immediately after the war. Knoch emphasized the spontaneous nature of this awareness-raising campaign, which has still not been widely studied. The objective of these information policies was to "stamp out the whole tradition on which the German nation ha[d] been built" and to teach democracy to the German people (PRO FO 371/3909, quoted by H. Knoch 2001: 124). From June 1945 however, after only five weeks of this news campaign, the Allies were forced to recognize the limits of these accusatory policies (H. Knoch 2001: 154). Knoch mentions several factors that contributed to the progressive disappearance of Nazi crimes from the media: the effects of the images were unclear; the Cold War and anti-communism contributed to a change in the Western Allies' news campaign; de-Nazification was complete; and the foundation of the FRG in 1949 meant that economic reconstruction took precedence over the past (H. Knoch 2001: 157).

Moreover, the use of emotion became somewhat suspect in intellectual spheres in the second half of the 1940s and the early 1950s. Arguments warning against this approach emphasized the role that emotion played in the rise of Nazism: intentionally used by the dictatorship in its propaganda and as a tool for the manipulation of the masses (Lüdtke 1993b: 550).

Yet the absence of emotion in the political field and the lack of empathy with the victims of Nazism were concretely translated into very restrictive laws and legal practices relating reparation to the victims (Lüdtke 1993b).[4] This can also be seen in the focus of official compassion for the "German victims" (in particular the widows of soldiers, considered victims of "Nazi propaganda"), through governmental laws that led to financial support being primarily reserved for these people. This tendency for Germans to set themselves up as war victims during the 1950s (H. Knoch 2001: 161, 225–37) also led to the emergence of a specific discourse that would reappear thirty years later in the *Betroffenheitspädagogik*. Throughout the 1950s the "never again" discourse was framed in terms of "this war that brought us so much unhappiness."

The new incidences of neo-Nazism in the 1970s made political leaders in the FRG realize that teaching facts alone was not enough to change political opinions. There was thus a return to emotion or empathy, in the tradition of the postwar news policies of the US and British Allies. They once again took on their dual role, both political and pedagogical. On one hand, they aimed to recognize the suffering of the victims of Nazism, and on the other, to halt the growth of neo-Nazism among the "young," thus becoming a tool for the "democratization" of society. The German precursors of "emotion" as a political and pedagogical tool belonged to the small circle of *Geschichtswerkstätten* (history workshops).[5] Since the 1970s, various kinds of history, *Alltagsgeschichte* (history of everyday life) (Lipp 1995; Lüdtke 1995a, 1998, 2006), *Subjektgeschichte* (subject history), and *Lokalgeschichte* (local history), or *Mikrogeschichte* (micro history) (Ginzburg and Poni 1985; Medick 1996: 13–38; 1999; Schlumbohm 1998) were mobilized in these workshops. There was also a political approach that aimed to give increased visibility to the victims of fascism[6] and to "account" for the individual significance of their suffering, often lost in the sheer number of victims. The explicit objective of many of the members of these *Geschichtswerkstätten* was close to that of the Allied politicians responsible for informing the German population after the war; they sought to provoke an emotional upheaval, *Betroffenheit*. The difference here was of course that the intended audience was now the children of those directly involved in the war. Alf Lüdtke has critically analyzed the implications of this approach to *Betroffenheit*, in particular concerning the "moral security" of its authors (Lüdtke 1995b). Inspired by Christa Wolff, he proposed the concept of *Anteilnahme* (empathy) as a replacement for *Betroffenheit*. According to Lüdtke, *Anteilnahme*, instead of aiming to change the perception of the other, aims to understand them, but also to understand oneself. By contrast, *Betroffenheit*, in particular as it is applied to German fascism, is seen as having a tendency to simplify historical complexity by studying "victims only (or pure victims)" instead of taking into account the usual simultaneity of shared responsibility and guilt (*Mit-täterschaft*) and the status of victimhood (*Opfersein*) (Lüdtke 1995b).

From the mid-1980s and despite the existing critique from professional historians, pedagogy adopted the objectives of *Betroffenheit* to apply them specifically to the teaching of the Nazi period in secondary school. Some even saw in this the beginning of a "new phase of antifascist education" (Reich and Stammwitz 1989: 106), which would try to take into account the students' emotions." The historian Falk Pingel, for example, considers that from the 1980s—which he sees as a period of the institutionalization of change or "securing the achievements" (Pingel 2000: 19)—the critiques expressed by historians against a treatment of Nazism that ignores the suffering of the victims, but also the responsibility of the majority of the German population, had been taken into account at least in school textbooks. Alongside this, a more intense treatment of the period between 1933 and 1945 emerged in history classes (G. Schneider 1991: 170). This intensification can be seen, for example, in the role given to this theme in the school textbooks (Schatzker 1992). The reasoning behind this project is the following: the more the students are able to identify with the individual actors[7]—and in particular the victims—the more they will be deeply affected by the teachings on the subject. The concept of *forschendes Lernen* (learning through research) is linked to the concept of *Betroffenheit*. Interpreted here in the sense of "being moved by," this approach hypothesizes that students will be more "concerned" (*betroffen*) by the past if they discover it for themselves in local archives or through interviews with those who witnessed it (see Dudek 1989; Kolinsky 1991, 1992).

Questions about the population's participation in the Nazi extermination policy, and thus the question of their guilt (C. Schneider 1998), becomes central here because from this perspective it represents a "learning opportunity" (Wenzel and Weber 1989: 133) to guide the students toward political responsibility. New resources in didactics, such as visits to the concentration camps, use of novels on the subject, and discussions with survivors are all considered means for provoking the sought-after empathy. Thus the "concept" of concentration camps as "sites of learning" was born. It was also considered important that both the study of the perpetrators and the suffering of their victims should take place on the sites of the crimes in order to better generate emotions (Gudehus 2006).[8]

Educational specialists called this "new pedagogy" *Betroffenheitspädagogik*. They emphasized two key objectives, which closely resemble those of the Allied reeducation policy. This policy was to be a remedy against neo-Nazism and the rise in xenophobic violence in Germany; it was also intended to ensure the students' engagement with history as a discipline, but also with democratic citizenship. The teaching of the Nazi past was thus implicitly assimilated to civic education. *Betroffenheit* became an indicator of *Demokratiefähigkeit* or the democratic abilities of the students. The teaching of the history of Nazism appeared to be nothing less than the key to the democratization process.

44 • When Will We Talk about Hitler?

This movement continues in Germany, in spite of the criticism it has attracted—since the mid-1980s—from several educational historians (see Eberhard 1986; Gagel 1985) who considered that the cognitive processes at work in the learning of history were underestimated by the *Betroffenheitspädagogik*. This pedagogy remains the subject of debate. The essayist Cora Stephan has criticized it (1993) for being a whole society's "cult of emotion" (*Betroffenheitskult*); the historian Horst Gies condemned it more particularly for its potentially dangerous consequences (Gies 1995: 140, in particular). By comparing the didactics used under National Socialism and in the GDR, Gies establishes a correlation between the weakening of scientific knowledge and the pedagogical use of emotion.

The Use of Emotion in the GDR

Without completely adopting this comparison, which could be problematic because of the normative judgment it implies,[9] it may be useful to pause over the pedagogical methods used in the GDR in order to "contextualize" the two empirical cases in Leipzig that are studied in this book. Didactic methods in the GDR emphasized the connection between "historical logic and emotion" (Schörken 1992: 99). The goal of this was to teach a "love of the GDR" (Wierling 2000). A focus on certain Communist heroes such as Ernst Thälmann explicitly emphasized the emotional aspect of this teaching. Although emotion was not used in the GDR to provoke empathy toward the Jewish victims, the approach was similar. To take just one example, Communist resister-fighters who had been interned in one of the camps were regularly invited to come and talk to the students in class about their experience. This was a pedagogic practice commonly used by many of the teachers. Communists, both victims and heroes, were particularly well situated to mobilizing emotions as part of the teaching of history. Ms Norte, a forty-year-old teacher at the *Gymnasium* Monnet in Leipzig, immediately mentioned "emotion" when asked about the similarities and differences in teaching about Nazism before and after reunification: "We have—always, when I think of my time in the GDR—relied a bit on emotions. And so, emotional classes, we have thought about them a lot, we began them with literature, poetry, or other things—we played songs."[10] The transposition of the emotional framework to another group of victims does not seem that problematic, even if certain teachers[11] in Leipzig insist on the need to broaden the students' emotional relationship to history—beyond just the Jewish victims. Ms Norte, for example, explained that she likes to teach National Socialism because "emotion, it always plays a big role. Even if [she pauses] we shouldn't only associate it with the Jewish policy (*Judenpolitik*), I think, but also with the fate of the soldiers."[12]

Education in the Service of Democracy • 45

Ms Norte was the program coordinator (*Fachleiterin*) for history at the *Gymnasium* Monnet and she found a way of combining different visions of history through the use of emotion. Indeed, identification with soldiers (particularly Soviet soldiers) was very common in the GDR; she transposed this to German soldiers in the context of reunified Germany.

> For example, letters from the front. Stalingrad. [Smiling, she goes on.] I have a large collection [of sources]—where they [she hesitates]—where it's the soldier—on the wrong side—the German soldier, who is posted outside Stalingrad, and who is also a human being, in the end. He was obeying orders. But as a human being, he suffered as much as the one on the other side, on the Russian side. And that—or, through the Jewish policy (*Judenpolitik*),[13] we can do important things.[14]

For Ms Norte, the key reference remains the Russian soldier (she also stressed that "we only talked about the Red Army in the GDR"[15]). But now, she was able to emphasize that "in the end" the German soldier "suffered just as much." This did not stop her from also drawing attention to the Jewish suffering, although she talked about it in less concrete terms, without referring to the sources that spontaneously came to her mind, such as letters from the front line. In Leipzig, the use of emotion in history class was another way for the teachers to facilitate the change between regimes. It represented a continuity in the pedagogic approach that enabled teachers to reuse knowledge acquired in the GDR after unification, by marginally adapting it to the new context (taking into account the Jewish genocide and enlarging the categories of victims). The success of the *Betroffenheitspädagogik* in Leipzig can be explained by its ability to bridge the pre- and post-1989 worlds.

This is how the category of the victims was extended to Jews and how the inclusion of the Holocaust in the emotional pedagogy was internalized without any difficulty by the teachers in Leipzig. Sometimes this even occurred without leaving any noticeable "traces," and sometimes without the teachers remembering differences with the official historiography of the GDR.

Mr Wolff, the principal of the *Gymnasium* Monnet in Leipzig, expressed his surprise at the lack of this subject in the GDR, saying that he does not remember it personally.

> Before, it wasn't—well, I read a comparison [between history textbooks from the GDR and the FRG]—I didn't want to believe it. It didn't play a role in GDR, the persecution of the Jews. Almost not at all. And that's what it's like when you look at the history books, it's not there. There's maybe a short paragraph. And it's not referred to as the Holocaust either. It's really, really, really minor. Otherwise, it's the major role of the antifascists and the Communists, of course presented as real heroes, and then logically the analysis is that they

[the Communists] should have power in the GDR. Because they played a decisive role. Today, it's not the same. . . . that doesn't play a role anymore.[16]

Mr Wolff, "couldn't believe" that the genocide was not mentioned in the history textbooks of the GDR, even though he used these manuals himself at the beginning of his career. He did remember the role of the Communists perfectly, however. Moreover, he did not fail to use the latter as an example to criticize the textbooks "from the West" that do not sufficiently cover the Communist resistance, to his mind. This is also a subject of discontent among the other teachers in Leipzig: the presentation of the resistance in the textbooks of the GDR sometimes seems to them more adequate than in today's textbooks.[17]

In Leipzig, emotion was also used in teaching the more recent past, that of the Communist regime, sometimes through an explicit comparison with the Nazi past. Underpinning this is the question of responsibility for these crimes; particularly the responsibility of parents and grandparents during the Nazi period, but also the responsibility of teachers and parents regarding the GDR government. After listing the things she saw as important, apart from the Jewish Holocaust, Ms Norte continued,

> I also look at [she hesitates] the comparison with the GDR. And we can ask parents. Or the students can ask their parents. When they're so quick to say, "Never the GDR, never. We never should have voted for them or we never should have done this or that." It's not the same, when you've lived in a system, experienced it, than when you say, with hindsight, "I can't understand. How could they [elect] a Hitler, or a Honecker," or whatever, isn't it?[18]

This comparison of the suffering and the responsibility between the Nazi regime and the GDR regime remains specific to the teachers in Leipzig. In Hamburg, none of the teachers propose a comparison between the Nazi regime and the USSR or the GDR in this context. This difference might be explained by the fact that for the teachers in Leipzig the "treatment of the recent past" may seem personally urgent in a way it is not for Hamburg teachers.[19]

The Goals of Teaching the Nazi Past

The ways the teachers interpret the Nazi past are connected to their definition of "democracy" and "good citizenship." Using the distinction between a regime of faith and a regime of reason that Jacques Lagroye (2006) established for the priests of the Catholic Church, it is possible to identify the characteristics that the teachers consider necessary in order to become a "good citizen" according to the regime they believe in. However, the two variants (faith versus reason) are not contradictory and may coexist within the teachers' discourses. The relationship toward democracy also allows us to understand the pedagogic tools used in the transmission of the Nazi past.

Regimes of Faith

What is commonly referred to as the duty of remembrance in English[20] is formulated in German as "it must not be forgotten." The debate about the "right" way to remember takes here, as elsewhere, the form of an order: do not forget. The German phrase *es darf nicht vergessen werden*, quite close to the other common English formulation "lest we forget," is constantly mobilized in the interviews and during the history classes, both by the students and by the teachers. It operates as though the fact of remembrance was the first (and perhaps the only) duty, a sort of prerequisite condition to prevent Auschwitz from "ever happening again," and to bring about that "never again." In this sense, "Auschwitz" becomes the crystallization, not only of the crimes of the extermination policy, but also of how they are remembered.

Mr Gerste, a forty-year-old teacher at the *Gesamtschule* Wiesi in Hamburg, explicitly described the active memory of the Nazi past as a duty (*Verpflichtung*). "Using," "revisiting," and "working through" the past—this is the "duty" of all Germans.[21] Mr Gerste made an opposition between a simple "act of remembering" and "truly working through the past." This mobilizes the notion of "duty of remembrance" as it was formulated by the German political scientist Gesine Schwan (1997), or by the psychologist Birgit Rommelspacher (1995). According to these researchers, who adopt a normative stance, citizens have a "moral obligation" to "intensely and honestly" confront their past. This "duty" becomes a "professional obligation" for teachers. "As teachers, we have a duty to cover and work on these subjects in the course of our history lessons," said Mr Gerste.

The common refrain of "we must remember" may also be sung because it weakens or masks the differences in the politics of memory between the former FRG and GDR. The categorical imperative of the fight against forgetting constitutes a common denominator for two interpretations of the past that start from very different places, yet which come together on this point: the Nazi extermination policy was condemned on both sides of the wall.

Thus, in spite of the differences that continue to exist between the two Germanies, a consensus seems to have been reached (including in the classroom) regarding the two "paradigms" of remembrance: the "never again" and the "duty of remembrance." For the teachers, the transmission of the Nazi past reflects a belief, the feeling that they are on a mission that will contribute

48 • When Will We Talk about Hitler?

to saving democracy and making "good citizens" who believe in and are committed to the political system, and who follow humanist values. We can call this collective belief a regime of faith.

"Duty of Remembrance" and "Never Again"

The moral imperative of "never again" (*nie wieder*), which the teachers mobilize, is the equivalent of a "categorical imperative" as formulated by Theodor W. Adorno, in reference to Emmanuel Kant, in the 1960s in the FRG: "Hitler has imposed a new categorical imperative upon humanity . . .: to arrange their thoughts and actions in such a way that that Auschwitz should never be repeated, that nothing of the sort should ever happen again" (Adorno [1959] 2003: xiv).

All the interviewees agree that the horrors of Nazism "have to be remembered," since evoking them would provoke intense and immediate repulsion. For the teachers, this can constitute a political lesson in itself of the affective and intimate conviction that this must "never happen again." On this point, Mr Schulze said,

> The theme of Auschwitz means: "that must never happen again. And you must, with all your senses, integrate [he hesitates] why it must never happen again. And that must stay in your memory for your whole life, what you saw at Auschwitz." And I think that is the case, for the people who have been there; I don't think I could forget what I saw. I don't think the students will ever forget either. I think I don't need to explain what it means to say "Auschwitz is political."[22]

Ms Neumeier, from the *Gymnasium* Monnet in Leipzig and Ms Seidel from the 100th *Mittelschule* both also explained that the classes on Nazism are intended to warn the students, so that "nobody can say that it couldn't happen again today."[23]

Underlying this idea of "never again" is the fear of a return to the conditions capable of making the Nazi extermination policy once again conceivable or even possible. Mr Hatze, a fifty-year-old teacher at Weinberg, expressed his concern over the students' lack of interest in history classes. He saw a difference in his representation of the importance of Nazism and the students' perspective. For him, the fact that he was "influenced by working through the past," which "created values, not only concerning this period, but in general," is both a weight and an opportunity. The constant presence of the crimes of Nazism in peoples' minds constitutes, for him, a guarantee of peace.

Ms. Neumeier, a teacher at *Gymnasium* Monnet in Leipzig, aged around forty years old, emphasized the political urgency of this process of "working through the past."

Education in the Service of Democracy • 49

Because—I think that lots of factors—that we know about historically—
are back: unemployment, loss of hope, and we can see it, the meetings, in
Leipzig, you've seen it! And we have lots of gangs. Not so much in our school.
We don't really have extreme-right gangs, with Doc Martens and so forth,
who [show themselves] in public—but they think it's good, even so! [She
suddenly lowers her voice.] And on the internet, there is really lots of stuff,
unfortunately. Medals, or brutality, in video games, I really find it abomi-
nable. And that's really very dangerous. We really need to be careful and be
responsible. Yes.[24]

Ms. Neumeier's discourse illustrates a slip from the concrete (the question of the students' admiration for Nazism in class) to a contemporary fear
of neo-Nazism (even if she admits that it is not particularly present in her
school), and ends with an evocation of internet violence, a medium that the
teachers do not master and therefore causes them anxiety. Neo-Nazism thus
becomes a sort of symbolic incarnation of the evils of society that the teachers
are wary of.

Fear of neo-Nazism and racism are thus present in the teachers' comments, possibly even more so in those schools where the actual occurrence of
extreme-right engagement of students is highly unlikely. At the *Gymnasium*
Weinberg, for example, the presence of a single neo-Nazi student in the
1980s still provoked animated discussion among the teachers twenty years
later—much more than in places like the 100th *Mittelschule* where the
extreme-right is more of a reality.

This fear is often based on concrete experiences. Mr Herzog, for example,
told me how some students from his class at Wiesi were attacked by skinheads
with baseball bats "because there was a black guy with us."[25] These are typical
anecdotes,[26] told by students as well as by teachers. They often take place in
the former GDR or overseas, always in exceptional situations (while traveling
for example). There are two main variations of this story, which sometimes
merge together. They seem to emphasize the interpenetration of the Nazi
past and the representations of the danger of contemporary neo-Nazism. The
first version is that told by Mr Herzog: the class was attacked by "neo-Nazis"
because one of them was perceived as being foreign. The second version is a
variation on this theme, most often happening in England, or sometimes in
other European countries such as Italy or France, and more rarely in Eastern
European countries or in Russia. In this version, the class is attacked by the
foreigners "because they are Germans, and therefore considered to be Nazis."[27]

Pre-existing frameworks for interpretation are projected onto the teachers'
narratives; the Nazi past and the "guilt" of the German people who are associated with it constitute as much a frame of interpretation for these anecdotes
as racism and neo-Nazism. Interpretations of the past merge with the danger
of the present in these typical narratives told by the teachers.

The symbolic effect of neo-Nazism is powerful enough to sometimes lead to the danger being over-estimated; some teachers see "racism" everywhere. Karen Werthe for example, was particularly uneasy about "gang fights."

> I hope that this time, with the intensive coverage of the subjects of the Jews and the camps (*das Thema Juden und KZ's*), [she hesitates] I hope that they will genuinely understand, that they will interiorize, really. And that they [she hesitates again] that they will understand the consequences and perhaps they will apply that, because our school is really multicultural. And that they manage to put that into practice, as well, in two or three years. [She hesitates again.] So that they don't so much—what is really common here is Afghans against Turks, against Kurds, against Iraqis. They make groups according to nationality. . . . and really the danger [is] the gang wars that happen here. And even the [she pauses] the lack of respect, because if someone comes—[she breaks off to reformulate her sentence] or to have more respect, because someone comes from a particular country.[28]

Karen Werthe wants to prevent "others" from being judged for belonging to a specific nation. Teaching students about the Nazi policy of extermination seems liable to break with this logic, which she considered racist and led to the fact that "when you arrive in class and you are Turkish or Afghan you are completely *in*. But if you are German, you have problems right away."[29] Here we are faced with the production of "inverse stereotypes," or even an operation reversing the stigma (Affergan 1987; Becker 1963): difference is valued by the students instead of denigrated. Karen Werthe combined two attitudes here, slipping one into the other in the middle of her phrase. She began by saying that she would like to prevent the devaluing of any particular nationality, and then interrupted herself, realizing that at Wiesi it is more a question of (over)appreciation.

This argument has to be put into relation with the fact that the "Turks" and the "Afghans" are often leaders in the playground. We might be tempted to think, as Karen Werthe does, that this is an example of inverse racism, constructed on the essential appreciation of "foreigners." However, if we look more closely, this argument does not hold. From the observation of these processes of valorization we can see factors other than nationality at work, including age, and the physical constitution of the students. The new Afghani students in this school generally came from comfortable socio-economic backgrounds because their parents were political refugees from the intellectual middle classes, who left Afghanistan when the Islamic regime came into power (in the mid-1980s, and up until the 1990s). The socio-cultural characteristics of these parents led them to set up certain strategies to help their children's integration into the school system. It was therefore common practice to lie about the children's ages, when they are over six years old,[30] in order to have them placed in lower grades in the hope that the linguistic difficulties will be more easily overcome. They also lost a year because they attended a German language course to enable them to participate in class. They were, therefore, two or three years older than their classmates, on average, when they integrated into regular classes. The students Karen Werthe referred to as "the Turks" were most often German nationals whose parents were Turkish migrant workers and therefore came from very disadvantaged backgrounds, cumulating social and linguistic handicaps. Like all children from disadvantaged backgrounds in the German system, these students were more likely to repeat a year (especially the boys) than students from more privileged backgrounds (Beaud [2002] 2003; Delcroix 2001). Thus, for different reasons, both Afghan and "Turkish" students were older and bigger than their classmates and tended to dominate physically. They had an advantage in the minor fights between adolescents, and even in verbal confrontations, given that boys whose voices have broken are more comfortable with speaking in public and tend to have a larger slang and/or coarse vocabulary. The fact that they had older family members in the same school could also have had an impact on their status within a group of adolescents.

Karen Werthe was therefore projecting the racism that she would like to combat onto groups of children whose interactions were, in fact, following other logics. The combination of the Nazi past with the danger of racism enabled her to give meaning to the teaching of Nazi history and provided her with social legitimacy.[31]

In Leipzig, the teachers also mention racism and neo-Nazism as a danger. From Mr Wolff's "brown quagmire" to Ms Neumeier's "Nazi danger," the "students' passion" for Nazism is interpreted as a "danger for society." However, it is the "school of the GDR" that is put forward as being the best barricade against neo-Nazism and not the teaching of the past. However, this did not prevent the teachers from emphasizing "the importance of teaching the genocide" so that it "never happens again." Ms Neumeier thus observed that: "Even if—I don't really understand: the generation that is so passionate about that [neo-Nazism] today, they also went to school in the GDR (*die DDR-Schule*)—through their parents [education]! There are questions that I can't answer."[32]

Having and Transmitting Faith in the Political System

Faith in the political system (in "democracy") constitutes the second pedagogic objective that teachers seek to transmit in teaching the history of Nazism. In an interview on the pedagogic goals of history classes in general and on his own classes[33] in particular, Mr Schulze, the principal of

Gymnasium Weinberg, explained the importance of what he calls "affective pedagogic goals" as compared to "cognitive pedagogic goals." According to him, teaching Nazi history requires this distinction. He said, "it is increasingly important to transmit affective pedagogic goals and to inculcate ways of behaving," because these things represent a means of countering the risk of neo-Nazism, which is never directly named but implicitly present throughout. Indeed, according to Mr Schulze, "it is not enough to have concepts to define totalitarianism or crimes against humanity; you also have to understand them affectively."[34] Therefore, the primary "affective pedagogic goal" would be "identifying with the fundamental laws that were violated," in other words with the democratic constitution of Germany. For Mr Schulze, Nazism is an "exemplary case" of this violation.[35]

Transmitting Nazi history thus means providing "moral education" to the students. The priority here is not knowledge of the past as much as civic values, and for Mr Schulze, the Nazi extermination policy is "particularly effective" in this respect.

> It's—education, and I say this very consciously, education, . . . the educational effects of history teaching are particularly effective and desirable concerning this subject [National Socialism] in particular. Transmitting the history of the ideology of Nazism is an education in values. We do not teach it simply to provide information about what the Nazis believed at the time or to understand what they did. That's important too, but it's not what is most important. Talking about Social Darwinism, the theory of peoples (*Völkerprinzip*) and these National Socialist ideologies, means systematically and explicitly talking about the *opposite world*. About a world with *opposite values*. And, generally speaking, they grasp that quickly. "Why is Social Darwinism indefensible?" "What would that mean in today's world?" "How would disabled people be treated?" Etc., etc.[36]

Here Mr Schulze constructs an opposition between two "worlds of values": Nazism on one side, human dignity and fundamental rights on the other.

The following stage of the process is based on the hypothesis that studying the National Socialist extermination policy and the process of identifying with the victims would automatically lead to the valuing of a legal system (or even an emotional attachment to it). The teachers and the students develop an emotional attachment to this system because, as Mr Schulze said, "it is seen as opposed in every respect" to that of Nazism, and is thus supposed to "protect" the victims. The ultimate objective consists in transmitting the principles that are protected by fundamental law (of the German constitution), and in particular the right to human dignity (Article 1).

Mr Schulze did not hesitate to compare the teaching of history to the teaching of religion: learning "opposing values" is a matter of belief, even faith. Becoming a "good democratic citizen" means internalizing "democratic values."

> For me, it's [the teaching of Nazism and the Jewish Holocaust]—especially in the last tenth-grade class I had—it was an hour of religion. Or rather hours of religion. We have a history in Germany that obliges us to do that. Basic questions of moral education, questions of togetherness—which can't be overlooked when we study the Third Reich in class.[37]

In his class, Mr Schulze talks about certain Christian values, such as loving their neighbor, which are part of this vision of a "democracy based on values."

The teachers in Leipzig have had to readapt to the new requirements of history teaching, and this has not always been easy.[38] But the use of emotion to transmit political values establishes a continuity that transcends the 1989 rupture, and in the interviews, certain teachers in Leipzig clearly saw it that way.

> *Can you describe the goals of teaching National Socialism (NS) before and after reunification* (Wende)—*what you wanted the students to learn?*
>
> Yes. The denunciation of NS. And—the realization that—the only possibility of resolving the problem was in transformation—or commitment to communism. That the GDR—was the only legitimate heir to the antifascist resistance, that in the GDR, all these proletarian goals . . . [She hesitates, lowers her voice, does not finish her sentence.] That was it, the goal of teaching in the GDR, and—with that of course, the FRG was degraded—yes—I don't know if I should put it so concretely . . .
>
> *Mmm* [encouragement]
> [She smiles slightly, her voice somewhat husky.] Now, it's exactly the opposite, with National Socialism: we still condemn it, but—now it is the FRG and democracy which are presented as the desired outcomes of World War II. And the GDR that is the error of history. [She continues to smile.] But [she suddenly becomes tense and dry] in theory it's still the same. [She laughs abruptly.][39]

The continuity that Ms Weinecke evoked here is above all a continuity in terms of the relationship to the state, which has consequences for teaching practices. Although the content is not exactly the same—she teaches the history of National Socialism in order to legitimize democracy rather than communism—the goal remains the same: teaching history to defend an ideological and political position. Ms Weinecke described a fundamental inversion of values—the celebration of the GDR and degradation of the FRG have been replaced by their absolute opposites. She described the teaching body as "priests" of "state ideology."

54 • When Will We Talk about Hitler?

Loving Thy Neighbor

The transmission of values of tolerance, refusal of antisemitism and racism—and sometimes, more rarely, awareness of homophobia and respect for disabled people—is the third "affective" pedagogic goal sought by the teachers. Behind this education for tolerance are the values expressed in the Universal Declaration of Human Rights. Mr Gerste, a teacher at Wiesi, mentioned this explicitly.

> We could see, very quickly, that the question of human rights—well, that interests them! And it's *really* already civic and political education. We *are not allowed* to do anything other than immediately come back to the fundamental law of Germany (*Grundgesetz*)! They raise the examples themselves—"and here, why—but it's against human rights!" and so forth. And so, you have to respond to these questions. And—use the wealth of history for that. It's related to political education. I wouldn't have any scruples in saying that that is the most important aspect of teaching history!—even if, of course, it must be factually correct, from a scientific perspective as well![40]

Mr Schulze explained that the choice of films that he shows in class is based on their ability to "combine political history with personal history, to teach the students that nothing is solely personal." He wants to transform the students into "citizens who are conscious of the political aspect of their daily choices."[41] The connections between civic education and emotional upheaval are very clear.

The hypothesis that tolerant behavior can be brought about by the rejection of Nazism constitutes the teachers' second wager, supposing an automatic transfer of affect onto civic and voting behavior. This objective is reflected first in the hope of breaking down stereotypes through teaching the history of Nazism. As the young Annika Klein, a teacher at Wiesi put it, "I would like for them to understand what stereotypes do, if they are maintained in a negative way. And what it can lead to when people—or groups—are excluded."[42]

Mr Herzog, also a teacher at Wiesi, aged around sixty, thus remarked that National Socialism is "particularly useful" because "exclusion and persecution reached a climax and so we can conceptualize and illustrate themes such as stereotypes, racism, and exclusion particularly well";[43] it is a "perfect" example to see "what exclusion policies can lead to." His colleague Ms. Inger, who is around the same age, emphasized the importance of learning "to respect minorities."[44]

Ensuring Political Commitment

Civic courage and commitment, and the active protection of the rights of others are all additional objectives of this teaching. Mr Gerste hopes to see the history of Nazism lead the students to ask questions, but also to act.

> And when you read the Declaration of Human Rights, you see exactly what was violated, and what must be protected. And it is important to make the connection with classes on ethics. What do we need in order to live together? And especially: should I intervene, when I observe something happening, when someone is mistreated?[45]

The question of civic engagement connects with that of political engagement. The ideal citizen is therefore not only a tolerant citizen, but also a committed and courageous one, able to defend the values of human rights—under a dictatorship, for example. This constitutes a utopian vision of teaching and a belief in the effectiveness of education.

At Wiesi, the much more international *Gesamtschule*, with thirty-three nationalities present among the students, anti-racism has a more practical dimension to it than at Weinberg, the *Gymnasium* where only a very small number of students do not have German grandparents. This is no longer just a matter of accepting abstract values and legal texts such as the constitution or the Declaration of Human Rights, but bringing an end to "gang wars," and making it possible for the high school students to "live together" in everyday life. Mr Stein, a teacher at Wiesi, aged around fifty, put it like this:

> As the Muslims say: "the Nazis smashed the Jews. Us Muslims, we're against the Jews too. So *Heil Hitler*." That's it. They [he breaks off] but they do generally realize, that it's a provocation. They know it is. They aren't serious, anyway. And they know, or they are sufficiently conscious, during the classes, that their kind (*ihre Art*) would not have been well treated under Adolf.[46] They do know that. And that's the conclusion too. That's the conclusion of my classes. And they accept it. Yes, racism means that you consider your own race to be the only good thing in the world and that you refuse all others. So that means that all of you, all of you who are here, you would be among them [the others]. And in reality, at the end, they aren't racist. It's—yes, the ideal is that at the end of my classes there are no racists. And generally, that's how it is. But sometimes we don't agree. Sometimes there are real ones [racists]. But we can still shake them up quite a bit.[47]

Here "Muslim" students become both the "danger" and the "solution" for racism and neo-Nazism. They are dangerous because "authoritarian" and "a priori antisemitic," but also "saved" by anti-racist education as well as by the increased awareness of their own status as "victims" and by the civic engagement that is supposed to result from this.

This belief in the usefulness of teaching is clearly interspersed with moments of doubt, and the conviction that "against a true racist, there's nothing I can do." It is essential to believe in the possibility of changing racist attitudes and influencing the students' civic behavior in order to continue to work in this difficult profession. We can see this need to believe in the following extract from the interview with Mr Stein. In one phrase, he expressed the possibility of change, and then he denied it in the next phrase, and then affirmed it again, and then denied it again (for clarity, the changes in his argument are marked with the symbol //).

You can't fight against racism. I mean, against someone, who is really convinced about it, there are no arguments. They'd need to look with a microscope: look at the genes, in fact, they aren't really different—but they're not interested. They want to believe. That all existed under National Socialism, measuring skulls and things like that, they did it! // Well, in the sense of racial purity, they had nothing. That old joke—as blond as Hitler, as strong as Göring—I mean, it's a joke because in terms of race, it doesn't hold up // But when you want to be prejudiced, you find proof // But it can be contradicted (*aufbrechen*). That still works.

It works?

Yeah // [He lowers his voice.] I don't want to rule out the possibility there might still be an antisemite afterwards. Yes. But at that point, my teaching would have been a failure, for that one (*mein Unterricht hätte versagt, an dem*).[48]

Mr Wolff, the principal of the *Gymnasium* in Leipzig had a very similar argument. Like Mr Stein, he stressed the importance of tolerance, anti-racist education, and political engagement, while still being conscious of the limits of his contribution in terms of education.

You're in a situation where you want to only analyze NS. Because that's what you're studying, you have to ask questions about that. But what happens with someone who is not a part of our Saxon school program. And who has never heard about fascism or NS. And who is still tolerant with those who think differently. What about him? What do you make of him? He exists too! How do you explain his existence? That there are some people who don't bash others? Who have never heard anything about history? I mean—of course, it's rare. But well, you have to—[he trails off]. That, that's our little contribution, that's what we can do. And I don't think it's much. It's just one part, among many, many others.[49]

Mr Wolff mentioned family, friends, and television as other factors outside the school. His lucidity concerned not only the limits of school-based education but also the limits of the interview. He saw that focusing on the teaching of Nazism has the effect of artificially accentuating this specific teaching compared to other classes. The distortion that results from this does not prevent the existence of a link between "democratic education" and the teaching of the past.

Regimes of Reason

The teaching of the Nazi past mobilizes regimes of faith in order to encourage the students to adhere to the established political regime in affective terms. But it also draws on regimes of reason and critical thinking. Being wary of politicians, the media, other peoples' discourses in general, and not believing everything seen and heard, seems to be the teachers' second main concern. Apparently contradictory with the use of affective pedagogy, regimes of faith and reason exist simultaneously in the teachers' discourses. Indeed, the force of the argument probably lies in the combination of the two, which constitutes faith in democracy. Believing in a political system, while retaining the possibility of "critical thinking" and "freedom of thought," as long as it exists within the context of a regime of faith (i.e., belief in democracy, solidarity, and civic engagement); this indeed constitutes the center of democratic civic education.

The "ability to become a good democrat" is also defined by the existence of a critical mind, from its most ordinary formulation (the ability to form one's own opinion) to the strongest concretization (resisting the orders of the state). It is then translated into political engagement, from the simple act of voting, to a militant commitment to a political party or an interest group, or even in social activities. The interpretations of Nazism that concentrate on a handful of political actors (Hitler and "the Nazis") are particularly suitable for transmitting this fundamental lesson on the importance of critical thinking.

"Critical Thinking"

For many teachers, the education of students represents a way to contribute to the spread of the Enlightenment: "like many in my generation, I wanted to become a teacher to do everything better. I wanted to enlighten (*aufklären*) the students, to show them the path so they could be good! That's it. That was my motivation."[50] Here, Ms Simone expressed the "vocation" that is implicit in many of her colleagues' comments. She is part of a generation that is unusual in that it lived through the years around 1968–1970, as an initiation to political and pedagogical engagement.[51] For the students to become "good" in her own words, they need to be "enlightened." The idea of the Enlightenment is very common in the interviewees' comments.

According to the teachers, the risk of Nazism can be contained. In order that the students become "aware" of the dangers of what their teachers call "seduction" or "manipulation"[52] (by politicians and the media), it seems necessary to increase their political awareness through the teaching of history. Nazism as a "counter example" also allows high school students to develop a resistance to political manipulation. Particularly sensitive "at this age, because they have particularly strong moral codes," they are moved by "the people who were seduced [implying the German people], or who were afraid [the resisters], or those who were persecuted [the Jews]." In this comment, Mr Hatze used the image of the German people as victims of "manipulation" by a small group of (Nazi) leaders to enable him to emphasize the importance of "critical thinking" in order to prevent history from repeating itself.

"Critical thinking" is made of different elements. Thomas, a fifty-year-old teacher at Wiesi, explained that it is important to be wary, to not "take everything that is said at face value."[53] In order to be able to be "wary," one has to have access to information. Ms Inge, for example, expressed her hope that her students would be able to consult different sources so that they are not "like those who voted for National Socialism."

> They [the students] must be able to gather as much information as possible concerning something, to use as many different sources as possible. The people who voted for National Socialism with such enthusiasm, they did it for short-term reasons. . . . If we could manage to get the students to make the link, and to say "no, that, that hasn't been sufficiently thought out!"[54]

Being "suspicious" primarily has a political meaning; in order to be able to vote, one must be able to "question what the politicians say."[55] Ms. Simone, a forty-year-old teacher at the *Mittelschule* in Leipzig, also mentioned a second meaning, this time relating to the media.

> When they consciously reflect upon (*das bewußte Nachdenken*), what is happening in the world, what I read about every day [she gets worked up], and don't take everything at face value, what they read in [the newspaper] *Die Bild*[56] or wherever. Or what they see on the TV. It's very often a load of rubbish! (*Da kommt wirklich viel Mist*) Even me, when I see the news, I think to myself—it's not possible! We can't leave it like that! . . . I think that media education is much more important than anything else today. Because—they watch, they absorb, and everything they see is true![57]

For Ms Inge, wariness also has a third, more self-critical, dimension: "the ability to be critical, including about oneself. You don't immediately believe the first thing that seems logical or plausible."[58]

The use of conflicting sources in class represents one of the ways of providing the students with the means to "question" what they learn. Mr Schulze emphasized that "it is especially important to observe the principle of contradiction in didactics (*kontroverse Didaktick*). Because it is important—at all costs—that a contradictory vision is present, at least in history classes. That's obvious. And it's especially that which will, in turn, be useful for political education—when we do it consciously."[59]

Reflection and Introspection

This critical ability should eventually lead to a "capacity for reflection"; these teachers want to teach their students to "think." Herbert Weise, the assistant principal at *Gesamtschule* Wiesi in Hamburg, emphasizes this objective for all teaching, but history in particular, while also recognizing that it is very ambitious.

> Thinking about solutions: what would be best?! How are things linked to each other? Why is it like that? And thinking and analyzing all the way, what people did, and finding other "solutions." So, knowing how to take a historical approach. Looking analytically: what really happened, in the past? And what solutions can we take from that, for the future? How should it be? For me that is the center of what history can do. [He hesitates] Hmm, but myself, as a student, I wasn't capable of that. I didn't have that awareness. It came . . . [he does not finish his sentence] In order to be able to make well-founded judgments and to develop independent opinions . . . [softly] it was quite a process. It lasted [he hesitates] probably two-thirds of my studies, I'd say.[60]

Annika Klein, one of his colleagues, aged thirty-five, is convinced that the study of history, by definition, teaches students "independent thinking"[61] because "history challenges the present." She had this "revelation" during her own studies and hopes to be able to transmit it to her students: "I would like to—particularly on this theme [National Socialism], even if I want to for other themes too—I really want them to think. I probably have [she smiles, slightly surprised] an Enlightenment approach (*aufklärerischen Ansatz*)! They must think! They must look and *think*!"[62] Another colleague at the same school, Klara Rohrsteg, went even further. For her, it is not enough to provide a variety of information, to critique it, to be able to position oneself in relation to it, and to construct independent thought. It is also necessary to "have the courage to speak your opinions aloud," even if you do not agree with your classmates.[63]

In order to form an opinion, the students must "take a good look at themselves and be open to self-criticism." Ms Weinecke, a forty-year-old teacher at *Gymnasium* Monnet in Leipzig, emphasized the ability for "self-reflection" with an argument based on her own religious beliefs.

Every day I have to look at the world with my ears pricked and my eyes open, to see what is happening. I realize that I won't reach everyone. But if I can reach one person in each class, that's already quite a lot, I think! And I also try—of course—I hope you won't laugh, I really do it—to use Jesus in my arguments. Because Jesus said: I can't change the world, but if I change, I change the world! I always think that that's a really great motto! If a politician were to say that one day, I would support them right away! Make everyone aware: I must start with myself! I can't always say others have to do this or that. No! It's me, who has to [act]![64]

Resistance to a Repressive State

Some of the teachers at *Gesamtschule* Wiesi were very politically active, both in unions and political parties, and they were even more demanding. They expected the students to not only stand up and defend their opinions in class, or to their friends, but also to be able to confront the state. They see immigrants as having a particularly important "responsibility to resist" state authority. Mr Herzog, aged about fifty, was a member of the Education and Science Union (Gewerkschaft Erziehung und Wissenschaft [GEW])[65] at the time of the interview and was previously a member of the SPD. His father, who was denounced by his then girlfriend for "expressing criticism of Hitler," was interned in several concentration camps during World War II. Mr Herzog's attachment to the "spirit of resistance" therefore possibly has familial origins. He proclaims: "Yes, defend yourself (*Wehr Dich*)! Resist against people who want to oppress you! Resist against people who are racist in the way they treat you! Resist against fascist tendencies, against violence, against whatever! Basically: show civic courage!"[66]

The context of legal understanding and support for the constitution provides Mr Gerste with cognitive and affective support when he expresses a genuine "call for resistance" that students would need to demonstrate in order to "be good citizens." He used an anecdote to help to explain his position. The mother of one of his students, an Afghani immigrant who had lived in Hamburg for fifteen years, was insulted by a police officer while returning from holidays—she was threatened with deportation for no valid reason. Following this incident, the mother, terrorized, asked Mr Gerste for advice. He was shocked by the behavior of the German police officer, which he described as "madness." However, the mother's "passiveness" seemed to pose more of a problem for him.

She said to herself—"it must be normal for her to yell at me, I must be worth less than the others" or something like that. Giving in, accepting, and not resisting, not opposing. I still find that [he hesitates] there is a link with the fundamental laws of our free democracy (*die freiheitliche demokratische Grundordnung*). These are higher values (*übergeordnet*) that we want to transmit, that we must transmit. And the fact of protecting one's personal rights, that's part of it. You have to understand that, during the time of National Socialism, they [the rights] were revoked, for a long time. Completely revoked. And [to avoid that happening again] you have to be aware of it from the very first signs [of state privilege]. Because we can oppose it. Right? It [the first signs] can be [state] violence. Violence is fascism too.[67]

Mr Gerste thus expects his students (and their parents) to be aware of the legal order (and in particular, individual freedom and dignity), to defend it actively, and to oppose all abuse of power. State agents who abuse their positions provide an opportunity to perform heroic acts of everyday resistance. Here Mr Gerste clearly did not take into account the power imbalance between an Afghani immigrant with poor German skills and officers of the state such as the police. In order to be "a good citizen," she "should have resisted." He did not explain how he imagined such an opposition would have unfolded, nor the potential consequences for this woman (presumably including deportation). His argument, in fact, implies that the weak are responsible for the abuse of power by the strong. The "inability to resist" the state is thus interpreted as a "democratic shortcoming."

Teaching the Genocide through and with *Betroffenheit*

The use of *Betroffenheit* in the classroom is specific to the teaching of the genocide of the Jewish population, even though the teachers talk about applying it to the whole period between 1933 and 1945. This disjuncture between their discourses and their teaching practices is linked to the fact that the genocide is, in the discourse of many teachers (and also students) the crystallization of Nazism, the war, and the whole 1933–1945 period. This explains the permanent shifts between different aspects (and periods) in the history of Nazism. In practice, the teachers essentially use this affective pedagogy in order to provoke the students' identification with the victims of the Nazi extermination policy and in particular with Jews.

A reason-based approach is thus applied to the way the class covers the causes of Nazism and the arrival and consolidation of power of the Nazi regime between 1933 and 1936. Faith in democracy and *Betroffenheit* remain important concepts when it comes to teaching the consequences and in particular World War II and the genocide of the Jews.[68] There is thus a clear difference between the theory of *Betroffenheitspädagogik*, which is applicable to history overall, and even teaching in general, and actual teaching practice, whereby teachers only, or primarily, use it to teach students about the genocide.

This approach uses two fundamental procedures in order to provoke the students' *Betroffenheit*: it evokes emotions and identification with the victims. These two aspects of the pedagogy of "emotional upheaval" aim to provoke a feeling of guilt in the students, in order to induce a sense of political responsibility, according to the teachers' implicit or explicit wager.

Virtuous Emotion

All the teachers, without exception, systematically mentioned the importance of "emotion" in developing the students' understanding of history. Their discourse closely associated the means, the use of "emotional upheaval," and the ends, civic education. The link between the two seems to have been fairly self-evident for the teachers. This chapter distinguishes between the means and the ends for the sake of clarity, but this distinction is not found in the comments themselves.

One of the most effective ways of provoking emotion among the students is found in the use of audiovisual materials, and in particular, fiction films. The audiovisual protocol is intentionally subjective, and the teachers consciously acknowledge this subjectivity. Mr Gerste, at *Gesamtschule* Wiesi, explained why the films were particularly useful for him: "I am used to using films. Or working from images, visual things. Or—listening to stories or reading something, a short story, for example, to begin with. To connect with what a person feels in a given situation, at a particular time."[69] The use of audiovisual material also corresponds to pedagogic goals: "it is so that they can feel, they can relive the past, so that they identify with the lives of individuals, and particularly the victims."[70] The "victims of history" can play an important role, to the extent that they are able to capture the students' interest and attention. The genocide of the Jews is a paradigmatic example of this approach because it emphasizes the victims who have become a symbol of suffering *par excellence* (Traverso 2005). The genocide is particularly well-suited to fulfilling two key teaching priorities: emotional upheaval and the connection to the present.

Ms Klein and Ms Werthe, both teachers at Wiesi and aged around thirty, co-organized a semester specifically for the teaching of Nazism, in which their classes had five consecutive hours of politics and history on Friday afternoon. They had a teaching module that ran every Friday from ten o'clock in the morning to five o'clock in the afternoon with a two hour lunch break in the middle, in order to conduct "independent study, which includes class trips, visits to museums, interviews, etc."[71] When I arrived in class, the two teachers were finishing the introductory session (two weeks or ten hours of class) during which they covered the end of the Weimar Republic, the NSDAP's (Nationalsozialistische Deutsche Arbeiterpartei or National Socialist) seizure of power (*Machtergreifung*), and the consolidation of their power. The rest of the semester (sixteen weeks or eighty hours of class) would be dedicated to independent research conducted in small groups of four or five students. In order to give the students ideas and to guide them in the choice of subjects, the two teachers presented Steven Spielberg's film *Schindler's List* (1993) because it is "a very, very personal story, through Oskar Schindler." Karen Werthe described the film as appropriate because it "has an impact."

> Lots of them were really speechless (*geplättet*), even if the teachers were perhaps a little more [she smiles]. But lots were shocked. And they were fascinated. By the violence that is shown. Even the boys—not always, some are still the same big mouths—but lots were really, really shocked by the brutality that the film represents. The film is relatively brutal. It's a film—there is that Commandant, or camp leader, who is on the balcony, and he just shoots a few Jews at breakfast.[72]

The fact that this film "manages to shock" the students, sometimes into tears, is essential in the eyes of this young teacher. Mr Wolff, who is a teacher in Leipzig, mentioned the same scene, a little amended, to argue that the shock provoked by this kind of scene can "make the students think."

> But what reasons can we have, like—like here in Auschwitz, the camp leader, who, for his child's birthday takes ten babies and throws them in the air and lets his kid shoot them. What reason can there be for that? That, a student will have to explain that to me. And an adult too has to try and explain it to me. And I say to myself: with that approach, you can do a lot. Not everything, but a lot. I don't think we can make the world a better place through history classes. But . . . we can make . . . them think. That's possible.[73]

Schindler's List is frequently used by the teachers, and it was the audiovisual material most often cited by the students and the teachers interviewed here.

In Annika Klein and Karen Werthe's class at Wiesi, one group had trouble finding a theme for their research project. Annika Klein told me that she helped them by "giving them a book—I don't remember the title—but there were lots of pictures. Because images are powerful. And that's why they have a strong impact on the students; they feel concerned (*angesprochen*)."[74] In addition to the use of images and audiovisual material, inviting "witnesses" into the class helps to provoke an emotional relationship with the past. Ms Rohrsteg, a teacher at Wiesi, aged around fifty, explained that the students were "terribly upset (*betroffen*) because they could ask someone questions. Suddenly the past was not so abstract. It became genuinely real; there was someone here who had lived it. And who—yes, who could tell what had happened."[75] These invitations, which have long been regular practice both in the East and in the West, are now encountering more resistance among teachers in Leipzig. Ms Naute, a teacher at *Gymnasium* Monnet, aged around forty, explained that she "no longer invites witnesses" because "before [in the GDR] each school had its official witness, its party comrade, resister, who came to tell the students about their life." If she wanted to invite someone today, she "wouldn't know whom to invite."[76] The most frequent pedagogic practice was inviting a former Communist resister as a legitimate spokesperson for the camps. These were often people who held a discourse that conformed to that of the Socialist Party (SED). After reunification, the Communist resisters lost their monopoly on the legitimate discourse of the history of the camps and found themselves confronted with intense competition from those talking about Jewish suffering. This shift was integrated into the classes by the teachers. However, the new illegitimacy of the former practice—the invitation of Communist resisters—often led to the whole arrangement being rejected. The assimilation of the "Communist witness" to the transmission of values linked to the GDR state and official historiography was perceived too strongly by teachers.[77]

In showing Spielberg's film to the students, these teachers, Karen and Annika, began the teaching of the 1933–1945 period by emphasizing the consequences of Nazism—the genocide and its victims—while also provoking emotion among the students. The two teachers set up a period of four weeks after the viewing of the films for the students to organize themselves in groups of three to five, to choose a theme to cover over the semester. They brought them a "box of books" so that each group could find a specific theme. When I arrived in the class to conduct my observations, this phase had just finished, and I did not have access to the "more than eighty books" selected, by Annika Klein in particular, to help the students choose their topics. Of the six groups, five ultimately chose to cover the Jewish genocide. Among them, two groups who initially wanted to cover "Adolf Hitler's rise to power" and "the major battles of World War II" ended up following their teacher's instructions (she considered these themes to be "problematic"). This "guidance" led the students to work on a subject related to the genocide. The final list of subjects was thus: "Antisemitism and the Holocaust," "The Neuengamme Concentration Camp," "Concentration Camps," "The Diary of Anne Frank,"[78] "Judaism (*Judentum*) in Europe," and "A Comparison between Adolf Hitler and Oskar Schindler." With the exception of this last group, the teachers strongly encouraged the students to "choose" the Jewish genocide as a subject to study over the sixteen weeks of independent work. The importance of the subject can be seen in the time that the students dedicated to its study.

The analysis of the five projects relating to the genocide shows the importance of the affective relationship to the subject in the grading practices. Indeed, two of these projects received a "good grade"—these were students that the teacher considered "good" and who demonstrated their intense emotional reaction to the subject. The use of a large number of photos and "personal reports" outlining the students' feelings during visits to museums or concentration camps, as well as the language used, all reflect this emotion. It seems that one of the paths to good grades here consisted in emphasizing one's personal and emotional reactions to the subject.

Identification with the Victims

Particular identification "with the victims of history" is a second requirement, linked very closely to the "need to provoke emotion." Mr Gerste explained the interest of the Neuengamme museum, near Hamburg.

> There are computers in the corner and you can look for names, really. [He lowers his voice.] "Ah,—and who is Mr Meier? And what happened to him? Ah, yes he did that." And so you discover the stories—you can even play detective a bit, and you can spend a lot of time looking! And then in one of the drawers you find an object that belonged to this Willi Meier. A watch that was his. And then you walk around and you see, "Ah, there are the bunks, that's where he slept." And you know, it's really very direct, very personal. It's well done.[79]

According to him, the museum allows the students to "step into the shoes" of a particular person, who they discover little by little as they go around. The involvement by practical discovery (opening drawers) awakens the students' curiosity, but it also provides them the possibility of entering into someone's life—going progressively deeper as though revealing the layers of an archeological dig one by one. The more the student uncovers the intimate details of a person's life, the more they will identify with that person.

An example of one of Mr Schulze's classes provides a good illustration of this process of identification.

A Ninth-Grade History Class, Taught by Mr Schulze, Gymnasium in Hamburg

Extracts from field notes: 12 December 2003–9 January 2004

In order to introduce the theme of Nazism, Mr Schulze has decided to show the film *Die Geschwister Oppermann*, directed by Egon Monk, from the book by Lion Feuchtwanger. As the film lasts more than three hours, Mr Schulze is dedicating two and a half weeks—five hours of history class—to showing the film to the students. The sessions take place in the TV room, where the students sit in a semicircle, with no tables, around the television. The boys choose to sit on one side of the room, the girls on the other. In general, Mr Schulze begins the session with questions on the extract that they saw in the previous session. He also generally stops the film at points that he considers key, to make sure that the students have understood the stakes and nature of the situation. These moments reveal the priorities of Mr Schulze's teaching practices regarding the history of Nazism. Two examples are particularly interesting concerning identification with victims. The first concerns a scene at the beginning of the film, which takes place in a classroom. One of the main characters, Berthold (the son of one of the Oppermann brothers and the same age as Mr Schulze's students) has a new teacher, an early supporter of National Socialism. The boys laugh at him when they see the teacher—one of them remarks, "he looks like Hitler!" Ridiculed by his misplaced authoritarianism, the new teacher terrorizes the students and in particular the young Oppermann, the only Jewish student in the class. Mr Schulze stops the film here and asks the students: "Imagine how you would have reacted here. Put yourselves in his place—what would you have felt?" He takes the time to do this, clearly demonstrating the importance that he places in the process of identification with the Jewish schoolboy. He asks Martha, a rather shy student. She refuses to answer, saying "it's too personal. I can't answer that here in front of everyone." Martha's refusal provokes an awkward but eloquent silence. The students are touched by the film; they don't necessarily want to share their feelings with their classmates. Karen, Mr Schulze's favorite student, tries to save the situation and says, "that teacher doesn't allow any possibility to respond freely." The discussion begins. Kai, who is a year older than his classmates because he repeated a year, finds the teacher "sadistic. He's just waiting for one thing, for me to make a mistake, so he can dump on me."

Kai's use of the first person here suggests to what extent the identification with the main character is effective. Indeed, Kai's own difficulties at school make the situation all the more understandable for him. As he later confesses in an interview, he also often had the impression that teachers were just "waiting [for him] to mess up."[80] Once the identification was established, thanks in particular to Mr Schulze's questions, the students were able to watch the film and put themselves in "Berthold's place." Mr Schulze encouraged them in this attitude, including the moment when the young man decides to commit suicide.

Mr Schulze stops the film just before Berthold takes his own life. With the intensification of the regime and the increase in antisemitic violence, the young man is having more and more difficulties at school. A brilliant student, he continues to stand up against his teacher who discriminates against him. Little by little the other students begin to avoid him. He is excluded from the class and attacked. One morning his best friend no longer wants to go to school with him. His teacher has prepared a public humiliation for him in front of the whole school. He decides to commit suicide. Mr Schulze stops the film at the point where the young man is alone, at night, in his room, beginning to write his goodbye letter, and asks his students: "Put yourselves in his place. How would you feel?" He takes ten minutes for a discussion among the students, each explaining what he or she would be feeling—humiliated by the teacher, ostracized by his friends, left alone by his parents who have other concerns, etc. The students are visibly touched by the young man's hopeless situation.

Mr Schulze questions them about what would happen after this—"How will Berthold react?" A heated discussion takes place in the class—"why doesn't the school principal help Berthold? He knows that he is a good student." "Are you stupid or what? He can't help Berthold, because the teacher has all the Nazi system behind him, and they could just shoot the principal!"

Mr Schulze asks his question again: "and you, how would you react?" "Me, I think that I would say sorry. Well, it's true, honor and all that, but still, I'd prefer a punishment." "I think he won't apologize. He'd prefer to go to a concentration camp." "Me, I'd just leave [the school]."

The students join in. They take Berthold's place and talk about what they would do if they were him. Some continue to talk about the character in the first person.

Another element used to reinforce the identification process can be seen here—the emphasis on adolescence. The reasoning behind this is simply that these young people will find it easier to identify with other young people. Klara Rohrsteg explained this approach: "One possibility [to motivate the students] is age. Looking in the past to see if there were children, how children felt this, or how life was for children. I think that there are still lots of things to do, in didactics of history, to be able to motivate the students differently."[81] Yet, although the teachers in both Hamburg and Leipzig used the example of children to illustrate their classes, differences remain. In Hamburg, the focus was particularly on child victims, often in the camps and sometimes, like in the case of Berthold, young Jews persecuted before their deportation. In Leipzig, however, the teachers more often referred to "young Germans" and their daily life. In this town, understanding the participation in the Hitler Youth Movement (that is, compared to participation in the Communist Youth movement under the GDR) sometimes seems more important to the teachers than identification with the victims. This difference is symptomatic of the East-West divide, the Holocaust being central to the FRG teaching of the history of Nazi Germany, but much less central in the GDR interpretation of that same history.

In this respect, Mr Wolff was rather atypical for Leipzig, to the extent that he adapted the *Betroffenheitspädagogik* to the Jewish victims in a very insistent way—as though he had integrated the new requirements particularly well[82] (or, perhaps he wanted to show the researcher from the West that he fulfilled these requirements?). He took the objective of identification very far. When he visited the Buchenwald concentration camp with his class, he asked each of his students in turn to come and stand in the place of the victims who were shot. One room in the museum is the "shooting place": a wall with wooden boards for measuring people's height, which conceals an opening through which the victim was shot in the neck. The victims would think they were in a doctor's office and be assassinated without realizing the situation. Mr Wolff asked his students to stand in front of the opening, and then he stood on the other side, in the place of the executioner. Most often, the students reacted with a certain discomfort, initially refusing to stand in front of the opening, sometimes turning around to try and "see the danger." Then they accepted the situation, as Mr Wolff had planned; the identification process was thus effective.[83]

At Wiesi, the *Gesamtschule* in Hamburg, where most students did not have German nationality (or whose parents did not), the teachers suggested that there is a "specific ability for upheaval." Mr Gerste, for example, thought that his students, who were sometimes personally confronted with anti-immigrant hatred, would be particularly open to *Betroffenheit* with regard to the victims of the past. The logic is simply that being a victim can facilitate identification with other victims. This is especially the case given that these "victims of the present" would have been "victims of the past" if antisemitism, racism, and xenophobia are placed on the same level (as both the teachers and the students were wont to do). The status of "victim" could thus sometimes be an "advantage" in this school environment, because it inferred a supposedly greater capacity for *Betroffenheit*.

In an informal interview I conducted after the class, Mr Schulze said that he was very happy about the way his class had interpreted the film (*wahrnehmen*): "the question of emotions is very important. They integrated it well, they respond well."[84]

Both schools and museums are sites dedicated to learning "appropriate" behavior. Students learn "good manners," those that are socially legitimate, "how to talk" about the past correctly (Gudehus 2006). The Jewish genocide has an important place here for the teachers (but also the museum guides), and particular attention is paid to the socially legitimate ways of talking about it. Beyond "appropriate behavior," this is a matter of transferring the teachers' attitudes to their students. The subject of the genocide appears to particularly affect the female teachers who express their own emotional upheaval in the way they talk about the subject. One of the teachers at *Gymnasium* Weinberg broke down in tears during our second interview, while talking about her visit to Theresienstadt. We were obliged to stop the interview while she let her emotions out. Another teacher at the *Gymnasium* in Leipzig, who does not come from a Jewish background herself, expressed her identification with the Jewish victims of the genocide by using the first person in the present tense in her comments.

> And then, I tell them that it overwhelms me, especially the image of that little girl—or the ramps, when we see the photos or the videos [she swallows] and the events—on the ramp, you went left or you went right. *And me, as a mother, I had no chance to save my child. I* could do nothing but take the child by the hand and lead her to the gas chamber. That was the only thing *I could do.* And to transmit through these examples, which touch me personally, the feeling that they don't see anonymous human beings, but that they try to step into their shoes. From simple examples like that. It isn't great, as a comparison, but *I often see myself,* when I watch a video with the students about that [she swallows] *I very often see myself, I'm not able,* like so many mothers under the Third Reich, *I* wouldn't have been able, if I'd lived at the time [she speaks more quickly] to save *my own* child. And that, you can perhaps transmit that to the students like that.[85]

This interviewee spoke as though she had seen the genocide herself, as though she had accompanied her child into the gas chambers. The tone of her voice and her repeated swallowing also suggest her personal involvement in the narrative and her own identification with the victims.

The logic of emotional upheaval is criticized however, in particular by the teachers who declare themselves "anti-68ers," and who see this approach as a "hypocritical left-wing attitude." Among the teachers that I interviewed, this critique is specific to Hamburg; none in Leipzig expressed this perspective toward this pedagogic approach relying on emotion, as we will see below. Ms Groß von Wilhelmshöhe, a teacher at the *Gymnasium* in Hamburg expressed her disdain like this:

> I am very careful—when people talk about NS and the upheaval [that it inspires], I distance myself from that, I'm a bit skeptical, and I say—this upheaval, this lyricism, well, I have them here. [She makes a gesture with her hand in front of her eyes.] Of course, I do it in class, of course! But I'm very careful about it. I say to myself: those who are not really upset make a lot of mistakes. They take on—a posture.

> *A posture?*

> Yes, for us, there is [she hesitates]—yes, [she hesitates again] antifascist intellectuals. And I really have it in for them! [She laughs.] It's unbearable! They are perfectly aware of the errors that our parents committed. Our parents' generation had it all wrong, and "they should have known!" It's just—clichés. And they—they simply apply them and that's why they are blind. And I've always tried to fight against that, saying "it's easy to talk, but first take a look at yourself."[86]

70 • When Will We Talk about Hitler?

The personal history of this teacher partly explains her position. Her Jewish father managed to obtain a false Aryan "passport" through his wife's family ("big *Junkers* from the east," as she calls them), but he died as a German soldier on the Eastern Front. He was saved as a Jew but died as a German. Ms Groß von Wilhelmshöhe could not stand the *Betroffenheit* of those who did not lose a loved one during the war; she considered it hypocritical.

But there is also a debate between "generational units that are pro- and anti-1968," a debate that structures and explains her comments. Indeed, there is a powerful generational configuration at the *Gymnasium* in Hamburg. With only two exceptions, all the history teachers at Weinberg were students at the University of Hamburg in the late 1960s and the early 1970s. Although they did not all know each other as students, their shared membership to groups like "Fritz Fischer students" or "Zechlin students"[87] seems to still constitute a powerful marker that helps to explain their oppositions today. Several teachers explained to me that they "knew when someone arrived for *Referendariat* (professional training) whether they came from Fischer or Zechlin."

The expression "antifascist intellectuals" used by Ms Groß von Wilhelmshöhe (herself a student of Zechlin), refers to the "pro-1968" generational unit, "Fritz Fischer's people." Her criticism of their "false *Betroffenheit*," which she sees as "just a posture," makes sense within the generational debate and the struggles around the "right pedagogy" to "break authoritarian relations." As a result, it is not surprising that this criticism is not found among the teachers in Leipzig; they are not part of the same generational group and the debate does not follow the same references in this context. The fact that this position is marginal in Hamburg can also be easily understood: the "pro-1968 generational unit" was clearly in the majority in both teaching and in the public service, in this traditionally left-wing town,[88] where the "events of 1968" were significant and had a strong impact on the students at the time. Ms Heide, who is a member of the next generation, makes an argument similar to Ms Groß von Wilhelmshöhe. Both refuse what they call the "politicization" of teaching, i.e., teaching history to defend specific political objectives through what they describe as "affective indoctrination." Moreover, in their eyes this "politicization" is incarnated by *Betroffenheitspädagoik*, which they reject as a contradiction to what they call "scientific neutrality."

The Limits of *Betroffenheit*

Although the classes on the Jewish genocide that I observed were saturated with *Betroffenheit*, the ways in which the past was discussed in class revealed the limits of this attitude, among the teachers as well as the students.

The Presence of Absence

When they refer to the genocide, the interviewees use expressions that remain abstract or vague. Mr Gerste and Ms Seidel use expressions such as "that" (*es*) or "something like that"; Ms Rohrsteg uses the term "such a thing." The students, but also some of the teachers, have trouble making "it" explicit. In the interviews, they often refer to the genocide as "what happened," sometimes mentioning "the horrors," "the evil that occurred" (*das was Schlimmes passiert ist*), or just "it." There is a profound difficulty, even an impossibility, in articulating killing, death, and extermination.

It is also important to question the rhetorical efficiency of imprecision. The term "it" allows everyone to fill the term with their own memories and associations, to pair the signifier with their own significations. In an article published as part of the debate between Martin Walser and Ignatz Bubis in 1998 in the *Frankfurter Allgemeine Zeitung* (*FAZ*), Klaus von Dohnanyi—a former mayor of Hamburg and SPD politician—mentioned the Holocaust in this cryptic expression: "German identity . . . is today defined by our common origin in that shameful time: the origin of those who did it, who defended it, who at least tolerated it" (*Die is taten, die es begrüßten, oder die es doch mindestens zuließen*[89]). The "es," the "it," is clearly used reflectively and rhetorically. This is an article written and published by a politician who would not leave such an important expression to chance. Yet he did not consider it necessary to specify "it"; he assumed that readers would know what "it" referred to when he wrote of "the shame of what was done." This quote is a good illustration of both the omnipresence of the genocide and its absence.

After an initial round of interviews, the difficulty associated with articulating the mass murders became very clear to me, as a difficulty of talking about a potentially "shameful" past through the methods of interviews (Lavabre 1994: chap. 2). Indeed, particularly in the interviews with the students, it was possible to talk about "it" for half an hour without ever specifying what "it" was. As I am accustomed to using the interviewees' own words and expressions in the interview prompts, it was possible to avoid specification entirely. In a second round of interviews I forced myself to ask them to be more specific, and the interviews then replaced "it" with other expressions.

"What happened with the Jews" or "what happened to the Jews" were among the most frequently used expressions, both for the students and the teachers, in both Hamburg and Leipzig. These expressions reveal a degree of imprecision, but also a degree of "euphemism." The extermination policy is both too well-known and too abstract to be able to articulate. The difficulty putting the murder and extermination policies into words constructs an emptiness, a void in the discourse, in spite of the omnipresence of the theme. Theodor W. Adorno and Max Horkheimer noted this same tendency toward

72 • When Will We Talk about Hitler?

euphemism in their interviews with people who directly witnessed the war, in its immediate aftermath. "We often remarked that moderate or euphemistic expressions were used [to talk about the genocide] or an emptiness was constructed in the discourse" (Adorno 1971: 32). The fact that this emptiness already existed during the 1950s among the parents and grandparents of my interviewees raises the question of its transmission. The psychoanalyst Serge Tisseron used the comic book *Tintin* to analyze the mechanisms of "secrets" within families. Among other things, he showed that the emptiness in language around the "secret" could be transmitted over generations. The question then becomes in what ways these conclusions can be transposed onto the mechanisms of transmission of the genocide (Tisseron 1992).

The second characteristic of the expressions used to refer to the genocide is their passive structure, the lack of direct actors in these crimes. The genocide "happened" to the Jews, as though it fell from the sky, like a natural disaster. It is extremely rare in the interviews that the respondents explicitly mention the actors when they describe the atrocities of the genocide. The language used therefore prevents the designation of the crimes and their criminals. The respondents found themselves in a situation where it was linguistically impossible to talk about the genocide, which remains unspeakable, and thus unthinkable. For example, when Mr Gerste talked about a museum close to Wiesi (a former school in which a doctor conducted experiments, with the support of the Nazi government, on Jewish children before assassinating them), he used passive sentences and very common euphemisms.

> There was a cellar—where—hmmm—there was a photo exhibition or something like that. And the rooms [he pauses, searching for words] where—the children, uh, [he struggles to find an appropriate expression] were kept (*aufbewahrt*). And where the *crimes happened.* The descriptions are very impressive. And the photo exhibition. It's not as good as at Neuengamme, but still, it's [he hesitates]—it's very impressive, because of what [he searches for the right words again]—because of *what happened there.*[90]

His choice of words here is revealing. *Aufbewahren*—to keep or store—is a word that ordinarily has a positive connotation, used for food or precious objects that are put away in a specific place. Here it is used for the bodies of dead children (or possibly not yet dead, in this place of imprisonment). This word, which he chose carefully, seems out of place given the reality of imprisonment and medical experiments. The following expressions "where the crimes happened" (*wo Verbrechen passiert sind*) and "what happened there" are symptomatic of the vague and unspecific way of talking about the Holocaust. The crimes just "happen"; they are formulated without definite pronouns (Mr Gerste did not specify the crimes, only "crimes," *Verbrechen*, although he assumed I knew what he was referring to). This expression sounds strange; in German, the lack of a definite pronoun is used to express doubt about the reality of something. We would normally expect this kind of formulation to be accompanied by a phrase expressing rumor or doubt, such as: "where it is said crimes happened" (*man sagt dort seien Verbrechen passiert*). Mr Gerste's expression thus linguistically suspends the reality of these crimes, even though he himself recognizes that reality.

This dual characteristic, the difficulty of explicit articulation and the use of the passive form, as well as the use of "euphemisms" in order to refer to the National Socialist extermination policy, all contribute to the absence of specific content in the "categorical imperative" of "never again." The requirement to remember thus remains somehow void.

Ultimate Incomprehension

The relative emptiness of expressions like "never again" or "duty of remembrance" and the difficulty in articulating the genocide or describing the atrocities of the National Socialist extermination policy produce an impression of "total horror" that ultimately remains "incomprehensible." This is exacerbated by the invisibility of the perpetrators, who remain completely absent from the interviewees discourses; the focus, of both the teachers and the students, is instead entirely on the victims. Klara Rohrsteg, a teacher at Wiesi, aged around fifty, declared, "I still don't understand . . . how it could happen."[91] Mr Gerste put his incomprehension in normative terms.

> It's mixed up with—how can I put it—irrational acts. And explanations— strange things. For example: medical experiments on children [he lowers his voice] for me, it's—it's . . . [He does not finish his sentence.] It's an area where there are still questions. [He raises his voice a little.] How could a doctor behave like that? That's a question. Doctors should all know that! Like me, I know that as a driver of a car, I do not have the right to run a red light, right? But it's—yes, it's inconceivable [he hesitates] and incomprehensible.[92]

We find this same feeling of incomprehension among the students. Almost all of them said that they could not understand how "such a thing was possible." The school system does not help the students in their interrogations: "the basic questions [how the genocide was possible] that I asked myself, I'm still asking them," said Magdalena, an eighteen-year-old student at *Gymnasium* Weinberg.[93]

Annika Klein, a teacher at Wiesi, said she studied the persecution of the Jews during the Middle Ages as part of her university studies, specifically because at school she had not found the answers to her questions about the origins of antisemitism.

74 • When Will We Talk about Hitler?

Well, yes, [what interests me is] the origins, the origins of—the incredible hatred against Jews, and the extreme persecution of Jews during the Third Reich. That's it. Because, as a student, I didn't really get it. I didn't understand anything. I don't know, what we did before the foundation of the Reich, and then Bismarck, who made the laws, I don't know, and then there was World War I, and a bit of Weimar as well, and then all at once all the Jews were persecuted and then they were all assassinated. It was completely bizarre, really, completely grotesque.[94]

It was only later, during her history studies, as part of a seminar on medieval history, chosen at random to fit in with her working hours that she covered the medieval pogroms against the Jews, and she became aware of the historical roots of the persecution.

And that was when I realized: well, well, let's see, in fact it didn't begin there [in 1933]. Of course, you don't understand! Why such a thing happened! Nobody ever told you anything about Jews! NEVER in history class! And then they were all assassinated! It's really weird this whole thing (*Komische Sache*)![95]

The discovery of the historical roots of antisemitism led her to begin research that lasted several years, and which led to her Master's thesis in history. Yet this intellectual undertaking did not help her find a satisfying answer to the fundamental question of the origins of this prejudice.

In my Master's thesis, I didn't cover that. Not at all. Well, it's a question that I kind of touched on, more or less. But it wasn't the main question. Because I don't feel like I can answer it. Because I don't understand. I don't understand! I just don't understand how a group, in completely different regions, should be perpetually exposed to the same accusations. And the more I found isolated responses—for a specific place, a particular event, a specific pogrom or something—the less it helped find an overall response. On the contrary it increased the questions, made them more pressing, still more surprising.[96]

If Annika Klein explained her initial lack of understanding by the lack of explanation about the historical context taught in school, and by the abstract nature of the sudden violence of the genocide, she recognized that in spite of her own research, her questions remained unanswered. Moreover, neither Klein, nor the other history professors referred to historiography or quoted a history book that might have helped this understanding. These questionings undoubtedly continued to lead them to dedicate an important place to this theme in their classes.

Betroffenheit as a Frame of Reference

As we have seen, the intricate interconnection between civic education and the teaching of history can be partly explained by the history of the project for democratic education in postwar Germany. This project, launched by the American occupying forces directly after the war, found expression in the development of a particular pedagogic theory, *Betroffenheitspädagogik*, the pedagogy of emotional upheaval, which developed from the 1970s and 1980s. This theory, initially conceived as a way of addressing the German population's apparent lack of empathy for the victims of Nazism, and in particular for the Jews, remained very influential in pedagogic practice up until the 1990s and 2000s, particularly in the teaching of the genocide. The combined use of emotion and identification with the victims form a common denominator between the former FRG and the former GDR, which enables them to overcome the political fracture of 1989 and find a common ground between two previously opposing historical explanations.

It may be suggested that the "categorical imperative" to remember (which is in fact an "invention of the West") is so vague, goes some way to explaining the ease with which the teachers in Leipzig have today adopted and incorporated the central nature of the Jewish genocide. It could also explain the continuity or even the unexpected post-unification increase in the omnipresence of this imperative "to remember," which is incessantly repeated in the newly unified Germany.

In the following chapters, we will see the different ways in which the students appropriate and mobilize the Nazi past. From time to time, we will observe the use of emotion, but this has little to do with the way this pedagogic framework was conceived by the politicians and the postwar administration or the way it was implemented by the teachers. Indeed, the students demonstrate what Lüdtke called *Eigensinn*: they develop their own logics of appropriating the Nazi past, which are clearly influenced by the pedagogic framework that they have encountered at school but only partially. It is these logics of appropriation and their functioning that will be the object of analysis in this book.

The objective here is therefore not to adopt "pedagogic" reasoning, in order to demonstrate whether or not this approach is "effective" in "transmitting the Nazi past," "encouraging the students to become interested in politics," or "becoming good democratic citizens." That is a task best left to specialists of pedagogy. Nor is the goal to establish whether or not the students identify with the victims and adopt the emotion prescribed by this pedagogic framework. However, the emotional approach constitutes a frame of reference as well as an operational framework through which to talk about (and appropriate) the Jewish genocide, and the Nazi past more generally. Indeed, it is as a framework that it is of interest to us here, because it is within this framework, which has become "self-evident" for the students, that they must take a position, react, and mobilize the Nazi past. The purpose here is to analyze their different utilizations and the social frames of these student practices.

In the next chapter, we will look at the different ways of talking about the Nazi past that are particularly compatible with the school framework and are thus seen by the teachers in a positive light. Academic success in history requires a certain number of techniques that can be acquired by the students and used in different ways to stand out in the class and/or to impress their teachers. But beyond the rules of behavior that are imposed by the school setting, the social trajectories of the students themselves influence their attitudes toward the school and also toward Nazism. We will therefore look at the social conditions that enable academic success in classes on the history of Nazism, but we will also examine the social resources that may contribute to this success, through three specific case studies.

Notes

Epigraph: Interview with Ms Simone, 9 April 2003.
1. In the transcription, italics (without brackets) in the interviewees' comments represent words the respondent emphasized when speaking.
2. The *Zentrum für politische Bildung*, a state publishing house, also publishes many informative magazines for use in history classes.
3. On the translation of Betroffenheit as emotional upheaval, see note 41 in the Introduction.
4. The first law for reparations was introduced by the US military government in 1949 to make payments to Jewish survivors. But from February 1952 in the new independent Republic (under Allied tutelage in matters of foreign affairs and defense), it was the actors and not the victims who were the primary focus of judicial activities. This was expressed through a series of amnesties for Nuremberg criminals and the "victims of de-Nazification" of the 1949–1953 period (Frei 1999). The first German law on reparations (1953) contained clauses that limited the conditions for filing a request (such as those concerning residency on German soil, or internment for one year in a concentration camp in order to be able to lodge a complaint). The restrictive nature of the legal application of these clauses prevented most victims from receiving compensation. The second law (1956) relaxed some of the conditions necessary to demand reparations from the state. A certain number of groups of people remained excluded from the principle of reparations however, until the 1980s, specifically forced laborers from overseas, Roma people, homosexuals, and even Communists (this was relaxed in 1967). Moreover, even for those who were eligible, the administrative procedure to obtain compensation was very long and difficult. (Lüdkte 1993b: particularly 563–71). For a chronological summary of the governmental decisions made on this question since the war, see Reichel (2001: 75–96).

Education in the Service of Democracy • 77

5. These history workshops are made up of historians and amateurs who often study the local history of their towns. Founded in April 1985, the *Geschichtswerkstatt e.V.* is a national organization that brings together local initiatives and publishes the journal *Geschichtswerkstatt.* History celebrations or parties, *Geschichtsfeste*, bringing together members of the local workshops, are organized every year.

6. This explicit politico-memorial objective can be explained by a commitment to change the names of streets and schools, erect plaques, monuments, and "sites of memory," in order to make it more difficult to forget and repress this past.

7. Hence the need to personalize this teaching, for example, by involving students in local level research on their own town.

8. To what extent these visits constituted a continuation of the Allies' policy after the war still needs to be studied.

9. One of the criticisms addressed to Gies is that a comparison between Nazism and the GDR puts the two regimes on the same level, thus "euphemizing" the first while "diabolizing" the second, and finally painting the third, the FRG as "ideal."

10. Interview of 15 October 2003.

11. It is worth noting here that among these teachers there are eleven women and one man. It is perhaps not entirely by chance that women rather than men mobilize emotion in class.

12. Interview of 15 October 2003.

13. This expression is used by Ms Norte to refer to the Nazi genocide policy.

14. Ibid.

15. Ibid.

16. Interview of 10 October 2003.

17. This is also the case for some of the teachers in Hamburg. The clearest example of this is Ms Reinhard, who grew up in the GDR and can still remember a presentation that she had to do in the ninth grade on the Communist resistance. Like Mr Wolff, she mentions this in order to criticize the textbooks used in Hamburg and their lack of emphasis on the Communists. A similar discourse can be seen in the comments made by Herbert Wiese, Thomas, and Mr Gerste, all three teachers in Wiesi, who were members of the Marxistischer Studentenbund when they were students. The MSB Spartakus was a West-German student organization (1971–1990) close to the DKP, founded after the Sozialistischer Deutscher Studentenbund (SDS) was disbanded in 1970. The first two teachers subsequently became members of the DKP.

18. Interview of 15 October 2003.

19. The way in which the teachers teach history is of course linked to their own socialization and the process by which they were trained and experienced teaching, factors that are all different between Hamburg and Leipzig. Elsewhere, I have analyzed the teachers' own relationship toward the history of Nazism (Oeser 2007a, 2009a). This chapter simply aims to remind readers of the pedagogic framework that they set up for the students, but it does not analyze the conditions in which this framework was produced, which can be found in the teachers' trajectories (see Oeser 2007a: chap. 3 and 4; 2009a), but also in the remembrance policies in the FRG and the GDR respectively (Oeser 2007a: chap. 1).

20. This is an important debate in France in particular; for the origins of the French term "devoir de memoire" see for example Lalieu (2001). For a critique in terms of the "abuses" of the term, see Finkielkraut, Todorov and Marienstras (2000), Todorov (1995), and also Ricoeur (2000) for analysis in terms of "duty to remember" versus "right to forget." These authors share the search for the "right use" of discourses about the past. For a complete bibliography as well as an in-depth critique, see Gensburger and Lavabre (2005).

78 • When Will We Talk about Hitler?

21. Interview of 20 October 2003.
22. Interview of 13 February 2003.
23. Interview of 1 November 2003 and also interview of 14 January 2004.
24. Interview of 1 November 2003.
25. Interview of 25 April 2003.
26. The fact that I refer to these as typical narratives is not meant to imply that they are not based on real events. What seems interesting, however, is the homogeneity of these anecdotes and their retrospective interpretation.
27. This is a variation of the discourse that is found only in Hamburg. Indeed, the teachers and students in Leipzig very rarely related disagreeable experiences with foreigners accusing them of Nazism because of their German appearance. We will come back to this point (see chapter 4).
28. Interview of 7 November 2003.
29. Ibid. The inversion of stereotypes is linked here to the question of what constitutes a "minority": the "foreigner" category includes nearly everyone. In Karen Werthe's class, possibly three out of the twenty-five student have parents who both have German nationality. It is therefore these students, who are considered "German," that are in the minority.
30. This practice is also frequent during adolescence. An immigrant child over the age of fifteen is considered an adult and no longer has the right to enter the school system and can therefore not sit the high school exams. Given that school in the country of immigration is often a key means of accessing a socially valued position, the pressure to ensure that the children can integrate the system is very high. One of the most efficient means to enable this is to lie about the children's real age.
31. To dispel all doubt, it is important to note that racism is a very real phenomenon in Germany, which leads to political, personal, and professional discrimination. However, there are also discourses that tend to see it as the basis for all social phenomena, to cast it as the incarnation of all "social evils," and to see it as the only priority in a political struggle. The discourses around the "duty of remembrance" sometimes tend in this direction.
32. Interview of 1 November 2003.
33. In Germany, all school principals continue to teach classes in addition to their administrative responsibilities.
34. Informal conversation of 9 January 2004. The two concepts mobilized by Mr Schulze are not insignificant, in fact his work in the classroom was centered around these two themes.
35. Even though Mr Schulze affirmed that this is an "exemplary case," it is in fact the only case of the violation of a democratic constitution in the history of Germany. When he referred to the violation of the German constitution, he was therefore clearly referring to Nazism.
36. Interview of 17 February 2003.
37. Interview of 17 February 2003.
38. Elsewhere I have studied the difficulties that teachers in Leipzig encountered in readapting to a new state after reunification (see Oeser 2007a).
39. Interview of 14 October 2003.
40. Interview of 13 February 2003.
41. Ibid.
42. Interview of 23 October 2003.
43. Interview of 25 April 2003.
44. Interview of 24 April 2003.

45. Interview of 20 October 2003.
46. Note the familiar and personalized expression.
47. Interview of 26 September 2003.
48. Ibid.
49. Interview of 10 October 2003.
50. Interview of 9 April 2003.
51. Elsewhere, I have analyzed the relationship between experiences of "1968" and methods of teaching history, among the teachers in Hamburg, see Oeser (2009a).
52. On the implication generated by the use of these terms and the imaginary that is associated with them, see chapter 3.
53. Thomas never told me his family name. I met him outside the school context through a friend. We were therefore on first name terms from the beginning. I refer to him by his first name (even though here it's a pseudonym) because it reflects the informal nature of the research relationship, which was unique in the context of this research and is essential in understanding Thomas's discourse.
54. Interview of 24 April 2003.
55. Ibid.
56. The most widely sold tabloid daily newspaper in Germany with political scandals making its headlines.
57. Interview of 14 January 2004.
58. Interview of 24 April 2003.
59. Interview of 13 February 2003.
60. Interview of 22 April 2003.
61. Interview of 23 October 2003.
62. Interview of 3 October 2003.
63. Interview of 20 October 2003.
64. Interview of 14 October 2003.
65. This is the main union for secondary teachers in Germany. The GEW is one of the sixteen components of the Deutscher Gerwerkschaftsbund (DGB) the German Trade Union Confederation.
66. Interview of 25 April 2003.
67. Interview of 20 October 2003.
68. The pedagogy of emotional upheaval emphasizes the victims. The use of the word "genocide" in this section to refer to the victims of the National Socialist extermination policy is a reminder of this pedagogic perspective, which partly erases the actors and their responsibility. For the teachers, the genocide of the Jews is both the symbol and the expression of the extermination policy and implicitly, silently, includes other groups of victims. The addition of the adjective "Jewish" is a reminder of this specificity that remains implicit in the teachers' discourse.
69. Interview of 20 October 2003
70. Interview of 17 February 2003
71. Interview with Karen Werthe, 23 October 2003.
72. Interview of 7 November 2003.
73. Interview of 10 October 2003.
74. Interview of 23 October 2003.
75. Interview of 20 October 2003.
76. Interview of 3 November 2003.
77. With the death of those who witnessed this period first hand, this practice is inevitably destined to be replaced by something else (invitations to political figures, writers,

children of witnesses, and so forth). Perhaps this will help the teachers in Leipzig return to the practice of inviting people from outside the school environment to speak to the students.

78. This project was not completed.
79. Interview of 20 October 2003.
80. Interview of 22 September 2003.
81. Interview of 10 October 2003.
82. Mr Wolff belongs to the "winning" generation of 1989. He has a job as a principal and has adapted particularly well to the new system. Indeed, upward social mobility and the defense of "values of the old FRG" go together (see Oeser 2007a).
83. Visit to the Buchenwald concentration camp with a ninth grade class, May 2004.
84. Informal Interview after class, 9 January 2003.
85. Interview of 3 November 2003, emphasis by the author.
86. Interview of 19 February 2003.
87. Fritz Fischer (1908–1999) was appointed Professor at the University of Hamburg in 1942. In 1961, he published his major book entitled *Griff nach der Weltmacht* in which he challenged the consensus among German historians regarding the non-culpability of belligerent countries in World War I and emphasized the responsibility of German political and military elites in this war because they consciously took the risk of starting a war (Fischer [1961] 1975). Fischer radicalized his theses over the years that followed with publications like *Weltmacht oder Niedergang* (1965) and *Krieg der Illusionen* (1969) in which he described German leaders as preparing for war from 1912. He also underlined the economic and social factors that pushed the elites toward war for reasons of "internal security" (the danger of socialism). He was attacked particularly ferociously by Gerhard Ritter (1888–1967), a well-established historian in the FRG at the time, and this criticism reached its peak at the Deutscher Historikertag in Berlin in 1964 and at the International Congress of Historians in Vienna in 1965. He was furthermore particularly criticized by Egmont Zechlin (1896–1992), also a professor at the University of Hamburg, and who worked on the same archives as Fischer. For an overview of the controversy around Fischer, see Husson (2001: 69–83) and Hallgarten (1969).
88. Hamburg continually had a Social Democratic government until the arrival of the Christian Democrats in 2001.
89. Klaus von Dohnanyi, "Eine Friedensrede, Martin Walsers notwendige Klage," *FAZ*, 14 November 1998.
90. Interview of 20 October 2003.
91. Interview of 20 October 2003.
92. Ibid.
93. Ibid.
94. Interview of 23 October 2003.
95. Ibid.
96. Ibid.

Chapter 2

TALKING ABOUT THE NAZI PAST IN CLASS AND SUCCEEDING AT SCHOOL

There are "right" ways of reinterpreting the Nazi past: those that are considered legitimate within the school system as well as outside it. They are acquired through multiple processes by which the Nazi past is reappropriated, both inside and outside school. The school is thus one of the institutions that contributes to learning the "right" ways of talking about the past. Some, who are privileged by their social background and their family socialization (teachers' children in particular) adapt more easily than others to the normative framework of school. This chapter aims to untangle the processes by which the "right" attitudes to the Nazi past are transmitted and to understand the social dispositions that help the "faultless" acquisition of these ways of behaving. In the first section of this chapter, we will show that the reappropriation of understandings of the past that are academically legitimate goes hand in hand with academic success more generally—if only because they are "rewarded" by the teachers. In the second section, we will focus on the study of the social trajectories of three students who, for different reasons, develop a relationship with the Nazi past that is considered legitimate in the school environment. These case studies will enable an analysis of the links between social trajectories and legitimate forms of reappropriation of the Nazi past. We will seek to understand the social conditions that provide opportunities for certain students to appropriate these academically legitimate forms of the Nazi past and transform them into resources that enable them to succeed at school, but also to be confident within their peer groups or pursue future careers.

"Good Students" and the "Self-Evidence" of Legitimate Discourse

First, it is important to underline a certain consensus in the discourse. Professors and students, in Hamburg and Leipzig, from bourgeois or working-class families, of various ethnic backgrounds, whether migrants or not, all agree on the central importance of the Nazi past and more particularly of the National Socialist extermination policy. The moral rejection of the genocide is unambiguous and unquestioned.[1]

The school therefore transmits ways of talking about the past that the students will adapt to in their own ways. In spite of a certain ambiguity about this past among the students, from ninth grade on, they learn how to talk about it in class according to rules that they internalize in different ways.

All the students were questioned about their personal relationship with German history through an open question: "if you think about German history, is there a period, an event, a moment that seems, to you, personally, in your own life, to be particularly important?" The aim of this general question was to establish the importance (or not) of the period under consideration for the historic consciousness of these young Germans. The overwhelming majority of students, both in Hamburg and Leipzig, in both privileged and disadvantaged schools, referred to the period between 1933 and 1945 as being the most important.[2] Fewer than twenty of the over one hundred students questioned did not mention it in the very first phrase. Among the other historical periods sometimes mentioned were the fall of the Berlin Wall and the Weimar Republic. Six children did not answer this question as it did not make sense to them (we will come back to this).

Most of the teachers interviewed (who were unanimous as to the importance of this period) also talked about the students' interest—or even passion—for this subject from as early as seventh grade. Over the last twenty years they have seen students ten, eleven, and twelve years old regularly ask in class "when will we talk about Hitler?" (*wann machen wir/kriegen wir endlich Hitler?*). Sometimes: "Can't we do Hitler today? Even just for ten minutes?" They are impatient to "learn about Hitler" and they want to "do Hitler in class" well before they reach that point in the curriculum. They want to know "what was so bad about Hitler" (*was war denn eigentlich schlimm an Hitler?*)—because they know that he was "bad" but not why—and they are interested in "how one becomes such an awful person" (*wie wird man so ein Schlimmer*). This "desire for Hitler" expressed by the students (*ich hab Lust auf Hitler*) is based on prior knowledge. At age ten, all or almost all of them have heard about this person and know that "he did very bad things." Hitler, the symbol of absolute evil, has a certain fascination for the students, which the teachers refer to by repeating their expressions. Karen Werthe,

aged thirty-five, for example, used their vaguely sexual expressions, emphasizing the erotic, narcissistic, and phantasmagorical nature of them: "They're
really hot on Hitler, they're really into him" (*die sind ganz heiß auf Hitler:
die fahren voll auf Hitler ab*).[3] Ms Reinhard, who is a teacher at *Gymnasium*
Weinberg put it like this:

> Well, yes, they often know a lot of things about Hitler as a person [before
> Nazism is covered in class]. The—yes, the stereotypes. And they know—the
> clichés (*Schlagworte*): the war, the persecution of the Jews. [She hesitates.]
> Most of the time, things that are not very precise.[4]

Other than the figure of the dictator, the genocide of the Jews also provokes particular interest among the students, in particular the girls (see chapter 3); it represents the crystallization of Nazism for them. The persecution
of the Jews symbolizes "the whole war"[5] and provokes the curiosity of the
children who wonder: "How was that possible?"

The importance of the Nazi past for the interviewees can be clearly seen
in how Maren (aged eighteen, from *Gymnasium* Weinberg in Hamburg)
responded to the prompt. In answering the general question on German
history, she spontaneously mentioned *The Diary of Anne Frank*, without her
comments being situated in a particular historical period, which is what the
question asked her for. The importance of Nazism is in fact so clear that, for
her, it does not need to be explicitly stated.

Thus, and unlike the other periods of history, covering Nazism in class
is first a "pleasure" for the students. Leonore, a sixteen-year-old student in
Leipzig, said this:

> Yes, and also, I saw the film *Hitler and His Women*. And I enjoyed it. And then,
> it was also for that, it was a pleasure to study World War II [in class]. . . . I was
> very happy that we were going to cover this period—I was very enthusiastic
> about the subject. That's also why it was really fun to do it in class (*das hat so
> richtig Spass gemacht*).[6]

Moreover, the students share certain knowledge about this past with each
other. Heidi, aged eighteen, a student of Mr Schulze at the *Gymnasium* in
Hamburg and passionate about history said that a certain number of images
from the period were going around and that "we know about them" (without
actually specifying who "we" refers to).[7]

> Well yes. There is this perfectly normal way of seeing things. We've seen films
> and we know these typical images or those books—there are children who
> lost their parents, things like that. Because someone somewhere was Jewish
> or something like that. And then we've read a bit—or—[she starts again] no,

a book, that's already too specific. I don't know—general public awareness (*das allgemeine* öffentliche *Bewußtsein*) about what happened. But what I'm implying, and what I know also from lots of my friends—even if we had it in history—is that we don't really know how they came to power exactly. Or—well, me neither, I couldn't really explain it. [She laughs.] Something happened, somewhere, and Germany lost the war, and there were six million Jews, or even more, who were assassinated, and then the Federal Republic was born or something like that. And then perhaps more or less exact details—like for example, they somehow made lamps out of them (*da ham sie dann irgendwie Lampen draus gemacht*) and other disgusting things like that. But otherwise, I think that we don't really know the details and all that.[8]

Heidi has put her finger on the phenomenon. The importance of this past for the students, and their "ordinary knowledge" does not prevent what the teachers call "significant lacunae"—on the contrary. Although none of the students are among those who "don't know what Auschwitz is," as some surveys have reported (Silbermann and Stoffers 2000), several do not know in which country to situate Auschwitz geographically, even though they describe it as "the biggest concentration camp."[9] Daniel (the son of a doctor and a high school teacher), aged sixteen, is a student at the *Gesamtschule* Wiesi who struggled academically at the *Gymnasium* and had to change schools. His academic difficulties influence his knowledge of history: he is convinced that he visited Auschwitz "in Berlin."[10] Asked to describe the place he visited, he said he did not remember very well because "it was closed, but there were huts and everything." Reiner (the son of a factory worker and a gardener, aged twenty, former student at the *Gesamtschule* Wiesi and an apprentice welder in a building company at the time of the interview) tells me that "the Jews were sent" to the concentration camps "to work," "when they were old and sick" were "disposed of" after a "medical exam" to be "put to death" under supervision by doctors. Christian, a student at the 100th *Mittelschule* in Leipzig, the son of a truck driver and a hairdresser, thinks that Hitler was "in the GDR." Although candidates for the *Arbitur* high school diploma show greater knowledge of the period than those in vocational schools, we encounter this "vague knowledge" with almost all students, especially the younger ones. But it does not take the same forms according to the school type and social origins of the children. We will examine the ways in which it functions in more detail below.

This vague, sometimes "inexact" knowledge by no means prevents the students from incorporating the major lessons of the history of the Nazi past, either in critical terms or in terms of beliefs. There is thus no automatic link between the degree of historical accuracy of the children's knowledge and the moral position they will adopt. They can be perfectly convinced that Auschwitz is in Berlin and reject Nazism as a criminal regime or believe in the German constitution.

Legitimate Ways of Treating the Nazi Past in Class

The family and the school function as sites in which the competences deemed necessary at a given time are constituted by usage itself, and simultaneously as sites in which the *price* of those competencies is determined., i.e., as markets, which by their positive or negative sanctions, evaluate performance, reinforcing what is acceptable, discouraging what is not, condemning valueless dispositions to extinction jokes that "fall flat," or though acceptable in another context, another market, here seem "out of place" and only provoke embarrassment or disapproval . . . ." (Bourdieu [1979] 2010: 170–171)

What Pierre Bourdieu has shown of the "market of school culture" compared to that of "general culture" (*culture libre*) also applies to inside the school. Indeed, there are legitimate and non-legitimate ways of talking about the Nazi past, in class as elsewhere. School, embodied in the figures of the teachers, negatively sanctions the non-legitimate (or "out of place") ways of talking about the Nazi past and encourages those which are "acceptable" according to the school rules. This part of the chapter will use the example of one tenth-grade class in Wiesi to look at the ways in which the teachers control the students' performance. We will observe the ways the students manage to adapt to this control by developing a specific language and a way of writing about the Nazi past which helps them obtain good grades.

In Annika Klein and Karen Werthe's tenth-grade class at *Gesamtschule Wiesi* in Hamburg the sixteen-year-old students chose the subjects they wanted to research in relation to the period 1933–1945. For six months they read around a subject and then "investigated" it—in libraries, museums, they visited a former concentration camp (Neuengamme), interviewed people in the street, etc.—and they covered the subject quite freely. Some wrote a written report, others made a film, and others set up a website. However, with the exception of one group, they all covered a theme linked to the genocide, thus conforming to the teachers (implicit) demands. The clear demonstration of a personal, "emotional" connection to the subject helped the students obtain good grades. The two best projects were those which contained the most elements to provoke emotion: images, "personal reports," diary entries that summarized the thoughts and feelings experienced during "the investigation." The language used to describe the camps reflected the emotionally sensitive state of the students.

The Right Images

In the students' projects there are images of the Neuengamme concentration camp, Ravensbrück, and other unidentified camps. The students used three

86 • When Will We Talk about Hitler?

main ways of representing them. First, they used images of the camp buildings, the train tracks, and what remains visible in Neuengamme today. Second, they added images of the sites of memory, the monument to the victims, tombstones, flowers, and a copy of the list of the names of those who died at Neuengamme. Third, they reproduced highly charged emotional images—emaciated bodies, men and women piled high in beds, bodies in mass graves, experiments. One student drew a series of gray buildings with a blue sky and gray clouds, a yellow sun with a sad face and crying eyes. At the bottom of his picture, he copied the symbols that the different detainees wore on their uniforms: the yellow star for Jews, the pink triangle for homosexuals, and so forth.

The yellow of the sun is the only bright color in this otherwise overwhelmingly gray drawing. Its crying face is expressive and gives emotional strength to the image.

Sandy[11] is considered a "fairly good" student by her teachers. In the text below she commented on the photos she took at Neuengamme.

> In the second image we can see a small house, which was a help house [she uses the word *Hilfsstation* but means *Revier*, infirmary], in which fifty or so detainees were piled on top of each other. You can't really say it was a help house because people didn't get better there. For example, if someone came with

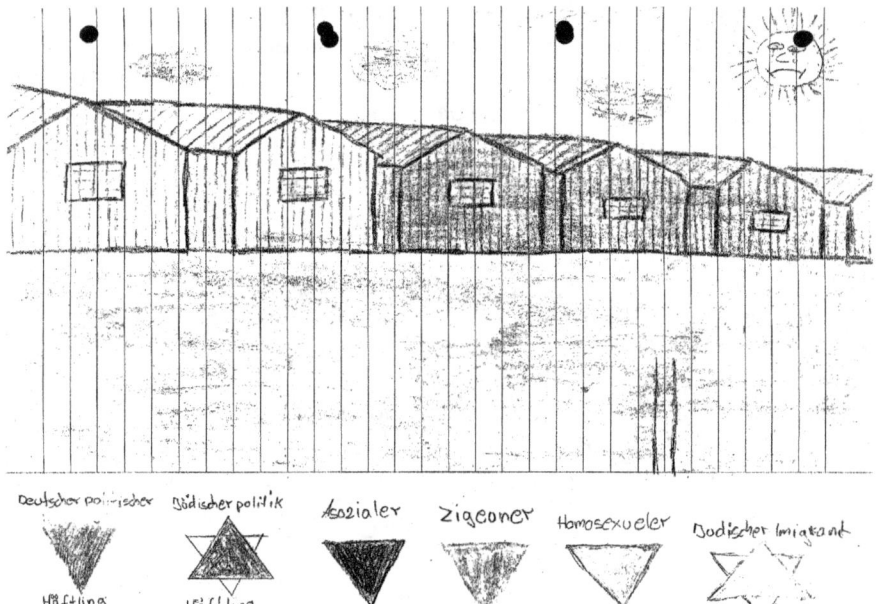

Figure 2.1 Student's drawing of the Neuengamme concentration camp.
Source: Author's private archives.

pneumonia, there was a strong possibility he would contaminate the others or that the others would contaminate him. Most of the detainees were very scared of ending up in that house, so they mostly killed themselves before going. The sick didn't receive any help, they were just quarantined, so as not to infect the others. The detainees called this the "house of no return."[12]

In this report on the camps, the description of the living conditions is omnipresent. Sandy did not hesitate to express her own feelings in the face of the victims' suffering, their sicknesses, and their deaths. Her classmate, Anna, also directly described the situation from the point of view of the victims. "If the women couldn't work, the Nazis took their children and shoot them [sic].[13] The ones who didn't want to work were shoot [sic], the ones who complained were shoot [sic] in front of everyone." She expressed her pity for the prisoners who "had to work day and night, and only had the right to sleep for two hours."[14]

Kevin and Martin also submitted a project on the concentration camp in Neuengamme. One page was particularly well appreciated by Karen Werthe (see Figure 2.2). It included two photos and a text on the housing and food of the prisoners. The photos show the bunk beds with prisoners crammed into them (the students' commentary was "the beds for sleeping"), and a mass grave (the student's comment here reads "dead prisoners simply thrown on the compost [Kompost]"[15]).

Translation of the German Text by Kevin and Martin

The food and housing in a camp (KZ). The housing in the KZ was not exactly pretty, on the contrary, it was cruel. There were three people in a little bed, which was about 1 meter long and so the people didn't really have room to stretch out their legs. With three people in a bed it was really hard and so there was even more risk of falling ill. Because there was only one tap to wash 10,000 people. You have to imagine. And the food was not great either, it didn't make the prisoners stronger. There were three meals a day, morning, noon, and night. In the morning, there was always a coffee or a clear broth. The lunch was clear turnip soup with little fat. In the evening, the prisoners ate a piece of bread with a bit of sausage. The food was already insufficient in 1940. Year by year the food at the KZ decreased even more, and sometimes the SS took the food for themselves, and so the prisoners had nothing and couldn't survive. The prisoners who didn't have any food got really thin and were insulted and teased by the SS for being "Muslims." In fact only those who managed to get food by other means or those who were classed [sic] as hard workers could survive because they had a bit more food.[16]

The first image probably comes from the camp at Auschwitz, the second from either Auschwitz or Buchenwald, at the liberation. It is certain that they

88 • When Will We Talk about Hitler?

Unterbringung und Verpflegung im KZ

Die Unterbringung im KZ war nicht gerade sehr schön, im Gegenteil es war grausam. Es waren ca. 3 Leute in einem kleinen Bett, das ca 1 Meter lang war, so dass die Menschen keinen richtigen Platz hatten um ihre Beine auszustrecken. Zu 3. in einem Bett ist schon sehr hart, so durch wurde auch die Krankheitsgefahr gesteigert. Denn es gab nur einen Wasserhahn zum Waschen für 10.000 Leute. Das muss man sich mal vorstellen. Und die Ernährung war auch nicht die beste, dadurch wurden die Häftlinge auch nicht stärker. Es gabs pro Tag 3 Mahlzeiten, Morgens, Mittags, Abend. Morgens gab es immer ein Kaffee oder eine dünne Suppe. Das Mittagsessen bestand aus wässriger Steckrübensuppe mit wenig Fett. Abends bekamen die Häftlinge dann ein Stück Brot mit etwas Wurst. Schon 1940 war das Essen nicht ausreichend. Von Jahr zu Jahr wurde das Essen im KZ nur noch weniger und die SS-Leute nahmen sich auch teilweise einfach das Essen so dass einige Häftlinge nichts bekamen und so auch nicht überleben konnten. Die Häftlinge die nichts zu Essen bekamen nahmen tierisch ab und wurden von den SS-Leuten als Muselmänner beschimpft und ausgelacht. Eigentlich konnten nur die Menschen im KZ überleben die sich auf anderer Weise Essen beschaffen konnten oder als Schwerstarbeiter eingestuft war da die etwas mehr zu Essen bekamen.

— Die Schlafbetten

Im Gegensatz zum „Aufbau des KZs" hast du hier viel eigenständiger formuliert. Hier merkt man, dass du verstanden hast, was du schreibst! Pri

Tote Häftlinge wurden einfach auf den Kompost geschmissen.

Figure 2.2 Text and image by Kevin and Martin on life in the concentration camps. Source: Author's private archives.

do not come from Neuengamme. The teacher had nothing to say, however, about the fact that the students illustrated their project on Neuengamme with images from other camps nor on the use of the word "compost" to describe the mass graves.

Instead, Karen Werthe's commentary praised the students: "you formulated this in your own words. Here we can see that you have understood what you are describing." The students put themselves in the prisoners' shoes describing their difficult lives, which is what the teachers asked of them.

Good Work

Five of the students added "reflection" pages to their projects, in which they described why they had appreciated the group work on the visit to the museum at Neuengamme. Karsten commented,

> In the exhibition, we can see documents, like a death certificate for example. And at the end [of the exhibition] there were the graves of people who died there. I learned lots of things in this exhibition: in books there are lots of things too, but when you see things like that in real life, you can imagine them much better.[17]

Karsten had a very vivid imagination. During his first visit to Neuengamme, when I accompanied them, he spent a lot of time watching the films that showed original sequences of workers at their duties or being transported in wagons. The photos showed their deplorable condition, in particular their wasted bodies and ragged clothes. These "typical" images of the camps were particularly violent. The other students wandered at length around the museum, while Karsten remained alone watching these images. He left the exhibition earlier than his classmates and said that he did not feel well, he wanted to throw up.[18] This difficult experience, which he did not want to discuss, was never mentioned in his report. Karsten wrote that he thought it was "good" to have been to the museum because he can now "imagine" how the prisoners died. He established an emotional relationship with the prisoners in the way his teachers had asked him.

The reflections of his classmate Anna are much more "emotional." She talks freely of the feelings that Karsten prefers to keep to himself. Anna observes that she found the subject of "the concentration camps," "interesting, but also sad." "There was everything we wanted to know: with lots of images of small children and lots of dead people." In particular Anna found the beds "very good, but also very cruel." And she repeats, "I found that very good, but also sad."[19]

How to Write about the Camps

Sandy's empathy is clearly expressed in her writing. She writes, "imagine, in a wooden hut, thousands of beds all lined up! It's HORRIBLE (*SCHRECKLICH*)!!!!"[20] The use of capital letters and exclamation marks is not enough to convey her indignation. She repeats the word horrible several times to describe the camp. Her final comments are indicative of her relation to emotion, and they also express the specific expectations concerning the discovery of these "horrors." Sandy emphasized that

> Obviously the camps have all been restored and are not as horrible as they were then. There is probably a reason that they are not as dark today. If they were still as horrible then maybe not as many people would come and visit. . . . When we go to a camp today, it's not really so shocking, because everything is so green, but when you see the exhibition, you can put yourself in the situation [of the detainees].[21]

The use of the first person, the adjectives to qualify feelings of horror and sadness, the repetition, the exclamations, the style used by the students all testifies as to an emotional sensitivity. The girls in particular expressed this freely and it is perfectly suited to the context of the pedagogy of emotional upheaval. There is a certain distance between this manifest emotional state and the actual visit to the camp that was "in fact, not so horrible," which underlines the students' ability to express a feeling of horror that they do not necessarily feel but is expected of them. Indeed, Sandy's disappointment suggests an emotional reaction that was pre-formed, because it was expected by the school institution as well as by the student herself. She thus feels the need to explain (and to explain to herself) why her "impression" was not "as dark" as she had expected. Her project satisfied her teachers' expectations and she received a good grade.

Socially Situated Moral Efficiency

The students' share their teachers' convictions about the importance of the "duty to remember." Almost all of them are convinced that "it is necessary to know what happened" to "avoid it happening again." They have thus integrated the underlying moral requirements in the teaching of the Nazi past.

The extraordinary status of this past is made explicit and justified in a more or less detailed way depending on the social origin of the student—given that language and argumentative skills are directly linked to academic success from as early as nursery school. Thus, the explanations and judgments vary, from the basic ethical response expressed in one or two repeated phrases ("we must not forget" or "it was horrible"), to the most sophisticated political and economic arguments. All these arguments correspond to the expectations of the teachers. The students who develop longer arguments are also those who get good grades. The older they are, the more they come from the "good schools," and the more they are considered "good students," then the more their formulations will be close to those of their teachers. For some, the reasons for the importance of the subject being self-evident remained obscure, such as for Magdalena, aged eighteen, the eldest daughter of two professionals. Magdalena considered herself "the worst student" in her advanced history class[22] at *Gymnasium* Weinberg.

> It's important because so many people died, and were hunted, and somehow, I think that it's, even under Hitler, during that time—it's in some ways quite important, and somehow [she hesitates, searching for words]—I think, you know, because it's negative, you know [she hesitates again]—it's quite extreme, how one person—can impose their will on everyone. And there were also lots of people who died, so, I think that it's quite—frightening in fact! And that's also why it's [she hesitates] the most important—in German history. It the most overwhelming event.[23]

Magdalena understood the importance of the subject: she mentioned the horror, the difficulty in understanding the Jewish genocide, and the fact that it is a "cataclysmic" event (*einschneidend*). However, although she perfectly adopted the emotional register (frightening, overwhelming), her reasoning remained circular, even tautological. Magdalena was an exception however.

Almost all the students evoke anti-racism and tolerance as the first lesson to take from the past. At Wiesi, the migrants, or children of migrants, applied this lesson directly to themselves and to the relations between the students at school. Joey, aged fifteen, was born in Afghanistan and immigrated to Hamburg at the age of seven; he puts it like this:

Can you explain why you find the period of Hitler important?
Because it teaches people how to live together, no matter what their skin color, their nationality, we have to live together. No matter where they come from, it's the person that counts. That means, it is not important what skin color you have, or if you're black or white. It's important how you are. Your ways of being, not the color of your skin.

Could we say that history—
[He interrupts] teaches us things. It teaches us to be better human beings. But also [to respect] foreigners, other cultures and everything. And that it's also interesting. [He pauses to consider.] Lots of other cultures are very interesting. It's a lesson that we should never forget.

And here, at school—
[He interrupts] yes, well, here—they [the students] are not so much like that.
[He hesitates.] They don't say [he hesitates], "Yeah—you, you're a shitty foreigner" (*Ja du, du bist jetzt 'n scheiß Ausländer*) or something like that. They
aren't like that! They're like [he searches] like us.[24]

Joey, the son of a former soldier and a mother who stays at home and are
political refugees in Germany, clearly understood the lessons about "tolerance" regarding "other cultures." However, he was still reasoning in terms of
"us" (foreigners) and "them" (Germans and children of Germans), although
these categories come together in his statement "they are like us." But Joey's
example shows to what extent everyone can find a way to apply the "great
moral lessons" from the Nazi past to their own situations.

Samira, who was seventeen at the time of the interview, is one of the
rare students at Wiesi who was going to sit the *Arbitur* exams. Her father
migrated to Germany from Nigeria in the 1960s to study medicine and, as
he did not finish his course, now works in an institution for handicapped
people. Her mother is a German social pedagogue in the same institution.
Samira explicitly expressed her belief in the importance of the school system
and the values that are transmitted there. She said that she "can't understand"
her classmates, some of whom "don't like Jews."

I think that the most important is that [National Socialism] never happens
again. I think it's less important [she hesitates] to know the exact dates of what
happened. It's more important to learn from it! It's no use to me if I can recite
all the historic dates by heart—but don't know what it means or the significance that that history can have for us today. That's what I think is the most
important.

And what exactly must not happen again?
[She pauses to think] that human beings close their eyes, that they react with
indifference to other humans [she pauses again]. For example, *Kristallnacht*,
where [she hesitates] for me, really it's [she struggles to find the words] my
reason tells me that I must try, as much as I can, to not do anything against
another human being, or something like that. And that we can—somehow
devalue a—a Jewish person, and not see them as a human being, but rather
as an animal or as an object, and then mistreat them or inflict physical and
psychological injury on them—that I can't understand.[25]

Samira, like many other girls, rebelled against the suffering inflicted on
the victims of history, who were dominant in her discourse formulating the
lessons to be learned from the Nazi past. The boys on the other hand, especially when they come from well-off families, tended to rely more on political
and economic categories and construct their reasoning at the national, and

even the international level. They also demonstrated a differential capacity to transpose the example onto other objects, events, and so forth.

When I interviewed him, René, the son of two secondary teachers, was eighteen years old and a student at the *Gymnasium* Weinberg in Hamburg. He says, "And so—we must—avoid forgetting, at all costs! Because—you can see it now too—it's because it's not really, not completely forgotten, that it still has an influence on government policy."[26] René was referring to the refusal of the Schröder government to participate in the second war in Iraq, a debate that was raging at the time of the interview.[27] The importance of this "duty to remember" and the observation of the presence of the past both in contemporary politics but also in broader society, all overlap in René's discourse.

> And [the Nazi past], it's present, in the way people think. For example, that they say, out of principle—war, no way! Things like that. I think that it's linked to our past. To the fact that we don't forget . . . It's that, I think, that's the most important, that we don't forget. But also, to take opposition [he hesitates], to be skeptical [he hesitates again] toward extreme movements.[28]

Hauke, a seventeen-year-old student at *Gymnasium* Monnet and the son of a shopkeeper and a bank manager, put the emphasis on the economy, of which he had a good understanding. His parents' professions undoubtedly had an impact on his perspective.

> I find that period interesting, because there are so many things that happened—and because we can learn lessons, for your own life too. And you see what you can improve, and it attracts our attention to the signs that a situation is deteriorating. And the points at which you have to pay attention, to what is happening, with yourself or with the country's politics.
>
> *And what are these "lessons"?*
> Yes, for example xenophobia (*Fremdenfeindlichkeit*), of course. But more generally [he hesitates] the economic recession that there was before 1933 inflation. They're the period during which you have to pay particular attention to politics.[29]

Hauke not only mentioned the "general lessons" to be learned from history, but was also able to apply them to the present situation and draw economic and political conclusions.

> At the moment, we're in a recession. Growth is at 2 percent I think, at the moment. And I think that if it continues like that, it will be easier for the extremists to get people enthusiastic about their radical ideas. Because people think, logically, that you need radical change to improve the situation. [He pauses to think.] It's easier to lead people in the wrong direction![30]

94 • When Will We Talk about Hitler?

Thus, for both teachers and students, Nazism is "still there, like a warning (*das mahnende Beispiel*) so that we're aware that it can still happen again if we're not careful" to use an expression from Benjamin (eighteen, student at *Gymnasium* Weinberg). Alexander (also eighteen, student at the *Gesamtschule* Wiesi, the son of two secondary teachers) added:

> We must always learn lessons from history. And—we produced enough shit (*Scheiße gemacht*) in history! [He laughs.] And yeah, forgetting it would lead us to make the same mistakes again. And I think it's really important to think about history and to learn from it. Yeah, yeah and vote for a party that isn't going to make the same mistake again![31]

Alexander was able to draw concrete lessons from his history class in terms of civic behavior (voting), and this corresponds to the objectives explicitly expressed by his teachers. Johannes, aged eighteen, a student at *Gymnasium* Weinberg in Hamburg, the son of a doctor and a high school teacher, explicitly stated what Alexander only implied: "in my opinion, this past is the basis for our historical responsibility that we all bear together as a generation."[32] For Johannes, this responsibility consists—beyond pacifism and "democratic votes" ("non-radical")—in "preserving Germany's image overseas."

> We have the duty [he hesitates], yes, to rectify our bad image (*unser schlechtes Licht gerade zu rücken*) somehow. I think that as a new generation, we must prove that we are not like that, that we don't stand out by being particularly National Socialist or fascist or—discriminatory or [he searches for words] inhuman, or something like that. [We must prove that] it's not [he hesitates] specific to Germans. But rather: it's all history now.[33]

These boys and girls "from bourgeois families" share with their teachers the belief that "without knowledge of history you can't have a well-founded opinion, because everything is [historically] connected."[34] This result is in keeping with studies on political socialization that show the cumulative effects of school and family in guiding the development of children's political opinions (Percheron 1977). But these students were also invested with a (masculine) mission. Their generation must "prove itself" at the international level to be recognized as "democratic." This desire has concrete political consequences. Hauke also affirmed:

> For me, concretely, that means voting red-green [he laughs], for example. And [he pauses to think] yes—having open immigration policies, for example. And [he hesitates, searching for words] and supporting—more or less— weaker countries, developing countries, things like that.[35]

Other than consequences in terms of foreign or internal policy, Richard, aged eighteen, from the *Gymnasium* Weinberg in Hamburg, the son of a law professor and a real estate business owner, expressed his expectations in politico-philosophical, even religious terms, evoking human rights and dignities.

> The Holocaust—this ideology full of contempt for human beings, racist laws, and for example, considering the Russians as subhuman—devaluing human beings, considering them as objects . . . It's in any case very good [to cover it in class or in the media] because it increases the democratic sentiment in society. Seeing that all human beings count as individuals, that each living being is valuable. And freedom: freedom of expression, of movement, of reunion (*Freizügigkeit*). That, and the constitution (*Grundgesetz*), human rights and all that. And I think that [knowing the Nazi past] helps a lot.[36]

The students therefore deeply integrated the moral expectations of their teachers, even though the justifications that they put forward vary according to their social situations and their cultural and academic capital, as well as according to gender.

An Ambiguous Relationship with the Past

Accepting the importance of the Nazi past and its political implications does not prevent these students from developing an ambiguous relationship with the past, linked to the feeling of being considered guilty.

> As Germans, overseas we're branded right away or something like that. Sometimes it upsets me, when you think that I, I had nothing to do with that [Nazism]. And my parents had nothing to do with it either [he hesitates]. They were too little too. And so every time, we're rejected, like the Germans, the Germans want to be big and strong again, want to control the world, things like that.[37]

Karl, whose father ran a small family business in which his mother occasionally worked, was nineteen years old and a student at *Gymnasium* Weinberg at the time of the interview. He was conscious of the stigma of history when he traveled overseas. In part, this is related to his feeling of being judged and found guilty without having committed any crime himself. He felt automatically associated with the National Socialists, this made the Nazi period important for him, but meant he had an ambiguous relationship with it. "The weight of the past" was heavy on Karl, "they" expected him to feel ashamed of being German. This feeling is diffuse (as we can see in his use of "they" and the passive voice). It is only after he was questioned directly on this "they" that he referred to "other countries," German politicians, and "some Germans." This ambiguity is also seen in other interviewees, more or less explicitly. In Hamburg, it was even directly incorporated into a strong feeling of "guilt in spite of themselves." The difficulty that the students in Hamburg had in expressing this guilt and shame can be felt in their generic and indefinite use of pronouns ("they" or "you").

> Ultimately, I would argue that—as much as [he hesitates] you can't be proud of Germany, you also can't—yes, in principle [he searches for words], you can't be ashamed of a past that you didn't live through (*sich für Vergangenes schämen wenn man selber nicht dabei war*). [He hesitates.] But it's true, that [he hesitates again, having trouble formulating what he wants to say] I think that I—[he considers and then takes the leap] yes, in any case, I am ashamed (*ich schäme mich dafür*). Overseas—when you arrive overseas and you know that . . . [he does not finish the phrase]. In particular when you go to Poland or . . . [he again does not finish his phrase]. We have a Polish cleaning lady. And it's true [he hesitates], it's true that you're ashamed. I think so, yes.[38]

In this quotation we can see that René, aged eighteen, student at Gymnasium Weinberg, did manage to express his feeling of guilt, albeit after much hesitation. Others however, simply repeated that it "isn't my fault," "I'm not obliged to be ashamed," "I have nothing to do with it," "I'm not guilty, I don't feel guilty." These declarations strongly suggest that they were struggling with a feeling of guilt that was indeed present but which was poorly expressed by repeated statements to the contrary.

Being ashamed of the national past is specific to the former FRG. Further on we will see the consequences of this kind of shame in the differences between Hamburg and Leipzig. For the moment it is important to bear in mind that the "good students" once again align themselves with their teachers, even in adopting a feeling of shame that they do not approve of. The past may therefore take on additional importance because the students experience it in a negative way, in particular through the prejudice that they are subject to "as Germans" (overseas for example).

Recovering Social Status through Legitimate Discourse

The process of adopting a legitimate relationship with the Nazi past is one of the means of accessing "citizenship," i.e., a system of political values defined, in part, at school and by teachers. It opens up possibilities for those who have specific resources, leading them to want to "get themselves out" through school, but also to those who use the past in order to assert themselves in their kin and peer groups. We will look at three examples that illustrate the social trajectories and the family configurations in which the adoption of legitimate school discourse on the past becomes a means to access a coveted social status. Steffen, a struggling student at the *Gymnasium* in Hamburg, was trying to reverse the slope of his social and academic trajectory, which was out of step with the other members of his family, and to "catch up." Marji, a "good student" at the *Gesamtschule* in Hamburg, wanted to use her success at school to leave her social milieu and her "immigrant" neighborhood behind and reverse the downward social mobility her mother encountered as a result of her exile from Iran. Michael, a student at the *Gymnasium* in Leipzig, was trying to protect his father who had been denigrated by the rest of the family. He adopted an interpretation of the Nazi past and a form of pro-liberal, pro-FRG political engagement, which valued the difficult trajectory of his father in the GDR and made him into a "hero."

All three of these students came to appropriate the dominant academic discourse regarding the Nazi past, word-for-word, and each in their own way adapted it to their family trajectory and social and biographical background. They did do so not for reasons of academic strategy, but for reasons that were primarily social, or familial, but also based on group dynamics.

Steffen, a Catch-Up Strategy

When I interviewed him, Steffen was seventeen; he was born in one of the deprived urban areas of Hamburg. His father trained as a doctor and was then working as a departmental manager in the local government of the *Land* of Hamburg (*Ministerialrat*). His mother was a housewife. He had four brothers and sisters. Like his siblings, he began his studies in a *Gymnasium*, but after repeating eighth grade, he was forced to change to a *Haupt- und Realschule*, where he completed ninth grade before changing again to *Gesamtschule* Wiesi. At the time of the interview, in 2002, he had spent a year at Wiesi, repeating ninth grade. Even before he began the interview, he told me that he "failed" the *Gymnasium*, which was, for him, extremely detrimental, particularly when faced with an interviewer who he assumed "succeeded brilliantly" in her education.[39] It was all the more difficult for him in comparison with the social status of his father and his four brothers and sisters who all remained at the *Gymnasium*. Listening to him, his discourse sounds like a confession; he admitted that he was "wrong," he let all his chances slide, even though he was given numerous opportunities. "The teachers were so adorable," they did everything to help him. He had refused. He accused himself of being "too lazy," saying "it's my own fault." He hoped to catch up through a *Gesamtschule* and sit the *Abitur*. Indeed, in hindsight, the *Gymnasium* seemed "great" to him, the classes "much more interesting." "We were taught to think, to work independently, it wasn't like here, where all we do is learn by heart." After this "awakening," he began to invest more in his schoolwork and quickly became one of the "best" students in his class. He also became involved in extracurricular activities; in 2002, he was the student representative for the school. That is how his teacher introduced him to me; he would be "particularly able" to answer my questions. Indeed, it seems that he corresponded quite well to her image of a "good student" and a "good citizen," able to give a "good image" of their school.

His discourse on the Nazi past very much conforms to the school requirements. We find the same figures of speech discussed above, "never again" and "duty to remember," which he mobilized in much the same way as his teachers. In response to the general prompt, he explained that he "right away thought of World War II because of the Holocaust" and that "it's important to know things about that subject." He then reiterated several times that he was very interested in "World War II" and in particular "the Jewish genocide." Because he repeated classes and changed schools, he has had two history courses on the subject. He emphasized the fact that, in spite of repeating a year, he was still interested: "I'm never bored with it, it's always interesting." When asked to explain why he found it so interesting, he launched into a long speech:

> I think that you have to know. What happened, you have to know, you know? What happened here in Germany, and in particular here in Germany. What Mao and Stalin pulled off (*was Mao und Stalin abgezogen haben*) was exactly the same, there were as many dead, I think. Perhaps a little less, but there were still lots too. Stalin had concentration camps too. Or rather work camps. Not with gas and extermination and all. But Saddam Hussein did that too, with gas. But here it's so extreme, and all this madness (*dieser Wahn*): reigning over the world and all that, I think you should know it. Well, there are people who aren't interested at all. You can't force them either, but I think that it's still important, to know things about the subject. . . . I think that you have to know really, when you live in Germany. I think. No?[40]

Steffen adopted a kind of reasoning that seems to come from outside. For almost the whole of his speech, he uses the generic "you" rather than the first person singular or plural. He was unable to say why it is important to "know things" about this period, which led him to repeat the ready-made expression "you have to know." Both times he used the first person, he reformulated the ready-made expression ("it's important, you have to know"), and adapted it without going any further in his reasoning. In other words, he said "I find it very important because it's important." This circular reasoning is of course evocative of his teachers who express the "duty of remembrance" without ever specifying its exact content. Everything happens as though Steffen simply adopted the discourse he heard repeatedly at school without ever having personal reasons for defending it. Moreover, Steffen, although he has adopted his teachers' discourse, did modify them considerably: insisting on the comparison with crimes committed in other countries clearly expresses his ambiguity about the subject and an implicit refusal to attribute guilt to the Germans alone. Although Steffen adopted a legitimate discourse, he implicitly and simultaneously questioned the specificity of the Jewish genocide and the National Socialist extermination policy, and thus the singularity of German guilt. In exporting the legitimate relationship to the past, that "you have to know" to other countries ("the Chinese have to know what happened with Mao, the Americans have to know what happened with the Indians"), he universalizes the legitimate discourse on the past asked of him at school and removes the guilt associated with it.

It is not by chance, apparently, that this student mobilized a discourse that conforms to school norms and yet is so specific. Certain students were critical of this discourse, particularly regarding the incessant repetition on the subject; others said that they did not feel concerned by it, a case that will be developed in the chapters that follow. Steffen was different. He openly regretted leaving the *Gymnasium*, and he was trying to "catch up" by perfectly espousing the school norms, word-for-word, including regarding the "appropriate" relationship to the past. He found a way to express the criticisms that others openly directed at the school by integrating them into the academically legitimate discourse, which he then "exported" to other countries. In this way, he was (belatedly) able to conform to the image that he thought teachers expected of him. His political engagement (as school representative) was part of this "catch up" strategy, which was in fact quite efficient. His teacher, for example, stressed that "Steffen is different, he is the student representative, he is interested." We will see below that in an academic environment that brings together students from very disadvantaged social backgrounds and represent significant academic difficulties, it is important to be "different" from the other students. This "difference," particularly regarding other students who struggle to appropriately adopt the academic discourse, provided these students with a degree of recognition from the teaching body, even though it often led to exclusion by their peers.

The use of generic forms in Steffen's discourse reflects the presence of social norms that he has not freely chosen but that correspond to the expectations of the group he wanted to return to, the students and teachers at the *Gymnasium*. The rest of the interview shows how comfortable he is in combining this discourse on the "duty to remember" with that of "everyone's necessary guilt," a discourse that is also widely present among the teachers.

And you think that we should know about it, here, because it was the Germans?
Yeah, right. And also because it was so extreme. You should also know about it if you're [he hesitates] English, for example, or Spanish. But for us, it was

still different because [he hesitates again], yes, because our grandparents per-haps contributed. Or our great-grandparents [he considers] or [he searches for words] other members of our family who were involved. It was impos-sible to avoid. You couldn't avoid it, everyone knows, it's obvious (*Umgehen konnte man das Ganze ja bekanntlich nicht, das is ja klar*). You couldn't not participate. It was very hard. But, I think, you should know. Just [he consid-ers] because, well, because there is the possibility that your grandfather was an SS or even just a soldier. You have to know and not close your eyes. Perhaps everyone does. But in lots of films that we have seen from the 1950s, 1960s, lots of people said "Oh no! We shouldn't talk about that so much!" I don't agree.[41]

The ambiguity of Steffen's discourse, characteristic of the whole interview, allows us to understand the interconnectedness, the overlapping and the simultaneity of the different interpretations of the past for this young man. In this passage, he affirms the guilt of grandparents who participated in Nazism and in the implementation of the extermination policy, whether as members of the SS or as simple soldiers. Yet he simultaneously states that they could not have avoided this participation. The dominant school dis-course exists here alongside a more personal one related to Steffen's family history. The coexistence of these two discourses testifies to the force of his dual affiliations—in both the school and his family—with these two affilia-tions combining and contradicting each other to doubly influence his inter-pretations of the Nazi past.

Conforming to academic norms does not automatically signify that they are the only ones to influence the students' relationship with the past. Steffen was conscious that the Nazi regime was supported by the population, and in particular by "people in the media" and "the economists," which also shows a certain understanding of how the Nazis came to power.

In any event, we had it at least twice at the *Gymnasium*. The topic of National Socialism, from the beginning to the end, how Hitler became powerful and all the developments, yes it was between [19]33 and [19]45, and how they rose up, and then also with [he hesitates] the people in the media and the economy and all that, how they supported Hitler and all, but yes, it was also a story! [He hesitates again.] And how they made Hitler rise up and all his partisans and all. [He hesitates.] Yes, and then there was also the program *Hitlers Helfer* on the ZDF [public television channel], that was . . . [He trails off.] So, yeah.[42]

What Steffen expressed here is a frequent and historically exact (albeit partial and simplified) interpretation of the rise of National Socialism. It was a response to the very neutral question of the interviewee's possible memories of the ways the subject had been covered at school. The source of this memory is not necessarily the school however, the program *Hitlers Helfer*[43] seems to have particularly marked this student who mentioned it in response to a question about his history classes at school.

Apparently, Steffen had learned (at school, on television, or elsewhere) the importance of the participation and support of "normal Germans" for the Nazi regime, which for him constituted sufficient reason to defend the "duty of remembrance." He had integrated this knowledge to the point he was able to express it consciously. However, it remained a painful reality, concretely implicating his ancestors through the "guilt of the German people." Indeed, at a different point in the interview, he changed his discourse, when talking about his grandfather.

> My Grandpa, I have to think, he was born in [19]22 [he hesitates] or, well, no, [19]21, Grandpa was born in [19]21. So, he wasn't that old in 1939, just seventeen or eighteen. At eighteen, he left with the submarines. [He raises his voice.] Well, not right away, I think that was in 1940, but [he hesitates] it was probably the Hitlerjugend before that. He did the HJ before. Yes, he did everything he was supposed to (*nett alles*), and then [he lowers his voice], well, you didn't think, really. It was before, before it was different, everything was so [he hesitates], well, [there was] so much propaganda. "Today we have Germany, tomorrow, the world!" and all that. You couldn't really know that something was going to happen, or if you did [he continues his train of thought] because Germany was really invincible—[he hesitates, not finishing his phrase, and returning to his grandfather]. He was just like any HJ who [he hesitates]—I don't know—was playing adventurer or something like that (*halt irgendso ein HJ, der eben, was weiss ich, Geländespiel macht oder so*).[44]

We can see the thought process as Steffen puts himself in his grandfather's shoes. At the beginning, he uses the third person, describing his grandfather's age and starts to analyze his actions during the war based on his joining the submarine corps in the 1940s. Then, after an initial hesitation (which reveals how sensitive the subject is), he begins again, raising his voice, to declare that his grandfather was a member of the Hitlerjugend. The "probably" (*wahrscheinlich vorher Hitlerjugend*) is misleading here. The following phrase shows, by its affirmative form, that this student is well aware that his grandfather was a member of the Nazi youth group (as were the vast majority of fourteen- to eighteen-year-old Germans after 1938), and he did judge him for that (*net alles*). This judgment is difficult, however, given the close family ties. He is trying to understand his grandfather by putting himself in his shoes. Steffen lowers his voice and changes his use of pronouns, thus expressing a clear break in his discourse. The second person plural is very rarely used to refer to a third person, more often to take some distance when talking about oneself (Pollak 2000: 238), which suggests here that the speaker generalizes his discourse and includes himself in it at the same time. The phrase "you didn't think really" (*da machst Du dir ja auch nicht so ne Gedanken*) is an active defense of his grandfather, who apparently joined the HJ and faithfully participated without thinking (and later fought in the war, which Steffen did not explicitly mention again, but which is nevertheless implied throughout his narrative). His defense of his grandfather becomes more explicit in the next phrase, which shifts the responsibility onto the period (it was "before"), to excuse the individual who could not reasonably have predicted such consequences (*wo man eigentlich nicht mit rechnen konnte*). His use of the neutral "you" (*man*) is a generalization that makes his comment normative. In the same situation as the one his grandfather lived through, no one would have been able to predict the historic events (total war and the Jewish genocide—and in particular the genocide on the Eastern Front). The last phrase, comparing the war to a game for the members of the HJ, is the most significant minimization of his grandfather's responsibility.

The ambiguity we have seen elsewhere is once again present in Steffen's analysis of his grandfather's concrete responsibility, which combines responsibility and minimization. The two may be associated with a "model" academic relationship with this history that conforms to the teachers' expectations and would most likely help Steffen improve his situation at school. These different extracts from a single interview also show the functions that different kinds of knowledge and the different frames of family and school can have for the students' complex interpretations of the past. Indeed, the pure knowledge of these historic facts as well as the adoption of the "great lessons" of history can form part of the *Geschichtbewußtein*, historical consciousness. Nevertheless, attempts to protect the family also allow us to perceive the *Geschichtsbild*, the historical image, to use Karl-Ernst Jeismann's (1988) conceptual distinction. These two notions have different functions. Adopting a relationship with the Nazi past that is considered legitimate in the school environment by no means prevents the parallel coexistence of other relationships with the same past, as well as discourses that are both complex and ambiguous. Our results here partly contradict the findings of Harald Welzer and his team ([2002] 2005)[45] who insist that grandchildren remove the burden of responsibility of family members' participation in the war. Indeed, if "de-responsibilization" discourse does exist, it exists in parallel with discourse on responsibility and the moral judgment of the same family members. It is the detailed analysis of single interviews and the follow-up of student's trajectories that permit us to understand the complexity of these discourses and not make over-hasty conclusions on generationally hegemonic discourses.

Marji, a Strategy for Upward Social Mobility

Marie-Claire Lavabre (1991) has emphasized the dual dimension of all relationships with the past, which is both a "choice" that provides resources and a "weight" that can be a social handicap. The case of Marji,[46] an Iranian immigrant now enrolled at Wiesi, demonstrates this dual dimension of the past through her ambiguous appropriation of what she considered to be "German."

Marji was born in 1985 in Tehran. Her mother (born in 1952) completed high school and began studying for a literature degree (which she did not finish) before marrying her first husband, a wealthy pilot close to the Shah. They had three children, a daughter (1972) and two sons (1976 and 1978). Marji apparently looked up to this man, she referred to him as "her father" at the beginning of the interview before correcting herself and explaining that she is in fact the daughter of her mother's second husband. Her mother's political activity with her first husband (who was apparently assassinated during the revolution) was the source of their difficult situation in Iran. Her mother remarried (not out of love according to Marji but because "in Iran you can't do anything if you're not married"). Marji's father left the family for political and personal reasons (conjugal issues) and moved to London to study medicine. The two elder children left the country first and then their mother followed with Marji and her younger brother. They spent a year in Turkey (1990)[47] before continuing their exile in Germany (1991). They arrived in a refugee camp in Munich and then moved to Frankfurt before ending up in 1992 in Hamburg in Wiesenbergshafen. Marji's older brother, her older sister, and her sister's fiancé were already established at Wiesi. Marji knew so little of her own father, who is now working as a doctor in England, she seemed to regard herself as fatherless. She was seven years old when she arrived in Hamburg.[48] She went to the local primary school and then *Gesamtschule* Wiesi where I met her in 2003 when she was eighteen.

Marji appropriated the Nazi past in order to "become German," which constituted a genuine "weight" for her, to the point where she felt discriminated against as a German (and thus as a Nazi) when overseas or in encounters with other immigrants. She did, however, express a latitude in this appropriation that allowed her to reject this past when it became too heavy. Indeed, this past also constituted a resource for her—knowing about the history of National Socialism and being committed to a political struggle against Nazism allowed her to earn recognition from her teachers at Wiesi. This was a step toward accomplishing her social ambitions, which involved "escaping" from her neighborhood and from her mother's immigrant status, which were particularly stigmatized in Germany. This, of course, is the third memorial dimension—neither "choice," nor "weight," but refusal—the past is still present in the xenophobia she continues to encounter. Marji doubly rejected this existence as an "immigrant," which represented nothing more than the actualization of Nazism in her eyes. On the one hand, she rejected it as a "good German citizen" politically committed to democracy, and on the other hand, she refused it as a "foreigner" who suffered discrimination for her "too Iranian" appearance.[49]

Marji was in eleventh grade and "well-known" at the school—I heard several different teachers talk about her before I met her in person. Thomas, a very politically active teacher, said to me as she walked by, "Look! There's a student who's different from the others. She has a political conscience. She is interested. [He laughs happily, affectionately.] But it's rare!"[50] She was considered a "good student," almost a "model" student—atypical in this school where "no one cares," where students were often described as "lazy."

Marji had indeed internalized this image of herself. During the interview she described herself several times as different because she "is interested in things," in "politics," in "history," including the history of Nazism, and in "school" generally. "I don't know if I'm an exception, because I'm so interested [in history] and [she pauses] I *wanted* it too! And others they don't even want it . . . exactly. Me? I *wanted it*!"[51] She was on friendly terms with several teachers and they helped her with her homework. "Oh, yes, that one [Mr Winter], he's an English teacher too. And because I'm pretty bad in English, and because I like him so much and he adores me, and we [she hesitates], well, he helps me, yes." Thus, Marji was able to establish privileged relations with teachers who gave her access to knowledge, a resource that she wanted to obtain at any cost in order to "break free." She was close enough to the teachers to even obtain "selective" information. "There were meetings [on this problem]—the teachers, they talk more openly to me [than to the others]. Normally they're not allowed to talk about the school council meetings." Indeed, being close to teachers is one way of overcoming shortcomings in family resources, when parents do not speak German, for example, as is the case here (Lahire 1995; Delcroix 2001: 176). Marji rapidly realized that "at home, they couldn't help [me]." Being close to the teachers was thus a first step to "getting ahead." Biographical studies in the German school context show that it is in particular students from disadvantaged backgrounds, whose parents have fewer economic and/or cultural resources to support their children in academic success, who turn toward their teachers in search of a referent (Graßhoff and Höblich 2005). We can nevertheless criticize these authors for talking in psychological terms of "incomplete, problematic families" (Graßhoff and Höblich 2005: 124) and classing them as "abnormal" instead of investigating the social conditions and resources available in these family contexts.

Meeting adolescents from outside the neighborhood was another way of getting out, as was political activism against xenophobia and neo-Nazism.

This activism in turn reinforced her teachers' admiration for her. In political terms, she corresponded to their expectations twice over: she was politically active (on the left) and she fought for democracy and against fascism. She had thus adopted a form of political behavior in perfect alignment with the memory policy defended by her teachers.

Leaving the neighborhood and being politically active are of course linked: at age fourteen, Marji joined the *Linksruck*, an antifascist association, which provided her not only contacts outside the neighborhood, but also brought her closer to her teachers and further away from her classmates. This was how she built her image as a "different" kind of student.

> [At the *Linksruck*, we can talk] about anything. . . . anything you want. Beginning with those who are interested in animals, or plants, or activities against Castor [nuclear] transport, everything! It's really important. [She hesitates, all of a sudden taking a serious and pedagogic tone.] I think I wouldn't have made such progress in politics and history, and wouldn't have my good grades, if I hadn't been in the *Linksruck*. Because—well, I got motivated on my own, because, well, you're there [in the classroom] and the teacher says something and you think "my God, I have to get away," and you go to the john and then you come back, but you don't listen, because—it's just so tiring! But when you make an effort, it even becomes fascinating! [Enthusiastically.] And then you read a book and you can't stop, until late at night and then [she pauses for a long while] and it changes—everything—everyone around you, your life (*dein ganzes Umfeld*)!

Marji mentioned being bored in class and her desire to get away, to a world other than "knowledge," including through her use of a familiar language,[52] phrases that are left unfinished, reminiscent of comic strips. She also used the second person singular to include me in her discourse, but also to more easily (and with fewer risks) refer to her (past) opposition to the school system. This makes way for an interest that is expressed through more sophisticated academic language, including at the beginning of the quote. Here Marji takes the point of view of her teachers. She talks about her own "progress" in history class and makes a link between her extracurricular (political) activities and her "success" at school, in particular in history. Marji adopted this "teacher's" perspective at several points in the interview. She thus noted that she was "sad" to not have started reading and being interested in politics earlier. She saw this interest as a synonym of "democratic" engagement and the rejection of the extreme-right (she considered that she started at fourteen, when she met a girl from the *Linksruck* on a bus). It was from this perspective that she said "I'd know so many more things today, if I was less stupid."

The appropriation of the expectations of the school and her teachers, including by putting Nazism at the forefront of her political concerns, as well as her proximity to the teaching body, made up her effective twofold strategy "to break free." She thus adopted a form of behavior that was linked to an upwardly mobile personal trajectory, aiming to compensate for the downwardly mobile trajectory of her family and in particular her mother. Although she was born into the intellectual and political bourgeoisie in Iran, her mother now has very few resources in Germany (at the time of the interview, she was dependent on welfare assistance and did not speak German like many of her compatriots). This situation clearly weighed heavily on Marji, who appeared to be haunted by the fear of unemployment, seeing her mother "waste her life." Only the dual logic of the acquisition of cultural capital and socially legitimate discourse, including on the past, and the act of distancing herself from her milieu and her neighborhood would potentially protect her. "Without that [the *Linksruck* and the help of her teachers], I would find myself without a diploma (*Hauptschulabschluss*) and—and unemployed. I'd be completely rubbish!" (*Wenn ich die nicht gehabt hätte, ich, ich säß hier mit'm Hauptabschulss und, und wär arbeitslos. Nee, ich hätt' nichts auf die Reihe gekriegt!*)

Indeed, the downward slope of her mother's social trajectory and undoubtedly the memory of a more socially prestigious family status were decisive for Marji's engagement. Indeed, both Steffen and Marji have experienced social "decline" (Marji more violently) and they were both yearning for a different social status. Thus, a (formerly) privileged social position can also be a resource and a basis for an upward trajectory, associated with the appropriation of legitimate discourses about the past. On the other hand, Marji's political involvement was in keeping with a family tradition of strong political engagement in Iran.

But what exactly did Marji want to "break free" from? She perceived her mother's social decline and the living conditions in her neighborhood as a threat. In her eyes, the other residents represented the "lower classes," which she wanted to avoid belonging to at all costs. She thus sought to set herself apart from the migrant workers, particularly Turks, whom she despised, by acquiring cultural capital adapted to the requirements of her new country. She hoped that this would allow her to access an upward trajectory and obtain the grades required to study medicine, which is subject to a quota. This upward trajectory is also dependent on her acquisition of "Germanity," which operates, among other things, through learning "the lessons from the Nazi past," in a political group and at school. Marji referred to those she did not want to be like as "the others" and "the foreigners."

And you wanted to tell me how you came to Linksruck?

Right. So there was a girl that I met on a bus—because there was a guy who wanted to chat me up (*weil mich so'n Typ angebaggert hat*)—like—like, a gross

Turk (*ekliger Türke*), right? And who thought I was hot. And it really got me angry, I, I [she gets angry] even today I have a problem with these [she hesitates, searching for words] with, with, with those [she pauses, breathes deeply, and blurts] those machos! And, and, the way the guys in particular behave, particularly when [she speeds up, speaking quickly] they're from oriental countries, well, Turks, Iranians, Afghanis, my countrymen too, and that time [she gets annoyed again] I got really angry, I raised my voice—"what the heck?" [She imitates her own voice, but quietly.] "Is that a Turkish custom or something? What are you thinking? You think I've got 'easy lay' written on my head or something?" And then she came up to me and she held me back, like "calm down, they're not all like that." [She goes back to her normal voice.] And then we started talking about—xenophobia, and we talked on the bus about the fact that not all foreigners are like that—obviously I'm a foreigner too and I'm not like that. That they're not all like that and that I shouldn't get worked up like that, and then well we talked politics and she said, if you're interested come with me. . . . Before the *Linksruck*, I was quite prejudiced, and I was pretty aggressive. I mean, I [she stumbles over her words, lowers her voice suddenly, looking at me] yes, it's anonymous, right? [She goes back to her normal voice.] I didn't like foreigners! There! I had to say it, you know! The—the Turks, the Afghans, the Iranians, with their stupid national pride, their gold chains and their leather jackets [she was getting louder and angrier] and who really think they're like kings! Yeah! And they just have to chat up anyone [she is searching for words, angry now] who crosses their path! And then I—I get told that there are reasons. That they're discriminated against here, excluded, and there are reasons that they develop this kind of group dynamic. And on the other side the—um, the Nazis, that there are also reasons for their behavior. That they're not born like that. Obviously.

What Marji deplored in "the foreigners" is primarily their "macho attitude." She "doesn't like them because they chat her up." The issue is once again social here. It is not so much the fact they "chat her up" but the forms that they use that offended her. It is to do with a lack of social ease, a sign of cultural resources and habitus specific to the well-off classes to which Marji aspires. This kind of chat up is the very incarnation of what Marji wants to escape from: her family's social decline. Thus Marji's preferences in terms of social relations are very much in keeping with the logics of distinction analyzed by Bourdieu.

Explicit aesthetic choices are indeed often constituted in opposition to the choices of the groups that are the closest in social space, with whom the competition is the most direct and the most immediate, and more precisely, no doubt, in relation to those choices most clearly marked by the intention (perceived as a pretension), of marking distinction vis-à-vis lower groups. (Bourdieu [1979] 2010: 127–28)

108 • When Will We Talk about Hitler?

But beyond the desire to distinguish herself from the groups closest to her, economic immigrants, particularly Turks, it was Marji's own trajectory at play here, in a dynamic process that was part of a genuine "life plan." "Hanging out" with these "foreigners" endangered her goal of regaining her family's lost social status. She thus declared, "I only hang out with Germans,[53] especially at college, my boyfriend's friends. He's studying history and politics." For Marji, upward social mobility and "frequenting the masses" are mutually exclusive. This evokes the issues revealed by the French sociologist Stéphane Beaud regarding the children of workers at Gercourt.

> What kind of compromise would enable us to be accepted by "the others" while not entirely joining in with them? How can we attenuate the effects of social segregation at school, how can information be gathered, in order to avoid falling into bad classes with "the others"? How and when should we "cut off" our relationships with friends from the neighborhood? (Beaud [2002] 2003: 28)

Marji found a radical solution: she broke off all contact.[54] This was made possible by her then boyfriend who was at university and his friends, who were all from outside the neighborhood. In order to achieve her social plan, she had to first disconnect from her milieu and find other resources that would allow her to find a place in German society. Her friend Omeira, the daughter of two Serbian workers who immigrated to Hamburg at the end of the 1980s did not understand, in Marji's words, "the danger she is in" when she "keeps hanging out with the others."

> She's an incredible woman—she is going to succeed in life! But not with that lot. If [she hesitates] if she doesn't let go soon—[she hesitates, and then has an idea] well, if she goes on to study she'll have to let go. But—she wants to know so much, and yet she lets herself get caught up with them! She—in spite of her intelligence, she is a little *Mitläuferin*.[55] . . . When she opens her mouth, you know right away that she's clever. She understands everything. . . . But she can—I think that if she broke away from those people, she could experiment and see so much more in her life. She goes to the museum sometimes, with her family, and does what normal people do. But she is way too fragile and exposed to insults. She gets hassled because she's a good student, she [gets an] A+ and she'll always be good. And so they're jealous, they treat her badly. But she doesn't see it because she has no one else, she only has them. If she didn't hang out with them—she's also someone who is very . . . [She hesitates, breaks off and begins again.] When you're here at school, right? And you're sensitive, emotional, and yes, a little unstable, you know? And easily [she hesitates]—and fragile, well, you can just give up right away.

Marji considered it important to be "strong" to "break free." But Omeira is not "strong enough," she is too "sensitive" to do what Marji has decided to do and cut off all contact with "the others." In order to "be strong" one must have resources outside the neighborhood that Omeira does not have according to Marji. This break from the "masses" was the condition required for Marji to achieve upward social mobility.

> I have a friend [Tatiana], she is a little like me, but she's Polish. She—she's always been a bit like, "that's not possible, all that." [She smiles.] And she's always asked questions. And then—she's kind of artistic, a dreamer! She is very individualistic and really an unusual being. And because she is not like the others, I noticed her, and she noticed me! You see. And [she hesitates] she had the strength and the vigor to break off from—the—the—masses. She was also a follower (*Mitläufer*) before, but she pulled herself away from them, from the masses, all by herself. And with her—she's the only one I get on with at school. Break time would be unbearable—if it weren't for her.

This process of "extricating" oneself from the influence of "the others," in the neighborhood where they live, from "Muslims," from "tradition," from "the poor," all go along with an attempt to "get closer to Germans," to adopt their past and their relationship with the past. Marji thus describes a linear process, an evolution between two poles. The negative pole was the Wiesi neighborhood and its residents, "Muslims and foreigners," unemployment, poverty, lack of cultural capital, and the impossibility of escape. This pole is described as a prison, a trap that she must get out of at all costs. The positive pole, by contrast, was upward social mobility: university, museums, the *Linksruck*, and "German things." It included having white skin, blond hair, "German culture," and in history and politics, "democratic" and anti-Nazi activism, academic success, and education in general. It also represents physical "freedom," ways of dressing (even transparent clothes, showing one's bra), movement (going out when and where you want), sexual freedom (having a boyfriend and showing affection in public, walking hand in hand, kissing), and freedom of thought (being an atheist, criticizing "the masses," and so forth).

In Germany, for Marji, upward social mobility was only possible by "being German," that is adopting a form of behavior that Marji describes as "German." "Germany" thus represented all the things that were positive for her—including social status—and that she wanted. The legitimate relationship with the Nazi past and the legitimate discourses about this past were part of these "German things" that provided the opportunity for her to "get ahead." This self-imposed process, which for the moment I would like to call Marji's "nationalization" operates in different ways. Succeeding at school and distancing herself from her "foreign" classmates are the first steps. The next will involve "going toward Germany." Here, Marji emphasized her "German friends," beginning with her boyfriend who is "German" and "blond with blue eyes." He was a history and politics student at Hamburg University where she hoped to study medicine. Her "access" to the student milieu was, at that time, based on him. She "hangs out" with his friends, who are "all Germans," and attended student parties. "Nationalizing herself" in order to access the positive end of her scale and "extricating herself" from the negative end were parallel processes for Marji.

> First, I'm an atheist. [She lowers her voice.] I don't believe in the afterlife (*das Übersinnliche*). And I have no national pride, either, and I don't have that—that [she hesitates]—I don't know, [she stops, starts again] I don't behave how an Iranian woman should behave. [She lists the items off, raising her voice and speaking more quickly] I wear what I want, I wear makeup, I wear my hair down, I look men in the eyes.

On the day of the interview, she was wearing a white skirt with a little pink top, over which she wore a transparent white blouse. She was wearing pink strappy sandals and her brown skin was visible through her shirt. Her black hair was loose and hung down to the middle of her back, with just a few strands held in place with clips. Her makeup made her dark eyes stand out; a line of black eyeliner and some pink-orange eye shadow. She was wearing earrings, several rings, and carried a small white leather handbag. She continued her list.

> [I'm different because] of my mindset, the way I do certain things. First, I'm not a Muslim, and that's a scandal here in Wiesi!! It's crazy how much people gossip about that here! (*Ey, das ging hier rum, das ist der Hammer gewesen!*) My mother had to talk to people she'd never seen before. [She imitates them.] "It's shameful, my God!" (*das ist eine Schande*). And then I—I also have a German boyfriend, which I don't hide, and I walk around freely (*freizügig*) with him—and—and you can see my bra!! [She feigns horror, imitating the criticism.] "Oh my God!"

Marji was, in her own words, "out of place" (*fehl am Platze*) in Wiesi, because she felt "different." Her boyfriend played a fundamental role in this process of constructing this difference, this "Germanization."

> I have a *German boyfriend*. [She feigns a critical tone.] That's why I'm excluded here. [Speaking quickly.] I don't have any friends here, because, well more than 80 percent of them are foreigners. Especially the ones I'm talking about. And, me, I only have German friends. And so, everyone asks me [she hesitates], says to me, a bit funny—"actually you're a German." You see.

This statement does little to hide Marji's ambiguities. She greeted a dozen people who walked by during our three-hour interview on the lawn in front

Talking about the Nazi Past in Class and Succeeding at School • 111

of the school. Sometimes she made a disapproving face, whispering that she "doesn't like" those people (almost always girls) and that she did not want to be seen, but sometimes she took the time to explain that she was doing an "interview" and that she would call them later. Marji talked to me, the interviewer, as a "young German," a doctoral student, the incarnation of the university sphere that she spoke so highly of, also the incarnation of her "way out." The distance she adopted from her "neighborhood" and her desire to "get closer to Germany" were also linked to her idea of my judgment of her. She was trying to get as close as possible to what she considered to be my milieu so that she might be appreciated in my eyes.

The ambiguity of this "Germanity" is linked to the Nazi past. The mention of this past is used by "the others" to discredit Marji, but it also allows her to justify her partial nationalization. "Being German" for her also means being immediately confronted with the Nazi past. Her description clearly shows just how much the two are inseparable.

[She whispers] I've heard it before, "You are German!" Like that. [She imitated a Nazi accent, a harsh intonation, ironically. We both laugh.] . . . Yes, sometimes it's said that I'm more German than . . . [she did not finish the phrase, but speeds up.] But then—then [she stumbles] that funny way,[56] "You are German!" Germany! [She took the same Nazi tone again and laughs.] Yeah, it's funny.

In what way is it funny?

Yeah—this—the—Hitler or Goebbels speeches or something like that. It's "Germany for the Germans." [She took the same tone again and we laugh.] The way they spoke, that's what's funny . . .

Yeah, and especially the—mmm—the Persians, they're Aryans right? [I laugh, surprised.] Yes, you understand—uh [she hesitates for a long while and returns to her classmates' comments] [they say] "Aryan pure blood" (*Vollblutarier*) and things like that [she laughs, not without pride]. Yeah, well degrading things too. . . . [one student] calls me "the one who is really trying to learn German."

The different levels of identification and rejection, and the search for a personal trajectory become meaningful in their interconnections. There is the Nazi past which, for Marji, is not her own except for in its "studied" form, the memorial past, incarnated in the anti-Nazi struggle of her political action. However, her classmates accused her of being "an Aryan" when she seemed to them to be "too German." This insult both evokes her "Persian" origin and her dual desire to set herself apart both as a student and as a German. Marji thus took on this accusation and recast it in a positive light, inversing the stigma. Throughout the rest of the interview she referred to herself in this way, not without underlying pride, even if the effects of her exclusion were very real. We can see here, once again, the coexistence of complex—even contradictory—relationships with the Nazi past, which are never exclusive. Marji can thus adopt an "academically expected" attitude toward Nazism and be proud of her "Aryan origins," even if this is a case of the inversion of a stigma into a sign of distinction and positive identification. The Nazi past is thus a weapon for the "others" and an unexpected "weight" for Marji, while simultaneously being a resource. Although her distinction by her "Germanity" and her school knowledge, two attributes that seem intricately connected both in her eyes and in those of the classmates who criticized her, provided her with a certain feeling of pride, they were also troubling for her. She wanted to stand out at the local level of her neighborhood, and rise up socially, but she was far from actually "feeling German" at a national level. Indeed, on several occasions she was subject to discrimination that she considered to be xenophobic and/or racially motivated.

> We were in the metro, and there was this old man who stood up in front of me, I didn't even realize, because I was doing something else or daydreaming or something, and he looked at me really nastily, brutally, apparently. And then my boyfriend's friend, who's this big beefy guy, a footballer, stood in front of him and said, "What's up, old guy?" And he was like, "nothing, I can't believe it" and all. And that's when I realized. I was so perplexed that he said something bad about me, like, "what's she doing here" and all that. And I was like, "what the heck?" and then, yeah. It's obvious those people, they're still attached to that period [Nazism]. But it's only the old ones, the young ones are ok. Sometimes they get taught that and so they're just as bad, but I've never had something like that from a young person.

Nazism becomes something else here, something foreign, specific to old xenophobic Germans who insult her in the metro or her boyfriend's grandparents who "have *Mein Kampf* on their bookshelf"—he is ashamed of them and wants to protect her from them. In times like these, she defines herself as much as she is defined as non-German and without any connection to this past. This led her to observe "anyway, no one really buys that I'm German,"[57] an affirmation that expresses her ambiguity toward this Germany and its past. She calls herself German here, even if no one believes her. Of course, "no one" doesn't really mean that, because her classmates at Wiesi accused her of being "too German." Here, she was referring only to socially legitimate Germans, i.e., those without a family history of migration, but also those with a socially acceptable family position, whose judgment and exclusion Marji considers legitimate because—in these moments—she also feels that she is not "really German." This legitimacy is limited however, by the attachment of the "old" people to the Nazi past, which undermines the value of their negative judgments on the young woman.

Thus, the parallel feeling of belonging and distance in relation to her "Germanity," represent both a handicap and a resource for Marji. This was also the case for her relation to the Nazi past. Experienced as something outside her own person, it was also nevertheless a possible weapon to value or denigrate her depending on the context.

Marji's struggle around her "nationalization" could bring her to identify with Germany, to the point where she felt discriminated against as a (Nazi) German in the United Kingdom, for example, and where she developed a sensitivity and feeling of guilt—which she describes as "stupid."

> It's this guilt that they carry. But not the young people, who say [she interrupts herself] uh, uh [she hesitates, thinking], I think it's stupid, to say today that a young person must feel guilty for what's happened. But when you arrive in England, I've heard stories already, they discriminate against you automatically because I am—because you are German. And because they automatically have the image of the Nazis in their heads. Uhh . . . but you shouldn't feel guilty, as a young person, for what happened. You can't do anything and [she hesitates], yeah, I don't know.

Her slight hesitation in the middle of the paragraph crystallizes the relation that Marji had developed with Germany's past. The "I am" becomes "you are" and expresses the flexibility of her relationship with her country and the Nazi past.

The acquisition of an "irreproachable" attitude, both as far as her political behavior was concerned, and the use of the German past in the school context, as well as her playing with this acquisition outside of school, allowed Marji to project herself into an upwardly mobile social trajectory, "to break free" from the loss of social status her mother suffered through her situation as a political immigrant. The legitimate relation to the Nazi past thus represented a resource for her—a weapon, but also a weight. Appropriating these legitimate discourses does not prevent them from becoming a burden, an inconvenience, and the basis for discrimination in certain contexts. Discourses on the Nazi past thus do not have any specific meaning in themselves. Analysis that neglects situating these discourses in the social context of the speaker's trajectory thus miss their point. They are socially structured and make sense within a trajectory and specific configurations and particular groups in a given context. They are also subject to permanent reinterpretation, which can take contradictory forms, according to the context in which they are spoken, the interaction that takes place, and what is at stake in that context.

Michael, a Militant Strategy

Michael was born in 1987 in Leipzig, his mother was a dental technician (*Zahntechnikerin*) and his father was an artist, opposed to the Socialist regime. Michael described his paternal grandfather, a pastor born in 1918, as a "Nazi through and through" (*durch und durch*), who continued to believe in Nazi ideology even after 1945 and after 1989. He died in 2003. His paternal grandmother, fifteen years younger than her husband, was a supervisor in a cotton factory and considered herself "apolitical." Michael, however, said that she had a tendency toward nostalgia in general—during the socialist period she sang the praises of Nazism, and after 1989, she sang the praises of the Socialist regime—all in the face of criticisms from her sons and grandsons. Both his grandparents were also very religious, but divorced in the 1970s. Thus as a child, Michael knew his grandmother and grandfather separately. His grandmother's second marriage was to a businessman, also quite critical of the regime, who immigrated to Canada soon after. After reunification, his grandmother had a third marriage with the youngest brother of her second husband (the businessman) who was more supportive of the Socialist regime. The political discord between the two brothers lessened with reunification.

His maternal grandparents, born in 1933 and 1939, were part of the GDR "construction generation." His grandfather, a driver for government personnel, and his grandmother who was a factory inspector, both subscribed to the values of the Socialist Party. His grandmother, the elder of the two, had also actively participated in the Hitler Youth organization for girls (BDM, Bund Deutscher Mädel), which her grandson considers "in keeping with Nazism" (*NS-konform*) and as being a "follower" (*Mitläuferin*) without taking into account the fact that she was only twelve in 1945.

The two families did not lack examples of "political conformity." Michaels' father represents an exception in this family scheme. He had difficulties as an artist in the GDR and was even forbidden to perform on stage. Obliged to change profession, he opened a bowling alley. This position as a "victim" and then (after 1989) as a "hero" were, in hindsight, particularly appreciated by his son, who appeared to consider his father as the only man in the family to have "genuine political convictions." This positive appreciation also led his son to join the German Liberal Party (Freie Demokratische Partei, FDP) at a very young age (fifteen years old).

> Politics has *always* interested me. And then, one day, there was this—"but—you can't do anything by yourself." So, I said to myself—a party! And then, I noticed the FDP, because this fundamentally liberal idea, freedom (*der liberale freiheitliche Grundgedanke*) [he hesitates] that gave me something. [He considers] and

Talking about the Nazi Past in Class and Succeeding at School • 115

then, I don't need unions—and all that. And religion—I can't get used to it! For me, all that, it's dogma, that shuts me up, dominates me, takes away my freedom (*das mich in meiner Freiheit unterdrückt*)! And that's why [I chose] the FDP.[58]

His political activities ran parallel to his appreciation of history lessons, which he interpreted in light of his desire for political and economic freedom. Thus, his response to the general opening prompt was particularly precise.

[He thinks for a long while.] For me, personally, it would be *Gleichschaltung* (Nazification[59]) under the Nazi regime. [He hesitates.] When all the fundamental rights (*Grundrechte*) were abrogated, things like that. [He considers.] Because you can see just how easy it is to wipe out democracy, and the long path from the Weimar Republic [he hesitates], the constitution, the government [he hesitates], in the end it was possible to erase them and [he hesitates] how many errors were committed!

Throughout the interview, freedom is at the heart of his political and historical argument. It is also the reason that he admired the United States so much, seeing it as an ideal "liberal state." The failure of the Weimar Republic and the rise of the Nazis were "symbols of the German inability to achieve democracy" for Michael. "They tried to create a democracy, with the Weimar Republic. But it didn't work. First we needed the Americans, and then the English, to come and teach us about democracy. And then it lasted a long time, it's still going!"

The collective pronoun (we) that Michael uses here refers to the FRG—as it was indeed the American, English, and French occupying forces that structured the FRG constitution in 1949. Michael had fully integrated the idea of state continuity between the FRG and reunified Germany. For him, the "democracy founded by the Americans" and the state in which he lived had become one and the same. The GDR, the Soviet occupying forces, and socialism have little place in this vision of things. He only mentioned them as negative examples, opposed to "democracy" in the FRG.

Democracy is managed by older generations. They still know, perhaps because of the GDR regime and all that, what it provides: freedom of expression and all that! But young people today—no, they don't at all! Because—what have they been through (*mitgemacht*[60])? Them? Nothing at all! They live here, now, in a perfect state, I call it that. You can say that, I think. There is everything, everyone has everything, if they need it. At least the most basic needs are covered. . . . But they don't have any political opinions and they do nothing! When you look at young people, they are all wound up in drugs and alcohol! [He hesitates.] And they complain about politics, because there are no apprenticeship positions, but ultimately, they do nothing! And when I meet someone who tells me: "Politics is boring!" I wonder: "Who is going to make it better, then?" (*wer soll es denn richten?*)

Michael's attachment to a pluralist system, to liberal ideas and political engagement can be explained by the opposition between his father and his paternal grandparents, but it can also be seen in his maternal grandparents' position after reunification. The former took a clear stance in favor of Nazism, in particular his grandfather, a position that led to numerous family conflicts.

My Grandpa, it was really difficult [to talk to him]. He was even more—I'd say Nazi and propagandist (*NS propagierter*) than my grandma. Well, he was in the Wehrmacht and everything was fine. [He hesitates.] It's difficult to talk to him about that. He can talk about, what it was like, at the time—well, how many people he killed! But killing people, for him, it's not "I shot someone." Instead, he'll say [he pauses, searching for the right words], "I eliminated sub-humans (*Untermenschen*). I saved the world!" [Silence.] He has *no conscience at all* about the fact that he killed *defenseless* human beings when he went into a town in Russia and shot people—women and children! For him, it's not that! He thought—"they were Russian subhumans," and he continues to think that, even today! [He hesitates.] And, every time I'm at his house, he says, "those bastard Ruskies! (*Der Scheißrusse*) Everything is their fault!" [He considers.] Of course they [Russia] weren't great either, and not *much better*, but he [Grandpa] still shot women and children! But he doesn't want to see that! Yeah, he talks about it as though it was a piece of *cake!* It's not bad at all for him.

His grandfather's claims were scandalous for Michael, as they were for Michael's father. The latter's opposition to the system was linked, among other things, to a permanent confrontation with his own father. The comparison between the GDR and the Nazi regime allowed Michael's father to affirm his political position, including in relation to his parents-in-law, who were ashamed that their daughter married "a dissident." The experience of reunification, which came as a relief—both in personal, professional, and political terms, lowering family tensions—was transmitted to Michael. The freedom to practice one's profession, be politically active, and especially to express one's opinion were all conversations around the dinner table; but they still provoked tensions—his mother was convinced that Michael's father lost his job due to a lack of "political responsibility." Subscribing to the new pluralist regime of the FRG was a way for him to stand up to his wife, for whom the political shift has been more difficult, particularly because of her parents' disappointment, which she has experienced vicariously. In joining the FDP, Michael took a stance not only in opposition to both sets of grandparents, but also in support of his father, against his mother. His appropriation of the

Nazi past (and his political activities) became a resource that allowed him to emphasize the shift in his father's trajectory: the "dissident" who lost his job became a "hero" after reunification. The rejection of Nazism and unconditional support for liberalism and the FRG were, for Michael, additional ways to cast this evolution in a positive light.

His engagement and interest in history also allowed Michael to defend his opinion in the family environment—to support his father, who was the object of collective family disapprobation. It also enabled him to assert himself in the group of young FDP militants whom he praised for their political commitment and their knowledge. Indeed, history was often discussed in this group, which "is used for thinking about politics." Knowledge was a necessary condition in order to be able to assert himself in this context and to take on his fellow members.

> We talk about it in the party too. But just politics really. So—we don't talk so much about—how the Jews burned (*wie die Juden verbrannt sind*), but we talk more about the *Gleichschaltung*, the constitution and all that. So more about how they [the Nazis] came to power.
>
> *Do you remember a specific discussion that you had?*
>
> One time we talked about the exceptional laws, under the Weimar Republic. And all that. Brüning and Schleicher . . . And it's really terrible, that someone came along and just revoked everything. He [Hitler?] also said that our democracy wasn't the right one! I see, once again, we're not able to construct a democracy, that's for sure! Others had to do it for us! Finally! And so, we say, us [the party], that's really serious, I think, that Germany couldn't get out of it by itself! And the Germans destroyed their own creation! And the [economic] conditions of Weimar, unemployment, are more or less coming back!

The questions that Michael raised in the interview were also often discussed within his group of activists. His historical knowledge helped him maintain his political repartee, to reflect on the system, democracy, laws, and even government policy. It is also why he put questions of economic policy at the heart of his reasoning, rather than questions to do with the National Socialist extermination policy. Indeed, the conditions for the rise of Nazism serve to establish direct connections to the current political situation (especially unemployment), which is an argument dear to his history teachers.

But it was not in the hope of pleasing them that Michael read history books. On the contrary, he took his success at school completely for granted, as a sort of secondary and inevitable consequence of his political and intellectual activities. This position also led him look on those who "cram" for history classes with a degree of contempt.

Almost no one is actually interested in it. Even in advanced history, they learn it all by heart. I find it hilarious when they get an A and I get a B. I don't cram for history class! For me, that's not what it's about, history. I'm interested because I like it, and because I really want to know things. But I find it so stupid. Of course, you have to know the date of the French Revolution. At least the year, but I find it so stupid, to learn—when did the National Assembly happen? I don't think that's what history is about, and I *don't learn* it! I don't do it! I don't even write the dates in my book. I prefer to read a book at home, and to read—sources or things like that. I find it much more interesting than this stupid rote learning!

Michael refused to adopt a strategic attitude to learning. Rote learning simply to get good grades was a "pathetic" attitude in his eyes, and he said he cannot understand "why people like that do history." Moreover, he also said he could not stand those who get bad grades "they should just do something else," he says, uncomprehending. Michael's casual attitude to knowledge is something that Bourdieu attributes to the upper classes (1979). It was in fact the resources outside the school system and his family, his militant resources, that allowed Michael to distance himself from the school system while still mobilizing an academically legitimate discourse. Indeed, his teachers did value his "genuine interest" in history outside of the school context, because it was in keeping with their own attitude toward knowledge. They valued it in spite of the fact that, unlike Steffen and Marji, Michael failed to mobilize the emotional register that was demanded in class. This register thus constitutes one way of succeeding at school among others; it is a particularly efficient, but not exclusive, means for students to demonstrate their interest in history to their teacher. Other means, like that of political activism or erudition, also provide possibilities for the students, in particular from the upper classes, to succeed in history class.

Michael's "personal" interest is particularly necessary to gain respect among his fellow activists at the FDP. Rote learning is associated with "uncritical thinking," which does not allow for "fruitful discussion." For Michael, academic success was thus the lesser, but still valuable, consequence of his genuine engagement in politics. His historical knowledge was a resource that enabled him to assert himself both among his activist friends and his family.

Giving Meaning to Legitimate Knowledge

There are academically legitimate discourses about the Nazi past that become "self-evident" after they are taught in school. Students therefore begin by learning appropriate ways of speaking about this subject, rather than knowledge or facts. Almost all of the students integrate these ways of speaking with relative ease; the moral requirements of the teaching of the history of Nazism become "second nature" for them. The moral efficiency of this teaching influences the way the academic market operates: "appropriate ways of speaking," "appropriate images," and "appropriate ways of writing" are rewarded by the teacher through good grades. An analysis of the material produced by the students reveals these requirements in terms of emotional engagement, but also the ways in which these requirements are appropriated by the students. There remain differences, however, in the way this academically legitimate discourse is justified. The more the students come from advantaged backgrounds, the easier it is for them to develop economic, political, and civic arguments to justify the moral requirements that they defend. Such arguments do not prevent them also developing an ambiguous relationship with the Nazi past however, linked to a diffuse feeling of guilt that they outwardly refuse.

The three case studies presented in this chapter have allowed us to identify a series of factors that are associated with the adoption of academically legitimate discourses by the students. Two of these three students adopt a belief in the school system and the possibilities of success that it can provide. Their discourses on the Nazi past are closely linked to this belief, which the sociologist Stéphane Beaud describes as specific to the lower classes. The young people who work with Beaud are similar in this to Marji and Steffen; they "imagine their future as a kind of basic alternative: either continue studying 'as far as possible,' or 'fail school' and run the risk of unemployment" ([2002] 2003: 10). However, Beaud worked with young people who experienced the democratization of the school system in France, which did not happen as quickly and massively in Germany. Marji, for example, more closely resembles the figure of the "scholarship student" described by Richard Hoggart ([1957] 2006) in chapter 8 of *The Uses of Literacy.* Indeed, although she does not have a scholarship, she does have very specific resources (coming from a family of political refugees who previously belonged to the intellectual bourgeoisie of her country of origin) and can expect a "return" on her academic investment in the form of professional success and social advancement (Beaud [2002] 2003:11). But this analysis also shows how students from more privileged backgrounds can adopt, under certain configurations, this same belief in the school—for different reasons (as was the case of Steffen, the son of a doctor and politician). Moreover, although faith in the school system is always accompanied by academically legitimate discourses about the past, the opposite is not always true. Thus Michael, who mobilizes a legitimate discourse about Nazi Germany for reasons that are linked to school, family, and political action, by no means shares Marji's and Steffen's faith in the school system.

120 • When Will We Talk about Hitler?

Although the school is quite efficient in transmitting a system of values and ways of speaking, it also shapes the students' appropriations of the Nazi past, albeit indirectly. In the next chapter we will look more closely at the gender differences that are visible in the appropriations of the Nazi past. We will explore the complex and paradoxical role of the school system in the reinforcement, but also in the temporary attenuation, of differences between boys and girls in this area.

Notes

1. The only exception to this are certain confirmed neo-Nazis, quite a small group, whose members sometimes deny, sometimes approve of the genocide. Given my research protocol, I only met one boy who openly declared he was a neo-Nazi, but he neither clearly denied nor approved of the genocide (see chapter 4).
2. In presenting myself to the interviewees, I told them that I worked on the academic transmission of history, not on Nazism in particular. The expression used by the students to refer to this period was for the most part "World War II," some also talked about "Hitler," and a few mentioned the "NS," or "'33–45."
3. Interview of 7 November 2003.
4. Interview of 7 November 2003
5. "[Nazism] is important. Because of the Holocaust and all that, the persecution of the Jews in general. The whole war you know." Interview with Steffen, student of the Hamburg *Gymnasium*, tenth grade, 12 March 2002.
6. Interview of 28 January 2004.
7. We will see later that that the students do not all have the same access to these images.
8. Interview of 21 January 2002.
9. Moreover, none of the students made a distinction between concentration camps and death camps. The fact that there is no abbreviation in German to say *Vernichtungslager* (extermination camp), an equivalent to saying *KZ* for *Konzentrationslager* (concentration camp), may also play a role in how the adolescents refer to the camps.
10. He emphasized the fact that he visited this place inside the town, he took the subway to get there. Any request for further information was met with the following answer: "Well, Auschwitz, the concentration camp, you know it (*sie wissen schon*)!" Interview of 14 March 2002.
11. One of the only students in the class to have both parents of German nationality. She was born in 1988 in Hamburg, and her father is a technician in a shopping center and her mother a pharmacist's assistant.
12. Project "The Concentration Camps" by Sandy, Anna, Kai, Karsten, and Sascha.
13. Anna uses the word *geschossen* (to shoot), rather than *erschossen* (shot).
14. Project "The Concentration Camps" by Sandy, Anna, Kai, Karsten, and Sascha.
15. The use of this word seems to indicate a certain disconnection between the students and the reality of the camps. Apparently, he meant to explain that the prisoners were treated like "garbage."
16. Project "The Neuengamme Concentration Camp" by Kevin and Martin.

17. Project "The Concentration Camps" by Sandy, Anna, Kai, Karsten, and Sascha.
18. Field journal, 2 December 2003.
19. Project "The Concentration Camps" by Sandy, Anna, Kai, Karsten and Sascha.
20. Ibid.
21. Ibid.
22. In the two final years of school, students can specialize by taking advanced courses (five hours per week each), which count double at the final exams. These advanced courses are made up of a maximum fifteen students.
23. Interview of 13 April 2003.
24. Interview of 29 September 2003.
25. Interview of 8 April 2003.
26. Interview of 3 November 2003.
27. The Nazi past was omnipresent in this debate. Some years previously, during the war in Kosovo, Joschka Fischer, then foreign minister, had declared "we must avoid a new Auschwitz" to justify the participation of German troops. This expression was reused later in other debates and in other contexts. At the time of the second Iraq War, the specter of Nazism, through the image of a powerful German army, served to defend the "impossibility of committing German troops to overseas intervention," a principle that is anchored in the Constitution of 1949.
28. Interview of 3 November 2003.
29. Interview of 3 November 2003.
30. Ibid.
31. Interview of 21 October 2003.
32. Interview of 22 February 2003.
33. Ibid.
34. Interview of 18 April 2003.
35. Interview of 22 February 2003.
36. Interview of 11 April 2003.
37. Interview of 20 March 2002.
38. Interview of 17 April 2003.
39. When they learned that I was preparing my PhD, several interviewees, both teachers and students, assumed that I was brilliant at school, which sets me apart from them. The distance that is thus established is particularly difficult to overcome when faced with students from low social and academic backgrounds (see introduction and chapter 5).
40. Interview of 12 March 2002.
41. Interview of 21 March 2002.
42. Interview of 12 March 2002.
43. The ZDF is the second major German public television channel. This program was very well known and hosted by historian and chief editor of the "History" section of the channel, Guido Knopp. Most students refer to this program as "very interesting." Knopp conducts many interviews with eyewitnesses from the period, who stimulate the students with their "vivacity" and their "emotionality." Guido Knopp, *Hitlers Helfer I* ("1. Rudolf Hess, the Deputy," "2. Karl Dönitz, the Successor," "3. Joseph Goebbels, the Pyromaniac," "4. Hermann Göring, the Right Hand Man," "5. Heinrich Himmler, the Executioner," "6. Albert Speer, the Architect"), *II* ("1. Martin Bormann, the Man in the Shadows," "2. Adolf Eichmann, the Destroyer," "3. Roland Freisler, the Executor," "4. Joseph Mengele, the Doctor of Death," "5. Joachim von Ribbentrop, the Henchman," "6. Baldur von Schirach, the Hitler Youth"), Universum, 320 min., 1997.
44. Interview of 12 March 2002.

122 • When Will We Talk about Hitler?

45. The original German version of this book (*Opa war kein Nazi*, Fischer Taschenbuch, 2002) was only partially translated into English. For the reader's convenience, we refer to the English version.

46. This section on Marji was the subject of an article published in slightly different form as "Marji et le passé nazi: Trajectoire migrante et relation ambiguë à l'Allemagne d'une jeune iranienne en ascension sociale," in *Comment transmettre la Shoah?*, ed. Jacques Fijalkow (Paris: Editions de Paris, 2009).

47. Marji therefore also learned Turkish along with Farsi, her mother tongue. This linguistic acquisition would help her in Germany. At school, she would ask her Turkish classmates to translate her homework. At Wiesi, the large number of Iranian immigrants led the school to appoint a teacher to teach Farsi as a second foreign language option (along with French and Spanish; English is the first foreign language). This teacher also works as a translator and interpreter in meetings with parents and is the key contact for both students and parents.

48. Like many children of immigrants who arrive at that age, Marji was two years older than her classmates. She spent a year in an "integration class" where she learned German before beginning first grade when she was eight years old.

49. Unless otherwise stated, Marji's comments in this section are taken from the interview I conducted with her on 22 April 2004.

50. Interview of 22 April 2003.

51. The italics in the text are her emphasis.

52. This can be seen in her use of the word *Klo* for the toilets for example, a familiar and oral term rendered by the American slang "john."

53. Implying people of German nationality whose parents and grandparents are also German.

54. At least she said she has. It is worth remembering that she knew lots of people in Wiesi. Because of my social status as a doctoral student and researcher, it is impossible for me to verify what she said about who she "hangs out" with outside of school. However, she was apparently the only one to affirm such a radical break with the "neighborhood," and the "milieu," indeed with "the others" in general.

55. See note 37 in the introduction for a discussion of this term. Given that this term refers to those who "followed along" with the Nazi regime, without being directly involved, the use of this term in this context is surprising to say the least. It may possibly be explained by the generalization of the reference to fascism as the "absolute evil." The evil here is "the others," the "primitive foreigners," as Marji called them. Her friend is a "*Mitläufer*" because she spends time with them instead of distancing herself and opposing them. By using this term, Marji was criticizing her friend for not resisting more against "the masses" of "others" who dictate her life, which forced the two friends to see each other in secret.

56. *Lustig*, in German means funny, but in this context it also means strange, difficult to understand.

57. *Mir kauft man sowieso nicht ab, dass ich ne Deutsche bin, von daher.*

58. Unless otherwise indicated, the citations from Michael come from the interview I conducted with him on 18 October 2003. I have italicized the words that Michael particularly emphasized.

59. *Gleichschaltung* has been translated as "bringing into line," "cooperation," but "Nazification" seems to be the most frequent translation. It generally refers to the six-month period after the Nazi rise to power when all institutions and administrations were brought into line with the Nazi ideology, when the Weimar constitution was abrogated,

and when the administrative and political personnel changed. It also refers to the rapid incarceration and subsequent murder of any opposition, from the German Communists to members of the SA (*Sturmabteilung*—paramilitary unit of the NSDAP, until it was dissolved in 1934 during the "night of long knives").

60. The verb *mitmachen*, literally means participate, but it can have a double meaning. Here it means both the experiences of older generations but also their suffering.

Chapter 3

GENDER, FAMILY, AND THE NAZI PAST(S)

Research in the sociology of education, both in the United States and in Europe, has long demonstrated the influence of gender on education (Arnot 2009; Arnot and Dillabough 2000). It has shown the impact of gender on students' experiences at school, on their achievements, on teachers' attitudes and attention to students (Francis 2000). It has also shown the influence of teachers on the construction of gender identities (Belotti ([1973] 1975) and gendered perceptions of academic ability. Indeed, from elementary school onward, children generally associate with others of the same sex (Maccoby 1990) and Barrie Thorne (1993) explains this tendency toward same-sex peer groups with the notion of "behavioral compatibility," through which the two sexes tend to turn toward different activities. This segregation is also potentially driven by different styles of play, with girls preferring coop- erative play and avoiding participation in boys' more assertive and physical play, which can be a way for girls to avoid being dominated within a group of boys (Chodorow 1978; Thorne 1993). There is also substantial research on the impact of this segregation in the form of single-sex or coeducational learning environments. Research in sociology of education has suggested that girls acquire greater self-esteem in single-sex universities (Miller-Bernal 1993; Smith 1990). Studies have shown that girls educated in single-sex envi- ronments move more readily into traditionally male-dominated professions (Tidball 1985, 1986), go on to earn proportionally more than girls graduat- ing from coed schools (Riordan 1994), and are ultimately more successful in their careers (Oates and Williamson 1978; Rice and Hemmings 1988;

Tidball 1980). Contrary to this, in coeducational settings (and from as early as preschool), girls are less active and have more difficulty affirming themselves (Maccoby 1990). Moreover, we know that inequalities still persist in terms of education (Foster, Gomm, and Hammersley 1996): although girls are more successful at school (through university) (Baudelot and Establet 1992; Reed 1999), their career perspectives are more limited and their salaries are lower.[1]

What role do these elements play in the processes of transmitting the history of Nazism at school? Is gender an important factor in how teachers evaluate students and their abilities in normative terms? Does it have an impact on the ways the past is used? How do these two elements interact? More specifically, what role does gender play in the transmission of the Nazi past and in the mechanisms of its appropriation? How do school socialization and family socialization interact to produce and reproduce gendered behavior around the appropriation of history? In order to respond to these questions, we need to look more closely at the different gendered interactions within the classroom, the content and nature of these interactions, and individuals' room to maneuver within them. These are all factors that remain essentially invisible in statistical studies (Canada 1995). We will also need to investigate the teachers' language practices, as well as family configurations and the influences they have on different forms of appropriation.

Actors and Victims: Learning to Talk about the Genocide

The teaching of the Nazi period is based almost exclusively on the *Betroffenheit* pedagogy, the pedagogy of emotional upheaval. This approach asks the students to identify with the victims, relying on the use of emotions and therefore temporarily breaks with the usual frames of pedagogical understanding. Indeed, according to the teachers, learning ancient history and the history of the Middle Ages requires other abilities—reason rather than emotion, rote learning rather than empathy—which the teachers tend to consider as masculine traits. According to the teachers interviewed in this study, democratic civic-mindedness requires specific abilities that are facilitated by emotional upheaval and "empathy" with the victims. The emotional involvement of the students is seen as representing a "guarantee" against "evil." Yet although affect is valued in this teaching context, it is also traditionally considered a feminine trait, and this attribution is at the heart of the *Betroffenheit* pedagogy and the role that gender plays in the teaching of the history of Nazism. In order to understand this interaction, we must first study the ways that students mobilize the past in gendered ways—even before the teacher is involved. The way the girls use the emotional frame almost exclusively leads

126 • When Will We Talk about Hitler?

to empathy with the victims, while the adolescent boys' uses of it very often lead to a fascination for the executioners or perpetrators. This follows a classic division between the public space (attributed to or reserved for men) and the private space (attributed to or reserved for women). These different uses of the emotional frame contribute to and reinforce gendered representations of learning abilities by the teachers. It is this representation, along with the objectives of the *Betroffenheitspädagogik* that lead to gendered grading practices, which in turn have a decisive effect on the ways in which boys appropriate this past, whereas they leave female appropriations unchanged.

Gender Differences in the Way Students Use the Past

The *Betroffenheitspädagogik*, with its specific emotional frame and emphasis on the victims, is introduced in ninth grade. In order to see the perceptions of the Nazi past that students have before this official pedagogy is introduced—and the role that gender plays in them—interviews were also conducted in eighth grade. From these interviews we can see that boys and girls differ in the way they use the past in at least two key ways. First, they gather information about the past using different materials, but in addition, both the themes they focus on and the ways they identify with historical actors also differ.

In these interviews we can see that girls and boys are not drawn to the same sources of information, nor do these sources provoke the same degrees of identification—a difference that can also be seen when they get older (in the interviews with eighteen and nineteen year olds). Girls tend to turn toward fiction to gather information on the period, which corresponds to female cultural practices: various national and international studies in thirty-five countries have shown that girls are more regular and more comfortable readers than boys (Baudelot, Cartier, and Détrez 1999; Baudelot and Establet 1992; Mullis et al. 2003; OECD 1995, 2001). Moreover, girls seem to be particularly attracted to novels, but the gender gap decreases when it comes to non-fiction reading practices (Richter and Brügelmann 1995; Schwippert, Bos, and Lankes 2004; Stanat and Kunter 2002). The girls that have participated in this study are selective in their choice of novels and autobiographies on Nazism: they focus on the genocide of the Jews and talk a lot about *The Diary of Anne Frank*,[2] *Friedrich*,[3] or the series written by Klaus Kordon.[4] They read these books voluntarily; they borrow them from the library, are given them by their parents, or lend them to each other.[5]

Katharina (eighteen years old, daughter of two senior executives, and a former student of Mr Schultze at Weinberg *Gymnasium*) explained to me that when she was thirteen or fourteen years old, she was passionate about everything to do with Nazism, and in particular the genocide of the Jews, an interest that waned as she got older. "I was always such a fan of those 'books about the Jews' (*Judenbücher*), I went to the library and [she laughs] I looked at everything there was about the Third Reich, and then I read it all."[6] Almost all the girls I interviewed mentioned going to the library to borrow books about "the Jews," among their favorite pastimes. This is particularly true for girls from privileged social backgrounds. Nevertheless, the difference between girls and boys on this point is also visible in the less privileged areas. This observation is echoed by the findings of Susan Dumais (2002) in the United States, which show that the libraries are more frequently visited by adolescents higher up the social hierarchy, but that for adolescents lower down the hierarchy, the library still constitutes the most significant cultural activity—before concerts, museums, or lessons in art, dance, or music. Dumais also shows that at age fourteen, girls go to the library more frequently than boys and that this difference increases at the lower end of the social hierarchy.

Heidi, for example, who is a friend of Katharina, described this phenomenon almost like a fashion: "all the girls read the same books, swap them around."[7] Beyond simply reading the books, the practice of lending them shows that the girls' discussions about "the Jews" are an important element in their adolescent socialization. Works of fiction can therefore play an important role in the processes of politicization, for these girls in any case.

Even though they are obliged to read the same books in their German literature class, the boys demonstrate a more reluctant attitude toward works of fiction. A good example of this is Peter, nineteen years old and in thirteenth grade (the last grade before *Abitur* exams in Germany). He was one of the boys in the advanced history class at Weinberg in Hamburg and the son of a bank worker and a mother at home. In response to me asking whether he reads novels he replied, "Oh no! No way! I don't read much and never on that subject." Boys also more frequently did not remember the content of the books they have to read for school (whereas the girls quote them in great detail) or said they find them boring.

Max, whose mother is a literature teacher and whose father is a local politician, is an example of this. At the time of the interview, he was in Mr Schulze's ninth-grade class. He said he "likes to read" in his free time, particularly "adventure" books like the *Lord of the Rings*.[8] He was one of the few boys who remembered the content of the books about the Nazi past that have been covered in class. He talked about the novel *Friedrich*.

It's about a boy, a Jewish boy, who is friends with a German boy. And—yes, how does it [the persecution] happen. I don't remember very well—it's . . . they live in a house, and the German goes to the swimming pool with the Jewish boy. And at one point they need the yellow stars (*Judensterne*). And the

German is shunned and he can't go to the pool with him anymore. And at the end there is a bombing—and everyone was there. And the guardian—or I don't know what he was—he was supposed to organize the air-raid shelter. And he was, well, a Nazi. And he wouldn't let the Jewish boy into the shelter, at the end. And the American planes [he lowers his voice], they passed overhead, and they killed him, Friedrich. Or—I don't remember who is called Friedrich, if it's the German friend or the other. Anyway, it doesn't matter, one of them.

And what did you think of the book?
Well—sometimes it was a little off the subject.

A little off the subject?
Yes! There were three chapters on how they walked in the woods, and it wasn't so—well, I don't remember that much. But it wasn't really on the subject. They didn't meet anyone either. And there wasn't much connection to the story afterwards. I don't know why there was that. But, well, I don't remember too well.[9]

In fact, Max did remember, but he remained unenthusiastic. The scene that he is referring to is a scene that the boys often criticized. It is one of the moments in the book in which the two friends talk about their perceptions of the world, but also about their friendship. The boys reading the story criticized the lack of "action," whereas the girls were much more enthusiastic about the passages on "human problems." For example, Annelore (eighteen years old, in thirteenth grade at Weinberg) described this same passage as being about "who believes what, and why, and who loves who and all that—I like that."[10] The content and the form are therefore very closely linked. This attraction for "action" is also expressed in the fact that the boys played video games more often than girls, which sometimes represent the Nazi past. They were also keener to gather information from television sources: documentaries and news reports. They were also very interested in cinema (particularly war films) and fiction.

Another boy named Michael, aged sixteen, the son of an actor and a dentist's assistant in Leipzig, chose a history specialization at *Gymnasium* Monnet and explained,

I watch news reports [he considers] like *Spiegel TV*, for example, or things like that. They mostly talk about the events of the war. For example, the pact between Stalin and Hitler and the reasons for it. Or Poland's role, for example. Things like that. I quite like it. I find it interesting.

And what is it that you find interesting about it?
[He pauses to think about this.] Well, yes, above all the [original] documents, because you don't see that very often. Because—who has the opportunity [to see that]?[11]

Michael emphasized aesthetic reasons for his interest, rather than the "content" of the images. The fact that these materials are rare seemed to increase their value for him—arguments that are scarcely ever found among the girls.

The boys also said they read newspapers more often than the girls, or news magazines such as *Der Spiegel*,[12] in which there are articles on the period, particularly on the figure of Hitler. Thomas, for example, said that he liked to read these articles at his grandfather's house, as an opportunity to talk about the past "between men."

In addition to drawing on different materials, male and female students also differ in two other interrelated ways: the themes that they are particularly interested in and their modes of identification with historical actors.

For the girls, there is an empathy with the victims and also with their own grandparents that goes hand in hand with a personalization of history. This corresponds to a specific interest in the everyday history of ordinary people and families, in a perspective that is not too far removed from that of the history of the everyday or *Alltagsgeschichte*. Indeed, the

> occupations and difficulties of those we often label with the evocative but imprecise term "little people" are at the heart of the research on the history of everyday life and its writing. We talk about their work and their leisure. We describe their ways of being at home and being homeless, their ways of dress and of nakedness, their ways of eating and going hungry . . . What is important are the lives and the survival of the unnamed actors in history, their daily struggles as well as their "occasional explosive release" [rather than], the deeds (and misdeeds) . . . of those who held secular and political power. (Lüdtke 1995b: 3)

Yet the two identification processes are not of the same nature. In the first instance, it is a projection onto the "weak," the "little people," the "victims" of history; in the second, the identification is with those who are close to oneself, grandparents, sometimes, but not always, considered "victims of history." This form of victimization can be associated with "hero-worship" (Welzer, Moller, and Tschuggnall 2005; Welzer, Montau, and Plaß 1997). The two—identification with "little people" and identification with family members—share a common form however: an interest in the history of the everyday, the history of private lives, family history. In both cases, the girls appreciate the narratives that remind them of crime or adventure novels: the flight and exile of the persecuted Jews; German populations fleeing before the Red Army, or hiding in basements while the Allies bombed. These processes of identifying with the "victims," the concentration on these specific aspects of victimhood, also mean that the *Täter*, those perpetrating the suffering, are consequently of secondary interest.[13]

This particularity of themes and modes of identification among the girls led them to associate Nazism exclusively with the experiences of the Jewish victims, as representative of all victims—as we can see in their use of neologisms such as *Judenthema, Judenbücher* (Jewish themes, Jewish books) to refer to books covering this period. These are terms invented by the students that official discourse refuses because of its analogy to the language of the Third Reich—the *lingua tertii imperii* (LTI)—described by Victor Klemperer.[14] The students were apparently not aware of this analogy.

Several girls talked about their ability to empathetically "relive" the situation of the characters in these novels. Heidi, age eighteen, was a former student of Mr Schulze, and explained that she was able to identify with people in the story to a point where she sometimes had difficulty dealing with their suffering.

> It's through the feelings (*gefühlsmässig*). Well, in particular when I'm very focused on a subject or reading a book that happened at that time [during Nazism], I realize that—how much I can identify myself with them, put myself completely in their shoes [the characters—*wie ich mich da reinsteigern kann*]. And I find it really horrible—and so oppressive (*beklemmend*)—all that, so much that I have to put the book down and have to consciously do something else, I do something else to disconnect from all that.[15]

This projection through pity seems necessary for Heidi to be interested in the story, even though the strength of her feelings led her to adopt a certain distance from this kind of reading.

In general, the connections between family history and "overall history" are what interest these girls. They appeared to be more interested than the boys in the possibilities "ordinary people," sometimes their own grandparents, had for resistance. Leonore, (aged fifteen, daughter of a retail worker, and a student at the 100th *Mittelschule* in Leipzig) was particularly affected by her maternal family history—she didn't know her father, he left when she was three. One of her great-grandmothers, on her mother's side, apparently "hid Jews" during the war; unlike the mother of her maternal grandfather who "followed along with the regime" (*Mitläuferin*). These different ways of confronting history led Leonore to ask herself a number of questions.

> Well, for me, what I find interesting is how they thought during that period. I try to—[she hesitates] yes, to put myself in their place, in the time. And then—I—it's also one of the themes that interests me: should we help the Jews? At the time I mean. Because they didn't have any rights and so on—and then I ask myself the question—would I have—helped [she hesitates] someone— well, if I'd had friends who were Jews—would I have helped them? And then, I should say, I came to the conclusion that [she hesitates] those who didn't

Gender, Family, and the Nazi Past(s) • 131

help, they were not really bad people.[16] But they were afraid for their families and—well, even if one person had decided to hide Jews—automatically all the family would have been sent to the concentration camp. And [she hesitates]— I can understand that they wanted to protect their families—I mean, I would have probably [she struggles to find the words]—even if you just gave food to the Jews you'd have been punished for that for sure! It happened. But—I think I would have done it . . . Because you had to do something.

And why do you think that you would have wanted to do something?
Well, because it's human I suppose.[17]

It is this "humanity" that is of interest to these girls. Other than their compassion for the victims, the girls seemed to want to put themselves in their grandparents' shoes and to question their own position in the face of the Nazi regime, but more particularly in the face of the victims. This double empathy can be found in the books that they read, they said they liked, and they remembered. Sometimes their interest and their identification took place through images. For example, Maren (sixteen years old, daughter of low-skilled workers, and a student at the 100th *Mittelschule*) explained how she became interested in the subject.

I think that at school we had this—this Jewish theme (*Judenthema*) where—or in general history I looked at the textbook and I quickly saw—there was a picture of Anne Frank. And underneath it mentioned her diary, and that—I could learn something about that. And so I thought—well, let's go—I often go to the library and everything—and so I went to the library and I borrowed it [the *Diary*], and I read it myself.[18]

The books that the girls said they liked are not only about the suffering and exclusion of the Jews but also about the possibilities of micro-resistance against the Nazi regime. They also tend to adapt an individualizing perspective that is particular to the history of everyday life. Annelore, for example, (aged eighteen and a student at Weinberg, her father is a manager in a petrol company and her mother is a schoolteacher) explained what she liked about the series of books by Klaus Kordon.

For me, it was fascinating to learn about what human beings thought during that period, or in any case the main character. I don't remember how old he was, twelve or something, fourteen, a boy, his father had been in the SPD, his big brother was a Communist, and his mother didn't get involved in anything. And he lives in a courtyard with lots of people—and also some young Nazis, together. And then he comes—he begins [she hesitates], he finally has work in a factory where he can start right away. And then, yeah, [she mumbles] yeah, they—they attract the attention of the two young Nazis, two young very militant Nazis and—they really finished him off (*die machen ihn wirklich fertig*). They lock him in a box and put it in the cupboard and say, "admit that you're a Red!" "We're gonna smash your face up!" (*wir polieren Dir die Fresse*) Or something like that. And I found it—my God, that really happened—how can someone develop so much hate, and—that was the part that affected me the most.[19]

The way that Annelore talked about the story shows just how much she connected with it. She did not have the same meta-discourse as Michael from Leipzig who was interested in the form, or the critical distance of Max in Hamburg, mentioned above. She identified with the main characters and especially the victims. The cultural practices of the girls were thus entirely in keeping with the political objectives of the *Betroffenheitspädagogik*. The books that they liked and the ways in which they related to the past fit well with the school curriculum. For their teachers, the empathy of these girls with the victims constituted the "first step" toward rejecting Nazism and thus toward "a commitment to democracy."

The destiny of the individual victims was not the boys' favorite subject, however. They were more interested in the war, in battles, and in weapons. They particularly focused on figures who were—to use Lüdtke's expression—at the "height of command" (*Kommandohöhen*), participating in the politico-military hierarchy, the government or the administration (often referred to by the interviewees as "the Nazis").[20] This focus is closer to "event history,"[21] typically defined as "political" and focusing on the figures that drive it, i.e., the "major actors" in history—specifically the *Täter*, the perpetrators of the Nazi extermination policy. This opposition between "political" history (that we see in films, television, and magazines) and "family" history (in novels) reproduces the division between the public sphere and the private sphere (Weintraub and Kumar 1997), which itself corresponds to a world order divided into male and female spheres.[22]

Thomas, aged fourteen, is the son of a chemistry professor at Hamburg University and a nurse. At the time of the interview, he was a former student of Mr Schulze and he enjoyed talking about his grandfather's experiences as a soldier on the eastern front. Here, he talked about the most recent film he had seen on this theme.

In fact, I prefer [he laughs, a little uneasy] to watch fiction films. But sometimes I watch things like that [documentaries]. Last time there was something on—on Rommel. What was it called, Phoenix, yeah, Phoenix [cable television channel]. There are often things on—on Hitler, Rommel—Hitler, Heydrich, and things like that. I don't remember . . . They showed how—I don't know—they didn't have any petrol because—Rommel—he went off driving in the desert (*der ist da in der Wüste rumgefahren*) with his tanks, and that it was a bit pointless. [He considers.] Or—for Himmler, I know, about him, they said that—he was as horrible (*schlimm*) as Hitler [he hesitates], like, well, if Hitler had died, he would have done the same thing. He was from the SS, I think, their "Führer" or something like that. And he shot loads of Jews. And Heydrich, or Himmler, I don't remember which one, I just remember the name, in any case he was a bad guy too, awful (*ein Fieser*) [he laughs].[23]

Like the girls, Thomas also talked about the genocide of the Jews. But unlike them, he focused on the "political actors," the "persecutors" of history rather than the victims. At the center of his narrative are the Nazi figures he knows by name. Several boys expressed their interest in the different tanks that were used and that they knew the details of.

Johnny, for example (the son of a painter and a cleaner, and a fifteen-year-old student at Wiesi), professed a veritable fascination for tanks.

I compare: I have my German *Tiger-Panzer* and the Russian *T34*. And which was better? [He is getting carried away.] Which one was stationed where? And what conditions did it advance best in? And in Stalingrad, did they have tanks like this? The Russians could make more *T34s*. But they didn't have a radio transmitter-receiver. So if they had an order, they went, and they couldn't encounter allies and things like that. Because there was no radio transmitter. But they were faster. And there were more parts for exchange. Yeah, and they were better on the ground. The German tank—in fact, the German tank was more technical in general. Radio transmitters. Loudspeakers and everything. Like a Hi-Fi stereo. But the *Tiger*, it had an 88mm, and that could take out any enemy tank. And it was super well-protected. The only weak spot was at the back. And it was too slow! 38 km per hour. When you're too slow, you're an easy target for planes. And that was the disadvantage. There was no perfect tank, [he lowers his voice] they all had their weaknesses.

They should have made a combination—
[He cuts me off.] Yeah, well there was one—the Panther! It was made for the T34. It was in 19 . . . [he hesitates] 1941. They said it was built in 1941. It came out in 1942. The end of [19]42! Almost at the same time as the Tiger. And it was built like a T34, because the Germans wanted to copy the T34. Because, in fact in 1941—Barbarossa—they didn't have tanks that were better than the Russians. And so they only won because they could communicate between each other, and because they were better tacticians. The tacticians of the *blitzkrieg*. That's why the Germans won. If they hadn't had to beat them tank against tank, they would never had arrived in Moscow—or Stalingrad.[24]

Johnny demonstrated very detailed knowledge here. He reconstructed battles to "replay the war" and understood strategic and military stakes, such as, how to arrive "outside Moscow" (*vor Moskau*). Although the girls never mentioned weapons or tanks, almost all the boys did—regardless of their socio-economic backgrounds. Boys from intellectual families were just as likely to be fascinated by the tools of war. Heiner (aged fourteen, son of two secondary school teachers and a student of Mr Schultze at Weinberg in Hamburg), for example, talked about how he saw a documentary on Arte[25] television that "fascinated" him.

> And then they talked about which tanks—how they built the tanks. And they had lots of eye-witnesses[26]—and yes, it's captivating when they talk about it: "here the tank came out of the water, and they shot my friend" and stuff like that. It affects and influences you (*das prägt*) and so you remember. Yeah.[27]

The boys, like the girls, developed an exclusive, almost obsessional relationship with this theme, and some developed a particular fascination for "the worst criminals," their murderous techniques, and military choices.

The twelfth-grade students in Ms Heide's advanced history class at Weinberg *Gymnasium* were all boys, and they insisted on covering the "military history" of the period, against their teacher's wishes. Peter explained why the subject attracted him "right away."

> Yeah, we asked to talk directly about the war. And I also wanted to do it because we haven't done it before in history [class]. And I don't know anything about how the war played out. Rather the—the [he hesitates] the framework (*Rahmenhandlung*)—I don't know [he laughs] how to say it. The period [he hesitates] like, at the beginning of the war, the Polish campaign, and then, how it continued, to Russia, Stalingrad and then the withdrawal. And things like that, we have never really talked about that before, what really happened. But not the atrocities and all that. That doesn't interest me at all, that, no [he laughs].
>
> *You don't really want to know?*
> No, I don't want to know [he speaks quickly]. I saw enough of that in the diary [of his grandfather].[28]

It was therefore not the violence of war that interested Peter but the "developments" (*Verlauf*) and the strategic choices of the military commanders.

Moreover, the male students appeared to be interested in questions of national and international politics, which is typically a component in "event history." Leif (aged eighteen, student at Weinburg *Gymnasium* in Hamburg, son of a policeman and an employee) put the question this way:

> What I'm interested in is, on one hand—how is it possible that Hitler came to power? And also—why didn't other countries react when Germany started to expand? Or, like, the war in Russia—that interests me too. For example, the Germans were just outside Moscow. So, how is it possible that Hitler—who

had to have been quite intelligent in spite of everything—he did have some very intelligent people under him! How is it possible that [he hesitates] yeah, all at once, because of a harsh winter, in Russia, that Germany was completely squashed, and because of that he more or less lost the war! Or like—the atrocities, for example, on both sides! In Russia, what happened, with cannibalism in the camps. But [he hesitates] on both sides! And how enemy soldiers were treated.[29]

Once again, his interest was clearly at the governmental and military levels, with the national and international leaders. He saw this as "real politics, where wars are decided." Several boys explained that the importance of World War II lies primarily in its influence on German geography, because the territorial outlines of the current FRG were drawn during this period. Both of Karsten's (the son of two self-employed shopkeepers) grandfathers "felt close to Hitler"; his paternal grandfather told his grandson about his "adventures on the Eastern Front," and his maternal grandfather told him about his "adventures in Paris as a Nazi spy in the 1930s." When asked why World War II was particularly important for him, he replied,

Yeah, I'd say—because so many people died. [He pauses to think.] And probably because—oh yeah, it changed all the landscape. [He thought again.] Because—[he hesitates] the map changed.

The landscape—?
Yeah, the map of Germany—it was—it became—the Germans attacked other countries, Poland and all that, and then—the map got bigger. And then, it got smaller. Yeah, and then, I'd say—yeah, through World War II—relationships were built with certain countries—for the better or the worse, yeah.[30]

The exclusive, recurring, and near-obsessional relationship the students have with the Nazi past seems to evoke a fascination for the threat of death in wartime. The intensity of this provokes particular interest and identification among both the boys and the girls—but they clearly use the past in very different ways. The usages these adolescents internalized are inscribed in a gendered world order broadly divided between "masculine" and "feminine," between "politics" and "everyday life." The transmission of this order is also gendered in itself: the interviews suggest, for example, that grandfathers talk about the war more often to their grandsons than their granddaughters.

However, the way the teachers react to this gender difference presents an unusual problem. Without mobilizing the division between the "political" and the "domestic," the teachers are focused on the role of "affect," which they frequently present to me as being a "feminine quality." But we cannot conclude (as the teachers do) that the boys are less "emotional" or "empathetic" in their relation to history—they were passionate about the subjects they discuss in the interviews. However, their interest in weapons, tanks, battles, and "major historical figures" (who, in this particular case, were criminals) is very problematic socially and difficult to accept in class.[31] Thus, when Ms Gerhard evokes the boys' "passion for war," she despaired rather than being pleased by this particular attachment, especially when it concerns the period between 1933 and 1945. This explains why this fascination for the figures of Nazism is not recognized as a legitimate feeling, and why it is presented as a "particular interest" of the boys, but never considered an affective relation to history.

Gender and Teaching Practices

Numerous studies suggest important effects of gender differences on teachers' practices (Arnot 2000; Fagot et al. 1985; Hall and Sandler 1982; Sadker and Sadker 1994). The discourses of the teachers interviewed here are also imbued with gendered representations—particularly concerning the idea of what constitutes a talented student. According to this frequent representation, girls "are not good at history" until ninth grade, and then they catch up. Boys, on the other hand, develop an interest in this discipline early on, which the teachers explain by their "natural militaristic tendency." Thus, history as a discipline is associated with war; this is "event history," which constitutes most of the school curriculum before the introduction of *Betroffenheitspädagogik*.

Mr Schulze, the school principal,[32] emphasized the boys' "superiority" in terms of "handling" the "historical material" for the period before 1933–1945. The boys, "history teachers," as he called them, already "know everything, they've already learned it all by heart."[33] He explained this by what he saw as the boys' superior "knowledge."[34] In Germany, the term *auswendig lernen*, which refers to rote learning of lexical knowledge (*lexikalischen Wissens*), evokes more the cerebral and the performance required for scientific reasoning imputed to boys. Gerhard Amendt (1996: 379) has analyzed the attribution of "feelings" to girls, and "performance principles" to boys by school teachers in Germany. By contrast, in other countries the notion of "hard work" is more associated with girls, and "talent" associated with boys. In France, for example, learning "by heart" is attributed to girls and less valued than what are considered boys' "natural abilities." Girls are seen as "hard-working," boys as "brilliant" (see Mosconi 1999), which reflects the distinction between "the worker" and "the talented" in categories of perception and social ranking (hard-working laborers, brilliant elites) (Bourdieu 1989: 33–34; Bourdieu and Passeron [1964] 1985). This research thus shows that not only sexual stereotypes are varying according to the country, even between European neighbors such as France and Germany. It also shows that they change according to age.

Indeed, in ninth grade this configuration changes radically, which Mr Schulze explained by the "disappearance of the girls' handicap." The history taught before ninth grade (the Middle Ages and ancient history, in particular) is taught "apolitically" (as the teachers in the East frequently explicitly put it[35]). According to Mr Schulze, this requires "knowledge" and "learning by heart" and therefore puts boys at an advantage. On the other hand, twentieth century history, and particularly the history of Nazism, is considered "political,"[36] i.e., useful in democratic and civic education and requiring other qualities, as we have seen.

Mr Schulze did not explicitly mention this change in how the students are evaluated. But his comments on one ninth-grade female student make it clear: "She takes it all to heart," "she burns [with enthusiasm]," he says admiringly. In teaching the history of Nazism, this attitude is particularly valued. When Mr Schulze evokes this student and her affective relationship to the subject, he is proud of her. Girls are considered "more able" to reason holistically in this sense—"not only with the head but also with the heart"— and as a result they are able to study political history that requires a certain "emotional" involvement.[37]

Mr Schulze's representations of what constitutes a "talented student" were not the same over the different stages of high school however. Although he considered girls to be "more emotional," and boys "more cerebral," his reactions to these stereotypes and what they meant for his idea of a "talented student" all changed between grade five and grade nine. The fact that girls were seen as "more emotional" was a handicap for them in grade five, but from ninth grade and the introduction of the history of Nazism, it becomes an advantage. In the teachers' words, the girls "got better" at history, but in practice it was the boys who "got weaker," as we can see in Table 3.1.

Out of twenty-eight students, a little fewer than half maintained the same grades over the two years—but this is true for many more girls than boys, eight out of eleven.[38] Only a small proportion of students improved their grades—three out of twenty-eight, two of whom were girls. But half the class obtained a grade lower than they had the previous year, and two-thirds of them were boys.

We can therefore consider that Mr Schulze's representations only partially correspond to his grading practices. He said that he appreciates the girls' work on National Socialism in ninth grade, but he did not necessarily give them better grades than he did in eighth grade. However, he did lower the grades of the boys if necessary. This could be interpreted as a form of punishment for the boys. They sometimes used the emotional framework of the *Betroffenheitspädagogik* to express their interest for the military and for Nazis,

138 • When Will We Talk about Hitler?

Table 3.1 Students' academic progress in history by sex for Mr Schulze's class (end of eighth grade, beginning of ninth grade).

Grades	Boys	Girls	Total
Improvement	1	2	3
Regression	10	4	14
No change	3	8	11
Total	14	14	28

Notes: This takes into account the students' grades at the end of eighth grade, the middle of ninth grade, and the end of ninth grade. "Improvement" refers to grades that were at least two points higher (out of fifteen) at the middle and end of ninth grade compared to the eighth grade. "Regression" refers to the students whose grades went down by at least one point. Those whose grades do not vary much at all (half a point) or initially increased and then decreased were put in the "no change" category.

which is not well accepted in the school context. Based on their grading practices, the teachers also unconsciously guided the boys to focus on a new object—the victims—which progressively led them to adopt the same frames of reference of the past as the girls and thus led to a homogenization of the students' discourses.

Uniformity of Discourse in the Final Year

From tenth grade, and then in particular in the twelfth and thirteenth grades[39] (the final year, just before the *Abitur* matriculation exams), the gender differences in the students' interest in the past progressively disappeared, making way for a remarkably uniform discourse. The boys' relationship to the past seems to have moved into line with that of the girls, although certain differences remained. Their interest in "politics" had become less pronounced, and made way for a progressive sensibility to the plight of the victims, with whom the boys began to develop an emotional connection. They still did not talk much about novels, but they did talk about visiting the concentration camps, which often had a profound impact on them. Even Daniel, a final year student who was sympathetic to extreme-right ideas, was visibly shocked by the experience. "And then, there's a very strange feeling (*merkwürdig*), like—when you go into these big halls—and you know that in these halls were assembly-line workers (*Fließbandarbeit*), and they dug these holes—and they died in there—really, it really gets to you, you know (*das geht einem schon an die Nieren*)."[40]

This experience was so important for him that it managed to momentarily shake his political representations. His otherwise strong tendency to minimize the importance of the genocide of the Jews disappeared entirely at this point in the interview, replaced by a strong identification with the victims—which is what the pedagogic context demanded.

The boys also talked a lot about films and documentaries, but the content had changed from the ones they watched in early secondary school. The themes no longer focused on Hitler and the war, but on the genocide; films such as Roberto Benigni's *Life Is Beautiful* or Steven Spielberg's *Schindler's List*. This subject provoked emotions that were so strong for the students that sometimes, like Daniel here, the words get stuck in their throats.

> They showed us films [he hesitates] on the refugees (*Flüchtlinge*) or the [he hesitates again], well not the gassing, of course [he lowers his voice], but like how they were piled into the camps and like how they were so thin! That, that's maybe the most gruesome image (*das grausigste Bild*) that I've ever seen [he hesitates again] when they pushed all the corpses into a big pile (*die ganzen Leichen auf einen Haufen gekehrt*) [he stops and begins again]. Really. That, that was the most horrible.
>
> *And do you remember your reaction?*
> I think [he considers], nothing. I was speechless.[41]

These experiences tend to take place during school excursions, and unlike those proposed in eighth grade, these later ones did provoke empathetic reactions. The boys in thirteenth grade remembered visits to the camps and watched the films again at home. They were emotionally affected, shocked, and expressed their compassion for the victims.

This change in attitude also concerns the girls, but in the opposite direction to the boys. Their fixation on the subject declines significantly with age. Although they remained interested, these older girls said they felt like they had "seen it all before." Senior students talked about their "past passion" for the question, "the time when I read everything in the library that had a title linked to Nazism, no matter what it was about."[42] This period of their lives seems far away from them now, and the subject is less important to them in their everyday lives.

The boys' acquisition of a legitimate relationship with the Nazi past in the school environment can be seen in a homogenization of the students' discourses, and particularly in their ability to acquire a normative "empathy" previously considered "specific to girls." This occurs in two ways; while the teachers see it as a "true understanding" of the subject, it is indicative of the transmission of their norms through teaching. Moreover, gender norms have a certain degree of flexibility; a certain amount of room for maneuver that allows boys to adapt (relatively speaking) to roles attributed to girls, when they are seen as positive. However, these differences do not seem to influence the teachers' representations of so-called "feminine" and "masculine" qualities in that they continue to read these dispositions in gendered terms even once the traditional gender lines have been blurred. Empathy, therefore, and affect more generally, is explicitly praised during the teaching of Nazi history (but not in any other history classes) including among the boys.

An informal conversation with Mr Schulze[43] also provided a vision of the norms that he applied to his students. He talked about "Victor, the difficult student," a young man who "does stupid things" at school. What shocked Mr Schulze in particular were "the jokes about Hitler" and behavior such as tagging Nazi slogans or symbols on the school walls (Victor had just been caught doing this, along with his friend Markus). The two boys also had the worst grades in history class. However, Mr Schulze considered Markus to be a "bad influence" on Victor—the former being a student who was "impossible to save."[44] For his teacher, Victor still had a chance, unlike his friend; he was "beginning to develop a real passion for the subject of Nazism" (by which he meant the victims). This shift led Mr Schulze to share with me his "increasingly affectionate appreciation" (*liebevoll*) for this student. We can see that the appropriation of legitimate discourses on Nazism can radically alter a teacher's appreciation of a student—to the point where his "stupidity" is attributed to the "true" responsibility of his friend.

Representations of the intellectual capacities of girls and boys have a strong influence on the grading system at school, broadly speaking. But one capacity in particular, "empathy," persistently associated with girls, is depreciated in early secondary school and then valued after ninth grade. This changes the way the students are evaluated, with the boys receiving lower grades because they are seen as "lacking this essential quality," or as using it in ways that are frowned upon (in their focus on the *Täter*, the perpetrators). Yet the teachers also depreciate this same characteristic—even scorn it—in the girls before they reach ninth grade.

There is therefore a certain stability in representations relating to the particular characteristics associated with "masculine" and "feminine," which reflects an opposition between rationality and affectivity. This coexists with the fluctuating judgments that the students are subject to (positive/negative evaluations). This variability does not seem to pose a problem for the teachers' system of reference, in which the "masculine" is still seen in positive terms. Indeed, for the girls, this change in judgment does not seem to have much influence on the way they are graded. However, the boys have more room for maneuver at their disposal: they are temporarily de-valued by the new grading criteria, and then they acquire the desired "feminine" qualities (interest in the victims), and thus succeed in making up lost ground.[45]

Moreover, positive and negative judgments relating to perceived "feminine" affectivity and empathy exist simultaneously for a given teacher depending on the age of his or her students, which is likely to provoke contradictory representations. Affect does not have the same status according to the gender of students. Initially criticized as a "natural handicap" for girls, and seen as inaccessible to boys, it then becomes a resource for the girls from the ninth grade onward, also adopted by the boys. However, in the representations of the teachers, it remains as an essentially "female" quality.

Finally, we can question the function of the *Betroffenheitspädagogik*, and more specifically the vision of empathy as "female" that it produces. We have seen that it seems to constitute the legitimate form of the adolescents' fascination for danger and death in wartime. Yet when this fascination is associated with voyeurism and violence, it becomes awkward and is considered by teachers to be inappropriate in a school setting. We can therefore suppose that as far as this fascination focuses on the victims, teachers consider it positive, as a sign of empathy, and as creating the dispositions favorable for non-violence. According to this logic, an interest in the victims and their suffering, rather than in the *Täter*, the perpetrators, should lead to a moral condemnation of repressive and police measures that are contrary to human rights—torture, violence, the death penalty and so on. Inversely, an interest in the Nazi actors (which is the case for most of the boys) is interpreted by the teachers as a sign of dispositions that are favorable to violence and intolerance, or even neo-Nazism and xenophobia. Conforming to social norms is impossible here, hence the need to reorient the boys' emotional connection to the past, and bring it into line with the girls' more socially acceptable reaction.

The creation of this conformity shows just how much the universalization of *Betroffenheitspädagogik* is more than just the sincere desire to recognize the suffering of the victims. It corresponds to a sheer impossibility to accept this fascination for death in wartime, which leaves room for only a partial reinterpretation as "empathy for the victims," and completely neglects the other implications (the fascination for the persecutors' violence). Moreover, it leads to an interrogation into the way in which universalist civic pedagogy can reinforce gender stereotypes and produce specific forms of discrimination.

Although the teachers intervene to homogenize the discourses between boys and girls and to attract all the students' attention to the plight of the victims, gender differences do persist—including among the teachers. Although less striking than those among the students, these differences can be seen in the way the teachers mobilize their different interpretations of Nazism.

Male Language and Transmission

Although all the teachers were unanimous about the objectives of teaching students about Nazism, their ways of presenting the subject, particularly

142 • When Will We Talk about Hitler?

their formulations, their syntax, and their expressions, were different between male and female teachers. Moreover, these differences were also observed in transmissions within the family environment.

The interpretations of Nazism in school textbooks that focus excessively on the figure of the dictator have been criticized by specialists of didactics of history for the last thirty years (see, for example, E. Kolinsky 1992; M. Kolinsky and E. Kolinsky 1974). We would thus expect that this personalizing vision of history in textbooks has influenced the teachers' practices, their ways of being, doing, and speaking. Yet this influence is unequally distributed among teachers. Indeed, there are gender differences in the teachers' discourses about the Nazi past, just as there are for students. For example, most of the male teachers I spoke to talked extensively about the figure of Hitler. He is an omnipresent figure in all of their discourses, either explicitly (as "Hitler" or "the dictator") or without being directly named (as "one man," "a man so small," "him," "he"). According to the teachers, directly discussing the "figure of Hitler" responds first to a strong demand on the part of the students, who are also interested in this figure, as we have seen. Beyond the students' non-negotiable interest, however, the dictator operates as a "linguistic shortcut" to talk about National Socialism. Although this is typical of men talking about the Nazi past, we do not see it—with one exception—in the women's discourses. Expressions such as "Hitler's rise to power," "Hitler waged war," or "Hitler's genocide" and other variations are almost systematic in the discourses of the male teachers. Hitler is often the only grammatical subject in their descriptions of the period between 1933 and 1945.

Mr Stein (forty-nine years old, teacher at Wiesi) thus affirmed:

Racism, for example. There's lots of that today. What does that actually mean, racism? You don't need to have a Hitler to explain to people what racism means. You can use Hitler, and his consequences, but never—"be careful, it's bad because it could lead to a Hitler." Because someone could say—"and if I stop just before, that's not bad?" Yes. Of course it is![46]

In these phrases, "Hitler" represents first, racism and antisemitism between 1933 and 1945; second, "his consequences," the death camps and planned murder of six million Jews;[47] and third, dictatorship in general and its consequences. The use of the indefinite pronoun "a" also has an effect of generalization. It suggests that there might be other "Hitlers" in various forms. Mr Winter (fifty-four years old, teacher at Weisi), compared "the nasty Machiavelli" to Hitler, and observed that

The motivations of people who go into politics, they're always the same. It doesn't matter if they lived in the fifteenth, or nineteenth or twentieth

centuries. For example, personality, the desire for power! Little Hitlers—
according to their possibilities—they also existed in the fifteenth century![48]

Through the use of the plural, we can see the same focus on the "major
actors" of history that we have already seen in the students' discourses. Even
when he was talking about the genocide of the Jews and of "evil" generally,
Mr Winter mobilizes political figures that he compares to each other using
the formulation "little Hitlers."

Beyond the vagueness caused by the frequent use of the dictator's surname
(sometimes replaced by his first name, a use that increases proximity between
the speaker and the dictator and is not observed among the women), this
use leads to a personalization of the Nazi regime and a personification of
the crimes committed between 1933 and 1945 into the sole figure of Hitler.
Hitler is thus presented as the sole person responsible for the political dictatorship as well as for the crimes committed. To take only a few examples,
Mr Gerste (aged forty-four, teacher at Wiesi) asked his students, "When a dictator like this is attacked and killed, someone who constantly kills people (*der
am laufenden Band Menschen umbringt*), is it murder? Is it acceptable?"[49] The
"dictator," Hitler, is described as someone who constantly kills people and the
German expression uses the idea of the factory and the conveyor belt to evoke
the speed and extent of the crimes. Alf Lüdtke has analyzed the depersonal-
izing effect of the image of machinery applied to the Holocaust, that renders
invisible the actors of the crimes (Lüdtke 1996). But the formulation used by
Mr Gerste suggests that Hitler himself committed them. Mr Gerste was of
course perfectly aware that Hitler did not kill that many people with his own
hands. His formulation suggests this implicitly, but probably unintention-
ally. This is how the image of isolated responsibility for the crimes committed
between 1933 and 1945 is transmitted. Through language, Hitler becomes
the sole historical actor. Mr Herzog (teacher at Wiesi, around fifty years old)
emphasized that "the main point is that it can happen again—that one man,
a dictator . . . [he does not finish the sentence]."[50] Mr Wolff (aged forty-five,
principal of *Gymnasium* Monnet in Leipzig) was more explicit; for him, it is
important that the students "know what an individual (*ein Einzelner*) can do
with seventy million people."[51] Mr Stein, (aged forty-nine, at *Gesamtschule*
Wiesi in Hamburg) in criticizing Israel's policy, nevertheless stressed that it
is "not comparable with what Hitler did with the Jews."[52] When confronted
with this contradiction, neither Mr Wolff nor Mr Gerste nor Mr Herzog nor
Mr Stein argued that Hitler was the only person responsible or even the only
actor in the National Socialist policy of extermination. Yet their everyday
formulations in the context of teaching—which only extended classroom
observation can reveal—conveyed a "Hitler-centric" vision of this period of
history to their students, who had been socialized to receive and reproduce it.

144 • When Will We Talk about Hitler?

Words and syntax, as vehicles of speech, can be contradicted by their contents, the historical vision that is conveyed. We can see this in an example from Mr Kamm (teacher at Wiesi, about sixty years old) who was talking about his studies at Hamburg University in the 1960s.

You said you wrote a thesis on Nazism, at university?
Yes, it was on—Hitler's coalition. To say that Hitler—never—even in the March 1933 elections, never had the majority of the population behind him. He was therefore dependent on a coalition. There were, therefore, a lot of people who refused to follow him. Only later, during Hitler's regime, there were different results—that's something else. But this vote, in March 1933—we can say that it was pretty democratic, it [his own university research] was about that, on the conditions—[he pauses to think, stumbles, makes a comparison] not many have [he breaks off and begins again]—yes, Adenauer obtained more than 50 percent, once, I think [he laughs]. So, he was not a Chancellor who had obtained the majority, even if he was in office.[53]

Grammatically speaking, Hitler is the subject of each sentence. Moreover, the regime and the coalition are "Hitler's," the possessive reduces the dictatorship to his individual status. The people are also "for" or "against" Hitler, rather than National Socialism, the NSDAP, or the ideology, etc. The vote is also presented as being "for" or "against" Hitler—even though this is historically inaccurate (the Chancellor is not elected by universal suffrage in Germany). The comparison with Adenauer reveals the personalizing tendency of the language outside the 1933–1945 period. In spite of this grammatical and linguistic focus on the person, Mr Kamm rightly emphasized "Hitler's" dependency (i.e., the NSDAP) on other parties for support in 1933. Raising this question meant emphasizing the shared and complex responsibility in the NSDAP's "rise to power." In a similar way, Mr Winter criticized the position of the revisionist historian Ernst Nolte during the *Historikerstreit* of the 1980s, accusing him of not taking "economic factors" sufficiently into account in the "explanation of the Third Reich"—or of Hitler.[54]

Mr Winter, like the other teachers quoted here, would admit that no historian wants to or can "explain Hitler." But the "Hitler" shortcut remains a powerful signifier. The comparison between the teachers' uses of the past and those of the students opens up other paths for analysis. The youngest students openly concentrated on political figures and completely ignored economic explanations or the *Alltagsgeschichte* of Nazism. This ignorance, not yet modified by teaching practices, enabled them to affirm their interests without reserve: they had not yet completely interiorized the "acceptable ways" of talking about the past. They could display their passion for tanks, weapons, and Hitler, which was tolerated by the teachers "because they're boys" even though it was frowned upon. In speaking about her advanced history class, Ms Heide explained that "there are only eight of them and they're all boys. And they are really—really—into weapons, military, all that stuff. And I don't know anything about it! We're going to look at the battles (*Schlachten*)—I promised them. I don't know—well, they are boys, right?!"[55]

What is tolerated in "boys" is no longer tolerated when they are adults—particularly when they are teachers. A history teacher professing his passion for tanks would undoubtedly make a "bad impression" among his colleagues and even among his students. The question is whether these male uses of the Nazi past, which do not conform to what is socially acceptable, remain present in language even though they appear to be absent—or erased—at a conscious level. Can the "success" of this discourse on the Nazi past by the male teachers be explained by the fact that it "resonates" with the male students' areas of interests?

Mr Gerste (teacher at Wiesi, aged forty-two) explained the choices he made to "make his class interesting."

> At the moment, we have—to take an example that's a bit dumb—the accusation that Schwarzenegger [he was talking about the actor's election as governor of California] has some connection to Hitler. At the moment we're looking at the taking of power (*Machtergreifung*). So we can think about it: are they comparable or not? And so forth.[56]

Mr Gerste used newspapers and current events in his class. At the time of the interview, 20 October 2003, certain newspapers had raised the question of the comparison between the two figures. This came in the wake of accusations by US media that Schwarzenegger had been an "admirer of Hitler" in his youth.[57] As absurd as this comparison may seem from a historical point of view (including to Mr Gerste), it was covered in class because it provided "good material for discussion." Indeed, it corresponds to the ordinary uses of the past by many students.

The teachers therefore anticipated the students' reactions (consciously and unconsciously) in constructing their classes, in particular adapting them to the boys' uses of the past by emphasizing political figures. Some, like Ms Reinhardt, (age sixty-two, *Gymnasium* Weinberg) were aware of this.

> What surprises me, really, for all those years, is that it is a discipline [history] that interests the boys more than the girls. Maybe it's because, I don't know, I'd like to understand if it's generally like that, or if it's just my way of teaching [she hesitates]. I don't know. In any case, I observe that it resonates more strongly with the boys. And yes, they work better, and they are, they also understand better I think. [She considers.] In any case [she pauses again], yes, they do work harder in class, and they're more successful as well. In history [she hesitates], yes, it's bizarre (*merkwürdig*).[58]

146 • When Will We Talk about Hitler?

While Ms Reinhardt questioned her observations, four other (male) teachers at Wiesi had a more active approach to counteracting the gender effects that they produce in the classroom. Mr Gerste explained that he was careful to choose "themes for both genders (*Geschlechter*[59])."

> What were the defenses like when they attacked the fort? It's perhaps more the boys who are interested in that, by their nature or something. I don't want to bring everything back to girls and boys [he hesitates], to gender specificities (*geschlechtsspezifisch*). But—sometimes there are, how can I put it, themes . . . [he does not finish his sentence]. So, I change them. For example, on one hand, there are those who are more interested in war themes (*kriegerisch*). And so, they can make a model of a soldier or something like that. And then, on the other hand, we can do—wigs, for example. During the French Revolution. Or in presentations, for example [they can choose] to present fashion, cosmetics, if they feel like it. Or the situation of women during the war. Love stories. What happened when a loved one (*der Geliebte*) was sent to the front. I've had that quite often too.[60]

Mr Gerste took this even further: he encouraged the girls to get interested in the war and the boys to be interested in love and fashion, to "reverse the roles" and "give them the opportunity to try something else." However, by his own admission, this has "not been very successful."

Mr Weise also covered what he calls "women's themes" in class. In particular, he mentioned the usefulness of studying "female emancipation" to "strengthen the girls" because "at home there are still a lot of stereotypes: you'll do the sewing and you'll repair the bike, you know."[61] These conscious attempts to counteract gendered history do not prevent these teachers from continually formulating subjects—especially when talking about World War II—in terms that reflect those used by the male students. For example, the choices of presentation subjects (outside the question of the Jewish Holocaust, which, as we have seen, is an exception to this) almost systematically propose a narrow biographical approach to "Hitler's life."

The fact that one young teacher at Wiesi, Annika Klein (aged thirty-five) refused to let a group of students work on "Hitler's rise to power" is revealing in this respect. She confided in me that this group, made up of three boys considered "difficult" by the history teachers, and their choice of subject were a source of "concern" for her. She considered it "dangerous," although she did not want to go into details about what she saw as the possible "undesirable" consequences. There is an implicit fear of the boys' "fascination" for the figure of Hitler, which is seen as inappropriate and resulting in a fascination for National Socialism, or even an "extreme-right" tendency among the young boys. This apprehension, expressed by several female teachers, systematically concerned the boys and in particular the "troublemakers" of the class. On the other hand, the teachers considered that the girls were "by definition" or "by nature" protected from this danger. Another group, for example, made up of three girls and a boy considered "a good student" were therefore allowed to prepare a presentation on "Hitler and Schindler, two comparative biographies." This led Annika Klein to comment enthusiastically—"I don't know what they'll come up with, but I'm curious. It's fascinating." The group considered "difficult" ended up presenting on the subject of the "concentration camps." The decision of the teachers, Annika Klein and her colleague Karen Werthe, might appear radical because of its extreme focus on the Jewish genocide—the course begins with the showing of the film *Schindler's List* and all the students except the group mentioned above ended up covering the genocide for their personal projects. The dictator and the regime remained almost absent from the class. This avoidance of themes considered too "masculine," reinforces an intentional "political" choice to focus on the genocide.

Female Figures

Although both male and female teachers tried to direct the boys toward subjects they considered more socially acceptable, focused on the victims of the genocide and the Jewish population in particular, the female teachers used different figures from their male colleagues to describe the Nazi regime.

Seduction

Although often absent from the female teachers' discourses, the figure of Hitler was nevertheless present in their teaching practices. Indeed, they had a greater tendency than their male colleagues to show films on the private life of Hitler. One of the films most often mentioned by the teachers was *Hitler's Women*, a television report by journalist Guido Knopp on the private life of the dictator.[62] The subject "Hitler and his women" evokes themes of manipulation, fascination, and seduction. Ms Norte (teacher at *Gymnasium* Monnet in Leipzig, aged around forty) explained why she often used the film *Hitler, an Overview*, the first section of which discusses the dictator as a private individual, and the second—entitled "The Seducer"—discusses his relationship with "his" women.[63]

Here at school we watched the film *Hitler, an Overview*. It's made up of six films where we see Hitler as a private man, at home in Berghof, how he spoke, how he behaved, with different women. Although the issue of women becomes secondary, but [she laughs] these differences between what happens on the private level and his politics. And that he could really be apolitical (*unpolitisch*), also, or just not talk about it. That contradiction.[64]

This emphasis on the "private sphere" echoed the female students' uses of the past, and unsurprisingly these teaching practices were welcomed by them. Leonore (age sixteen, 100th *Mittelschule*) began her interview by talking about why she mentioned Nazism.

I've seen documentaries, on the period and all—for example, *Women of Hitler* or something like that. And my mother can tell me lots of things too, yeah.

Your mother?
Yeah, she's read lots of books. And I talk with her about everything, all the time!

And the films you've seen, you said Women of Hitler?
It was a documentary. On Hitler's women, who he went out with, or had an affair with. It was a documentary—it was screened—I don't know, every Tuesday, I think. There were eight women or something like that. I don't know anymore. In any case, it was every Wednesday—on one woman or something. And I watched them all.[65]

Both Leonore and her classmate Annabelle were happy to have changed teachers: "I didn't like the other one," said Annabelle. "It was always battles (*Schlachten*) and dates and things like that." The girls appreciated the fact that their teacher, Ms Naute, showed films that also deal with "stories of the heart." "It's much more fun," they said.

There is an emphasis on seduction here. The girls often wonder, "How could he have attracted so many women?" Ms Naute (teacher at the 100th *Mittelschule* in Leipzig) explained to her students the effect of a dictator on the people "who adore him," "they throw their children into his arms."[66] This image of seduction is often associated with female admirers.[67] Women, in particular, are seen by the teacher as objects of this seduction, which is supposed to work not only by his image of power but also by his status as a "strong man." Here we see the emergence of the stereotype of the "weak woman," with no willpower, who lets herself be seduced by Hitler.

The other major figures of weakness who are subject to the seduction of the dictator and his men are the poor and the unemployed (men and women). Ms Weinecke (forty-eight years old, *Gymnasium* Monnet) emphasized the "danger" that she sees in Europe: the rise of "strong men" such as "Zhirinovsky or Le Pen."[68] Her explanation of the power of seduction is based in economics: "when people are struggling, and there is someone who knows what he wants and he sells it well, there is a danger that they will fall for it (*daß sie drauf reinfallen*)."[69]

> Well, people who voted for the National Socialists, they did it for short-term reasons (*kurzfristige Motive*). They were really in the shit (*es ging ihnen sau-schlecht*). And they [the Nazis] promised them stuff, and they [the people] got carried away by it. And the rest, they didn't want to know about it (*den Rest haben sie dann ausgeblendet*).[70]

Ms Inge (a teacher at Wiesi, around fifty years old) suggested that the people's lack of resistance to "mean politicians" is due to the weakness and trust of "the poor" using a rhetoric that is quite similar to the "feminine dispositions" mentioned above.[71] Her colleague, Klara Rohrsteg, who is the same age, also emphasized the "consequences of poverty" on human behavior.

> It comes from distress (*Not*), I think. It's often like that, when I'm having trouble (*Not*), I join a group and I oppress (*unterdrücken*) other people. Those kinds of mechanisms. It's the only explanation I can find for what happened. And that, I think it is important that the students learn it. What would happen to me if I was in a difficult situation (*in Not*)? We can see it today all over the world. Almost all acts of aggression are the result of a situation of penury (*Not*).[72]

People are capable of discriminating against other people, imprisoning or assassinating them, in situations where they themselves have been deprived of essentials and need to be valorized once again. Ms Rohrsteg, concluded that this leads to "the poor" being more receptive to racist theories. This interpretation, based on a condescending vision of the working classes, does however allow her an identification; Ms Rohrsteg used the first person—"when I am in a difficult situation"—to evoke the weakness of the poor. This also seems to be a female process of identification or a homology of positions in power relations. Indeed, although some of the male respondents did evoke the poor, they did not use the first person to describe them.

Manipulation

A variation on the idea of an explanation based on the seduction of the weak is that those who are seduced are also manipulated. These two explanatory schemas share the passivity of the object in the face of the strength or magic of a manipulator or seducer (the first connoted more negatively than the second). One of the only male respondents to develop this figure was Mr Hatze (a teacher at *Gymnasium* Weinburg in Hamburg, aged around fifty years old), who had been actively engaged since the 1970s in the fight for equality between men and women.

Could you explain what you think is particularly important for classes on this period?
Yes, I'd say seduction (*die Verführung*).

Seduction?
Yes. Well—how—how people can be manipulated. [He hesitates] because—I think that it's important today too [he hesitates again]. Mmm . . . well not in the form [he laughs softly] that Goebbels adopted obviously. But we can still be incited to influence citizens in a certain way. Or, how we can realize . . . how that works. What mechanisms are used, what words, how to read between the lines. How we can question it, how we can be attentive to what is going on. And we can see that through this example [National Socialism] when catastrophe strikes. And learn from it. . . . How we—how we can—in these aspects—manipulate human beings [he sighs], and what that can lead to, yes.[73]

Goebbels is generally mentioned as the "hero" or the "magician" of manipulation. Citizens are presented as passive beings who allow themselves to be manipulated by him and his power over words. National Socialism becomes the symbol of the consequences of such a manipulation when applied to the contemporary political field: "what [manipulation] can lead to if we don't pay attention."

There are specific teaching practices that correspond to these figures of seduction and manipulation. In history (or literature) classes, the teachers in Leipzig almost systematically used the book *The Wave*, by US writer Morton Rhue (the pen name of Todd Strasser), translated into German in 1984, or the film of the book.[74]

Morton Rhue, *The Wave* (Puffin Books, 1981)

The novel, a fictionalized account of an experiment conducted in a high school in California in 1967, tells the story of a role-play exercise that gets out of control. As part of a history class focusing on how ordinary Germans came to accept Nazi ideology, a high school teacher sets up a group called "The Wave" that is characterized by a system of strict rules and behavior, a military organization with a specific ideology that must be absolutely adhered to, and a system of surveillance and denunciation through a hierarchy of positions among students. This group begins in his particular class and spreads rapidly throughout the school. The "heroes" of the book are two adolescents who are also initially drawn into their teacher's group, but who begin to question these practices when they are confronted with their own violence. Resistance to manipulation is thus strongly valued in the book.

Ms Seidel (a teacher at the *Mittelschule* in Leipzig, around forty years old) put it like this: "I put a lot of emphasis on ethics—I always use *The Wave* as an example, because they always say 'It [Nazism] couldn't happen today.' To show them that we can be very easily manipulated. And that we are all manipulated. I don't exclude myself."[75]

Ms Seidel emphasized manipulation in class with a specific pedagogical intention: to warn students about the current dangers of two forms of manipulation. The first is manipulation by politicians or by the media. Indeed, there is another figure of explanation implicit in the theme of manipulation: "it's the media's fault." Ms Seidel emphasized the Nazi control of the media, in particular the radio. The media is seen as dangerous for the students. The way the female teachers in Leipzig used this novel raises the question of their own experience of living under dictatorship. The revelation of what they considered their own "manipulation" has particularly strong resonance with this book.

Mr Gerste is the other male respondent who raised this theme of manipulation (and seduction, because the two are linked), and he also used *The Wave* in class. Both he and his wife are militant feminists, and he discussed the need to reinforce young girls' awareness of male domination and to encourage them to adopt more "masculine" perspectives. This is perhaps one of the reasons why the "male" and "female" figures of explanation of the Nazi past, the presence of Hitler in his discourse, and the use of the figures of seduction and manipulation as explanatory figures are combined in his discourse.

The female teachers, although they did emphasize the themes of seduction and manipulation (of women), also talked more willingly about their own feelings, such as fear, which led them to be prudent about the past. Ms Heide (a teacher at *Gymnasium* Weinberg in Hamburg, around thirty years old), explained why she was convinced she "wouldn't have been in the resistance."

> [I try to convey] what it means to live in a totalitarian state. That is—I think [she searches for words] I don't know how other colleagues do it, but I think it is important! Personally, I don't think, given what I know about myself, I don't know, but I'm pretty sure I wouldn't have been among the first resistance fighters, I would have been scared too. My husband is completely different. He probably, I can see him as an armed resister. He wouldn't have given a damn [about the danger]. [Fighting] for something, right. But [she lowers her voice] me, I would have been afraid, I think. I would have been easily intimidated.[76]

If we can see Ms Heide's husband as the "war hero" so dear to the young boys, we can also see how the women can depict themselves as "weak women." They are not expected to be "heroic," which is a trait more often characteristic of "male virility." The girl students expressed doubts that echo those of their female teachers, but they were not always accepted among the adolescents as a group. They expressed these hesitations in individual interviews rather than in the classroom. Elisabeth (aged sixteen, student

152 • When Will We Talk about Hitler?

at *Gymnasium* Monnet in Leipzig, daughter of a real estate agent and an employee in commerce), for example, explained that she did not enjoy being continually confronted with this theme, because it made her question herself when faced with the past.

> On one hand, I would like to help, but [she hesitates], on the other hand, I would be really too scared: what might happen to me?! But when you think about it [she hesitates], for the people that you really like—or for your family or your friends, or people you love in some way, you'd say [she gets worked up] you'd throw yourself in front and say: "Take me, don't shoot them! Me! Take me!" [She goes back to her normal tone.] But with people you don't know—yes, I don't know, perhaps, you can understand that people say, "No, I wouldn't have done it [I wouldn't have helped them]."[77]

The identification with the victims, the sentimental tone and the references to fear are specific to the girls' comments. The female teachers can therefore find an echo in the girls' attitudes toward the past.

The school's role in the transmission of history and in the practice of gendered history is highly mediatized. Yet as Annick Percheron noted (particularly 1977, 1978, 1981, 1984, 1993), it is very often the family configuration (but also peer groups) that influence the ways adolescents appropriate the past. Its influence is found in dinner table discussions, in the kitchen, in shared social practices such as sports, or games, reading material, family media consumption but also in housework and other informal activities. It is also important to make the connection between gendered practices and family configurations to understand the role that gender can play in the construction of appropriations of the past.

Family Configurations and Gendered Forms of Appropriation

As a site of primary socialization, the household and its members structure the practices and the habitus of individuals from their early childhood. "Household" is used here in the sense of the French notion *maisonnée* defined by Florence Weber (2005; Weber, Gojard, and Gramain 2003), as a group of domestic production that is temporary and in constant evolution, and which is defined by the shared objective of mutual assistance and organization of daily life. Attitudes toward the past and toward politics are closely linked and find their first sources of construction in this environment. Within the descent group—defined as an ensemble of people who are related or who feel collectively responsible for the image of the group (Billaud et al. 2015; Firth 1956; Rivers 1910; Willmott and Young [1957] 1986)—factors such as social and geographic situation, individual trajectories, kinship relations (in particular between brothers and sisters), and positions within the household all influence the processes by which the family past is appropriated.

Gender plays a particularly important role here, specifically in the construction of positions between brothers and sisters within the family configuration. It will therefore be necessary to analyze more closely the ways in which the positions within these configurations lead to different ways of appropriating the family past, paying close attention to the role that gender might play in this. We will look both at the progressive construction of gendered worlds in which the division of space, practices, and representations interact to contribute to representations of the past that reflect these gender divisions. We will then examine the role of objects in the transmission of family histories.

> When I talk to my grandma, about that [the Nazi past], or with my mother, it's a lot about—the oppression of the Jews—or about—the German population, how much they suffered, or how they lived during the war and things like that. With my father—it's more—everything to do with event history (*Ereignisgeschichte*).[78] When I talk about what we're doing in history, like at the moment, the role of the United States, how they put themselves forward as the saviors of the world—and then you go back and compare: what was it like at the time? And here, how did they behave here? And right away, it's always events.
>
> *And with your mother and grandmother, it's more feelings?*
> [She cuts me off.] Yes! Yes! Yes! [She stops to think.] It's funny in fact—the gender separation (*Geschlechtertrennung*) [she laughs happily].[79]

Heidi (aged eighteen, student at *Gymnasium* Weinburg in Hamburg, the daughter of a management consultant and a nurse) was very perspicacious in remarking what she called "gender segregation." This segregation—with female family members transmitting a very different perspective on history to male family members—can be seen on several levels and leads to and operates within gendered spheres in the family.

First, there is a clear separation of spaces and activities between the sexes, whether in terms of domestic labor or leisure activities; men and women do not engage in the same activities in the same spaces. Pierre Bourdieu described the separation of spaces and activities between men and women in Kabyle society ([1979] 2010; [1998] 2001). In order to explore the ways in which these spheres operate, the way they are reproduced, used, and modified by family members, we will look at the situation of one young woman in particular.

Leoni was a student of Mr Schulze at Weinberg and fourteen years old at the time of the interview. Her father, born in 1954, studied information

154 • When Will We Talk about Hitler?

technology at Hamburg University before becoming an IT consultant. At age twenty-six, he married a literature student, four years his junior, who later became a primary school teacher. They had a son, born in 1986. In 1989, Leoni and her twin sister were born. Leoni and her brother both attended the *Gymnasium*, but her sister had more trouble at school and enrolled in the nearby *Gesamtschule* for students refused entry to the *Gymnasium*. At the time of the interviews, Leoni's older brother had just left to study in the United States for a year, which would come to have an important impact on the gender configurations in the family.

In Leoni's family, the division of labor between the sexes, the gendered division of domestic space, and the gendered division of worldviews seem intricately connected. For example, in the eyes of all family members, politics was reserved for the "men of the family," the father and his son. They talked about it at the table and during the television news; but these were conversations that were not intended for the female family members, who were busy preparing the meals, serving, and clearing the table.

Second, this separation, which consists of gendered spaces and activities, also determines interactions that are separated by gender, by and through the family configurations: the men talk to the men about particular subjects and the women talk to the women about other things. The family therefore becomes a space for the production and reproduction of traditional male and female roles: politics, like history, belongs in this case to the male sphere. Leoni explained this by invoking a lack of interest in politics among the women in her family, who stay together, and therefore are not likely to find themselves in a conversation about politics. "Yeah, my mother, she's not interested in politics. She always votes like my father. And my sister, even less! Me neither actually. Politics is not for me!"[80]

Third, this threefold separation of spaces, activities, and practices, and interactions is the source of a gendered division of the themes discussed—including the past in general and the Nazi past in particular, as we can see in the quotation from Heidi above. It plays out on the gendered appropriation of the past by the students. The girls tended to talk to their mothers and grandmothers (for example, in the kitchen) about "women's history": daily life during the war; the bombing, hunger, expulsions from Eastern Europe; and the return (often on foot) to the "Reich" before the end of the war. For example, Annabelle (aged sixteen, a student at the 100th *Mittelschule*) explained that she learned the story of her paternal grandmother who "hid Jews" during the war, from her aunt and not from her father.

Karen Werthe (a teacher at Wiesi, aged around thirty), recalled her vivid memories of the stories transmitted to her by her paternal grandmother and her grandmother's friend, whom she considered a second grandmother.

Gender, Family, and the Nazi Past(s) • 155

Among the stories transmitted by these two women to their granddaughter is a "meeting with Hitler."

> And there he was, standing up! Apparently in a white cabriolet on a clifftop and he was looking down on the masses below! A bloody great scene (*auch ganz geil inszeniert*), if you think about it. And they were down below and him above. And they were saying—I have an adopted grandmother, she was there too—and the two grandmas were saying, "We got shivers down our backs because the man was so impressive!" And I was thinking, "what can be so impressive about this guy?" [She laughs.] A little dwarf like that—and then, not my type, so . . . But they—they thought he was super classy! [She sounds a little surprised.] And they were both—extremely fascinated by strong men. They also loved Hans Albers![81] And this other guy from the 1940s with steel blue eyes—what's his name—also a macho like that, a super macho! Well—these men with really a lot of power, they really found them exciting! And this wanting to let yourself be led. It was clear that both of them thought it was really good. And they also shut up when my grandfather was talking.[82]

We can also see here the transmission of ways of talking, a language, as well as areas of interest. As is often the case in the interviews with women, and unlike those with men, Hitler is not named here. Karen Werthe used the pronouns "he" or "him" (or the "dwarf") to refer to him. She emphasized idealization of the figure, his ability to impress "women" who "love strong men." The German people, who were seduced by this figure, are once again depicted as "a weak woman" unable to affirm themselves in the face of a man in a white cabriolet on a clifftop. It is interesting that Karen's grandfather, who was present at the time, remains entirely absent from this passage that exclusively describes the reaction of the two women to the figure of Hitler. The granddaughter reproduces the gendered division of roles in her interpretation and reappropriation of the story, even though she was openly critical of the two women. The grandfather only appears at the end, not as a citizen who has been seduced, but as a dominant man on the same level as the dictator who reduces these "women who want to let themselves be led" to silence when he talks. The feminine weakness put forward in this image naturalizes the fascination of the "dictator up on high" (in an almost divine reference) for the "people down below." The sexual connotation is explicit here and the women are seduced not by Nazism, nor by the ideology, ideas, or rhetoric, but by Hitler as a man. In this version of Hitler as a demiurge, this appears as a sort of male sorcery which has the effect of exonerating the people and associating the responsibility for Nazism's success wholly on the seducer. We can see this as an inversion of the classical image of the femme fatale, seductive and dangerous, responsible for the man's unhappiness.

It is also worth noting that typically these conversations take place between protagonists of the same sex. Here two grandmothers were talking to their granddaughter, who had never heard her grandfather tell this story. Boys, on the other hand, tended to say they talked to their fathers and grandfathers about "men's history" (weapons, battles, military strategies, and international politics). Thomas (age fourteen, student at the *Gymnasium* in Hamburg) talked about how he read *Der Spiegel* with this grandfather, but also that this exclusive interaction with his grandson encouraged his grandfather to begin talking about "men's stories."

> And my grandfather—with whom I always read *Der Spiegel*—sometimes he told me stories too. It was [he hesitates, looking for the words] I know [he still struggles to find the words] he was at the elite school for Nazis, in Plön. That much I know. He told me. And he liked it. Because he could—you could ride motorbikes, things like that—shoot [guns] and things like that. In fact, everything that boys like doing, really.[83]

"What boys like doing" is something shared between fathers, grandfathers, and their sons and grandsons—if they have any. If we return to the example of Leoni, we can see this schema at work. Her brother, for example, filled the same role for their father as Thomas did for his grandfather. He was the one, among the children, who was "interested in politics," which had a profound influence on the attitude that his younger sisters developed toward the subject.

When I first met Leoni, in the spring of 2003, she was in eighth grade and "terrible at history." She herself said it was a subject that did not interest her.

> History, it's not really my thing. It's more my brother. He's a real freak in history. He loves everything about the past, wars, events, strategy—[she hesitates]—politics too. He's very involved. He had a scholarship and was part of the youth parliament (*Jugendparlament*). Not me. He's like my dad. They talk a lot about all that at dinner in the evening during the *Tagesschau* [TV news]. Me, I've got nothing to say. And I think the *Tagesschau* is boring.[84]

Leoni felt that she was not competent enough to engage in the male-dominated family discussions about "politics" and "history" during the news. This self-censorship was possibly reinforced by her twin sister's difficulty at school: "me and my sister, we aren't like my brother. Learning is not really our thing."[85] Academic ability operated alongside male domination in Leoni's family in a way that was particularly unfavorable to the two sisters.

However, these gendered interactions are potentially flexible and can evolve according to the family configuration. This is particularly clear in the favorable evolution of Leoni's position in the family. When her brother left for the United States, she took his place at their father's side for conversations on politics and history during the television news.

During one interview, almost a year after our first meeting, Leoni observed, "Yeah, in fact, I've changed. I enjoy talking about history now. [She considers.] Since my brother left, my father asks me many more questions."[86] She also said she enjoyed watching the news with her father, while her sister helped her mother do the cooking. "I learn a lot, because he explains things to me. I can ask questions too," she said.

This was the year in which they studied the period 1933–1945 in history class and the teacher, Mr Schulze, noticed this radical change in Leoni, saying, "She has made remarkable progress. She participates more and more."[87] This change in Leoni was also due to the parallel evolution of family and school configurations. The treatment of the Holocaust in class, which as we have seen, encourages girls' interest in history, was paralleled by a closer and more positive relationship with her father. This new relationship led to a valorization that helped her to feel authorized to explore spaces that she previously saw as reserved for men. This small example illustrates the fluidity and possible evolutions of students' relationships to the past according to the evolution of gender divisions within the family and of family configurations, as well as their interdependence. It also underlines the importance of gender in configurations of power relations. If Leoni was able to explore these "male" spaces and activities both at home and at school, it was not because the separation of gendered spaces had changed, but because she had temporarily taken the (male) role of her brother alongside her father, leaving her twin sister to fulfill the (female) roles alongside their mother. We might also consider that gender roles include some flexibility according to evolutions of family configurations and that the (male) role temporarily seized and occupied by Leoni in her brother's absence might durably change the family configuration upon the return of the brother.

The ways in which the family past is discussed in the home echo the way the teachers speak in class. We see the same gendered separation of topics and interests among the parents that we observed among both students and teachers. It is less explicit because it is expressed above all through their use of language and their explanations of the Nazi past: the women emphasize the history of everyday life and suffering, the history of the victims and their feelings; the men stress "event history," major actors, military and international themes. This is the source of the strength and continuity of the gender separation of attitudes toward the history of Nazism—the school and the family cumulate their influences to produce and reproduce explanatory schemas of the present world and of the past.

Objects of Shame and Pride: Gendered Objects, Evocative Objects

Objects—medals, letters, diaries, sometimes weapons, but also furniture, jewelry, photographs, and clothes—can also be a means of transmitting the past or a specific relationship to it. Although the transmission of these objects has been studied in detail by anthropologists (see, for example, Segalen 1987), the role that they play in shaping and transmitting a specific relationship with the past is yet to be analyzed. These objects can provide access to the family past that is otherwise inaccessible, as in the case of working-class families (Billaud 2005) or in certain male environments that are difficult to access through direct speech. In addition to the fact that they also contain and convey "family history," the objects that are transmitted in this way are also gendered. A knife or a medal from the war, for example, are typically masculine objects that are transmitted between men, whereas jewelry tends to be transmitted between women as a more feminine object. Other objects are less obviously gendered; diaries and letters, or photographs can be transmitted between the sexes. It seems that gender is not related to the nature of the object but rather to the way it is used. Once again it is the gendered interactions of family members that will determine a gendered use of the objects. Grandfathers pass their war diaries on to their grandsons to whom they tell their stories and experiences, while grandmothers pass their love letters on to their granddaughters.

The interview with Peter (aged eighteen, son of two bank employees and a student in his final year at Weinberg) shows this kind of communication and transmission between men. His grandfather was born in 1914 and was a soldier until 1945, when he became a low-level public servant in the Hamburg municipal administration. When he died, Peter's grandmother (a tailor, born in 1918) moved to a new house, and "all these things from the past reappeared." Peter and his father were responsible for "cleaning up" his grandfather's things, as his older brother was elsewhere at the time. During this episode, Peter's father told him about his grandfather's war diary, which would accompany the grandson throughout his adolescence and which he would study in detail when he later covered World War II in advanced history at high school. His grandfather also left a collection of photographs, which Peter's father decided to burn in the fireplace of the grandfather's house. His son did not ask him any questions about this. His father's remark—they were "not very nice"—was enough for him.

And did you ask him why he burned the photographs?
Yes, and he said that—that some of them were—not [he hesitates] not very nice [he smiles awkwardly]. But—I don't know, what [he hesitates] what the photos were of. But he thought they were really not cool.

Do you know if they were photos from the war?
Yeah, yeah, they clearly were. Everything that was photographed during the war—I don't even know if they were all photos by my grandfather. If he took them. Or—[he hesitates for a long time] I don't know! Because I didn't see them!

And you didn't ask him?
No [quietly]. I don't know if it was really necessary to burn them or if we could have kept them. [Very low] I don't know. [A little louder] I should ask really![88]

This was clearly a sensitive topic. Although it was raised several times during the interview, Peter began to laugh each time it was discussed. The content of the photographs visibly made him uneasy. Although we can imagine that they perhaps depicted scenes of wartime atrocities, he had trouble formulating this, laughingly repeating that they were just "not very nice"— undoubtedly a euphemism. The psychoanalyst Serge Tisseron (1992) has examined this difficulty—or impossibility—of expressing in words an experience, either lived or transmitted, a situation that generates family secrets and that may be a source of psychological problems. He explains the paradoxical communication in the case of family secrets transmitted to children. The child is thus faced with having to "correspond to two contradictory requirements . . . 'there is a secret that it is forbidden to know, but you transmit the fact that there is a secret that it is forbidden to know'" (Tisseron 1992: 133). Objects can also serve to transmit this kind of secret. But beyond this purely psychoanalytic reading, a reflection on this act of destroying traces of the wartime past, performed between men (the father, the son, the late grandfather) also testifies to the shared nature of the family past and the impossibility of speaking about it. Peter was aware of the highly symbolic nature of the act: burning photographs is in no way the same as throwing them away. It implies creating distance from the past through purification by fire. The meaning of the act seems to have been transmitted to the son, but he remains ignorant of the reasons for such distancing. These two factors have contributed to creating a deep unease—perhaps greater than the exact knowledge of a shameful past would have done. Peter could only imagine the content of the photographs. Peter did not see the pictures, so it is not clear if they were documentary-style evidence of the type used in textbooks or if these were Abu Ghraib-style evidence of his grandfather participating in torture. Alternatively, it could have been pornography of a kind that made the son (Peter's father) uncomfortable, so he burned them. Neither Peter nor us will ever know what these pictures represented. But Peter suggests that they are from the war, even though he has not talked about this with his father or grandfather. The collective images that the students generally retain from this period (in particular they refer to the liberation of the camps, but also the "mountains of bodies"), might have fuelled Peter's imagination with a reservoir of "possible" images that could only conjure up the worst possible horrors. The fear of what the answers might be cannot be understood without that reservoir of possible images, outweighing the desire for knowledge and hence creating the impossibility of asking questions. Along with this uneasiness, there is a (masculine) complicity and the feeling of belonging to a (paternal) family line, which are also created by these transmissions and non-transmissions. The grandfather's diary, along with the burned photographs, provide access to the late ancestor's past, while also preserving the family honor—and purifying it by guarding the "secret" of the burned photographs that Peter did not see. These acts also reinforce the links between father and son. With his silence, Peter was protecting his father and his decision to burn the photographs and thus fulfilling the trust placed in him as the witness to the act "destroying traces of the past."

Objects as traces of the past can transmit both pride and shame at the same time. Before his grandmother moved to a new house and his father burned the photos, Peter found his grandfather's medals in the basement, although he "didn't really look at them much." The fact that he found them in the basement shows this dual dimension. Although they were kept, they were hidden from visitors. Only family members had access to the basement. As testimonies to the everyday lives of ancestors, it is personal attachment that makes these objects valuable (even though they might also be politically significant) and sometimes leads children and grandchildren to treasure them in spite of their Nazi political connotations.

Ms Neumeier, a teacher at the *Gymnasium* in Leipzig, was born in 1953; her father was born in 1903 and made his career in the Nazi Party in the early 1930s, becoming a political leader in a ministry before becoming director of an insurance company. Her mother, born in 1924, worked in local administration, both under the Nazi regime and under the Communist Party SED. Ms Neumeier has an older half-brother, the son of her mother, born in 1945, but who left for West Germany in 1961 and whom she did not see between 1961 and 1989. She thus grew up among women. Her younger sister is a bookshop owner and her half-sister, by her mother and twenty years her senior, is a doctor. At the death of her father in 1980, her mother left for West Germany to join her son. So the father's eldest daughter (because there was no son) inherited a collection of Nazi objects belonging to him: his passport, medals, photographs taken at various official occasions, newspaper articles praising his work in the ministry, a *Gaudiplom* (see Figure 3.1), a Nazi distinction of honor for the contribution of his company to the "war effort in 1940–41."

The fact that Ms Neumeier was personally very involved in the East German Communist Party did not prevent her from keeping these objects

Figure 3.1 The *Gaudiplom* belonging to Ms Neumeier's father. Source: Author's private archives.

carefully in a drawer by her bed and, she confessed, from looking at them from time to time. This ambiguity, between shame and pride, expresses the ambiguity of the relationship that children (or grandchildren) have with their family past. This past, both hidden and preserved, takes shape—sometimes painfully—through objects.

The exceptional example of Thomas[89] (fifty-four years old, teacher at Wiesi) illustrates the ongoing violence in the familial and generational confrontations surrounding the parents' Nazi past. Objects can symbolize, reveal, and express this violence, but also give voice to subjects that are otherwise unspeakable.

Thomas was born in 1949 in Bremen. His father, born in 1911 in Silesia, became a helmsman (*Steuermann*) at sixteen before joining the army. From the end of the 1920s, when he was already a member of the NSDAP, the rise of Nazism brought him undreamed of career possibilities. He joined the Waffen-SS, and then the *Leibstandarte*, Hitler's bodyguards. In Paris, he met Thomas's mother, Heydrich's personal secretary. He spent the war in Paris, a particularly "enchanting" period for him, as he experienced both professional recognition and romance there, along with great *joie de vivre*. He practiced horseback riding and got married in 1944, the year Thomas's elder brother was born (his brother later became an architect and worked for the Hamburg city council as an urbanist). After the war, the father took a position in the municipal administration.

Thomas's parents' memories of the war are at odds with their son's expectations. At the beginning of the interview, he mentioned "the conflicts at home. My father was a Nazi, and then—questions came up. And this conflict led me to be more interested in history."[90] But it was not easy to discuss it. Each time Thomas mentioned his father during the interview, he started scratching frenetically with his keys at the tree trunk he was sitting on. He said just a few words before quickly changing the subject. Yet Thomas was also one of the few interviewees to explicitly distance himself from his father, who he referred to as a "Nazi" or a "mega-Nazi" (*Obernazi*). This distance presented an opening for me to ask questions that I would not have otherwise been able to pose. This (exceptional) possibility was also facilitated by the research relationship we had established. I met Thomas through a friend of a friend working at Wiesi, and we had all eaten lunch together at the school several times before I asked him if he would participate in the study. He spoke informally to me at once and introduced himself with this first name—I never knew his surname. For him, I was first and foremost a friend of a friend, before being a PhD student or a researcher, just as for me he was first and foremost a friend rather than an interviewee. This relationship of mutual trust, as well as Thomas's willingness to talk, enabled me to ask questions relatively openly.

Thomas's story is based on a series of objects that symbolize the political opinion and commitment of his father. When he could not talk about his father's discourse, he mobilized objects or the newspapers that he read.

As a child—I have a vague memory of my father—[he hesitates for a long moment] somewhere, he said some things—that I found strange. And then I remember the magazines, national newspapers that he subscribed to. *Der Freiwillige*, that was the newsletter of the HIAG, the *Hilfsgemeinschaft auf Gegenseitigkeit der ehemaligen Angehörigen der Waffen-SS e. V* [the mutual support group for former members of the Waffen-SS], which were always lying around our house. At first, I wasn't interested in them at all, but at some point [he lowers his voice] I realized that they were very [he hesitates, lowers his voice again] national, these papers [he breaks off, does not finish his sentence. When he begins again he changes the subject].[91]

This first passage shows just how uncomfortable he was talking about his father's involvement in the Waffen-SS. His tone, which ended up as a whisper, and the change of subject are the first signs of the real difficulty Thomas had in putting this subject into words. There are two ways that he expressed his father's "shameful" involvement: his deliberately provocative denomination of him as a "mega-Nazi," and the objects that crystallized his relationship with the past, such as *Der Freiwillige*, a typical Nazi paper. Later, Thomas mentions the "editors, publications" that "substantiate" (*untermauern*) the "lie of Auschwitz" (*die Auschwitzlüge*), that his father "subscribed to" and that "he read." "That's where he got his arguments from," he said.[92]

When I asked him about it, he said "it was impossible to talk about it as a family." It also seemed difficult to talk to an interviewer; it was only by successive references that Thomas was able to formulate the—painful—role that this past played in the configuration of his family.

At the beginning, he only discussed his own position, his inability to openly confront his father, which led to him to isolate himself and physically avoid the latter. But there are objects that symbolize the break between father and son that words seem unable to express. Thomas talked about how his father broke an LP record into "a thousand pieces" because the American singer was praising the *deutsche Fräulein*, alluding to the relationships between German women and the occupying forces—considered a "national shame" by the father. This broken record was also the beginning of the break between father and son.

It was in the 1960s, when the two sons went to university, physically left the family home, and symbolically left their social milieu, that they joined the DKP (German Communist Party, the successor of the *Kommunistische Partei Deutschlands*, KPD, outlawed in 1956). The political break with the father was also accompanied by a social and cultural break; the two sons

164 • When Will We Talk about Hitler?

obtained university degrees, one became a teacher, the other an architect. Their involvement in communism provoked violent reactions from their father, who initially attempted "to convince his sons."

> Because there are letters (*da gibt es Briefe*), that he wrote to us, in which he accuses the school that "seduced" us (*verführt*) [he laughs, shortly and sharply], that didn't educate us properly (*aufgeklärt*), and all that. He tried that up until quite recently. Again and again. But it came from his side—right—we didn't try and change him. Well, we didn't try and engage him in a discussion. It wouldn't have been possible in any case.[93]

Once again Thomas used objects to evoke his fathers' political position, and he had trouble evoking the content of "these letters." The passive formulation "there are letters" expresses the distress of the son faced with these objects that are an unmerciful testimony to his father's political engagement and that the son must confront, even if he does not reply. Even though he could not tolerate it himself, he tried to explain it, as though after talking about the letters he felt obliged to provide explanations to avoid harsh judgment:

> He had his reasons. He came from a very poor background, he grew up under Nazism [he was 22 in 1933], he became someone there, and that's it. He went to Paris, he met my mother there, he had a horse, went riding, had a super life, and that's it. And then afterward—at the end of the war, he was just a little man and that always irritated him (*das hat immer an ihm gekratzt*). And that's why it was not even possible—[he hesitates] to think, about what happened during that era. Well, you know.[94]

It is only after my incessant questions that he confided in me what he found so difficult about his father and what constituted the basis of the family breakdown, which he, in vain, attempted to avoid:

> *And when you say that he wanted to convince you [in his letters] he wanted to convince you of what exactly—of National Socialism?*
> Mmmhmmm. Yes. [Silence.]
>
> *What does that mean?*
> That—that it was all good. In other words—he was not even able to see what had happened. And—yes, the [he hesitates, stumbles]. In his eyes, the mass exterminations didn't happen. It was a lie made up by the enemies. Just like that. And everything was good. [Silence.]
>
> *And what were his arguments? What was so good about all that?*
> Yes—yes, he—well, he tried—but that's going too far, it's not our subject here—he tried—I don't know, if you've already done some research on this, but there are a number of editors, publications—in this area, that try and

Gender, Family, and the Nazi Past(s) • 165

prove the lie of Auschwitz. And it's still like that today. And that, he—he read them, he subscribed, to these magazines, books. But only after we left home. It wasn't like that before. It got stronger and stronger in him. Well—these publications, he always [he hesitates] tried to get his arguments out of them.[95]

Once again, objects symbolize and embody the past—publications, books, magazines. The written word is a testimony and helps stabilize the past, but also—like letters—helps to approach the past indirectly without using speech and interaction. It also allows us to discuss in the interview the political opinions of the father that are so unbearable for the son, by attributing them to others: to revisionist historians, editors, and journalists. The son can thus talk about his father's opinions while still protecting him from the overly curious researcher.

The example of this interview with Thomas raises the difficulties of studying the family relationships that are articulated around the transmission of the past. What has often been referred to as a "family silence" about the Nazi past should rather be seen as revealing a difficult communication within the family. It is therefore even more difficult to observe as an outsider, who can only access the "positive," "heroic," and "speakable" stories. What goes unsaid, or what cannot be said, not publicly in any case, remains inaccessible to the observer using sociological research methods (Pollak 1986, 1993, 2000).

Moreover, Thomas's case reveals the possibilities that objects provide for the study of family transmission. Not only do objects sometimes give us access to discourses about the past, but they can also facilitate speech itself— by symbolizing that which is otherwise difficult to express. The interview with Thomas and the discussion of the objects (particularly his father's letters) also questions the classical idea of the "collective hero-worship of parents" (notably Welzer, Moller, and Tschuggnall 2002). It seems that family transmission is plural and complex. Thomas's story teaches us just how difficult it is to determine the existence or the absence of a "familial confrontation" (Auseinandersetzung). We have seen to what extent Thomas himself considered that in his family "discussions about the Nazi past were impossible" and that he had never had an "open discussion" with his father. Yet the letters exist; there was an exchange between father and son that had consequences for the whole family, which are difficult to evaluate through explicit statements, especially by a person outside the family.

Research Relationships: The Unsaid and the Unspeakable

The interview with Thomas also poses ethical questions regarding research practices and provokes reflection on the limits of research. Over the course of the interview, Thomas hinted several times that I was overstepping the boundaries of politeness and impinging on his intimacy with my questions. His remark "that would take us too far" was a discrete indication that this was a subject I was not authorized to ask about so brutally, in an interview that was not intended for this (I had told my interviewees that I wanted to talk about the teaching of history at the school and their professional biography). A little afterwards, when I continued to ask him questions about his family, and his mother, he gave me a more explicit sign to change the subject: "I told you, the Nazi past was never discussed (*das war nie ein Thema*) in my family!" So I changed the subject and we finished the interview talking about the school and the problems associated with the transmission of Nazism in class.

But the relationship of trust had suffered—the interview ended ten minutes later in a tense atmosphere. Although Thomas remained kind and polite when we met, our complicity disappeared after this interview. One day, in the playground he stopped me and bombarded me with questions, a little aggressively: "And who do you vote for? And your parents, who do they vote for? And who did they vote for before that? And today? And why?" He did not let me respond—besides which I was too surprised to stammer out an answer. But he made me understand the aggression that he had felt with my questions about his family. In the interview, I had betrayed his trust with my position as a "scientific" investigator. I created the conditions required to steal from him his trust, his intimacy, and his family pride (Schwarz 1999). Thomas's example shows the cynicism of this approach. As the friend of a friend, Thomas was not an interviewee like the others. I encouraged him to reveal to me what was painful but also unspeakable, and I did not "return" this "openness" by giving of myself as he had done, and as a friend might do in such an exchange. I therefore betrayed his trust, and he subsequently made this clear to me in our abrupt exchange.

In terms of gender, the objects of Thomas's narrative are not neutral. They symbolize male confrontation: the two sons confronting the father. The break with the father is embodied in the letters. It was the father who took it upon himself to seek to convince his sons politically. The mother remained curiously in the shadows of this interview—even though she was Heydrich's secretary. Gender plays a double role here; the mother and the two grandmothers are considered "apolitical" by the son. This representation is both the reason that "you don't talk politics" with women and also contributes to the social reproduction of this attitude.

And the family conversations on the past—was that only with your father? Did your mother participate as well?
My mother stayed completely out of these conversations. She didn't get involved. Umm [he pauses to think]—even though my mother was one of

Gender, Family, and the Nazi Past(s) • 167

Heydrich's secretaries. [He laughs a little.] But she always behaved as if she was completely apolitical. [He hesitates for a long while.] I think that was true. [He hesitates again.] I think so, in fact, even though she was probably not completely ignorant [of politics]. But I don't think that she really thought about it [politics]. She just—she did her job (*Tätigkeit*), without really thinking about it. [He raises his voice.] After the war she was not politically active either.[96]

His mother was not political—so she was not "politicized"—she did not leave objects that could testify to her engagement. She did not write "political" letters or read newspapers—at least, her son assumes she did not. Her gender, the female attributes that her son projects onto her, protect her from blame; because she is a woman, she is considered both apolitical and not responsible. This is also true for his paternal grandmother.

My father's parents [he yawns]—were also Nazis. And the father, he was killed by lightning during the war, I never knew him, he was apparently a mega-Nazi (*Obernazi*), who had a lot of influence over my father. And my paternal grandmother—she never said anything about politics (*hat sich politisch nicht geäußert*). That's all.[97]

Here Thomas painted a picture of a paternal family line that was marked by male political heritage, traced back to his paternal grandfather, who he referred to as a "mega-Nazi," like his father. The attribution of responsibility is clear—Thomas suggests that the Nazi political opinions of his grandfather were transmitted directly to his father. His paternal grandmother played the same role as his mother, both seen as "apolitical."

However, the gendered attributions of parents' political engagements change depending on the family configurations and interactions, which are also gendered. Klara Rohrsteg was born in 1956 and was a teacher at the *Gesamtschule* in Hamburg when I interviewed her. Her father was born in 1914; he was self-employed before becoming a solider, and he died in 1995. Her mother was born in 1922, worked as a sales assistant, and was very active in the BDM (Bund Deutscher Mädel). She would have liked to join the NSDAP, but her father would not allow it. Klara has an older sister, born in 1952, who did not go to university and who does not work. She also has a brother by marriage, her father's step-son, much older (over sixty) and an engineer. At the time of the interview, Klara was married, with two sons, aged twenty-seven and twenty, and a ten-year-old daughter.

Her mother's involvement with the BDM is a problem for Klara. She suspects her mother of being antisemitic, which bothers her.

My mother was relatively young. Not my father, but he, he was never a Nazi. But my mother was. She was young, born in [19]26, but she was very active in the BDM (überzeugtes *BDM Mädchen*). And I realize—even today, it's a subject [we talk about]. I realize, that there are situations—even if she completely refuses it—there are sides of her that reappear, where I think, "oops, watch what you're saying there!" For example, on the Israel-Palestine conflict. She often says "oh, it's because of the Jews" . . . It's her way of saying it, you see, which is really awkward (*das ist so ganz fatal*)! Well—she'd never admit it, but—I can tell from the way she says it.[98]

The conversations between Klara and her mother are described as awkward and difficult, just as they are between Thomas and his father. In this case it was not objects but "ways of talking" that gave the daughter clues as to her mother's supposed political affiliations. The form and content of the speech diverge, providing the daughter with material to objectify her mother's discourse. Like the objects, the form of the mother's language is marked by the past, constituting a trace of her Nazi activities and past political convictions, while remaining open to interpretation by her children. Thus Klara did not really believe her mother when she insisted on her ignorance of the genocide of the Jews—"that's what my mother always says, that she didn't know! But me, I can't believe that.[99]

Klara said she had "girl'" conversations with her mother: the latter talked of her friendships with Jewish children at school or in her building and then they "disappeared." This is a continual point of incomprehension between mother and daughter.

How is it possible (*wie kann das angehen*) that you didn't realize that in your house the Jewish children, who you played with, were taken! You must have questioned that! (*das must Du doch in Frage gestellt haben!*) Ok, right, she didn't know they were killed, but she saw it [that they disappeared]! Yeah, I say, at that point, you'd have to wonder! It's not possible otherwise (*das kann doch nicht angehen*)! But no! But they didn't [ask questions]. That's how it was.[100]

During the interview, Klara recounted a recent conversation with her mother (imagined or real). The political disagreement was explicitly expressed, and even the source of repeated disputes between daughter and mother. However, Klara did not talk about the Nazi past with her father.

And with your father, have you talked about [the Nazi past]?
Yes, well, he can always hide behind the fact that he was never a Nazi. It's probably true—he was always able to hide behind the fact that he was Communist, and ultimately, I didn't talk about it that much with him . . . no, it was more with my mother. It's linked to the relation that I have with my parents. I have a different connection with my mother. And him, he never really told me, at the time. He died a while ago now.[101]

Even if Klara, by her own account, was "skeptical" about her father's Communist involvement, it was her mother's past that was the real source of her concern. Their intimate relationship made her mother's Nazi involvement unbearable for the daughter. The father's attempts to recount his experiences as a soldier were not so interesting to his daughter—"yes, he was a soldier—right." She was not interested in her father's tales and critiques of weapons, nor battles won and lost, nor in experiences on the frontline.

It is therefore the intimate relationships that enable both transmission and non-transmission of objects, anecdotes, and family stories about the past. Along with language and anecdotes, objects play the role of objectification and incorporation as well as assisting transmission and discussion. As both vehicles and symbols, objects are shaped and used in social context, sometimes according to gendered practices that render them gendered too.

Gender, School, and Family: Intersecting Spaces of Analysis

We have seen here that the uses and appropriations of the Nazi past differ according to gender for both students and teachers. This observation has its origins and its explanations in family configurations and in primary socialization. Children learn to take their "place" within the household, to build a role for themselves within the gendered worlds and configurations they are exposed to. But gender is not the only factor, as we can see in the case of Leoni. Different social factors contribute to the perpetual reconstruction of the family configuration, one of which is notably the relationship between siblings. In Leoni's case, there needed to be a boy in the household for the girls to take the role of "girls." Sometimes roles that have long been considered "male" can potentially be filled by girls. Gender—or rather gendered representations that divide the space and the practices, and therefore reinforce representations—thus create roles to be fulfilled. These roles are positions or possible positions within the family configuration that the members of the family can both occupy but also construct. The conversations, practices and spaces shared between members of the same sex, as well as family stories—and the objects that symbolize them—are told and transmitted differently according to gender. The shared intimacy, practices, and spaces between members of the same sex create group behaviors, i.e., both homogeneity and alterity based on gender and therefore differences between the sexes. Girls become girls, and boys become boys (Martschukat and Stieglitz 2005). In becoming a boy or a girl, they adopt the ways of doing, speaking, and being interested in the past that are modeled by their elders, siblings, as well as parents and teachers.

These categories, including gender categories, are not set in stone. They evolve, are constructed, and reconstructed on a daily basis. The example of Leoni shows us both the construction and the fluidity of all categories and the various possibilities for fulfilling them, building them or dismantling them, interpreting and appropriating them. But this example also shows us the importance of gender as a variable in interactions and in the ways in which it organizes space, practices, and representations. Varying the scale and the focus of the analysis (rather than the space analyzed) allows us to consider these two dimensions together. Indeed, an analysis in terms of categories emphasizes the existence of social facts outside individual experience. But the evolution of Leoni's experience over time shows that these social facts are both constructed and reappropriated by social agents. Leoni's (female) role evolved according to her place within the family configuration and was a result of the places occupied by other members of the family. But this evolution does not pose a problem for an analysis in terms of gender categories, which describe the relationships between men and women as social facts. It is not because Leoni is able to adopt a more typically male role in her brother's absence that would make the divisions of male and female space or gendered representations disappear. But it does show their complexity. Indeed, it is because an analysis in terms of social categories focuses on the prior existence of social facts that it has trouble analyzing the social construction of these facts, as well as the role of social agents in this construction.

These gendered divisions of the world (of space, practices, and representations) can be reinforced at (and by) school, where these same divisions are replayed. Yet school, as we have seen, can in certain cases also play against these divisions. Indeed, when certain representations, certain interests, and certain practices do not conform to scholarly norms, the school (in the form of the teacher) sanctions them (often via grades, sometimes with disciplinary sanctions). In the case of the National Socialist past, it is the representations and leisure activities of the boys that do not correspond to academic expectations. Their interest in military themes, national, and international policy, strategy and "grand" historical figures, led them, in the context of the history of Nazism, directly to an interest in the *Täter*, the perpetrators, historical criminals. This specifically male form of fascination for death and danger in wartime, which is socially unacceptable, was sanctioned by the school and the teachers because it was in contradiction to a specific pedagogical objective: civic and moral education. These sanctions seem to have been most effective in the two *Gymnasium*, among the students from the most privileged backgrounds, those who would have the longest formal education. In this context, the boys modified their discourses and their interests, and thus moved closer to the more feminine forms of appropriation, adopting the *Betroffenheit* toward the victims. Although the boys' exclusive interest in the *Täter* progressively broadened to take into account the victims, the difference between boys and girls did not disappear as we can see in the analysis of the discourses and practices of the teachers. Language in particular, but also teaching practices, are marked by gendered appropriations of history.

Other factors operate alongside and in interaction with gender to influence the appropriations of the Nazi past among these adolescents. In the following chapter, we will look at the social trajectories and belongings of both the students and their parents, and the effects of their social backgrounds on their positions within configurations in both the family and school. We aim to shed light on the ways in which these engagements and positions influence the ways in which the adolescents appropriate the Nazi past.

Notes

A more condensed version of this text was previously published in French in Oeser (2007b).

1. The gender pay gap between men's and women's salaries in Europe, even if decreasing slowly, is still at 16.5 percent in the EU member states in 2016, close to 12 percent for Germany, according to Eurostat: http://ec.europa.eu/eurostat/statistics-explained/index.php/Gender_pay_gap_statistics. See also Reed (1999: 36).

2. Anne Frank, *Anne Frank: The Diary of a Young Girl*, trans. B.M. Mooyaart (1947, trans. 1952; New York: Bantam, 1993). The German edition was published as *Das Tagebuch der Anne Frank* in 1950.

3. Hans P. Richter, *Friedrich*, trans. Edith Kroll (New York: Puffin Books, 1970). This is the story of a friendship between a Jewish boy and a non-Jewish boy in the 1930s, and the progressive exclusion of the former seen through the eyes of his friend.

4. Klaus Kordon, *Die Roten Matrosen, oder ein vergessener Winter* (1984); *Mit dem Rücken zur Wand* (1990); *Der erste Früling* (1993), all published in Weinheim by Beltz and Gelber. This trilogy tells the story of a family in 1918–1919 during the revolution, then in 1932–1933 before the Nazi rise to power, and then in 1945 at the liberation of Berlin. In the second volume, the progressive exclusion of Jews from German Society is a central theme.

5. Along with the novels covered in the German literature class, which are compulsory for all secondary school students.

6. Interview of 26 December 2001.

7. Interview of 27 December 2001.

8. J. R.R. Tolkien, *The Lord of the Rings* (London: Allen and Unwin, 1954). The German edition was published as *Der Herr der Ringe* in 1972.

9. Interview of 13 April 2003.

10. Interview of 3 April 2002.

11. Interview of 18 October 2003.

12. *Der Spiegel* has the largest print run of the national weekly news magazines in Germany.

13. In German, the term *Täter* refers to those who commit a crime, while *Tat* literally refers to the act (not necessarily criminal) and the verb *tun* means to do or to act. In English, the term "persecutor" has a negative normative connotation absent from *Täter*, but it has the advantage of being the direct opposite of "victim" as in the German. Perpetrator is more neutral, but, unlike the German, implying the idea of a fault being committed and it also reflects the active quality of *Tat*.

14. Victor Klemperer (1881–1960) was a professor of philology and prohibited from occupying an intellectual profession under the antisemitic policies of the NSDAP from 1935. After the war, he published the notes that he made on the progressive exclusion of Jews from German society and the establishment of a racist ideology, including by the use of language specific to the Nazi government. In 1957, Klemperer became interested in the perpetuation of this ideology through language ([1957] 2006).

15. Interview of 28 January 2004.

16. In sophisticated language, the word *unmöglich* means "impossible." But in oral and informal speech, it can express moral disapproval as it does here. We have opted for this free translation to try and reflect the familiar tone of the comment.

17. Interview of 28 January 2004.

18. Interview of 7 January 2004.

19. Interview of 3 May 2002.

20. Soldiers constitute a particular and somewhat intermediary category, which can attract the boys' attention, particularly through family histories (of grandfathers). Their dual status as both heroes and victims probably helps the boys' interest in their fates.

21. Girls talk about "politics" when they refer to this aspect of history; boys call it "strategy."

22. The notion of politics is clearly more complicated and involve more than "actors on the political scene." Indeed, everyday life has an important political dimension. However, although the analytic separation between, the "political" public sphere on the one hand, and the "a-political" private sphere on the other, has been criticized by feminist thought over the last thirty years, it persists in the representations of the students. The use of quotation marks around "political" allows us to maintain a critical distance regarding their use of this term.

23. Interview of 16 April 2003.

24. Interview of 25 April 2003.

25. Arte is public television channel specializing in the history and culture of France and Germany funded by the governments of the two countries. Its goal is to improve cross-cultural understanding and targets a primarily intellectual audience.

26. The adolescents place a lot of value in eye-witness accounts, which seem to reflect what they define as "historical truth."

27. Interview of 30 September 2003.

28. Interview of 21 April 2003. Although this diary seemed very important to Peter, I did not manage to convince him to show it to me.

29. Interview of 22 February 2003.

30. Interview of 16 April 2003.

31. Indeed, the boys' interest in the *Täter*, the perpetrators, is suspected of being the expression of a tendency to see them as "heroes" or even as the expression of a violent temperament. It is as though, in the teacher's eyes, being interested in Nazi figures automatically implies a danger of being or becoming a Nazi. The teachers make a connection between this fascination of the perpetrators and "extreme-right wing" political opinions (particularly among the boys), just as they do between the fascination for the

victims and "democratic" political opinions (particularly among the girls). The fact that the *Täter* (and Hitler in particular) are widely covered on television and in the media, in no way prevents these assumptions about adolescents' interests. It seems that the teachers interpret this interest in different ways depending on the age and sex of the people manifesting it.

32. The fact that he is a school principal put him in a position clearly superior to mine. This meant that he was less obliged to control his discourse and more able to put forward generalizing explanations and this should be taken into account in analyzing his comments.

33. Informal conversation after history class, 15 January 2004.

34. Mr Schulze used the German expressions *lexikalisches Wissen* and *Stoffhuberei*. They are translated here as "knowledge," which expresses the aspects of work and learning in German terms. We can also distinguish these forms from cultural capital or forms of knowledge inherited "without effort."

35. Under the Communist regime, the overwhelming majority of twentieth-century history taught in schools focused on the Russian revolution and the Communist party in power in the GDR, the SED. This was clearly civic education for the benefit and value of the party. Some teachers, who refused to join the party, for example, were forbidden from teaching this period; instead they taught the history of the Middle Ages or ancient history, for example, which were considered "apolitical history" (see chapter 2). The way Nazism is taught shows that in the FRG and in unified Germany today, this difference is still valid, even though it is less explicit than it was in the East in the past.

36. Contrary to the way it is used above, teachers use the term "political" to refer to the normativity of civic education.

37. In Germany, oral expression is seen as very important in secondary and senior school. It makes up 60 percent of the final grade (40 percent for written expression). This emphasis on speaking might facilitate the expression of emotion.

38. This could be seen as a surprising result. In theory, the grading scale is from one to fifteen. But in practice the grades range from six to twelve, which explains the large number of grades that do not change.

39. At the time of the study, the matriculation exams were held after thirteen years of study in the old *Länder*, and after twelve years in most of the new *Länder*, including Saxe, where schooling has always lasted only twelve years. In 2008, a decision by the KMK (Kulturminister Konferenz) established the number of hours of secondary teaching required to sit the *Abitur*. Some of the old *Länder* (including Hamburg) moved to twelve years, others remained at twelve and three quarters years, such as the *Land* Rhineland-Palatinate.

40. Interview of 18 April 2002.

41. Interview of 8 April 2003.

42. Katharina, *Gymnasium*, final year, interview of 26 December 2001.

43. On 9 January 2004.

44. On this category of students, see the section entitled "'Left Behind' in History Class" in chapter 5.

45. This maneuverability is dependent on social origins. It is the boys from the most socially privileged backgrounds who are able to adapt their uses of the past to this emotional framework. Later on (chapter 4), we will analyze how the obstacles faced by young people from less socially privileged backgrounds in acquiring legitimate attitudes to the Nazi past may turn out to be insurmountable.

46. Interview of 29 September 2003.
47. In the teachers' comments, the Nazi genocide is a direct reference to the Jewish Holocaust—hence the evocation of six million, which is the number generally agreed on by historians for the victims of the Holocaust, not including the other categories of victims of extermination and persecution. These other categories included prisoners of war (particularly Russian), political prisoners, intellectuals (especially Polish), homosexuals, Roma, Jehovah's Witnesses, handicapped and disabled people, Christians, and forced workers in Eastern Europe, etc. For the historiographic debate on the figures, see Benz (1991).
48. Interview of 7 April 2003.
49. Field notes, 20 October 2003.
50. Interview of 25 April 2004.
51. Interview of 10 October 2003.
52. Field notes, 29 September 2003.
53. Interview of 23 April 2003.
54. Interview of 7 April 2003.
55. Informal conversation before class, 26 February 2003.
56. Interview of 25 April 2004.
57. See "Arnold Schwarzenegger—ein erotomaner Nazi?" *Die Welt*, 4 October 2003; "Schwarzenegger dementiert Hitler Bewunderung" *Der Spiegel*, 3 October 2003.
58. Interview of 9 April 2003.
59. I have translated the teacher's term, *Geschlecht*, as gender in English. In German, the term has two meanings: it refers to both social and grammatical gender. In German, the term *Geschlecht* is also frequently used in militant spheres, which is the second reason it is used here. At the time of the interview, Mr Gerste and his wife were actively involved in feminist movements. At several points in the interview he talked critically about "gender differences" (*Geschlechterdifferenz*).
60. Interview of 20 October 2003.
61. Interview of 7 April 2003.
62. Guido Knopp, *Hitlers Frauen*, television series: "Eva Braun, die Freundin" (the friend); "Magda Goebbels, die Gefolgsfrau" (the companion); "Winifred Wagner, die Muse" (the muse); "Zarah Leander, die Sängerin" (the singer); "Leni Riefenstahl, die Regisseurin" (the director); "Marlene Dietrich, die Gegnerin" (the opponent) *Dokumentation des ZDF*, Universum Film, Germany, Austria, 1995 (306 mins).
63. Guido Knopp, *Hitler eine Bilanz*, television series: "Der Privatmann" (The private man); "Der Verführer" (The seducer); "Der Erpresser" (The rackateer); "Der Diktator" (The dictator); "Der Kriegsherr" (The military leader); "Der Verbrecher" (The criminal), *Dokumentation des ZDF*, Universum Film, Germany, Austria, 1995, (306 mins).
64. Interview of 15 October 2003.
65. Interview of 28 January 2004.
66. Interview of 17 December 2003.
67. This is reminiscent of a Nazi propaganda photograph, frequently cited by both teachers and students and mobilized in the four textbooks used in the schools. In this photo, in the midst of a crowd, Hitler bends down to receive a bunch of flowers from a little girl (perhaps six years old, in her Sunday best, with blond plaits). He puts his hand on her cheek and smiles at her, and the girl looks back at him admiringly and very proud.
68. Vladimir Volfovitch Zhirinovsky (born in 1946) is a Russian journalist and politician, founder of the Liberal Democratic Party of Russia, considered an extreme-right

party. Jean-Marie Le Pen is the former leader of France's extreme-right party the *Front National*, well-known for his revisionist comments. The party is now led by his daughter, Marine Le Pen.

69. Interview of 14 October 2003.
70. Interview of 24 April 2003.
71. It is interesting to note the implicit elements in this comment: in translating from the German it is necessary to add the subjects (the people, the Nazis) that are not stated explicitly. Ms Inge also does not explicitly state what it is that "people" did not want to know—presumably the Jewish genocide or war crimes.
72. Interview of 20 October 2003. The German word *Not* has different English meanings.
73. Interview of 18 February 2002.
74. The German film of the book, *Die Welle*, was directed by Dennis Gansel and came out in 2008.
75. Interview of 14 January 2004.
76. Interview of 18 February 2003.
77. Interview of 4 November 2003.
78. This is a very scholarly term in German.
79. Interview of 21 April 2002.
80. Interview of 14 April 2003.
81. Hans Albers (1891–1960) was a German actor and singer; he was very well known in Hamburg where he was from.
82. Interview of 7 November 2003.
83. Interview of 16 April 2003.
84. Interview of 16 April 2003.
85. Ibid.
86. Interview of 18 February 2004.
87. Informal conversation, 10 February 2004.
88. Interview of 21 April 2003.
89. I met Thomas through a friend of mine, and we called each other by our first names from the beginning. In order to keep as close to the field as possible, I thus use his first name (a pseudonym) in the book.
90. Interview of 22 April 2003.
91. Interview of 22 April 2003.
92. Interview of 22 April 2003.
93. Interview of 22 April 2003.
94. Ibid.
95. Interview of 22 April 2003.
96. Interview of 22 April 2003.
97. Interview of 22 April 2003.
98. Interview of 22 April 2003.
99. Interview of 20 October 2003.
100. Interview of 20 October 2003.
101. Ibid.

Chapter 4

THE NAZI PAST AS AN EVERYDAY RESOURCE FOR ADOLESCENTS

There are uses of the Nazi past that are considered illegitimate in the school environment. This chapter will cover a minority of students (14 out of 105) who use their knowledge[1] to re-appropriate the Nazi past in ways that do not always (or do not at all) correspond to teachers' interpretations. They develop their *Eigensinn*[2] to give meaning to the Nazi past in their everyday lives, both in and out of school. When the students mobilize discourses or practices that are not well received by their teachers, they are not necessarily taking a political position,[3] nor can we assume that they are adhering to Nazi or neo-Nazi values. However, there are also more specifically political uses of the past that exist among some of these students, which put their values into practice.

There is a significant danger in overestimating the political signification of most of these illegitimate practices directed against the school as an institution. Considering these students simply as neo-Nazis devalues their historical knowledge and their opinions and underestimates the complexity of their practices. This kind of a priori judgment can obscure our vision and prevent analysis of the uses of the past. Indeed, political and ideological judgment cannot be the basis of a sociological study; politological classifications on "left–right" scales can be only the beginning of the analysis and never its endpoint. In his analysis of the far right in France, Patrick Lehingue rightly emphasizes the danger inherent in our uneasy reactions, our disgust or our indignation, which make it difficult to distance ourselves from the research object (Lehingue 2003: 249). Indeed, according to him, these reactions can lead to an "unflattering, pessimistic and alarmist portrait of National Front voters, this type of reductionism proving once again that good intentions are not sufficient to produce enlightened analysis" because they tend to invalidate it through caricature (Lehingue 2003: 251). These dangers and the ways of escaping them are also described by Martina Avanza (2008) in her article on the conditions of the study on the Lega Nord in Italy.

This kind of invalidation reflects a separation between legitimate and illegitimate practices that Richard Hoggart sheds light on in his book *The Uses of Literacy* ([1957] 2006). In his preface to the French translation, Jean-Claude Passeron (1970) emphasizes the risk of sociological studies falling prey to legitimist positions, "condemned, by the way they pose the questions of their analysis, to find the specificity of popular attitudes only in failure or insufficiency, in 'lack of motivation,' lack of interest, or lack of aspiration" (Passeron 1970: 19), a miserabilist trap that Hoggart manages to avoid (see also Grignon and Passeron 1989). Jacques Revel further pursues this critique in an article on the "uses and abuses" of the notion of "popular culture." He reveals the dual opposition underlying most historical analyses of this theme in France between the 1960s and the 1980s, which resulted in a separation between "legitimate" and "illegitimate" culture and thus contributed to the construction of the problem of popular culture in terms of what is "lacking" (Revel 1986).

The analysis of the transmission of the Nazi past is also vulnerable to this trap because it refers to representations of Nazism solely in terms of political tradition and civic engagement. The result is an equation according to which "legitimate" discourses on the Nazi past reject Nazism and (automatically) subscribe to democracy; the systemic consequence being that "illegitimate" discourses on the Nazi past are also those that subscribe to Nazism, and thus automatically reject democracy. Such an equation is clearly simplistic—other combinations are worth considering.

In fact, there are a whole range of uses of the Nazi past that do not have a direct political signification. The opposition between "legitimate and illegitimate," although it allows us to situate the use of the Nazi past within a normative framework, makes it difficult to provide a complex description of the extra-institutional uses of this past. In the rest of this book, I will refer to the uses and interpretations of the Nazi past that can be found among the teachers and in textbooks and official documents as being "academic" or "school-based." I also discuss the "students' uses" of the past that may conform, partly conform, or oppose teachers' expectations; I will then refer to them as "academic," "anti-academic," or "extracurricular." These uses may be resistant, indifferent, political, or apolitical, but they are always multiple, complex, and based on *Eigensinn*. The uses of history can therefore serve to claim a particular form of belonging (Avanza and Laferté 2005; Brubaker 2001). This belonging is sometimes (but rarely) national; it can also refer to peer groups, friendship groups or the family. These uses of history can serve to construct a position in the class group, for example, to forge a form of legitimacy and create a reputation for oneself (as a "rebel," "a good student," "a comedian"). It can also be a way of proving one's "good intentions" cultur-ally or setting oneself apart, with the teachers and/or other students rejected as being "other." This "process of othering" refers to a process of externaliza-tion, symbolic and material localization, of setting apart what appears to be close to oneself in spatial, cultural, or even temporal terms (Le Bihan 2007). It contributes to self-esteem. In social psychology, Henri Tajfel and A. L. Wilkes (1963) also observe a systematic relationship between otherness and self-esteem. According to them, the process of devaluing and rejecting the "outgroup" reinforces self-esteem due to in-group favoritism. This con-nection has also been observed by Norbert Elias and John Scotson ([1965] 1994).

School is also the place where adolescents construct an image of themselves and others, both along with and in relation to their families. However, this is a complex space, where several fields of play with specific rules overlap and intersect. What is discouraged by teachers may be encouraged by classmates; what the teacher does not laugh at, one's "pals" might—even if that laughter might be muffled or only partially displayed. This chapter will attempt to show how defending interpretations of history that are considered academi-cally illegitimate may simultaneously increase the status and reputation of those who "dare" to speak these words repressed by the institution. This kind of use of the past can also—in the family context—serve to distinguish one-self from one's parents, construct one's own life, provide a certain autonomy, and an image, both within a group but also for oneself. Students, particularly during puberty, use school as a site for experimentation, which allows them to escape from the frame of the family in order to build their own personal-ity. Knowledge acquired at school can also serve to gain recognition or to set oneself apart from one's parents. The school is a key site for recognition: this may come in the form of academic success incurring awards or good grades, or the construction of a "deviant career" (Becker 1963) recognized by the peer group, or indeed infinite combinations of these two extremes. School is a place for students to acquire knowledge, but it is also a place for them to implement strategies for socialization, recognition, interaction, and pleasure. These issues will be the central concern in this chapter.

Analyzing the transmission of the Nazi past in the school environment would not be possible without mobilizing the notion of legitimacy (academic or political). Indeed, the school is organized hierarchically, which tends to impose a certain understanding of knowledge, society, and also the political system. In the specific context of history class, the teachers' interpretation of the past is clearly inscribed within a legitimate, state-controlled framework, which must be conceived as such and which organizes the way the Nazi past can be used by students and teachers. There is thus an academic definition of the legitimate uses of the past, i.e., those which are profitable and rewarded on the academic market, which will directly or indirectly influence the way the students use it. This definition constitutes one of the frameworks for interaction with and appropriation of the past by the students.

In this fourth chapter, we will look at the ways in which some students appropriate historical knowledge strategically. How do they use it? In what context? With what purpose? The students all developed their own visions and understandings of the Nazi past, sometimes by altering their academic knowledge, but always by appropriating it. What are the conditions that allow them to do this? How can the Nazi past become a resource for contemporary economic, political, and social claims? How can it be used to justify "anti-system"[4] positions that are critical of the politico-economic system of governance? In the first part of this chapter, we will focus on five students who share (in addition to a certain number of social characteristics) a similar way of mobilizing the Nazi past, which constitutes a positive reference for them, in critical opposition to the current system of governance. In the second part of the chapter, we will look at nine other students from the final year of the *Gymnasien* in Hamburg and in Leipzig. Unlike students discussed in the first section, the Nazi past remains a negative reference for them. But their appropriations are also used to criticize or to support both the political economic system and the school system of the FRG. Setting themselves apart from their teachers' and parents' generation through their different appropriations of the past, while still remaining within the academic rules established by the teachers is one of the strategies of these *Gymnasium* students to combine academic success with the construction of their own vision of the past.

Economic Difficulties and Criticism of the FRG

If it is difficult to interview "bad students," it is almost impossible to speak to those whom their classmates describe as "neo-Nazis." Because this position is so difficult to defend within the school environment, the young people with extreme-right tendencies systematically avoided me. I was not able to meet any adolescents who regularly attended organized extreme-right or skinhead groups. However, I was put in contact with five students who openly expressed interpretations of the past that were directly opposed to those promoted by their teachers. The issue here is not to affirm their political belonging, which is difficult, particularly because of their age, but rather to question what is awkwardly referred to (sometimes by the professional blindness of researchers in political science) as the "political" dimension of their statements and behavior. Indeed, these students voice a certain number of opinions that can be easily attributed to the political extreme-right (in particular the denial of the Jewish genocide, positive attitudes toward the Nazi regime, antisemitism, and xenophobia) without explicitly belonging to a political organization. Instead, these are individuals whose political positions are not necessarily stable or well-defined. Therefore, those who refer to their classmates as "neo-Nazis" invoke a priori judgments, the expression being often used to stigmatize and identify a marginalized other. Moreover, this designation, too specifically political, does not necessarily correspond to the positions described and experienced by the students themselves. For these reasons, I will not use the term "neo-Nazi" to refer to these students.

The five students discussed in this section share an interpretation of Nazism that can be described as both illegitimate and "oppositional" in relation to the discourses in the school sphere, in the sense that they explicitly take position against the school rules and the norms of what constitutes "legitimate speech" (S. Hall 1973). This dual dimension is situated on two distinct levels. Historically, this has meant interpreting the Nazi past in a positive way, praising its "achievements," whether political, military, or social, particularly the increase of territory and the construction of a "strong power," but also "the decrease in unemployment," and the creation of jobs through major public works. At the same time, this position involves minimizing, or even denying, the criminal aspects of the Nazi regime and, in particular, the extermination policies. This denial is accompanied by pronounced antisemitism and xenophobia and is directly opposed to the interpretation of Nazism put forward by teachers particularly in history classes.

Alongside this, the students proclaim critical discourses on contemporary social and economic policies (even if these discourses are not necessarily consciously "political" in the classical sense of the term). They rely on the Nazi past as a counterexample, a reference, to devalue or even delegitimize the FRG. This position is also in opposition with the discourse of the teachers because it throws into question (at least in their eyes) the civic and democratic education proposed by the school.

These criticisms sometimes concern the regime and political policies of the government itself, but more often target the social and economic conditions of the students' everyday lives—which are difficult, sometimes unbearable. Two central criticisms are put forward against the current regime. They concern the economic system of the FRG and unemployment. These adolescents attack the welfare state, with its "hand-out policies," which they see as leading to "a lazy society," because "nobody wants to work if they can have money without doing anything." They also criticize the immigration policy of the FRG, because "foreigners are stealing our jobs"—whereas Hitler would have "got[ten] rid of the immigrants."

Individuals who publicly express (in class but also in the interviews) taboo positions (including the denial of the genocide) are not representative of the population who share their ideas, without necessarily using them as we describe here. Most of these people prefer to remain silent and do not express these opinions publicly because their social environments would not tolerate such statements.[5] The specificity of the interviewees must therefore be taken into account in the analysis. The five students who agreed to speak to me and who are the focus of this first section of the chapter share specific social characteristics: Johnny and Jürgen are students at the *Gesamtschule* Wiesi in Hamburg. Wolfgang is a student at the 100th *Mittelschule* in Leipzig. Thomas is a student at *Gymnasium* Weinberg in Hamburg. Domenico is an apprentice in a construction company and a former student of the *Gesamtschule* Wiesi.

It is undoubtedly not by chance that they are all boys. Although it is difficult to meet young people who openly affirm opinions that value certain aspects of the Nazi past, these young men more easily manifest their open opposition to the school order. Adolescent girls have more difficulty openly affirming opinions that are so clearly in opposition to "school norms" and so politically "incorrect." If they had such opinions, they did not show me. This reflects the hypothesis put forward by Patrick Lehingue that women are more likely to not express a vote considered taboo, such as a vote for the National Front, which would reduce the gender gap in the extreme-right vote without completely erasing it (2003: 275).

They all have encountered difficulties at school (four out of five did not sit the *Abitur*) and four out of five come from families in which parents were manual workers, tradesmen, or low-level employees. I made a special effort to contact these students upon the suggestion of their respective teachers who said "it could be interesting" for you.[6]

It is likely that opinions similar to those expressed here may be defended by some girls, or by certain students from less disadvantaged backgrounds, with more significant cultural capital. Indeed, we know that the "nationalist" vote, which mobilizes some of the arguments presented by the students here is sociologically distributed among all social classes (Schubarth and Stöss 2001). However, the discourses of these students who agreed to talk to me are interesting even though they are socially situated, because they provide clues to understanding the forms of "oppositional" mobilization or demands relating to the Nazi past, which transform the latter into a resource in specific contexts.

In Search of the Lost "Great Germany"

Johnny, aged fifteen, is the eldest of three children. He was born in 1988 in Wiesi, where he has spent all his life and done all his schooling. At the time of the interview, Johnny's father, born in 1960, was a painter in a small business, run by his father before him (also born in Leipzig, in 1942). His paternal family fled to Hamburg at the end of the war, where Johnny's grandfather met his future wife, born in Hamburg in 1944, who had a stationery shop. Both Johnny's father and his paternal grandfather obtained the *Hauptschulabschluss* (a middle school graduation certificate) and no additional qualifications. His mother, who was also born in 1960, sat the *Realschulabschluss* (a junior high school graduation certificate) and worked as a cleaning lady in the prison administration. Through her marriage, she experienced downward social mobility, both professionally and socially, compared to the trajectory of her own parents. Her father, born in 1919 and married to a dental assistant (born in 1928), was employed in a bank after the war. Between 1933 and 1945, he had been a member of the Nazi Party and participated in the "battle for Stalingrad"—as his grandson, in whose eyes he remained an important figure, told me proudly.

Both of Johnny's parents are politically close to the Social Democrats (SPD). Johnny said that he would vote for the Nazi Party—NSDAP—if he could, but failing that he would vote for the German People's Union (*Deutsche Volks Union*—DVU, at the time of the interview one of the three far right parties in Germany, along with the *Nationaldemokratische Partei Deutschlands*—NPD, and *Republikaner*) as soon as he was old enough. Almost all the students I met at Wiesi knew that Johnny has an oversized swastika flag that covered a whole wall in his bedroom. At school, his friends shared this information with those who do not know him personally.

In Johnny's discourse, his grandfather's past as a soldier engaged in war, which he considers "glorious," is in striking contrast with his present situation and that of his parents. His description of the Federal Republic evokes misery and boredom.

> And when you look, after World War II: giant buildings made of concrete! Everything is gray! It's all gray now! I don't know . . . And the new cars, square boxes, there is no style anymore, nothing is special. And, it's boring. And the Federal Republic, for me, it's boring too, because it's now. It's as simple as that! What is exciting, is after 1939. With the war. That's what's exciting."
>
> *You're a bit like Patton[7] who said that we are bored without war* [he had mentioned this expression earlier in the interview].
> Yes.[8]

In contrast to the boring present, Nazi history represents the "heroic" past of Johnny's maternal grandfather, associated with a positive image of a powerful, "exciting" Germany. This positive perspective is also linked to the (socially and financially) higher status professions of the maternal side

The Nazi Past as an Everyday Resource for Adolescents • 183

of the family. It is the war itself that interests Johnny, because it provides an escape from everyday life and a feeling of connection to his grandfather's "adventures."

> My parents always say: "enough, stop with that! You could be interested in something else!" But [he hesitates], I don't know, if I didn't have that [books about war, tank games etc.], I wouldn't know what to do. I would be bored.[9]

The feeling that the situation in the FRG has declined explains much of these interviewees' positive discourses on the Nazi past. We can observe certain similarities with the characteristics of extreme-right voters: "their exceptional degree of pessimism, mistrust of others, the apprehension that they feel regarding their own and their family's futures" (Lehingue 2003: 270).[10] Downwardly mobile social trajectories, family tensions, and professional insecurity all contribute to this feeling of apprehension. But for Johnny, the return to the Nazi past also enables a return to the maternal side of his family—skipping his parents' generation—which helps him to forget the downwardly mobile trajectory of the family and the anxiety of his present and future.

Wolfgang was fifteen years old at the time of the study, born in 1988, a student at the *Mittelschule* in Leipzig, and his parents provide another example of downward social mobility. His father, born in 1961, was an electrician, and his mother, also born in 1961, a secretary. They both lost their jobs after reunification and have been unemployed for more than ten years. Wolfgang has one older sister, aged eighteen, who had just obtained the *Abitur* and wanted to study music, and another, aged twenty-one, who was studying orthopedics in Berlin. Both his older sisters are thus on strong upwardly mobile trajectories, while he himself, having dropped out of the *Gymnasium* to go to a *Mittelschule*, was having trouble keeping up.

Wolfgang clearly and directly expressed his admiration for "Hitler." He said that he agrees with his parents' political opinions and considered, like them, that the CDU is a "left-wing party." His parents discussed current political problems around the themes of unemployment and immigration. Wolfgang had an eventful childhood. By age fifteen, he had already moved seven times. When I arrived in Ms Seidengleich's ninth-grade class in the 100th *Mittelschule* in December 2003 to attend her classes on the history of National Socialism and interview her students, Wolfgang had only just arrived. He had had to leave the *Thomasschule*, the most prestigious *Gymnasium* in Leipzig, for academic and disciplinary reasons. His teachers claimed he did not have "the required level," but he had also attracted their disapproval with his political opinions, considered to be on the extreme-right. Unlike Steffen, who we met in chapter 2, he was not trying to return to the *Gymnasium* (even though it is important to take into consideration the fact that he had only just arrived when I interviewed him and that it is entirely possible that his position changed later[11]). Already identified by Ms Seidengleich as a "difficult student," he in fact reinforced his opposition to the school environment when he arrived at the *Mittelschule*. The most significant source of this opposition came from the mobilization of the Nazi past. In his interview, for example, he outlined the "good sides of Nazism."

> Lots of people think that Hitler was bad, but—yes, but me, I don't think so! He also did lots of things, that were not all bad!
>
> *Like what for example?*
> Yes, well, for example, he allowed painters (*Maleragentur*) to also have holidays, things like that. And before, painters didn't have access to that at all! And—he also created several public holidays too.[12]

In referring to the "good things" that Hitler allegedly did, Wolfgang gives meaning to this past, which allows him to first find a positive identification figure; second, provides him a basis upon which to found his political opinion; third, facilitates his critique of present-day problems; and last but not least, gives him the opportunity to provoke his teachers and sometimes also his classmates (see below). In particular, he criticized "the others" for having been sucked in "by the TV" where "there is only coverage of the camps. What he [Hitler] did other than that is never shown at all. It's completely disappeared."[13] Interestingly, his discourse includes forms of source criticism reflecting things he had learned at school on different subjects. He therefore very intelligently constructs his critique using legitimate forms of expression. At the time of the interview, Wolfgang agreed with his parents politically, who "also think that Hitler was great—well, perhaps not necessarily great, but who [think that he] was not so bad after all."[14]

The family reading of the Nazi past in opposition to the dominant reading at school, can also be found in Johnny's discourse who, although he was initially quite critical of "Hitler," was so for reasons that are incompatible with his teachers' discourses. In his eyes, Hitler apparently prevented the greatness of the nation to express itself. Through his poor military and strategic decisions, he deceived the German people and made them suffer:

> Because—it was really a terrible thing [World War II] (*war schon ne schreckliche Sache*). Because—yes, when you're logical about it, [he hesitates] I don't know, on one hand, the World War II is linked to World War I, I think. Because, the Germans lost the first war. And then, they really wanted another war, they wanted to wage the ultimate war! Yes, and then Hitler came to power. A little later, in [19]33. Yes, and then, of course, he first tried to promise the people everything. And "I have a solution for everything" (*ich mach*

alles gut). Yes, and afterwards, there was the war. And sometimes, I think, that he—he really fucked Germany (*Er hat Deutschland verarscht*). Because first he said that he was the perfect man who was going to make everything alright (*ja er ist der gute Mann, er macht alles*). And then, he—all of a sudden, he said, yes, "Poland attacked us, right." That was propaganda and all (*alles dann so mehr propagandamäßig*). And then, I think, yes, sending the sixth army to Stalingrad, and fighting to the last man, even though it didn't make sense anymore. Sacrificing all those men, and there were so many people, thousands, who died as prisoners of war, that, that wasn't really necessary (*das müsste eigentlich nicht sein*).[15]

Here Johnny is adopting the point of view of his grandfather, a soldier on the eastern front and a member of the Nazi Party (NSDAP), who talked of his disappointment with a regime that he had believed in. This disappointment was also a military one. Hitler would have sacrificed the Germans to his military ends, without taking the necessary precautions to save "German lives." Johnny's grandfather's concern was not for the civilians and the criminal acts of the regime, the Nazi extermination policies, or wars of destruction. It was the poor military calculations that concerned both grandfather and grandson. Here we can see the influence of discourses on "Germans as the victims of Hitler's war" popular in the FRG in the 1950s. He mobilized the well-known saying, "history is written by the victors," in order to underline the "good sides" of Nazism, too often overlooked, according to him.

In this sense, he would like to be able to rewrite history, to be able to "be proud without having a bad conscience." But it is indeed specifically the military defeat that is so unbearable for him half a century later.

Perhaps I would have left everything as it is, as history really is. And then just militarily, I would make the Germans [he hesitates], it would be good, you know, if the Germans had succeeded everything they undertook. Russia would have surrendered, England would have surrendered. The United States would have done nothing, would have withdrawn. And Europe would have become a fortress (*Festung*) and Germany would win. The NSDAP would be celebrated. But then, after, I would make it so that the people would oppose the German occupation. And that the Germans would realize on their own: "we can't stay here." Because the civilian people are against us! So, we will draw back. Without being beaten by the enemy. So, they withdraw, until they are inside their own country. But they don't lose their own country! So, there is no battle around Berlin! That's what I would have done . . . That we—that we withdraw by ourselves into our country. And that—what was destroyed (*kaputt gemacht*) would be fixed (*heile gemacht*). Except that the German Reich would still exist! Maybe we would still have the German Reich, if it had been like that.

And why do you think it would be good if the German Reich still existed? What would be better, if it did?
I don't know. On one hand, Germany would be bigger. And [he hesitates], yes, Germany would be bigger. We—we could also say, I dunno, with a good conscience, we could say: the German Reich and everything that existed before [1933 to 1945] was good.[16]

This passage shows Johnny's search for a "lost great Germany" but also his attempt to construct an original and interesting version of history and build an image of himself as different from the others, to make himself unique. Rewriting the end of the war, allows for a reconstruction of history in which his grandfather's "military victories" remain victorious. His desire to "fix" the German "destruction" reveals Johnny's search to restore honor to Nazi Germany, without the period between 1933 and 1945 being a breaking point. In spite of everything, this passage also shows the strength of the transmission of a certain number of school (or family) values. Although Johnny says he would want to vote for the DVU (extreme-right party), and although he wants to be positive about "Hitler" and "the Nazis," if he could he would nevertheless first rewrite history into a less criminal history, less bloody, and "reconstruct" or repair some of the criminal actions of the Germans in order to be able to build this positive image. The use of the very childish expression *heile machen*, literally "to make whole," which also contains the word *Heil* (benediction) and the verb *heilen* (to heal) strongly suggests this childish desire that there be no negative traces of the German presence overseas.[17] In his vision of the "ideal history," he does not imagine an imperialistic Germany, but rather a "reasonable" Germany, which, after the "popular uprisings," would understand "by itself" that it must "withdraw" from occupied countries. Johnny wanted to remove "a historic shame" in order to rebuild "a national pride" free from risk. But the interview speaks volumes by what it omits: although Johnny said he wants a voice for the peoples of the occupied countries, he did not mention the genocide or the Jews in his alternative version of German history. He only talked about that question when I asked him about it directly, later on in the interview, as we will see in the section below.

The fact that it is forbidden to speak "positively" of Nazism at school is incomprehensible but also painful for this student. "Why can't we talk about Hitler anymore? He was Chancellor. We can talk about Emperor Wilhelm, even though he did World War I. I say, 'Kaiser Wilhelm' and that's fine. But if I say 'Hitler,' I have to shut my mouth. Why?"[18]

It is possible that the discrepancy between the oral history transmitted to him by his grandfather and the history he received at school is the foundation of his incomprehension. In order to understand the tension between his own historical interpretations and the expectations of his teachers, he mobilized an explanation based on his vision of the political orientations of the latter: "they're all greenies, all hippies, right. At home, they all walk around with flags with *peace* written on them in giant letters!"[19]

The historical reconstruction of a "great Germany," a posteriori, can take more ambiguous, less obvious forms. The case of Domenico, an apprentice welder born in 1984 in a disadvantaged area south of Hamburg to Greek parents, may serve as an example of the possible coexistence of an academic version of the Nazi past and an appreciation of German military strength.

Domenico's father, born in 1937, was a welder at the time of the interview. He immigrated to Hamburg in 1964, when he worked in a shipyard in the port, until it went bankrupt. He tried to open a sausage stand but quickly went bankrupt, and then became a factory worker in a company making wardrobes. His mother, born in 1938 in Greece, immigrated with her family to Hamburg in 1963, where she met Domenico's father. As an unskilled worker with no diploma, she worked in various factories around Hamburg and then as an interim worker until the birth of her four children (Domenico is the youngest). She then became a housewife. Domenico went to German school and sat the *Hauptschulabschluss*, but still attended Greek nursery and primary school in the afternoons and the evenings until he was twelve. When he was sixteen, he moved to *Gesamtschule* Wiesi, where he spent two years without managing to pass the *Realschulabschluss* vocational certificate. He did odd jobs before beginning his apprenticeship in industrial mechanics, while attending a vocational school. Domenico says he is "not very interested in history," but "what comes to mind first, what would probably come to mind for everyone, is World War II." This event appears to him the "biggest" in German history.[20] The aspects that interest him the most relate to the situation in Greece during the war. The invasion of "our home," civil war "in our home," are events that his parents have talked to him about when the subject was covered at school. Thus, as is often the case during the interviews, it is the school that is the catalyst for family narratives that are inscribed in great detail in the memories of the interviewees. Domenico remembers vividly what his father told him about his youth.

> The village is at the bottom of the mountain. It's not so big. There's a river too. And the German troops had their base camp behind the river, in front of the mountain. And my father also said that they had—well, he was little, my father, he was about six, or five maybe, five or six years old—and he said that he saw everything, and when he saw the Germans, he looked at them and they looked at him, wide-eyed and everything, and he saw the technical knowledge they had, all the weapons and everything, they showed them too. And my father told me that they even had a bakery, just for their base camp. They were so advanced, technologically advanced, that we, we were in front of them, just

amazed, because we thought we were in a time machine. And that we had gone maybe a hundred or maybe twenty or thirty years into the future. Everything that they had! Such a small base camp, and they had their own bakery and everything! And us, the little village, we had to go to town and all that. It was really very different, for my father, when he was little.[21]

This passage reveals Domenico's very strong identification with his father's stories and thus with "his country," Greece, particularly through the use of the personal pronoun "us." The Germans, with their more advanced techniques (in particular their weapons, which fascinate Domenico), seem to come from the future. But this fascination does not prevent him from strongly identifying with the people in the village, who observe this prowess with surprise. Even though he respects the technical prowess of these "foreigners," he also clearly considers them invaders. Over the course of the narrative, they progressively become enemies who kill arbitrarily. He recounts in detail the "accidental" murder of a young girl from his father's village by the German soldiers. The son thus becomes the depositary of his father's lived experience and the family past ensures a certain distance from the German troops. Torn between his respect for the strength of the latter and his identification with Greece, Domenico alternates between critical and heroic interpretations of the German army. He relates the events that he learned about at his Greek primary school in Hamburg.

Yes, and then, Italy tried, in [19]42 I think, to come to Greece, by sea, with boats, and Greece said no. And—we call it "the day we said no," because we said, "no, you can't come in our country. We will rise up." That's it. And so, we rose up against the Italians, and the Italians withdrew. They said, "no, we can't do it." And so, German troops, lots of German troops were obliged to come. And then Greece, it's a little country, against the German Wehrmacht, at the time [he makes a gesture of powerlessness] and so, they were already inside. Yes, and that's why they took what they wanted. So, they said, "this is ours, and that too is ours, and yes, over there we'll make a base camp." And it was like that in the village there. Well, my father, he said that life went on, pretty much normally. Well, they didn't do anything to hurt us, they even helped us really. That's what he said.[22]

In this discourse we can see that Domenico not only admires the German military and technical strength, he also likes to talk about his father's "swaps" with the soldiers (some soldiers regularly gave him their "bakery" bread in return for the fish he caught). Domenico describes these soldiers as "nice guys." Domenico combines various sources in his discourse: classes from his Greek primary school, family history, and classes at his German high school. Greek national history is thus intertwined with family history and

German history learned in school. Although Domenico, unlike Johnny and Wolfgang, is neither provocative nor anti-school, his amazement at the "technological advances" of Nazi Germany constitutes a selective vision of the past which seeks, just like Johnny's and Wolfgang's discourses, to reconstruct a "lost greatness" for Germany. The coexistence of this amazement and a negative vision of the German soldiers who kill an innocent girl indicates the flexibility of the uses of the past in these adolescents' discourses, as well as the fluctuations in their emotional reactions to the Nazi past.

The Construction of a Position: Partial Reappropriation of TV Programs

Johnny, like his classmates, gets most of his information from television. Like many of them, Guido Knopp is one of his favorite documentary filmmakers. This "TV historian," on the second German public television station (ZDF), attracts between 15 and 21 percent of the prime-time audience with his programs about Nazism (Kansteiner 2006: 110), a combination of archival footage and reconstructed fiction, cut with interviews from "witnesses" who Knopp often manages to make cry in front of the camera. This filmed emotion provides an echo to the pedagogy of emotional upheaval used at school to transmit the Nazi past. Thus, Knopp's programs are somewhere between classical historical documentaries (in the use of archives, witnesses, and explanatory voice-overs), and the hybrid genre of the "docufiction," between fiction and documentary, which uses actors to represent historical figures.[23] Knopp himself considers that he makes "documentaries," not "docufictions." He also considers himself a "historian," a description challenged by his critics who are often academic historians.[24]

The success of these televised products is remarkable. Not only is Knopp the only one to be able to screen "his" documentaries directly after the TV news, a prime-time slot attracting a large audience, but his programs are also appreciated by both teachers and students, particularly boys from disadvantaged social backgrounds.[25] The audience, therefore, far exceeds the number of television viewers. History teachers use these documentaries to support or replace a class (an episode lasts forty-five minutes, which is the duration of the school class in Germany; "it's practical" several teachers told me). Indeed, although they do not systematically use them, not one of the thirty-three teachers I interviewed really criticized Knopp, who is "so well-loved by the students." Moreover, some programs are supported by the Minister for Education in certain *Länder* and included on the list of programs to be used in schools.[26] The US historian Wulf Kansteiner, in an analysis of German postwar memory policies, dedicates part of his book to the role of television in the transmission of memory policy (Kansteiner 2006: section 3). He explains that Knopp's success is due to his ambiguities (2006: 175–80). He thus emphasizes the fact that Knopp uses visual aids that allow the television viewer to "identify with," or even to "play" the Nazis, while emphasizing the detestable nature of the Nazi regime in a very politically correct voiceover (2006: 176, 177). By mobilizing Nazi propaganda from the 1930s and 1940s and updating it with twenty-first-century cinematographic techniques (speed, color, dramatic music[27]), he makes it attractive to the eye of the contemporary viewer. This commercial success—Knopp and his team of historians are the only ones to be able to compete with the private TV channels in prime-time slots—is well established today. Knopp plays on what Kansteiner calls "transgressive" pleasure. The success of these programs among adolescents, in particular boys, is found in the staging of emotions that are socially constructed as masculine.

The most common critiques of Knopp fall into two categories: form and content.[28] In terms of form, historians criticize him for combining archival sources and reconstructed fictions without giving the viewer the means of distinguishing between them. He is also accused of "working" the archives when they do not correspond to the vision that the historical team of the television station would like to give of the period. In terms of content, critics say Knopp shows the German army in a "too positive" light, in particular in his documentaries from the 1990s. These two criticisms are the foundation for the doubts that are expressed about the negative side effects of these programs "for a young audience." From a moral and political standpoint, Kansteiner thus expresses a fear that is widely shared among Knopp's critics: "perhaps young people will not get over their temporary identification with ordinary soldiers and the political elites of the Third Reich" (Kansteiner 2006: 179). He is thus concerned that "the youngest" lack the experience, and the political and aesthetic dispositions necessary for critical (re)interpretations. How can they question their own usage of transgressive pleasure? Yet, while he affirms (without any genuine proof) that "no other vision of history has been so successful in constructing the collective memory of Nazism in Germany," Kansteiner himself questions whether Knopp's programs actually have a structuring effect on television viewers, particularly for the oldest among them.

These doubts are confirmed by the study conducted here. Indeed, not only is the fascination with the actors of Nazism not incompatible with an empathy toward the victims and an open refusal of Nazism as a political regime (fascination with these images is not the same as political attraction), but it apparently leaves few long-term traces, particularly among adolescents from disadvantaged backgrounds. Their difficulty in remembering the content of history lessons is also true for the content of a historical film.

The students' uses of Knopp's programs are manifold. There are, roughly speaking, two categories of students who make close reference to Knopp. The "good students," who also adopt their teachers' discourses once the subject is covered at school; and students who mobilize discourses of opposition that are critical of the ways the Nazi past is taught at school, who have specific knowledge of the subject, and who use Knopp selectively to reinforce their political positions. Johnny, like most of his classmates, likes these documentaries because they seem credible: "there are witnesses, they won't lie, right." They tell "how it really was," which sets them apart in the students' eyes from "fiction films, because there, it's not always the whole truth."[29] He said that his favorite program was the one on the general Erwin Rommel.[30]

> Rommel was a Marshall—in North Africa. [He hesitates] yes, he fought against the English, in fact. With very few means, he pushed them back to Cairo, almost. And then, in El Alamein he stopped and had to go back. And yes, I thought Rommel was good, because, well, okay, he was a general, and he fought for the Nazis, okay, but he wasn't a Nazi himself. He was just a soldier. And yes, he knew what humanity was (*Menschlichkeit*). When you look at other generals, they take prisoners and "what will we do with them?"—[They] shot them, didn't they? And he, he looked after them as he did his own men. I think that's good. And then, he was crafty too.[31]

Rommel is a figure who can provide an adolescent with numerous possibilities for identification. In his own trajectory, there are many elements that these adolescents can use to project upon him their own dreams of chivalry. The "knightly" aspect of the "Desert Fox" has indeed been staged in several films. He does not present the "Nazi" criminal (like Himmler or Goebbels), but rather the image of an "honorable" soldier who was targeted because of his association with the 20 July plot. The various myths that circulate about him are testimony to this. Although he has been accused of crimes against humanity, his African corps was not actively involved in the Jewish genocide on the eastern front. In his trajectory, his military successes during World War I and II are often emphasized (he won several medals). It is probably not a coincidence that Johnny prefers Rommel to any other figure of the period. In Johnny's reconstructed history, in which the Germans become "honorable," Rommel is useful in embodying his dreams of honor and military success projected onto the Nazi past.

Johnny is not alone in his attraction to this general. A British scandal demonstrates that the figure of Rommel has lost none of its attraction even on the other side of the Channel, particularly for young men. In January 2005, Prince Harry (of Wales) dressed up as Erwin Rommel for a costume party entitled "Colonials and Natives," which shocked the British media and dominated headlines for two weeks. The scandal forced the younger prince to publicly apologize and admit that it was "a poor choice of costume."[32] Harry—like Johnny—chose Rommel rather than Himmler or Hitler: the ambiguity of the general is seductive for these adolescents. It allows them to play with the past and with norms. Harry, like Johnny, was trying to test the limits of what can be said and what is possible, while still remaining on the side of what is acceptable (more or less), thus seeking to be provocative, to reinvent himself, to make people laugh, and to take pleasure in playing with history. However, Harry, as a representative of the royal family, does not have the same freedoms as Johnny does in Hamburg and was forced to make a public apology.

Knopp's documentary also reflects this ambiguity, and we can assume that it is partly responsible for the attraction of this figure. Rommel's military "adventures" are commented on by witnesses and the critical testimonies of the soldiers are reinforced by Knopp's voiceover, explaining that Rommel's units had taken more prisoners and caused more dead and wounded than the other units of the Wehrmacht. The ambitious side (*karrieresüchtiger Hazardeur*) of the general is also emphasized. These "critical" comments are alternated, however, with more positive testimonies. Rommel's military qualities and the fact that he was concerned about his troops' well-being is also emphasized. These testimonies are particularly convincing due to the report by a British veteran who specifically stated that Rommel ensured honorable treatment of not only his own troops, but also those of the enemy.

In spite of the comments that are critical of Knopp, Johnny stands firm in his image of Rommel solely based on positive testimonies, describing him as a hero who was "not very Nazi" and "a true soldier." A positive image of certain Nazis therefore seems very much compatible with Knopp's documentaries, nevertheless insisting that these figures are not "real Nazis," thus preserving a negative image of Nazism in general, while transforming Rommel into a hero. But this is not the only possible interpretation. Johnny is particularly attached to Rommel as a war hero; a well-organized strategist, standing alone. He therefore takes from the program only what is useful for him to build his position and to enrich the knowledge he has acquired elsewhere. We can see that these adolescents use the information they have selectively, with the selection depending on the information they have at their disposal and the positions that they build for themselves. Family histories, books, school classes, and television programs all intertwine and mutually influence each other.

Moreover, as we have already seen, selecting information and constructing a position that uses the Nazi past allows the students to formulate a certain number of criticisms, particularly regarding the public policy of the FRG government. These criticisms do not automatically or directly translate into partisan positions.

Challenges to Contemporary Public Policy

An interest in the Nazi past, and in particular positive attitudes toward it, can therefore help to escape a feeling of boredom with everyday life and provoke excitement in adolescents' lives, by transgressing dominant norms. But this may also be associated with—and reinforce—a more coherent opposition to the state and public policy. In the students' discourses, we can indeed see the interconnection of elements linked to the Nazi past and to contemporary demands (relating to economic policy and immigration), both of which are based in a fear of unemployment. For reasons of clarity, I will cover them separately here, but it is important to bear in mind that in practice these discourses are very closely connected.

Economic Policy and the Fear of Unemployment

The arguments that Wolfgang used in defending his vision of the Nazi past (which emphasizes the "good sides") are primarily economic.

> Yes, okay, maybe it's not a good example, but—he [Hitler] built a lot of roads. They were used afterwards for other things, but, he created lots of jobs. It was just for the war, but—there was work. [He falls silent, he does not want to keep talking.][33]

His parents, like 17.5 percent of the population of Saxony in 2004, were unemployed, which clearly played a role in the construction of his vision of the past. Indeed, the themes of unemployment and immigration constitute the core of the critique of the present and a positive image of the Nazi past in his discourse, as they do in those of his classmates. Johnny also questions the economic consequences of the Nazi's rise to power.

> Yes, because, I think that [he hesitates] okay, Hitler, if we hadn't had him, what kind of a guy would we have had (*was hätten wir dann für einen bekommen*)? Who would have taken power? What would have happened? Perhaps we would have had other things, here—recession again! So [with Hitler], we had economic expansion. Right, building the highways and all that. Everything he did for the country, it was good! Up until the war. That was bad. If you only look at that. Then yes.[34]

The separation of time into separate periods ("before the war," "after the war") enables a positive image of the past, which does not take into account the fact that the "economic success" of the regime was based on a war economy and that the two are intrinsically connected. This separation

194 • When Will We Talk about Hitler?

between an "economic dimension" and a "political dimension" of the regime means the former can be opposed to the economic policies of the FRG, which are criticized by the students. One of the explanations for the fact that their discourses are so concentrated on economic policies seems to lie in the fact that, with only one exception, the students come from very socially disadvantaged families. Their criticisms thus reflect their everyday reality.

Thomas, aged nineteen at the time of the study, is the son of a skilled worker in a furniture company, and a secretary, who stopped working when her son was born. The only *Gymnasium* student who positioned himself "on the extreme right of the political spectrum" and who agreed to talk to me, Thomas expressed well-argued political positions. He was the only student who began the interview by mentioning the "economic miracle of Ludwig Erhard,"[35] which he compared to that "of Hitler." He put a lot of emphasis on the latter's "success in reducing unemployment." In so doing, he engaged a dual process: on one hand, he minimized the importance of the regime's crimes, and on the other, he criticized the FRG and expressed his opposition to the state in which he lives.

> Hitler succeeded, with means that were a bit banal—let them dig and fill it in later—but people had something to do, they earned money. [He hesitates.] And then they didn't waste the state's money [he hesitates again], and more, they had something to do, they did something for their money. Yes, they were relatively happy with that, I think. I see that as one of the reasons that explains why Hitler got where he did. Because he motivated the masses. There were so many people unemployed and unemployment was going to disappear.[36]

The comparison between Erhard's liberal policies and the major works of the Nazi regime is historically and economically not very coherent. Thomas only resorted to it in order to compare both to the current government, which had not managed to reduce unemployment (at the time of the interview it had climbed to above 10 percent in Germany and 15 percent in Hamburg). This approach is also frequent in the interviews: any aspect of the present that is considered negative (political, economic, or other) is compared to a positive vision of the past.

The economic argument can also be turned around to serve the same ends; criticizing current-day Germany by comparing it (rather than by opposing it) to the Nazi regime. Jürgen defined himself as politically right-wing but contrary to the students mentioned before, he clearly condemned rather than praised the Nazi regime. At the time of the interview, he was eighteen years old and in ninth grade at *Gesamtschule* Wiesi in Hamburg. The son of two high school teachers, he comes from a family with a high level of cultural capital but has nevertheless fallen seriously behind on his schoolwork. He lived with his mother and her new partner, who is also a teacher and a high

The Nazi Past as an Everyday Resource for Adolescents • 195

school principal. When I met him, his experience at school had already been marked by several failures: he repeated two years before abandoning the *Gymnasium* and moving to the *Gesamtschule*. He was very nervous during the interview. He laid his hands on the table and was sitting up very straight. He was careful to give "the right answers." He said he was interested in the foundation of the FRG (he got the date wrong, situating it in 1948) and the creation of the welfare state, not to hold it up as an ideal model, as most of his teachers do, but on the contrary, to critique it. For him, it was the source of the future economic catastrophe for Germany. He therefore criticized the "social policy" of the FRG, particularly the support for the unemployed and other "welfare fraudsters," comparing it to National Socialism and socialism. This student considered these three "regimes" as being part of "the same economic system" and contrasted it to the capitalism of the United States.[37] "So that everyone can't go to the state and say, 'Hi, I have nothing, give me something.' Real capitalism, you know. He who is stupid will stay stupid. Everybody is responsible for themselves. Only those who manage to sell themselves will succeed in having something."[38]

Jürgen mentions the Nazi past in order to emphasize "the catastrophe" of 1945, which he interprets, by revising history, as "the ultimate economic failure of the National Socialist social state," a failure that would soon cause great suffering in the FRG. The Nazi past therefore serves as an example to be avoided but also simultaneously as an argument or a negative example that helps to criticize the current political and social system.

The overlapping of xenophobic, antisemitic and economic arguments, both linked to the question of unemployment, can be seen in an extract from the interview with Domenico, mobilizing ordinary stereotypes.

I only know that they [the Jews] didn't work, but they had heaps of money (*die hatten voll das Geld*), you know, they were all loan sharks (*Kredithaie*) or something like that. But I don't know exactly what they did. [He hesitates, thinking.] I just know that the Jews were bloody rich (*voll reich*), man, and that they were recognized, a people that was recognized, by everyone and they had a lot of jewelry shops (*Juwelierläden*). [He hesitates.] And Hitler, he got obsessed with them. I'm not a hundred percent sure why. [Very softly] I don't know. [He hesitates for a long time.] I only know that they—apparently they were very rich, and Hitler [he hesitates, and then has an idea] maybe he didn't want to let them spread here (*dass die sich hier ausbreiten*), so to speak. He said, "no, I won't allow that" or something like that. "That they can take over here (*sich breitmachen*) and that they are full of money (*voll das Geld*) and all that, and that, that's not possible (*das kann doch nicht angehen*)! We, we work—or the Germans they work—and they, they open jewelry shops and this and that, and they have all the money and everything." I think that it was perhaps one of the reasons he wanted to get rid of them.[39]

When he talks about the Jews, Domenico changes the register of his speech. He gets carried away by his feelings. His very familiar use of the adverb *voll* (full, fully), systematically used with the noun money or the adjective rich (*voll reich, voll das Geld*),[40] reveals an increased proximity with the content of his narrative. Sometimes, inversely, Domenico corrected himself, stressing the uncertainty of information or adding an "apparently" or a "maybe," which also indicates a certain distancing. This gets lost toward the end of his discourse, when he explained why "Hitler wanted to get rid of" the Jews. At this point, he changed perspective entirely. Although the collective "we" had been used up until then only to describe the Greeks, he now used it to refer to the German population with whom he is identifying. This identification is linked to the construction of an opposition between "the Germans who work," a population in which Domenico includes himself, and "the Jews, rich, jewelry shop owners" who "invaded" Germany. For Domenico, the Jewish genocide thus becomes understandable because it was a move against the economic injustice of an unjustifiably rich "people." Domenico, like many of his classmates, therefore sought to construct a "logical argument" to explain the Nazi examination policy. Although his teachers' arguments did not convince him, he tried to find his own "reasons" as to why a whole people might be exterminated, and he found them in the most common stereotypes, that combine antisemitism and xenophobia.

The overlap between the Nazi past and contemporary politics that is at work here is almost systematic in the interviews: antisemitism and xenophobia intertwine around the problem of unemployment.

Immigration Policies

The link between contemporary immigration policy and that of the 1930s leads to the superposition of the figure of the Jew and the Muslim in a xenophobic construction of otherness. This results in a distortion or even a negation of German war crimes and a desire to ignore the Jewish genocide: "it doesn't interest me too much. I don't know much about it." It was only after my insistent questions that, at the end of the interview, Johnny, for example, began to talk about it, combining classically antisemitic explanations and more contemporary xenophobic explanations.

Um—on that, I haven't really thought about it, about the Jews. Because—I think, that the people, *they* needed to have a baddie. And it was the Jews, because they were rich, they had everything in gold. And they worked at the banks. Because their religion didn't forbid stealing. Almost all religions forbid stealing. Yes and, and, *they* simply needed a scapegoat (*Buhmann*), to whom they could say, "yes, *we're* not doing too well, *we* have no work, because of the

Jews." And that means that the Jews had to leave, they had to disappear. That's how I explain it to myself.[41]

The historical stereotype of the rich Jew, working in the financial sector, and stealing from the poor mentioned in the first part of the above quote, makes way for the more current stereotype of those who "steal German people's work," a stereotype that is usually evoked in discourses about migrants. The shift from "they" used to describe the historical reasoning that Johnny attributes to the German people, to the more personal "we" illustrates this shift from historical reasoning toward a more contemporary approach ("we're not doing well etc."), transposed onto the past by simply replacing contemporary foreigners with "Jews." The more contemporary argument, "the need to make them leave," is therefore transformed into historical explanation, "the need to make them disappear."

These two overlapping reasonings, historical and contemporary, which combine to justify the Jewish genocide, can be found in several interviews. Johnny argued that Hitler, knowing that he would wage war, could not "kick out" the Jews, because he would "get them back" in occupying Poland, Russia, and so forth. He was therefore "obliged" to kill them. And, so that it was not too bloody, "he used gas."

> Once I saw, [on television?], there was Himmler, he was the head of the SS. And it was the SS who did it, the gassing. And then, I saw that Himmler visited and attended one of the executions. So they shot the Jews. And then, they said [on the television?] that Himmler was uncomfortable, when he saw how his men had killed the Jews. Even though it was him who had ordered it, right! And so, they thought about how they could do it so it wasn't so bloody. First, [by using] exhaust gas from cars, but it was too expensive, for Hitler, because of the petrol. And so they took another sort of gas. Yes, and that's what they used to kill them. I don't know exactly if it is Hitler's fault or his men's. Maybe he had a personal hatred. Yes, I understand, when you've had a bad experience with them. I understand! But I don't know much about it.[42]

Johnny was not alone in saying he "doesn't know much" about the Nazi extermination policy. The subject clearly ran the risk of shaking his convictions.

When questioned on why the Jews were deported, Domenico, like Johnny, said he doesn't really know.

> The Jews, we didn't do that [in class]. I learned that afterwards. Okay, there were images, with the concentration camps, and all that. How were treated, but nothing else. What uniforms they had, what signs, with the triangles. So they could be recognized as Jewish. And that they were taken prisoners, and

that they worked too. [He pauses to think] The Jews, we didn't learn much about that.[43]

Yet his visit to the concentration camp in Dachau nevertheless had an impact on him. He confirmed that he "felt pain" when he saw the ovens and felt very uneasy with the idea "that there were people who were killed, just like that, without any reason, from work and all." When Domenico talked about Dachau, he said it was "terrible, what they [the Germans] did, there was someone, who went into their gas chamber and outside there was a little boy, and they said to him: 'look, come here, I'll give you a lolly,' and so he went and he was gassed. It's terrible what they did with those people."[44] In this passage, Domenico includes arguments in his discourse that are close to that of his teachers, although he confuses forced labor and extermination. This visit to the concentration camp and his condemnation of the killings (even though the scale of them is apparently unimaginable for him—he seems to imagine them killed one by one) is disconnected from the opinions that he expressed elsewhere. Oppositional and legitimate discourses about the past go hand in hand in Domenico's representations of the past, even though they might seem contradictory. They are not necessarily mutually exclusive and can exist in parallel to each other, depending on the context in which they are spoken.

Xenophobia and antisemitism can be observed in discourses of other interviewees. For the students who constructed discourses that were not academically legitimate, or in opposition to school discourses, these were almost always associated with the negation or minimization of the Nazi extermination policies, while also including legitimate ways of talking about the past. Thus, although some of them said certain aspects of these crimes were revolting, they considered their teachers' discourses "exaggerated." Thus, Wolfgang believed that: "we could have found other solutions. Oh yeah, for example, in the Middle Ages, we just sent them out of the towns, the Jews. We could have maybe, I don't know, sent them away. Instead of killing them."[45]

Mobilizing a religious argument, Wolfgang combined Judaism and Islam in a process of othering that allowed him to set them in opposition to Christianity, "the true religion of Germany."

Yes, so the problem is that the—that he [Hitler] wanted to kill all the Jews. So that Judaism (das Judentum) died. But, that's not really necessary (das muss ja nicht unbedingt sein). Judaism can continue to live. Just, not necessarily in Germany."

But why should they leave?
Yes, well, for me it doesn't bother me if there are a few Jews or people—some—the Muslims. As long as they—they don't try to eradicate Germany's

true religion. And—I don't know how many—how many Muslims there are in Eu—in Germany, perhaps a thousand? Maybe two thousand? Scattered throughout the whole country. And [he hesitates] it's not possible that [he hesitates again] that they can come, maybe twenty-seven of them, to build a giant mosque! Well, they can build it, but they can't build a tower next to it where they call for prayer five times a day! And that is, that's really . . . [he trails off and starts again]. It doesn't fit with our landscape at all (*das passt einfach nicht in unsere Gegend rein*)![46]

Although it might initially seem that Wolfgang's argument resembles the Nazi argument of the time, the vocabulary that he used, in a very familiar language, was far removed from that of the LTI (*Lingua tertii imperii*, the language of the third Reich), analyzed by Victor Klemperer ([1957] 2006), which instead suggested that the "vital space" (*Lebensraum*) must be "free of Jews" (*judenfrei*). In all of these interviews it seems that the central question is not the past but the present; here, it is the fear of foreigners.

Wolfgang considered other religions dangerous. A German Jew or a Muslim is therefore not a "true German." What was initially a religious refusal thus becomes xenophobic. This distortion plays out on two levels, religious and national, which are interconnected. In this discourse we can see the age-old question of the definition of the nation, in this case Germany, and the questions of belonging associated with it. The identity dimension remains the principle basis in the students' construction of two different (but independent) forms of otherness: that of the contemporary "foreigner" (national and religious, but also linguistic) and that of the historical "foreigner." We might ask if the ease of this essentialist argument is based on the widely shared acceptance (including by the intelligentsia) of the idea of the nation, which by definition implies a more or less closed identity (Noiriel 1991, 2001).

Wolfgang expressed the traditional fear of Übervölkerung (overpopulation) and used an argument based on thresholds: a country can only "absorb" a certain number of "foreigners," before being "adulterated."

And do you really think that there is a danger today that the Jews and the Muslims could push the Christians out of Germany?
Yes. I think so yes.

And how do you see this danger?
Well, for example, this story about Frankfurt. Where they built this huge mosque. And now—yes. . . . In most of the big cities, they're building mosques now. . . . Well, there have always been a small amount. But sometimes I have the feeling that [it] is getting beyond us (*dass das übergreift*) and that—that they try, by force, to increase that amount. That it's no longer 0.2 percent but 20 [percent], something like that.

And how do they do that, by force?
Well, by building everywhere, wherever they have a little community, they build a great big mosque!

And how will they increase their community by building a mosque?
Well, quite simply, when they're there, and—yes, at that point, when they have the mosque, someone walks past and thinks, "there is another mosque!" And then, the Christians will automatically clash with them. And yes. And like that, they hope others will join them.[47]

The confusion between the problems of the present and the interpretation of the past leads to the definition of Muslims as permanently "foreigners" and "dangerous."[48] When I asked questions about the Jewish genocide, Wolfgang talked about contemporary immigration. His fear of Islam as a religion, associated with the assignation of responsibility for unemployment onto "foreigners," made him believe in the need to close German borders, or more precisely European borders, before sending immigrants back to their countries. This is what Germany should have done with the Jews in the 1930s and 1940s, according to him.

When Wolfgang related the conversations that he has had with his parents, he also emphasized the connections between the Nazi past and contemporary politics.

[The conversations with my parents], it's not always about Hitler, directly, but more generally—that for example [he hesitates] that foreigners are allowed to come in without any regulation. For example, I know through friends, their neighbors are foreigners. And in the space of two years, they have constructed an apartment building, for several families. And things like that. And they don't speak a word of German! And—I don't know, me, that is not possible for me, is it! [Silence.] A German works all his life, to have a little house [annoyed]. And they, they build a whole block of flats in two years![49]

Wolfgang expressed his irritation at the idea that foreigners might benefit from a more advantageous economic situation than his own parents, who have been unemployed for a long time. He was particularly offended by the idea that the state spends money "on foreigners." According to him, this "bad policy" is a direct result of losing World War II. Stricter immigration policy would be impossible in Germany: "otherwise, the whole world war thing would come up again."[50]

Wolfgang is a typical example of the mobilization of a discourse in opposition to the past, which can sometimes take the form of the political discourse of the new East German right. His parents' economic downgrading and unemployment, his own failure at school, which is closing the very doors by which he might "get out," led him to turn to the Nazi past as a solution.

This discourse has the advantage of combining a conception of Germany as "heroic," because "large and militarily strong," with a degree of political provocation that is attractive for adolescents because it verges on being illegal. But the illegitimate or oppositional forms that these discourses on the Nazi past sometimes take can also be accompanied by more mainstream discourses, which closely resemble the teachers' positions, and for some students, can coexist.

At the end of a more or less long and convoluted chain of interdependencies, these perspectives seem to essentially be the result of the family trajectory of the students. Their nostalgia about Nazism as a political regime that eradicated unemployment is clearly not unrelated to their parents' unemployment. Their denunciation of political and economic instability and their nostalgia for a clear order seems objectively linked to endlessly moving and the highly problematic (at this age) construction of a coherent and well-structured vision of the self. The improvisation of adolescents' constructions of the self and their appropriations of the Nazi past are thus essentially explained by their family relations. For these boys, it is more specifically their relations with their fathers and grandfathers that structure their appropriations. Moreover, these are articulated with strategies that allow the adolescents to situate themselves within a family line (maternal or paternal) in which they can construct a positive vision of the group from which they descend. Yet these examples also illustrate the permanent interaction of these groups of primary belonging, here the family with peer groups. Adolescent peer groups and friends indeed provide the other frame of reference (with or against, in relation to, in extension of, or in opposition to the family) that allow for positive self-esteem based on these positions. The interconnectedness of these different spaces of reference, the family and peer group, structure the processes by which the Nazi past is appropriated within a larger process of self-construction.

The importance of family trajectories explains the differences in perspectives according to the social situation of the students, but also the difference between the students in Hamburg and those in Leipzig. We will now explore this in more detail in the second part of the chapter. What are the illegitimate perspectives of students who are socially and academically privileged? What are the strategies for the appropriation of the Nazi past, taking positions, and constructing a self-image, that are specific to them?

Cultural Capital, Academic Claims, and "Anti-system" Positions: Differences between Leipzig and Hamburg

Let us now look at how oppositional appropriations of the Nazi past function at the other end of the social hierarchy. Indeed, political critique and

202 • When Will We Talk about Hitler?

anti-school positions are not specific to socially disadvantaged students. However, among students from more socially advantaged backgrounds with more cultural capital, opposition to teachers' discourses does not take the same form as it does for students who are struggling in school. How can we understand these differences? How do students with high cultural and academic capital use these resources to contest teachers' discourses? How do they appropriate the Nazi past and what meanings do they give to it in these contestations? On this side of the social hierarchy, the differences between Hamburg and Leipzig continue to play an important role, which was not the case for the students discussed in the first part of this chapter. How can we understand this specificity?

In the *Gymnasium* schools in Hamburg or in Leipzig, the students did not openly defend Hitler as some in the *Mittelschule* or the *Gesamtschule* did. A student's overt engagement with the extreme right is so rare in this environment that it is remembered long afterwards (the students involved having been expelled from the school), as we can see in this anecdote from *Gymnasium* Weinberg in Hamburg.

Extract from Interview with a Teacher from *Gymnasium* Weinberg

13 February 2003
[After a question on neo-Nazism in Weinberg, Mr Schulze, who had previously said "that doesn't exist here," told me this anecdote.]
In 1986, we had an incident (*Affaire*), here at school. There was a new student, who had changed schools and who arrived here in eleventh grade. Shortly afterward, it turned out that he was part of an extreme-right organization, the FAP [*Freiheitliche Arbeiterpartei*, Free German Workers' Party]. This party used lots of Nazi symbolism. The student appeared wearing boots and dressed in leather. But, otherwise, not much else . . . And then, one day, when he was already quite sure of himself, he came into the cafeteria in a leather jacket, with an emblem on the shoulder. It was nothing less than the former symbol of the Hitler Youth, with the arrow and—not exactly a swastika, but black, white, and red. And on that day, I was there, in the cafeteria with Mr M. who said, when he saw it, "If you don't do something right now as the principal, I'm leaving the school tomorrow." It reminded him of his youth—he was called up to fight when he was eighteen. I hadn't even noticed. I went up to him and said, "What's that you have there?" He said, "Yeah, it's the expression of my attachment to my homeland (*Heimatverbundenheit*)." There was *Gau Hansa* written on it. I said, "Did you know that this is the original symbol of the Hitler Youth?" "No, that's not possible!" I said, "I'm a history teacher, I have books, I can show you it, it's exactly the same." He started to have some doubts

[about how to react]. Of course he knew. And then, he asked me, even though he knew, if I was the principal. I [said,] "You have to take it off right now." [He said,] "Is that an order (*Befehl*)?" I said, "Yes." I hesitated (*geschluckt*), first, I had only been principal for five years, and I had never had to [he raises his voice, ironic and amused] to give an order to anybody. Never had anyone asked me what I "ordered" so to speak, and it has never happened since. I said, "Yes, that's an order." [And he added, a little ironically, toward me,] I did my service at the Bundeswehr, I know what an order is [he smiles]. And, well, to my surprise, he took off his jacket and removed the emblem and put it in his pocket. For him, it was over. He just wanted to know if it was an order.

This student was eventually expelled after his involvement in violence against "antifascist" students and after having made antisemitic comments in the schoolyard.[51] This anecdote was told to me by all of the teachers at Weinberg twenty years after the incident, as though it happened yesterday. They insisted that "there has never been anything like it since." At the *Gymnasium* Monnet in Leipzig, the situation was much the same. The teachers also remembered an anecdote involving "neo-Nazi" students that happened in the early 1990s. "There aren't any more of them here now," they said. Indeed, the students of the two *Gymnasiums* did not tend to openly refer to the Nazi past in positive terms, which makes these "events" all the more exceptional when they do happen.

On the other hand, history classes on Nazism were challenged by students in different ways. Some of the themes evoked in the first part of this chapter were observed: the question of national pride, for example, was equally central for these *Gymnasium* students, both in Hamburg and in Leipzig, although they expressed it differently on either side of the former border. Finally, among the students with high levels of academic and cultural capital, we also observe criticisms of public policy, but these tended to be based on civics rather than economics.

"German Guilt" and "National Pride"

The differences between the students at the *Gymnasium* in Hamburg and those in Leipzig are linked to the different school requirements on either side of the former border. Although the official curriculum is similar, there are differences between these schools, which are particularly explicit concerning the way the teachers present the past and the role that they would like it to play in the everyday life of their students. To analyze the position of the students, it is therefore necessary to take into account the position of their teachers, who represent one of the frames through which the students appropriate the past.

We have seen (in chapter 2) that the question of the "responsibility" of future generations is intermingled with the question of past generations' "guilt." This was one of the subjects that was systematically covered in the first minutes of the interviews with the students in Hamburg. The link between teaching the Nazi past at school and a vague feeling of guilt was expressed by all students over age sixteen from upper-middle-class backgrounds. In the next chapter, we will see the reasons that contribute to confining this discourse to the upper echelons of the social scale. For now, let us focus on the East-West differences between Hamburg and Leipzig.

In talking about his visit to a concentration camp, Karl, who is the son of a doctor and a high school teacher, said, "As a German, you don't feel very good, well, me, I didn't feel very good. . . . You still feel guilty, even if really (*eigentlich*) we didn't have anything to do with that. You still feel ashamed, a bit."[52]

We have seen that throughout the interviews, other students also repeated "it's not my fault," "I shouldn't have to feel ashamed," "I have nothing to do with all that," "I'm not guilty, I don't feel guilty." This strongly suggests that they struggle with a feeling of guilt, although their words express the opposite. These students thus develop a very aggressive and defensive discourse, as though they felt they were being attacked. They spoke to me of their experiences overseas (in England, France, Italy, Spain, and Poland), which particularly affected them. As soon as they were identified as Germans, the jokes began, often ending in the classical insults, such as "Nazi" or the *Heil Hitler* salute. It is also because the students felt a kind of confused guilt that they were particularly sensitive about these remarks, which brought up their own doubts.

However, the students in Leipzig did not talk about feeling attacked in their travels overseas, nor about their feelings of guilt. An initial explanation for this could come from the "official" antifascist discourse of the GDR, which established the "external guilt" of capitalism, at the same time providing self-justification for the GDR and its inhabitants as the inheritors of the Communist resistance. However, several studies have shown the very limited influence of this "official" discourse in terms of family appropriations of the past, both during the GDR (Eschebach 1997; Niethammer, Plato, and Wierling 1991) and even more after reunification (Wierling 1999). It seems that the discourses on "national belonging" are not quite the same on either side of the former wall. We might wonder to what extent the definition of the nation in terms of "class" rather than in terms of "ethnicity" complexifies the connection between "national pride" and the shameful Nazi past.

Indeed, the students in Leipzig seemed to be just as "proud" to be German as their teachers were. Although teachers in Hamburg actively struggled against patriotic sentiment among the students, teachers in Leipzig considered such feelings to be "normal," even necessary. Mr Wolff, a teacher in his forties, said this:

And for me, the result [of teaching about Nazism] must be, I still think [he hesitates] is, for me I call it a little like, a liberation (*Befreiung*) for my students. But it isn't the right word. The result has to be that—I always do it a little provocatively. I write it on the board: "I am proud to be German." And for me, at the end, that the result has to be yes, we can be. This generation.[53]

The position of his colleagues in Hamburg was almost diametrically opposite. Mr Stein, a teacher in his fifties, said:

That would be good—I would be happy that a student learns that it's not because you're born in an ethnic group that everything that group does is good and must be defended. But they come to me and say, "I'm Turkish, Mr Stein, you have to understand!" And I say to them, "No! Being Turkish doesn't make me understand anything! A critical person can still think about whether everything that the Turks do is good!" "Yes, but you, you are proud too, to come from Germany, to be German!" [He speaks quickly] and when I tell them "not at all," there is a deathly silence. For several seconds. "Really not?" [The students ask.] "No, really not. I was born here, I have a passport, and my father, if he had been born a little later, he would have been a citizen of the GDR. And my mother is Austrian. But they were born in the German Reich (*Großdeutsche Reich*) and I don't know what I could be proud of! You can be proud when you run a hundred meters really quickly and you trained for it. [He smiles] Or when you pass your exam, you can be proud. But otherwise, there's no reason" [he lowers his voice].[54]

For teachers in Hamburg, national pride is inconceivable. Individualist reasoning trumps "collective pride." "I don't see what we can be proud of" is the negation of all rational and emotional foundations of patriotism, a feeling that the teachers consider as "blameworthy," "dangerous," and something they despise. For Mr Stein, patriotism is the first step toward racism, particularly "dangerous for the poor, who do not have a very pleasant life," who have nothing other than national pride to feed their self-esteem.

On this point, the teachers in Hamburg are quite different from their colleagues in Leipzig. For both Ms Norte and Ms Weinecke, national pride is happily self-evident.

Being proud or not proud, was that an issue?
No—because we were proud! Of course, we were proud! There were no questions to ask ourselves! [She laughs a lot, and continues to laugh while speaking.] Yes, but staying true to certain things, that were defined [by the state].

And what were they, these things?
Well, me, yes, I was proud to wear the blue scarf, for example [she bursts out laughing, short, but very happy] and also of the Freie Deutsche Jugend (FDJ),[55] and all that—and globally, of everything socialism achieved (*Errungenschaften*)!

A teacher, Ms Weinecke, walked by and overheard the last phrase and added, before continuing on her way, "and the party days (*Parteitage*)!" [The three of us laugh.] Ms Norte continues.

Yes! And the construction of social housing! Yes! [She continues to laugh until she was wiping away tears, and says ironically] and the main objective: the unity of economic and social policy! [She is still laughing.] See, some of it is still there . . . [lots of laughter].

And today, how do you see that? With pride?
I think so, yes. [She continues to laugh softly.] Yes, there are lots of things Germans can be proud of. Like there are lots of things, in other countries, that other people can be proud of.[56]

For Ms Norte, pride means above all pride in socialism, that of the ex-GDR. Even though the teachers speak ironically, making fun of their own pride in the past, this is nevertheless a genuine feeling, which is not unambiguous. They have preserved this feeling of pride in belonging to a country and consider that feeling legitimate. They see this pride as being opposed to a feeling of guilt, associated with the FRG and crystallized in the action of German Chancellor Willy Brandt, who knelt in homage to the uprising in the Jewish ghetto in Warsaw in 1970.

The country is beautiful. We have beautiful buildings, which represent traditions, about which we may disagree, but we must make do. I think that we have a lot of good people—researchers, writers, and who knows what else! The classical age, for example, Weimar, and Leipzig, the city of books, the Book Fair, there are so many things—why would we not be proud! Everyone else is proud of their country. Why not Germany? And, of course, as I already said, some things need to be seen in a positive light. And being aware, obviously [of the past]. But I don't think that we need to permanently kneel down (*dass man noch ständig diesen Kniefall machen sollte*).

Kneel?
Kneel. Willy's kneeling (*Kniefall*). No, that was quite ok, really, but—not all Germans are automatically fascists! Not at all![57]

The students at the *Gymnasium* in Leipzig agreed with their teachers. National pride is not a "problem" in these interviews, unlike those conducted in Hamburg. It is not even a subject of conversation, except in the rare cases where I explicitly ask the question.

Memory policy on the Nazi past in the FRG is crystallized around repentance, expressed in Chancellor Willy Brandt's gesture. Indeed, nearly all the teachers in Hamburg I spoke to mentioned this as a positive reference. The need to apologize, which is essential for this generation, appears less urgent for their students, who feel that Germany has "atoned" for its past and who seem to feel a sense of guilt that they cannot clearly understand themselves. Magdalena, an eighteen-year-old student at the *Gymnasium* in Hamburg, said that sometimes she envies her boyfriend whose grandfather is Turkish and who therefore has the right to say, "me, I'm allowed to be proud to be German. Because I'm Turkish." The inability to express patriotism is therefore socially and territorially situated. It contributes to the expression of criticism toward academic teaching, but also toward the politico-economic system of the FRG.

What Past for What Present? Support for and Challenges to the FRG

In certain areas, the differences between the ex-GDR and the ex-FRG have more powerful effects for those in the higher levels of the social hierarchy. The feeling of ongoing economic and cultural privileges, along with professional and social security, are specific to the upper classes of the former FRG. Although the generation of parents and teachers in the ex-GDR, including the most privileged, experienced a very significant political and personal upheaval in the middle of their lives, with the end of the GDR and reunification (for better or worse), the most privileged populations in the former FRG enjoyed economic and professional success that was not disturbed by the change in regime. This is particularly true for public servants, who as we have seen make up a large percentage of the parents in both of these *Gymnasien* schools. The children of the upper classes of the former FRG, born in the 1980s, are therefore different in terms of their life experience from all the other adolescents because of their additional economic political and personal security. To use the expression of one student, they had a childhood and an adolescence that was particularly "sheltered" (*behütet*). Although their parents perhaps experienced the doubts and fears of the previous generation (their grandparents, who experienced the war, and the hunger and fear of the postwar period), these students rely on their experience of the security associated with the economic growth that ensured the upward social trajectory of their parents.

However, reunification had a destabilizing effect on the GDR, including for the more privileged classes. It overturned the social hierarchy and job security—including for public servants—and led to a complete inversion of social values, which made them more uncertain, more unstable, and more

208 • When Will We Talk about Hitler?

fragile. Students in the former GDR, born between 1988 in 1989, began their lives in an atmosphere of political insecurity and an uncertain future, which weighed heavily on their parents. This feeling of insecurity had demographic effects, the birthrate dropped dramatically from 1989–1990 in the ex-GDR territory, which meant that at the time of the study high schools were being closed. It was only toward the end of the 1990s that the birthrate returned to the level it was before the 1980s.

The role of this differential experience of economic, professional, and affective security/insecurity among the most privileged populations of the ex-FRG and ex-GDR is at the heart of this section of this chapter. This difference in experiences is expressed through a different attitude toward the politico-economic system and toward peace.

The Politico-economic System

The different socialization of teachers in Hamburg and Leipzig is based on contrasting attitudes to the politico-economic system. These differences constitute the framework in relation to which the students position themselves. For teachers in Hamburg, "democracy" remains a fragile system, something that must be protected at all costs against the threat of fascism, totalitarianism, or against the political positions of individuals. Most often teachers in Leipzig experienced the shift toward a pluralist regime as something that was imposed upon them from the outside, although some celebrated the end of the Communist regime. Their relationship with the state that is their employer is therefore more ambiguous, marked more by discontinuity than continuity. This leads to a deep generational difference between teachers and students in Hamburg, which is much less pronounced in Leipzig.

In Hamburg, the students opposed their teachers' political pessimism. Indeed, nearly all of the students over sixteen that were interviewed in the *Gymnasium* in Hamburg considered the political regime to be very stable. Even those who were more critical of the "capitalist" and "parliamentary" system did not envisage any change. Parliamentary democracy and the liberal economic system were considered the only politically viable system, by almost all students. Hence the total absence of concrete fear regarding a return to dictatorship. René, aged eighteen, expressed it like this:

No, I don't think that—[he hesitates] that that would be possible [a return to Nazism] no. It's there, it's embedded, Nazi thought, it's clear that it exists—but I don't think that it would be possible. First, because young people, for example—or even also [he hesitates] even the older people, even the ninety-year-olds, who were there, I don't think that they would want that again (*dass die nicht noch mal Lust drauf hätten*). No![58]

The Nazi Past as an Everyday Resource for Adolescents • 209

For the students in Hamburg, fascism seems marginalized in Germany, and a return to dictatorship is considered unimaginable. Faith in the system runs deep among the students whose parents occupy social positions that are both economically and professionally stable, and most of whom have been public servants for more than a generation. Both of René's parents are high school teachers, and he grew up in a context of job security and an economically carefree situation. This has been the norm in his maternal family for several generations. His maternal grandfather (born in the early 1920s) was a public servant in the Ministry for Transport; his maternal grandmother (born in 1925) was a nurse before working as an employee in a social security company. His paternal grandfather (1923) studied to be an engineer before becoming an airline pilot; his paternal grandmother (born in 1920) worked in a bank.

However, the students I interviewed in Leipzig (like their teachers) had a much more ambiguous relationship with the current regime, and their challenges to it may have been partly based in a degree of valorization of the GDR regime. This is particularly visible within the parents' and teachers' generation; the first "FDJ" generation, born in the early 1950s (Wierling 1999, 2000, 2002). We also see this argument in comments made by Mark, the son of two journalists and a student at *Gymnasium* Monnet in Leipzig.

Those who went to school in the GDR, they learned very different things. And some things stay. You see, West German citizens didn't exactly learn the same things at school as a citizen in the GDR. It's obvious. They read Marx and Engels, and so they have a different vision of the world. They are—I think that East Germans see the world as it is today with much more critical eyes because they still have all these extreme-left opinions in their heads, because they were obliged to learn them. . . . I see, for example, my parents, particularly my father, they see all that very critically. It's not nostalgic, like he says he wants to go back to the GDR, but—even for me—it's the same. When you've known all that [the history of the GDR and socialist readings], you see our current state as a capitalist country, very critically. And because I'm very interested in the GDR, and I read the books that they read then—and not just about the GDR as the Stasi state—but also about the ideas that they were trying to achieve. And when I look at that, I realize quite a lot of things. . . . Capitalism's hostility toward people was criticized [in the GDR]. And capitalism is sort of cold, and impersonal, particularly in Germany. Everything is bureaucratic, here. The way people are treated, very impersonally. For example, the unemployed, at the unemployment office (*Arbeitsamt*). They're treated like things. And that, I think, that the East Germans are very critical of it. Especially because they are struggling more than the West Germans. In terms of unemployment and things like that. Because these *Länder* are poorer. Yes.[59]

The experience of another political, economic, but also ideological system, based on a different system of reference and explanation of the world, opens up the field of possibilities in terms of political imagination. As a result, it facilitates the development of critical positions for the generation of these students' teachers and parents. The students themselves, although they were born at the moment of reunification, have nevertheless inherited this experience of political upheaval, which marked their very early socialization. Mark's position is therefore not unrelated to his parents' support for the Communist regime, in particular his father's. Moreover, reunification presented a significant biographical turning point for this young man, and for his parents, who divorced in 1989 and lost their jobs shortly afterwards. Mark grew up with his mother's new husband, who is also a journalist, and who also became unemployed after reunification. Mark's three parents found work in journalism or communication, but his father's social trajectory was once again seriously thrown into question at the end of the 1990s. He was accused of spying on his army comrades during his military service in the GDR and working with the Stasi.[60] He was threatened with dismissal from his job as a journalist on a public radio station. Thus, in spite of the high cultural capital of the family, economic and political insecurity has affected Mark's parents several times since reunification. The comparison of their situation before and after reunification is a frequent topic of family discussions. The capitalist system therefore appeared to Mark to be one possible system among others. Considering the GDR past as a real political alternative to capitalism minimizes the importance of the Nazi past in his discourse, replaced by the past of the GDR as the reference and basis for his political reasoning and his criticisms of the current reunified German political regime. The fact that students in Leipzig accorded less interest to the Nazi past explains why they differed from students in Hamburg concerning the themes of guilt and responsibility. Their questions around their immediate past—and the political and economic positions of their parents—erase or perhaps submerge questions on the past that came before it.

However, almost all the students in the *Gymnasium* in Hamburg demonstrated an inability to think in opposition to the system and a very profound integration of the values of their pluralist regime. René expressed this in terms that were very close to those of his teachers: "We are against [he hesitates] against extremes. We're not as open to extremes [as before]."[61]

René himself explained the lack of success of "political extremes" in Germany (as can be seen, among other things, by their lack of political representation, at least in the older *Länder*[62]) as being due to a generational effect and, more specifically in his case, the political position and history transmitted to him by his parents.

I think that for young people that is the case [they are no longer that extreme] but I think that our parents showed us the way, those who are fifty—who went through [19]68. They're the ones who [he hesitates], yes, well, I dunno so much about that, the history of the [19]68 movement, but I know that through my parents' stories—that—[he hesitates] well that there was—[he breaks off, starts again]. In theory, the movement was not really constructed around the "anti-right" slogan or something like that, but it was more against authority, I think. That's what it was, really. [He pauses to think.] Yes, and that the—that people became very reticent about authority, against a strong authority, I think, because—you didn't really want to be governed, because in particular in Germany, you knew the consequences, when someone has so much power.[63]

For René, what his parents fought against, both in terms of representations (belief in authority) and in terms of power mechanisms (authoritarian hierarchies at university, at school, etc.) has disappeared. As a result, abuse of power no longer represents an immediate danger. His optimistic belief in the political vigilance of the German people and his support for the system can also be seen in the discourse of nearly all of his classmates. Moreover, the way these students spoke about Nazism is very close to the comments of their teachers. Johannes, for example, an eighteen-year-old student at the *Gymnasium* in Hamburg, the son of a doctor and a high school teacher, said this:

> That's the most important thing. That we don't forget, but that we are against— that we're a bit skeptical about extremist movements. And we should make the most [of the lessons of the past] so as to be not only open to other people and other cultures, but also more friendly (*freundlicher*) with them. We should treat the foreigners who are here normally. We should work toward [equality], so there's no more discrimination toward anyone.[64]

Johannes seems to have thus internalized two major lessons (tolerance and critical thinking) promoted by the school. However, like most of his classmates over sixteen, he considered them self-evident in the FRG of the early twenty-first century.

In Leipzig, the past of the GDR has been transformed into a resource used to position oneself in a family group, a peer group, or in relation to one's history teacher. It is used to criticize reunified Germany, and can serve to promote the current political regime. This is how Michael used the Nazi past. He was one of Mark's classmates and the son of an actor and a dental assistant. He used the Nazi past to discredit the past of the GDR, in a discourse about the political instability of democracy, which involves an attitude toward the Nazi past that is close to the teachers in Hamburg, but which he is sometimes obliged to defend against his own teachers in Leipzig.

> Last Friday, in social science class (*Gemeinschaftskunde*), my teacher wanted to convince me that we can't compare the GDR regime with Nazism. That it

was much better, and ultimately, it was a democracy! But—I find that terrifying, because—for me, a democracy is not defined by the fact that I imprison all the opposition and I don't have freedom of the press, and things like that! And then, she said, "there was an opposition, the National Front." And then I said, "There were FDJ [Communist Party Youth] leaders in it. They were all just associations that were really run by the SED. And there weren't elections at all! Ninety-five percent—that's completely unrealistic as an electoral result!"[65]

We can see that for the students in Leipzig, their attitude toward the political regime of reunified Germany is much more influenced by their interpretation of the GDR regime, than by that of Nazism, which is a compliment to the former. Michael considered the new regime to be fragile: "We cannot make stable democracies, others had to do it for us, both in 1945 and in 1989." His grandparents' positive attitudes toward the Nazi past, along with some of his teachers' and his grandmothers' praise for the GDR constituted a challenge to the political and economic regime of the FRG, which contributed to Michael's impression of its instability. However, his father, a performance artist, suffered from the lack of freedom of expression imposed by the SED. For him, reunification was a genuine "liberation," which might potentially explain his son's enthusiastic attachment to the new regime. We have already seen to what extent Michael's family history has been marked by internal political and social oppositions.[66] This discontinuity may have contributed to his search for political stability.

Civil Peace

In Leipzig, the presence of neo-Nazis is considered tangibly dangerous due to the annual extreme-right demonstrations at the *Völkerschlachtdenkmal*,[67] and their parallel "counter-demonstrations." Some students at the *Gymnasium* Monnet participate directly in these demonstrations, but for many the debates around this issue are salient even if they are not politically active themselves. Students in Leipzig tend to express a physical fear associated with demonstrations and mention the violence that they have experienced, a feeling that is entirely absent from the interviews in Hamburg. This was the case for Else, whose parents are both teachers.

Have you been to any counter-demonstrations?
No, it frightens me (*mich schreckt das ab*). A long time ago, two years ago, there were guys in school, who were ostentatiously walking around with stickers saying "anti-Nazi." And the others, with their boots and their jackets. And their haircuts. And when they confronted each other—yes, it was two years ago, during the big demonstrations, with the water cannons and all that. And I heard what happened! And when there are demonstrations, I

The Nazi Past as an Everyday Resource for Adolescents • 213

don't go outside, on principle. You never know. Before, they used to say, "or maybe a bullet" (*Oder Kugel, sagte man früher*). [Today] it's not so bad, I mean something could happen to us anywhere. But I avoid that kind of demonstration.[68]

For the students in Leipzig, it is possible to envisage the civil peace being threatened, possibly because this experience exists in their family histories. Fear of state repression through violence is present in many of the interviews with the teachers, when they talk about the "Monday demonstrations" in Leipzig that preceded the fall of the Berlin Wall, for example. Fear of imprisonment or even armed intervention was very present in their minds—hence Else's use of the expression "or else a bullet." The experience of having been subject to a regime change is all the more violent for her parents because they are both public servants (secondary school teachers) attached to the current regime. Her maternal grandparents, born in the 1930s, were also secondary school teachers in the GDR. Her paternal grandfather, born in 1930 in Leipzig, was a lawyer. The generation of Else's grandparents lived through the war as children and adolescents. The GDR provided them with an upward social trajectory and job security, which were thrown into question for Else's parents during reunification. In her research on this subject, Dorothee Wierling observed a fear of war in the generation born around 1950 (the generation of the parents and teachers of the students), which she attributes, among other things, to the memories of the war, but also to the presence of the ruins of war in the urban environment (which lasted longer in the GDR than in the FRG) (Wierling 1999).

However, civil peace is taken for granted by students in Hamburg, which sets them apart from their parents and grandparents and their teachers. Moreover, in *Gymnasium* Weinberg, students have almost no contact with neo-Nazism. This also contributes to their feeling of political security. Benjamin, aged eighteen, the son of a radio director and a primary school teacher, was very sociologically astute in his analysis of the fact that he did not meet anyone who actually defended "anti-system" political opinions and particularly extreme-right opinions.

This is a phenomenon that has to also be explained by education. And I think that—apart from working at McDonald's—I must say that I find myself in a fairly elite environment—well, that's perhaps not the right expression—but I have grown up in an environment with a very high level of education and in which people think a lot. That is not the case everywhere! And I think that's why when you grow up, like, here in Weinberg, sheltered and well educated, we don't have contact with people like that in private, until we enter professional life. And that's the reason why I can't name an example, where I could say: here, I met some people who thought that [Nazism] was cool or something like that. Because, I simply have no contact with people like that. Apart from at work [at McDonald's].[69]

Benjamin mentioned "education" (*Bildung*), which for him explains his attitude toward the Nazi past but also toward the current political regime. This is a form of intellectual elitism, a way of setting oneself apart from both the lower classes and from the neo-Nazism he associates with them. Although he works at McDonald's to make some pocket money, Benjamin is condescending of his workmates who spend their lives there through economic obligation and who do not obtain the education required (according to him) to avoid falling prey to nationalist temptations. But this elitist vision of the past and of society also genuinely protects him from the fear of the collapse of the politico-economic system. His little world is indeed "sheltered," protected from all political, economic, and/or ideological threats.

Play and Provocation: Challenges from within School Discourse

The politico-economic security that the students experience does not prevent some of them from expressing political critiques of the "capitalist system," however. Benjamin, for example, was the "best student" in Ms Heide's final year advanced history class at the *Gymnasium* in Hamburg. Appropriations of the Nazi past, political critique, and historical learning all overlap in this young man's constructions of his political vision.

An adolescent "punk," Benjamin first became interested in politics around age fourteen, through challenges to the political regime, but also in opposition to the neo-Nazi movement. At age eighteen, he had maintained his critical perspective of the system. "I find the system today—well, ok, it works, but ultimately—personally I think that recently, it is not social enough anymore. We don't take those who live in more disadvantaged conditions than our own enough into account! And that's a shame!"[70]

He was not satisfied with his former position however, which he describes as simply "negative" at the time of the study and based in the simple refusal of the system, accompanied by a focus on Nazism, the single historical reference "to avoid." This is why he expressed a certain "weariness" about a theme that is no longer the basis for a political alternative.

Benjamin slowly and progressively constructed a "positive," even "utopic" vision of politics, an ideal. From there came the progressive replacement of Nazism by the Weimar regime, as his reference, defined not as the "prelude" to the "Third Reich" (as often is the case in history classes), but as an alternative attempt at "democracy" or "socialism."

The event that had the most impact on me, and which I became the most interested in, is in principle the—the revolution of 1918–1919 in Germany. I found that really fascinating, and I could also identify with it.

Identify, how do you mean?
Yes, well I think that [he hesitates] that idea, after the collapse of the *Kaiserreich* during the war, to [construct] something radically democratic, and not like today, but with really socialist tendencies, I find that really interesting. And it's a shame that it didn't work. Because I think that socialism deserved a chance.

And that's what Weimar is for you?
Yes, in particular at the beginning. There were the same ideals behind it, that I would have in terms of politics.[71]

Benjamin expressed his desire to "identify" with history. He was not interested in the past for the past, but sought to appropriate it in order to reposition himself in the present, within his peer group, in relation to his teachers and parents. He also sought to construct an interesting personality, a positive image of himself in different spheres. Benjamin's strategy was very close to that of the students in the *Mittelschule* who were mentioned in the first part of the chapter. However, unlike them, Benjamin was never positive about Nazism. Indeed, if he appropriated the Nazi past in a positive way, he would have been in grave danger of losing his good grades. Students discussed in the first section of this chapter because they had neither good grades nor a good reputation at school, did not consider these factors as having a potential influence on their behavior in school or their interpretation of Nazism. However, these different appropriations of history and the strategies implemented have the same function: they defend a position in a given configuration of power.

Constructing Weimar as a political alternative means abandoning a historical reading in which Nazism becomes a "prism" through which all political references are to be seen (to paraphrase an expression of Jürgen Habermas in reference to culture rather than politics), and in this way separate the study of the Weimar Republic from Nazism. For Benjamin, his interest in Weimar crystallizes the way in which he expressed his desire to construct a political utopia, but also to construct a persona for himself. At school, he used this to set himself apart—while still accepting the political regime as it is—both from his teachers ("conservative") and from his classmates ("mostly ignorant antifascists") in order to adopt a position as both a "rebel" and the "best student." At home, he tried to set himself apart from his parents and brothers in order to break out of his sheltered family environment. His "political difference"—which he expressed through physical difference (his multicolored hair)—allowed him to create a persona, to challenge without completely rejecting. He worked at McDonald's, but at the same time he criticized "the capitalism of the FRG."

Benjamin's transgression remains constrained. He was careful not to cross the boundaries of what is considered academically legitimate, which could threaten his good grades. He is a "punk," but he is still "the best student," and his interest in Weimar allows him to bring these two together. His emphasis on the beginning of the Weimar Republic, his study of the years 1918–1919, and in particular the role of the soldiers' and workers' revolutionary councils (*Räte*) are symptomatic of this ambivalent position.

> I find the collective aspect (*gemeinschaftlich*) really very important. The eco-nomic reforms too. We should take a little bit of power away from the multi-national companies and big business, too. I think that's important. And then, in general I lean toward left-wing opinions. And—the more we give power to the people, the better it works, the state. It is important to give people the impression that they're important as citizens. And that we give them the impression that their services are essential. And that it's not only every four years you vote, and then us, we do the rest. I think that's very important.
>
> *And you had the impression that Weimar . . .*
> [He interrupts me] Yes, I have the impression that their ideas, at the begin-ning, were going in that direction. With the soldiers' and workers' councils and all that. And that representatives could be called back at any time, with this system of councils, that's essential, I think. So, it's not, he has a mandate for four years, and afterwards we'll see if he did well or not and whether we vote for him again. But that there is a permanent exchange between represen-tatives and their electorate![72]

By criticizing the political system without entirely rejecting it, he remains within the rules of the political field but also within the rules laid out by the teachers. This allows him to mobilize historical references to justify a politi-cal opinion, but also to criticize the system in a way that remains acceptable to teachers. Benjamin's strategy means he can construct his own historical world. He is quite successful at it; he manages to become "the best student," while rebelling against the political system. In so doing, he avoids the vision of his parents and teachers focused on Nazism, and reinvents his own twofold opposition: he is hostile to Nazism and authoritarianism, but he is especially against capitalism and the FRG, which is "not egalitarian and collective enough" in his opinion. He also manages to express this without mentioning the GDR in his historical vision, which is a reference too ambiguous to be useful to him in the academic environment of Hamburg.

Students from the most privileged social backgrounds in Hamburg there-fore differ from their counterparts in Leipzig in the ways in which they subscribe to the political system and the links that they create with the Nazi past. Although the students in Hamburg consider Nazism as part of the past, the students in Leipzig (who are in more direct contact with neo-Nazi demonstrations and more inclined to consider political systems other than pluralism as possibilities) use the Nazi past to better define their fears about the present, and thus echo their teachers. This difference does not prevent the students in Hamburg from integrating the major lessons to be learned from the Nazi past: "tolerance" and "critical thinking." Unlike the teachers and their fellows in Leipzig, however, they seek these lessons more through the mobilization of pasts other than Nazism or the GDR, which both remain present in the discourses of the students in Leipzig. Nazism therefore loses its status as the unique and primordial historical reference for students from privileged backgrounds in Hamburg. It is replaced by periods prior to 1933. However, for the students in Leipzig, the past of the GDR remains in close interaction and even overlaps the Nazi past. This process of negotiating and appropriating different perspectives on German history, including the Third Reich, the GDR, and the FRG, interact intricately with the students' own critiques of the present politico-economic system.

The Social Frameworks of Political Uses of the Past

A student must have information and resources in order to be able to construct "alternative discourses" to those provided in the school environment or to give his or her own meaning to the past, whether at school or in everyday life. These appropriations are constructed differently depending on the social origin and resources—cultural, academic, family, economic—that the students have at their disposal. These resources constitute social frameworks that articulate the appropriations of the Nazi past. But it is also the academic and family configurations of these appropriations that influence the way the students use the Nazi past, the ways in which they transform it into a resource (political and critical), but also in order to position themselves in relation to their family, their school, their peers, and the political world. For and/or against their teachers, for and/or against their parents, to affirm and to construct an image of themselves.

This book is methodologically based on a multitude of comparisons: East-West, economic status, academic levels, social environments and territories. The results underline the fact that the uses of the Nazi past do not occur in a social vacuum. Social conditions and concrete family configurations combine and articulate the appropriations of the past. For a sociologist it comes as no surprise (yet is frequently neglected in current research) that coming from a family of history teachers, a family of migrant workers, or a family of now unemployed former SED leaders, has a resounding impact on the forms that the appropriation of this past will take. Yet in order to understand how the students use the Nazi past, it is also essential to take into account the configurations that enable them to give meaning to the Nazi past in their everyday lives. The resources that allow them to position themselves within the school environment influence the ways in which they mobilize the Nazi past and the discourses that they construct around it. It is thus the complex interaction of school, family, and peer groups that result in appropriations of the Nazi past that make sense in the everyday lives of the students.

Attitudes toward history, to the past (both in the school and the family), but also toward politics, are therefore constructed both outside of and prior to history teaching at school. This is even more the case for the more politicized families. Whether they are right-wing or left-wing, pro- or anti-system, the family environment and the peer group provide the frameworks for the construction of political affiliation. The school, in bringing young people from different backgrounds and political opinions together, only has an indirect impact on the mechanisms by which attitudes toward the past (legitimate or not) are appropriated. This however, also provides additional elements that contribute to the construction of discourses around the past, in particular in terms of knowledge. It can also encourage students who are not used to being interested in politics, to acquire a taste for it.

In all the students' strategies for appropriating the Nazi past there is an element of playfulness. Playing with the Nazi past is thus a way for the students to challenge the school rules, but also a more serious way to affirm a sense of self within their environment and to construct their personality. Caught between enjoyment and vital issues (economic, political, personal), the forms of appropriation of the Nazi past are only one element in the political socialization of these adolescents.

It is the male students who are struggling at school who most easily transgress the school rules surrounding the interpretation of the past, using their appreciation of the Nazi period to criticize the current political regime. Taking fewer statutory risks by transgressing institutional taboos, they therefore transform their status as academic outsiders into a source of prestige among their peers, a classic strategy for outsiders (Elias and Scotson, [1965] 1994). The "good students" will not risk their grades by adopting interpretations of the Nazi past that have no value on the academic market (the denial or the minimization of the Nazi extermination policies, for example), even if such comments may have a certain value in the peer group. They, therefore, find other ways to oppose the academic order without overtly challenging it; pushing limits and setting themselves apart from their classmates, teachers, and parents, while still constructing a personality within the boundaries of what is permitted.

Moreover, girls and young women interviewed here were also less likely to adopt opinions on the Nazi past that would be sanctioned at school. There is both a greater hesitation to express opinions that are radically opposed to the school market and a lack of female peer groups that would validate this kind of appropriation (in the same way the male peer groups validate transgression). This undoubtedly encourages more academically legitimate forms of appropriation among the girls. Indeed, the transgressions we have seen here are also an expression of virility for the boys: by evoking the Nazi past in ways that are considered illegitimate in the school environment, the boys play at being soldiers by proxy, a stance which is less socially valued in a female peer group. We also know that girls tend to be more academically successful in terms of grades, at least until the final high school certificate (Baudelot and Establet 1992). As a result, they have more to lose by transgressing academic norms and less to gain in extra-academic contexts.

Criticizing economic and immigration policy allows students from the *Mittelschule* and the *Gesamtschule* to set themselves apart from their teachers, but also from "immigrants," and to construct an "ideal" image of the republic that would be more "favorable" to them than the republic is today. The civic and academic critiques voiced by students from the *Gymnasien* also provide a double distinction: they thus set themselves apart from the "generation" of their parents and teachers, but also from "those who are not interested in history." There is a social attraction for "history in the name of science," which is perhaps expressed through the interest some students have in Marxism.

Discovering a taste, an interest, or even a passion for history in general and for the Nazi past in particular seems linked to the fact that in-depth knowledge allows students to construct their own image of the past—whether that is in keeping with the vision of parents, teachers, and classmates, or not. Being able to use the Nazi past to develop strategies to integrate it into one's discourses or one's everyday practices requires academic, cultural, and social resources. The strategies that the students implement in practice transform the past into a resource and help them position themselves in relation to it. But the past cannot be a resource for everybody. There are limits as to how it is appropriated. Indeed, some students remain deaf to academic discourses and this will be covered in the next chapter.

Notes

1. These are students who are interested in the Nazi past and who are, on average, rather better informed than their classmates.
2. See the introduction for more information on the notion of *Eigensinn*.
3. By political position I mean a position within the political field that is permanently defined and redefined by the struggles of actors belonging to the field, but also more

broadly by the engagement of a group that participates (through militant action, for example) in the struggle for definition.

4. I have borrowed this term from a neologism systematically used by Emmanuel Wallerstein.

5. The studies on the extreme right have shown a significant gap between the opinions expressed in surveys and the vote itself. There has been significant evolution on this question in the last fifteen years. It has become easier in Europe, and also in Germany, to express extreme right political positions publicly (see preface to the English edition 2019). The gap is thus even stronger here, since the fieldwork was done shortly after the millennium and before the creation of the AfD (Alternative für Deutschland, Alternative for Germany) in Germany, which has contributed to legitimizing extreme-right opinions in the public sphere. The students interviewed in this chapter would now be in their late twenties; it would be interesting to see their political evolution.

6. Meetings with Mr Schulze, principal of the *Gymnasium* in Hamburg, with Mr Bertelsman, English teacher at Wiesi, and with Ms Nieter, principal of the *Mittelschule* in Leipzig.

7. George Smith Patton (1885–1945), US Army General during World War II.

8. Interview of 5 December 2003.

9. Ibid.

10. There are of course limits to this comparison. Here, these are adolescents whose pessimism and mistrust are influenced by failure at school, which is the foundation of their fear of the future (the fear of unemployment is palpable). They could not vote at the time of the interview and will most likely not all vote "extreme right" once they reach voting age.

11 I tried to re-contact Wolfgang in 2008 for follow up research (published in Oeser 2015). Although he did not agree to be interviewed again, I was able to discover that he had moved to the western part of Germany, former FRG, and was in the process of sitting the *Abitur.*

12. Interview on 13 January 2004.

13. Ibid.

14. Ibid.

15. Interview of 25 April 2003.

16. Ibid.

17. Like the expression *kaputt machen*, this is an everyday word. A child who breaks her toy, tells her parents, *kaputt machen*, and asked if it can be fixed, *heile machen.* The expression is also used to tell a child that her minor injury, or boo-boo, will heal quickly. The word also evokes a German nursery rhyme, *heile, heile, Segen* (holy, holy blessing), which is sung to comfort children or to put them to sleep.

18. Interview of 25 April 2003.

19. Ibid.

20. Ibid.

21. Interview of 17 February 2002.

22. Ibid.

23. The origin of docufiction is controversial. A certain number of cinema experts claim that it has existed since the 1920s, and that Robert Flaherty, a US documentary filmmaker is its "spiritual father." Others claim that Flaherty did not make docufictions but rather historical fictions, which did not aspire to be documentaries and therefore differ from docufictions by their clearly fictional nature. In either case, the BBC has made many docufictions since the 1970s.

The Nazi Past as an Everyday Resource for Adolescents • 221

24. Some custodians of historical monuments and concentration camps also criticize Knopp. However, high school teachers appreciate his ability to engage adolescents.

25. Many students say they find the interviews with the eyewitnesses stimulating, for their intensity as well as their emotional impact. "Sometimes they cry, when they talk about that, you can really see that it affects them" (interview with Domenico, 17 February 2002). We can see here the characteristics of the "ordinary reading" and identification processes.

26. In addition to this official authorization, all of the teachers in Hamburg, and nearly a third of those in Leipzig, regularly record these programs and use them in class, whether legally or not. Television is thus a regular part of school teaching without any ministerial control.

27. The overrepresentation of Wagner's music in Knopp's documentaries has also drawn criticism from academic historians. If we observe that Knopp uses common cinematographic techniques to make his documentaries "attractive," criticism from professional historians focuses specifically on the use of these techniques, and particularly the use of emotion in documentaries that aim to be historical or non-fiction.

28. In a press conference in Cologne in June 1988, university professors and historians of the television channel publicly expressed their opposition to Knopp's program. Particularly strong criticism came from historian Ulrich Herbert, who accused the television station of producing "Nazi kitsch." See for example, Thomas Gehringer, "'NS-Kitsch': Fernsehen und Zeitgeschichte, eine Auseinandersetzung," *Tagesspiegel*, 16 June 1998.

29. The interview with Johnny tends to lend support to Kansteiner's argument when he presumes that Knopp "doesn't change opinions" but that his programs will be liked by people from the political far right, who interpret them as reinforcing their political positions (letters from viewers to the television station attest to this). This does not mean, however, that they are appreciated by that audience alone, or that they create extreme right tendencies.

30. Guido Knopp, *Hitlers Krieger, part 1, Rommel-das-Idol.*

31. Interview of 25 April 2003.

32. See, for example, *Spiegel online*, 13 January 2005, "When Harry Met Hitler," http://www.spiegel.de/international/scandal-in-britain-when-harry-met-hitler-a-336667.html (last accessed 4 April 2019).

33. Interview of 13 January 2004.

34. Ibid.

35. Ludwig Erhard (1897–1977) was a liberal FRG politician. He was Minister for the Economy (1949–1963) under the Adenauer government and then Chancellor (1963–1966). He is considered the father of the postwar "German economic miracle."

36. Interview of 14 February 2002.

37. He also situated "Islam" among the "socialist systems," which, in his eyes, explains its opposition to the United States. This categorization also allowed him to simultaneously denigrate "Islamist" foreigners.

38. Interview of 23 February 2003.

39. Ibid.

40. The word *voll* (literally "full") is used as a filling adverb in German, much as it is in some forms of colloquial English. For readability, we have used "bloody" instead, which is more common in different forms of English and which reflects the same tone of conversation.

41. Interview of 23 February 2003.

42. Ibid.

222 • When Will We Talk about Hitler?

43. Ibid.
44. Ibid.
45. Ibid.
46. Ibid.
47. Interview of 27 January 2004.
48. In German, there is a play on words between "stranger" (*Der Fremde*), which is used where in English we would use "foreigner," and the adjective "strange" (*fremd, fremdartig*), which has a double meaning. It is strange in the sense of foreign, as well as strange in the sense of different from others, with a slightly negative connotation. The verb *befremden* (to disconcert or irritate), which comes from the same root, refers to a feeling of irritation in the context of another's "abnormal" behavior, indicating that what is *fremd*—which provokes the reaction of being *befremdet* (annoyed) or the feeling of *Befremden* (negative surprise)—are outside the norm. However, the students much more often use the term *Ausländer* (as opposed to *Inländer*), which refers to a person who is born outside the country, when talking about those who have other nationalities, religions, or languages.
49. Interview of 27 January 2004.
50. Ibid.
51. The student cried "hep, hep, hep" toward a group of students. This is an antisemitic expression from an early nineteenth-century fraternity (*Burschenschaft*) meaning *Jerusalem est perdita*, Jerusalem must be destroyed.
52. Interview of 10 March 2003.
53. Interview of 17 October 2003.
54. Interview of 26 September 2003.
55. The FDJ was the youth organization of the SED (Socialist Unity party).
56. Interview of 2 December 2003.
57. Ibid.
58. Interview of 17 April 2003.
59. Interview of 17 October 2003.
60. The Stasi was the secret police force of the GDR, *Ministerium für Staatssicherheit (MfS)*.
61. Interview of 17 January 2003.
62. The political success of the radical left (PDS, follower of the SED) was geographically limited to the new *Länder*. Moreover, the German communist party (DKP), and the extreme right political parties had relatively little success in terms of political representation in the political landscape of the post-war FRG.
63. Interview of 17 January 2003.
64. Interview of 22 February 2003.
65. Interview of 18 October 2003.
66. For Michael's biography and family history see chapter 2, "Michael, a Militant Strategy."
67. Also known as the Battle of the Nations, this historic monument commemorates Napoleon's defeat near Leipzig in 1813.
68. Interview of 18 April 2003.
69. Ibid.
70. Ibid.
71. Ibid.
72. Ibid.

Chapter 5

THE SOCIAL AND CULTURAL LIMITS TO APPROPRIATIONS OF THE NAZI PAST

We have seen how certain students adapt to their teachers' expectations by identically reproducing[1] legitimate discourses on the Nazi past that combine political and civic content. For other students, however, the processes of appropriating the Nazi past led to mobilizations that either do not fit well in the school context or are even opposed to the school as an institution or to the teacher's discourses, as we saw in the previous chapter. There are certain students who refuse this past altogether, who "don't want to hear about it," who demonstrate their total indifference, or their difficulty in appropriating it. These reactions will be explored in this chapter. It seems important to emphasize that a study of ordinary ways of appropriating this past must necessarily involve the limits to these appropriations. Not everyone wants to (or is able to) appropriate everything, all the time. There are indeed students who do not want to, or who cannot, appropriate academic discourse on the Nazi past. Once again, the purpose here is not to "judge" this non-academic behavior. This chapter will be focused on analyzing the elements that prevent, or which constitute obstacles to, the appropriation of the Nazi past. These obstacles are linked to the students' cultural practices, which differ according to the social origins and cultural capital of the families. We will, therefore, look at ways in which these different dimensions—social origins, cultural practices, and cultural capital—interact to organize students' appropriations and construct the social forms of the limits to ordinary appropriations of the Nazi past. We must also seek to understand under what conditions the Nazi past can—or cannot—have meaning in the everyday lives of adolescents.

Certain students adopt an "anti-school culture," a refusal of everything associated with the school environment. Based on a study of children attending school in a low-income public housing area in a developing industrial region in France, Stéphane Beaud observed a similar phenomenon: "the 'most left behind at school,' those who are unhappy in high school, develop attitudes and express varying degrees of refusal of school. . . . Even within the school institution, there is an inversion of school values, the manifestation of an anti-school culture within the high schools on the edges of the city." (Beaud [2002] 2003: 24). This phenomenon has consequences for the forms of appropriation of this past because the refusal of school can also imply the refusal of what is transmitted at school. However, we must be cautious in attributing this kind of culture exclusively to disadvantaged areas: "anti-school culture" and "anti-intellectualism" can also exist in privileged high schools, although they take different forms. In any case, adopting a discourse of refusal, in its different forms, still seems to require certain resources (for example, the formation of a group that supports such a discourse, formulating and expressing it openly, etc.).

Yet those most "left behind" academically do not necessarily have the resources either inside or outside the school to construct a genuinely "oppositional" or "anti-system" discourse. It is therefore necessary to distinguish between those who have alternative resources and those who do not. The first explicitly refuse the legitimate discourse on the Nazi past; the others simply remain indifferent to it because it has neither meaning nor significance for them.

Students develop different ways of partially or completely resisting the teaching of the Nazi past—from indifference to open refusal, but also including "saturation"—and they express these socially. We will see that the students who are "in substantial academic difficulties" and who lack social and family resources, do not develop the same logics of resistance as the "good students" and those from very affluent social backgrounds.

"Left Behind" in History Class

The students who face "substantial difficulties" at school pose specific methodological problems for the researcher. First, it is very difficult to meet them, particularly in the school context. Gérard Mauger points out that some of those who are "the most intimidated, who are also probably the most disadvantaged, have no other choice than to refuse to participate in the study and to remain 'among themselves'" (1991: 134). However, I was able to convince some of the students to participate by remaining in their class long enough to earn their trust and, with the help of their teachers who suggested

The Social and Cultural Limits to Appropriations of the Nazi Past • 225

that I interview them during class time, these students were allowed to play "truant" without being punished. Of course, these are very particular interview situations, but they are "neither more nor less artificial or unreal than those necessarily produced, by any survey on legitimate culture in a working-class milieu" (Bourdieu [1979] 2010: 84–85). Once they were in front of me, it was also extremely difficult to have the students talk about history, a subject that for them was not interesting and intimidating. They were afraid of "making mistakes" or "saying the wrong thing." On top of "the interviewer's explicit definition of the interview situation as a situation of communication must be superimposed an implicit definition of the situation as a symbolic relation of power" (Mauger 1991: 129). These difficulties, already present in any interview situation in a working-class area, were exacerbated by the fact that I was a PhD student and thus a representative of the university, a world that was inaccessible for most of the students. Moreover, I contacted the students through their history teacher, to interview them inside their school environment,[2] on a subject in which the gap between my knowledge and their knowledge was particularly substantial. I was therefore the representative of the school system, their school, and their history teacher. As a result, the interview situation must be taken into account, in as much detail as possible, in order to analyze the interview as a social situation.

"I Don't Understand What You're Saying!"

The way in which I chose to begin the interviews contains an element of bias. Asking young people and adolescents if there is an event from history that seems particularly important, implies that this question is meaningful to them. It supposes that history has not only academic meaning but also meaning in their lives. Confronted with students who are considered academically "weak," who have not adopted their teachers' reasonings, and whose families sometimes have no link to German history, my question appeared not only inappropriate, but also meaningless and uninteresting. Indeed, several students simply did not understand the question.

You already know that this is about history, about the way the school teaches history. And maybe you could tell me [I hesitate]—*I wanted to talk about—first about German history, but also other histories* [in other countries]. *I'm interested in your personal opinion. What you personally feel. Is there, in German history, an event, a period, a moment that seems to you to be particularly important?*
Umm [he hesitates for a long time]. For example? Can you give me an example?

There's nothing that seems particularly important? When you think it about Germany, German history?

There's nothing that comes to mind. . .

No?
Mmmnnn [negative interjection].

That history—maybe something that's more interesting to you than other things, or something about which you think that—
I don't understand what you mean. What exactly do you want to say?

Well, there are events and periods in history. Is there one event that is more important than the others?
No [he sighs].

There is none.
No.
[Irritated] *and—um—and history in general, is there something that—that . . .*
Tell me what you want. I don't understand what you want![3]

This was the first interview that I conducted with a student at Wiesi. It was only when I formulated the initial prompt, by then well-rehearsed,[4] that I realized that the context had changed and my question had become problematic. The interviewee was a young man aged sixteen, named Moher. He was born in Hamburg and lived with his two sisters (one aged seventeen, one aged eleven) and his mother (born in 1967 in Afghanistan). His mother had come with her parents to Germany as an adolescent and met the father of her children. She never went to school and has worked as a shop assistant since her divorce in 1999. His father, born in 1956, had been able to begin his studies in Afghanistan before emigrating in the 1980s. He then worked as a taxi driver, but wanted to open his own business. Moher has both German and Afghani nationalities and speaks both languages perfectly. He proudly declared his Afghani heritage to me when we first met. Without knowing his history, I can assume that this migration was linked to the political issues of the time, as it was for most of his compatriots. Given the existence of almost entirely negative stereotypes associated with Afghanistan in Europe (for him, his classmates' knowledge is limited to "war, the Taliban, and drugs"), Moher can only expect negative reactions from me concerning his origins. That is why he was on the defensive at the beginning of the interview. Communication was immediately difficult. My hesitations and the difficulty I had in formulating the prompts clearly reveal my unease. In addition to the problem of social distance and differences in habitus (social and national), there is also a methodological problem. I realized as I was asking the question that it was inappropriate. It assumed that the student had an interest in German history. But perhaps he had an interest in Afghani history, which he began to talk to me about as we walked toward the cafeteria where the interview would take place. This sudden idea led me to reformulate the prompt, as soon as I mentioned that I was interested in German history, to add that I was also interested in the history of other countries, but first I wanted to talk about German history. Uneasy with the idea of assuming that he would be more interested in Afghani history than with that of the country he was born in, Germany, I found myself determined by social reasoning powerful enough to suggest that I bring the interviewee back to his geographical origins, in spite of my convictions to do otherwise. This is an approach that is used by the teachers at Wiesi and which I have heard and criticized[5] many times since the beginning of the study. In vain, I tried to take refuge in the formulation based on my interest in the person of the interviewee (independent of any nationality), hence my insistence on the phrase "about your personal opinion, what you personally feel." Yet, this formulation reveals my tendency as a researcher to extrapolate from my own situation (I have my own personal opinion on history) and to impose it on the interviewee.

Moher did not help me to overcome my discomfort. He did not understand and therefore asked for more details. I realized that it is possible to not be interested in history at all, and I therefore reformulated my question in the negative structure: "there's nothing that you find interesting in German history?" He did not find anything interesting. But I did not want to end the interview on this negative. I therefore persisted (a researcher must find something!). The discomfort only increased the more I insisted. I reworded the question: "if there is nothing that is really important, perhaps there is a hierarchy of events that are more important than others?" My incredulity in the face of Moher's negative response then made him uncomfortable. Instead of insisting on his negative response, he behaved as any "insecure" student would behave in a school context: he assumed that he misunderstood the question and once again affirmed his inadequacy ("I don't understand what you want").

I reformulated the question, he understood it perfectly, and once again answered in the negative, sighing, clearly aware that this answer was not satisfactory to me and that I would continue to ask this meaningless question, which of course I did. I was still driven by the desire to complete this interview and I was unable to question my approach in the heat of the moment (given that my research study focuses specifically on the importance of history in the lives of German people). It was therefore extremely difficult for me to realize that my approach was based on an assumption (social and professional) that is to suppose that history (German, but also more generally history as a discipline) is interesting to everyone. I persisted, asking him if he was (at least) interested in history in general. He responded with his only alternative to "no!," which was "I don't understand!"

This example is typical of what we call a failed interview. Indeed, the mutual incomprehension between two actors belonging to worlds too far apart from one another reveals more about the social relations between us and my relative inexperience as a doctoral student at the time of the fieldwork, rather than anything about the relation the student has with history. I had reached the limits of my research question, wanting to study the "reception" or the "appropriation" of legitimate culture (of which history is not only a part, but an important pillar) by those who lack cultural capital. Like school itself, through my research I imposed a type of knowledge, a specific form of history (written, European, scientific), onto these students. It was the form of my approach (interviews) that was inadequate here. I would have not had this problem had I been able to integrate into the group of students over a long period of time; but their peer groups (where they talk also about history) were all male and more than ten years my junior. Participant observation would have been difficult in this context. Nevertheless, my observation of playground interactions allowed me to identify situations in which history (German, and that of Nazism) was indeed meaningful to the students (see below). But this could not be demonstrated through interviews.

Power relations and the misunderstandings that result from them are found in all four of the interviews conducted in this group of "weak" students in Mr Stein's class, as well as in three interviews conducted in the 100th *Mittelschule* in Leipzig. It is extremely difficult to conduct interviews on history with students who are completely uninterested in the subject, whatever the reasons for this lack of interest may be (family history, academic difficulty, language problems, other cultural or intellectual practices, etc.).

The relationship established between the interviewees and the interviewer in the school environment makes it difficult for others to interpret their comments. They must be understood as formulations of what these students believe to be "my expectations," in other words, academic expectations. This is also true for students who are socially and academically more privileged, but it is particularly exacerbated for students who have very few social, cultural, or academic resources, due to the number of factors that separate us (academic status, social situation, age, gender, race, sometimes nationality).

The interview conducted with Omer, a student in the same class as Moher, Mr. Stein's tenth grade class, also clearly shows how little importance German history has in his life. He was born in 1987 in Hamburg and he has German nationality. His father, born in 1958 in Kabul, fled his country during the Soviet occupation in 1980 and arrived in Germany to open a car parts business. His mother, born in 1961 also in Kabul, became a housewife. His older brother sat the *Abitur* exam and completed his civil service. His older sister got married after passing her vocational certificate (*Realschulabschluss*) and was unemployed at the time of the interview. Omer does not know his grandparents who stayed behind in Afghanistan, a country he has never visited. This interview, like that conducted with Moher, is also laden with

The Social and Cultural Limits to Appropriations of the Nazi Past • 229

misunderstandings, even though I had taken additional precautions and reformulated the introductory prompt in a different way

You know that I'm interested in history and the [students'] *relationship to history. I'm interested in your opinion, your personal opinion. What is important for you. And when you think of history, and in particular German history, I'll begin by asking you if for you, there's an event, a period, which seems particularly important.* For me? [Surprised. Silence.]

You don't understand?
No.
[I speak slowly, watching Omer to see if he understands.] *If, in German history* [Omer said "yes"] *there is a period, an event, a time* [Omer said "yes"] *an era, a moment, that seem to you to be particularly important.*
Ah! Yes. [He considers.] When I was little [he hesitates] it was better!

When you were little?
Yes, better.

Why was it better?
Because, you're a child. You are more [he hesitates] much more, I want to say [he hesitates again] how can I put it, much more—well noticeable.
[I suggest] *You mean noticed more?*
Yes. Yes. And now less.
[I smile] *And now, you're less noticed?*
Yes. Not so much now. When you grow up, and then [he hesitates] because [he searches for words] . . . Harder and harder, it's—[he does not finish his sentence].

Today is more difficult?
Yes, that's it.[6]

Omer clearly did not understand the question. History, for him, is the history of his own life. And he wants to tell me how difficult his life is, more difficult as an adolescent than as a child. The divide between my question on the meaning of history in his life, and his response on the difficulty of his life is considerable. It is linked to the fact that history, as I see it ("political" history, from the distant past, written and scientific) has no existence or meaning in his everyday life; it is therefore difficult for Omer to give meaning to his history lessons. This difficulty is increased in Omer's case because of his language difficulties. He does not speak German very well, makes lots of mistakes when speaking, and even more in writing. As a result, he has trouble meeting his teachers' expectations.

The misunderstandings in Moher's interview were resolved when I listed a series of examples: reunification, famine, war. He thought for a long time. Then he had an idea: "Oh, yeah. What happened with Hitler." I asked him, as I had done for the other students, why he thought this event was particularly interesting, without taking into account that he just explained to me at length that he was not interested in anything about history. He drew an answer from the academic canon of the pedagogy of emotional upheaval: "Yes, he wanted to attack the entire world. Lots of people died, right, and especially a lot, a lot of Jews."[7] This was the only piece of information that Moher gave me about this period in the whole interview. It was impossible for me to make him say any more about it.

The Nazi Past, Historical Knowledge, and Cultural Practices among Students with "Substantial Academic Difficulties"

The impossibility to have these students talk about the theme of National Socialism is connected to a lack of knowledge about dates, facts, and events. Omeira, unlike Moher, "likes history" and tries to explain to me what it is that she likes. Born in 1986 in Yugoslavia (Serbia), her parents left the country as soon as the borders were open in 1989 to move to Germany. Her father, who was a builder, found employment in a cleaning company, where he is now the foreman. Her mother is a skilled worker in the same company. Omeira has two brothers, the eldest left school at fifteen. At the time of the interview, she was eighteen years old and, like several other students, was two years behind. She has experienced a number of significant family upheavals: her maternal grandparents were expelled from Germany a few months before the interview and were forced to return to Serbia after living in Hamburg for fifteen years. Her paternal grandfather, who is divorced, had been expelled to Macedonia a few years earlier. Her paternal grandmother, who married a German, was the only one to remain in Hamburg, the last local family contact Omeira had. The young girl's academic difficulties made conversation on history almost impossible. Although she spoke a lot, and loudly, her knowledge was so vague that it was difficult to understand what she was talking about. She mixed up time periods, apparently remembering facts to do with the suffering of people in disadvantaged positions or persecuted minorities. In her discourse, she therefore confuses "slaves," those persecuted "by Hitler" (she does not mention Jews), the victims of the war in Iraq, and victims in general of unknown nationality; she only remembers that they suffered. It is slavery in particular that seems to have marked her as a terrifying historical fact. Therefore, all victims of history, including Jews in concentration camps, become "slaves."

> For example, lots of people—for example, with Hitler and all that—they were slaves. And—and with [she hesitates, searching for words] for example that the

The Social and Cultural Limits to Appropriations of the Nazi Past • 231

Germans were waging war against the others, and all that, and didn't have help or anything. . . . Yes. And he [Hitler] forced a lot of slaves and all that. And he murdered lots too, and all that (*er hat auch viele umgebracht und so*).

And why do you think that's important?
I don't know. [Her tone changes.] Because it's interesting, how people lived before. That's all. And today, it's not like that. Ummm—yes before, with the slaves, all that. That doesn't exist anymore, like that.[8]

In her discourse, Omeira has a vague idea that Hitler "forced people," she does not really know what he forced them to do, but she makes a not altogether illogical link to slavery. For her, Hitler is a slaveowner who "murdered a lot." The lack of historical context is not problematic for Omeira. Her own history lacks depth, dates are mixed up, she is unable to say in which period, or even in which century the event happened. When I asked questions about chronology or dates, she responded simply "before" (*früher*).[9] Everything that is not in the present (defined in relation to her own life) is categorized in a homogenous temporal otherness, which perhaps we should describe as an "other" that is situated outside space and time. "Before" therefore means "before I was born." She repeated several times that history is interesting because "before it wasn't the same"—to which we should add "as today, in my current life." The geographical or temporal specificity of the past as well as its "contextualized" coherence have no clear signification for her, but are only useful in comparison to her own life. For her, it is sufficient to know that the events she speaks of occurred in the past, the period is of little importance. Nazism and Nazi extermination policy are therefore also a part of this atemporal elsewhere, along with slavery, the war in the former Yugoslavia, or "Bin Laden." Omeira constructed no hierarchy between these events; no one was more important or more striking than the others, which is perhaps linked to the fact that she did not really know much about any of them.[10]

Christian was born in 1988 in Leipzig. At the time of the interview, his father (born in 1958) was a truck driver and his mother (born in 1960) had worked first as a cashier and then as a hairdresser. Both parents left school after the tenth grade. This student, who was in Ms Seidengleich's class at the 100th *Mittelschule* in Leipzig, was quite loquacious, like Omeira. He said he was interested in history, particularly "the time of Adolf Hitler." In fact, he said as much in his first sentence.

German history. So, first the—well, the time of Adolf Hitler, when he—well, yes, with the Jews—how can I put it—well, he wasn't really their friend, well, he hated them, rather, in fact, and all that, well, and he wanted to kick them out, and then he killed himself, of his own free will, with poison in his drink, or something like that, wine or something, as you do—[he falls silent, a long silence].

Can you tell me why it's important?
It was also the time—with the wall. No? Was it the—[he does not finish his sentence, looks at me, questioning.]

What do you mean, with the wall?
Yes, it was built, during that time? Was that it? [He is not really sure, looks to me. I do not answer, just say "mmm."] There was, well—there [he hesitates, pronounces it as though it was a foreign word] the F-R-G—is that it? Yes, I think, FRG and that [he hesitates for a long time, does not find the phrase he is looking for]. I don't remember the name—here—the FRG and—[he looks at me].

[I help him.] *The GDR?*
Yes exactly. That they were separated, and the power was—Berlin was in the FRG, I think, no? And—all around, there was the GDR—and Hitler, he wanted control, during that time—

Of what? What do you mean?
The—[he hesitates, looks at me questioningly] the GDR, I think! Yes. And they felt excluded, the Berliners, because they had the wall around the country. Around the town, and they couldn't come into the GDR anymore, and vice versa. And then, there was a lot of smuggling, on one side and the other, and it came from outside too, there were lots of people who came to the GDR, and they smuggled stockings and cigarettes and things like that.

And when you say, Hitler wanted to have power over the GDR, where was he then? [I am trying to understand.]
In the GDR! [He smiles].

You said that Hitler's time, it was important, because there was a separation. Can you explain why it was important? For Germany or for you?
So [he sighs], it was an important time for Germany. They were separated. And then, after fifty years, the wall fell down already. And Germany was reunified again, Hitler was dead, and I—I think there was Lenin who took power, no? In the middle of the period that [I cough]. And the wall—everyone was happy that the wall fell down. That they could go everywhere, at the time, and that products from the West could come into the East, and the products from the East could go into the West.[11]

We can see that Christian's understanding is more than vague here. He does not know the geographical borders between the GDR and the FRG, he does not know the difference between Nazism and the GDR, he has heard of Hitler and Lenin, but remains unable to situate them in space or time. The result is a kind of collage with names, people, and events that appear without meaning. Where others fall silent and say that they do not know, Christian embarks on developments that quickly lead him into a whirlwind of uncertainties, and in which he becomes lost.[12]

This interview with Christian shows how difficult it is for some of the students with low levels of academic capital to construct a link between their family history and history as it is presented at school, or in the media, or cinema. Indeed, some of the information mobilized by Christian seems to come from a film he had recently seen (*Sonnenallee*). Illegal smuggling to the GDR was one of the themes in the film: an uncle of the main character regularly "brings in" stockings and cigarettes. Christian, when he talks about the film, systematically confuses the GDR and the FRG, thinking that "in the FRG, they didn't have anything, they weren't doing very well," so the uncle "brought things in from the GDR." However, he very clearly situates his parents' childhood in the GDR and mentions how they were lacking "things." Yet he clearly could not make the connection between his parents' childhood and a film like *Sonnenallee*, or the political and governmental reality taught at school. Hence his permanent uncertainty about his discourse on the FRG and the GDR, expressed in his hesitations, and formulations such as "I think that it was in the FRG." We can also see the clear superposition of the Nazi past and the more recent past of divided Germany, which interferes in his constructions of representations of Nazism. We can also see how certain images from the film have marked this student, allowing him to integrate them into his discourse on the Nazi past, by shifting "Hitler" into the GDR. These superimposed images, an operation Harald Welzer, Sabine Moller, and Karoline Tschuggnall ([2002] 2005) have called *Wechselrahmung* (framing transfers), are only possible if there is a lack of specific knowledge, unstructured chronology, and historical vagueness that can be modified when needed.

We can therefore understand why history does not seem to be an asset in the school environment for these students. A lack of family resources and knowledge prevents them from appropriating it. It has no meaning for them in their everyday lives. The fact that their families have sometimes lived through a past other than that of Germany, can make this process of appropriating the Nazi past, and German past more generally, all the more difficult. But this is not an entirely sufficient explanation, as we can see in Christian's example, but also in the "counterexample" of Marji (see chapter 2).

Their difficulties in correctly imagining and speaking about the past do not in any way prevent the students retaining the "major lessons" at school. In spite of their lacunae, these students who are struggling academically are indeed able to name World War II and Hitler as "particularly important." Omer's comments are testimony to this.

Yes, so [he hesitates] at school, it's something that you have to learn. And so, there are things, and themes that come out, and you have to—how can I

234 • When Will We Talk about Hitler?

explain that—well, a history like that, you have to know it, what happened before, or why Hitler—Hitler did such bad things. It was [he hesitates] it wasn't good! We want to know that, why he did it.

And what was not good? You said that it was bad. What was bad?
He destroyed everything. The ge—[he breaks off] um, well, he—he destroyed everything, people who he didn't like, and he—it wasn't good, right?

And you know why he did that?
No, I don't have an explanation. No, I don't know. No.

And do you think you will talk about it at school?
I think so yes. You have to know! Once you begin on this subject, you want to know things. Why? Why he did it. You have to know. Otherwise, there's no point in beginning the subject.[13]

Omer has integrated certain school "rules." He knows that it is a place where "you have to learn" and he believes that these rules are "right." He also knows his own difficulties and he knows that he has a lot of "work" to do if he is to conform to school expectations. History is therefore "a school thing"; the history of Nazism is "an important subject" that "you have to know." But this past remains external, as though imposed on him. Moher submitted a homework piece on "European Judaism in the Nineteenth Century," which almost exclusively focused on the Jewish genocide (reproducing, in chronological disorder, dates linked to the extermination of Jews), which he clearly copied from somewhere. However, this nevertheless shows that the students have indeed interiorized the academic importance of the Nazi past.

In spite of the difficulties that they had at school, both Moher and Omer were curious about the Nazi past. Beginning to learn about the atrocities of the Nazi extermination policies raised the question of "why," and thus the question of responsibility. They believe that school knowledge is not gratuitous; it must lead to an understanding of what remains incomprehensible, both for them and their classmates.

This incomprehension was explained by some of the students and constitutes a critique of the school system by students who, in spite of their considerable difficulties at school, still expect the school to provide an answer to their questions. Karsten, for example, was born in 1988 in Leipzig and, at the time of the interview, was living with his mother, who was an optician's assistant but who has been unemployed since reunification (his father left shortly after he was born). He was a student at the 100th *Mittelschule* in Leipzig and he explained what he expects from the school.

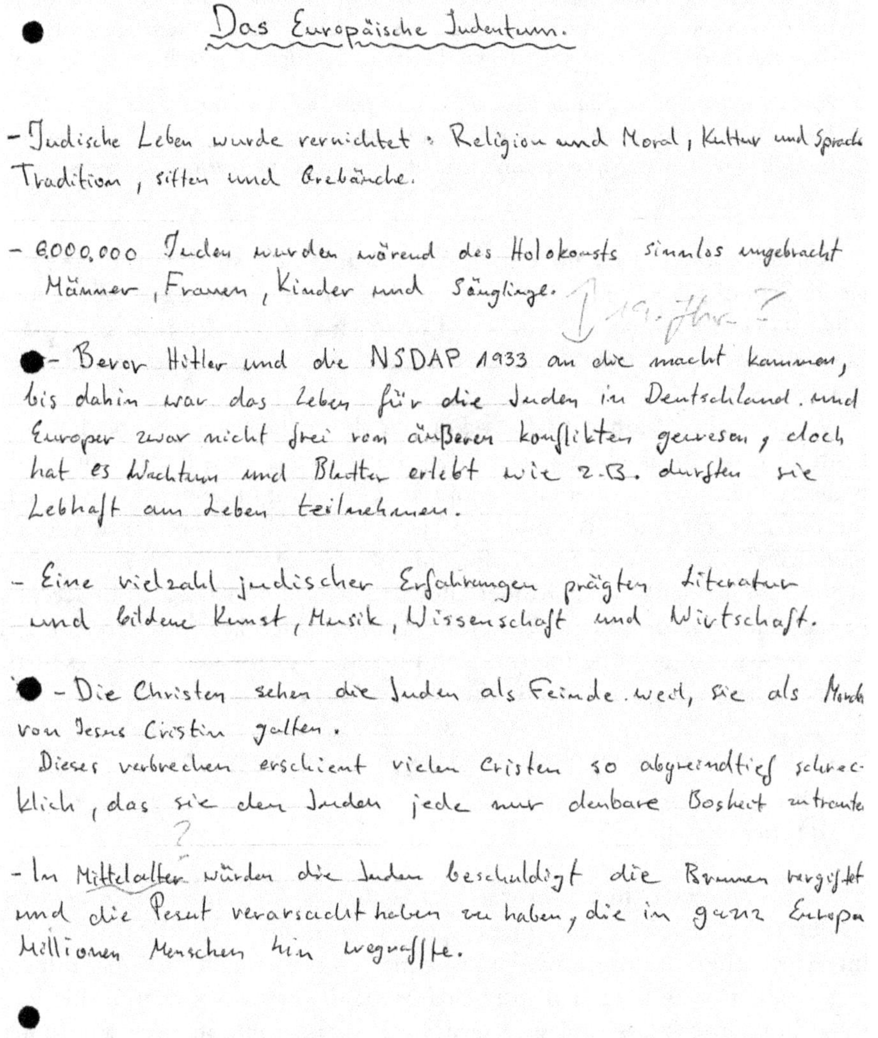
Das Europäische Judentum.

- Judische Leben wurde vernichtet : Religion und Moral, Kultur und Sprache Tradition, sitten und Grebäuche.

- 6000,000 Juden wurden wärend des Holokausts sinnlos umgebracht Männer, Frauen, Kinder und Säuglinge. 19. Jhr. ?

- Bevor Hitler und die NSDAP 1933 an die macht kammen, bis dahin war das Leben für die Juden in Deutschland. und Europer zwar nicht frei von äußeren konflikten gewesen, doch hat es Wachtum und Blutter erlebt wie z.B. durften sie Lebhaft am Leben teilnehmen.

- Eine vielzahl judischer Erfahrungen prägten Literatur und bildene Kunst, Musik, Wissenschaft und Wirtschaft.

- Die Christen sehen die Juden als Feinde. weil, sie als Mörder von Jesus Cristin galten.
Dieses verbrechen erschient vielen Cristen so abgrundtief schreck-klich, das sie den Juden jede nur denbare Boshest zutrauten ?

- Im Mittelalter würden die Juden beschuldigt die Brunnen vergiftet und die Pesut verarsacht haben zu haben, die in ganz Europa Millionen Menschen hin wegraffte.

Figure 5.1 Extract from Moher's homework: "European Judaism in the Nineteenth Century." Source: Author's private archives.

Translation of the German text: "Jewish lives were destroyed: religion, morals, culture and language, tradition and rites. Six million Jews were assassinated during the Holocaust for no reason: men, women, children, and babies. Before Hitler and the NSDAP came to power in 1933, the lives of Jewish people were not without external conflict, but there were improvements, for example they had the right to participate actively in working life. A great number of Jewish experiences influenced literature and art, music, science, and economics. Christians saw Jews as enemies, because they were perceived as the murderers of Jesus Christ. This crime seems so horrible to many Christians, that they imagined the Jews capable of all sorts of atrocities. In the Middle Ages, the Jews were accused of having poisoned wells and causing the plague, which killed millions of people all over Europe.

I don't really know—he [Hitler] did something with the Jews—he had something with the Jews even if—even if he was one himself and—he killed a lot, at the time he tried to take over the world, if—if I understood right.

And when you say, he had something with the Jews, what do you mean?
He—he had a lot of them killed. From what I understood. But—he was one himself—well, I don't really understand very well (*ich versteh das irgendwie nicht richtig*)![14]

Karsten expressed his hope that school would help shed light on the subject.[15] School is the place that contains (legitimate) knowledge, which most students consider necessary in life. But for many, this knowledge remains inaccessible, even if they attend class and believe in the importance of access to knowledge.

When I asked Moher if what he knows about the Jewish genocide comes from his history class, he explained that they "haven't done it yet," but that he had seen "serious documentaries, not like RTL, things like that, but very serious documentaries on TV" on the subject.[16] His insistence on "serious documentaries" was intended to convince me of how serious his own practices of acquiring knowledge were. Moher knows that certain media are not accepted in the school environment. RTL, for example, which is a commercial television station, but also the internet, fall into this category—in the eyes of the interviewees in any case. Moher therefore told me,

On the internet, I don't watch things like that [to do with history].

What do you watch then?
I'd better not tell you.[17]

The Internet is thus a media source that is used for exploring extra-academic subjects that cannot be spoken of in the context of a "serious" interview. These "transgressive" adolescent practices are all the more difficult to talk about with a woman, particularly for the boys. My relationship with these boys, the "class dunces" (regardless of their nationality) was indeed very different in class and in the interviews. In class, when they were physically distant from me and among their peers, they regularly provoked me, making jokes yelled from the back row, particularly sexual jokes; they asked if they could meet me at night, if I was married; they spoke loudly and they laughed a lot. However, as soon as they were alone (or in pairs) in the interview, the interaction was calmer and more controlled. The ambiguity disappeared entirely to make way for a very "serious" attitude; they were concentrated, attentive, academic, and they tried to answer my questions as best they could. The separation between the school space and the male peer group, which became a space of masculine games, was clearly visible in their interactions with me and with their classmates. It is this separation, which is at the heart of their difficulty in giving meaning to the past in an academic sense and leads them to their playful attitudes toward the Nazi past (see chapter 6).

This separation is also present in the way these boys devalue books, which are seen as the symbols of the school space. "At school, it's all books. Loads! (*mengen-weise*)," Moher complained. When I asked him if he liked to read novels, he said, alarmed, "No!!!"[18] Many students at Wiesi gave reasons that included "not having time" or "not being able to read because of exhaustion" to explain their difficulties with books. Moher went even further in his analysis. He explained to me quite clearly that "maybe it's because—I don't know. Well—my parents don't have—they didn't get me used to reading books, when I was little."[19] For him, books remained relatively inaccessible.

Sometimes, we have to read. I read a book at school. *Die Welle* (*The Wave*[20]). But I found it boring.

It was boring?
Yes. I couldn't imagine it.

Did you managed to finish it?
Yes, we had to.

And why do you say that you couldn't imagine it?
[He considers.] Maybe I don't have enough imagination? I don't know. Anyway, when you read something like that, you have to be able to imagine it, how they are, where it is, what they are doing.

And when you can't, it's boring?
[He hesitates.] "Well, me—I do it like that, I read, I read, I read. But I don't learn anything. I don't understand anything. I just read. And I don't know what, after [what I just read].[21]

The difficulties that these students from modest social backgrounds have in reading represents a major obstacle to the appropriation of knowledge about history. Moher did not only struggle with "scholarly reading," which is based on the idea that reading is justified by an interesting text that can be valued in the school environment.[22] It was also "ordinary reading" that he found hard, reading that uses "the text as an instrument toward external ends" (Baudelot, Cartier, and Détrez 1999: 163), such as amusement, for information, or to identify with, which enables young people to become invested in the books they read. The distinction between "scholarly reading" and "ordinary reading," which we have borrowed from Christian Baudelot, Maire Cartier and Christine Détrez, is based on the differentiation between "aesthetic reading" and "ethical reading" established among others by the German philosopher and literary theorist Hans Robert Jauss, who was notably inspired by the work of Erwin Panofsky, Michael Baxandall and Brigitte Hilmer. Jauss's theory has recently been put into context with his SS-membership and Nazi past. It was used by Bourdieu ([1979] 2010) long before the discussion of Jauss's criminal past came to light (Westemeier 2015) to distinguish two orders of disposition. Baudelot, Cartier, and Détrez prefer the term "ordinary" because it emphasizes the fact that this "kind of reading has a much more universal status than we might believe from the discourses that relegate it, to better disparage it, to juvenile or popular categories. Indeed, this form of reading often overflows substantially, both historically and socially, from these two categories of readers. That is why we describe it as ordinary" (Baudelot, Cartier, and Détrez 1999: 161). Moher had not acquired a taste for reading because he could not invest himself in the book nor "imagine it." As a result, reading in general, both "ordinary" and "scholarly," remained out of his reach.

As for Omer, he had begun to enjoy reading over the last year. Strongly encouraged by his teachers, he read in order to acquire the language skills he was lacking. He went to the library and borrowed books to read every night.

> *Do you read books?* [Yes] *Novels for example? Or what kinds of books?*
> Oh, well—I read kids' books! I have to, because my German is not very—readable. Not very good, you know. So, I have to read so that it gets better.
>
> *And so you read to improve your language skills?*
> Yes, exactly, yes.
>
> *And do you do that at school or—?*
> Well, Mr Stein has said it a few times. My teacher told me a few times and for—[he hesitates] about a year, I read, very often, always, when I go to sleep—an hour, half an hour, I read. And after, I sleep.
>
> *And what kinds of books do you read?*
> Sometimes novels. Sometimes also—*Goosebumps* books, scary ones. Books like that.
>
> *And is it boring to have to read every night? Or do you like it too?*
> "I like it! [Very decisively.] You should always [do it] when you want to. When I want to, I do it too. And when I don't want to, I don't.[23]

Of course, Omer started reading because he became aware that his difficulty at school was due to his problems with the German language. Yet, like many young people from working-class backgrounds, he read young adult fiction or science fiction that is not in keeping with school culture, primarily

The Social and Cultural Limits to Appropriations of the Nazi Past • 239

because of less parental guidance in reading practices (Baudelot, Cartier, Détrez 1999: 119–23). This reading may indeed help Omer to improve his language skills, but it will not provide him with (academically) useful information about history.

These students come up against three main obstacles to reading. Mostly male, they are "behind" at school and come from low socio-economic backgrounds (see, Baudelot, Cartier, Détrez 1999: in particular ch. 8). For some of them, German is not their first language, which increases their academic difficulties. They are among the 15 percent of students that have substantial difficulty with reading, writing, and written expression. We must remember that these students are streamed into specific schools, due to the tripartite structure of the German school system. At Wiesi therefore, only about 3 to 7 percent of students obtain the *Abitur.* All the teachers at Wiesi and at the 100th *Mittelschule*, without exception, mention the difficulties posed by the students' trouble concentrating, the fact that they are "behind," their problems with the German language, and more generally with acquiring reading and writing skills. These conditions also influence the mechanisms by which these students appropriate the Nazi past. Indeed, when books are not (or only rarely) among the sources of information about the past, knowledge must be found elsewhere.[24]

Moher therefore referred to "serious documentaries" on television to gather information about Nazism. Students in general, but more particularly those in the two schools in disadvantaged areas, both in Leipzig and Hamburg, regularly watch TV "programs," and documentaries. We know that cultural practices vary in terms of social belonging. Based on time-use studies conducted by the French institute for statistics (INSEE) between 1986 and 1998 Philippe Coulangeon observed that, for France, the "average time spent watching television is correlated to cultural capital. At its maximum for non-high-school graduates, it is at its minimum among those with a higher degree" (Coulangeon 2003: 287). Those of the students who were more easily able to remember the names of these documentaries[25] confirmed that they particularly like those made by Guido Knopp (see chapter 4).

Although Moher and his classmates told me that they "really like" watching Knopp on television (as much as their fellows in the *Gymnasien*), they had trouble remembering the content of the programs, unlike the students from more socially and academically privileged backgrounds or more politically active students. The fewer academic and family resources available to them is a hindrance to their familiarization with historical discourse and also hampers the construction of "oppositional" or "anti-system" historical discourses. Moher, aside from statements like "there were lots, lots of Jews who died," had no opinion on the Nazi past.

Between Indifference and Refusal: Rejections of Academic History at the *Gymnasium*

Among students from more privileged backgrounds, and those at the *Gymnasien*, I also occasionally observed an opposition to school, or a difficulty or refusal to appropriate the Nazi past, which took different forms to those encountered by academically struggling students from less privileged families. At *Gymnasium* Weinberg, Markus, one of Victor's friends, was failing at school, was not interested in history, and had no desire to be "subjected" to an interview. Born in 1988 in Weinberg, he is the son of a real estate agent (born in 1951) who inherited his real estate business from his own father after graduating from high school. His father married a shop assistant (Marcus's mother, born in 1955) who became a housewife after she had children. His mother obtained a vocational certificate and occasionally worked in his father's business. Marcus comes from a family background that is much more economically privileged than students at Wiesi or at the 100th *Mittelschule*, even though, in Weinberg he was among students whose families have much higher cultural capital than his own and was therefore in a situation of relative disadvantage. His older sister was sitting the *Abitur* in the same school. Markus was not able to situate his parents, his grandparents, or his sister politically. Clearly politics was not a subject that was discussed at home.

It took me nine months to convince Markus to agree to an interview.[26] I met him in a cafe (given Markus's opposition to school, I thought it was a good idea that we speak outside this environment), but the atmosphere was strained. When he arrived, I offered him a coffee and ordered one for myself. He refused, asking me directly and aggressively "what I wanted from him" because "history is not his thing" and that he really "doesn't know why I insisted on speaking to him" since he has "nothing to say to me."[27] The interview lasted no more than twenty minutes and he remained in a position of refusal throughout, with his arms folded in front of him, turning his shoulder to me and looking at the window, from time to time leaning backward on his chair. Several times he repeated that he "doesn't give a shit" about history. My attempts to reassure him remained in vain, I explained that my study was as much on students who were not interested in history as those who were, and that his contribution was particularly valuable in this respect, because he could help me to understand the reasons for his disinterest. I tried to introduce the questions in other ways, talking about what he enjoyed, books, films, and asking what he was interested in. Markus relaxed a little, for a brief moment when he spoke about music, particularly German rock. But as soon as I asked about the past or about politics, both of which for him represent the school that he hates, I faced refusal. There was nothing for it. I abandoned the idea of continuing the interview that neither of us was enjoying.

Markus was among the students who not only opposed the school system, but also rejected everything that is valued at school to construct an identity around concerns that are external to this environment (such as music). These concerns can, of course, have a political form (Markus had a fondness for political songs) and may even involve representations of the past. Although these forms of interest in history are beyond this research on the school environment, it seems essential that they be investigated in the context of studies on the reappropriation of the past through sources such as music (Löding 2009).

We have seen that the appropriations of the Nazi past are limited, and there are students who encounter obstacles that make such appropriation difficult in the school context. However, the same students (often struggling in school) can sometimes mobilize other resources to give meaning to that past, which are not necessarily recognized at school. Markus's interest in music could become a resource for him in the appropriation of this past, perhaps it already was, but it remained inaccessible to me because of our inability to communicate. Among some of the students at Wiesi, family migration history as well as experiences of discrimination and xenophobia, can be transformed into a resource to give meaning to the past in a more personal way. This observation allows us to differentiate and complexify the image of a simple refusal of the Nazi past based on school difficulties and lack of cultural and family resources.

Giving Meaning to the Past through Personal Experiences of Migration

Students who have experienced migration have a particular way of giving meaning to the Nazi past, reinterpreting it in light of their own personal experiences. Joey was born in 1987 in Kabul. He was sixteen at the time of the interview. His father, born in 1939, had wanted to pursue his studies after his high school degree. Joey insists on this ("my father went on to study"), but does not know what he studied, and later confessed that his father quickly had to stop to join the army, a position that became difficult after the Taliban's rise to power. He left for Germany in 1994, but once he arrived, he never managed to find work. Joey's mother, born in the 1940s, never went to school and never worked. Joey said that his father is "retired." Given that his father never worked in Germany, we can imagine that Joey's family lives on welfare. Joey has seven brothers and sisters, aged between 22 and 37, scattered throughout the world. At the beginning of the interview, he immediately made a comparison between World War II and the war in Afghanistan.

German history, huh! [He hesitates] Yes, what should I say? German history—
that's yes, of course, the history of Hitler. That's it [he hesitates again]. Yes,
that, that's interesting.

Yes, and why is it interesting?
Yes, because lots of people, like in our country, lots of people were murdered
by that. And then—the enthusiasm and all that [he smiles].

And when you say, "in our country" what do you mean?
Yes, in our country there was—there was also a lot of people who died.

And which is your country?
Afghanistan!

Afghanistan. And did a lot of people die?
Yes. In the war.[28]

The connection that Joey makes between Nazism and the war in
Afghanistan allows him to forge a personal connection to the history of
World War II. First, he experienced war when he was seven. The permanent
presence of war, fear, the use of children during conflict, are all personal experiences of combat, although they occurred early in his life. He remembers
these experiences, the deaths, but also the escape, the exile, and the family
separation that he experiences every day. Second, his father was a soldier. His
father's experience of the war, its political role in Afghanistan, and political
emigration are all a frame through which Joey interprets and reads the Nazi
past and World War II. These connections are essential in giving meaning
to the Nazi past, to constructing its signification in the everyday. This is not
a question of mentioning the past for the past's sake, but using the past to
understand and interpret the present, in this case, a family history of migration and dispersal.

However, the comparison between the Nazi past and experiences of war
in other places is only one way of doing this. Many students evoke everyday
racism and xenophobia to establish a link between the Nazi past and their
own experiences.

In Mr Stein's Class, a Discussion Develops among the Students

Field notes: 22 October 2003
Student 1: Yes, today, with the foreigners, it's the same—as with the Jews.
Student 2: Yes, they just made an effort, to have a job.
Student 1: But I don't understand. They haven't done anything. They just did
their job.
Student 2: It is the same today. They do the cleaning, and everyone is against
them.

The Social and Cultural Limits to Appropriations of the Nazi Past • 243

Establishing a connection between xenophobia toward foreigners who "do the cleaning" and the Jews who were killed in the Nazi camps is not necessarily historically appropriate. However, this is about making information tangible, providing a non-historical signification, an operation that requires active construction on the part of the students. The modifications of the past that result from this have their own meanings, as we can see in Joey's case.

[I ask myself] the question, for example: how many people died? And—for [he hesitates] why so many Jewish people died? What was the reason? Yes, questions like that.

Do you find answers? To why so many Jewish people died?
Yes! Because the [he speaks slowly, carefully articulating his words] Hitler was against—[he hesitates] he was against foreigners, right. Well, he wanted to [he hesitates again] for Germany to be occupied by Germans. So, no Blacks [he does not finish his phrase]. And that's why he killed a lot of Jews and black people too.[29]

Joey did not know that African immigration is very recent in Germany and that the Jews assassinated in the 1940s were neither "foreigners" nor "immigrants." Here, historical interpretation is used as a tool to understand racial hatred and xenophobia; inversely, the current day is blended with history. This deeply ahistorical reasoning is necessary to make the teaching of history useful and to give it meaning, which can also sometimes lead to confusion. For example, Joey said, "We watched a film, last week: *American History X*.[30] There was Hitler, and everything, and they beat up Blacks, and all that. It was—I thought wasn't good."[31]

This is a film about racism and neo-Nazism in the 1980s on the east coast of America. Omer, like Joey, thought it took place "in Hitler's time."

Yes, so, there is a black guy, who robbed the house, Hitler's—[he broke off] yes, or, Hitler's people. And after he, the little brother of the brother, he woke up. And he said: "Come on, there are heaps of Blacks." He goes out and kills one (*hat erst mal einen abgeknallt*). And shoots another, in the leg, he falls down. And then—in his mouth and everything—and bang. . . . Yeah, and then [he stammers] afterwards, yeah, when he was the boss. And they got him (*sie haben ihn gekriegt*)! He—he got five years in prison. And afterwards, when he came out, he said, "It's not good," still [he begins again] he went back to normal, and he said, "I won't do that anymore."[32]

Like several of his classmates, whether they come from families with a history of migration or not, Omer speaks in broken phrases when he tells a story. He does not use verbs. His narrative occasionally resembles a comic strip, with sounds ("bang!"), and unfinished phrases. His use of language expresses a certain distance from the academic sphere. He employs words specific to his social environment, he changes the syntax, the vocabulary,[33] echoing the speed and movement of images, action and pace are the priority. The rhythm and images in Omer's discourse reflects the pleasure he felt in watching the movie. The screening is used by the students in their own way: the critical distance and historical contextualization of the film are secondary to the personal and contemporary meanings that link the film to the students' lives, but also to cultural practices (reading comics, for example).

Several factors may explain the confusion between "Hitler" and the United States. First, the fact that the students did not see the historical meaning of the film as being particularly important, and the difficulty that they had establishing a chronology and placing the events in space and time. Second, the fact that the students watched the film in history class dedicated to Nazism. However, this might also be simply a figure of speech; "Hitler" may not be a reference to the historical figure, but rather to a symbol of evil. Talking about "Hitler's guys" or "Hitler's house" might also be a way of referring to neo-Nazism and more generally something to be disapproved of, without necessarily believing that the action takes place in the Nazi period. Such usage is not specific to the students: "Hitler" is very often evoked in media discourses, particularly to create an opposition between "good" and "evil," or to efficiently denounce a political adversary. George W. Bush, John McCain, and Arnold Schwarzenegger have all been compared to the dictator, for example.

These different ways of interpreting the Nazi past are indeed connected. Given the fact that the past is "decontextualized," and there is an inability to situate it in time and space, history can be more easily mobilized as an ahistorical value reference. Moreover, some of the pleasure associated with watching the film and the meaning the students attribute to it come from implicit or explicit comparisons with the past and the moral judgments that allows the students to effectively condemn the experiences of xenophobia and racism that they are subject to.

This first part of the chapter has attempted to show that students in "substantial academic difficulty" develop their own specific ways of appropriating the past. The discrepancies between cultural practices in their families and peer groups, and academic practices and discourses are responsible for their difficulties at school, which does not prevent them from giving meaning to the past in their own way. In order to do this, they draw on their own daily or past experiences, which are not always in keeping with the school's expectations.

However, there are different ways of opposing school discourses. In the next section, we will see how "good students" from very comfortable backgrounds with high cultural capital, develop alternative ways of refusing school

The Social and Cultural Limits to Appropriations of the Nazi Past • 245

discourses. We will also see that some of these logics in the construction of meaning and appropriation of the past are similar to those we have seen here.

"Bored" with History Class

That's enough
It's so annoying
It's everywhere, all the time
It never stops
After a while, you get saturated
It was too much
Shouldn't go overboard [with the treatment of the subject]
Leave me alone with all that
They stuffed our heads full of it

This theme has followed us around at school for an eternity, in almost all subjects
We were force fed it
We had to chew it up and spit it out
We did the Jews, the Jews, and even more Jews
I'm totally over it.

There are so many different expressions through which all (or almost all) of the interviewees over age sixteen at *Gymnasium* Weinberg in Hamburg expressed a feeling that can be described with the ancient German word *Harthörigkeit* (difficulty listening). *Harthörig* means to have "a hard ear," literally to be hard of hearing, to not be able to "differentiate tonality and words."[34] But in the school context this can also refer to people who do not want to hear. We should not be fooled, however, by the systematic presence of various elements from the teachers' discourses on the past in their students' discourses; among these adolescents there are figures of *Harthörigkeiten* that run alongside academic discourses. In other words, the forms of appropriation that we cover separately here are not mutually exclusive: a student may indeed be passionate about the Nazi past, for example, and develop an academically legitimate discourse in front of his or her teacher, while also defending a different position with their peers. Or they might opt for an academically legitimate discourse at age fourteen, but change that discourse by age sixteen, which is very often the case with students from the *Gymnasium* in Hamburg.

This *Harthörigkeit* results in an exasperation with the feeling of "omnipresence" of this subject that they "see everywhere," and they have a desire "to move onto something else," or—to use a negative and aggressive expression often seen in public debates—a desire "to draw a line under it" (*Schlußstrich ziehen*). The media and certain academics have described this phenomenon as Übersättigung (saturation)[35] and it has often been criticized as specific to the third postwar generation. It has been attributed to the fact that living testimony is becoming rarer, and thus to the shift from what the Egyptologist Jan Assman (1997) calls "communicative memory" to "cultural memory"— in other words, the shift from living memory, maintained through oral testimony, to memory institutionalized through writing. However, we may wonder at the heuristic power of such a binary opposition.[36]

There are several reasons for doubting this. This phenomenon concerns a very particular social population. It is specific to students from families with high levels of cultural (and to a lesser degree economic) capital. It is situated in a specific period of the students' schooling, when they are between sixteen and twenty years old, and it was observed in one specific school, the *Gymnasium* in Hamburg. Indeed, with one exception, the students in Leipzig did not express this same feeling of boredom. In the previous chapter we saw some of the explanations for the differences between East and West Germany, which may help understand the relative lack of this phenomena in Leipzig. In this section, we will look more closely at the differences in social origin. How can we explain that this form of *Harthörigkeit* toward the teaching of the Nazi past seems specific to students from privileged social backgrounds, particularly with high levels of cultural capital? Indeed, among the twenty-two parents of the students cited here, who most openly express this feeling of boredom, seven are teachers or educators (mostly in the secondary system, but also in higher education and primary), one is a journalist, one a doctor, nine are senior managers (three in the public sector), one is a nurse, one a secretary, and one a white-collar employee. The last two left their jobs to dedicate themselves to their families. These are families who combine economic capital (most often from the father, who works in business or as a doctor) and cultural capital (often on the side of the mother, who works in teaching or in cultural fields). Moreover, the elder siblings of those students who have brothers and sisters are at university; three studying medicine, one studying economics, and one literature. These are also students who know how to precisely situate their parents on the political scale and who are generally more well-informed about political parties than their classmates. Four of them situated themselves "on the left," voting SPD or Green, like their parents (and most often like their fathers). Only one of them said he felt close to the PDS, which at the time of the study had not yet joined with the dissidents from the SPD in *Die Linke*. Two of the students said they were right-wing, voting CDU like their fathers. Finally, there were two students and their parents who can be considered very well informed about political issues and "critical of power"; they change their votes depending on the context and develop sophisticated strategies to systematically oppose the government.[37] These people are political virtuosos, most often encountered only in textbooks or in films. Indeed, since the now famous studies by Paul Lazarsfeld and his team at the University of Columbia (Lazarsfeld, Berelson, and Gaudet [1944] 1952; Berelson, Lazarsfeld, and McPhee [1954] 1986) in the 1940s, the sociology of voting has demonstrated that voters are not always as rational and well-informed as democratic theory would wish them to be. On the whole, they tend to be less interested and less well-informed on candidates and electoral issues, and their decisions depend more on the social groups to which they belong than on the information that they receive during the campaign. Elections are not only the expression of political opinion, they are also a social ritual. "Political virtuosos" are indeed extremely rare.

With the exception of one family, the mothers tended to vote more left-wing than the fathers. Overall, these are children with a divided habitus, both in political terms (political discord between the parents) and in socio-economic terms (economic capital and employment in management or business versus cultural capital and employment in the public sector, notably education).

Before attempting to identify the social projects that can explain the link between this phenomenon of boredom developed by the students and their socio-economic, cultural, and political capital, we can quote Richard, a final year student at *Gymnasium* Weinberg. His father is a professor of law and a researcher at the Max Planck Institute, and his mother is a politics and literature teacher in a secondary school. He explained his relationship with the history of Nazism at length, mentioning many of the social logics that are relevant here, without necessarily naming them as such.

Interview with Richard, a Final Year Student, in a Cafe in Hamburg, 11 April 2003

I like to read history novels, but on that period [Nazism] it doesn't interest me anymore. It's that effect that I mentioned before. It's— [he did not finish his sentence].

Saturation (Überdruss)?
Yes, saturation, yes.

And when you were younger?
I think, perhaps Härtling. Peter Härtling.[38] It was about a cripple, who had to get out when Germany was destroyed or something like that. It was not directly about Nazism, but it was a book for children that covered that. I think that it was one of my first conscious experiences on the subject. I have to say, I have a biography of Hitler—I never started it—it's lying around in my house, and I would like to read it, but ultimately, somehow, it's not interesting, that subject. That's what is the most present, because it is everywhere, but from a historical perspective, I think that it's—well, I wouldn't want to, when I'll study history, which I'll probably do, I wouldn't want to have to confront it. Because I don't think I could. I'm too involved.

You couldn't?
Because I'm too involved. Because I—I grew up in Germany, and so I have this bizarre relationship that Germans have with their past [he lowers his voice].

248 • When Will We Talk about Hitler?

What do you mean by bizarre relationship?
Yes, what I've been describing for the last half an hour. Germans, with this subject—everything is emotional. A scientific approach—scientific and critical, that's not possible, I think. When you are German. No?

[I laugh.] *That's not very encouraging for me!*
No—really, that's what I think. I think [he hesitates] it's—I would find it boring, because the roles are too defined. That the Germans did terrible things, it's been proven. And so—to prove moral things—whose fault it is—it's already been done. When you see these images of Auschwitz, the liberation, euthanasia, and their—war crimes. Personally, I'm just not interested anymore. I don't know.

And so for you this is a subject that can only be treated emotionally?
It's—between the two. Because of—the euthanasia—I find that really horrible, and it's through that that I have a personal relationship with the subject [he has a brother who is disabled]. But otherwise—war—it's horrible, of course, but—you can imagine two people dead or one person dead, even if they were assassinated. But 20 million—it's just a number, nothing more. For me, World War II is incomprehensible because of the number of human victims. And so, [he hesitates] the emotional connections don't exist, for me. And well, you always say [he hesitates] somehow [he hesitates again], it's an "emotionality" that we have been trained in (*antrainiert*) somehow.

*Is that how you've been taught (*Anerzogen*) or would you say it has been hammered into you (*Reingeklopft*)?*
Yes—[he hesitates, not completely agreeing with the German expression *Reingeklopft*, which evokes a hammer pounding nails]. Well [he explaines], it's horrible. I can say it. And this relationship that Germans have with the past—to do it so pathetically or so theatrically, I think that's—not ideal. Because—it doesn't matter how human we are or how much we can put ourselves in someone else's shoes, 20 million dead, it's not possible. Human comprehension stops there. I think it already stops at twenty people dead. Or thereabouts. Twenty people killed, we can already not really understand the suffering—what suffering each one felt as a person. That's what I find distorted in this discussion. That we make it so emotional, when the subject is so abstract somehow, it's beyond us. . . . I don't know how to put it. I think that [he hesitates for a long time]. Yes [he hesitates again], it's a historical subject where you have to be very careful about what you say. For example, if I say that—because of the Treaty of Versailles the French and English have a certain shared responsibility in World War II. Historically, that's relatively well recognized by academics, as at least one of the factors that contributed. And if I say that, publicly, for example, as a politician in a speech, well, at the next elections my words will be reinterpreted and I will have a problem. Or in economics. In general, in public life. And I think that there is still a very ambivalent relationship. And we are very careful. And so, I think that it's too present. I don't know if it's the televised documentaries or German cultural life that does that or both. And so, for me, the theme is not interesting, because I'm too involved.

The Social and Cultural Limits to Appropriations of the Nazi Past • 249

Isn't that a contradiction, to say that "it's not interesting because I'm too involved"?
Yes, but I find it difficult to express myself. As a German, we have complexes on the subject. We can't help it. There is scientific or rational study possible, but it's [he hesitates, begins the phrase again]. Even if we have nothing to do with this past, like me, or you, because we were born after the war, it's still a relation that is very—yes, very emotional, somehow. Perhaps our generation is the last one that will experience this, because our grandparents experienced it directly. In any case, that's how it is for us. That's why—the relationships, our relationship to history, in particular twentieth century history, is ambivalent. [He hesitates for a long time]. Yes. . . . we need time for the subject to be sufficiently removed from everybody, to the point where there are no personal relations anymore.

And at that point will it be interesting once again?
Yes—not for me. [He laughs.] Because I'm not far away enough. I really think so, because I'm part of the historical development, and so [he does not finish his sentence].

And for you, the theatricality, the exaggeration of the opposition, that only exists in the media and in politics, or does it also exist at school?
I want to just clarify: you can't not be opposed. I want to take back the expression "exaggerated opposition." Of course, it's atrocious, and you have to be opposed to it. But what happens at school, when we cover it so often, but superficially, and the events are only commented on from the German perspective—it's boring. . . . I think that—how can you deal with facts, for example, how can you teach that objectively, as far as interpretation is concerned. When you are—emotionally affected. Of course, it has to be thematic. But I think that it's covered in a way [he hesitates], already at school, they make us clearly understand that [he hesitates again, begins his phrase again], of course we're guilty. Or the Germans are guilty. But I think that they really emphasize that a lot, at school. In the teacher's comments, for example."

Do you remember anything specific?
No, but you feel it, when they give us presentations or in what they value. For example, when you speak in a tone—or you say emotional things. [He hesitates.] I think that anybody, if they really study this theme, will arrive at the same conclusion. I'm certain of it. It's so obvious. It's really evil. But the problem lies in the fact that in Germany, people can't discover it for themselves. We're inculcated with it. I think. It's not like in political science, when we talk about contemporary politics, and everyone can judge. There are facts, but—the teachers try not to involve their political opinions. And even if the teachers' opinions are not wrong, as far as Nazism is concerned. But it's the theme where you always clearly see the teachers take a political stance, and aggressively. So, I'm criticizing the way they do it, rather than what they do [he hesitates]. . . . I just think that, I don't know if it's good, pedagogically. To transmit an opinion. It's politics, past politics, everybody has to find their own way to access it. That's what doesn't exist in Germany. So there you go, for me, the subject

is uninteresting. Because people, it's like with my grandmother. Or with my parents. There is a consensus and the consensus is transmitted from generation to generation, and so it's not exciting. [Silence.] On one hand, I think we have to transmit. And avoid, in practical terms, that people again fall victim (*zum Opfer fallen*) to such an ideology, fascism. Actively or passively. But the question that arises, is: is it normal for a country to be completely caught up in its past? Is it normal that all the institutions, all the schools, all the educational institutions, all the culture, force each human being into a particular position? From birth!

There are different ways of appropriating the past. We can see in Richard's discourse that emotion has a fundamental role to play in understanding the phenomena of "I don't want to hear about this past anymore." The quantity and repetition, the moral tone, the lack of scientific rigor, the emotional link, the link with democracy, Richard covers many explanatory elements in his own ambiguous relationship with the Nazi past and the *Harthörigkeit* that he develops. Unlike those who are "behind" in history class, this concerns the other extreme of the academic hierarchy: the "good" or "very good" students, who come from socio-economically comfortable backgrounds.

But like their less privileged classmates, it is the cultural practices of the family that open numerous potential avenues through which to analyze these students' attitudes toward the Nazi past. Structural homologies between cultural, familial, and academic practices, and gaps between academic historical interpretations, and historical interpretations within the family (by the grandparents) constitute factors that may help explain this specific form of *Harthörigkeit* among these more privileged students.

From "Too Much" to "Too Little": The Ambiguity of the Feeling of Saturation

Magdalena, an eighteen-year-old student at the *Gymnasium* in Hamburg, the daughter of two senior engineers (her father in the private sector, her mother in public administration at the Ministry for the Environment), talked about the teaching of Nazism, a theme that she used to be passionate about.

> During the period when we studied the subject in middle school, I read things outside of the textbooks. But as we went on it was—we started in ninth grade and then, we continued in tenth, eleventh, we did it again, and at one point, I'd had enough, of repeating it again, somehow. Of course, it was *the* subject, and that's important, of course, to cover it. But if we did it for two years or more, it's like—well "now it's enough." And we would like to do something else. There was also really a lot of repetition, all the time, and at one point, it's enough.[39]

The Social and Cultural Limits to Appropriations of the Nazi Past • 251

This impression of "déjà vu" or "repetition" is mentioned in nearly all[40] of the fifteen interviews conducted with the students over age sixteen in the *Gymnasium* in Hamburg. Several students expressed a feeling "of too much" in terms of quantity. Heidi, a former student of Mr Schulze in the *Gymnasium* Weinberg in Hamburg, is the daughter of a management consultant in an audit company and a pediatric nurse working in a childcare center. She explained more specifically the content of these classes that "bore" her.

> In history, in particular, when we did it with Mr Schulze, when he put a lot of emphasis, almost exclusively, on the persecutions of the Jews and all that, what they weren't allowed to do, what people did to them and all that. [She hesitates] and that, I think that was interesting, *of course*, and in any case, I wouldn't want to minimize it, of course, it's one of the most important aspects. But for example, Hiroshima and the atomic bomb, we never talked about it in history class! And if I hadn't learned it—I don't know, through my general knowledge, from my parents and grandparents, I would still not know! [She laughs.] You see! Because—at school, really, it was never covered, because we kept going over (*darauf herumgeritten*) this thing with the Jews—the persecution of Jews. And we did a lot on that, and that's probably good, also, but I think that the rest, that's part of it too. And also, the direction of the war, who did what, when and things like that, we never learned about it. You had to appropriate it by yourself. And I think that's a bit of a shame.[41]

Although Heidi began specifically talking about Mr Schulze's class, she quickly generalized her comments. From using the indefinite pronoun *man* she moved on to more passive structures (*es wurde darauf hermumgeritten*) to describe an excessive focus on the teaching of the Jewish genocide. At the beginning, Heidi's discourse targets the priorities of one particular teacher (Mr Schulze), but she quickly expands her range to talk about "history class" in general, and at the end of the extract, "the school" has become the object of the critique. In this kind of generalized statement, any actor with a specific discourse disappears behind passive formulations such as "we never learned it." We also observe this kind of formulation of the problem among other students. The use of the impersonal pronouns and passive structures are frequent in evoking saturation, which corresponds to this vague feeling of the subject being omnipresent, without however being able to define the specific sources of discourses on the past. The probability of encountering the subject of the Nazi past is indeed very high for these students.

In the introduction, we saw the quantitative frequency of the Nazi past in the national media. The example of the analysis of programs on the ARD television station can also tell us about their quality (in terms of depth). We can group the programs into three main categories according to the time that they dedicate to the subject (Figure 5.2).

252 • When Will We Talk about Hitler?

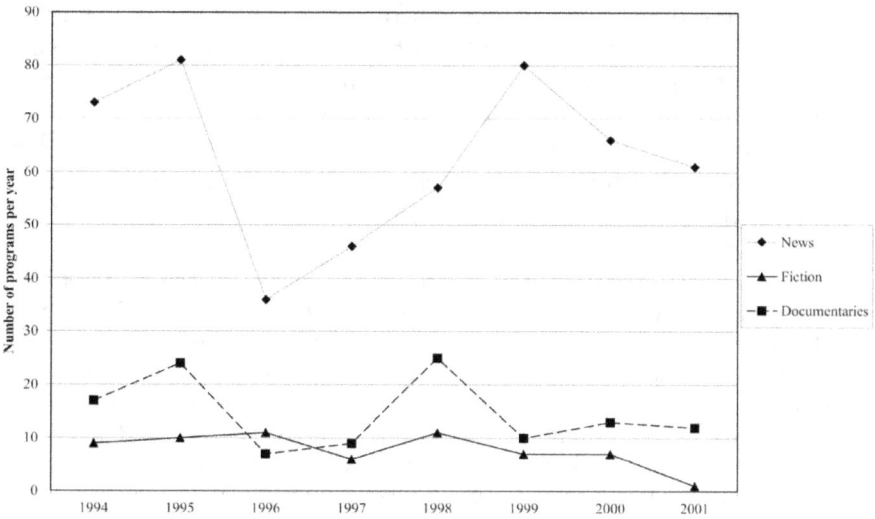

Figure 5.2 Presence of a subject mentioning the Nazi past on the first German television channel (ARD) according to the program type (1994–2001). Figure created by the author.

The first category contains the programs mentioning National Socialism among other themes. This is, for example, the case of television news, which mentions the periods in the context of current societal and political debates.[42] We have also included talk shows in this category, which is the largest category of programs (74 percent on average of all programs). The second category contains documentaries specifically on this particular period (17 percent of programs), and fictional productions make up the third and smallest category (9 percent).

Although, unsurprisingly, documentaries make up a substantial proportion of programs covering this historical subject, the presence of the Nazi past on TV news and talk shows reveals just how important this theme is in current debates in the politico-media sphere. Figure 5.2 also shows us that there is a very high probability of encountering the subject "unexpectedly" on TV, mentioned quickly and superficially, buried under other themes. This probably has an impact on the impression that young Germans in Hamburg with high cultural capital (and who watch the television news) describe of "seeing Nazism everywhere." Heidi explained,

And when you say that everyone talks about the [Nazi] past, who is everyone exactly?
Yes. [She considers.] It's so present, probably—I don't know, somewhere [she hesitates], it's sort of used as an instrument, I think. By politicians too. To say

The Social and Cultural Limits to Appropriations of the Nazi Past • 253

something. And there are always debates, among intellectuals or others, which explain a new opinion on the subject or which talk about the ways we should deal with the past in the public sphere (*Öffentlichkeit*). And there are always new studies that are being talked about. You don't really have the impression that one day it will decrease or that it will stop. But, of course, it's not really necessary that it stops. But [she laughs], I think that there is no reason to be worried at the idea that it is decreasing. And otherwise—yes, there's the media.

And when you talk about intellectuals, are you thinking of anyone in particular?
No, I can't really remember, it's been a while now. But there was—[she hesitates] between Paul Spiegel and all that—I think [she hesitates] that played a role too—what was it again?—[She pauses to think] I don't know—something like "instrumentalization of German shame"—but I don't remember, if it was him or Walser or whoever—all these people I don't remember their names. So, that's the last concrete example I remember. But even though I don't often read newspapers that write about it, and I don't know much about it, I simply see them as always talking about it, and very often, on TV, for example, things like that . . . I think that's strange, in fact—you have the feeling—well, I have the feeling that it's [Nazism] is present everywhere in the media, and that everybody talks about it, but I never meet anyone [who talks about it]. Between us, with friends. And I think that [she laughes, a little irritated, and does not finish her sentence]. But [she hesitated, thinking, and then found an idea]. Except, perhaps, books, in bookshops, I dunno, another biography of Hitler or something like that. Or [she hesitates] documentaries. I really think that's completely stupid. *Hitler and His Women* or something like that. Or, at one point, there were very short programs. It's so annoying, on RTL,[43] when there is a five-minute program![44]

Heidi's attitudes toward "public" information is interesting here. She seems to know a lot more about the debates than many of her classmates, but her knowledge remains vague. She had heard of Paul Spiegel, the then president of the Central Council of Jews in Germany, and of the debate in 1998 between the writer Martin Walser and Ignatz Bubis (Spiegel's predecessor), on relations to the Holocaust, from which she has remembered the phrase "the instrumentalization of German shame," which is, perhaps not by chance, one of the most often cited from the debate (the other being "the moral cudgel of Auschwitz"). Heidi, who was fourteen during the debate, did not take a position in the interview with me, which took place three years later. She had trouble situating the protagonists (whose names she could only partly remember) and their respective positions. Without exactly understanding the issue, she has remembered one thing that has stayed with her: Nazism is being discussed over and over again.

Moreover, she emphasized the fact that it is not important for her that an intellectual takes a position for or against "the way of treating the past."

254 • When Will We Talk about Hitler?

What matters is the debate itself, not its content. And it is precisely the lack of detailed information on the content that leads her to the impression that it is always the same debate. It is therefore the combination of too much information (and feeling like they hear it everywhere) and the lack of specific knowledge ("superficial" five-minute programs) that make up the first element in this impression, among the *Gymnasium* students in Hamburg, of endless repetition with each new debate. This ambiguous relationship between "too much" and "too little" explanation about the Nazi past has its origins in family configurations and the cultural practices of the students, and the structural similarities between their family practices and the school requirements.

"My Sister Taught Me . . .": Family Configurations and Attitudes toward the Past

The first signs of boredom I observed in the ninth-grade class in Weinberg, which I followed for more than a year, emerged toward the end of the school year during a session that I organized with half the class to "evaluate their teacher." Some students began by saying that they would like to cover something else now, it had being "too long," although without using words that suggested the same real "exasperation" as their older schoolmates.[45] One year before, in an interview in eighth grade, all of these students had expressed curiosity and a strong desire to study this subject in class. It therefore seems obvious that the discourse of saturation is directly linked to the teaching of the subject in school. Students who wanted to "absolutely do Hitler," who even spent their holidays looking for novels or documentaries on the theme, were "sick of it" by the end of ninth grade. This is not specific to one teacher or a particular school. The feeling of boredom is found in the other *Gymnasium* schools in Hamburg, where I carried out approximately twenty interviews in 2002, as well as in letters written to Martin Walser (Schirrmacher 1999). But beyond school or the media, it is family configurations that play a role in the creation of this feeling of boredom.

The analysis of the roles played by brothers and sisters in the transmission of academic knowledge in general, and more specifically knowledge of the Nazi past, show to what extent family and school configurations interact. Having older brothers and sisters who talk about their history classes "at the table," can arouse the interest of younger siblings.[46] Peter, for example, aged eighteen, was a student at *Gymnasium* Weinberg, and the son of a manager and a bank employee, who was a stay-at-home mother at the time of the study. He said, "Yes, well, my [older] brother, he also took advanced history, and he really liked [the classes] and he always talked about his history class.

It was with Mr Krull, and I think his anecdotes had a lot of influence on me. For him as well, it was cool, it was fun."[47] But older siblings' stories can also increase the "déjà vu" effect. The discovery of Nazism at school is disturbing enough for many children, and it becomes a subject of interest in families who talk about history "at the table" (see Keppler 1994). Thus it is transmitted "before time" to younger children. If the children go to the same school, which is often the case, they will have already seen their brothers' and sisters' history books or read their novels. They may not have the same teacher, they will study the same material. Although this is the case for all of the subjects for these younger siblings, it is the fact that this particular subject becomes a topic for "family conversation" that leads these students to want to learn more about it and therefore to discover Nazism very early.

Johannes, aged nineteen, the son of a doctor and a secondary school teacher, became interested in history through his two older sisters, both also passionate about the subject. The elder sister, Anna, aged twenty-seven, became a doctor, and the second, Merle, aged twenty-three, was studying literature at the time of the interview. Like them, Johannes chose to take advanced history. He observed that it was a subject that was regularly discussed among the three children. "What Anna talks about, what Merle talks about, yes, it was very present. [And Nazism] yes, yes, we talked about it too. Quite simply because Anna has always talked about everything, everything that comes into her head [he laughs]. Yes."[48] Thus, when Johannes read *When Hitler Stole Pink Rabbit*[49] in English class, he was not particularly enthused.

> You know it so much, by heart, you've read it a thousand times. Well, it wasn't bad, but—I have two older sisters, and the subject has already been talked about twice over dinner. It wasn't—well—[he laughs]. I already pretty much knew everything [about the book]. So, well she's a bit like "now, it's the little brother's turn! Be careful [he laughs] you do that, and that, and that . . . And you have to do it well!"[50]

When they are interested in history, older brothers and sisters can thus contribute to their younger siblings' overexposure to these themes. Moreover, the cultural practices of their parents also contribute to this overexposure.

"Let's Visit a Concentration Camp!"

Students who are bored with history class are particularly familiar with the political-media discourses on the Nazi past through their family origins and their cultural practices. Indeed, the students' parents are predominantly from the upper classes, and in intellectual professions. Among the students I spoke to at the *Gymnasium* Weinberg, over two-thirds of their fathers and almost half of the mothers belong to the upper classes or upper middle classes and in particular to liberal and intellectual professions. Half of them are secondary school teachers (see Table 1 in the introduction). With parents who work either professionally or voluntarily (donating their time as assistants, supervisors, in the library, or the cafeteria, for example) in school environments themselves, it is not surprising that they have perfectly interiorized academic discourse. The sociologists Kent M. Jennings, Lee Ehman, and Richard G. Niemi (1974) have shown the importance of homogeneity and political values between parents and teachers in the efficiency of transmission of political opinions. More specifically, Annick Percheron has shown, for the French case, that when parents are themselves teachers, the reproduction of political choices between parents and children increases from an average of 56 percent to 74 percent (Percheron 1977).[51] At Weinberg, social and cultural homogeneity between students and parents can be seen first in their level of education: among all of the students that I mention, only one mother did not graduate from high school and only one other did not go on to higher education. All the others have at least an undergraduate or a master's degree, and some have a PhD. We also observed the high number of parents who are themselves teachers. Their children said that at least one of the two parents generally vote for left-wing parties, like the teachers in Weinberg. In terms of the transmission of Nazi history, we can see the homogeneity between parents and teachers in the importance that they both accord to this particular historic period in the education of the children. Richard told me how he heard of the subject for the first time.

> The first time [he pauses to think]—I think it was when I was four or five years old. My father went to a concentration camp in Dachau with my brother [six years older than him]. We lived in Bavaria, at the time. It seemed that my father wanted to show my brother [he hesitates] what happened there. And I remember very clearly, that I didn't understand why I wasn't allowed to go. And he said to me, that it was very bad (*schlimm*). I think that was the first time that I was consciously aware of something to do with the NS period.[52]

At four or five years old, Richard was unable to understand what this was about, but in a very confused way he was already confronted with the fact that there was "something very bad, that happened, that was linked to Nazism." This is not an unusual experience. Visiting the camps is a frequent activity (on "holidays") in middle and upper classes, particularly for teachers, but many of the students in Weinberg talked to me about family visits: "we were on our way to Spain, and we saw the sign [to Bergen-Belsen] on the motorway, and so we stopped."[53] Working-class families do not go away for

The Social and Cultural Limits to Appropriations of the Nazi Past • 257

holidays as often, and so the opportunity for a visit, even an impromptu one, is less likely to arise. Such a trip would have to be planned in advance, but rarely is, because of time and money, but also cultural priorities. None of the students at Wiesi or at the 100th *Mittelschule* talks to me about a family visit to concentration camps, even though I systematically ask the question.

Cultural practices thus influence relations to the past and lead to a higher degree of exposure to information about Nazism among the children of the upper classes, who therefore develop a relationship with the past in the family environment that is close to the one developed at school (visits to concentration camps are only one example of this). Of course, this does not mean that students from more modest backgrounds do not encounter the Nazi past in their families, or that they have no connection to history. We have seen that they appropriate it in their own specific ways. However, they do not encounter the past in its academic form like the students from more privileged backgrounds do (particularly those who are children of teachers). To take another example, none of the students at Wiesi or from the 100th *Mittelschule* visited an exhibition on Nazism outside the context of school, whereas several students from the two *Gymnasien* made these kind of visits with their families (in particular the exhibition on the Wehrmacht, in Hamburg, but also the Buchenwald camp in Weimar, near Leipzig[54]). Johannes therefore talked about his parents' "desire to educate," and in particular his mother who not only regularly took him to the museum, but also talked to him about books that she considers essential.

> My mother [he hesitates] yes, well, she always told us things [about the past] or about writers, and so early on, during the holidays, we had to visit things, and so on. For example: "that man, he wrote this" and "that book's about this," and "here, at the time, there was that" . . . She wanted to transmit her own passion for these things to us. On the one hand, books. But also [my parents] they [he hesitates] yes, when we were together [during family discussions] (*beisammen saßen*)—they told us things [about the past, literature]. They wanted to teach us [he laughs], for us to learn about these things.[55]

This desire to transmit "culture" (that is, "academic" culture using what teachers prioritize such as books and museums) in which history is one element among others means the students have more exposure to this theme than their classmates from less privileged families, even before they study it at school. It is worth noting however that these are not specifically family narratives. Students in the two *Gymnasien* made a distinction between their grandparents who talked about their experiences in the war, and the parents who talked more about "grand history" and, in particular, the Jewish genocide and the "horrors of the past" by taking them to a camp or buying them novels—or encouraging them to read those in the "family library." It is this discrepancy between cultural and academic practices on one hand, and the grandparents' history on the other that contributes to the *Harthörigkeit* of students from privileged social backgrounds.

Yes, Grandpa Was a Nazi, but What Kind of a Nazi?

Most students from comfortable social backgrounds belong to families whose grandparents were difficult to categorize in terms of "fervent Nazis" or "resistance fighters." The grandparents belong to the vague category of the *Mitläufer*, who accepted the regime, sometimes profited from it, and, in any case, did not oppose it. They also quickly adapted to the new political regimes (GDR or FRG) after the war. These "normal Germans" pose particular problems for their grandchildren once the latter have become aware of the atrocities of the Nazi regime, which is the case for the "good students." Indeed, through books, visits to museums, and at school, the students learn about a past that is "too horrible" but also "too remote" to imagine that their grandparents were involved.

Difficulties Speaking

All of the interviews reveal the extent to which family conversations on Nazism are not easy. Taking an active approach to gathering information about the family history from one's grandparents is sometimes an insurmountable obstacle. These students ordinarily have difficulty asking their grandparents questions about the past, but there is a specific difficulty here due to the violence of the Nazi past and the extermination policies. Events like these typically constitute collective secrets because they are

> situations in which a large number of participants from the group are involved and yet the group as a whole was never able to deal with. The event thus remains "without memory" and the family is both actor and victim of the collective silence, both suffering from it and reproducing it, for want of words transmitted through the group with which the event could be spoken of. (Tisseron 1992: 106)

Indeed, the interviews showed that although there are multiple manifestations of public discourses referring to the Nazi past, to which these students from privilege social backgrounds are particularly exposed, the extermination policies, the Jewish genocide, and the atrocities of war remain cloaked by the family omertà.

The Social and Cultural Limits to Appropriations of the Nazi Past • 259

When I spoke to René (aged eighteen, a student at Weinberg in Hamburg, and the son of two secondary school teachers, both members of the SPD), about his grandparents, he rapidly mentioned that his maternal grandfather had been a pilot in the Luftwaffe before becoming an airplane mechanic after the war, and then moved on to his paternal grandfather whose "history is much more interesting, because he was the mayor of a small town and he opposed [Nazism]. He went to jail too." Although René knew the details of this history, he remained silent about the past of his maternal grandparents.

> I don't know much about it unfortunately. I should learn one day (*Müsste ich eigentlich noch mal rauskriegen*). I don't really know why. [He considers.] No, I think [he hesitates] I think that very often, that's how it is. I don't know if that's the case here, but—that's how it was in the years after the war. They didn't talk about it. People started working again, and they silenced it (*totgeschwiegen*). I think it was also like that here. We don't talk about that anymore, I think. A taboo subject. There you go.[56]

René talks about the "general silence" to explain his own lack of conversation about the past with his maternal grandparents. He does not dare talk about the specific reasons why he has not questioned his grandparents, and why they themselves have never broached the subject. Some students encounter an explicit refusal to talk about the past, like Benjamin, aged eighteen, student in Weinberg, the son of a radio director and a primary school teacher. He talked about the reaction of his grandmother, a retired secretary. "The war is a period that she doesn't like to think about, and she doesn't really want to talk about it. And so, I leave her alone. Everyone has to know themselves [how to deal with it]."[57]

Most of the students, however, have not dared to ask their grandparents for information. Several factors can explain this lack of initiative on the part of the students. The dual fears of "hurting" the grandparents by mentioning a difficult period in their lives or discovering a shameful past (a typical configuration in the construction of family secrets) are strong enough to prevent the grandchildren from breaking the silence that protects their grandparents. Indeed, once they have learned about the Nazi past, these students are afraid of what they might discover.

Magdalena, whom we encountered earlier,[58] evoked the reluctance of her maternal grandfather, a retired postman, to talk about his past as a soldier in the Wehrmacht on the Eastern Front, which was "a taboo theme." Her mother explained this reaction by the terrible experiences her father had during the war and the fact that he lost two brothers on the front line. Magdalena, although she repeated this interpretation, also expressed her doubts.

Well, I don't know how it happened. I can only imagine that the escape at the end, the permanent fear, being with no food—that it was difficult for him. And to have lost two brothers, and all that, it's overwhelming. But I don't know to what extent [she hesitates] he was in the NSDAP or what—I don't know at all. I mean—at any rate, they all had to be members, but I don't know, to what point he—it was really [she hesitates] it was really their opinion, I don't know. But I can't imagine talking to him about it. He is already so withdrawn in any case.[59]

The fear of awakening painful memories is therefore accompanied by the fear of discovering Nazi belonging or beliefs, which today constitute a social and political stigma. The fact that parents and grandparents are silent about this past reinforces the students' reticence to ask questions. The silence allows them free rein to imagine the worst, as we can see in Benjamin's case.

The problem is that he [the grandfather] was never very talkative, if you didn't go toward him. Apparently, he was a prisoner of war with the Russians. And he always talked about his war wound, how he got it, it was a grenade, I think. But there was also a time—I was fourteen or fifteen years old and I was very, very left-wing, had a mohawk and things like that. And for me, anybody who had anything to do with this war was a criminal—well [he does not finish his sentence]. But I couldn't understand that at all—and I just said, "no, how could you go to war, and especially for the National Socialists." And [he hesitates] I don't know, I had had trouble managing all that . . . . The fact that he—yes, I don't know if [he hesitates] actually, he still did follow this ideology, which was for me, at the time—he [he begins his sentence again] even today, it's quite incomprehensible for me personally. But I don't know, you can't generalize like that. At the time, [when I was an adolescent], it was very simple: all those who lived in the state and who didn't oppose it are, by definition, criminals.[60]

The more clues there are as to a probable participation of grandparents in Nazi crimes, the more difficult conversation with the grandchildren is. The critical ability of the latter seems to be inversely proportional to the seriousness of the facts. The more likely it is that the grandparents were not only merely uncritical "spectators" of the murders, but were in fact personally active in the Nazi extermination policies, the more difficult it is to talk about these things in the family, and the more it becomes almost impossible to have a "partially critical" discourse. Richard talked for three hours and told me several stories about his grandmothers and his maternal family, before telling me, at the end of the interview, and in a completely different context (regarding the exhibition on the Wehrmacht), about an episode that resembles an active participation by his grandfather in the mass shootings of Jews on the Eastern Front, the first stage of the Jewish genocide.

I heard that [in the exhibition on the Wehrmacht] scientifically, the images were faked (*gefaked*). And that's why [he hesitates] that it was more the SS or—and not the Wehrmacht, in any case. Even though—I have to say—my grandfather told me that when he was in the Baltic states, in Lithuania, during World War II, the SS invited the Wehrmacht—more exactly the company under his command—they invited them, to participate in an execution of Jews![61]

The anecdote remains inevitably vague, in spite of my numerous questions in the remainder of the interview and the fact that it is an anecdote that was repeated several times, both by the grandfather himself and his wife. Several times, Richard expressed his belief that his grandfather "refused to go" without being able to explain how that happened exactly. We can see the students' difficulty in talking about (and accepting) a loved one's possible active participation in the genocide, for the students who are now well aware of the historical atrocities. However, this does not prevent him from being critical toward the same grandparents, nor from observing a "general participation" in the Nazi war effort. It, therefore, seems necessary to relativize the observation made by Harald Welzer and his team involving the hero-worship of grandparents by grandchildren. Indeed, my fieldwork does not confirm Welzer's results. The appropriation of the history of the Nazi past and family histories are both complex and can be paradoxical or contradictory. The discourses of these adolescents are very rarely homogenous, as Welzer and his team would have us believe. Although they indeed have difficulties admitting (at least in an interview) that their grandfathers actively participated in the genocide and they also use vague stories (as Welzer and his team show), these practices of avoiding a grandparent's guilt are very often accompanied by a critical attitude toward the same grandfather, his political position, or his active support for National Socialism. Things are therefore not as straightforward as Welzer, who assumes that grandchildren are generally less willing to confront the past than their grandparents, suggests. Rather than a generational opposition, there are socially distinctive ways of dealing with the past, which never exclude critique. In this respect, my fieldwork with "good" students instead demonstrates that for them, Grandpa was indeed a Nazi, but we do not know what kind of Nazi he was.

Everyday History versus Political History

When grandparents do begin to talk, a gap emerges between their memories and these well-informed adolescents' interpretations of the past, which adds to the communication problems. This configuration brings the students closer to the history teachers who experienced similar problems with their own parents. Indeed, whether students or teachers, family discussions of the past, without exception, are very rarely political. Everyday history, feelings, fears, adventures, or misfortunes are transmitted, but there is very little discussion about political positions or reflections on the Nazi extermination policies.

> Yes, my grandfather often talked about these themes [the past]. My grandmother not so much, because she didn't really experience the war—well, yes, she did consciously live through the war, but she was only in Hamburg (*die war ja nur in Hamburg, saß die ja*)! Yes, well, she also talked about that she had to go and hide in the basement, or when she was on a school bus and a bomb exploded next to it, and they all had to get out, etc. But—[he hesitates] yes, it's more my grandfather who really talked a lot about World War II.[62]

Leif (an eighteen-year-old student at Weinberg, the son of a police executive and an employee, both right-wing, like their children) considered the stories of his grandmother's everyday life as not very typical of the war that "she did not really experience."[63] However, he considered that his grandfather, as a soldier, "experienced the war," even if the stories the latter told are as much a part of "everyday life" as those of his wife. As a man, the grandfather thus seems to be more legitimate in speaking about "war experiences" than the grandmother. Gender is again clearly at work here in the definition of what is associated with war. In Leif's eyes, war is clearly defined as "men's business."

> Grandpa talks a lot about World War II, even if he didn't have that many experiences on the front line . . . . Above all, he always talks about the period after the war, and how he met my grandmother. Or how he was a cook, and at the end, he had to leave to go to the front in France. But he only [tells] the funny stories (*die lustigen Geschichten*), how they stole schnapps, over there. Yes, and every time, he gets all enthusiastic about the English family who took him in when he came out of prison in 1946. He didn't even want to go back to Germany. He wanted to stay there. He still kept in touch with that family by letter, until very recently.[64]

When they mention their grandparents, the interviews overflow with stories and adventures of this kind, which it would be interesting to be able to present in detail, as has been done in research specifically centered on the family (see Welzer, Montau and Plaß 1997; Welzer, Müller and Tschuggnall [2002] 2005).[65] The past is transmitted through everyday life, disconnected from the political context of the time and in particular from the atrocities of the Nazi extermination policies. This disconnection can also lead to intergenerational conflict with grandchildren who are particularly politicized and

The Social and Cultural Limits to Appropriations of the Nazi Past • 263

historically well informed, like Richard, who talked about his inability to speak to his grandparents.

> I avoid talking to them. Well—no, I don't avoid it, but I do it much less, now. Because—after fifty years, they have established their role. They were part of the generation that was active at the time –my grandmother is eight-five, and she was very conscious of the war, and she was able to situate [the events] politically. And of course, she built herself a protective wall (*Schutzwall*). That's why we can't really talk anymore. I know how she lived through that, and it must've been horrible, of course. She lived here in Hamburg, the war, the bombs, the fire. And so [he hesitates] I think that because she was a victim herself, in this war [he hesitates] yes, still, *she was also* a victim, we can't really talk about it, because she lives all of that very subjectively. She was [too] involved.[66]

Richard's hesitation reveals his position here. Indeed, he has difficulty presenting his grandmother's "apolitical" interpretation as is. Having passed a vocational certificate, his grandmother was a housewife and then an employee in his grandfather's business. The expression "victim" does not seem quite appropriate to him, which is why he quickly nuances his statement by implying that she was also something other than a victim, even though he does not say exactly what. The grandparents' stories create a narrative of the experiences of war from the point of view of civilians, or even from the point of view of soldiers, and are out of step and sometimes in contradiction with the academic interpretations of their grandchildren, particularly in socially privileged environments. "The sites of their own experiences and thus of their socialization are diverse. Through the different roles that they take on, children become aware of different principles of organization at work in society and can partly test the norms and values that they have learned" (Percheron 1978: 41).

Learning at school and in the family can therefore reinforce each other, but they can also be in conflict, as they are for Richard here. He had trouble tolerating his grandmother's narrative of the war because he was interested in war specifically in political and academic terms.

> For example, she told me that she went to the center of the town on a bike with my uncle, he was two or three years old, and there was fire everywhere, and my uncle was yelling, "Don't go too close to the fire, Mummy!" And so, you can't talk about it. Because [he hesitates] she blocks it (*blockt ab*), a bit. I think that it's generally very widespread, in this generation.[67]

I only spoke to four families (out of 120) in which the children talked consciously and voluntarily about the role of the Jewish genocide in the political positions of their grandparents. They are rare cases of the political explanation of the past. In order to avoid painful breakdowns or awkward silences, the Holocaust is excluded from conversations with the generation who lived through it. Richard explained why he is critical of his grandmother.

Yes, because—my grandmother, I have to say—it's annoying—well, it does annoy me a bit—this ignorance, because—it is a difficult subject after all. And we hear it everywhere in the newspapers every day and it bothers me that she pretends: yes, we didn't see anything. That they hunted the Jews. Even though she knew some herself, a few Jews and a Jewish girl in her class who was also taken away, apparently. And she never asked where they took them, or why, why she disappeared. Like the racist laws. They never challenged them. Well, she said it was a mistake [the Jewish genocide], but you can see that she doesn't want to—[he hesitates]—to really confront it.[68]

Grandparents not necessarily prepared to justify themselves to their children and grandchildren, often arguing that the latter "can't understand," and the latter are also not always ready to question their grandparents, even when they have the means to do so. That does not prevent them from partially criticizing or doubting the accuracy of their memories, like Richard regarding his grandmother, for example.

Although among the 120 interviewees there is one case of a violent confrontation between a father and a son during the latter's adolescent politicization, such direct confrontation seems more difficult between grandparents and grandchildren. The children, who construct their own identity during adolescence (which may take political forms), are able to confront their parents with violence, but their relationship with their grandparents seems both more distant, but also (as a result?) less conflictual. When I asked Richard if he argued with his grandmother because she never questioned the fate of her Jewish classmate, he responded,

Yeah, well, like I could fight with my granny (*so wie ich mich mit der Oma streiten könnte*). Not really—it's stupid, but [he smiles, a little awkward] well, it stays very calm. But—well, I change the subject at that point, because—there's no point. I don't think that it's on purpose, or that she has bad intentions (*das ist keine böse Absicht*) or that—[he hesitates] well, it was just her youth, and she doesn't want to take responsibility for that. It was sixty years ago [he lowered his voice], that's her perspective . . . I wouldn't say that my grandmother is rightwing, but it's—it's not very nice, to have to confront these subjects, or perhaps even admit a certain guilt. So, it's better to repress it. That annoys me a bit. Gets me angry too. So yeah. But at eighty-five years old, maybe it's normal.[69]

Other than the desire not to openly confront his grandmother, Richard's social environment may also play a role here. When Richard mentions the fact that he cannot argue with his grandmother, he has not only interiorized the norm of respecting elderly people but also that of "not raising once voice," "remaining calm." Open conflict thus appears even more difficult to imagine in this bourgeois milieu in Hamburg, than it is for example in working-class families in the Ruhr, questioned by Lutz Niethammer and Alexander Von Plato on the same subject (1983–1985).

Although Richard said he was able to understand his grandmother's repressed "guilt," which consisted in not asking questions about the deportation of the Jews, it remains unimaginable for him to argue with her. Communication is even more complicated with his grandfather, who was probably directly involved in the extermination of Jews on the frontline, as we saw in the half-confessed participation (or refusal to participate?) in at least one shooting, mentioned above. Of course, it is easier to accept passive behavior or a lack of criticism in the face of Nazi extermination policies than it is to accept the active participation of one's grandfather.[70] Asking for justification would mean taking stock of the crime, which may risk destroying the family. Rare are the children and grandchildren who would provoke such conflict—and accept the emotional consequences—not only with their grandparents, but also (and perhaps especially?) with their parents. Parents would be implicitly criticized in any interrogation of grandparents, because this would mean challenging the silence of the former. It is therefore important to relativize the results of Harald Welzer's research team: although the students questioned here were aware that "Grandpa may have been a Nazi," indeed sometimes they clearly affirmed that "Grandpa was indeed a Nazi," they tried to save face for their grandparents, and reconcile the irreconcilable, academic history with the family history of their grandparents. Sometimes, if this reconciliation is difficult, the discrepancy between the two versions of the past too contradictory, this can contribute to the feeling of boredom. Pursuing questions of Nazism in the family throws into question the honor and respect of one's elders, the psychological and family tensions are too important here; the price to pay is too high, and the students develop their own form of *Harthörigkeit*.

Differences between Hamburg and Leipzig: From Family Trajectories to School Lessons

The students experiencing this specific kind of boredom that we have called *Harthörigkeit* are not only students from a Gymnasium, coming from socially well-off families. The phenomenon is also specific to Hamburg. The comparison between Hamburg and Leipzig will complexify further the comparison between students from socially advantaged families and those that come from a working-class background.

The fact that the students in Leipzig did not express this same feeling of boredom with the subject can be explained by family configurations that are specific to East Germany, which we have seen in the previous chapter, and which we will only briefly discuss the impact of here. This lack of boredom can also be explained by teaching practices that are specific to Leipzig, a point that we will see in more detail in this section. First, as we saw in the introduction, most of the students in Leipzig belong to the fourth postwar generation. It was their great-grandparents who lived through the Nazi period, which increases their distance from Nazism. The second explanation lies in their parents' (and grandparents') experiences in the GDR, a theme which appears incomparably more urgent than that of Nazism. These two "accursed" periods overlap in my interview with Hauke, a student in his final year at the *Gymnasium* in Leipzig and the son of a shopkeeper and a bank director.

> My grandma doesn't want to understand anything. Either National Socialism or the GDR, "yes that happened, it wasn't good, but it wasn't all bad either! Adolf also built the highways" and "you can't see it like that." Yes, she is becoming—inflexible because of her age, also, I think. With the GDR it's the same. But in the GDR, both of my grandparents were much more active—as [he hesitates], well, the FDJ (Communist youth), I don't know what they call that, *Bezirkleiter* (district leader),[71] and Party members. Everywhere they could participate, my grandparents *participated*. It doesn't matter if it was good or bad. [He hesitates again.] In the GDR, it was really extreme, because my Grandpa, he wanted to study, and for that, it was better to be in the Party! And so, once again, *Mitläufertum* (following along). . . . Yes, and then, today, they still say, it wasn't all bad! Everybody had work and everything! And my grandma, she is not the type to go traveling everywhere. Maybe to the Czech Republic at the most. And she could have done that then anyway. And [he imitates the sound of her voice] "it wasn't so bad at all, really." And when we say, "yes, but now you can buy bananas," she responds, "yes, but we survived, without bananas." There you go, typical old people attitudes. I think it's quite widespread![72]

Although Hauke criticizes his grandparents' positions in relation to Nazism, it is their participation in the Communist regime that poses more problems for him—without him trying to compare these two regimes— possibly because it has contributed to a conflict between his mother and her parents. It seems that the students in Leipzig were less focused on the subject of Nazism, when it comes to family history, which may contribute to the fact that they were less overwhelmed by the subject when they encountered it intensively at school. We also saw in the previous chapter that they perceived the current regime as being more "in danger" than their peers in Hamburg did. The intensive teaching of Nazism at school may therefore seem to them more justified than it does to the more privileged students in Hamburg, who consider democracy to be self-evident.

Finally, the different pedagogic practices in Hamburg and Leipzig also play a role in the production of these differences.

An analysis of the subjects on the *Abitur* exam at Weinberg since 1983 shows how rare the treatment of the historical period of 1933–1945 is after the eleventh grade.[73] The substantial freedom given to schools in Hamburg allows each teacher to choose the curriculum in twelfth and thirteenth grade (the only constraint being the obligation to cover at least one subject in contemporary history and one subject in modern or premodern history). Depending on the periods covered, a teacher can propose three subjects for the *Abitur*, from which two will be chosen for his or her students (and only them) by a delegate from the ministry. The students from the same school therefore answer different questions for the *Abitur*, depending on the teacher that they have had in class. The three subjects reflect the three semesters of the class over the two years prior to the *Abitur* (twelfth and thirteenth grade). They therefore give us indications about what has been covered in class between 1983 and 2004. Examining the figures, the importance of Nazism is minimal and ultimately quite recent.

In comparison with other themes, the difference is striking: out of 190 subjects from the *Abitur* exam since 1983, Roman history has been far more frequently posed than any other subject (slightly more than one out of five, thirty-nine times in total), followed (but far ahead of) the Middle Ages (slightly more than one out of seven, twenty-eight times). The French Revolution and Prussia are in a similar position (one in eleven, seventeen and eighteen times respectively) and it is only in the third group of subjects (once in twenty-one questions) that Weimar appears (nine times), appearing for the first time in 1987, behind German or American imperialism (eleven times), but before the United States (eight times) and as often as colonialism. Nazism has a very marginal place (three times), along with antisemitism (appearing only once on the *Abitur*) and the Cold War.

Subjects on the period of National Socialism were proposed by two different teachers, first in 1995 by Mr Hatze (between 1983 and 1995 the subject was not proposed at the *Abitur*), a second and third time by Ms Heide in 2002 and 2003. This teacher, interviewed on her unusual treatment of the subject in the last two years of high school, argues quite simply: "the subject is part of the curriculum, so I cover it." Unlike other teachers in this school, she does not let the students choose whether they wish to study this theme.[74] However, between 1995 and 2003, there was only one student who actually chose to answer this question for the exam (there are always two subjects to choose from).

None of the other schools allowed me to access the archives. It is therefore impossible to systematically compare how the subject is treated in different schools. However, observation allows me to say that the teachers in Leipzig tend to scrupulously follow the curriculum. When I arrived in 2003 at the *Gymnasium* Monnet, the four classes of ninth grade as well as the four classes in twelfth grade were studying National Socialism. "[The subject is on] the curriculum in 12.1 [first semester of twelfth grade], which allows us to cover it quite quickly in ninth grade, because we will really go into detail later [in final year]," Ms Gerte told me. Mr Wolff emphasized the fact that the teaching of Nazism has been broadened, particularly to be able to cover it in the final year in comparison with the GDR. "And that's good,"[75] he observes. He also explains that the way of covering the subject is completely different between middle school and high school.

> Yes, well, here, in our school, we try to cover it more emotionally rather than rationally in ninth grade. . . . Because afterwards, in high school, we will have much more time to really study the laws. To study the enabling act (*Ermächtigungsgesetz*). I can't do that in ninth grade. I can say, quite quickly, that Hitler took full control in 1934, and that there were two or three elements that led to it, but I can't look at the text of a law. But that's what I mean. In twelfth grade, I really have time, I have six months on National Socialism, I can go into it in-depth. I can really work in detail. With historical facts, contacts and links, with different people, and I can work on specific motivations. I don't have the time to do that in ninth grade.[76]

The students in the final year of school in Leipzig did not complain of feeling bored with the subject nor did they consider that the lessons at school "taught them nothing new," nor was it seen as "too much"—even though objectively they spent much more time on that subject because they covered it not only in ninth grade, but also for six months in twelfth grade.[77] In this respect, the curriculum in Leipzig is quite close to what Ms Heide does in Hamburg; a longer approach in high school allows for a different perspective to that in ninth grade. Moreover, in Leipzig, beyond the family reasons already mentioned, the treatment in ninth grade is perhaps not long enough to allow for the development of a *Harthörigkeit* comparable to that of the students in Hamburg.

The students in Hamburg who chose to take advanced history, who had an interest in the subject, and who expressed a feeling of annoyance had generally not covered National Socialism in junior or senior year. Indeed, the *Harthörigkeit* expressed by the students was taken seriously by most of their teachers. Some think that it is counterproductive to make the students "disgusted" with the subject, "because they're so sick of it." Others consider, like the students, that it is not very historically interesting. Ms Gerhard told me,

The Social and Cultural Limits to Appropriations of the Nazi Past • 269

for example, that she finds "Weimar much more interesting than National Socialism," because the latter theme does not really allow for "an interesting analysis." As in any dictatorship, she said, "everything is played out in advance," there are "no surprises." That is why she said she thinks it is good to teach it in ninth grade but not in junior or senior year. Most of her colleagues share this analysis.

It seems quite possible to overcome the feelings of annoyance, as we can see when looking at the eight students who attend Ms Heidi's advanced history class. They are an exception at the *Gymnasium* Weinberg because she forced them to study the period in their senior year, initially against their will. Indeed, she is one of two teachers who obliged her students to study this period in their final year in advanced history, in spite of their protests and their claims that they "already knew everything about the subject." Let us look more closely at this exception.

Nazism in Its Historical Context: Giving Meaning to the Past through Its Historicization

The treatment of the period between 1933 and 1945 in their senior year in Hamburg surprised the boys[78] in Ms Heide's class and was sufficiently powerful to counteract their feelings of boredom. Covering Nazism "in detail" in the senior year provides the students with an understanding of the subject that they could not have acquired in ninth grade. Going beyond simplistic emotional explanations also allows students to extricate themselves from the feeling of vague guilt and move toward a better understanding of the historical reasons for the genocide. Their *Harthörigkeit* was progressively replaced by renewed interest. Ms Heide's class illustrates the fact that boredom is not simply to do with "too much," but a combination of "too much" quantity and "too little" quality for students from socially privileged backgrounds with high cultural and academic capital. Moreover, these classes illustrate what is at stake in the use of emotion with this specific public. The students were expressing their fatigue at encountering the subjects in the same repetitive emotional ways without obtaining an understanding of the scientific and historical issues. Johannes described the evolution of his own attitude toward the history of Nazism.

> Up until tenth grade, it was really good. And then, yes, the eleventh and the twelfth, there was a certain annoyance with the Third Reich (*Drittes Reich-Verdruss*), we said, "oh no, not that again, and again (*nicht schon wieder, ständig*), we know all that already." But now, in thirteenth grade, we have studied it completely differently. And doing it now, it's not at all the same thing, we have

all understood that now. It's much more—exact, with more details. And it's really something else, and it's really good. In thirteenth grade, we do it much more intensively than in tenth grade. And you realize a lot of things, we're much more interested. [He hesitates] Yes—me, I also understand more things than back then, in tenth grade. Perhaps we weren't always listening either.[79]

The eight students in Ms Heide's advanced history class are different from the other students in the final year because of their personal interest in pre-1933 history. Only one of them mentioned Nazism at the beginning of the interview, six others mentioned Weimar and/or the 1918 revolution, and the last mentioned the revolution of 1848 as the theme that appears the most important to them. The enlargement of their historical repertoire and increasing distance from the Nazi past in a first step has allowed them later on in their lives to return toward this same past, regarding it with fresh eyes.

Yes, ultimately, everything comes back in advanced history class. It allowed me to really understand a lot of things. Perspectives on history, that I didn't have before. In principle, before, I never really thought. I always said, "National Socialism, that's shit. It shouldn't have happened." But I never really thought about why it happened, and why it could also happen [again]. It was just, "that's it, it's bad," and that was all for me. And that has really changed. . . . And I never thought [in fact] that antisemitism did not come out of nowhere with the NSDAP and when Hitler came. But it's something that existed for hundreds of years before. And retrospectively, I had a very limited point of view (*eingeschränkte Sichtweise*).[80]

René spoke of how becoming aware of historical complexity and the treatment of Weimar in senior year helped him to understand the NSDAP's rise to power in a specific historical conjuncture, which up until then had remained obscure to him. "Now, we study it [the history of Nazism] in a very comprehensive way, and it's also lots of things that happened in the two years [before Nazism] or in the year of the 1923 crisis, all that."[81]

Covering the Weimar Republic in detail in class helps the students to understand the history of the Nazi past. Nazism thus changes in status. It goes from being an incomprehensible horror, to being a historical event produced by human beings in a specific social and political configuration. Horror and rejection are replaced by an acceptance of this human and political reality, of which the causes must be understood.

I think Weimar is particularly important. The revolution. And retrospectively—yes, the mistakes, perhaps, that were committed. Because there were lots of things that were created from that. Hitler took power, and the history of the twenty or twenty-five years that followed were influenced by that.

And when you stay mistakes, what you mean?
First [he hesitates], the articles—I think it was Article 48 in the Constitution. The emergency decree (*Notverordnung*). And then, the SPD joined the Conservatives—took a step toward them, and the revolution wasn't finished. That they moved toward moderation, toward reform, and so they didn't make any profound changes. The structure wasn't changed. And so, for example, the army leadership was still—in place. And they remained in contact with the government. . . . In principle, there wasn't a real rupture between—the old and the new principles. And—for reasons of political power, in order to have the army behind them, they contacted people like Hindenburg. Or Ludendorff.[82]

Inserting Nazism into its historical context thus allows the students to create distance from it. It allows them to be interested in other periods of history in more depth and to develop a personal relationship to German history before the war without generating anxiety. This new interest then allows them to rediscover their taste for the history of Nazism and to appropriate it in their own way.

School-Based Constructions of Likes and Dislikes

Some students, as we have seen, do not have the necessary resources to appropriate the Nazi past, and may simply miss the point of the school discourses, or develop a certain *Harthörigkeit* toward them. Yet others are more inclined—and more able—to construct their own interpretation of the Nazi past and make sense of history and the stories they use in their everyday lives to construct one or several positive image/s of themselves.

The discourses of the students and the teachers are closely related. The scientific interpretive framework corresponds more to expectations of students from privileged social backgrounds with high levels of cultural capital, while the moral interpretive framework corresponds more to students from disadvantaged social backgrounds, because it interacts with their own likes and dislikes, as well as their resentment, caused by personal experiences of discrimination or xenophobia.

Students who are "in significant academic difficulty," "left behind in history class," and the "good students" who are "bored with history class" nevertheless share difficulties in making history meaningful in their everyday lives and making sense of what they learn at school. As a result, there are certain forms of *Harthörigkeit* that are specific to each of them. For the first group, language difficulties, low levels of cultural family capital and family cultural practices that are out of step with school practices, all make it difficult for them to access history as it is taught at school. History therefore often remains a series of punctual events, that are positioned as contemporary, without depth or spatial and temporal diversity. In the students' lives, "history" is sometimes simply opposed to "the present," as it was for Omeira. Although Joey is one of the students who went the furthest in trying to compare World War II and the Afghanistan war in particular, he lacked the knowledge required to make such a comparison.

Among the students from more advantaged backgrounds, family cultural practices and school practices are very similar. The information that the students acquire in their families, through their older brothers and sisters, at family discussions around the table, visits to museums, reading newspapers or young adult novels, but also through television programs, all strongly resemble what they learn at school—hence a feeling of "déjà vu" and hostility to their "overexposure" to the subject.

The academic difficulties of those who are "left behind in history" are responsible for a significant disconnection between family history and school history. The students often struggle to establish a connection between what they learn "in books," or "in films," and the lives of their parents and grandparents. The lack of temporality is once again essential here. Not being able to establish a chronology of historical events makes it difficult to place their parents or grandparents "in history."

In contrast, for the students who are "bored with history class," the resemblance between parental and teachers' discourses is part of what makes history so unattractive to them. Moreover, they clearly know how to situate their grandparents in history. Specific knowledge of dates, in particular of atrocities, leads them to fear the active involvement, or at least passive complicity, of their grandparents in the crimes. In addition, history classes at middle school do not provide them with the essential information they need to understand these atrocities, which are thus relegated to an "absolute evil." It is therefore difficult, even impossible, for these adolescents to identify their grandparents as actors of history (as it is presented at school), which is why they reinterpret it.

Students whose parents come from other countries do not encounter (or only very rarely) the history of these countries as part of the school curriculum. The history of Afghanistan is not included in the courses, the image of the country does not move beyond negative Western stereotypes (drugs, war, fundamentalism). In order to analyze the attitudes toward history of students whose parents come from Afghanistan, for example, it would be necessary to begin with the history of Afghanistan, in order to see how they construct connections between that history and the history of Nazi Germany. This is also true for students who come from Eastern European countries, from Asia or from Africa. The eurocentrism that is inherent in the secondary school system therefore has clear repercussions on the choice of this research subject and its analysis. Although it is not possible in the context of this book, an experiment in a class with students from very diverse origins, able to make parallels between the histories of their countries of origin and the country of arrival would be a very interesting avenue for future research. Some teachers indeed try to do this, but it remains an exception for two main reasons. First, there is a lack of training on non-European history, and second, there is such a wide diversity of national origins among the students (thirty-three nationalities are represented at Wiesi). In France, David Lepoutre and Isabelle Cannoodt (2005) took steps in this direction with their school-based study focusing on family histories, conducted with students from migrant families over four consecutive years during a writing activity, and combined with documentary research on family memory in tenth-grade classes at Pointcaré middle school in La Courneuve, near Paris.

Family histories of migration, however, although they are not frequently present in teaching per se, are nonetheless mobilized by the students to give meaning to the academic history of the Nazi past. Thus, the students' own experiences of war, or those of their family, but also their experiences of xenophobic or racist discrimination in German society can be mobilized to give a personal meaning to the history they see at school. These adolescents therefore transpose these experiences onto the Nazi past, transforming them and appropriating them as a "past in the present." The temporal and spatial compression of history into an amalgamation, in which events and figures float unattached, facilitates this operation: historical references are mobilized freely, in a potpourri of stories that primarily serve to pass moral judgment both on the past and on the present. This judgment, although it is made on grounds different from those of their teachers leads to a structural homology in likes and dislikes toward the past and the present. This homology finds its basis in an emotional approach to the past.

Students in the *Gymnasium* in Hamburg, on the other hand, rediscovered their appetite for the past by establishing a distance from it, through its historicization and its inscription in a broader historical context. The fact that they are being taught by a teacher who is herself from the third generation, for whom it is important to distance oneself from moral judgment and adopt a historicizing approach, creates once again a homology of likes and dislikes between the teacher and the students. This homology, however, is based on a scientific approach rather than an emotional one.

The phenomenon of *Harthörigkeit* is therefore socially situated and can be overcome in different ways depending on the social environment and the academic and social capital available to the students. Adopting an emotional or a scientific attitude toward the past allows the students to once again develop their interest in it.

Here we have looked at the school and the family as frames that influence the appropriation of the past. The next chapter will specifically focus on peer groups and their role as a frame in the more practical and playful uses of the past.

Notes

1. It is important to remember, with Alf Lüdtke, that "the mechanical execution of an order or a prohibition is impossible. There are only permanent (re-)interpretations (*[Um] deuten*) that ensure survival" (1991a: 14).
2. Although in the more well-off suburbs of Hamburg and Leipzig it was possible to meet interviewees in nearby cafes, this was impossible in the two low-income areas, because there were neither bars nor cafes.
3. Interview of 30 September 2003.
4. By the time I arrived at Wiesi, I had already done more than thirty interviews with students in Weinberg.
5. At Wiesi, teachers often explained deviant behavior among students in terms of national groups or origins, suggesting that "Turks or Afghans are more violent" and so forth. This use of nationality as an explanation for behavior considered unacceptable by the institution clearly leads to discrimination.
6. Interview of 30 September 2003.
7. Ibid.
8. Interview of 29 September 2003.
9. Although Omeira's vocabulary was quantitatively limited, she did not have the same language difficulties as her classmate Omer.
10. Several teachers talked to me about this difficulty that students with low cultural capital have situating events in time and in space.
11. Interview of 31 January 2004.
12. We might hypothesize that Christian had never really thought about the borders between the GDR and the FRG before in his everyday life, and that the discourse he produces here is entirely linked to the interview situation, which forces him to produce a discourse on reality that has very little real meaning for him. He behaves in the interview as he does in class—he tries out something and looks at me, as he looks at his teacher, to see if he is on the right track. Since I do not give him any indications to stop, as a teacher would in class, he continues.
13. Interview of 30 September 2003. Omer has problems with spoken German, he makes grammatical errors, particularly with gender. These have not been reproduced in the translation given that the re-transcription of errors brings little to the interpretation here.
14. Interview of 12 February 2004.
15. It is striking to note that for almost all the students, even after they have covered Nazism in class, and regardless of their social belonging or academic success, this question of "why" the genocide happened remains entirely intact. The school provides them nothing in the way of satisfying explanations.
16. Interview of 30 September 2003.
17. Ibid.
18. Ibid.
19. Ibid.
20. See the discussion of this book in chapter 3, in the subsection on Manipulation.
21. Interview of 20 September 2003.
22. According to Christian Baudelot, Marie Cartier, and Christine Détrez, it is this scholarly reading that constitutes one of the explanations (among others, including adolescent socialization) for the decline in reading among French adolescents (particularly boys) between middle school and high school.

The Social and Cultural Limits to Appropriations of the Nazi Past • 275

23. Interview of 30 September 2003.
24. Although Baudelot, Cartier, and Détrez emphasize the proximity between the worlds of books and images for high school students, this is only true for those who read. Indeed, those who do not read turn exclusively toward audiovisual media, and there are many of them among the students mentioned here.
25. The students' difficulties remembering the names of authors and producers are connected—both for reading and for other media—to this "ordinary" way of reading.
26. Interview of 26 February 2004. I was able to interview Markus only because I spoke to all the students in the tenth grade class in Weinberg. I also used this argument to convince him to speak to me. I told him that my thesis depended on him, that if I did not speak to all of the students my results would be biased.
27. Field notes, 26 February 2004.
28. Interview of 30 September 2003.
29. Ibid.
30. *American History X*, directed by Tony Kaye (Burbank, CA: New Line Cinema, 1998).
31. Interview of 3 September 2003.
32. Ibid.
33. Omer, in addition to this informal, colloquial, sometimes slang, "youth" language, has a genuine difficulty with spoken German.
34. This German term is similar to the English expression "hard of hearing." However, where in English we would equate this with the beginning of deafness, the German does not necessarily reflect a physical affliction, but rather a difficulty listening/hearing, that may or may not be physiological. "Harthörig: daher kommt es, dasz . . . ein harthörichter den klang und die worte nimmermehr recht zu unterscheiden weisz," *Das Deutsche Wörterbuch von Jacob und Wilhelm Grimm in 16 Bänden*, Leipzig, S. Hirzel, 1854–1960, *Quellenverzeichnis 1971* 10, no. 513 (available online: http://woerterbuchnetz. de/cgi-bin/WBNetz/wbgui_py?sigle=DWB&mode=Vernetzung&lemid=GH02814# XGH02814). I would like to thank Alf Lüdtke for directing my attention to the conceptual usefulness of this term.
35. The media's use of this term is extremely normative and does not help us to clarify the phenomena. As a result, I will not use it here.
36. The theoretical issue of the opposition between the written and the oral, not very useful in the analysis of representations of the past, has been dealt with, notably in the introduction.
37. In Germany, each citizen has two votes in the legislative elections, one for a party list to achieve proportional representation, and the second one to directly elect a representative in a first-past-the-post vote. Most people vote for the same party but it is possible to vote in two different directions, which is what these interviewees do almost systematically, justifying this practice with arguments that demonstrate their in-depth knowledge of political stakes and mobilizing the language of the political field.
38. Peter Härtling, 2000. *Reise gegen den Wind* (Fly against the wind), Weinheim, Basel, Beltz.
39. Interview of 13 April 2003. The interviewee emphasized the word that is italicized.
40. Here, as elsewhere, there is one exception.
41. Interview of 27 December 2001.
42. For example, the debate in the early twenty-first century around the compensation that German companies should pay to forced laborers, whom they exploited under the Nazi regime.
43. RTL is a commercial television station in Germany.
44. Interview of 26 December 2001.

45. Objectively speaking, the treatment of Nazism did take a long time: from October 2003 to December 2004. The students spent over a year studying this theme. The "collective evaluation" session (I called it a brainstorming, so as to not intimidate the students) took place in June 2003, after eight months of class on the subject.
46. The contrary is also possible, as we have seen for Leonie, whose older brother monopolized conversations on history and politics with the father until he left for the United States (chapter 3). The effect of age combined with that of gender was particularly disadvantageous in Leonie's family.
47. Interview of 21 April 2003.
48. Interview of 22 February 2003.
49. Judith Kerr, *When Hitler Stole Pink Rabbit* (New York: Coward, McCann & Geoghegan, 1971.)
50. Interview of 22 February 2003.
51. Although there are many teachers among the population of parents at the Weinberg school, for whom Percheron's analysis seems to still be valid, the children of doctors and lawyers also seem to have similar experiences. Can we conclude that there is a left-right consensus in the academic treatment of the period? Other studies on the parents' voting practices and the treatment of Nazism would be necessary to confirm this.
52. Interview of 11 April 2003.
53. Ibid.
54. We will see below why students from privileged social backgrounds in Leipzig do not have the same reactions of boredom as those in Hamburg do.
55. Interview of 22 February 2003.
56. Ibid.
57. Interview of 18 April 2003.
58. See chapter 2, section "Legitimate Ways of Treating the Nazi Past."
59. Interview of 13 April 2003.
60. Interview of 18 April 2003.
61. Interview of 4 November 2003.
62. Interview of 22 February 2003.
63. It is interesting to note this definition of war used by the interviewees, which is almost always limited to the battlefield. It is also important to explore the reasons why a broader and more everyday definition of war seems inconceivable to the interviewees. This might help us to understand the gaps and breakdowns between the school and media political discourses on the Nazi past on one hand, and the family discourses on the other.
64. Interview of 22 February 2003.
65. Although such a presentation is beyond the scope of this book, an in-depth study on the mechanisms of family transmission, based on monographs of European families, is planned for a future publication.
66. Interview of 11 April 2003.
67. Interview of 13 April 2003.
68. Ibid.
69. Interview of 11 April 2003.
70. Here I am specifically referring to the Jewish genocide, because it is the subject that these German students are most concerned with and which they say they have trouble talking with their grandparents about. There are, of course, any number of other taboo subjects, such as the execution of civilians, the treatment of prisoners of war, forced labor, et cetera. But these are never mentioned by the students; the taboo therefore remains intact, unlike the Jewish genocide. The students mention this as a "problematic subject" for their

The Social and Cultural Limits to Appropriations of the Nazi Past • 277

communication with their grandparents, probably because it is covered in such detail at school, in the books that they read, and the museums they visit.

71. In the GDR, the districts (*Bezirke*) were administrative units between the state and the *Landkreis*. In 1952, fourteen *Bezirke* were created in the GDR, which is roughly equivalent to the *Regierungsbezirke* in the FRG, to which East Berlin was added in 1961. They did not have the same political autonomy as the *Länder* in the FRG. The *Bezirksleitung* was the administrative level of the SED that governed the *Bezirke*. The secretary-general of the *Bezirksleitung* was a member of the *Zentralkomitee* of the SED and sometimes even a member of the *Politbüro* of the *Zentralkomitee* of the SED, the highest political body of the Party. As members of the *Bezirksleitung*, Hauke's grandparents held positions of significant administrative and political responsibility, even though they were not secretary-generals.

72. Interview of 3 November 2003.

73. To obtain these figures, I analyzed the archives of the *Abitur* exams in the basement of *Gymnasium* Weinberg. The school principal, passionate about history, had kept all the school archives since his arrival, and generously allowed me access to the basement where they were preserved, completely disordered, and under a thick layer of dust. I was thus able to sort through all of the *Abitur* exam questions conducted since 1983. I had hoped to be able to study in detail the exam questions on the 1933–1945 period carried out by the students since 1983, but I found, to my great surprise, only one exercise written on the subject in twenty years. As a result, I chose to quantitatively study the subjects proposed by the teachers. I constructed categories based on the questions formulated in the exam.

74. In Hamburg, the curriculum in history from the eleventh grade is very free. Lots of history teachers propose a series of subjects to the students and decide with them will be covered.

75. Interview of 10 October 2003.

76. Interview of 10 October 2003.

77. There is one exception among the students interviewed in Leipzig: one girl in twelfth grade says that they could "reduce" the number of classes on Nazism.

78. There are only boys in Ms Heide's class.

79. Interview of 22 February 2003.

80. Interview of 23 April 2003 with René.

81. Interview of 22 February 2003.

82. Interview of 22 February 2003.

Chapter 6

PEER-GROUP DYNAMICS AND PLAYFUL
USES OF THE PAST

The Nazi past is a serious subject, especially at school. It evokes feelings of guilt, regret, "absolute" horror, and dismay. The National Socialist extermination policy is a subject that "cannot be joked about." There was too much suffering, too much cruelty, and too much violence leading up to the rationalized extermination of millions of people for the Nazi past to be anything other than somber and solemn. The dignity of the victims and the gravity of the Nazi atrocities make this essential. Beyond the moral requirements, very specific attitudes must be maintained out of respect for the victims and their families without losing sight of the political system and the values of human rights that were so brutally violated. As a result, the school, and history teachers in particular, require an "intensive" treatment of the period between 1933 and 1945. They also ensure that the students react to it with respect.

All pedagogical relationships impose rules for behavior (sitting still, being silent, etc.) that are exerted within the framework of a relationship of domination between the school as an institution, its representatives (the teachers), and those who are subject to these constraints (often against or outside of their own will). This also applies, and perhaps particularly applies, to the teaching of the Nazi past. Indeed, as we have seen, the teaching of National Socialist history is often explicitly compared to "religious education" by some teachers. As in church, specific moral behavior is expected: no laughing, no whispering, complete attention and respect, and so forth.

Yet, although the adolescents indeed learn "how to behave" when confronted with this past, this does not prevent them from developing their own ways of using it. Often these are parallel uses, in the sense that they are neither intended nor predicted by the teachers. When the Nazi extermination policy is covered in class, the teachers regularly complain about jokes, but also about the war games that mobilize the Nazi past, particularly through the use of toy weapons and other military accoutrements, especially among the boys. This chapter will focus specifically on these jokes and games, but also on the students' "teasing" and insults that make reference to the Nazi past. These uses of the past may appear shocking, particularly because they are reminiscent of antisemitism, with which they are sometimes imbued. Here, we will particularly focus on the social functions that such jokes may fulfill within the school as an institution, and we will deconstruct the diversity of their meanings.

Although some of the students discussed here indeed develop close links to the political extreme right, others are less (or not at all) politicized. However, they all share the fact that they have invented tactics that allow them to test the limits of legitimacy, to partially challenge it, to stir up the institutional framework in order to be able to cope with it on an everyday basis. These students are most often male and are generally also having difficulty academically or are openly hostile to the school system; but there are also some "very good students" who may participate in theses collective practices. Faced with the constraints of the school system, the students are forced to adapt: they try to get around the rules, they may openly confront them, or they may ignore them. These practices are attempts to appropriate time and space within a constraining institution, as much as they are attempts to create new rules, which will alter their position within an adolescent peer group. Michel de Certeau makes a distinction between two notions: he talks about "strategies" to refer to practices of positioning and of rules being defined by dominant figures or technocrats on one hand, and on the other, "tactics" to refer to everyday practices constructing meanings and alternative interpretations among the dominated. He uses this distinction to emphasize that some do not have their own space for expression and action and thus are only able to take a position within a pre-existing structure. The tactics therefore introduce other rules into a field defined by "technocratic (and scriptural) strategies that seek to create places in conformity with abstract models" (Certeau [1980] 1988: 29). The difference between strategies and tactics is essential for our analysis. Tactics create "a space in which he [the individual] can find ways of using the constraining order of the place or the language. Without leaving the place where he has no choice but to live, and which lays down its law for him, he establishes within it a degree of plurality and creativity. By an art of being in-between he draws unexpected results from his situation" (Certeau [1980] 1988: 30).

Certain appropriations of the Nazi past in the academic environment correspond exactly to the tactics that de Certeau describes, or to Alf Lüdtke's notion of *Eigensinn*.[1] They create a space for games within an existing institutional structure (here the space of the school), which provides some of the rules of the game, to which the students' tactics must adapt. Norbert Elias uses the analogy of the card game to understand social operations (Elias [1978] 1984). Participation in a game can be thus analyzed from the point of view of "I" (the gaze of the player), of "you" (the gaze of the spectator or another player involved in the game), or of "they" (the gaze of an observer outside the game and its players). There is a double game here. The students, creating their own game within the social space, play by double rules: school rules, established by teachers and the institution, and the rule of their own position in a social space among their peers, but also in interaction with the teachers.

The teachers develop their own strategies to "hold on to" the students, to get them interested in the content of their classes, to make them participate, to prevent them "doing silly things," and to teach them the appropriate position regarding the rules. Moreover, they attempt to inculcate the "correct discourse" regarding the Nazi past. In return, the students develop practices that allow them to assert themselves, have fun, and pass the time by creating spaces of everyday freedom. They write notes to each other, they whisper, they make jokes and laugh at their teachers or their classmates—in other words they develop their *Eigensinn* in order to appropriate the space and sometimes the content of the teaching that is imposed upon them.

These practices are useful for the students. In addition to the fact that they provide a distraction and a defense against the threat of boredom, they also challenge the authority of the school. Certain students build an image of themselves as "rebels" to reinforce their situation in their peer group. The reactions of the teachers, and other students (which can take the form of frowning and disapprobation, but also sometimes more or less explicit applause) to this "transgressive" or even "deviant" behavior provides satisfaction to some of the students. Indeed, they allow the students to make themselves stand out, gain recognition and notoriety (even if somewhat dubious) through the process of constructing a self-image specific to a particular in-group. David Lepoutre, in his book *Coeur de Banlieue* (Heart of the ghetto) analyzes adolescent street culture in these terms, describing it as "an ordered ensemble of practices, a unified system of personal attitudes and relations, ultimately a cultural system" (Lepoutre [1997] 2001: 198).[2] He observed the importance of mastering the language, codes, and rituals of street culture (particularly jokes and mockery) that allow certain students to dominate others: "the domination of the best is sometimes so strong that any exchange with them is generally hopeless. The 'victim' doesn't even attempt a reply . . . and the exchange inevitably comes to an abrupt end" (Lepoutre [1997] 2001: 198).

Deviant practices and dominance within the group thus often go hand in hand. These initiatives, these responses allow the student to broaden their space for maneuvering within the group. The Nazi past is only one aspect of the curriculum among others, but it provides the students with tools that are particularly efficient in engaging conflictual relations with their teachers, to test the limits of what is possible, and to situate themselves "politically" and (especially) socially within the class. Indeed, the Nazi past presents a double advantage here: the taboo, which is consecrated in the legal prohibition of certain practices and signs (the swastika, Nazi symbols, Nazi salute, positive public references to the Nazi past, etc.), makes using these references "dangerous" because they are forbidden in the eyes of the students. It is like playing with fire. These themes are considered interesting because they are dangerous, and this "danger" increases the attraction. All the young people between twelve and fourteen years old interviewed here, with very rare exceptions, said they were interested in the period, even though the ways they used it did not necessarily conform to academic canons.

Playing with the Nazi Past: Strategies, Everyday Practices, and Tactics

Field notes: 20 October 2003
The students are excited as I enter Mr Gerste's class at the *Gesamtschule Wiesi* in Hamburg. They whisper, giggle, and talk among themselves. A group of guys gathers around Osman, talking excitedly: "Go on, you go." Osman is sixteen and is repeating tenth grade to be able to sit the *Fachabitur* (professional diploma) and then the competitive exam to join the national police force.[3] He is the class clown in many ways. He is very tall (1.90 m) and stocky. He wears his dark hair quite long; he has very dark eyes and olive skin. His imposing build gives him a physical advantage over his classmates, which is reinforced by the fact that he is a year older than most of them. He sometimes gives the others orders, particularly to some of the boys who are smaller than him. Children of Afghan parents are the majority in this class group, five or six of them often form a group with children from Turkish backgrounds. These two nationalities constitute the majority of the student body in the school. They have also accumulated a specific symbolic capital due to two Afghan "gangs" that are well-known in the neighborhood, because they often fight each other (one or two students from the school, but not from this class, are members).[4] The students (but also some of the teachers) express a certain "respect," even some fear, of these "groups." As is often the case in this *Gesamtschule*, there are only one or two students from this class whose parents both have German nationality. The group who has gathered around Osman this morning is thus a reference group, or in any case, a dominant group in the schoolyard.

Mr Gerste comes into the classroom. Osman goes up and plants himself in front of him (he is two heads taller than the teacher). The teacher looks at him in silence. "Heil Hitler!" says Osman suddenly, performing the Nazi salute. A few moments of silence follow, and then Osman, who is trying to keep a straight face asks innocently: "If we welcome you like that every day, Mr Gerste, will you get angry?" The teacher looks at him and calmly answer, "I hope that when we have covered the subject in class, such behavior will no longer occur. Go and sit down." The students burst out laughing. They all talk at once. The tension drops."Explain it to us, we don't understand," says one. "Why is it forbidden?" says another, but the question is drowned in the hubbub.[5]

We could interpret this interaction as a scene staged for my benefit as a researcher, as I was present in the classroom. But this possibility does not prevent us also analyzing it in terms of the interaction between a teacher and his students and within a group of students. Osman and his classmates—because here this was clearly a collective action—were using the Nazi past to challenge the balance of power with their history teacher.[6] They did not instigate direct confrontation with him, aware that they would lose. Nor was this a conscious valorization of the Nazi past. They were simply playing with the rules, momentarily transgressing, with a "joke"—the Nazi salute (*Hitlergruß*)—before immediately returning to the legitimate form of power relations, a student asking the teacher a question, abiding by the rules, a legitimate everyday action in the school context. The "trick" consists in transgressing the rules from within the framework of the rules themselves, which limits the teacher's power to sanction. Mr Gerste, attributing their behavior to their youth and lack of information, responded by reducing them to their status as immature students; the relationship of dependency was thus re-established. The students had their moment of pleasure—the curiosity of what would happen to Osman—and the twofold relief that led them to burst out laughing: relief both that Mr Gerste "took the joke well," and that order had been re-established in the form of the institutionally legitimate power balance. If these "little tests" are designed to destabilize the teacher, they are not, at least not here, designed to reverse the hierarchy. Indeed, the respect for this hierarchy lies in the fact that this joke is disguised as a simple question. Through such actions the students create a space for play, temporarily reversing ordinary relations: the ball is in the (surprised) teacher's court and he or she must adapt, react to the students' initiative and restore the order that will allow the class to function. The power relations between students and teachers can therefore not simply be defined as a bipolar hierarchy. Considering them in relational terms, exerted within a "force field" (Thomson 1978), allows us to underline the interdependence of those who dominate and those who are expect to obey within a system of domination.[7] The actions of the dominated, far from simple obedience or the execution

Peer-Group Dynamics and Playful Uses of the Past • 283

of orders, oblige the dominants to react on a daily basis, to establish and re-establish the institutional order in practice (Lüdtke 1991a, 1991b). These practices (which also play out through directives and their reinterpretation by the agents to which they are directed) thus participate in the perpetuation and reinvention of this social order on an everyday basis.

Mr Gerste attempted to explain the students' behavior.

> They are provocations [he hesitated]—I would not even say they are always blunders (*Entgleisungen*). I think it's the lack of knowledge that leads to that, and the fact that they have not really been confronted (*auseinandergesetzt*) with the theme. . . . Well, but I have never [he hesitates] punished anyone for that, in any case, you can't, not for that, can you![8]

Depriving the students of their "little pleasures" may also run the risk of provoking lasting revolt. Mr Gerste said that he is able to tolerate these challenges, more than he is obliged to. Indeed, punishing the students or getting angry about a collective joke would also make him ridiculous in the eyes of the class that launched the challenge. He has to keep a cool head and find adequate repartee, otherwise he runs the risk of losing control over the class until the end of the year. Knowing when one can accept a challenge is part of the implicit rules of how the school should function and helps the teacher gain the students' respect. Mr Gerste is aware that he runs fewer risks by letting the students laugh, while still bringing them back to their place in the school hierarchy than he would in taking too firm a stance against Osman and punishing him. He demonstrates as much flexibility as the students who are playing with the school rules. This double game helps the order at school function smoothly. Just as the factory's acceptance of the moonlighting practice of *la perruque* described by de Certeau ([1980] 1988) or Lüdtke's descriptions of "Coffee breaks and horseplay" (Lüdtke 1986a), or "Games in the workplace and 'escape' from the factory" (*Spielereien am Arbeitsplatz und "Fliehen" aus der Fabrik*) (1986b). These practices are accepted by the factory hierarchy because they are useful for the continuing establishment of order necessary for efficient production. Similarly, the temporary creation of spaces for games at school can have a beneficial effect on teaching, by easing the tension accumulated by the students (if the teacher does not become completely overwhelmed by the students). Thus *Eigensinn*, the everyday appropriation of the space, the practices, and the tactics of invention, games, and escape actively participate in the power structure. The teacher realizes the playful nature of the students' actions and also takes into account the difficulties they experience at school. These actions, which he referred to as "a casual attitude toward the theme [Nazism]," seem "strange" (*merkwürdig*) to him in light of the painful, serious, and frightening reality of Nazi crime. Yet he also admits that the students do not have the same references as he does (nor do they have the same needs in a classroom), whereas he analyzes this past as a teacher and an "intellectual."

> It's nothing more than a "yes, Hitler" or—or—or sometimes "if I draw a swastika like that, is it bad?" [He imitates a student drawing.] "Could I go to prison?" It's things like—well, graffiti, things like that. Sometimes someone will have written "Rudolf Hess was here." They've seen it somewhere. They're thinking about it. And well, it goes into the young people's jargon, in all their ways of behaving (*das ganze Gehabe*).[9]

Defining these acts as the products of a "youth" (sub)culture "which they'll grow out of," means admitting an adolescent parenthesis in the institutional sphere, so that there might be only minimal disturbance to the class program (at the beginning of the lesson). These acts also establish a link between the peer space (the schoolyard) and the school space (the classroom), that teachers must "work with" in order to maintain the "school order." This interaction can be understood as a kind of relay (of the symbolic scepter of power) between the head of the schoolyard (Osman) and the head of the classroom (the teacher). These practices allow for the transformation of the deviant uses of the past, integrated into adolescent culture, into (risky) resources.

Thus, certain uses of the Nazi past participate in the daily battles and power games in the hierarchical relations and authority stakes between teachers and students. These usages can be sometimes shown to be a resistance against a "duty to remember," which is expected of students in the context of attempts to impose a legitimate relation to the past or represent a reaction against the school's inculcation of "democracy." Sometimes these reactions may be part of an "anti-system discourse," which may be coherent and constructed as we have seen in the previous chapter. However, there is also an aspect that is playful and fun, drawing its efficiency from the repertoires of humor teachers may disapprove of. Such usages of the Nazi past are one demonstration among others of the tactics that the students develop to create a partially autonomous world within the school environment.

Indeed, the teachers know that the practices they observe cannot necessarily or always be situated in a political space. Mr Herzog said he is aware of the importance of the protest and confrontation aspects of the students' behavior.

Interview with Mr Herzog, 23 April 2003

They had positions like that—pro-Nazi: "Hitler wasn't all bad," etc. etc.—and they were always drawing swastikas on the board. And they found a pamphlet: death to the Reds (*Rotfront verrecke*) that they stuck on my car, things like that. But from what I know—real Nazis, no they don't exist here—because of the environment. All the Muslim students—Afghan, Iranian—or the Polish and the Russians—they all have their history and they know it. It's not like in the neighborhood nearby—there are real neo-Nazis there. But they don't dare come here. They would know, if ten of them come, there'd be eighty Afghans waiting to smack them up! So, yeah. That's why there aren't any here. Except—certain fashions sometimes, sort of waves. We don't know where it comes from and who it is. But sometimes we see swastikas and things like that. But it's not a problem. . . .

And then they have a position—well, it's a protest identity. Like for example: "the teachers are all left—so I'm against them." I see that very differently today, with ten or twenty years' hindsight. There was one guy, who I never saw again. But two others—well, they were actually quite nice guys—they told me about it afterwards. They wanted to protest, they wanted to be noticed—they wanted to be different. Like us, back then, we wanted to be different too. We had long hair [he laughs softly]. And we had to defend our long hair against the protests of parents and teachers.

Mr Herzog makes a distinction between "real Nazis," which he situates in a nearby working-class neighborhood with a smaller immigrant population, and the students at Wiesi, who are, for him, merely protesting. He therefore puts the swastikas they draw on the board and their calling him a "leftist" on the same level. According to Mr Herzog's reasoning, if the teachers at Wiesi were right-wing, the students would confront them from the left, just as he had confronted his teachers and parents in the 1960s. So, he sees the students' behavior as intra-academic, a generational struggle, rather than as a political position as such. According to him, children of immigrant parents cannot be "real Nazis." Yet antisemitism and xenophobia are not absent from countries such as Poland, Russia, Afghanistan, or Iran, although they take different forms. In Mr Herzog's reasoning however, the fact that these students are potential victims of xenophobic acts must, to a certain extent, immunize them against what he calls "neo-Nazism." This artificial construction of a group of students reduced to their status as foreigners also encourages him to seek apolitical explanations for the students' behavior.

School Space and Teenage Togetherness

Outside of the power relations with the teachers, there is a second battlefield, a second playing field, on which the students must take position every day: the peer group. At this time in their lives, finding a place in a group of adolescents is vital. Exclusion from a group can represent a more fundamental threat for certain students than a bad grade at the end of the year.[10]

Finding Your Place

Jokes are common at school, sometimes in class, but most often in the school-yard. Some students, generally (but not exclusively) boys who are "behind" at school or those who have repeated a year, enjoy making jokes about Nazism. There are "jokes about Hitler" on one hand and "jokes about the Jews" on the other. Karsten, from the 100th *Mittelschule*, was generally "up to date" with his schoolwork.[11] He explained that "other" students (but he also put himself in this group) tell "jokes about Hitler and the Jews," which is why he cannot talk seriously about Nazism with them, because he would appear ridiculous. Thus Karsten, in order to take part in the game, must accept part of the rules established by the "more academically deviant" in the group. However, in his interview with me, he emphasized that there is a difference between his own practices and the antisemitic or xenophobic affirmations made by his classmate, Karl.

And do you talk about the Nazi past with your classmates?
No, not really, because—they, they make jokes about it. In fact, me too, a bit, I joke about it with them. But not—not "Jews out" or stuff like that. That's what the others say. I don't say things like that.

And who says "Jews out"?
Like Karl, the one who always sits at the back. And Michael Kerte—him a bit less, but he does it too. And then—then Eberhard—the one who just arrived, who sits at the very front—he's also a Karl type of guy. Who—well, yeah, he, he's always doing stupid things.

And what does that mean to be a "Karl type of guy"?
Well, yeah, he disturbs the classes, you know, he talks all the time. Karl, he's the worst in the class now. Every year we lose the worst, each time. And him, he's our new class clown.[12]

Karsten created a hierarchy of these practices, at least that is what he told me, the representation of the school institution in his eyes. He clearly condemned the excessive and systematic transgression of the school rules in terms of behavior, such as open opposition during classes (in the form of whispering, showing disrespect, etc.). It is difficult to tell whether Karsten presented this discourse merely because he was trying to conform to my expectations, or because he genuinely disagreed with his classmates, but in either case, his discourse shows a strong awareness of the separation of spaces and different rules to be observed in each. It also revealed his own significant ability to adapt, an impression that seemed to be reinforced by the fact that, unlike his classmate Karl, he was doing quite well academically and was successful in the peer group. This was partly because he was able to join in the jokes and "play along" in the schoolyard. Karl unfortunately refused to talk to me; an interview with him would have helped shed light on the gap that seems to exist between these two boys. However, the interviews with the other students confirmed Karl's position, or at least his reputation as the "worst" and the "class clown."

These two positions seem to be linked. It is only possible to accept the position as the class clown once almost everything has been lost academically, or because the chances of surviving another academic year are low. Investment in the peer group thus replaces investment in the academic space, which in turn encourages the transgression of school rules in order to assert oneself in the adolescent space. But this is risky behavior because those who transgress the school rules too regularly will not be able to avoid sanctions, repeating classes and ultimately expulsion. The consequence of this is a temporary and then permanent exclusion from the group, a destiny that Karl will probably face. Conversely, Karsten was clear about the very real risks of disobeying the school rules (he says "every year we lose the worst"). This lucidity allowed him to play on both levels. He paid attention in class, he was "up to date" with his schoolwork, and he was pursuing a specific objective, passing the *Fachabitur*. However, the schoolyard jokes allowed him to also join in with his classmates and to take his place among the "bad boys" in the schoolyard, while respecting certain limits: he partially refused to participate in openly xenophobic discourses (at least in front of the teacher and myself), but tolerated it among his friends. He could thus condemn these practices while still partially imitating them, in the form of jokes. He manages to combine both acceptance of and opposition to the institutional rules and the alternative uses and tactics surrounding the Nazi past, in order to play within two configurations that are clearly distinct but heavily interdependent. He contributes to the construction of a space for play among his peers that obeys its own rules but remains embedded in the school space.

The students clearly distinguish between the rules of the peer configuration, and the school rules. Christian,[13] one of Karsten's classmates, who was also in the group that hangs around Karl, said that he finds his teacher's arguments about the "jokes about the Jews" quite convincing.

Our teacher, she also talked about it [Nazism]. Because in the class there were people who made jokes. And she said that that was really serious, that they shouldn't tell jokes about that.

And what did she tell you? What was so bad?
Because of the Jews, and what he [Hitler?] did. Because of—shooting, I don't know. Yeah.

And what were the jokes?
I don't remember. Those students have left now. I don't know.

And you, what do you think about all that? Did you think it was stupid what she said, or good? Was it convincing or not at all?
It was convincing, that's for sure. Well, she explained why it's not funny. And—yes, I think it's obvious.

What convinced you?
Well, she told us that he had—[he hesitates] he began the war. Or—yes, and because of the shooting, especially because of that.[14]

In the interview, Christian expressed his "understanding" for his teacher's position. He could explain why these "jokes" not only do not make her laugh, but are "out of place" and unacceptable in the context of the rules laid down by the school. He was able to mobilize institutional language perfectly and use it in conversation with me. This ability to adapt to (and adopt) expected academic discourse did not prevent him from continuing to joke with his friends, as he explained later in the interview; but he was careful to not be overheard by the teachers. However, the evolution of the peer group, and particularly romantic attachments were progressively leading these boys into a more feminine world and seem to be, among other things, responsible for most of the changes in the attitude of older boys regarding these jokes. David Lepoutre, in his study on a French *banlieue*, notes an evolution of adolescent street culture between junior and senior high school. He writes, "entry into adult life, which corresponds to a projection of oneself into a social and professional future, . . . for most young people, this corresponds to a clear abandonment of street culture and the correlated development of very different forms of sociability, more in keeping with those of the middle and upper classes" ([1997] 2001: 29, 30). Indeed, the deviant humor between boys will lose its importance in the construction of an identity that is more based on sexual experience, or being in a relationship (Clair 2007), or having a professional career, etc. This evolution does not prevent these practices and jokes from surviving in male social space, hence their derogatory name *Stammtischwitze*[15] (locker room jokes). It is also important to note the adolescents' ability to adapt their discourse, practices, and language to their environment.

Jokes are part of the ordinary, everyday use of the past, but there seems to be a hierarchy among them.

And the jokes, what are the jokes that you tell?
Well—uh . . . uh . . . about—[he has trouble telling me] well—jokes about Hitler (*Hitlerwitze*). Yeah. About the Jews and the gas chambers. Stuff like that.

Is there one that comes to mind? I don't know any jokes about Hitler.
Uhh . . . [he was quite disturbed and thought for a while]. "Why did the gas chamber have eleven holes? [I don't know] Because Jews only have ten

fingers to put in them." That's for the gas chambers, for example [he laughs softly], well—I'd have to ask Karl because he, he knows lots, really! [he laughs openly].[16]

This particular "joke" seems widespread in Germany. It was told to me both in Hamburg and in Leipzig, by both children from disadvantaged backgrounds and those from more comfortable ones, by children of immigrants and those whose grandparents are German. Yet it is also quite clearly gendered. None of the people who told me this joke were girls, and in the groups that came together to tell it in the playground the girls did not stay to listen. This joins the results of David Lepoutre, who also notes that the peer groups that he observed on the street are always single sex, and if there are groups of girls, they only rarely meet in the streets ([1997] 2001: 131). The wide reach of this joke in particular and this kind of joke in general seems to be linked to their circulation online. There are specific websites specializing in humor relating to Nazism,[17] and an appearance (or reappearance?) of specific German words to refer to them (*Judenwitze, Hitlerwitze*) (Korte and Lechner 2013; Lauterwein and Strauss-Hiva 2009). Jokes about Jewish people (and the term used to describe them, *Judenwitze*) are part of a traditional antisemitic repertoire. Yet these are not simply antisemitic jokes. Their particularity lies in the fact that they do not mock the Jews in themselves but rather the genocide and the extermination process (Steir-Livney 2017). These specialized actors, spaces, and language reflect a certain institutionalization[18] of these illegitimate uses of the Nazi past.

The use of these jokes is limited, as we have seen, to specific spaces. Thus, Karsten not only knows how to play on both fields within the school, he also knows how to distinguish the peer group, where such jokes are permitted and can be a source of pleasure and social positioning in the group, from family or private spaces, where such jokes would be "out of place."

> For example, I would never tell them to my family, because I know that lots of people in my family, at the time, in the war, they di—[he starts over] During Hitler's time, they died. And so in my family, I wouldn't. But at school, sometimes, now we're studying it, sometimes we tell jokes too, about it.
>
> *During break time?*
> Yeah, but not so much.[19]

We can see that inside the family sphere, Karsten obeyed still another set of rules. This is not a matter of a hierarchical relationship with an institution that can destroy his chances for a future career, but a relationship (that may also be hierarchical) with his elders. His primary concern is not hurting his family members, but although he emphasizes his sensitivity to his family's feelings, Karsten also knows that these discursive tactics provide recognition among his peers and not in his family.

It is different for Johnny,[20] however. The strong reputation he has among the others as a "neo-Nazi" also comes from a construction that goes beyond the schoolyard and the students' play. The Nazi flag that hangs in his bedroom can be seen as a form of provocation against his parents (who vote Social Democrat), who regularly ask him to become interested in something other than Nazism. But it can also be seen as a coherent form of self-presentation in the face of a group of friends who refuse to acknowledge him. The students who whisper "Nazi Johnny" when he walks by do not include him in their everyday interactions in the schoolyard. He is therefore obliged to build himself another, more solitary, space that remains linked to the space of his peers.

Emotion in Public: Saving Face

From a Goffmanian perspective, these jokes can also allow the boys to distance themselves from the emotion generated by the confrontation with the Jewish genocide (and its images). When they feel moved in spite of themselves by the images showing scenes of the victims suffering, using irony can also allow them to "save face" and to cement their place in the peer group.

I was present for the lesson in which Annika Klein's tenth-grade class watched *Schindler's List* in a large projection room at Wiese. A group of boys, congregating around Ivan, immediately sat at the back. I sat next to them. When the film began, the students quickly became quiet, drawn in by the scenario. However, from time to time the boys made comments "oh, yeah, that one again," and sometimes laughed. Then there was a violent scene where one of the camp commanders came out onto his balcony to "shoot some Jews for breakfast." Kevin, one of Ivan's friends, said "yeah, go for it," a little too loudly, and began laughing. Ivan said nothing. Martin, another in the group, also started laughing, a little uncomfortably.

One girl left the screening in tears. One of the teachers, Karen Werthe went out to join her. She explained to me afterwards in the interview that, "Melanie was really weeping, tears running down her face. She is Polish and was born there, and because it happened in her region—well. She was overwhelmed. She couldn't stop crying. I tried to console her."[21]

The boys and girls reacted differently to the film and to their own feelings. While Melanie could cry to express her discomfort, to the point where she was obliged to leave the classroom, the boys apparently did not have that option. As we know, laughter has social functions (Katz 1999; Kuipers 2006; Zijderfeld 1983). In this context, laughter, like jokes, is also a way for the students to relieve tension. Jacqueline Frisch-Gauthier emphasized this function in her 1961 study of laughter in the workplace: "laughter is linked to a certain freedom from what bothers, tires or irritates you" (Frisch-Gauthier 1961: 294). It allows workers to step back from a job that is risky, difficult, physically dangerous or exhausting. "All jokes . . . liberate a bit of nervous tension when it is too strong" (Frisch-Gauthier 1961: 296).

In the school environment, Melanie's reaction is much more easily accepted than Kevin's. Through her tears, she sets herself apart from the peer group but she creates a space for togetherness with the (female) teacher who comes out to talk to her. Mutual understanding, support and the creation of a kind of intimacy constitute a female space that conforms to the school rules about appropriate behavior. Melanie's tears fit perfectly into the logic of *Betroffenheitspädagogik* (pedagogy of emotional upheaval) that the teachers expect regarding images of World War II (Knoch 2001) and the violence of the scenes of Nazi extermination and its victims. The boys' laughter, however, frequent during their confrontation with these violent images, is rejected by the institution. Some teachers are anxious about it, interpreting it as a "lack of maturity," and a "lack of emotion." Yet we know that laughter is by no means a stranger to emotion. Alfred Reginald Radcliffe-Brown (1952) emphasized the fact that laughter can conceal, master, or codify hostility or aggression in interactions in certain primitive societies. Here, it allows the boys to control their emotions, to prove that they are not overwhelmed "like a girl" and to emphasize "self-control" as a way of asserting themselves in the group and "saving face" (Goffman [1967] 2005).

Ivan was born in 1986 in Russia and arrived in Germany when he was nine years old. His parents left Russia as part of the wave of immigration of "German Russians" in the mid-1990s.[22] His father, born in 1941, has no formal qualifications. He was a train driver in Russia and was working as an unskilled worker in a warehouse at the time of the interview. His mother, born in 1941, was the daughter of a German Communist worker who immigrated to Russia during World War II. Ivan's mother has a university degree and worked as an engineer in Russia. She had her only son at age forty-five. When she arrived in Germany, she returned to study and now works as a nursing assistant in a retirement home. Ivan, at eighteen years old, is one of the oldest students in the tenth-grade class. He is tall, 1.85 m, and very stocky and is blond with gray-green eyes. In spite of (or perhaps because of?) the fact that he is behind in the curriculum, he is one of the "good students" in the class, one of the few who are aiming to sit the *Abitur*, because he wants to work in "information technology." In the configuration of the small group of boys, which Kevin and Martin are part of, Ivan clearly dominates. In the work that they do together, he is the group leader, makes the decisions, and takes control, partly through his computer skills.[23]

Kevin does not hide his admiration for his friend. Small and thin, he seems to be the opposite of Ivan. His hair is mid-length and dark, his eyes brown; Kevin is two years younger than Ivan and barely comes up to his shoulder. He usually underperforms academically compared to Ivan, and his teacher, Annika Klein, thinks he will repeat the year. Kevin was born in 1988 in Hamburg, his father was then unemployed and without formal qualifications, his mother is a housewife and left school in tenth grade. Kevin has no family resources that could help him to succeed at school, unlike Ivan, whose mother has significant academic skills. Group work with Ivan has helped him at school but also makes him dependent. Because of his difficulties in balancing the relationship by returning academic assistance, he does not miss any opportunities to try and attract Ivan's attention and respect and to assert himself in the peer group via jokes, as soon as his tall friend is nearby.

The jokes about the film did not have the desired effect with Ivan however. Martin, who has an intermediary role in the group, laughed uncertainly, between Ivan's silence and support for Kevin. The joke, which Kevin used to hide his emotion and save face by affirming his virility and his position in the group, was no less embarrassing for the others. Martin felt obliged to laugh, in order to save Kevin from ridicule, as well as himself and others.

> A person ... will have two points of view: a defensive orientation toward saving his own face, and a protective orientation toward saving the others' face ... In trying to save the face of others, a person must choose a tack that will not lead to loss of his own; in trying to save his own he must consider the loss of face his action may entail for others." (Goffman [1967] 2005: 14)

Therefore, we can see the need to consider the situation, specifically the interaction between the three boys, their individual dispositions, the academic and social resources that make up the configuration of the group, and finally the possible axes that their interactions might take. The power relation between the three boys and the group configuration are central here. They guide the possible appropriations of the film about the Nazi past. The ideological or political positions play a certain role here (because it is not possible to laugh about everything), but they interact with strategies for the presentation of the self within a specific configuration of power. The self-image (Goffman 1959) that is built in this way, the demands for self-control, but also the resources that enable this construction, consolidate certain attitudes toward Nazism that the boys stage in this way.

Between *Nazischwein* and *Judensau*: Broadening the Repertoire of "Jokes"

The term *vanne*—which is popular and more or less slang in the way it is used—refers both to all sorts of virulent remarks, derogatory banter, and teasing exchanged in humorous tones between people who know each other, or at least share a certain complicity. The principle of this teasing is fundamentally based on the symbolic distance that allows interlocuters to make fun of or insult each other without negative consequences. (Lepoutre [1997] 2001: 173–174)

One of the frequent particularities of the way young people "playfully tease" each other is the obscene nature of their jokes. Lepoutre established a very full repertoire of the direct jokes (directly aimed at an individual) and indirect jokes (which run through a reference to a family member, often a parent and particularly the mother) of the Parisian suburbs. His study is particularly useful for us here because it reveals two essential aspects of these adolescent practices, competition and confrontation, but also playfulness and shared laughter. In the context of schools in the suburbs of Hamburg and Leipzig, the adolescents "tease" each other all day. There is a German specificity in this however that must be mentioned: the students make abundant reference to the Nazi past, particularly in direct jokes, but the indirect equivalent also exists (son of a Nazi, son of a Jew, etc.). This past is highly compatible with the provocative connotations of this humoristic culture. Jokes drawing on the parents' sexuality, particularly the mother's, are thus used alongside those mobilizing a serious past, which cannot be used in humoristic or insulting tones without transgressing social and academic norms.

Field Notes, 15 November 2003

I go into the hall at Wiesi. It is 9 a.m., the students are in class. I meet a small group of five boys in an empty corridor. Two of them are talking about something I didn't hear. "Dirty Turk," says one. "Stop being an idiot," says the other. "Yeah, but you're still a dirty Turk, admit it!" "And you, you're an asshole!" "Well, you should just go back where you came from!" "Ya Nazi pig!" (*Du Nazischwein, Du*) "Ya dirty Jewish sow!" (*du Dreckige Judensau*) "Fuck you!" "Son of a bitch!" The two boys start fighting, but to my surprise, they stop very quickly and leave the school laughing and patting each other on the back.[24]

The untrained observer (such as myself, a researcher at the beginning of my investigation) could be forgiven for thinking this was a conflictual situation.[25] In fact, it is merely a verbal jousting match between close friends (Lepoutre notes, "you can't insult just anyone's mother"). We could also interpret (as some teachers do and as I did at the beginning of the study) this passage as an attribution of identity on the part of the boys. The "German" calls his classmate a "Turk" and the "Turk" responds by calling the other a "Nazi," which produces an antisemitic insult in return. The joust leads to vulgar sexual insults. Observations of "ordinary xenophobia" often appear self-evident in this, but the tendency to reduce the person to their "national" and/or ethnic origins is easy to misinterpret. Indeed, this situation can be easily reversed.

Field Notes, 23 January 2004

In Mr Stein's classroom, the students are waiting for the teacher to arrive. Kevin, from another tenth-grade class, comes into the room. Omer welcomes him with, "Hi there, ya potato eater." Kevin replies "Hi, ya son of a Turk." Omer responds, saying "Hey, asshole, don't insult my mother!" To which Kevin throws back, "Dirty Nazi!"[26]

Here the roles are reversed. Omer calls his friend a "potato eater" (*Kartoffelfresser*), a provocative term for the Germans, but Kevin responds by calling him a "Turk," when Omer's mother is in fact Afghan. The fact that Omer feels insulted by the attribution of a Turkish nationality to his Afghan mother is criticized as a fascist attitude by Kevin, who has the last word in this exchange. This is by no means accidental. Indeed, the Afghan students, or those whose parents are Afghan immigrants, almost all arrived with the wave of political immigration in the 1980s and are therefore part of the liberal intellectual bourgeoisie. They take pains to distinguish themselves from their Turkish classmates, whose families were economic migrants and almost exclusively working class. In Germany, calling an Afghan (or the child of an Afghan) a "Turk" must thus be seen in the internal hierarchy of nationalities in migratory movements. Hence Omer's indignant reaction, considering that his mother has been insulted. Called an "asshole" Kevin takes it up a notch, calling Omer a "Nazi" (in order to challenge the hierarchy of nationalities that Omer refers to perhaps?). If Kevin refers to the fact that Omer is not "really" German, the fact that he then describes him as a Nazi a few second later as part of his tactics of one-upmanship, is clearly not related to his German nationality. This is in fact a verbal exchange in which "everything is false by definition." The insult, as a signifier, is disconnected from the identity it signifies. This is an imaginary joke, which is not pertinent because it has a relation to "reality" but rather is efficient because of the "gap" between the "facts" and the statement. Indeed, jokes have a ritual aspect, which sets them apart from "insults." Nor do they have a specific political content. It is not because students tease their classmates using Nazi or antisemitic insults that they are "neo-Nazis" or even "antisemitic," even if sometimes they may indeed be involved on the extreme right. But there is no direct or automatic link between the content of these jokes and political involvement.

However, these jokes must be considered attempts to situate oneself in a group, by proving one's creativity and rapid wit. Insults can have the same function in a configuration of rivalry between boys, as we can see in the interview with Karsten, a student at the *Mittelschule* in Leipzig. They may be used to carve a place for oneself in the group and to affirm one's superiority, but also to intimidate the weaker members of the group.

And "Jews get out"—why "Jews get out"?
I don't know.

Who says that?
Hitler, because he didn't get along with the Jews.

Do you know why?
"No. And Karl, he doesn't like Jews either apparently. He tells everyone: foreigners get out. And—at the time, there was one in the class, Juan, he has repeated a year now, and [Karl] always told him "foreigners get out."

He was a foreigner?
His father was a foreigner. Even if he was born in Germany, I think that [he hesitates and changes his mind] so, he's German by birth, then?

That depends on what you call German. If he has the nationality, the passport, then he's German in any case. It's possible to apply for a passport. I don't know.
Well, actually, I don't really know either.

But everyone made fun of Juan?
Yeah.[27]

Karsten shows his uncertainty here. He seemed to not really know what it means to "be a foreigner" or to "be German." Nor did he make a distinction between "foreigners" and "Jews." He noted that Karl laughed at Juan, insulting him, calling him a "foreigner" or a "Jew" and admits he has doubts about how relevant these attributes are in relation to Juan (or his father). Thus, although Karsten is aware of Karl's tendency to speak badly about Jews and foreigners, which he explains in political terms, the link established with the "victims" of these insults is more than vague. We can hypothesize that the boys around Karl teased Juan because of his subaltern position within the group. This is a process of inferiorization, not necessarily or exclusively linked to the nationality or religious belonging of his paternal grandparents. Juan is the only student mentioned who might have had Jewish grandparents. I was not able to talk to Juan, as he had already left the class. None of the students I interviewed is Jewish; there are very small numbers of Jewish students in the schools of Hamburg and Leipzig, cities where the Jewish communities have remained a small minority after their murder during the Nazi genocide. Therefore, I was not able to ask any Jewish students how they felt about these exchanges. More generally, in these exchanges, the Jewish population is the absent referent. The effectiveness of this humor and these insults,[28] including in friendly banter, is constructed on the basis of xenophobic and antisemitic references. But Karl would not have insulted Juan in this way if the latter had been in a structurally superior position in the social group (Ivan is never insulted as a "Russkof" or a "foreigner," for example).

Although teachers tolerate the banter, the insults are more difficult to accept. The sociological clarity that leads them to grasp the strategic stakes of social position when it comes to joking is missing when the symbolic violence increases and the word play sometimes becomes physical confrontation between students. The teachers are more inclined to give a political interpretation to an act of violence, which leads to a moral condemnation of students described as "right-wing." This political interpretation is closely linked with secondary teachers' political socialization as a whole, understood as participating in "the democratic construction" of Germany.

> There was a student who was forcibly transferred into my class because he had tattooed or scratched (*geritzt*) a swastika with a knife on a girl's—a left-wing girl's—skin. Yes. [Silence.] And with a pen he'd written "Nazi"—no, it was "dirty Jew" (*Judensau*) on her forehead or something.
>
> *And—what can you do with a young man like that?*
> You try and shoot him down (*Den setzt man unter Feuer*). In fact—you mustn't believe, as I said before—that you can educate him or make him a democrat or a leftist or anything else. It's hopeless. We don't touch them, those ones.[29]

The boy's physical violence toward his classmate only slightly destabilized Mr Herzog; he did not linger over this story, which would have had completely different consequences in a *Gymnasium* like Weinberg; perhaps because teachers at Wiesi are more used to physical violence between students than their colleagues in *Gymnasium*, and their indignation only lasts until the next incident. However, his vivid condemnation results in a political interpretation of the student's motives. Mr Herzog hesitates over this story as he is telling it: he does not remember well whether it was "Nazi" or "dirty Jew" that was written on the girl's forehead. As he is in doubt, he says it was an antisemitic insult. Given that, for Mr Herzog, this was a "young man on the extreme-right, not democratic" and a young "left-wing girl," he must have insulted her as a "Jew" and not as a "Nazi" for his "logical" political interpretation to function. On the other hand, it is also remarkable that in contemporary Germany, both terms, Nazi and Jew, work as a credible insult

Peer-Group Dynamics and Playful Uses of the Past • 297

(for the teacher) and are often employed in the same context, becoming even interchangeable, thus showing clearly that the condemnation of the Nazi past (turning the adjective into an insult) can leave the antisemitic reasoning perfectly untouched, so that it continues to be socially effective.

In the discourse of the teacher, the encounter between the two students remains vague. Was it really a political disagreement? Or was it more a personal disagreement? Is it the humiliation of a student through violence, an attack on her personal security, regardless of the historical signification of the words used (Nazi or Jew) that is at stake here? It is important to note that, like "jokes about Hitler" and "jokes about the Jews," both identities (Nazi and Jew) serve as insults here and are put on the same level by the teacher. The possibility of considering them together relies on old antisemitic traditions (we need only to insert "Christian" in place of "Jew" to understand why this does not work as an insult for the students). Non-political antisemitism is the framework within which these insults function.

As for Mr Herzog, he shifts from one explanation to another very smoothly, without considering them to be mutually exclusive. Thus, it is perhaps the seriousness of the action, or the availability of a political explanation (which of course simplifies the interpretation—an extreme-right boy and a left-wing girl), which leads Mr Herzog to mobilize it. Yet the political interpretation and the interpretation in terms of power and positioning in a group overlap and interact and are by no means exclusive.

Political Position and Peer-Group Position

Jokes about the Nazi past can clearly be a more specifically political resource in order to draw attention to oneself or build status within the group. It is not rare that attitudes toward the past become an issue of political belonging, particularly when these groups define themselves in political terms. René, a student at *Gymnasium* Weinberg, the son of a secondary school teacher and a doctor, defines himself as "left-wing." In the interview, he explained the configuration of the two "opposing" groups in his school. The "capitalists" stand against the "anti-capitalists" (or, as René put it, "leftist intellectuals"). These are social and economic oppositions (one of the stakes is the money the adolescents have, or rather that their parents have given them, to buy a car, clothes, etc.) that overlap with political oppositions and can lead to a mobilization of the Nazi past. René thus compared "the others" (on the "right," the "capitalists") to Nazis, in order to discredit them.

Yes, and sometimes it is the same thoughts, the same schema [as for the Nazis]. I really believe that. Even if the Nazis didn't really like capitalism in itself. In any case, there were similarities. It's a little bit [he hesitates] the same. Just discipline. And the attitude to work [he hesitates] "In Germany you have to work." That for example. And "He who does not work is worth nothing."[30]

Even though René is encouraged to make this comparison in the context of an interview on the Nazi past, and though he himself describes it as "a little extreme," the interpretation of the past is used to identify different groups of belonging. This identification serves to reject those in the "other" group. When there is no "opposite group," however, the designation of the "other" as a Nazi can lead to exclusion.

This is the case of both Thomas, a student at *Gymnasium* in Hamburg, as well as Wolfgang, before he left the *Gymnasium* in Leipzig for a *Mittelschule*.[31] The two students struggled to defend their position, which was stigmatized as being "far right" in both schools. This is linked to the fact that it is very much a minority opinion in both schools where, if the student bodies are at all politicized, they lean to the left. Thus, Wolfgang explains how he was criticized by his "far-left" classmates."

> *And when you say that lots of them think that [Hitler was all bad], how do you know? Did you talk with the others?*
> Yes, I was in another school, which was really extreme left. The *Thomasschule.* And as soon as you said something that could be interpreted as praise for Hitler, which wasn't really the case, there you go [he does not finish his sentence]. And then, people talk about it.
>
> *And when you say that the school was extreme left what do you mean?*
> Oh well, yeah, everything that leans toward the right—tear it down!
>
> *And when, for example, they say that Hitler created holidays?*
> Yeah, exactly. Straightaway labeled right-wing.[32]

This is how Wolfgang came to have an "extreme-right reputation," partly in spite of himself. Although ambiguous because it is a source of problems with his classmates (including physical confrontations), this reputation has nevertheless made him distinctive.

Similarly, Thomas is conscious of his "unusual" position, which, in spite of or because of the fact that he had trouble being accepted, became a source of pride.

> I see that in relation to World War II. Economic history interests me more than the rest of history, [he hesitates] and what I say might seem a bit radical but I've also found that in those times [he hesitates again], eh, Hitler, he managed to resolve unemployment. And the economy was good, well, in quotation marks, you know, at the time. And then, with the destruction it was all fucked.[33]

Thomas therefore constructed an identity around provocation in the school environment. Among his peers he was seen as "radical" (*kraß*), as the one who breaks the rules of good behavior and the legitimate discourse on the Nazi past. The consequence of this behavior was both dual and ambiguous. Thomas felt excluded from the class he was in, "everyone says, oh look at him."[34] Stigmatized in this way, he then found himself alone. However, having integrated this position, he turned it to his advantage by constructing an image for himself as a "rebel." He thus described himself as "the only one who says things, the others, there are lots who agree but they don't dare talk." Similarly, Wolfgang considered himself "the one who says aloud what the others are thinking."

Do you remember when you classmates asked you about it for the first time?
Yes, someone asked me what I thought. And so I told him. And then he told me that he thought exactly the same, but that you can't say it aloud. [He hesitates.] Because—well, yes, there were perhaps two or three of us, and then yes, there weren't just two or three of them but many more!

And afterwards what happened?
It's strange in a way. Yes, there are others who see it like that, we're not alone.

And so everyone knew?
Yes, it got out [he hesitates]. Other people asked me, when they realized and then they talked. It's like that, gossip. Yes—they're apparently—labeled extreme-right, our comments.

And were you able to talk about it?
No, they're too set on the idea that it is really extreme-right, what we think.[35]

Although the "extreme-right" label only half satisfied these boys, it did allow them to occupy a marginal position, to increase their notoriety and be seen as "different." This position was frowned on by their teachers, and sometimes even provoked aggression on the part of their peers, but it could also operate as a resource, making their opposition to the school system more efficient through a reasoning that aimed to be "political." Ivan Bruneau (2002) has shown, through the analysis of the social trajectory of a miner's son, how this position as an outsider in school can lead to a particular involvement in the extreme-right National Front in France. The strategy of "reverse stigmatization" that led Bruneau's interviewee "A" to proudly accept his nickname "Adolf" in the schoolyard and invest in history books on World War II seems similar to Wolfgang's. Born to a father who is an electrician and a mother who is a secretary, Wolfgang (unlike interviewee "A") in fact wants to distinguish himself from his two sisters. The schoolyard is also a space that compensates for his lost status in the family, given that his academic difficulties are all the more difficult to accept because of his sisters' success at school and university.

300 • When Will We Talk about Hitler?

Wolfgang's construction of a "Nazi identity" and nickname, recognized by others, can provoke confrontation with teachers, which is considered "courageous" by his classmates. The politically "notorious" thus become boys who are secretly admired by the others because they dare to publicly oppose the school system and authority of the teachers.

Alongside individual political positions, are the positions of a whole group, which the students adopt as is. Wolfgang, for example, belongs to a group that he himself calls a "sect." It is a small organization, that he joined through a "friend," and which mobilizes "Christian" values to construct a political position praising the Nazi past. Wolfgang mobilizes this argument that reveals genuine reflection on the reasons for antisemitism.

> Finally—yes, Hitler was also a Christian. And—true Christians, they're a little bit extreme because they think, or they're convinced, that the Jews crucified Jesus. And that's the reason—that's their vengeance. That's why they did that [the genocide of the Jews].
>
> *And so you think that Hitler had Christian reasons?*
> Yes, well [he hesitates]—already in the Old Testament, it was written that— some thousands of years ago—that Christ would be crucified. By the Jews. And so you can't say that they are the great sinners. Of course, they made a mistake (*Sie haben das falsch gemacht*). But [he hesitates again] in principle they did what was written.
>
> *I don't understand. You said that Jews were not sinners because they did what was written?*
> Yes. But in reality, they killed Jesus.
>
> *So, they are still sinners?*
> "Oh, well yes. Of course! But—well, it's the other way around. That they did what was in the Scriptures [long silence]. Because it was just meant to be (*weil es halt so kommen musste*).[36]

Fragments of this explanation, in shortened form (Hitler killed the Jews because the Jews killed Jesus), exist in the discourse of other students, without necessarily being accompanied by political positions as decided as Wolfgang's. For the latter, his need to adopt the point of view of the group to which he belongs can be felt throughout the whole interview. He repeatedly quoted his friend, particularly when he mentions the reasons for the genocide. His conversations with this friend "made [him] understand lots of things." The process of *Aneignung*, reappropriation of interpretations of the past, therefore operates on two levels. On one hand, the individual process of appropriation and reappropriation, and on the other, collective processes in which specific groups (here Wolfgang's religious group) appropriate practices, symbols, and ideas in order to build their specific identity.

Playing Cowboys and Indians: The Nazi Past as a Barricade against Loneliness

The example of Johnny[37] illustrates the ways in which the boys extend these playful and transgressive attitudes toward the Nazi past into the private sphere, as well as the strength of the peer group configurations, which have a significant impact on inclusion and/or exclusion even outside school. Johnny is "well-known" in his school because he has forced a specific and conspicuous image for himself as a "neo-Nazi." But his "fascination" for the past has above all helped him challenge the school rules. Moreover, it also remains a source of pleasure and a pastime at home. The association of informative, playful, and transgressive uses of the Nazi past provide enough pleasure for it to become a passion in a universe that is rather lacking in other cultural practices.

> *When you think about history, is there a moment, a period, which seems particularly important, for you, personally?*
> Yes, yes, World War II. [He hesitates.] Yes because—I don't know—because it interests me, what happened then. Especially military history!
>
> *And what do you find interesting about that?*
> Yes, well, what interests me above all is the—the cars (*Fahrzeuge*)! Because—it came from building models (*Modelbau*) and then—I got more and more interested. And then, later, outside Stalingrad, there was the invasion, and then, I wanted to know more and more. And then, to give you an example of what interests me: how many divisions did they march with, in which—what year was it? And how many died, and how long were the supply lines—all that, I'm interested in all that!
>
> *Do you remember the first time you ever discovered this theme?*
> I don't know. Perhaps because I—with my father—I always watched cartoons in the evening. But I think, that it was especially because of the models. I made (*bastel*) model tanks, and there was always a little booklet that came with them—when they were constructed, to do what and I always read all that.[38]

Through building models and watching cartoons, Johnny discovered World War II in a playful, non-serious way. It was playing with objects he himself had created and the physical relation he developed with them that provoked his curiosity and his desire for knowledge. The recognition of a medal on a model would lead him to research it, to consult "books."

And then I thought, hey, I know that, I know that medal. And then I looked in other books. But the medal was from the Eastern Front. And so, I wanted to know, and I delved into it more and more.

What kind of medal was it?
Uh—yeah, it was a division medal, with a little key on it. It was from the [he hesitates] the Waffen-SS.

And where did you find it? Were there books in your house?
Yeah, my parents had old history books. And, yeah. [He hesitates.] Yeah, I don't know—in a film I saw as well. And then once I was at a museum in Munster, in a tank museum (*Panzer Museum*). And there I saw it everywhere. And then when I knew that it was—for example, that that's the Waffen-SS. So I bought a book about the Waffen-SS and it just continued like that.

And do you remember what book it was that you read about the Waffen-SS?
Yeah, it was a small book, Waffen-SS, by—I don't remember the author. But [he thinks a little and remembers the publisher] published by Steinmetz or something like that. Yes, and there they described how—how the SS was created. And how later it became the Waffen-SS. And Hitler's Black Order, etc. etc. Yes, and I read all that. Yes, I don't know if that [he hesitated] made me more intelligent or not.[39]

Johnny's interest is much like that of almost all the other fourteen-year-old boys I spoke to, except that he made it into his hobby. At the time of the interviews, he spent his time collecting Nazi military insignia and the Waffen-SS was the focus of his attention in particular. He bought model tanks online, and regularly spent whole afternoons in costume shops trying on military costumes, bringing his Waffen-SS medals and looking at himself in the mirror (he did not have enough money to buy or even rent the uniforms). Later in the interview, faced with my insistent questions about these objects, he admitted that he spends a lot of energy in living his hobby, given that Nazi insignia is prohibited in Germany (it takes him some time to admit that these activities are defined as illegal). He is forced to procure them in the Netherlands (on the Internet) or to buy them in secret in flea markets. He has also spent time looking for a copy of *Mein Kampf* online, but has not been able to buy one. He said that his greatest pleasure was a trip to Poland where he was able to buy toys and Nazi medals in a market.[40]

World War II was the end of the German Reich, and [the transformation] into the Federal Republic. Yes, in principle, it was the last period that was different, in Germany. Before, there was Emperor Wilhelm, the German Reich and when you go back further, Charlemagne or others . . . Yes, and then there was the Reich. And then, all of a sudden, the Federal Republic. And the Federal Republic, for me, it's—I don't know, everything works and—it's boring! Nothing important ever happens! There is one chancellor, then another. And always more taxes. And me, I want to go back in time, to World War II. There, there was action—a spark (*Flimmer, Flammer*), excitement, you know, action! Yes, and then, in theory, Germany before World War II was really a different

Peer-Group Dynamics and Playful Uses of the Past • 303

country than after the war. Yes the war changed everything. And that's what I find interesting.[41]

The opposition between the action of World War II and the boredom of the Federal Republic reflects Johnny's own boredom. He is often alone in his bedroom, in a neighborhood where the only pastime is football between friends, an activity that he is quite contemptuous of. There are no cafés and no cinemas in this area separated from central Hamburg by a large ring-road. The nearest shopping mall is a twenty-minute bus ride away. The only place where teenagers can come together is the local library, which is in the same building as their school. Johnny prefers to escape to his imaginary world, constructed around World War II.

If someone asked me, seriously—well, in fact it's something I haven't told my parents yet—but if someone asked me if I wanted—if I could go back in a time machine, to World War II, and I knew I'd be a soldier and had to go to the front, I'd do it. I'd do it for sure.

And where would you go on the front?
I don't care. Somewhere not too cold [I smile]. So, Siberia or the Eastern Front, that's out of the question! But not too hot either, so the desert's out of the question too. France! The Western Front. But Russia is a beautiful country too . . . I'm attracted by it [war]. Because, partly because [he hesitates] I dream of driving an old tank. And I know that at the time they existed! So I could—that would be wonderful, for me, to be in a war, during World War II, and to drive around, as a tank commander in a battlefield. That [dreamily] would be the best thing for me. Even if I know I could die, but [he hesitates] I don't know. That's normal, in wartime."

You're not scared?
Yes, I am scared. But [he hesitates] of course I'm scared, when you know that you could die. But [he hesitates again] I want—I mean, if I was fighting! In a war! I wouldn't even think about it! I would just think: you have to do what you have to do.[42] And so you do it! And it's just bad luck if you get hit by a bullet. You can't change anything about it! That's what I would think. There are people who find that horrible. It is horrible too. But [he considers] I don't know, I'd still do it.[43]

The fear of death disappears behind the feeling of serving, or being useful for, a higher purpose. This is the idea of following the order of things, which he has no control over even up to his own death, in order to become a hero. Johnny does not want to suffer needlessly. He does not like the idea of the discomfort linked to war—the cold, the heat—he wants to live (and die) heroically on the battlefield, preferably as a commander and not as a mere soldier. In this sense, this fantasy could reflect a concern about his

304 • When Will We Talk about Hitler?

professional future, vaguely felt as a future that must be carried out without him having control over it—the opposite of a heroic commander in a motorized battalion.

Again, this fascination for the battlefield and the dream of heroically driving a tank are shared by many boys his age. But Johnny goes further than many of his classmates in identifying Nazi war heroes specifically and in opposing this bellicose universe to his personal life, which seems boring by contrast. Building models takes time and requires precision. Johnny also shows his perfectionism when he carefully assembles the Nazi accoutrements that help him dress up in a costume shop from time to time. Dedication (*Hingabe*) to a well-accomplished task is combined here with the transgressive aspect of social norms that bring Johnny's solitary games into contact with the humoristic uses of the Nazi past in the schoolyard. Johnny is excluded from the other boys' jokes and has built his own way of playing with the past, transgressing school and family norms, and enjoying a freedom of interpretation that he would not have in the group he is excluded from. For Johnny, the alternative to collective pleasure is found in solitary imagination. He plays alone at "cowboys and Indians," adapting this traditional war play to an omnipresent and available past—Nazism.

Conceptualizing Configurations and Forms of Reappropriation

The analysis of the playful and humoristic uses of the Nazi past by adolescents, both inside and outside the school environment allows us to understand the social functions of references to this past. These references may be individual or collective, political or playful, take place in school or outside it, or any combination of the above. They make sense on an everyday level in the configurations in which the students find themselves; the relationships they build with their entourage, including teachers and classmates, but also family, parents and grandparents. These practices can be a challenge to the authority of the school, or be used to construct a new self-image, either "rebellious," "macho," "courageous," or "political," or have many other significations, serving to reinforce their position within the peer group. These initiatives allow the students to increase the room for maneuver within the group, but they can also be used to escape from the boredom of everyday life, in class or at home. Finally, jokes can also constitute an entrance into politics in working-class areas, a form of political learning that is specific in its transgressive nature. Coming up against social norms means becoming aware of those norms, and thus taking a position that can also sometimes take a political form. Therefore, any mobilizations of the past that are not legitimate in the school environment, including jokes, teasing, and even drawing a swastika or saying *Heil Hitler* to the teacher, have a range of meanings and must be interpreted according to the concrete situation and its configurations.

It is in the configuration of the group, through its mechanisms of inclusion and exclusion, that students must make a place for themselves in order to save face, to build self-image, or to restore their status after an exclusion from the group or marginalization by the academic institution. Therefore, it is group configurations that are the driving force for the students' various uses of the Nazi past. The classroom, but also and especially the playground, constitute the social spaces in which group configurations are established: hierarchies, recognition, contempt, and fights to impose oneself and find a space within the group. They are also the space for masculine friendships, complicities and camaraderie, all contributing to the establishment of these configurations. These evolve over time, obviously, and construct the adolescents' forms of appropriation and mobilizations of the Nazi past.

Within these configurations, the Nazi past is used in ways that often have little (or no) resonance with the academic expectations of the institution and its representatives (teachers), yet the two are closely interconnected; school group and peer group, configurations inside and outside class, they cannot exist without each other. The position that is defended in the peer group is highly dependent on the one that is acquired in class, in relation to the teacher or to school configurations and expectations. Concretely, it is impossible to "get good grades," be "a dunce" or "the best student" without that influencing the place one holds within the peer group configuration and the strategies implemented to preserve, challenge, or transform that place. Mobilizing the Nazi past, reappropriating and reinventing it—according to newly invented rules, which must be constantly reinvented and defended—is part of the repertoire of strategies that can be exploited to assert oneself in the peer group. But the forms this mobilization and reinvention takes also depend on the place one occupies in the class and the school status one can, wants to, or is supposed to defend.

This chapter deals with the playful uses of the Nazi past by students from relatively disadvantaged social backgrounds, in suburbs in Hamburg and Leipzig. It is important to note that these uses of the past also exist in the *Gymnasien* (certain interviewees attest to this), although I did not observe them directly. The fact that the students told me about them in the interviews but held back from performing them in my presence can be attributed to the stricter behavioral rules imposed on children from more privileged neighborhoods. Thus, a student who had been caught "tagging" a swastika on a school wall at the *Gymnasium* in Hamburg would have been very severely sanctioned: called before the principal and punished (made to clean the wall, expulsion if repeated). The difference in the treatment of "deviant" behavior between institutions reflects not so much the behavior of privileged and less privileged students, but rather the way teachers appropriate dominant pedagogic or academic norms in their implementation of sanctions. This can, in turn, be explained, among other things, by their own socialization and social trajectories.

Finally, jokes and humor as an initial encounter with politics in working-class areas constitute a potentially rich avenue for research, but one that is beyond the scope of this chapter and this book. It his however important to emphasize that throughout this study the social spaces of interaction—political and social, academic and playful, family and friends—are in constant interaction and are by no means exclusive from each other. Chapter 4 deals more explicitly with the political uses of the Nazi past, but in this chapter we have focused on the importance of games, fun, and playful teasing, but also pleasure, in the ways in which the Nazi past is appropriated in the everyday. Taking these playful uses of the past seriously also allows us to understand the interaction dynamics that help adolescents give meaning to the Nazi past, both through group configurations and within them.

Notes

1. For a discussion of this concept, see the Introduction, "School Experience: Between *Eigensinn*, Social Frames, and Reappropriations."
2. Lepoutre's study was based on ethnographic observation of young people in the disadvantaged public housing projects of the *Quatre Mille* in the outskirts of Paris.
3. Osman's father was born in 1951 in Kabul, Afghanistan, but left when he was eighteen to begin a long voyage across Iran, Turkey, and Poland to Germany, where he arrived in the mid-1970s. He had a shop selling oriental carpets and, along with his two brothers, founded a museum on Afghanistan in Hamburg. His mother, born in 1965 also in Afghanistan, had studied to be a primary school teacher before emigrating in the early 1980s to Germany where she met her husband.
4. On Easter 2003, the "fights" between these two groups reached such proportions that the police were called and a scandal erupted, which ended up in the local papers. The students told me proudly who belonged to which group, even though the physical confrontations took place outside the school and only a small minority of students were involved.
5. Field notes from 20 October 2003.
6. My presence may have incited them to do this in a particularly provocative way, to "prove" their creativity or to "shock" the researcher. But the teacher also told me that this kind of interaction is not rare in class generally, even when I am not present.
7. For the difficulties in translating notions such as *Kräftefeld* and *Herrschaft* and the implications for the vocabulary of Bourdieu, see the Introduction.
8. Interview of 20 October 2003.
9. Mr Gerste, interview of 20 October 2003.

Peer-Group Dynamics and Playful Uses of the Past • 307

10. The importance of group acceptance and the catastrophic consequences of exclusion are wonderfully described by Robert Musil, in *Die Verwirrungen des Zöglings Törless*, Vienna, 1906 (translated as *The Confusions of Young Törless*, 2001).

11. I use this expression and its opposite, a student who is "left behind," following Baudelot, Cartier and Détrez (1999). For Karsten's background, see chapter 5, section "The Nazi Past, Historical Knowledge, and Cultural Practices among Students with 'Substantial Academic Difficulties'".

12. Interview of 12 January 2004.

13. Christian was born in 1988, in Leipzig. His father is a truck driver (born in 1958) and his mother (born in 1960) worked first as a cashier, then as a hairdresser. Both parents left school after tenth grade and had no further education. At the time of the interview, Christian was a student at the *Mittelschule* in Leipzig and very talkative. He said he is interested in history and in particular "the time of Adolf Hitler," which he made clear in the very first phrases of the interview.

14. Interview of 21 January 2004.

15. The *Stammtisch* is the regulars' table at the local bar. In Germany the *Stammtischrunde* is an exclusively male social practice that is very working-class: friends meet once a week on a given night (every Thursday for example) to have a beer. The female equivalent is the *Kaffeekränzchen*, which traditionally takes place in the afternoon. The idea of the closed male-only space is found in the English term "locker room" jokes.

16. Interview with Karsten, 12 January 2004.

17. One student told me that jokes about Hitler are even on the radio sometimes, but that is not the case for jokes about Jewish people.

18. If we adopt a very broad, Durkheimian, definition of this term, referring to ways of doing, feeling, and thinking that have become crystallized, constrained, constraining, and distinctive for a particular social group (Durkheim [1895] 1966). For a critical analysis of this notion in the social sciences, see Revel (1995b).

19. Interview of 12 January 2004.

20. For Johnny's background, see chapter 3, section "Gender Differences in the Way Students Use the Past".

21. Field notes of 8 October 2003 and interview of 7 November 2003. The boys' and girls' different reactions in the face of these images were also observed in other classes. Watching *Life is Beautiful* by Roberto Benigni (1997), in which a father tries to make his son believe that the concentration camp they have been deported to is a game, another girl, Judith, wept with her mouth open and her hands in front of her face. At the same time several boys started laughing and making jokes about the "sentimentality" of the film.

22. After the opening of Soviet borders, Germany accepted all those who could "prove" they had a "German" ancestor as immigrants.

23. This group submitted their "end of year report" on the school intranet and produced a sophisticated digital presentation. Ivan was responsible for resolving technical problems to the admiration of his classmates and teachers.

24. Field notes, 15 November 2003.

25. For an outside observer, it is always difficult to tell the difference between playful banter and actual conflict.

26. Field notes, 23 January 2004.

27. Interview of 12 January 2004.

28. It is important to remember, following Lepoutre, that these two practices overlap and are not always easy to distinguish, particularly for someone outside street culture.

29. Interview of 12 January 2004
30. Interview of 12 January 2004.
31. For the biographies of Wolfgang and Thomas, see chapter 4, section "Economic Difficulties and Criticism of the FRG".
32. Interview of 13 January 2004.
33. Interview of 30 March 2002.
34. Ibid.
35. Interview of 13 January 2002.
36. Ibid.
37. For Johnny's biography, see chapter 4, section "In Search of the Lost 'Great Germany'".
38. Interview of 25 April 2003.
39. Ibid.
40. This passion for weapons is quite widespread among fourteen-year-old boys and is not necessarily associated with an "oppositional" discourse on the Nazi past. Johnny's passion (which he shares with some of his classmates) is different from those who defend a more "legitimate" position, in that he concentrates exclusively on the NS insignia and particularly on the Waffen-SS, illegal in Germany. Moreover, he does not hesitate to display them (like the flag in his bedroom for example).
41. Interview of 25 April 2003.
42. Johnny uses the German verb *erfüllen* (fulfill), generally used with the term obligation or duty (*eine Plicht erfüllen*). Even though he uses it here with the noun *Sache* (thing), this verb suggests a situation where he acts without thinking in order to adapt to a clear norm or execute an order. The English expression clearly reflects this sense of obligation.
43. Interview of 25 April 2003.

CONCLUSION

From Memory to Appropriation(s)

This research has demonstrated that the ways in which adolescents in Germany appropriate the Nazi past are far more complex than the debates in the public and media spheres would lead us to believe. One of the main problems that this book has tried to avoid lies in the closed-circuit between the media-intellectual sphere and academia. Journalistic debates mirror academic studies and vice versa. The academic sphere's lack of independence on topics concerning memory leads to a polarization of the issue: they lament both "too much memory," seen as leading to saturation and a refusal to confront the Nazi past, particularly among "young people," and paradoxically also "too little memory," described as the cause of ignorance and forgetting in the same population. In both cases, this is a simplistic diagnosis that does away with the need to examine different practices more closely.

The past is appropriated in ways that are complex, even paradoxical. Among young people, we see saturation, rejection, and ignorance, sometimes at the same time. However, we also see adolescents who are very well informed, who can turn their backs on the past after having been passionate about it, or who return to this same past after having previously rejected it, depending on their age and the social context in which they are embedded. Thus, the binary opposition, and the public policy "choice" between "too much" or "too little" memory, overlooks the social stakes in these appropriations. As a result, it is fundamental to understand the multiple and complex forms that these appropriations can take, in order to draw conclusions relating to public policy on the past. Indeed, although important, it is not sufficient to focus on actors in the "upper echelons" of the public sphere if we wish to understand the functioning of these policies. It is the grassroots approach, through ordinary appropriations, which opens new perspectives on what is too often described as "national collective memory."

The past is appropriated socially. This may appear banal, but given the binary opposition already mentioned, it is important to reiterate it. In a scientific context in which the notion of generation in social and historical sciences in Germany has seen a revival in the early 2000s (Jureit and Wildt 2005; Schüle, Ahbe, and Gries 2006; Schulz and Grebner 2003), existing studies, particularly in Germany, cultivate the opposition between "too much" and "too little" by concentrating on the oppositions between generations.

They set the second generation in opposition to the third with a homogenizing discourse about "young people" and their inability or disinclination to speak or hear about the Nazi past. The existing studies on families that analyze the transmission of this history (Kohlstruck 1997; Leonhard 2002; Welzer, Montau, and Plaß 1997; Welzer, Moller, and Tschuggnall [2002] 2005) most often adopt a "generational" perspective, in other words a vertical "top-down" transmission, which prevents us from considering the household as a space for the circulation of representations, past and present. Moreover, this research often remains blind to social differences. In France, however, most studies of family memory that make intrafamilial social differences the center of their analysis (Coenen-Huther 1994; Déchaux 1997; Jolas and Zonabend 1973; Le Wita 1994; Muxel 1991, 2002) do not give much attention to the role of historical events in the transmission of family memories. Given that the focus of the analysis is different on both sides of the Rhine, it is important to combine these two national research traditions (Werner and Zimmermann 2004) in order to broaden our questioning and obtain a theoretical enrichment that allows us to identify the multiple connections between relations to the past and adolescents' age, gender, social origin and trajectory, family configurations, and peer groups.

Existing studies on this highly political and symbolic question are often burdened with moral and normative judgments. This research demonstrates that ordinary uses of the Nazi past must be contextualized in order to understand adolescents' practices. Indeed, this past may allow adolescents to conform to the expectations of school institutions, or of their peers, or to set themselves apart. It may also help them build an image of themselves, form a political opinion, share a sense of complicity with a friend, make a place for oneself in the peer group, in the family, or with a teacher. The past may constitute a tool for them to defend themselves, or promote themselves, to play but also to learn. It therefore seems essential to avoid constructing oppositions between political and social uses of the past, and instead focus on how

Conclusion: From Memory to Appropriation(s) • 311

they are interconnected. Indeed, the political is socially constructed, and in order to understand the meaning (political, playful, personal, but also social) that adolescents give to the past on an everyday basis, we must analyze the different layers of meaning that overlap, interact, and contradict themselves in these uses of the past.

Inspired by the work of Maurice Halbwachs, this research has therefore aimed to analyze ordinary representations of the past, by ordinary people, and in particular adolescents, in context. This choice was also inspired by the desire to reintroduce sociological analysis into memory studies, which tend to oscillate between intellectualism and psychological normativity.

Indeed, existing studies suppose that the terms of the debate in the intellectual space can be considered a natural frame that would apply to the whole population in the same way. Yet the sociology of culture has long shown that cultural production is not consumed or perceived in a homogenous way. Cultural practices differ according to social origin and trajectory, gender, age, group belonging, and so forth. Intellectual and media debates on the Nazi past unfold in a public sphere that is restricted to a small number of people with very high cultural capital. The fact that the great majority of secondary school history teachers (twenty-nine out of thirty-two) interviewed in this study do not refer to these debates at all, even though they are socially and professionally predisposed to be interested in this question, demonstrates their limited reach. Most of these teachers are unable to reproduce (and indeed are not interested in reproducing) the main lines of the debates that concern the community of academic historians, and as a result they do not teach them. Instead, their discourses, including on the Nazi past, remain structured by the debates that were dominant when these teachers were young, and particularly during their university studies (especially 1968 for the teachers in Hamburg) or moments of major personal, professional, or political upheaval (such as 1989 for teachers in Leipzig).

For the students, this observation is far less surprising. There is a near-total lack of familiarity with the terms and structures of the academic and political debates (with the exception of a very small minority of students with very high cultural capital) and this makes the everyday uses of the Nazi past all the more interesting. It means that they clearly reveal the influences of other spheres, which were explicitly discussed in the interviews: the family, but also peer groups and hobbies. However, it does not mean that public debates have no effect. It is possible that their effects are indirect and play out in the long-term, by influencing a small population of young people who are culturally exposed to them, and whose political and cultural practices will perhaps remain marked by the fact that they are young. These debates and positions will therefore perhaps be carried into the journalistic and political spheres when this generation grows into them. It therefore seems all the more important to study young people and adolescents in order to understand their relations to politics and to the past—which are often closely interconnected—and this may also shed light on the way these relations operate for adults.

Given this, we may wonder how memory policies impact upon populations with lower levels of cultural capital. It seems that at least three possibilities emerge from our study. For students with low levels of economic and sometimes also cultural capital in their families, but who can mobilize other resources (such as being involved in an organization, particularly a political or a union organization), investing in school history classes can be "a way out" of their neighborhood, their social condition and provide hope for a better future. Conforming to academic expectations can therefore also constitute a sign of academic and social goodwill, which is part of a strategy of upward social mobility. However, these students can also use the past to construct a project for themselves in opposition to the legitimate interpretations of history. Rebellion against academic interpretations of Nazism, particularly in constructing the Nazi past as a positive reference, can represent a particularly provocative means (thereby considered efficient) of challenging the government and its public policies. Transforming the Nazi past into a positive reference constitutes a way for them to transgress the rules of the political field by transposing the political stakes of the present (particularly unemployment) onto their reading of the past and devaluing the political system of the FRG. Moreover, there are, of course, those who explicitly remain outside the public and academic discourses on the Nazi past. However, these individuals can find other ways to refer to and use this past, through music, jokes, and everyday interactions, for example. It is precisely because this is a subject that is present in both the public sphere and at school that it is mobilized by the students, even if these mobilizations do not always conform to the expectations of the institutions responsible for transmitting it.

Deviant practices sometimes result from this, the most visible of which are the provocative references to Nazi symbols in class or in the schoolyard. These adolescent practices can be, but are not necessarily, associated with political positions defending the extreme right. Indeed, when a student draws a swastika on the board before the teacher comes in, this may obviously indicate the student's affiliation to the extreme right. However, this research has shown the multiplicity of meanings this kind of behavior may have: provoking the teacher, pleasing the peer group, setting oneself apart, or opposing one's parents. These are all typically adolescent attitudes and all factors that play a role in the students' behavior; they therefore complicate political positions more than they refute them. This behavior may reveal far right ideology and still serve as a critique of the government, public policy, or a friend's political opinions, or be used to attract attention to oneself within the class or the school, and so forth.

Conclusion: From Memory to Appropriation(s) • 313

In this we can see another unexpected effect of public policies on memory. The presence of the Nazi past in political and media discourses, along with the consensus on its condemnation (particularly regarding the extermination policies) even for the most deviant students that I spoke to, makes the transgressive uses of the past all the more efficient. Paradoxically, it is therefore the acceptance of a norm—the refusal of the Nazi past—that encourages the students to transgress it when they wish to position themselves against the various institutions that surround them (academic, political, family, etc.). This is why describing such behavior as "neo-Nazi" or as showing "a lack of understanding of the genocide" overlooks a fundamental element: it is only because they understand the horror of this past (while remaining vague as to its content) and accept the taboo that this kind of deviance can operate.

Among other things, this paradox is made possible through the lack of content associated with the "duty to remember." The students have indeed internalized the need to remember, but this "duty" seems just as abstract as the "it" of the Jewish genocide. The expression "you have to remember" has no object—remember what? To remember (*Sich erinnern*) is a transitive verb in German (*sich an etwas erinnern*): to remember something. The expressions "we must remember," "we have a duty to remember," as well as the negative formulations "lest we forget," "we must not forget" (*wir dürfen nicht vergessen*) are constantly used in the intransitive form by both the teachers and the students. Sometimes "it" (*es*) is added, to avoid grammatically incorrect constructions (*wir dürfen es nicht vergessen*). But what, exactly, must be remembered? What must not be forgotten? In the face of the horror of the genocide, the "it" symbolizes "absolute evil," and this question remains unanswered. It seems as though self-evidence prevents any questions, even to the point of concealing the meaning of this "duty of memory." This lack of content also allows a very broad consensus on the categorical imperative—everyone can interpret this obligation to memory in their own way. This consensus simultaneously constitutes the efficiency and the weakness of this "duty of memory." The students, while readily accepting this "duty," may just as easily challenge it, because it remains too abstract to have a specific meaning in their own lives. It is easier to play with this "duty of memory"—and particularly in a humorous way—because its content is so vague. Provocation is not primarily directed against the suffering of the victims (although, among certain students, antisemitic or xenophobic elements can emerge) but rather against the categorical imperative to remember, which remains unexplained. This is perhaps also one of the reasons that the older students use these humorous practices less often, in addition to the fact that socialization contexts change, and they leave the world of street culture and peer groups. For those who manage, in spite of these difficulties, to conduct personal study on the Nazi past, an understanding of elements of this past makes the "duty of memory" policy less abstract and they may sometimes develop a new interest for this period of history. For others, leaving school means leaving the world that imposed this "duty to remember" on them, a duty that remains incomprehensible, even though it has been fully internalized and accepted, and has become a civic reflex for almost all.

Moreover, this study demonstrates the importance of context: students who laugh at a Nazi joke with their classmates can perfectly understand that this would be out of place in the family or in front of the teacher, and adapt their behavior to different social situations. It is therefore important to take into account these contexts in interpreting the different layers of meaning in adolescent behavior. The use of a comparative study, taking into account belonging to two political spaces (former GDR and former FRG) as well as two socially distinct neighborhoods in each of the two cities (contrasting "bourgeois" neighborhoods with "working class" neighborhoods), enabled me to explore the links between different social spaces: school, families, peer groups, and neighborhood contexts. Rapidly, however, other analytic factors emerged, particularly in relation to gender and family histories of migration.

Constructing an empirical study within four school institutions allowed me to focus more closely on the adolescents who are the target of memory policies, education policies, and the teaching of history. It was important to be able to extract them from the place they are assigned in "public debates" and by the adults that surround them, in order to focus on their ability to be the actors of their own education. Focusing on the meanings that they give to the Nazi past meant considering these "young people" as individuals, with their own originality, and with all of their shortcomings and clumsiness. It meant seeing them for what they are, teens who are growing, with their adolescent everyday concerns, their love affairs, their pride, their friendships and falling outs, their hopes and fears for the future, their projects and anxieties of failure. This is the time of life when children become adults; they construct political consciousness, group belonging, projects for the future. It is particularly interesting to study the appropriations of the past at a time when the foundations of future directions of their lives are being constructed. This is one of the reasons why members of the "second postwar generation of the FRG," who dominate the political, media, and intellectual spheres, are so keen to influence "young people's" relation to Nazism. They are attempting to transmit their own relation to the Nazi past and politics, influenced by the relationship they had with their own parents (C. Schneider 1998), but also by their political socialization in the 1970s (Oeser 2009a). In turn, the adolescents of the 2000s are building their own attitudes to politics in another historical context. Focusing on the meanings that these adolescents give to the Nazi past in their everyday lives allows us to observe this progressive construction of political meaning at a key point in their lives.

Conclusion: From Memory to Appropriation(s) • 315

However, taking adolescents as a research object to study the appropriations of the Nazi past supposes deconstructing the homogeneity of this group. Because, although this is indeed a central moment in the political construction of the individual, it has neither the same signification nor the same form, depending on gender, ethnic background, family migration history, and social class. These appropriations also differ depending on the young people's friendships and peer groups, their schools and neighborhoods, and they are influenced by intrafamilial configurations such as relations between brothers and sisters, parents' trajectories, neighbors, and the broader family, etc. Shifting our gaze from macro sociological oppositions to micro sociological functioning not only allows us to refine the analysis and move beyond binary oppositions, but it also reflects the fact that these macro oppositions are constructed and reconstructed on an everyday basis by social agents and their interactions. This shift in our gaze, the taking into account of different levels of analysis, from micro to macro, from local to international (Revel 1996), therefore allows an analysis of domination (*Herrschaft*) not as an overarching factor, external to individuals, but as social praxis (Lüdtke 1991a). The focus on the micro level is therefore not to be seen as desociologizing the analysis or obscuring power relations but rather as focusing on how these are constructed and fabricated, as well as focusing on their renewal in everyday life. In concrete terms, this means that the processes of transmitting the norms by which the Nazi past is interpreted cannot be reduced to them simply being internalized or rejected by adolescents. It is the whole range of reinterpretations and reappropriations that makes norms meaningful and gives them their lasting power. Thus, the acceptance of the "duty of memory" and its simultaneous challenge by deviant or transgressive behavior contributes to perpetuating this duty as an unavoidable norm in dealing with the Nazi past. In other words, it is not only the legitimate interpretations of the past, but also those that transgress or contest that legitimacy that contribute to defining what is institutionally acceptable in the school, the family, or the peer group. The micro and the macro are therefore not binary opposites, neither at the theoretical level, nor at the empirical level; instead they are complementary analytical perspectives. The interplay of these sociological levels offers us a way out of the alternative between structuralism and interactionism, in order to understand how social agents contribute to the social functioning of power relations, which also shape the processes of transmission of the Nazi past. Focusing on adolescents and their interpretations of the Nazi past allows us to conduct this analysis based on political constructions of the past and socially situated norms that contribute to shaping power relations.

This book has aimed to be cumulative. Like the layers of an onion, each chapter has added a new dimension to the analysis, shifted perspective, taken a different angle or point of view on the same object. In the first two chapters,

I sought to identify the academic interpretations of the Nazi past. This began with the teachers, from the perspective of civic education, combining a belief in the liberal political system (whether it is well established such as in Hamburg, or newly acquired such as in Leipzig) with a twofold engagement for education and for the state. It then continued with the students who, depending on their trajectory, gave meaning to the Nazi past through the perspective of academic integration, upward social trajectory, personal or familial challenges, or political engagements. Academic success cannot be analyzed without situating it within the trajectory of an individual and their family. The Nazi past contributes to constructing the meaning of this success. The third chapter returned to the theme of interpenetration between school and the family environment from the point of view of gender, combining the perspectives of students, teachers, and parents (of both students and of teachers). The interaction between different levels, the interpenetration of school and family spaces, the gendered construction of representations of space, domestic roles and tasks, school activities, and pastimes all contribute to articulating the gendered appropriations of the Nazi past. This chapter also constitutes a turning point in the analysis because it introduces the differentiation between legitimate and illegitimate uses of the Nazi past and paves the way for the following chapters that concentrate on uses of the Nazi past outside of school and particularly those considered illegitimate by the institutions.

The last three chapters are interdependent and focus on a minority of adolescents who defy academic norms. Focusing on the illegitimate uses of the Nazi past allows us to achieve a closer analysis of the meanings that these boys (and more rarely girls) give to the Nazi past both outside and in opposition to the school framework. The fourth chapter covers the ways in which the Nazi past is transformed into a resource, particularly a political resource, by the students. The fifth chapter analyzes the limits to the possibilities of these appropriations and the forms of difficulties hearing and/or appropriating the past (*Harthörigkeiten*) that students sometimes encounter situations in which they cannot or will not speak about the Nazi past. Finally, the sixth chapter studies the playful dimensions that may be associated with the Nazi past in games, banter and insults, jokes and interactions, particularly among boys, sometimes within the class but most often in the playground and out of sight of the teachers.

On a theoretical level, this study has progressively abandoned analysis in terms of "collective memory" (Halbwachs [1950] 1997) in favor of "social frameworks of memory" (Halbwachs [1925] 1994)[1] and "multiple reappropriations." In conclusion, it now seems possible to reintroduce the temporal dimension into this study by reversing the perspective. Instead of posing the question of the students' relations to the (Nazi) past, it is perhaps relevant to once again shift our outlook and focus on their relation to the future. Or, to use François Hartog's now-famous expression, we ought to think in terms of "regimes of historicity" that provide a framework for the students' "experiences of time" or their "ways of articulating the past, present and future—and giving them meaning" (Hartog [2003] 2015: 118). Because attitudes toward the future and the present seem to indeed play a role in the ways in which the students give meaning to the Nazi past, we have tried to shed light on how this past acquires meaning in students' constructions of their future and their present. Reflecting on the articulation between regimes of historicity and students and teachers' experiences of time therefore allows us to situate our analytic perspective at a more macro level, in order to inscribe the adolescents' different uses of the past in their political and state context.

History teachers' experiences of time differs from those of their students, due the fundamental break from Nazism that led to the postwar boom during their adolescence and young adulthood and contributed to the construction of a belief in the future of democracy (liberal or socialist). Transmitting the Nazi past is seen as an attempt to ensure the future of a society that is fairer and more egalitarian: utopian in the FRG in 1968 and incarnated by the very real socialism of the GDR in the 1970s. This belief in a better society to be constructed through teaching (the past) has of course lost some of its utopian nature in the twenty-first century, but the teachers' experience of time and the way in which they articulate the past, present, and future remain marked by their political socialization and the period of their own education. The history of Nazism and its transmission constitute a central element in their attitudes toward politics; breaking away from the past remains the standpoint from which they must envisage and construct the present and the future. But the teachers' political socialization is also marked by the bipolarity in world politics that crystallized around the division of Germany. The interpretation of the Nazi past is fundamental for justifying the regime in which the teachers live and work, and which they try to transmit to their students through civic education. Western interpretations of totalitarianism that create a continuity between Nazism and Communism, serve (among other things) to transmit a love of liberal democracy and tend to identify the countries of the Soviet bloc and particularly the GDR as "enemy number one." The antifascist interpretations in the GDR, creating a continuity between Nazism and (fascist) capitalism serve (among other things) to teach a love for socialist democracy and tend to target the countries of the capitalist bloc, and in particular the FRG, as "enemy number one." Nazism is not only the starting point for this bipolar reasoning, it is fundamental to it. This mirror image on both sides of the wall is a powerful one, and it is structural to the political experience of the teachers, whether they adopt it or whether they oppose it. Of course, there are teachers who criticize this dichotomic caricature of the world. One remarkably efficient way of opposing this separation, which we observed at the Wiesi school in Hamburg, consists in mobilizing interpretations from "the other side of the wall," emphasizing the role of capitalism in the rise of fascism, in history classes in the FRG, for example. However even if it is challenged, this separation remains central, and requires a study of the period between 1933 and 1945. The fundamental, even unavoidable, position of the Nazi past in the teachers' experiences of time, both politically and professionally (and for some of the students' parents too) is linked to family situations and their relationship with parents who are assumed to be "Nazis." It is also linked to the political framework, the state organization of the present, the past and the future, or in other words, state thought.

After reunification, Nazism was partially replaced by the past of the GDR, which became the key historical reference to be overcome, particularly for of the *Ossis* of the "new *Länder*." In the FRG, political continuity led to the reinforcement of the totalitarian interpretation of the Nazi past, particularly applied to the "new *Länder*." Transforming the citizens "of the East" into liberal democrats through education required a rejection of the GDR's past, for which the comparison between Nazism and Communism was useful. As a result, it was mobilized broadly by teachers in Leipzig in an attempt to adapt to the new state thought. It was criticized by some teachers in Leipzig, who opposed this inversion of the dominant worldview, the polar opposite of the values that had governed their own socialization.

The students cannot possibly have the same experiences of time as their teachers or parents, who lived through the "German miracle"—economic above all, but also political—that was the Cold War. The book must therefore be understood through their relation to the future. Indeed, being born in reunified Germany clearly presents new historical references. The end of the bipolar world also means the end of political certainties. In Germany, the end of the division of the country represents the end of the Other—the enemy behind the wall—but also the model against which it was so easy to construct oneself, on both sides. The Nazi past, which was central in the construction of these opposing political visions and maintained its importance for the generation that was socialized under this bipolar vision of the world, has therefore lost part of its centrality for adolescents in the early twenty-first century. The new millennium is a time of uncertainties, political, economic, and ideological, and it is above all the uncertainty about the future, rather than about the past, which governs the experience of time and the political experiences of these adolescents. In other words, the Nazi past is no longer essential to building an image of oneself, a political opinion (of rebellion or acceptance) or a position in a group (political, peer, or even family). Generational oppositions persist, but in different forms: they extend beyond the limited framework of genealogical generations (such as they are often considered by studies

Conclusion: From Memory to Appropriation(s) • 319

on the family transmission of Nazism) and are written more broadly into the political and social organization of the world.

Adolescence is a key moment in the construction of the self in relation to social, political, and academic norms. The students interviewed here are constructing themselves both by appropriating these norms and by playing with transgression in a process that is specific to adolescents. We have seen to what extent the Nazi past is central to the relation to the state and to politics for this generation of teachers and parents. This is a very powerful norm, which manifests itself in various ways and requires adolescents to take a position.

It seems that a well-formed life project can help an individual appropriate the Nazi past in ways that are considered legitimate and then become an aspect of this project. Fear of unemployment, failure at school, and professional uncertainty all involve an anxiety about the future that requires more oppositional or contesting uses of the Nazi past. Growing up in political economic and financial familial stability, as the children of public servants in the FRG are able to do, gives them a secure attitude toward their political and professional futures and a belief in the political system. However, for parents in the GDR, the break in 1989 challenged their belief in the political and ideological system, which in turn led to repercussions for the place of the Nazi past in their children's lives. These different attitudes toward the present and the future influence the perceptions of the past. A future dictatorship seems plausible for students in Leipzig, for example, but not for those in Hamburg, which influences the importance that they grant to past dictatorships.

In a general climate of insecurity and threat, the feeling of political and economic security persists among certain students, at certain points in life, and in certain contexts. This feeling is dependent not only on the trajectories of parents, but also on those of the students themselves. The year 1989 plays a central role because it inverted social hierarchies in East Germany and destabilized the elites of the former GDR, but experiences of unemployment, poverty, or migration can have similar effects. Gender differences also have a place in this analysis. Girls, often better suited to the requirements of the school system, tend to be more at ease in constructing a life project that includes a legitimate reading of the Nazi past. They are also less likely to oppose school rules, among other reasons because they are less likely to be members of peer groups that value the transgression of these norms, which is the case for some non-mixed groups of boys that value certain forms of exhibited virility.

Therefore, although generational opposition does exist, it is only one of the factors that structures appropriations of the past, among many others. It is indeed the interaction between these different factors that has been at the heart of this research. One of the phenomena that is most often explained in generational terms is "saturation," the fact that the younger generation has "had enough" of talking about Nazism. Although there are reasons to believe that the Nazi past has lost some of its importance for adolescents in the 2000s because of socio-political factors, this research shows that "saturation," or rather a period of *Harthörigkeit*, a desire to no longer listen, only affects a very small, socially privileged minority at a specific age. "Saturation" is therefore not so much a generational phenomenon as a specific period in the life of certain adolescents, often those who were intensely interested in the Nazi past around fourteen and 15 years old and by age sixteen, say they are "sick of it." Moreover, these same students regain interest in this topic by age eighteen. This is a population that comes from a very privileged background whose modes of opposition to school norms exclude any possible positive reference to Nazism or other behavior proscribed by the institution, such as open opposition to the teacher. Adolescents who aspire to academic success will not take the risk of losing any prestige they might have at school by opposing academic norms too openly—and interpretations of the Nazi past are an integral part of these norms. These students find other forms of opposition, including the expression of "saturation," which allows them to accuse the school institution as responsible for their disinterest and to disguise their opposition as critique (more or less constructive), or the students focus on other historical periods such as the Weimar Republic. These indirect "oppositional" strategies are relatively efficient and more accepted in the school context, particularly when they come from "good students." Indeed, we have seen how teachers in Weinberg have abandoned the idea of covering the period of National Socialism in senior school. By adopting the recognized academic language of critique, students manage to transform their opposition into a resource and combine a critique of the political and school system with their own academic success. Moreover, the media and political spheres continue to construct debates from a generational perspective, which demonstrates the social efficiency of this strategy. Indeed, these students (who are an exception) are also those who manage to make their voices heard in the media and intellectual scenes to the point that their behavior is projected onto the whole generation.

Students with low cultural resources, or those who are not overly successful at school, do not express the same forms of *Harthörigkeit* and never appear "saturated." We can understand this if we consider the gap that exists between their cultural practices and the school discourse, but also because their academic reputations (such as they are) are not so valuable to them, meaning they can resort to positive visions of the Nazi past, behavior forbidden by teachers. Indeed, these class "dunces," who have "no hope" of succeeding in the school institution, abandon any strategy of adopting the norms since they have already little to lose given that they are considered by

Conclusion: From Memory to Appropriation(s) • 321

both themselves and the institution as being "lost causes." As a result, it is easier for them to turn toward more provocative discourse.

We can see the social efficacy of the dominant discourse, and the contrast between the social diversity of discourses and the homogenizing vision in the media and academia in these socially differentiated forms of opposition to norms regarding the past. Indeed, attempts at opposition that do not mobilize the codes of academic language are excluded from the media and political field, or stigmatized as being "extremist" and rejected into illegality.

This is also the case for the forms of *Hörigkeit* (not wanting to listen) and *Gehorsamkeit* (obedience), as well as the forms of opposition. Behavior that corresponds to academic norms can be, occasionally, a sign of adopting the teachers' frameworks of interpretation. There seems to be a form of obedience in the "duty to memory" that may be entirely compatible with the lack of obedience in the interpretations of the details or a reinterpretation of the past for personal ends, group affirmations, or promotion of political opinions. Therefore, obedience and opposition are not necessarily incompatible. What is true for the "dunces" of the class is also true for the "good students." They may combine different interpretations of the past and oscillate between submission and transgression. Moreover, there is a whole range of legitimate reinterpretations of the Nazi past that are not only used to obtain good grades at school, to please one's teachers or parents, but also to construct an image of oneself, to share a political opinion with a group (an activist group, for example), to reconstruct family history or to break with a downward trajectory. This book has therefore sought to disentangle this complexity in order to contribute to a scientific approach to the transmission of the Nazi past, moving beyond the current debates that are weighed down by normative professional unity and an oversimplification of forms of reappropriation due to a lack of empirical study. In order to address the questions raised in this book, the analysis of different forms of appropriation and their social foundations requires a collective approach to the institutionalization of interdisciplinary studies on ordinary reappropriations of culture, history, politics, and the state.

Note

1. Paradoxically, the English translation of Halbwachs's "social frameworks of memory" is "collective memory." On the notion of frame analysis, see, though much later, Goffman (1974).

Appendix 1

THE GERMAN SCHOOL SYSTEM

The school system in Germany is federal. Decisions are made autonomously by each state, or *Land*, which means there are significant differences in each of the sixteen *Länder*. As a result, the length of schooling varies from twelve to thirteen years depending on the state, which explains the difference between Hamburg, which at the time of the study was still using the thirteen-year model, and Leipzig, where the twelve-year system of the GDR was maintained. The *Länder* are also responsible for deciding on the school curriculum and which textbooks to be used in class. That is why there is such a large number of school textbooks authorized in Germany. At the federal level, the Conference for Ministers of Education and Cultural Affairs (Kultusministerkonferenz—KMK), decides on the main guidelines of the education system. As Table A.1 shows, the three-part system leads to an institutional separation of children at age ten. The *Hauptschule* involves nine years of schooling and a diploma at age fifteen, the *Hauptschulabschluss*. The *Realschule* involves ten years of schooling and a diploma at age sixteen, the *Realschulabschluss*. Finally, the third option, the *Gymnasium*, traditionally involves thirteen years of schooling—since reunification has progressively been reduced to twelve years depending on the *Land*—and a diploma at age eighteen or nineteen, the *Abitur.*

In the 1970s, certain *Länder* controlled by the SPD, such as Hamburg, set up schools that brought the three types of schools into a single institution (*Hauptschule, Realschule,* and *Gymnasium*) in order to attenuate the effects of social segregation. These institutions were called *Gesamtschulen*. Politically controversial, they were never able to replace the other institutions, which is why they exist in parallel to the other three types of schools. In Hamburg, these *Gesamtschulen* were established in working-class and disadvantaged neighborhoods, which is why I chose to study Wiesi rather than a *Haupt-* or a *Realschule* in this neighborhood.

The GDR made the opposite decision, based on system with a single school, the *Polytechnische Oberschule* (POS), which was open to all students until the age of sixteen. It was possible to leave the POS after eight years of schooling (without a diploma) in order to begin an apprenticeship. Only the last four (or two) years prepared a portion of a given age group for the *Abitur*, in separate institutions, the *Erweiterte Oberschulen* (EOS).

After reunification, most of the new *Länder* adopted the three-part system of the FRG, with certain modifications. In Saxony, a compromise between the three-part system and the *Gesamtschule* model was found in the creation of a two-stream system: with a *Mittelschule* (which combines *Haupt-* and *Realschule*) and *Gymnasium* (see Table A.2).

Although there is no institutional separation between middle school and senior high school, this separation nevertheless exists within the *Gymnasium* and corresponds to the shift from the intermediate *Mittelstufe* (eighth through tenth grade) to the advanced grades *Gymnasiale Oberstufe*. *Mittelstufe* ends with an official exam that is the equivalent of the *Realschulabschluss*. Students who want to leave the *Gymnasium* at age sixteen will do so with a diploma called *Mittlere Reife*, if they pass the official exam.

Table A.1 Summary table of the school systems in the FRG and the GDR. Graduation exams in bold.

Type of school			Age of students	FRG				GDR	
Primary/elementary school			6	*Grundschule*				*POS*	
			7	1st grade				1st grade	
			8	2nd grade				2nd grade	
			9	3rd grade				3rd grade	
				4th grade				4th grade	
Secondary school	Junior			*Hauptschule*	*Gesamtschule* / *Realschule*		*Gymnasium*		
			10	5th grade	5th grade		5th grade	5th grade	
			11	6th grade	6th grade		6th grade	6th grade	
			12	7th grade	7th grade		7th grade	7th grade	
	Middle (or Junior High school)		13	8th grade	8th grade		8th grade	8th grade	*EOS*
			14	9th grade	9th grade		9th grade	9th grade	
			15	Apprenticeship	10th grade	Apprenticeship	10th grade	10th grade	10th grade
	Senior (or High-school)		16				11th grade	11th grade	Apprenticeship
			17				12th grade	12th grade	
			18				13th grade		
Qualification/Exam			High school diploma	**Hauptschulabschluss**	**Realschulabschluss, Mittlere Reife**		**Abitur**	**Abitur**	**Mittlere Reife**

Table A.2 Comparison of the four schools participating in the study.

Town	Hamburg		Leipzig	
Name/Type of school	*Gesamtschule* Wiesi	*Gymnasium* Weinberg	100th *Mittelschule*	*Gymnasium* Monnet
Junior/Middle school (or Junior High school)	*Hauptschule*	5th	5th	*Haupt-schule*	5th	5th
		6th	6th		6th	6th
		7th	7th		7th	7th
		8th	8th		8th	8th
		9th	9th		9th	9th
	Hauptschulabschluss		*Hauptschulabschluss*	
High school	*Realschule*	10th	10th	*Realschule*	10th	10th
	Realschulabschluss/Mittlere Reife			
	Gymnasiale Oberstufe	11th	11th		11th
		12th	12th		12th
		13th	13th		
Final Diploma		*Abitur*	*Abitur*		*Abitur*

Appendix 2

STRUCTURE OF INTERVIEWS WITH STUDENTS

These are not so much questions as themes that were covered in the interviews. There were not necessarily formulated in these exact words nor presented in this exact order.

Presentation

I am a history student studying the transmission of history in schools. How do teachers teach history, and what do students think about the history and about the teaching? I am interested in the personal experiences with history of students and teachers at school, in families, and among friends.

General prompt

I want to talk to you about history. German history. Is there, in German history, an event, a moment, a period, that seems to be particularly interesting for you personally? Or that is particularly important to you, personally, in your life?

First, let the interviewee speak and encourage the students to elaborate with further questions:

- What is he/she talking about?
- Which facts are they familiar with? Which are mentioned more than once?
- What are the student's questions regarding history?
- Chronology? Important dates?
- Context of period mentioned – follow-up questions on related subjects.

If they do not mention the subjects of their own accord, prompt:

- Nazism
- 1989

School

- History teacher: one, several?
- Have the student talk about the teacher to put them at ease.
- History class: what themes emerge?
- Discovery of Nazism, genocide: discussed in which class(es), how many times, for how long (weeks, months). In what other classes: German, ethics, religion, English, *Gemeinschaftskunde* (civic education) etc.?

Family

- Who do they talk with: parents, grandparents, men/women?
- How often (frequently, never)? Does it go well? Badly? Tensions or not, etc.?
- When was the first time, on what occasion, how did it happen?
- Who brought up the subject initially (children, parents, or grandparents)? What was the occasion?
- Anecdotes: encourage them to tell stories that have been told in their family, Who talks about them, when?
- Reactions and emotions.

Cultural practices

Books (about history)

- Children's books, which ones: precise memories or not. Have them tell the story as though I did not know the books.
- Where do the reading sources come from: family, gifts, friends, school, library?
- How many (one or several, over a particular period etc.)?
- Reactions and emotions.
- Are they still interested in them today?

Media (about history)

- Films.
- Documentaries.
- Television. Which stations (Arte, RTL, etc.)?
- Surfing channels or looking for specific things?
- Today, do they especially look for historical films or watch them by accident
- How many times have they watched one? What was the last film/documentary they saw and when? Can they tell the story of it?
- Today: do they watch more or less than before? Have they changed their attitude as a viewer or not?
- Reactions and emotion.

Newspapers

- Which newspaper? Family subscription or not? Read or not? Purchased or not?
- Which articles? Do they read them or not? Have them talk about an article they read recently.
- Debates on history in the media – if they have not been mentioned, talk about them at the end of the interview (Walser, Goldhagen, exhibition on the Wehrmacht, Berlin monument).
- Reactions and emotions.

Museums, camps

- Have they visited or not?
- If yes, talk about a visit to a museum or a camp: When? With whom (family/school/friends)? Whose idea was it (compulsory/not)? What occasion? What was it like?
- Reactions, emotions.

Friends

- Do they talk about history? About Nazism? About the camp visits (if they visited any)? About the books they read or the films they saw?
- When? On what occasions?
- Links to the present or not?
- "Imposed" (by school) or not?

Attitudes

- Toward Jews.
- Toward foreigners.
- Toward Germany.
- Feelings of belonging, patriotism, guilt.
- Pride, shame, guilt, ambiguity.
- Experiences overseas.

Political opinion

- Vote.
- Militancy/activism.
- Political opinion (toward the government, public policy).
- Family political discussions: When? On what occasion? About whom?
- Sensitive issues, interests.

Social characteristics and trajectory

- Age.
- School (still the same?): Which neighborhood? *Gymnasium, Gesamtschule, Haupt/Realschule?*
- Did they do an apprenticeship?

Parents

- Parents' professions.
- Their birthdates.
- Their place of residence.
- Experiences of 1968/1989.
- Particularly close to one or the other? Which one, in what way?
- Shared activities/hobbies.
- For all the cultural practices mentioned: ask with whom—role of parents?

Grandparents

- Grandparents' professions.
- Their birthdates.
- Their role during the war?
- How much does the student know about this and how (who told them)?
- Nazi or not?
- Combatants or not? If yes, on which front?
- Prisoners or not?
- Date of death: in relation to the age of their grandchildren.
- Experience of 1989.

Siblings

- Age.
- Activity.
- School.
- Interest in history.
- Relations between brothers and sisters.
- Particularly close to siblings?
- Shared activities/hobbies.
- For all the cultural practices mentioned: With whom—role of brothers and sisters?

Questionnaire
(completed at the end of the interview with the student)

Birthplace:

Date of birth:

Place of residence (from birth to eighteen years old):

School (name, place, type):

Subject specializations:

Predicted date of graduation:

Religion:

Do you believe in God?

Do you attend church, mosque, synagogue: once a week/month/year?

If there was an election tomorrow, would you vote if you had the right to? For which party?

Are you a member of a political party? If yes, which one?

Are you a member of an association organization? If yes, which one?

Family

Father

Place and date of birth:
Place of residence and dates of changing residences:
Qualifications:
Profession(s):
Date of marriage:
Divorce:
Political opinions/vote:
• Before 1989:
• After 1989:
Religion (faith, attendance etc.):
Death, date, reason:

Mother

Place and date of birth:
Place of residence and dates of changing residences:
Qualifications:
Profession(s):
Date of marriage:
Divorce:
Political opinions/vote:
• Before 1989:
• After 1989:
Religion (belief, attendance etc.):
Death, date, reason:

Brothers and sisters

(If married: same questions for the husband or the wife)
Place and date of birth, sex:
Place of residence and dates of changing residences:

Qualifications:

Profession(s):

Date of marriage:

Divorce:

Political opinions/vote:
* Before 1989:
* After 1989:

Religion (belief, attendance etc.):

Death, date, reason:

Paternal grandparents

Place and date of birth, sex:

Place of residence and dates of changing residences:

Qualifications:

Profession(s):

Date of marriage:

Divorce:

Political opinions/vote:
* Today:
* Before 1989:
* After 1989:

National Socialism:
* Combatant?
* Which front?
* Prisoner of war?

If you had to describe your grandfather/grandmother, would you say that during the war they were:
* An active member?
* *Mitläufer* (follower)?
* Persecuted?
* Resister?

Religion (belief, attendance etc.):

Death, date, reason:

Appendix 2: Structure of Interviews with Students • 333

Maternal grandparents

Place and date of birth, sex:

Place of residence and dates of changing residences:

Qualifications:

Profession(s):

Date of marriage:

Divorce:

Political opinions/vote:

- Today:
- Before 1989:
- After 1989:

National Socialism:

- Combatant?
- Which front?
- Prisoner of war?

If you had to describe your grandfather/grandmother, would you say that during the war they were:

- An active member?
- *Mitläufer* (follower)?
- Persecuted?
- Resister?

Religion (belief, attendance etc.):

Death, date, reason:

Great-grandparents, if relevant

Place and date of birth, sex:

Place of residence and dates of changing residences:

Qualifications:

Profession(s):

Date of marriage:

Divorce:

Political opinions/vote:

- Today:
- Before 1989:
- After 1989:

National Socialism:

- Combatant?
- Which front?
- Prisoner of war?

If you had to describe your great-grandfather/great-grandmother, would you say that during the war they were:

- An active member?
- *Mitläufer* (follower)?
- Persecuted?
- Resister?

Religion (belief, attendance etc.):
Death, date, reason:

Appendix 3

SUMMARY TABLE OF TEACHERS

Table A.3 Summary table of teachers (social origins, age, place of study, sex).

SPC of teachers' parents	Hamburg					Leipzig				
	Weinberg		Wiesi		Total 38	Monnet		100th *Mittelschule*		Total 26
	Father	Mother	Father	Mother		Father	Mother	Father	Mother	
Managers, intellectual professions (of which teachers)	3(1)	1(1)	3(1)	2(1)	9(4)	2(0)	1(1)	3(1)	0(0)	6(2)
Artisans, shopkeepers, business owners	2	0	3	0	5	1	0	2	0	3
Technicians and associate professionals	0	1	2	0	3	0	2	0	0	2
Employees	0	1	1	5	7	0	3	0	2	5
Manual workers	0	0	3	2	5	5	2	0	3	10

336 • Appendix 3: Summary Table of Teachers

Table A.3 Continued

Age of teachers in 2002	Male	Female	Male	Female	Total	Male	Female	Male	Female	Total
Unknown/deceased	2	1	0	0	3	0	0	0	0	0
Housewives	0	3	0	3	6	0	0	0	0	0
50–65 (1937–1952)	6		8		14	1		1		2
	3	3	6	2		0	1	0	1	
40–50 (1953–1963)	0		2		2	6		4		10
	0	0	1	1		1	5	0	4	
30–40 (1963–1973)	1		2		3	1		0		1
	0	1	0	2		0	1	0	0	
Total Men/Women per school	3	4	7	5	19	1	7	0	5	13

Teachers' place of study	Male	Female	Male	Female	Total	Male	Female	Male	Female	Total
Hamburg or Leipzig	2	2	7	5	16	1	5	0	4	10
Elsewhere in FRG/GDR	1	2	0	0	3	0	2	0	1	3
The "other side of the wall"	0	0	0	0	0	0	0	0	0	0
Total per school	7		12		19	8		5		13

Appendix 4

LIST OF TEACHERS INTERVIEWED

Organized by school and alphabetical order

Hamburg, *Gymnasium Weinberg*

- Ms Groß v. Wilhelmshöhe, 19 and 20 February 2003 (3 hours).

  History and English teacher.

  Born in 1942 in Berlin. *Abitur*, 1961. Master's degree in history (supervised by Egmont Zechlin), English and biology at the University of Hamburg, 1969. Married to a university history professor, no children. Member of the Socialist youth (*Jusos*); also a member of the SPD, which she left in 1972. Member of the *Deutscher Philologenverband*, a faction of the Independent Union Deutscher Lehrerverband (DLV).

  Father: born around 1910, Jewish. His parents died in 1929, managed to obtain an "Aryan" family tree during World War I. Soldier, died during the war. A large part of his family died in the camps.

  Mother: born around 1910. No formal qualifications. Mother at home.

- Mr Hatze, 18 February, 11 and 15 April 2003 (5 hours).

  History and physical education teacher.

Born in 1949. *Abitur*, 1968. Master's degree in history and sports at the University of Göttingen, 1978. One brother, a bank employee. Married, one son.

Father: (1925 in western Germany–2001) *Volksschule*. Artisan painter. Was a soldier on the Eastern Front.

Mother: born in 1926 in western Germany. *Volksschule*. Mother at home.

• Ms Heide, 18 February and 23 April 2003 (8 hours).

History and Latin teacher.

Born in 1971 near Bonn. *Abitur*, 1990. Master's degree in history (supervised by Klaus Hildebrand) and Latin, 1997. Abandoned her PhD project to become a teacher. Employed in a library in Cologne before finding a position in 2002 at the *Gymnasium* Weinberg. A practicing Protestant, attends church two or three times a year. Recently married, her husband has a degree in agricultural studies and works for the government agency for agriculture and food (*Bundesanstalt für Landwirtschaft und Ernährung*). No children yet.

Father: Born in 1933 near Aachen. Studied in a monastery. Catholic priest. Librarian in the monastery where he was studying. PhD in history at the University of Aachen, where he met his wife. Left the Catholic Church to get married in 1966. Today he is an atheist.

Mother: born in 1939 near Wuppertal, graduated in history and modern languages, secondary school teacher. FDP sympathizer. Practicing Protestant.

• Ms Reinhard, 9 and 16 April 2003 (4 hours).

History and German literature teacher.

Born in 1941. Lived in the GDR until age fifteen, for one year alone, before joining her parents in the FRG in 1957. *Abitur*, 1962. Master's degree in history and modern languages at the Free University of Berlin, 1969. Member of the GEW union, as an organizer.

Father: (1903–1972) *Volksschule*, commerce secondary school (*Handelschule*), apprenticeship. Public servant, town inspector (*Stadtinspektor*). A volunteer in 1939, fought on both fronts (East and West), interned until 1955 in an English camp before returning to the public service in the FRG. Jehovah's Witness.

Mother: (1910 in Bohemia–1981) Middle School certificate, apprenticeship in a deaconesses' boarding school. Dental assistant and then nurse.

Left the GDR in 1956 to join her husband, who had been released from the English prison, in the FRG,

- Mr Richter, 20 and 23 February 2003 (6 hours).

History and German literature teacher.

Born in 1940, *Abitur* 1960. Master's degree in history (supervised by Fritz Fischer) and German studies (*Germanistik*) at the University of Hamburg, 1968. One brother, born in 1926, who volunteered in 1941, and became a member of the SPD and took up his father's business. Married to a secondary school teacher, one child.

Father: (1904–1968) *Volkschule*, small business owner. Was not a combatant.

Mother: born in 1905, *Volkschule*, dressmaker. Mother at home after the birth of her children.

- Mr Schulze, 13 and 17 February 2003 (8 hours).

History and German literature teacher.

Born in 1943 in a small village now in Poland. *Abitur*, 1962. Master's degree in history (supervised by Fritz Fischer) and German studies (*Germanistik*) at the University of Hamburg, 1969. One brother, died in a car accident as a child. Married to a primary school teacher, no children. Member of Amnesty International.

Father: born in 1914 in Hamburg. Professional certificate. Joined the war in 1939. *Abitur* and university studies in architecture after the war. Independent architect.

Mother: born in 1915. *Abitur*. Worked at the employment office of the Reich (*Reichsarbeitsdienst*) between 1933 and 1940, then mother at home.

- Ms Simone, 9 April 2003 (45 minutes).

History and English teacher.

Born in 1951. *Abitur*, 1971. Master's degree in history and English at the University of Hamburg in the early 1980s. Married, two children.

No information about her parents.

Hamburg, *Gesamtschule Wiesi*

- Mr Gerste, 20 October 2003 (3.5 hours).

Politics (including history, geography and *Gemeinschaftskunde*), philosophy and English teacher.

Born in 1961. *Abitur*, 1982. Master's degree in philosophy, English and pedagogy (as a specific subject) at the University of Hamburg, 1988. Worked in marketing (*Marktforschung*), as a project manager. In 1991, became a secondary teacher. One brother (a teacher) and two sisters (a sales person and a nurse). Married, twelve-year-old daughter.

Father: (1925 in Silesia–1994), *Realschule*. Skilled worker, machine technician. A soldier on the Eastern Front from 1942. Lived in Lübeck after the war.

Mother: born in 1923 in Kiel. *Hauptschule*. Unskilled worker in an arms factory. Mother at home after the war.

- Mr Herzog, 25 April 2003 (2 hours).

  Politics, ethics, and religion teacher.

  Born in 1949 in Hamburg. *Abitur*, 1971. Master's degree in history (supervised by Fritz Fischer) and pedagogy in 1975 at the University of Hamburg.

  Member of the SPD until 1978 and the GEW until 1983. One sister, social pedagogue. One daughter aged twenty-eight.

  Father: born in 1906. *Abitur*. Worked as a public servant and in national administration before 1933. SPD supporter before, during, and after the war. Spent four years in a concentration camps for defamation (*Verächtlichmachung*) of Hitler. First in Buchenwald, then Neuengamme, and then a third camp. Sent to the Eastern Front in 1944, was then a prisoner of war held by the United States. After the war, became president of the Sophie Scholl Association in Hamburg.

  Mother: born in 1916 in Pomerania. Daughter of a farmworker. No formal qualifications. Before the war she worked as a day laborer (*Tagelöhnerin*); afterwards, as a salesperson in Hamburg. Was first married to a butcher who died during the war.

- Ms Inge, 24 April 2003 (2 hours).

  Politics and ethics teacher.

  Born in 1948 in Rostock, left to live with her parents in Hamburg in 1952. *Abitur*, 1968. Master's degree in history (supervised by Fritz Fischer) and pedagogy at the University of Hamburg, 1972. Member of the SPD and the GEW. Married, no children.

  Father: (1923 in Mecklenburg–1997) *Realschule*, apprenticeship. Employee.

  Mother: born in 1922 in Mecklenburg. No formal qualifications. Mother at home.

Appendix 4: List of Teachers Interviewed • 341

- Mr Kamm, 23 April 2003 (1.5 hours).

  Politics, ethics, and religion teacher.

  Born in the 1940s. Degree in engineering sciences in Hamburg, then in political science. Lives in Wiesi. Married, two children. Adopted a daughter from the school. Her brother "comes with her." He therefore has four children and left the neighborhood to live in a house close by.

  Father: born in 1917 in northern Germany. Worker. Conscripted in 1939.

  Mother: born in 1919. *Volkschule.* Mother at home.

- Annika Klein, 23 October 2003 (4 hours).

  Politics and German literature teacher.

  Born in 1968 in Hamburg. At age twelve, she joined a "Catholic cult" and wanted to become a nun. At age seventeen, broke with both the cult and with Catholicism. *Abitur,* 1988. Master's degree in history and modern languages, 1995. During her studies, she worked as social worker "on the streets" (*Sraßensozialarbeit*). Taught for two years in a Catholic private school before obtaining a position at Wiesi, in 2000. One brother (social pedagogue) and one sister (secondary school teacher).

  Father: born in 1936 in Breslau. Fled in 1945 with his parents to northern Germany. Apprenticeship, miner in the Ruhr, sat the *Abitur* at night school, before doing studies in engineering. Became a secondary school teacher like his father, a historian with a doctoral degree who died in the war in 1945. His mother was a secondary school teacher until her marriage.

  Mother: born in 1939. University degree. Secondary school teacher.

  Both parents practicing Catholics, attend church every Sunday (mother slightly less frequently).

- Klara Rohrsteg, 20 October 2003 and 15 January 2004 (3 hours).

  Politics and German literature teacher.

  Born in 1956. *Abitur,* 1976. Obtained a Master's degree in modern languages at the University of Hamburg, 1982. A sister, born in 1952, who has no formal qualifications or profession. One half-brother, the son of her father, much older (over sixty years old), who is an engineer. Married, two sons, aged twenty-seven and twenty, and one daughter, aged ten.

  Father: (1914 at Stettin–1995) arrived in Hamburg in 1939. High school certificate, apprenticeship in marketing/publicity. Self-employed at the end of his life. Was a soldier.

Mother: born in 1926 in Hamburg. *Realschulabschlus*, apprenticeship. Employed in a hotel (*Hotelkauffrau*). Very involved in the BDM as a teenager, would have been a member of the NSDAP if she had been older, in spite of her father's opposition.

- Mr Stein, 26 September 2003 (2 hours).

Politics and German literature teacher.

Born in 1954. *Abitur*, 1973. Master's degree in modern languages and political science at the University of Hamburg, mid-1980s. Unemployed, apprenticeship in IT. IT worker in the private sector until 1992, professional experience that allowed him be employed at Wiesi. Was apparently involved in extreme left activities. Two brothers, one a senior high school teacher, the other a farmer (after having studied agriculture at university). Single.

Father: (1912 in Magdebourg–1987) *Abitur*, apprenticeship. Employed in sales. Joined the army in 1931–1932. Became a captain of the Wehrmacht. Was on the Eastern Front, and then in Africa. Prisoner of war held by the Americans. After the war, a member of the CDU and town council in an average size town in northern Germany.

Mother: (1921 in Austria–1989) involved in the Nazi movement before 1938, became a leader of the BDM. Prisoner in Germany 1946. Master's degree. Primary school teacher.

- Ms Stern, 24 April 2003 (2 hours).

Politics and ethics teacher.

Born in 1949. *Abitur*, 1969. Master's degree in sociology, history, political science, and economics at the University of Hamburg, 1976. Member of the GEW (Gewerkschaft Erziehung und Wissenschaft, Education and Science Workers' Union). One sister seven years older, librarian. Married without children.

Father: (1914 at Paderborn–1991): engineer. Left for Western Prussia in the mid-1930s. Soldier in Greece, taken prisoner.

Mother: born in 1917 in Western Prussia. *Volksschule*, with an apprenticeship in "domestic economy" (*Hauswirtschaft*). Nazi sympathizer during the war and active in the BDM. After the war, housewife.

- Thomas (family name unknown), 22 April 2003 (45 minutes).

Politics, ethics and German literature teacher.

Born in 1949. *Abitur*, 1968. Master's degree in psychology, sociology and pedagogy at the University of Hamburg, 1976. In the 1970s, he was a member of *Spartakusbund* and then a member of the DKP until 1989. Member of the GEW. One brother, born in 1944, an architect, also a member of the DKP until 1989. Married, two daughters.

Father: born in 1911 in Silesia. High school certificate. Professional soldier, became a captain, member of the Waffen-SS and member of the *Leibstandarte Adolf Hitler*. Fought on the Eastern and Western fronts, prisoner of war in 1945 held by the Americans, escaped shortly afterwards. Later worked in the municipal administration in Hanover.

Mother: born in 1918 in Berlin. Telephone worker, and then private secretary to Heydrich until 1945. Mother at home after the war.

• Herbert Wiese, 22 April 2003 (4 hours).

Politics and English teacher.

Born in 1950. *Abitur*, 1969. Master's degree in history and English at the University of Hamburg, 1976. Vice principal at Wiesi. Was a member of the Socialist youth (*Jusos*) for a short time, member of the *Spartakists* in the 1970s, but also a member of the SPD. After "radicals" (especially Communists) were prohibited from working for the state by the SPD government in the 1970s (*Radikalengesetz*), he left the party and joined the DKP until 1989. After reunification, he considered joining the PDS. An active member of the GEW since 1973. One sister, a pharmacy assistant and single mother, today seriously ill. Married to a high school teacher who has become a housewife, two children.

Father: born in 1928. *Volksschule*. Member of the HJ, soldier at age sixteen (in 1944), and prisoner of war, held by the English. After the war, incomplete apprenticeship in the railways, and then builders apprentice. Toward 1948–1949, public servant in the administration of the Fire Department. Unionist.

Mother: (1926 in Western Prussia–1999) *Volksschule*, apprenticeship in a school. Active member of the BDM. Refugee in 1945 with her parents. Secretary until 1956, then housewife.

• Karen Werthe, 7 November 2003 and 24 January 2004 (5 hours).

Politics and German literature teacher.

Born in 1968. *Abitur*, 1988. Apprenticeship in sales, 1991. Master's degree in political science and modern languages at the University of Hamburg, mid-1990s. Worked in advertising and freelance journalism before finding a position at Wiesi at the end of the 1990s. Two older brothers (one a lawyer). Married to a public servant in administration, no children yet.

Father: born toward the end of the 1930s. *Realschule*, sales apprenticeship, self-employed.

Mother: born toward the early 1940s. *Realschule.* Works in her husband's business.

- Mr Winter, 7 April 2003 (3 hours).

  Politics and English teacher.

  Born in 1949. *Abitur*, 1969. Master's degree in English (to teach at the *Volks-* and *Realschule*) at the University of Hamburg, 1975. Return to studies in history in 1985 while teaching; Master's in history (to teach in *Gymnasium*), 1990–1991. One sister, born in 1943, died aged thirteen in an accident. Single, one adopted daughter, who is a very devout Muslim and a doctor. Member of the Greens, then the SPD until the early 1980s.

  Father: (1915–1998) working-class industrial family, left school at the beginning of the economic crisis and found himself unemployed. Apprenticeship as a welder. Joined the army in 1937. After the war, a member of the KPD, until it was banned in 1956.

  Mother: born in 1915. *Hauptschulabschluss*, saleswoman.

Leipzig, *Gymnasium Monnet*

- Ms Gerste, 12 and 26 January 2004 (2 hours).

  History and German literature teacher.

  Born in 1965 in Leipzig. *Abitur*, 1983. Master's in history and modern languages at the University of Leipzig, 1988. Member of the DFD (women's union) in the GDR and a unionist. Married, three children.

  Father: born in the 1930s. Engineer, and leader at the SED (ruling party of the GDR). Left his family in 1968.

  Mother: born in 1935 near Breslau. Fled in 1945 with her parents. Apprenticeship, social work.

- Ms Neumeier, 3 November, 1, 4, and 18 December 2003 (12 hours).

  History and fine arts teacher.

  Born in 1953 in Leipzig. Student at the *Klingerschule* (elite school in Leipzig). *Abitur*, 1970. Master's degree in history and fine arts from the University of Leipzig, 1976. Worked in a metalwork factory during and after her studies. One younger sister, librarian. One half-brother, born in 1945, electrician, left in 1961 for the FRG. One half-sister, twenty years older, doctor.

Father: (1903–1980) *Realschule,* employed in commerce. Member of the NSDAP. Manager of an insurance company.

Mother: born in 1924. *Volksschule.* Works in the town administration. Orphan. After the death of her husband, left for the FRG to join her son.

- Ms Mertens, 3 November 2003 (1 hour).

  Russian and history teacher.

  Born in 1951, in high school and senior school she specialized in Russian, apprenticeship in shipbuilding, a profession she maintained during her holidays when she was at university. Master's in Russian in history at the University of Leipzig. She has two brothers and one sister. Two are electricians, one was a soldier in the Volksarmee. One half-sister, housewife, left for the FRG in 1957 at age sixteen.

  Father: born at the end of the 1920s. Railway worker.

  Mother: born in the early 1930s. Railway worker.

- Ms Norte, 15 October and 2 December 2003 (4 hours).

  History and German literature teacher.

  Born in 1960 in GDR. *Abitur,* 1978. Master's in modern languages and history at the University of Leipzig, 1982. Today she is the history coordinator (*Geschichtspädagogische Leiterin*). Married, three children.

  Father: born in 1933 in Brandenburg. Apprenticeship. First as a miner, then as a skilled worker in mechanics (*Facharbeiter*). Member of the SED and Deputy Mayor in his small town until 1989.

  Mother: born in 1932 in Western Prussia, fled in 1944 to Berlin with her parents. *Volksschule.* Skilled worker in a factory, then dressmaker. After 1989, sales worker.

- Ms Meerstein, 2 December 2003 (2 hours).

  History and fine arts teacher.

  Born in 1963 in a village in the GDR. *Abitur,* 1982. Master's in history and fine arts at the University of Leipzig, 1986. After reunification, returned to study painting between 1990 and 1993. Two brothers in commerce, one of whom is a member of the SPD. Married, two children.

  Father: born in 1933. Surgeon.

  Mother: born in 1941. Primary school teacher.

- Ms Meisenau, 18 December 2003 and 8 January 2004 (4 hours).

  History and German literature teacher.

Born in 1953, was not able to pursue to studies of her choice (German as a foreign language). Master's in modern languages in history at the University of Leipzig, 1976. Refuses to teach contemporary history. Has tried unsuccessfully to leave teaching. Married to a writer, one son.

Father: born in 1921. Locksmith, then studied technology. Prisoner of war in Italy.

Mother: born in 1921, *Realschule*. Employee. One sister in the FRG.

- Ms Weineck 15 and 16 October 2003 (4 hours).

History and English teacher.

Born in 1955 in Leipzig. *Thomasschule. Abitur*, 1973. Involved in Christian movements, refused to be a member of the SED, which prevented her from studying psychology. Master's degree in Russian and history at the University of Leipzig, 1977. Junior high school teacher until 1985. Forbidden from teaching contemporary history. Left teaching after the birth of her second child to work in a museum as an assistant pedagogue. She was then an assistant professor at the University of Leipzig, as part of a contract to do a PhD in pedagogy of foreign languages, prevented by reunification. Return to study, Master's degree in English (to replace Russian) in 1992, return to high school. One sister, involved in the artistic sphere in Berlin. Married to a writer who had an important position in the GDR and traveled a lot, two children. Father-in-law is a Protestant pastor, used his position to critique the regime, which led to a threat of expatriation.

Father: (1913–1961) blacksmith, worked in commerce. Member of the SPD before 1933. Soldier in France and prisoner of war.

Mother: (1916–1997) saleswoman in a butcher shop owned by her first husband, who died at Stalingrad. Raised two children alone. One maternal uncle by marriage was a Communist resister under Nazism, and a prison warden in the GDR.

- Mr Wolff, 13 and 17 October 2003 (5 hours).

History and German literature teacher.

Born in 1958 in Thuringe. *Abitur*, 1976. Master's degree in modern languages and history at the University of Leipzig, 1982. In 1985, he returned to university to begin a PhD. He wrote for two years, and then stopped because of reunification. Married to a high school teacher, who is today a mother at home, two adolescent daughters.

Father: born in 1936. *Volksschule*, locksmith.

Mother: born in 1938. No formal qualifications. Worked in a grocery shop.

Leipzig, *100th Mittelschule*

- Ms Härtig, 12 January and 3 February 2004 (3 hours).

  History and German literature teacher.

  Born in 1961 near Magdeburg. *Abitur*, 1979. Master's degree in history and modern languages at the University of Leipzig, 1983. Refused to join the SED several times, despite pressure from her father. Divorced, one son.

  Father: born in 1936 in Berlin. Engineer and secondary school teacher in technical schools. Member of the SED, after 1989 the PDS, which he only recently left.

  Mother: born in 1938. *Polytechnische Oberschule.* Building worker. Joined the SED after her marriage.

- Ms Naute, 17 December 2003 and 7 January 2004 (4 hours).

  History and English teacher.

  Born in 1982 in Saxony. *Abitur*, 1980. Master's degree in Russian and history at the University of Leipzig, 1984. Return to study after 1989 to complete a Master's degree in English (to replace the Russian). Member of the GEW. Has two sisters, a baker and a saleswoman, and one brother, a manual worker. Married, two children.

  Father: born around 1943. Officer in the *Volkssarmee* (army of the GDR), member of the SED (ruling party of the GDR). After 1989, became a real estate agent.

  Mother: born in 1938. *Polytechnische Oberschule.* Apprenticeship as a turner, and then librarian. Member of the SED.

- Ms Mett, 12 January 2004 (1 hour).

  History, ethics, and English teacher.

  Born in 1951 in northeast Germany (in the "valley of the ignorant"). *Abitur*, 1970. Master's degree in history and Russian at the University of Leipzig, 1974. After reunification, returned to studies in English (to replace Russian) and ethics. Member of the GEW.

  Father: (1913–1991) sailor, apprenticeship as head cook. Worked in a bakery. Soldier in Norway. One sister and one brother in the FRG.

  Mother: born in 1926 in Western Prussia. Fled in 1945 with her family. No formal qualifications. Unskilled worker.

348 • Appendix 4: List of Teachers Interviewed

- Ms Seidel, 14 January 2004 (3 hours).

  History and fine arts teacher.

  Born in 1963 in Saxony. *Abitur*, 1981. Master's degree in Russian history at the University of Leipzig, 1985. Considered to be the next principal of her school, joined the SED in 1987–1988. Today she is the history coordinator (*Fachleiterin Geschichte*). One brother, engineer, also a member of the SED. Married, one son.

  Father: born in 1936. *Volksschule*, then night school. Farmer. Head of production in a farming collective (*Landwirtschaftliche Producktionsgenossenschaft, LFP*) member of the SED. Self-employed after reunification. Joined the PDS initially, then left in the mid-1990s for the CDU.

  Mother: born in 1938 in Poland. No formal qualifications, farmworker.

- Ms Seidengleich, 17 December 2003 (2 hours).

  History and geography teacher.

  Born in 1962, in Saxony. *Abitur*, 1980. Master's degree in geography and history at the University of Leipzig, 1984. Member of the SED until 1989. One younger brother, unemployed gardener. One older sister, formally an IT worker, has worked in a bank since the 1990s. Married, one son.

  Father: born in 1939. Engineer and manager at the SED. After 1989, opened a tourism agency.

  Mother: born in 1939 in Saxony. No formal qualifications, sales person. After 1989, had several casual jobs.

Appendix 5

LIST OF STUDENTS INTERVIEWED

Organized by school and alphabetized by first name. This appendix only contains students that are mentioned in the text, in order for the reader to be able to refer to their trajectories. This is the reason why there are more students appearing in the tables of the introduction than listed in detail here.

Hamburg, *Gymnasium Weinberg*

- Alexander, 21 October 2003 (2 hours and 30 minutes), twelfth grade, student of Mr Winter.[1]

  Born in 1986 in Hamburg, he wants to sit the *Abitur* at Wiesi. He has one sister aged twenty-one who is beginning studies in psychology, one half-sister aged thirty, his mother's daughter, who is a German and Spanish teacher, and one half-brother on his father's side, aged thirty-six, a gardener.

  Father: born in 1941 in Hamburg, secondary school teacher.

  Mother: born in 1952 in Hamburg, secondary school teacher.

- Annelore, 3 April 2002 (two hours), thirteenth grade, student of Mr Schulze.

  Born in 1984 in Hamburg, only child.

  Father: born in 1945, was commercial director for Esso. He died in 2000.

  Mother: born in 1950, was previously an educator, but now works in sales.

350 • Appendix 5: List of Students Interviewed

- Benjamin, 18 April 2003 (4 hours), thirteenth grade, student of Ms Heide.

  Born in 1984 in Saarbrücken came to Hamburg in 1991. He has one brother, born in 1987, and one sister born in 1990.

  Father: born in 1961 in Prague, manager in a regional radio station.

  Mother: born in 1963 in Saarbrücken, sat the *Abitur* and completed an apprenticeship in commerce before working in a bookshop. She has returned to studies to become a kindergarten teacher.

- Caroline, 23 September 2003 (30 minutes), ninth grade, student of Mr Schulze.

  Born in 1988 in Hamburg, has a brother aged sixteen, enrolled at the nearby *Gesamtschule*. He left for the United States at the time of interviewing.

  Father: born in 1955 in Hamburg, doctor in a hospital.

  Mother: born in 1960 in Hamburg, a history, French, and politics teacher.

- Daniel, 14 March 2002 (1 hour 30 minutes), tenth grade, student of Mr Herzog.

  Born in 1984 in Hamburg, he left the *Gymnasium* after struggling academically, and moved to *Gesamtschule* Wiesi. He repeated two separate year levels.

  Father: born in 1950 in Hamburg, doctor.

  Mother: born in 1955 in Hamburg, secondary school teacher.

- Elizabeth, 27 September 2003 (45 minutes), ninth grade, student of Mr Schulze.

  Born in 1990 in Hamburg, she has one brother, born in 1986, who also studies at Weinberg and who sat his *Abitur* in 2005. He is also doing an apprenticeship as a chemist in preparation for studying chemistry.

  Father: born in 1942 in Hamburg, English and French teacher in a *Gymnasium*.

  Mother: born in 1952 in Hamburg, chemistry teacher and biology teacher in the same school as her husband.

- Heidi, 27 December 2002 (2 hours 30 minutes), thirteenth grade, former student of Mr Schulze.

  Born in 1984, in Hamburg, has two younger sisters.

Father: born in 1950, business auditor.

Mother: born in 1949, nurse, now works as a kindergarten teacher part-time.

- Heiner, 30 September 2003 (1 hour), ninth grade, student of Mr Schulze.

  Born 1989 in Hamburg, he is a member of a sports club where he plays football and tennis. His older sister, aged eighteen, wants to sit the *Abitur* at Weinberg. His younger sister, aged ten, began her schooling at Weinberg in 2004.

  Father: born in 1956 in Hamburg, has a Master's degree in sports and management, was a secondary school teacher and today works in the administration of the education department (*Oberstudienrat*).

  Mother: born in 1959 near Hamburg, has a Master's degree in German, is a teacher in the secondary school system (*Haupt-* and *Realschule*), now teaches economics and cooking.

- Johannes, 22 February 2003 (2 hours), thirteenth grade, student of Ms Heide.

  Born in 1984 in Hamburg, two sisters, one born in 1980, studies theology and literature to become a teacher at high school, the other, born in 1978, studies medicine. Both are in Hamburg.

  Father: born in 1952, doctor.

  Mother: born in 1952, literature and political science teacher in a high school.

- Judith, 29 September 2003 (1 hour 30 minutes), ninth grade, student of Mr Schulze.

  Born in 1989 in Hamburg, two younger sisters, one born in 1992, who began school at Weinberg in 2003, and the other born in 1996.

  Father: born in 1960 in Lübeck, medical studies, private practitioner.

  Mother: born in 1965 in Hamburg, began architectures studies but stopped them to become a physiotherapist, profession she continues to this day.

- Kai, 22 September 2003 (2 hours), ninth grade, student of Mr Schulze.

  Born in 1987 in Hamburg, Kai is two years older than his classmates because he repeated eighth grade. He has a younger sister, born in 1989, who is also studying at Weinberg, in a lower grade.

  Father: born in 1945 in Lübeck, he sat his *Abitur* by attending night school while working during the day. He studied economics, works as a consultant and is today a senior manager in the Axel Springer media group. Separated from Kai's mother, he does not live with Kai.

Mother: born in 1958 in a village near Hamburg, she came to Hamburg as a child. She studied music and worked as an opera singer.

- Karen, 12 April 2003 (2 hours), eighth grade, student of Mr Schulze.

  Born in 1989, in Hamburg. Her older sister (born in 1981) did a sales apprenticeship and now works as a secretary. Her older brother (born in 1984) sat the *Abitur* at Weinberg and wants to study law.

  Father: born in 1950 in Austria, studied chemistry to become a teacher, but did not finish his studies and became a salesman insurance company. He is also a volunteer firefighter (*Freiwillige Feuerwehr*).

  Mother: born in 1953 in Hamburg, she sat the *Abitur* and did an apprenticeship in sales. She worked in finance administration and was then self-employed. Since her children were born, she has worked part-time in a toy shop.

- Birgit, 26 December 2001, (2 hours), thirteenth grade, a student of Mr Schulze.

  Born in 1984, no brothers and sisters.

  Father: social worker, managers a home for young offenders.

  Mother: works for the Minister of Health, Employment and Social Affairs.

- Karsten, 16 April 2003 (2 hours), eighth grade, student of Mr Schulze.

  Born in 1989 in Hamburg, one older sister, born in 1985, who attends a different school, and one brother, born in 1983, who changed school after repeating a year and is now studying at Weinberg as well.

  Father: born in 1950 in Hamburg, *Hauptschule* degree and apprenticeship as an electrician. Self-employed, he took over his father's electrician business.

  Mother: born in 1959, in Hamburg, sat the *Abitur* and studied commerce. First a secretary, she now works in her husband's shop.

- Kerstin, 13 April 3 (1 hour 30 minutes), eighth grade, student of Mr Schulze.

  Born in 1989 in Hamburg, she has one older brother, born in 1994, who is in the *Gesamtschule* next to Weinberg.

  Father: born in 1960, studied engineering. He worked in mechanical construction. No information about the father's parents.

Mother: born in 1962 in Hamburg, she sat the *Abitur* and began studying law. She stopped her studies to become a salesperson in insurance company.

- Leoni, 14 April 2003 and 18 February 2004 (4 hours), eighth grade, student of Mr Schulze.

  Born in 1989 in Hamburg, she has a twin sister and one older brother, born in 1986, who left for the United States around the time of the first interview and who is a member of the youth parliament.

  Father: born in 1954 in Hamburg, has a Master's in information technology and now works as an IT consultant.

  Mother: born in 1958 in Bremen, studied mathematics and sport in Hamburg, now works as a primary school teacher.

- Leif, 22 February 2003 (1 hour 30 minutes), thirteenth grade, student of Ms Heide.

  Born in 1984. One sister, born in 1981.

  Father: born in 1955, policeman.

  Mother: born in 1962, employee.

- Lisa, 29 September 2003, (1 hour), ninth grade, student of Mr Schulze.

  Born in 1988 in Hamburg, she has a thirty-year-old brother, who obtained his *Abitur* and is now a video producer, a sister who is twenty-seven years old, who worked for their father before becoming a mother at home, and twenty-one-year-old sister who studied German at Hamburg University to become a primary school teacher. She also has a younger sister, aged twelve, who is also studying at Weinberg.

  Father: born in 1945, self-employed (he has a shop that sells large appliances).

  Mother: born in 1949, was a nurse before becoming a childcare worker.

- Magdalena, 13 April 2003 (1 hour), thirteenth grade, student of Ms Simone.

  Born in 1985 in the south of Germany, came to Hamburg in 1987. She has one brother, born in 1982, who sat the *Abitur* in 2002 and joined the Navy to study economics.

  Father: born in 1952 in northern Germany, has been an engineer and businessman in the United States since 1992, when he divorced his wife.

Mother: born in 1954 in a small town in northern Germany, chemical engineer, now works in the administration of the Ministry for the Environment.

- Maren, 13 April 2003 (1 hour 30 minutes), eighth grade, student of Mr Schulze.

  Born in 1989 in Hamburg, one older brother aged sixteen, also a student at Weinberg.

  Father: born in 1956 in Hamburg, studied law, now works as a lawyer but also has a real estate business.

  Mother: born in 1956 in Hamburg, *Realschule* and then apprenticeship. Physiotherapist, but since Maren's birth she has been a mother at home.

- Martha, 24 September 2003 (2 hours), ninth grade, student of Mr Schulze.

  Born in 1988 in Hamburg, only child.

  Father: born in 1948 near Dortmund. Lived in Berlin before coming to Hamburg. He studied literature to become a teacher but became a librarian.

  Mother: born in 1946 in the Ruhr region. Studied psychology in Berlin. She is now a public servant (psychologist) at the employment office (*Arbeitsamt*) in Hamburg.

- Markus, 26 February 2004 (30 minutes), ninth grade, student of Mr Schulze.

  Born in 1988 in Hamburg, he has an older sister, aged eighteen, who was sitting the *Abitur* in Weinberg at the time of the interview.

  Father: born in 1952 in Hamburg, *Abitur*, took over his father's real estate business.

  Mother: born in 1956, *Realschule*, works in her husband's business sporadically.

- Max, 13 April 2003 (2 hours), eighth grade, student of Mr Schulze.

  Born in 1988, in Hamburg, has one brother born in 1992.

  Father: born in 1944 in Berlin, studied history and politics in Hamburg, worked in a bookshop before becoming a professional politician, party staffer at the SPD in Hamburg.

  Mother: born in 1958 in a town the Ruhr district. Studied pedagogy, now a secondary school teacher in a school for disabled children.

Appendix 5: List of Students Interviewed • 355

- Peter, 21 April 2003 (2 hours), thirteenth grade, student of Ms Heide.

  Born in 1984 in Hamburg. One brother, born in 1979, who studies medicine at the University of Hamburg.

  Father: born in 1945 in Hamburg, obtained the Abitur and did a commercial apprenticeship. Now works in a bank.

  Mother: born in 1950 in Hamburg, *Realschule*, did an apprenticeship in a bank. Since the birth of her children, she has been a mother at home.

- René, 17 January 2003 (2 hours 30 minutes), thirteenth grade, student of Ms Heide.

  Born in 1984 in Hamburg, one sister born in 1988.

  Father: born in 1952 in Hamburg. Teachers sports, biology, and IT at Weinberg.

  Mother: born in 1954 in Hamburg. Teaches literature and mathematics in a vocational high school.

- Richard, 11 April 2003 (3 hours), thirteenth grade, student of Ms Simone.

  Born in 1984 in Hamburg, two brothers. The elder, born in 1978, was also a student at Weinberg. He began studying law but then changed to study medicine. The youngest brother, born in 1982, is disabled.

  Father: born in 1949 in Hamburg, lived in the United States and in France. He teaches law and works at the Max Planck Institute (research institute).

  Mother: born in 1950, managing director of a real estate company.

- Tilman and Tim, twin brothers, 19 and 22 September 2003, (1 hour each), ninth grade, students of Mr Schulze.

  Born in 1989 in Hamburg, they have one older sister, also a student at Weinberg, who was born in 1986.

  Father: born in 1953 in Hamburg, obtained his *Abitur* and studied engineering. He took over his father's IT business.

  Mother: born in 1954 in Hamburg, multilingual secretary. After a period where she stopped working to take care of her children, she returned to work as a secretary in her husband's business.

- Thomas, 16 April 2003 (1 hour), eighth grade, student of Mr Schulze.

  Born in 1988 in Hamburg. Has one sister aged seventeen, who left for the United States when interviewing started, one brother aged six and another brother aged three.

Father: born in 1960, has a PhD in chemistry, and is a professor at the University of Hamburg.

Mother: born in 1960 in Bremen, obtained the *Abitur,* and is a midwife and nurse.

- Victor, 18 February 2004 (1 hour 30 minutes), ninth grade, student of Mr Schulze.

  Born in 1988 near Hamburg, he has a brother, two years older than him, who is in a private school and who would like to attend a technical *Gymnasium.*

  Father: born in 1950 in the Ruhr, who came to Hamburg as an adolescent. He studied medicine and is now a surgeon. His parents are separated. Victor does not see his father very often.

  Mother: born in 1952 near Hamburg, she obtained her *Abitur* and is now a secretary in hospital.

- Vincent, 13 April 2003 (1 hour), eighth grade, student of Mr Schulze.

  Born in 1988 in Hamburg. He has one older brother, aged nineteen, who sat the *Abitur* in Weinberg and would like to study medicine.

  Father: born in 1946, studied social pedagogy and is now professor at a technical university in Hamburg (*FH-Fachhochschule*).

  Mother: born in 1946 in Hamburg, social pedagogue, works in a drug dependency clinic.

Hamburg, *Gesamtschule Wiesi*

- Domenico, 17 February 2002 (1 hour 30 minutes). Former student of Wiesi, works in a construction company.

  Born in 1984 in Hamburg. Domenico has Greek nationality. He attended Greek primary school until fourth grade (the end of primary school) at the same time as he attended German primary school. At Wiesi, he completed the *Hauptschulabschluss* (after ninth grade) and attempted at the *Realschulabschluss* (after tenth grade) but was not successful. He is doing an apprenticeship in mechanical processes in a construction company.

  Father: Greek immigrant, unskilled worker in a factory near Hamburg.

  Mother: Greek immigrant, unskilled worker in a factory near Hamburg.

- Ivan, 22 February 2004 (1 hour 30 minutes), tenth grade, student of Annika Klein and Karen Werthe.

Born in 1986 in Russia. Came to Berlin at age nine, then moved to Hamburg. He wants to sit the *Abitur* and work in information technology. He has one sister, aged fourteen, who is also a student at Wiesi.

Father: born in 1940 in Russia, but is of German origin. He was a railway worker in Russia. Today he works as a forklift operator.

Mother: born in 1941 in Russia, has a degree in engineering. When she arrived in Germany, she retrained to be a care-giver in a retirement home.

- Joey, 29 September 2003 (1 hour), tenth grade, student of Mr Stein.

  Born in 1987 in Kabul (Afghanistan). He arrived in Hamburg aged seven. He would like to become a mechanic. Joey is the youngest of eight children. The eldest brother is a dentist in London, the second a taxi driver in Hamburg, the third is unemployed, also in Hamburg. His elder sister studies in Hamburg, the second was a secondary teacher in Pakistan, the third sat the *Realschule* in Hamburg and the youngest is in San Francisco. All four sisters are married and now housewives.

  Father: born in 1938 in Kabul. He was a commander in the army. He immigrated to Germany in the 1990s with his family for political reasons. He no longer works.

  Mother: born in 1947 in Kabul. She never went to school. She is now a housewife.

- Johnny, 25 April 2003 (3 hours), ninth grade, student of Ms Inge.

  Born in 1988 in Hamburg, he has one sister, born in 1991, and a brother, born in 1994, both students in Wiesi.

  Father: born in 1960 in Hamburg, tradesman (painter).

  Mother: born in 1960 in Hamburg works as a cleaning lady in the court buildings.

- Marji, 22 April 2003 (3 hours), twelfth grade, student of Mr Winter.

  Born in 1985 in Teheran. She was five years old when she fled Iran with her mother and her brother, going through Turkey where she stayed for a year and learned Turkish before arriving in Germany. She is a member of the far-left political organization *Linksruck*. She has a half-sister aged thirty-one, who finished her high school certificate in Iran and now works as a hairdresser in Hamburg. She has a half-brother, aged twenty-seven, who is a machine operator, and another half-brother, aged twenty-five who is doing an apprenticeship to become a police officer, both of whom are in Hamburg.

Father: studied medicine in England, where he works as a doctor. She does not know him.

Mother: born in 1951 in Teheran, she sat the equivalent of the *Abitur* and began studying literature, but she did not finish. She was married to a man close to the Shah who died in prison, the father of her three older children. She remarried Marji's father.

- Moher, 29 September 2003 (45 minutes), tenth grade, student of Mr Stein.

  Born in 1988 in Hamburg, he has two sisters, one aged seventeen, the other aged eleven, both are students at Wiesi.

  Father: born in 1956 in Afghanistan, where he began his studies, before immigrating to Germany in the early 1980s. He works as a taxi driver in Hamburg, but would like to open a shop to become independent. After his separation from Moher's mother, he remarried in 2003.

  Mother: born in 1967 in Afghanistan, she never went to school. She came to Hamburg with her parents, where she met her husband. Separated since 1999, she worked as a salesperson at the time of the interview.

- Omeira, 23 October 2003 (40 minutes), tenth grade, student of Mr Stein.

  Born in 1986 in Serbia, she came to Hamburg with her parents aged three. She has two brothers, one born in 1987, the other born in 1982, both of whom are also students at Wiesi.

  Father: born in 1967 in Macedonia, he was a builder, but now works as a cleaner in a cleaning company.

  Mother: born in 1970 in Serbia, she works in the same company as her husband.

- Omer, 29 September 2003 (1 hour), tenth grade, student of Mr Stein.

  Born in 1987 in Hamburg, he has one sister aged twenty-three, who is a housewife (she obtained the *Realschuleabschluss*) and one brother, at age nineteen, who sat the Abitur and did his civil service with disabled people.

  Father: born in 1958 in Kabul (Afghanistan), he immigrated to Germany in the 1980s, after the arrival of the Soviet army in his country. He owns an automobile business.

  Mother: born in 1961 in Afghanistan, she arrived in Hamburg with her husband and their eldest daughter. She is now a mother at home.

Appendix 5: List of Students Interviewed • 359

- Osman, 21 October 2003 (45 minutes), tenth grade, student of Mr Gerste.

  Born in 1987 in Hamburg. He would like to repeat his tenth grade to try and sit the *Fachabitur* (professional certificate) and become a police officer. He has one sister, who will sit the *Abitur* and wants to study psychology.

  Father: born in 1951 in Afghanistan. At age eighteen, he immigrated to Germany via Iran, Turkey, and Poland. He sells oriental carpets, and has also opened a museum about Afghanistan in Hamburg with his two brothers.

  Mother: born in 1955 in Afghanistan, she was a teacher. Since the 1980s she has lived in Hamburg where she met her husband. She no longer works.

- Samira, 8 April 2003 (2 hours), eleventh grade, student of Ms Inge.

  Born in 1986 in Hamburg, she is an only child. She has both German and Nigerian nationality.

  Father: born in 1948 in the village not far from Lagos in Nigeria. He immigrated in the 1960s to study medicine in England, but he did not finish. He works as a nurse in an institution for disabled people. Samira has not seen her father since her parents' divorce in 1990.

  Mother: born in 1949 Hamburg. Social pedagogue. She works in the same institution for disabled people as her ex-husband.

- Sandy, 23 December 2003 (1 hour 30 minutes), tenth grade, student of Annika Klein and Karen Werthe.

  Born in 1988 in Hamburg, she has one twelve-year-old brother, also at Wiesi.

  Father: born in 1961. He completed *Realschule* and an apprenticeship. He is a technician.

  Mother: born in 1962 in Hamburg, she is a pharmacist's assistant.

- Steffen, 12 March 2002 (1 hour 30 minutes), tenth grade, student of Annika Klein and Karen Werthe.

  Born in 1985, Steffen was initially a student in Weinberg. He repeated eighth grade and had to change schools in ninth grade for a *Haupt-* and *Realschule*. He changed schools again at the end of ninth grade to come to Wiesi, where he wants to sit the *Abitur*. His four brothers and sisters are all at the *Gymnasium*.

Father: born in 1949, doctor, appointed to a ministry (*Ministerialrat*).
Mother: born in 1950, housewife.

- Volker, 23 October 2003 (45 minutes), ninth grade, student of Mr Gerste.

  Born in 1987 in Hamburg, he has one older sister, aged seventeen, also at Wiesi.

  Father: born in 1955 in Hungary, he is head chef. Separated from his wife in 1998.

  Mother: born in 1960 in Hamburg, she is an interior designer, but does not work.

Leipzig, *Gymnasium Monnet*

- Alice, 26 January 2004 (1 hour), ninth grade, student of Ms Meerstein.

  Born in 1988 in Leipzig, she has a twenty-three-year-old brother.

  Father: born in 1960 in Leipzig. He initially worked in real estate, and then for the police force.

  Mother: born in 1959 in Leipzig, she is a member of the police force.

- Christiane, 2 February 2003 (2 hours), ninth grade, student of Ms Gerte.

  Born in 1988 in Leipzig, she has one sixteen-year-old brother who attends a *Mittelschule.*

  Father: born in 1954 in Brandenburg, studied German literature. He is now an actor in the theater and a director in the theater company.

  Mother: born in 1956. Studied history and works as an archivist.

- Daniel, 2 February 2004 (1 hour 30 minutes), ninth grade, student of Ms Gerte.

  Born in 1988 in Brandenburg, he is an only child.

  Father: born in 1956 in Saxony. He is a teacher at the *Gymnasium,* and also teaches at the university.

  Mother: born in 1960 in Saxony. She is a geography teacher at *Gymnasium* Monnet.

- Else, 3 November 2003 (2 hours), twelfth grade, student of Ms Norte.

  Born in 1987 in Leipzig, she is an only child.

Father: born in 1958 in Leipzig. He was an engineer but returned to study after the reunification of Germany and is now a secondary school teacher.

Mother: born in 1960 in Leipzig, secondary school teacher.

- Elizabeth, 4 November 2003 (2 hours), twelfth grade, student of Mr Weinecke.

  Born in 1985 in Leipzig, she has a sixteen-year-old brother who is also a student at *Gymnasium* Monnet.

  Father: born in 1958 in a town close to Dresden. He completed a PhD in economics and now runs a real estate business, while lecturing at the university (*Dozent*).

  Mother: born in 1954 in Saxony, she was a sales assistant. After the reunification of Germany, she returned to study economics and then social pedagogy. She is now the manager of a counseling center for children and families (*Kinder- und Familienberatungsstelle*).

- Franziska, 3 February 2004, (2 hours), ninth grade, student of Ms Gerste.

  Born in 1988 in Leipzig, she has an eleven-year-old brother.

  Father: born in 1954 in Berlin. He was a salesperson in a shoe shop. He returned to university to study theology. He opened a wine shop. Since 2003, he has been a company manager.

  Mother: born in 1966 in Saxony, POS, was not allowed to sit the *Abitur* because her father was a pastor. She is a nurse.

- Hauke, 3 November 2003 (1 hour), twelfth grade, student of Ms Weinecke.

  Born in 1984 in a town in Saxony, he has only lived in Leipzig for two years.

  Father: born in 1962, he is a shopkeeper.

  Mother born in 1963, she is a bank manager.

- Heike, 17 October 2003 (2 hours), tenth grade, student of Ms Norte.

  Born in 1986 in Leipzig. One sister, who is "in her late 20s" and studies history and journalism in Leipzig.

  Father: born in 1958 in Leipzig. He has done many different jobs: taxi driver, sales, and now has a tobacconist shop.

  Mother: born in 1958 in Leipzig, she is a pedagogue.

362 • Appendix 5: List of Students Interviewed

- Jessy, 4 November 2003 (2 hours), twelfth grade, student of Ms Weinecke. Born in 1986 in Leipzig, has one sister, born in 1992.

  Father: born in 1961 in Saxony. Came to Leipzig in the 1980s. He obtained his *Abitur*. A career army officer, he became an engineer after completing his studies with the army. He is now a businessman.

  Mother: born in 1964 in Leipzig, she is an opera singer.

- Mark, 17 October 2003 (3 hours), twelfth grade, student of Ms Norte. Born in 1987 in Berlin, he came to Leipzig in 1998. For a time, he was a member of *Antifa*, an antifascist group. He has a nineteen-year-old brother who is doing an apprenticeship after the *Mittelschule* to become a mechanic.

  Father: born in 1960 in Berlin, he is a journalist and works for a radio station.

  Mother: born in 1963 in Berlin, she is also a journalist and works in a communication agency.

- Marianne, 26 January 2004 (1 hour 30 minutes), ninth grade, student of Ms Meerstein.

  Born in 1988 in Leipzig.

  Father: born in 1960 in Leipzig, he is an engineer.

  Mother: born in 1963 in Leipzig, she studied economics and is a company manager.

- Melanie, 2 February 2004 (2 hours), ninth grade, student of Ms Gerste. Born in 1988 in Halle. She has one sister aged thirteen, and a baby half-sister aged five months, who is the daughter of her mother and her mother's new partner.

  Father: born in 1966 in Leipzig, an actor in the theater. Returned to study after reunification, to study social pedagogy. Her parents divorced in 1994, shared custody.

  Mother: born in 1964 in Dresden, biology teacher in *Gymnasium*.

- Michael, 18 October 2003 (3 hours), twelfth grade, student of Ms Norte. Born in 1987, member of the FDP and the young liberals. Only son.

  Father: born in 1960 in Leipzig. Studied theater, is an actor. After having been forbidden to perform by the regime, he opened a bowling center.

Mother: born in 1963 in Leipzig. After the EOS, completed the *Abitur* and an apprenticeship and became a dental assistant.

- Sarah, 15 October 2003 (2 hours), twelfth grade, student of Ms Norte.
  Born in 1986 in Leipzig, she has a half-brother and a half-sister, the children of her mother and her mother's new partner, who are six and four years old respectively. She also has a half-brother aged twenty, the son of her father.
  Father: born in 1960 in Thuringia, he is an electrician. Her parents separated in 1993.
  Stepfather: born in 1962 in Saxony. He was a builder but returned to university to study architecture after reunification and was finishing his studies at the time of the interview.
  Mother: born in 1962 in Saxony, she was a nurse. After reunification, she returned to study to become a secondary teacher.

- Sebastian, 30 January 2004 (1 hour 30 minutes), ninth grade student of Ms Gerste.
  Born in 1988 in Leipzig. Parents separated in 1990.
  Father: born in 1955 in Leipzig, geography teacher at the *Gymnasium*.
  Mother: born in 1965 in Leipzig, studied economics, runs a restaurant.

- Silvester, 17 October 2003 (2 hours), eleventh grade, student of Ms Norte.
  Born in 1987 in Leipzig, he has an older brother, aged twenty-one, who is an architect.
  Father: born in 1961 in Leipzig, he is a locksmith.
  Mother: born in 1960 in Leipzig, she is a waitress.

Leipzig, 100th *Mittelschule*

- Annabelle, 7 January 2004 (2 hours), tenth grade, student of Ms Naute.
  Born in 1988 in Leipzig.
  Father: unknown.
  Mother: born in 1965, worked in communication but had been unemployed for more than four years at the time of the interview.

364 • Appendix 5: List of Students Interviewed

- Annika, 7 January 2004 (1 hour), tenth grade, student of Ms Naute.

  Born in 1988 in Leipzig, has two brothers, one aged thirteen who is also at the 100th *Mittelschule*, and the other, aged twenty-three, is studying architecture.

  Father: born in 1944 in Saxony, he is a chef, but has run an ice cream shop for the last ten years.

  Mother: born in 1955 in Leipzig, she was initially a secretary, then a dressmaker. Today she is self-employed and delivers meals to elderly people.

- Christian, 31 January 2004 (1 hour), ninth grade, student of Ms Seidengleich.

  Born in 1988 in Leipzig, he has two sisters, one aged twenty, a supermarket cashier in Leipzig, and the other, aged twenty-six, was a nurse but who has been a housewife since she became a mother six years ago.

  Father: born in 1958 in Leipzig, POS, truck driver.

  Mother: born in 1960 in Leipzig, POS, she was a supermarket cashier, but is now a hairdresser.

- Karsten, 12 January 2004 (2 hours), ninth grade, student of Ms Seidengleich.

  Born in 1988 in Leipzig, has a one-year-old half-sister.

  Stepfather: his mother's partner (no information on biological father). Born in 1977 in Leipzig and is studying history.

  Mother: born in 1966 in Leipzig, she is an unemployed optician.

- Leonore, 28 January 2004 (2 hours), ninth grade, student of Ms Seidengleich.

  Born in 1988 in Leipzig.

  Father: unknown.

  Mother: born in 1969, sales worker.

- Maren, 7 January 2004 (1 hour), ninth grade, student of Ms Naute.

  Born in 1988 in Leipzig, has one brother aged twenty-two, and two half-sisters, children of her father, with whom she has little contact.

  Father: born in 1951 in Thuringia, he is a tradesman (painter).

  Mother: born in 1958, she was a nurse, but is today a housewife.

- Meike, 27 January 2004 (1 hour), tenth grade, student of Ms Naute.

  Born in 1987 in Leipzig. Has one thirteen-year-old sister, who is also a student at the 100th *Mittelschule*.

  Father: born in 1966 in Leipzig, he is a trained chef, but today works as a florist.

  Mother: born in 1957 in Leipzig, she worked in a laundry company, but has been unemployed since reunification. She occasionally cleans houses.

- Merle, 26 January 2004 (1 hour), ninth grade, student of Ms Seidengleich.

  Born in 1987, has three brothers. The first was born in 1968 and was not able to study because of his religious involvement. He works as a forklift driver and is divorced. The second brother, born in 1969, is slightly disabled and works as a postman. The third brother, born in 1974, trained as a housepainter, but today works in sales. He is married.

  Father: born in 1947, he is an artisan.

  Mother: born in 1951, she is a nurse and educator for disabled people.

- Michaela, 3 February 2004 (1 hour), ninth grade, student of Ms Seidengleich.

  Born in 1988 in Leipzig, has one brother, aged twenty-one, who is a builder and today in the army. Her other brother, aged twenty, dropped out of school at age fourteen and is unemployed. Her twin sister is in the same school, but not in the same class.

  Father: born in 1957 in Leipzig, he is a builder, unemployed since 2000.

  Mother: born in 1959 in Leipzig, she is sales woman, unemployed since 1999.

- Sophie, 14 January 2004 (1 hour 30 minutes), ninth grade, student of Ms Seidengleich.

  Born in 1988 in Leipzig. Parents separated in 2003.

  Father: born in 1964 not far from Leipzig, was an officer in the NVA (army of the GDR). After reunification, he lost his job, became a bus driver, and then returned to study information technology, and has now worked in an IT business for the last five years.

  Mother: born in 1964 near Leipzig, she was a skilled worker, retrained several times after reunification, worked in communication, then in an architect's office, before losing her job. Has been unemployed since.

- Wolfgang, 13 and 27 January 2004 (4 hours), ninth grade, student of Ms Seidengleich.

  Born in 1988 in a small town in Saxony, Wolfgang came to Leipzig in 1995. He has two sisters aged eighteen and twenty-one. The youngest wants to study music, the eldest is studying to be a speech therapist.

  Father: born in 1961, he is an electrician, now unemployed.

  Mother: born in 1961, she is a secretary, now unemployed.

Note

1. The name of the history teacher is mentioned, because the students often keep the same history teacher for three or four years.

References

Adorno, Theodor W. 1971. *Erziehung zur Mündigkeit, Vorträge und Gespräche mit Helmut Becker 1959–1969*. Frankfurt/Main: Suhrkamp.

———. [1959] 2003. *Can One Live after Auschwitz? A Philosophical Reader*, trans. Rodney Livingston and others, ed. Rolf Tiedman. Stanford, CA: Stanford University Press. (German original: *"Ob nach Auschwitz sich noch leben lasse": Ein philosophisches Lesebuch.* Leipzig: Suhrkamp.)

Affergan, Francis. 1987. *Exotisme et Altérité: Essai sur les Fondements d'une Critique de l'Anthropologie*. Paris: Presse universitaires de France.

Ahlrichs, Johanna, Katharina Baier, Barbara Christophe, Felicitas Macgilchist, Patrick Mielke, and Roman Richtera. 2015. "Memory Practices in the Classroom: On Reproducing, Destabilizing and Interrupting Majority Memories." *Journal of Educational Media, Memory, and Society* (JEMMS) 7(2): 89–109.

Amendt, Gerhard. 1996. "Genderaspekte im Schüler-Lehrer-Verhältnis." *Leviathan* 24(3): 372–86.

Anderson, Benedict. 1983. *Imagined Communities: Reflections on the Origins and Spread of Nationalism*. London: Verso.

Ansart, Pierre. 1981. "Manuels d'histoire et inculcation d'un rapport affectif au passé," communication au colloque "Manuels d'histoire et mémoire collective," 23–24–25 avril 1981, université Paris 8.

Arnot, Madeleine. 2000. *Reproducing Gender? Essays on Educational Theory and Feminist Politics*. London, New York: Routledge.

———. 2009. *Educating the Gendered Citizen*. London: Routledge.

Arnot, Madeleine, and Jo-Anne Dillabough. 2000. *Challenging Democracy: International Perspectives on Gender, Education and citizenship*. London: Routledge.

Assmann, Aleida, and Ute Frevert. 1999. *Geschichtsvergessenheit, Geschichtsversessenheit. Vom Umgang mit deutschen Vergangenheiten nach 1945*. Stuttgart: Deutsche Verlagsanstalt.

Assmann, Jan. 1997. *Das kulturelle Gedächtnis: Schrift, Erinnerung und politische Identität in frühen Hochkulturen*. Munich: C.H. Beck.

Avanza, Martina. 2008. "Comment faire de l'ethnographie quand on n'aime pas "ses indigènes"? Une enquête au sein d'un mouvement xenophobe." In *Les Politiques de l'enquête:* Épreuves *ethnographiques*, ed. Didier Fassin and Alban Bensa, 41–58. Paris: La Découverte.

Avanza, Martina, and Gilles Laferté. 2005. "Dépasser la 'construction des identités'? Identification, image sociale, appurtenance." *Genèses* 61(4): 134–52.

Baudelot, Christian, Maire Cartier, and Christine Détrez. 1999. *Et pourtant ils lisent. . . .* Paris: Le Seuil.

Baudelot, Christian, and Roger Establet. 1992. *Allez les filles! Une révolution silencieuse*. Paris: Le Seuil.

368 • References

Baudelot, Christian, and François LeClercq, eds. 2005. *Les Effets de l'éducation*. Paris: La Documentation française.

Beaud, Stéphane. 1996. "L'usage de l'entretien en sciences socials." *Politix* 35: 226–57.

———. [2002] 2003. *80 % au bac . . . et après? Les enfants de la démocratisation scolaire*. Paris: La Découverte.

Beaud, Stéphane, and Florence Weber. 1997. *Guide de l'enquête de terrain*. Paris: La Découverte.

Becker, Howard. 1963. *Outsiders: Studies in the Sociology of Deviance*. London: The Free Press.

Belotti, Elena Gianni. [1973] 1975. *Little Girls: Social Conditions and Its Effects on the Stereotyped Role of Women During Infancy*. London: Writers and Readers.

Bendix, Reinhard. 1964. *Nation Building and Citizenship: Studies of Our Changing Social Order*. Berkeley: University of California Press.

Benrath, Ruth Johanna. 2005. *Kontinuität im Wandel: Eine empirisch-qualitative Untersuchung zur Transformation des didaktischen Handelns von Geschichtslehrkräften aus der DDR*. Idstein: Schulz-Kirchner Verlag.

Bensa, Alban, and Didier Fabre, eds. 2001. *Une histoire à soi: Figurations du passé et localités*. Paris: Editions de la MSH.

Benson, Rodney, and Eric Neveu. 2005. *Bourdieu and the Journalistic Field*. Malden, MA: Polity Press.

Benz, Wolfgang. 1991. *Dimensionen des Völkermordes, die Zahl der jüdischen Opfer des Nationalsozialismus*. Munich: Oldenbourg Verlag.

Berelson, Bernard, Paul Lazarsfeld, and William McPhee. [1954] 1986. *Voting: A Study of Opinion Formation in a Presidential Campaign*. Chicago: University of Chicago Press.

Bergson, Henri. [1869] 1911. *Matter and Memory*. Trans. Nancy Margaret Paul and W. Scott Palmer. London: George Allen & Unwin LTD. (French original: *Matière et mémoire*. Paris: Presses Universitaires de France, 1993.)

Bertaux, Daniel. 1980. "L'approche biographique: sa validité méthodologique, ses potentialities." *Cahiers internationaux de sociologie* 69: 197–225.

———.1981. *Biography and Society: The Life History Approach in Social Sciences*. London: Sage Publications.

———.1997. *Les Récits de vie*. Paris: Nathan.

Billaud, Solène. 2005. *Passation de biens et pratiques de mémoires familiales dans l'espace domestique: une approche monographique. Le cas d'une famille issue de la petite agriculture, mémoire de DEA* sous la direction de Florence Weber. Paris: ENS/EHESS.

Billaud, Solène, Sibylle Gollac, Alexandra Oeser, and Julie Pagis. 2015. *Histoires de familles. Les récits du passé dans la parenté contemporaine*. Paris: Editions de la rue d'Ulm.

Bloch, Ernst. [1935] 1977. "Nonsynchronism and the Obligation to Its Dialectics," trans. Marc Ritter. *New German Critique* 11: 22–38.

Borries, Bodo (von). 1995. *Das Geschichtsbewußtsein Jugendlicher: Eine repräsentative Untersuchung über Vergangenheitsdeutungen, Gegenwartswahrnehmungen und Zukunftserwartungen von Schülerinnen und Schülern in Ost- und Westdeutschland*. Munich: Juventa.

Borries, Bodo, Hans-Jürgen Pandel, and Jörn Rüsen. 1991. *Geschichtsbewusstsein empirisch*. Pfaffenweiler: Centaurus.

Bourdieu, Pierre. [1979] 2010. *Distinction: A Social Critique of the Judgment of Taste*, trans. Richard Nice. London: Routledge.

———. 1979. *Algeria 1960: The Disenchantment of the World. The Sense of Honour: The Kabyle House or the World Reversed: Essays*. Cambridge: Cambridge University Press.

———. [1980] 1995. "Youth is Just a Word." In *Sociology in Question*, trans. Richard Nice, 94–102. London: Sage.

References • 369

———. 1986. "L'illusion biographique." *Actes de la recherche en sciences sociales* 62–63: 69–72.

———. 1989. *La Noblesse d'État: Grandes écoles et esprit du corps*. Paris: Minuit.

———. [1998] 2001. *Masculine Domination*. Stanford, CA: Stanford University Press.

Bourdieu, Pierre, and Roger Chartier. [1985] 2003. "La lecture: une pratique culturelle. Débat entre Pierre Bourdieu et Roger Chartier." In *Pratiques de la lecture*, Roger Chartier, 277–306. Paris: Payot & Rivages.

Bourdieu, Pierre, Alain Darbel, and Dominique Schnapper. [1969] 1991. *The Love of Art: European Art Museums and Their Public*. Stanford, CA: Stanford University Press.

Bourdieu, Pierre, and Jean-Claude Passeron. [1964] 1985. *Les Héritiers: Les étudiants et la culture*. Paris: Minuit.

Bourke, Joanna. 2005. *Fear: A Cultural History*. Berkeley: Counterpoint Press.

Brink, Cornelia. 1998. *Ikonen der Vernichtung: Öffentlicher Gebrauch von Fotografien aus national sozialistischen Konzentrationslagern nach 1945*. Berlin: Akademie Verlag.

Brown, George Isaac. 1978. *Gefühl und Aktion: Gestaltmethoden im integrativen Unterricht*. Frankfurt/Main: Flach.

Brubaker, Rogers. 1992. *Citizenship and Nationhood in France and Germany*. Cambridge, MA: Harvard University Press.

———. 1996. *Nationalism Reframed: Nationhood and the National Question in the New Europe*. Cambridge: Cambridge University Press.

———. 2001. "Au-delà de l'identité." *Actes de la recherche en sciences sociales* 139: 66–85.

Bruneau, Ivan. 2002. "Un mode d'engagement singulier au Front national: La trajectoire scolaire effective d'un fils de mineur." *Politix* 57: 183–211.

Canada, Katherine, and Richard Pringle. 1995. "The Role of Gender in College Classroom Interactions: A Social Context Approach." *Sociology of Education* 68: 161–86.

Certeau, Michel (de). [1980] 1988. *The Practice of Everyday Life*, trans. Steven Rendall. Berkeley: University of California Press.

Chartier, Roger. [1985] 2003. *Pratiques de la lecture*. Paris: Payot & Rivages.

Chodorow, Nancy. 1978. *The Reproduction of Mothering: Psychoanalysis and the Sociology of Gender*. Berkeley: University of California Press.

Clair, Isabelle. 2007. "La division genrée de l'expérience amoureuse: Enquête dans des cités d'habitat social." *Sociétés et représentations* 24: 145–62.

Coenen-Huther, Josette. 1994. *La Mémoire familiale: un travail de reconstruction du passé*. Paris: L'Harmattan.

Cohen, David William. 1994. *The Combing of History*. Chicago: University of Chicago Press.

———. 1997. "Further Thoughts on the Production of History." In *Between History and Histories: The Making of Silences and Commemorations*, Gerald Sider and Gavin Smith, 300–310. Toronto: University of Toronto Press.

Confino, Alon. 1997. "Collective Memory and Cultural History: Problems of Method." *The American Historical Review* 102(5): 1386–1403.

———. 2004. "Telling about Germany: Narratives of Memory and Culture." *The Journal of Modern History* 76: 398–416.

———. 2005. "Introduction." *History & Memory* 17(1–2): 5–11.

———. 2006. *Germany as a Culture of Remembrance: Promises and Limits of Writing History*. Chapel Hill: University of North Carolina Press.

Connell, R. W. 1989. "Cool Guys, Swoots and Wimps: The Interplay of Masculinity and Education." *Oxford Review of Education* 15(3): 291–303.

Coulangeon, Philippe. 2003. "Le poids de la télévision dans les loisirs. Évolution de 1986–1998." In *Regards croisés sur les pratiques culturelles*, ed. Olivier Donnat, 283–301. Paris: La Documentation française.

370 • References

Coutant, Isabelle. 2005. *Délit de jeunesse: La justice face aux quartiers*. Paris: La Découverte.

Curapp. 1998. *La Politique ailleurs*. Paris: Presses universitaires de France.

Cusset, François. 2005. *French Theory: Foucault, Derrida, Deleuze et Cie et les mutations de la vie intellectuelle aux Etats-Unis*. Paris: La Découverte.

Creet, Julia, and Andreas Kitzmann, eds. 2011. *Memory and Migration: Multidisciplinary Approaches to Memory Studies*. Toronto: University of Toronto Press.

Darras, Éric. 1995. "Le pouvoir médiacratique? Les logiques du recrutement des invités politiques à la télévision." *Politix* 30: 183–98.

———. 2003. "Les limites de la distance: Réflexions sur les modes d'appropriation des produits culturels." In *Regards croisés sur les pratiques culturelles*, ed. Olivier Donnat, 231–53. Paris: La Documentation française.

———. 2008. *L'Indissociabilité du processus de communication: Des productions aux appropriations télévisuelles et inversement. Mémoire d'habilitation à diriger des recherches en sciences socials*. Amiens: université de Picardie Jules Verne.

Déchaux, Jean-Hugues. 1997. *Le Souvenir des morts: Essai sur le lien de filiation*. Paris: Presses universitaires de France.

Delcroix, Cathérine. 2001. *Ombres et lumières de la famille Nour*. Paris: Payot.

Déloye, Ives, and Olivier Ihl. 2008. *L'Acte de vote*. Paris: Presses de Sciences-Po.

Deutsch, Karl. 1953. *Nationalism and Social Communication: An Inquiry into the Foundation of Nationality*. Cambridge, MA: MIT Press.

Deutsche Nationalbibliographie (DNB) (1972–2002). Sachgebiet 01.00, Allgemeines. Nachweis der deutschen Literaturproduktion: Bücher, Karten, Hochschulschriften. Anbieter, Deutsche Bibliothek, Buchhändler Vereinigung.

Dimbath, Oliver, and Michael Heinlein. 2015. *Gedächtnissoziologie*. Paderborn: Wilhelm Fink.

Donnat, Olivier. 1998. *Les Pratiques culturelles des Français: Enquête 1997*. Paris: La Documentation française.

Donnat, Olivier, ed. 2003. *Regards croisés sur les pratiques culturelles*. Paris: La Documentation française.

Dudek, Peter. 1989. "'Aufarbeitung der Vergangenheit' im Schulischen Unterricht?" In *Erziehung nach Auschwitz*, ed. Hanns Fred Rathenow and Norbert H. Weber, 4:109–16. Pfaffenweiler: Centaurus Verlagsgesellschaft.

Dumais, Susan A. 2002. "Cultural Capital, Gender and School Success: The Role of Habitus." *Sociology of Education* 75(1): 44–68.

Durkheim, Émile. [1893] 2014. *The Division of Labor in Society*, trans. W. D. Halls. New York: The Free Press [first translated 1984].

———. [1895] 1966. *The Rules of Sociological Method*, trans. Sarah A. Solovay and John H. Müller. New York: The Free Press. (French Original: *Les Règles de la méthode sociologique*. Paris: Presses universitaires de France, 2002.)

Duru-Bellat, Marie. 2002. *Les Inégalités sociales à l'école: Genèses et mythes*. Paris: Presses universitaires de France.

Eberhard, Wilms, ed. 1986. *Geschichte, Denk- und Arbeitsfach: Heinz Dieter Schmid zum 65. Geburtstag*. Frankfurt/Main: Hirschgraben-Verlag.

Elias, Norbert. [1978] 1984. *What is Sociology*, trans. Stephen Mennell and Grace Morrissey. New York: Columbia University Press.

Elias, Norbert, and John L. Scotson. [1965] 1994. *The Established and the Outsiders: A Sociological Enquiry into Community Problems*. London: Sage.

Eschebach, Insa. 1997. "Zur Umcodierung der eigenen Vergangenheit. Antifaschismuskonstruktionen in Rehabilitationsgesuchen ehemaliger Mitglieder der

NSDAP, Berlin 1945–1946." In *Akten. Eingaben. Schaufenster. Die DDR und ihre Texte. Erkundungen zu Herrschaft und Alltag*, ed. Alf Lüdtke and Peter Becker, 79–90. Berlin: Akademie Verlag.

Fabel-Lamla, Melanie. 2006. "Biographien von DDR-Lehrern der 1950ger Geburtsjahrgänge." In *Die DDR aus generationengeschichtlicher Perspektive. Eine Inventur*, ed. Annegret Schüle, Thomas Ahbe, and Rainer Gries, 193–216. Leipzig. Leipziger Universitätsverlag.

Fagot, Beverly I., Richard Hagan, Mary Driver Leinbach, and Sandra Kronsberg. 1985. "Differentiated Reactions to Assertive and Communicative Acts of Toddler Boys and Girls." *Child Development* 56(6): 1499–505.

Fassin, Éric. 2002. "La parité sans théorie: retour sur un débat." *Politix* 60: 19–32.

———. 2005. "Trouble-genre: Préface à l'édition française." In *Trouble dans le genre*, Judith Butler, 5–19. Paris: La Découverte.

Finkielkraut, Alain, Tzvetan Todorov, and Richard Marienstras. 2000. *Du bon usage de la mémoire*. Geneva: Éditions du Tricorne.

Fischer, Fritz. [1961] 1975. *World Power or Decline: Controversy over Germany's Aims in the First World War*. Little Hampton Book Services *Griff nach der Weltmacht*. Düsseldorf: Droste Verlag.

Firth, Raymond, ed. 1956. *Two Studies of Kinship in London*. London: Athlone Press.

Foote Whyte, William. [1943] 1993. *Street Corner Society: The Social Structure of an Italian Slum*. Chicago: University of Chicago Press.

Foster, Peter, Roger Gomm, and Martin Hammersley. 1996. *Constructing Educational Inequality: An Assessment of Research on School Inequalities*. London: The Farmer Press.

Francis, Becky. 2000. *Boys, Girls and Achievement: Addressing the Classroom Issues*. London: Routledge Falmer.

François, Etienne, and Hagen Schulze. 2001. *Deutsche Erinnerungsorte. 3 Bd.* Munich: Beck.

Frei, Norbert. 1999. *Vergangenheitspolitik: Die Anfänge der Bundesrepublik und die NS Vergangenheit*. Munich: Deutscher Taschenbuch Verlag.

Frisch-Gauthier, Jacqueline. 1961. "Le rire dans les relations de travail." *Revue française de sociologie* 2(4): 292–303.

Gagel, Walter. 1985. "Betroffenheitspädagogik, oder politischer Unterricht? Kritik am Subjektivismus der politischen Didaktik." *Gegenwartskunde* 4: 403–14.

Gaxie, Daniel. 1978. *Le Cens cache: Inégalités culturelles et ségrégation politique*. Paris: Le Seuil.

Gaxie, Daniel, Nicolas Hubé, and Jay Rowell. 2013. *Perceptions of Europe: A Comparative Sociology of European Attitudes*. Colchester: European Consortium for Political Research Press.

Gaxie, Daniel, and Patrick Lehingue. 1984. *Enjeux municipaux: La constitution des enjeux politiques dans une* élection *municipal*. Paris: Presses universitaires de France.

Gaxie, Daniel, and Michel Offerlé. 1985. "Les militants syndicaux et associatifs au pouvoir? Capital social collectif et carrière politique." In *Les Élites socialistes au pouvoir: 1981–1985*, ed. Pierre Birnbaum, 105–38. Paris: Presses universitaires de France.

Geertz, Clifford. 1973. "Thick Description: Towards an Interpretive Theory of Culture." In *The Interpretation of Cultures: Selected Essays*, 3–30. New York: Basic Books.

Gellner, Ernest. 1983. *Nations and Nationalism*. Ithaca, NY: Cornell University Press.

Gensburger, Sarah. 2010. *Les justes de France: politiques publiques de la mémoire*. Paris: Presses de SciencesPo.

Gensburger, Sarah, and Marie-Claire Lavabre. 2005. "Entre 'devoir de mémoire' et 'abus de mémoire,' la sociologie de la mémoire comme tierce position." In *Histoire, mémoire et épistémologie: À propos de Paul Ricoeur*, ed. Bernard Müller, 75–96. Lausanne: Payot.

Georgi, Viola. 2003. *Entliehene Erinnerung: Geschichtsbilder junger Migranten, in Deutschland.* Hamburg: Hamburger Edition.

Gies, Horst. 1995. "Die Rolle der Gefühle im Geschichtsunterricht des Dritten Reiches und der DDR." *Geschichte in Wissenschaft und Unterricht* 46(3): 127–41.

Ginzburg, Carlo. [1976] 1980. *The Cheese and the Worms: The Cosmos of a Sixteenth-Century Miller*, trans. John and Anne Tedeschi. Baltimore, MD: John Hopkins University Press.

———. [1979] 1980. "Signes, traces, pistes: racines d'un paradigme de l'indice." *Le Débat* 4: 116–42.

———. 1993. "Mikro-Historie: Zwei oder drei Dinge, die ich von ihr weiß." *Historische Anthropologie: Kultur, Gesellschaft, Alltag* 1(1): 169–92.

Ginzburg, Carlo, and Carlo Poni. 1985. "Was ist Mikrogeschichte?" *Geschichtswerkstatt* 6: 48–52.

Goffman, Erving. 1959. *The Presentation of the Self in Everyday Life.* New York: Anchor Books.

———. [1967] 2005. *Interaction Ritual: Essays in Face to Face Behavior.* New Brunswick, NJ: Aldine Transaction.

———. 1974. *Frame Analysis: An Essay of the Organization of Experience.* London: Harper and Row.

Gollac, Sibylle. 2005. "Faire ses partages: Le règlement d'une succession et sa mise en récits dans un groupe de descendance." *Terrain* 45: 113–24.

Graßhoff, Gunther, and Davina Höblich. 2005. "Lehrer-Schüler-Beziehungen an Waldorfschulen: Rekonstruktionen zum Verhältnis von Selbstverständnis der Lehrerschaft, Lehrer-Schüler-Interaktionen im Unterricht und individueller Schulkultur." BIOS 18(1): 115–27.

Grignon, Claude, and Jean-Claude Passeron. 1989. *Le Savant et le populaire: Misérabilisme et populisme en sociologie et en literature.* Paris: Gallimard, Le Seuil.

Gudehus, Christian. 2006. *Dem Gedächtnis zuhören: Erzählungen über NS-Verbrechen und ihre Repräsentation in deutschen Gedenkstätten.* Essen: Klartext.

Halbwachs, Maurice. [1925] 1994. *Les Cadres sociaux de la mémoire.* Paris: Albin Michel. (English translation of some of the texts, with a preface by Lewis A. Coser: *On Collective Memory.* Chicago: University of Chicago Press, 1992.)

———. [1939] 1997. "La mémoire collective chez les musiciens." In *La Mémoire collective*, Maurice Halbwachs, 19–50. Paris: Albin Michel.

———. [1941] 1971. *La Topographie légendaire des* Évangiles. Paris: Presses universitaires de France. (English translation of some of the texts, with a preface of Lewis A. Coser: *On Collective Memory.* Chicago: University of Chicago Press, 1992.)

———. [1950] 1997. *La Mémoire collective* (édition critique établie par Gérard Namer). Paris: Albin Michel.

Hall, Roberta, and Bernice R. Sandler. 1982. *The Classroom Climate: A Chilly One for Women?* Washington, DC: Project on the Status and Education of Women, Association of American Colleges.

Hall, Stuart. 1973. "Encoding and Decoding in Television Discourse." CCCS polycopié n°7. (This article has been reworked in a French translation in 1994: "Codage/décodage." *Réseaux* 68: 27–40.)

———. 1980. "Cultural Studies: A Paradigm." *Media, Culture and Society* 2: 57–72.

Hallgarten, George W. F. 1969. "Deutsche Selbstschau nach 50 Jahren: Fritz Fischer, Seine Gegner uns Vorläufer." In *Das Schicksal des Imperialismus*, 57–135. Frankfurt/Main: Europäische Verlagsanstalt.

Hartog, François. [2003] 2015. *Regimes of Historicity, Presentism and Experiences of Time*, trans. Saskia Brown. New York: Columbia University Press.

Hartog, François, and Jacques Revel, eds. 2001. "Note de conjoncture historique." In *Les Usages politiques du passé*, 13–25. Paris: éditions de l'EHESS.

Hilberg, Raul. 1992. *Perpetrators, Victims, Bystanders: The Jewish Catastrophe, 1933–1945.* New York: Aaron Asher Books.

Hirschman, Albert O. 1970. *Exit, Voice and Loyalty: Responses to Decline in Firms, Organizations and States.* Cambridge, MA: Harvard University Press.

Hoggart, Richard. [1957] 2006. *The Uses of Literacy: Aspects of Working Class Life.* London: Penguin.

Husson, Édouard. 2001. *Comprendre Hitler et la Shoah: Les historiens de la République fédérale d'Allemagne et l'identité allemande depuis 1949.* Paris: Presses universitaires de France.

Isnenghi, Mario. 2006. *L'Italie par elle-même: Les lieux de mémoire italiens, 1848 à nos jours,* Paris: Editions ENS Rue d'Ulm, Italica.

Jauss, Hans Robert. 1972. *Kleine Apologie der Aestetischen Erfahrung: Mit kunstgeschichtlichen Bemerkungen von Max Imdahl.* Konstanz: Universitätsverlag Konstanz.

Jeismann, Karl-Ernst. 1988. "Geschichtsbewußsein als zentrale Kategorie der Geschichtsdidaktik." In *Geschichtsbewußtsein und historisch-politisches Lernen, Jahrbuch für Geschichtsdidaktik,* ed. Gerhard Schneider, 1–27. Pfaffenweiler: Centaurus.

Jennings, Kent M., Lee Ehman, and Richard G. Niemi. 1974. "Social Studies: Teachers and Their Pupils." In *The Political Character of Adolescence: The Influence of Families and Schools,* 207–27. Princeton, NJ: Princeton University Press.

Jolas, Tina, and François Zonabend. 1973. "Gens du finage, gens du bois." *Annales ESC* 1: 285–305.

Jouvenceau, Maxime. 2018. *Produire des valeurs scolaires dans toutes les classes? Flux et fictions dans l'enseignement et les établissements: Thèse de sociologie.* Nanterre: Université Paris Nanterre.

Jureit, Ulrike, and Michael Wildt, ed. 2005. *Generationen: Zur Relevanz eines wissenschaftlichen Grundbegriffs.* Hamburg: Hamburger Edition, HIS.

Kansteiner, Wulf. 2006. *In Pursuit of German Memory: History, Television and Politics after Auschwitz.* Athens: Ohio University Press.

Katz, Jack. 1999. *How Emotions Work.* Chicago: Chicago University Press.

Keppler, Angela. 1994. *Tischgespräche: Über Formen kommunikativer Vergemeinschaftung am Beispiel der Konversation in Familien.* Frankfurt/Main: Suhrkamp.

Klemperer, Victor. [1957] 2006. *The Language of the Third Reich.* New York: Bloomsbury Academic.

Kmec, Sonja, Benoit Majerus, Michel Margue, Pit Peporte, ed. 2008. *Lieux de mémoire au Luxembourg.* Luxembourg: Ed. Saint Paul.

Knigge, Volkhard. 1996. "Vom Reden und Schweigen der Steine: Zu Denkmalen auf dem Gelände ehemaliger nationalsozialistischer Konzentrations- und Vernichtungslager." In *Fünfzig Jahre danach. Zur Nachgeschichte des Nationalsozialismus,* ed. Siegrid Weigel and Birgit R. Erdle, 101–13. Zurich: VDF Hochschulverlag.

Knoch, Habbo. 2001. *Die Tat als Bild: Fotografien des Holocaust in der deutschen Erinnerungskultur.* Hamburg: Hamburger Edition.

Knoch, Peter. 1986. "Geschichte und Gestaltpädagogik. Einige experimentelle Erfahrungen." In *Didaktik der Geschichte: Aus der Arbeit der Pädagogischen Hochschulen Baden-Würtembergs,* ed. Uwe Uffelmann, 73–105. Villingen-Schwenningen: Neckar Verlag.

Kohlstruck, Michael. 1997. *Zwischen Erinnerung und Geschichte: Der Nationalsozialismus und die jungen Deutschen.* Berlin: Metropol.

Kolinsky, Eva. 1991. "Geschichte gegen den Strom, zur Darstellung des Holocaust in neuen Schulgeschichtsbüchern." *Internationale Schulbuchforschung* 13(2): 121–45.

———.1992. "Remembering Auschwitz: A Survey of Recent Textbooks for the Teaching of History in German Schools." *Yad Vashem Studies* 22: 287–307.

Kolinsky, Martin, and Eva Kolinsky. 1974. "The Treatment of the Holocaust in West German Textbooks." *Yad Vashem Studies* 10: 149–216.

Korte Barbara, and Lechner Doris eds. 2013. *History and Humour: British and American Perspectives*. Bielefeld: Transcript Verlag.

Kuipers, Giselinde. 2006. *Good Humor, Bad Taste: A Sociology of the Joke*. Berlin: Mouton de Gruyter.

Lagroye, Jacques. 2006. *La Vérité dans l'Église catholique: Contestations et restauration d'un régime d'autorité*. Paris: Belin.

Lahire, Bernard. 1995. *Tableaux de familles: Heurs et malheurs scolaires en milieux populaires*. Paris: Le Seuil.

Lalieu, Olivier. 2001. "L'invention du 'devoir de mémoire,'" *Vingtième siècle: Revue d'Histoire* 1(69): 83–94.

Laqueur, Thomas. 1992. *Making Sex: Body and Gender from the Greeks to Freud*. Cambridge, MA: Harvard University Press.

Lauterwein, Andréa, and Colette Strauss-Hiva. 2009. *Rire, mémoire, Shoah*. Paris: Éditions de l'éclat.

Lavabre, Marie-Claire. 1991. "Du poids et du choix du passé, Lecture critique du 'syndrome de Vichy,'" in *Histoire politique et sciences socials*, ed. Denis Peschanski, Michael Pollak, and Henry Rousso, 265–78. Brussels: Complexe.

———.1994. *Le Fil Rouge: Sociologie de la mémoire communiste*. Paris: Presse de la Fondation nationale des sciences politiques.

———. 2000. "Usages et mésusages de la notion de mémoire." *Critique internationale* 7: 48–57.

———. 2001. "Peut-on agir sur la mémoire?" *Cahiers français* 303: 8–13.

Lazarsfeld, Paul, Bernard Berelson, and Hazel Gaudet. [1944] 1952. *The People's Choice: How the Voter Makes Up His Mind in a Presidential Campaign*. New York: Columbia University Press.

Le Bihan, Yann. 2007. *Construction sociale et stigmatisation de la "femme noire." Imaginaires coloniaux et sélection matrimoniale*. Paris: L'Harmattan.

Le Goff, Jacques. [1977] 1988. *Histoire et mémoire*. Paris: Gallimard.

Le Wita, Béatrix. 1994. "La mémoire familiale des Parisiens appartenant aux classes moyennes." *Ethnologie française* 14(1): 57–66.

Lehingue, Patrick. 2003. "L'objectivation statistique des électorats: Que savons nous des électeurs du Front national?" In *La Politisation*, ed. Jacques Lagroye, 247–78. Paris: Belin.

Leonhard, Nina. 2002. *Politik- und Geschichtsbewußtsein im Wandel: Die politische Bedeutung der nationalsozialistischen Vergangenheit im Verlauf von drei Generationen in Ost- und Westdeutschland*. Münster: LIT Verlag.

Lepoutre, David. [1997] 2001. *Coeur de banlieue: Codes, rites et langages*. Paris: Odile Jacob.

Lepoutre, David, and Isabelle Cannoodt. 2005. *Souvenirs de familles immigrées*. Paris: Odile Jacob.

Levi, Giovanni. [1985] 1989. *Le Pouvoir au village: Histoire d'un exorciste dans le Piémont du XIIe siècle*. Paris: Gallimard.

Levi, Primo. [1958] 1996. *Survival in Auschwitz*, trans. Giulio Einaudi. New York: Touchstone (first translation 1986).

Lindenberger, Thomas. 1999. *Herrschaft und Eigen-Sinn in der Diktatur: Studien zur Gesellschaftsgeschichte der DDR*. Cologne: Böhlau Verlag.

———. 2015. "Eigen-Sinn, Domination and no Resistance." *Docupedia-Zeitgeschichte*, 3 August 2015, http://docupedia.de/zg/lindenberger_eigensinn_v1_en_2015.

Linenthal, Edward T. 1995. *Preserving Memory: The Struggle to Create America's Holocaust Museum*. New York: Columbia University Press.

Lipp, Carola. 1995. "Histoire sociale et Alltagsgeschichte." *Actes de la recherche en sciences sociales* 106–107: 53–66.

Löding, Ole. 2009. "Deutschland Katastrophenstaat: Die Auseinandersetzung mit dem Nationalsozialismus im politischen Song der Bundesrepublik von 1964 bis zur Gegenwart." PhD diss., Universität Köln.

Lüdtke, Alf. 1984. "Le domaine réservé: affirmation de l'autonomie ouvrière et politique chez les ouvriers d'usine en Allemagne à la fin du XIXe siècle." *Le Mouvement social* 126: 29–52.

———. 1986a. "Cash, Coffee-Breaks, Horseplay: *Eigensinn* and Politics among Factory Workers in Germany circa 1900." In *Confrontation, Class Consciousness and the Labor Process*, ed. Michael Hanagen and Charles Stephenson, 65–95. New York: Greenwood Press.

———. 1986b. "'Deutsche Qualitätsarbeit,' 'Spielereien' am Arbeitsplatz und 'Fliehen' aus der Fabrik: industrielle Arbeitsprozesse und Arbeiterverhalten in den 1920er Jahren." In *Arbeiterkulturen zwischen Alltag und Politik*, ed. Friedhelm Boll, 155–97. Vienna: Europa-Verlag.

———. 1991a. "Herrschaft als soziale Praxis: Einleitung." In *Herrschaft als soziale Praxis*, 9–63. Göttingen: Vandenhoek & Ruprecht.

———. 1991b. "La domination au quotidien. 'Sens de soi' et individualité des travailleurs en Allemagne avant et après 1933." *Politix* 4(13): 68–78.

———. 1992a "Perpetrators, Accomplices, Victims: Further Reflections on Domination as a Social Practice." CSST working paper n°85, 1992, retrieved 6 April 2016 from https://deepblue.lib.umich.edu/bitstream/handle/2027.42/51247/481.pdf?sequence=1&isAllowed=y.

———. 1992b. "The Appeal of Exterminating 'Others': German Workers and the limits of Resistance," *Journal of Modern History* 64: 46–67.

———. 1993a. "Einleitung." In *Eigen-Sinn: Fabrikalltag, Arbeitererfahrungen und Politik vom Kaiserreich bis in den Faschismus*, 9–22. Hamburg: Ergebnisse Verlag.

———.1993b. "'Coming to Terms with the Past': Illusions of Remembering, Ways of Forgetting Nazism in West Germany." *Journal of Modern History* 65: 542–72.

———. 1994. "Geschichte und Eigensinn." In *Alltagskultur, Subjektivität und Geschichte: Zur Theorie und Praxis von Alltagsgeschichte*, ed. Berliner Geschichtswerkstatt, 139–53. Münster: Westfälisches Dampfboot.

———. 1995a. *The History of Everyday Life: Reconstructing Historical Experiences and Ways of Life*, trans. William Templer. Princeton, NJ: Princeton University Press.

———. 1995b. "Introduction: What Is the History of Everyday Life and Who Are Its Practitioners." In *The History of Everyday Life: Reconstructing Historical Experiences and Ways of Life*, ed. Alf Lüdtke, trans. William Templer, 3–40. Princeton, NJ: Princeton University Press.

———. 1995d. "What Happened to the 'Fiery Red Glow'? Workers' Experiences and German Fascism." In *The History of Everyday Life: Reconstructing Historical Experiences and Ways of Life*, ed. Alf Lüdtke, trans. William Templer, 198–251. Princeton, NJ: Princeton University Press.

———. 1995d. "Glossary." In *The History of Everyday Life: Reconstructing Historical Experiences and Ways of Life*, ed. Alf Lüdtke, trans. William Templer, 313–314. Princeton, NJ: Princeton University Press.

376 • References

———. 1996. "Ouvriers, Eigensinn et politique dans l'Allemagne du xxe siècle." *Actes de la recherche en sciences sociales* 113: 91–101.

———. 1998. "Alltagsgeschichte, Mikro-Historie, historische Anthropologie." In *Geschichte. Ein Grundkurs*, ed. Hans-Jürgen Goertz, 557–78. Hamburg: Rowohlt Taschenbuch Verlag.

———. 2006. "Alltag: Der blinde Fleck?" *Deutschland Archiv* 39(5): 895–901.

———. 2016. *Everyday Life in Mass Dictatorship: Collusion and Evasion*. New York: Palgrave Macmillan.

———. 2017. "Lebenswelt: verriegelte Welt? Überlegungen zu einem Konzept und seinen Verwendungen." *Werkstattgeschichte* 75: 115–124.

Maccoby, Eleanor. 1990. "Le sexe, catégorie sociale." *Actes de la recherche en sciences sociales* 183: 16–26.

Mannheim, Karl. [1928] 1970. "The Problem of Generations." *Psychoanalytic review* 57(3): 378.

Marshall, Thomas Humphrey. 1950. *Citizenship and Social Class and Other Essays*. Cambridge: Cambridge University Press.

Martschukat, Jürgen, and Olaf Stieglitz. 2005. *"Es ist ein Junge!" Einführung in die Geschichte der Männlichkeiten in der Neuzeit*. Tübingen: Diskord.

Mauger, Gérard. 1991. "Enquêter en milieu populaire." *Genèses* 6: 125–43.

Mauger, Gérard, and Clause Fosse-Poliak. 1983. "Les Loubards." *Actes de la recherche en sciences sociales* 50: 49–68.

Medick, Hans. 1996. *Weben und Überleben in Laichingen, 1650–1900: Lokalgeschichte als allgemeine Geschichte*. Göttingen: Vandenhoeck & Ruprecht.

———. 1999. "Mikro-Historie als Historikererfahrung und als Geschichtsarbeit: Rede zur Verleihung des René Kuczynski Preises 1997." *Zeitschrift für Sozialgeschichte des 20. und 21. Jahrhunderts* 14(1): 190–99.

Memmi, Dominique. 1985. "L'engagement politique." In *Traité de science politique*, vol. 3, ed. Madeleine Grawitz and Jean Leca, 310–67. Paris: Presses universitaires de France.

Michel, Johann. 2010. *Gouverner les memoires: Les politiques mémorielles en France*. Paris: PUF.

Michelat, Guy. 1975. "Sur l'utilisation de l'entretien non directif en sociologie." *Revue française de sociologie* 16: 229–47.

Mierow, Jürgen. 1991. "Geschichtswissen durch Geschichtsunterricht: Historische Kenntnisse und ihr Erwerb innerhalb und außerhalb der Schule." In *Geschichtsbewusstsein empirisch*, ed. Bodo von Borries, Hans-Jürgen Pandel, and Jörn Rüsen, 53–109. Pfaffenweiler: Centaurus.

Miller-Bernal, Leslie. 1993. "Single-Sex versus Coeducational Environments: A Comparison of Women Students' Experiences at Four Colleges." *American Journal of Education* 102: 23–54.

Mosconi, Nicole 1999. "Les recherches sur la socialisation différentielle des sexes à l'école." In *Filles et garçons jusqu'à l'adolescence: Socialisations différentielles*, ed. Yannick Lemel and Bernard Roudet, 85–116. Paris: L'Harmattan.

Mosconi, Nicole, and Josette Loudet-Verdier. 1997. "Inégalités de traitement entre les filles et les garcons." In *Variations sur une leçon de mathématiques*, ed. Claudine Blanchard-Laville, 127–50. Paris: L'Harmattan.

Mullis, Ina V., Michael O. Martin, Eugenio J. Gonzalez, and Ann M. Kennedy. 2003. *PIRLS—2001 International Report, IEA's Study of Reading Literacy Achievement in Primary School in 35 Countries*. Boston: International Study Centre.

Mütter, Bernd, and Uwe Uffelmann, eds. 1992. *Emotionen und historisches Lernen: Forschung, Vermittlung, Rezeption*. Frankfurt/Main: Diesterweg.

Muxel, Anne. 1991. "La mémoire familiale." In *La Famille: l'état des savoirs*, ed. François de Singly, 250–61. Paris: La Découverte.

———. 2002. *Individu et mémoire familiale*. Paris: Nathan.

Neumann, Erich P., and Elisabeth Noelle-Neumann. 1993. *Allensbacher Jahrbuch für Demoskopie* 9: 1984–1992.

Niethammer, Lutz, and Alexander Von Plato. 1983–1985. *Lebensgeschichte und Sozialkultur im Ruhrgebiet 1930–1960, 3 vol.* Berlin: Dietz Verlag.

Niethammer, Lutz, Alexander Von Plato, and Dorothee Wierling. 1991. *Die Volkseigene Erfahrung: Eine Archäologie des Lebens in der Industrieprovinz der DDR*, Berlin: Rowohlt.

Noiriel, Gérard. 1988. *Le Creuset français, Histoire de l'immigration XIXe–XXe siècles*. Paris: Le Seuil.

———. 1989. "Pour une approche subjectiviste du social." *Annnales ESC* 44(6): 1435–1459.

———. 1991. "La question nationale comme objet de l'histoire sociale." *Genèses* 4(4): 72–94.

———. 2001. État, Nation, Immigration, *Vers une histoire du pouvoir*. Paris: Belin.

———. 2007. *Immigration, antisémitisme et racisme en France (XIXe–XXe siècles): Discours publics, humiliations privées*. Paris: Fayard.

Nora, Pierre. [1984–1993] 1997. *Les Lieux de mémoire, 7 vol.* Paris: Gallimard.

———. 2002. "Pour une histoire au second degree." *Le Débat* 122: 24–31.

Oates, Mary J., and Susan Williamson. 1978. "Womens Colleges and Women Achievers." *Signs: Journal of Women in Culture and Society* 3(4): 795–806.

———. 1980. "Comments on Tidball's 'Women's Colleges and Women Achievers Revisited,'" *Signs: Journal of Women in Culture and Society* 6(2): 342–45.

OECD. 1995. *Littératie, économie et société: résultats de la première Enquête internationale sur l'alphabétisation des adultes*. Paris: OECD.

———.2001. *Connaissances et compétences: des atouts pour la vie: premiers résultats du programme international de l'OCDE*. Paris: OECD.

———. 2005. *Apprendre aujourd'hui, réussir demain—Premiers résultats de PISA 2003*. Paris: OECD.

Oeser, Alexandra. 2007a. *La Transmission du passé nazi en Allemagne: Étude comparative de quatre écoles à Hambourg et Leipzig, thèse de doctorat en sciences sociales*. PhD diss., EHESS/ENS Paris and University of Erfurt.

———. 2007b. "Genre et enseignement de l'histoire." *Sociétés et représent*ations 24: 111–28.

———. 2009a. "'1968' als Filter der NS-Vergangenheit: Hamburger Geschichtslehrer und die Erziehung zu ‚mündigen Bürgern'im Geschichtsunterricht." In *Eine Welt zu gewinnen! Formen und Folgen der 68er Bewegung in Ost- und Westeuropa*, ed. Klaus Bachmann, Falk Breschneider, Hanco Jürgens, and Jacco Pekelder, 135–63. Leipzig: Universitätsverlag Leipzig.

———. 2009b. "Marji et le passé nazi: Trajectoire migrante et relation ambiguë d'une jeune iranienne en ascension sociale." In *Transmettre la Shoah*, ed. Jacques Fijalkow, 68–90. Paris: Editions de Paris Max Chaleil.

———. 2015. "Le mur dans la famille: Emotions et appropriations historiques dans la fratrie entre RDA et RFA." In *Histoires de famille: Les récits du passé dans la parenté contemporaine*, ed. Solène Billaud, Sibylle Gollac, Alexandra Oeser, and Julie Pagis, 97–114. Paris: Editions de la rue d'Ulm.

———. (ed.). 2017a. "Penser les rapports de domination avec Alf Lüdtke." Special issue of *Sociétés Contemporaines*: 99–100.

———. 2017b. "Introduction: Penser les rapports de domination avec Alf Lüdtke." Special issue of *Sociétés Contemporaine*s 99–100: 5–16.

378 • References

Oeser, Alexandra, and Sibylle Gollac. 2011. "Comparing Family Memories in France and Germany: The Production of History(ies) Within and Through Kin Relations." *Journal of Comparative Family Studies* 3:385–98.

Passeron, Jean-Claude. 1970. "Présentation à la traduction française." In *La Culture du pauvre,* ed. Richard Hoggart, trans. Françoise Garcias, Jean-Claude Garcias, and Jean-Claude Passeron, 7–25. Paris: Minuit.

Passeron, Jean-Claude, and Jacques Revel, eds. 2005. *Penser par cas.* Paris: Éditions de l'EHESS.

Peneff, Jean. 1990. *La Méthode biographique.* Paris: Armand Colin.

Percheron, Annick. 1977. "Transmission des préférences idéologiques au sein de la famille." *Bulletin de la Société française de sociologie* 4(9): 41–52.

———. 1978. *Les Dix-seize ans et la politique.* Paris: Presses de la Fondation nationale des sciences politiques.

———. 1981. "Âge, filiation, génération," Actes du congrès de l'AFSP, 22, 23, 24 octobre 1981, table ronde n° 2, "Génération et Politique," rapport n°14.

———.1984. "L'école en porte à faux." *Pouvoirs* 30: 15–28.

———.1993. *La Socialisation politique.* Paris: Armand Colin.

Perks, Robert, and Alistair Thompson, eds. 1998. *The Oral History Reader.* London: Routledge.

Petzold, Gottfried, and George Isaac Brown, eds. 1977. *Gestalt-Pädagogik: Konzepte der integrativen Erziehung.* Munich: Pfeiffer.

Pilcher, Jane. 1994. "Mannheim's Sociology of Generation. An Undervalued Legacy." *The British Journal of Sociology* 45(3): 481–95.

Pingel, Falk. 2000. "National Socialism and the Holocaust in West German School Books." *Internationale Schulbuchforschung* 22(1): 11–29.

Pollak, Michael. 1986. "La gestion de l'indicible." *Actes de la recherche en sciences sociales* 62–63: 30–53.

———. 1993. "Mémoire, oubli, silence." In *Une identité blessée,* 15–40. Paris: Métailié.

———. 2000. *L'Expérience concentrationnaire.* Paris: Métailié.

Prochasson, Christophe. 2008. *L'Empire des emotions: Les historiens dans la mêlée.* Paris: Demopolis.

Pudal, Bernard. 1989. *Prendre parti: Pour une sociologie historique du PCF.* Paris: Presses de la Fondation nationale des sciences politiques.

Radcliffe-Brown, Alfred Reginald. 1952. *Structure and Function in Primitive Society.* London: Cohen and West.

Reed, Lynn Raphael. 1999. "Troubling Boys and Disturbing Discourses on Masculinity and Schooling: A Feminist Exploration of Current Debates and Interventions Concerning Boys in School." *Gender and Education* 11(1): 93–110.

Reich, Brigitte, and Wolfgang Stammwitz. 1989. "Antifaschistische Erziehung in der Bundesrepublik? Von den Schwierigkeiten einer pädagogischen 'Bewältigung' des Nationalsozialismus." In *Erziehung nach Auschwitz,* ed. Hanns-Fred Rathenow and Norbert H. Weber, 98–108. Pfaffenweiler: Centaurus Verlagsgesellschaft.

Reichel, Peter. 1995. *Politik mit der Erinnerung: Gedächtnisorte im Streit um die nationalsozialistische Vergangenheit.* Munich: Fischer Taschenbuch Verlag.

———. 2001. *Vergangenheitsbewältigung in Deutschland: Die Auseinandersetzung mit der NS Diktatur von 1945 bis heute.* Munich: C.H. Beck.

Revel, Jacques. 1986. "La culture populaire: sur les usages et les abus d'une notion." In *Las culturas populares,* 223–39. Madrid: Editorial Universidad Complutense.

———. 1995a. "Ressources narratives et connaissance historique." *Enquête* 1: 43–70.

———. 1995b. "L'institution et le social." In *Les Formes de l'expérience*, ed. Bernard Lepetit, 63–84. Paris: Albin Michel.

———. 2000. "Histoire vs Mémoire en France aujourd'hui." *French Politics, Culture & Society* 18(1): 1–12.

Revel, Jacques, ed. 1996. *Jeux d'échelles: La micro-analyse à l'expérience*. Paris: Le Seuil.

Rice, Joy K., and Annette Hemmings. 1988. "Womens Colleges and Women Achievers: An Update." *Signs: Journal of Women in Culture and Society* 13(3): 546–59.

Richter, Sigrun, and Hans Brügelmann. 1995. "Jungen und Mädchen lernen verschieden." *Beiträge zur Lehrerbildung* 13(1): 75–76.

Ricoeur, Paul. 2000. *Mémoire, histoire, oubli*. Paris: Le Seuil.

Riordan, Cornelius. 1994. "The Value of Attending a Women's College: Education, Occupation, and Income Benefits." *Journal of Higher Education* 65(4): 486–510.

Rivers, William Halse. 1910. "The Genealogical Method of Anthropological Inquiry." *Sociological Review* 3: 1–12.

Rommelspacher, Birgit. 1995. *Schuldlos-Schuldig? Wie sich junge Frauen mit Antisemitismus auseinandersetzen*. Hamburg: Konkret Literatur Verlag.

Sabrow, Martin. 2009. *Erinnerungsorte der DDR*. Munich: Beck.

Sadker, Myra, and David Sadker. 1994. *Failing at Fairness: How Our Schools Cheat Girls*. New York: Touchstone.

Sayad, Abdelmalek. 1991. *L'Immigration, ou les paradoxes de l'altérité*. Brussels: De Boeck.

———. 1999. *La Double Absence: Des illusions de l'émigré aux souffrances de l'immigré*. Paris: Le Seuil.

Schatzker, Chaim. 1992. "Was hat sich verändert, was ist geblieben? Analyse von seit 1985 in der Bundesrepublik Deutschland erschienenen Geschichtslehrbüchern für die Sekundarstufe I und II bezüglich ihrer Darstellung jüdischer Geschichte." In *Deutsch-Israelische Schulbuchempfehlungen, Zur Darstellung der jüdischen Geschichte sowie der Geschichte und Geographie Israels in Schulbüchern der Bundesrepublik Deutschland. Zur Darstellung der deutschen Geschichte und der Geographie der Bundesrepublik Deutschland in israelischen Schulbüchern*, 42–71. Frankfurt/Main: Georg-Eckert-Institut.

Schiele, Siegfried, and Herbert Schneider, ed. 1991. *Rationalität und Emotionalität in der politischen Bildung*. Stuttgart: Metzler.

Schirrmacher, Frank, ed. 1999. *Die Walser-Bubis-Debatte: Eine Dokumentation*. Frankfurt/Main: Suhrkamp.

Schlumbohm, Jürgen, ed. 1998. *Mikrogeschichte Makrogeschichte, komplementär oder inkommensurabel?* Göttingen: Wallstein Verlag.

Schneider, Christian. 1998. "Schuld als Generationenproblem." *Mittelweg 36* 7(7): 28–40.

Schneider, Gerhard. 1991. "Der Nationalsozialismus und die deutsche Einheit: Über die neue Aktualität eines traditionellen Unterrichtsgegenstandes." In *Dialog in Deutschland: Geschichtsunterricht im Vereinten Deutschland auf der Suche nach Neuorientierung: Teil II*, ed. Hans Süssmuth, 169–85. Baden Baden: Nomos Verlagsgesellschaft.

Schörken, Rolf. 1992. "Didaktische Mechanismen im DDR-Lehrbuchwerk, Geschichte 5–10", *Geschichte in Wissenschaft und Unterricht*, 43(2): 93–110.

Schubarth, Wilfried, and Richard Stöss, eds. 2001. *Rechtsextremismus in der Bundesrepublik Deutschland: Eine Bilanz*. Bonn: Leske & Budrich.

Schüle, Annegret, Thomas Ahbe, and Rainer Gries, eds. 2006. *Die DDR aus generationengeschichtlicher Perspektive. Eine Inventur*. Leipzig: Leipziger Universitätsverlag.

Schulz, Andreas, and Gundula Grebner. 2003. "Generation und Geschichte: Zur Renaissance eines umstrittenen Forschungskonzepts." *Historische Zeitschrift* 36: 1–24.

Schulz-Hageleit, Peter. 1987. *Geschichte erleben-lernen-verstehen*, vol. 44. Düsseldorf: Geschichtsdidaktik: Studien, Materialen.

Schwan, Gesine. 1997. *Politik und Schuld: Die Zerstörerische Macht des Schweigens*. Frankfurt/ Main: Fischer Taschenbuch Verlag.

Schwartz, Olivier. 1990. *Le Monde privé des ouvriers: Hommes et femmes du Nord*. Paris: Presses universitaires de France.

Schwippert, Kurt, Wilfried Bos, and Eva-Maria Lankes. 2004. "Lesen Mädchen anders? Vertiefende Analysen zu Geschlechtsdifferenzen auf der Basis der Internationalen Grundschul-Lese-Untersuchung IGLU." *Zeitschrift für Erziehungswissenschaft* 7(2): 219–34.

Segalen, Martine. 1987. "Objets domestiques de la vie ouvrière: Transmissions et ruptures dans les familles de Nanterre, 1920–1960." *Ethnologie française* 17: 29–38.

Sider, Gerald and Gavin Smith. 1997. *Between History and Histories: The Making of Silences and Commemorations*. Toronto: The University of Toronto Press.

Silbermann, Alphons, and Manfred Stoffers. 2000. *Auschwitz: Nie davon gehört? Erinnern und Vergessen in Deutschland*. Berlin: Rowohlt.

Smith, Daryl G. 1990. "Women's Colleges and Coed Colleges, Is There a Difference for Women?" *Journal of Higher Education* 61(2): 181–95.

Spivak, Gayatri Chakravorty. "Can the Subaltern Speak? Speculations on Widow-Sacrifice." *Wedge* 7/8: 120–30.

Stanat, Petra, and Marieke Kunter. 2002. "Geschlechterspezifische Leistungsunterschiede bei Fünfzehnjährigen im internationalen Vergleich." *Zeitschrift für Erziehungswissenschaft* 4: 28–48.

Steir-Livney, Liat. 2017. *Is It Ok to Laugh About It?: Holocaust Humour, Satire and Parody in Israeli Culture*. London: Valentine Mitchell.

Stephan, Cora. 1993. *Der Betroffenheitskult: Eine politische Sittengeschichte*. Berlin: Taschenbuch.

Strauss, Anselm L. [1959] 1997. *Mirrors and Masks: The Search for Identity*. New Brunswick. NJ: Transaction Publishers.

Tajfel, Henri, and A. L. Wilkes. 1963. "Classification and Quantitative Judgment." *British Journal of Psychology* 104: 101–14.

Thiesse, Anne-Marie. 1984. *Le Roman du quotidien, lecteurs et lectures populaires à la belle époque*. Paris: Chemin vert.

Thompson, Edward P. 1978. "Eighteenth-Century English Society: Class Struggle without Class?". *Social History* 3: 133–165.

Thorne, Barrie. 1993. *Gender Play: Girls and Boys in School*. New Brunswick, NJ: Rutgers University Press.

Throssell, Katharine. 2015. *Child and Nation: A Study of Political Socialisation and Banal Nationalism in France and England*. Oxford: Peter Lang.

Tidball, Elizabeth. 1980. "Women's Colleges and Women's Achievements Revisited." *Signs: Journal of Women in Culture and Society* 5: 504–17.

———. 1985. "Baccalaureate Origins of Entrants into American Medical Schools." *Journal of Higher Education* 56(4): 385–402.

———.1986. "Baccalaureate Origins of Entrants into American Natural Science Doctorates." *Journal of Higher Education* 57: 606–20.

Tisseron, Serge. 1992. *Tintin et les secrets de famille*. Paris: Aubier.

———.1999. *Comment l'esprit vient aux objets*. Paris: Aubier.

Todorov, Tzvetan. 1995. *Abus de la mémoire*. Paris: Arléa.

Traverso, Enzo. 2005. *Le Passé, modes d'emploi: histoire, mémoire, politique*. Paris: La Fabrique éditions.

Weber, Florence. 2005. *Le Nom, le sang, le quotidian*. Paris: Aux lieux d'être.

Weber, Florence, Séverine Gojard, and Agnès Gramain. 2003. *Charges de familles: Dépendances et parenté dans la France contemporaine*. Paris: La Découverte.

Weber, Max. [1921] 1976. *Wirtschaft und Gesellschaft: Grundriss der verstehenden Soziologie*. 5th revised edition. Tübingen: Mohr.

Weitz, Eric D., and Geoff Ely. 1995. "Romantisierung des Eigen-Sinns? Eine email Kontroverse aus Übersee." *WerkstattGeschichte* 10: 57–63.

Welzer, Harald, Robert Montau, and Christine Plaß. 1997. *"Was wir für böse Menschen sind!" Der Nationalsozialismus im Gespräch zwischen den Generationen*. Tübingen: Diskord.

Welzer, Harald, Sabine Moller, and Karoline Tschuggnall. [2002] 2005. *Grandpa Wasn't a Nazi: National Socialism and the Holocaust in German Memory Culture*. New York: American Jewish Committee. (Partial translation of the German original: *Opa war kein Nazi: Nationalsozialismus und Holocaust im Familiengedächtnis*. Frankfurt/Main: Fischer Taschenbuch Verlag).

Wenzel, Birgit, and Dagmar Weber. 1989. "Auschwitz in Geschichtsbüchern der Bundesrepublik Deutschland." In *Erziehung nach Auschwitz, Geschichtsdidaktik*, ed. Hanns Fred Rathenow and Norbert H. Weber, 4:117–35. Pfaffenweiler: Centaurus Verlagsgesellschaft.

Weintraub, Jeff, and Krishan Kumar. 1997. *Public and Private in Thought and Practice: Perspectives on a Grand Dichotomy*. Chicago: University of Chicago Press.

Werner, Michael, and Bénédicte Zimmermann, eds. 2004. *De la comparaison à l'histoire croisée*. Paris: Le Seuil.

Westemeier, Jens. 2015. *Hans Robert Jauß, Jugend, Krieg und Internierung, Wissenschaftliche Dokumentation*, Universität Konstanz, Geiselhöring, retrieved 28 March 2019 from http://kops.uni-konstanz.de/bitstream/handle/123456789/30994/Westemeier_0-290927. pdf?sequence=3&isAllowed=y.

Wierling, Dorothee. 1999. "Nationalsozialismus und Krieg in den Lebens- Geschichten der ersten Nachkriegsgeneration der DDR." In *Eine offene Geschichte: Zur kommunikativen Tradierung der nationalsozialistischen Vergangenheit*, ed. Elisabeth Domansky and Harald Welzer, 35–56. Tübingen: Diskord.

———. 2000. "Über die Liebe zum Staat-der Fall der DDR." *Historische Anthropologie* 8(2): 236–63.

———. 2002. *Geboren im Jahre Eins: Der Jahrgang 1949 in der DDR. Versuch einer Kollektivbiographie*. Berlin: Christoph Links Verlag.

Willmott, Peter, and Michael Young. [1957] 1986. *Family and Kinship in East London*. London: Routledge.

Wolfrum, Edgar. 1999. *Geschichtspolitik in der Bundesrepublik Deutschland: Der Weg zur Bundesrepublikanischen Erinnerung 1948–1990*. Darmstadt: Wissenschaftliche Buchgesellschaft.

Zijderveld, Anton C. 1983. *The Sociology of Humour and Laughter*. London: Sage.

INDEX

the *Abitur* (school), 14, 267
absence, presence of, 71–73
activism, against neo-Nazism, 104–5, 111
actors versus victims, of Nazism, 125–26, 132–33, 141, 190
adolescent boys. *See also* students, with illegitimate interpretations of Nazi past
  on books about Nazism, 127–28
  on concentration camp visits, 138–39
  emotions of, 290–92
  on films, 132–34
  in history classes, 136–38, 140, 144–46
  on Hitler, 146–47
  on military history, 134–36
  Nazi past jokes of, 288–89
  on perpetrators, of Nazism, 129, 132, 170–71, 172n31
  relationship with Nazi past, 138–39
  on television about Nazism, 128–29, 134
adolescent girls
  on books about Nazism, 126–27
  emotions of, 290–91
  empathy for victims, 125–26, 129, 131–32, 139–40
  on history and politics, 156–57
  in history classes, 136–38, 140, 144–46
  identification with victims, 129–30, 152
adolescents, 319
  appropriation of history by, xv–xvi
  appropriations of Nazi past by, 6, 33, 309
  born after fall of Berlin Wall, 6–7
  contextualized uses of Nazi past by, 3–4
  historical knowledge, lacking, 2–3, 9
  interview methods, for views of, 25–27, 165–66, 224–30

on Nazi past, xi–xiv, 25–26, 315–16
peer groups, 279, 289, 297–300
playful uses of Nazi past, xiv
reappropriations by, 7–11
transmission of Nazi past to, 2–3
on Walser, xi
Adorno, Theodor W., 48, 71–72
AfD. *See* Alternative für Deutschland
Afghani students, 50–51, 241–42, 281–82, 294
Alexander (student), 94
Alltagsgeschichte, xvi, 129
Alternative für Deutschland (AfD), xii–xiv
ambiguity, 95–96, 98–100, 102, 119, 250–54
Amendt, Gerhard, 136
Aneignung, 10
Annabelle (student), 148
Annelore (student), 131–32
Ansart, Pierre, 8
Anteilnahme, 42
antifascists, 42–43, 105, 204
anti-racist education, 55–56, 91
anti-school culture, of students, 224
antisemitism, 73–74, 92, 195–98, 294–96, 300
anti-system discourse, 33, 213, 224, 284
appropriation, of Nazi past, xv–xvii, 116–17. *See also* playful uses, of Nazi past; reappropriation, of Nazi past
  by adolescents, 6, 33, 309
  gendered forms of, 152–57, 171
  by immigrants, 103–4
  oppositional, 201–2
ARD, 2, 4, 251–52

Aryans, 111–12
Assman, Jan, 245–46
Auschwitz, 47–48, 63, 87–89
Avanza, Martina, 177

Beaud, Stéphane, 108, 119, 224
Benjamin (student), 213–15, 260
Berlin Wall, fall of, 6–7, 24
Betroffenheit, 42–43, 69–70, 75–76
Betroffenheit, in teaching Jewish genocide, 61
    films for, 62–67
    as frame of reference, 75–76
    identification with victims, 65–70
    limits of, 70–74
    virtuous emotion in, 62–65
Betroffenheitspädagogik, 32, 37n41
    empathy and, 141
    in FRG, 39–44
    in Leipzig, 45, 67–68
    Lüdtke, 40
    in ninth grade, 126
    politicization of, 70
    in teaching history of Nazism, 125–26
    teaching practice and, 61–62
Bloch, Ernst, 12
books, about Nazism, 126–28, 131–32,
    150–51
Bourdieu, Pierre, 9–10, 85, 107, 118
boys. *See* adolescent boys
Brandt, Willy, 206–7
Bruneau, Ivan, 299
Bubis, Ignatz, xi, 71
Buchenwald, 41, 68

Cannoodt, Isabelle, 273
capitalism, 209–10, 214
categorical imperative, 48, 75
CDU. *See* Christian Democratic Union
de Certeau, Michel, 279–80, 283
Chemnitz, xiv
choice and weight, in relationships with the
    past, 103–4
Christian (student), 231–33, 274n12,
    287–88, 307n13
Christian Democratic Union (CDU), xiii
citizenship, 8, 46–48, 96
civic education, 39

civic engagement, 54–56
civil peace, 212–14
classrooms, 10–11, 27–29, 63–64, 85–90.
    See also history classes
coeducational learning environments,
    124–25
Coeur de Banlieue (Lepoutre), 280
collective memory, 5, 7, 316
Communist resisters, 64
Communists, 46, 173n35
concentration camps, 43, 86–90, 138–39,
    198, 256–57
Confino, Alon, 5
critical thinking, 57–59
cultural capital, 106, 202
cultural memory, 5, 245–46

Daniel (student), 138–39
democracy, 46–48, 52–53, 57, 60–61,
    115–16, 208
democratic values, 52–53
dictator, 147–52. *See also* Hitler, Adolf
discrimination, against immigrants,
    103–4
DKP. *See* German Communist Party
Dohnanyi, Klaus von, 71
Domenico (student), 187–89, 195,
    197–98
Dumais, Susan, 127
duty of remembrance, 47–51, 73, 90–91,
    93, 98, 101, 313–14

economic difficulties, in criticisms of FRG,
    179–81
economic policy, 193–96
education
    antifascist, 42–43
    anti-racist, 55–56, 91
    civic, 39
    gender in, 124–25
    sociology of, 124
    studies on, 8–10
educational qualifications
    of parents of students at 100th
        Mittelschule, 23
    of parents of students at *Gymnasium*
        Monnet, 22

of parents of students at *Gymnasium*
Weinberg, 16–17
of parents of students at Wiesi, 20
Eigensinn, 11–13, 279–80
Elisabeth (student), 151–52
emotion. *See also Betroffenheitspädagogik*
of adolescent boys, 290–92
of adolescent girls, 290–91
in German reeducation, 41
pedagogy and, 32, 37n41, 51–52
in politics, 40, 42
rationality and, 3
in rise of Nazism, 41
of students, viewing films, 62–64, 139
in teaching Nazi past, 40
use of, in GDR, 44–46
virtuous, 62–65
empathy, 40–42, 75, 90
Betroffenheitspädagogik and, 141
as "feminine," 140–41
for victims, 125–26, 129, 131–32,
139–40
enlightenment, 57
Erhard, Ludwig, 194
Erlebnis, 4
extermination policy, 1–2, 34n3
condemnation of, 47
euphemisms for, 71–73
German guilt for, 99–100
Hitler and, 143
moral rejection of, in schools, 82
perpetrators of, 132
students on, 197–98
teaching, 50, 52
extreme right-wing
AfD, xii–xiii
demonstrations, in Leipzig, 212–13
far right movements, 176–77
pessimism of, 183
students, xiv, 179–80, 202–3, 298–300,
312

family, 13, 165, 169–71, 246–47, 259
family configuration, 152–57, 254–55
family history, 27, 100–101, 129–30, 132
difficulties speaking about, 258–61
of Domenico (student), 187–89

everyday versus political, 261–65
gendered transmission of, 153–57
of Johnny (student), 184–86
objects, in transmission of, 158–65
of Rohrsteg, 167–69
of Thomas (student), 162–67
far right movements, 176–77
fascism, threat of, 208–9
FAZ. See Frankfurter Allgemeine Zeitung
FDP. *See* Freie Demokratische Partei
Federal Republic of Germany (FRG), xii,
xiv, 14, 32, 314
Betroffenheitspädagogik, in teaching
National Socialism in, 39–44
economic difficulties and, 179–81
former, 207–8
German guilt in, 96, 206–7
Nazi past and, 180, 182–83, 195
in reunified Germany, 115
female teachers, 147–52, 155, 218–19
feminism, 151
films, 243–44
about Hitler, 147–48
about Nazism, 54, 62–68, 132–34
students' emotions viewing, 62–64, 139
for teaching Jewish genocide, 62–67, 139,
147
Fischer, Fritz, 70, 80n87
Fischer, Joschka, 121n27
foreigners, 49–50, 91–92, 222n48, 243,
295
Marji (student) on, 104, 106–8, 122n54
Wolfgang (student) on, 199–200
forschendes Lernen, 43
Frankfurter Allgemeine Zeitung (FAZ), xi–xii,
71
freedom, 115
Freie Demokratische Partei (FDP), 114–17
FRG. *See* Federal Republic of Germany
Friedrich (Richter), 127–28
Frisch-Gauthier, Jacqueline, 291

GDR. *See* German Democratic Republic
gender, 174n59
in appropriation of Nazi past, 152–57,
171
differences, 13, 33, 126–36, 139–40

gender (*cont.*)
    division, of spaces and activities, 153–54,
      157
    in eduction, 124–25
    male teachers and, 145–46
    in mobilization of past, 125–26
    norms, 139–40
    politics and, 166–67
    school, family and, 169–71
    segregation, 153
    teaching practices and, 136–38, 152
    in transmission of family history, 153–57,
      168–69
gendered objects, 158–66
generational position, xi–xii, xv, 2–3, 36n29,
    310, 319–20
genocide. *See Betroffenheit*, in teaching
    Jewish genocide; extermination policy;
    Jewish genocide
German army, 188, 190
German Communist Party (DKP), 163–64
German Democratic Republic (GDR),
    xii–xiii, 207–8, 277n71, 319
    antifascist discourse of, 204
    capitalism and, 209–10
    construction generation, 114
    emotion in, 44–46
    Leipzig students, on past of, 211–12
    nostalgia for, 24
    school system, in 1950s and 1960s,
      36nn26–27
    students on, 209
    teachers in, 9
    teaching NS in, 44–45
German guilt, 49, 95–96, 99–101, 203–7,
    265
German history. *See* Nazi past
Germanity, 106, 109–13
German language, 29–30, 72–73
German reunification, xiv, 24, 40, 44–45,
    115, 207–8, 210, 318
Germany, xii, 13, 41, 185–86
Gerste, Mr, 54, 143, 146, 151, 281–84
the *Gesamtschule* (school), 14
Gesamtschule Wiesi, in Hamburg, 17,
    20–21, 50, 55, 58, 281–82. *See also*
    Klein, Annika; Werthe, Karen

immigrant students on, 91–92
Marji (student) at, 103–13
physical violence at, 296
teachers at, 18–19, 60, 68, 239
Geschichtspolitik, xiii–xiv
Geschichtswerkstätten, 42
Geschlecht, 146, 174n59
Die Geschwister Oppermann (1983), 65–68
Gestalt pedagogy, 40
Gies, Horst, 44
girls. *See* adolescent girls
Gleichschaltung, 115, 117, 122n58
Gleichzeitigkeit des Ungleichzeitigen, 12
Goebbels, Joseph, 150
good citizens, 8, 46–48, 53
"good students," 82–84, 91, 98, 104, 191
grandparents, Nazism of, 258–66, 276n70
"Great Germany," 181–89
guilt, German, 49, 95–96, 99–101, 203–7,
    265
the *Gymnasium* (school), 14
Gymnasium Monnet, in Leipzig, 21–22,
    44–45, 48–49, 203–7, 268
Gymnasium Weinberg, in Hamburg, 15–17,
    19, 49, 55, 273
    Abitur exam, 267
    advanced history class, 91
    extreme right-wing student in, 202–3
    Harthörig at, 245–46
    on neo-Nazism, 213–14
    rejections of academic history at, 240–41
    saturation, in teaching of Nazism,
      250–51, 254
    Schulze's history class in, 65–68
    Steffen (student) at, 97–102
Gymnasium Weinberg, in Hamburg,
    students
    on civil peace, 213–14
    German guilt of, 204
    on Nazi past, 94–96
    against political extremes, 210–11
    as upper class, 255–56

Halbwachs, Maurice, 5–7, 311
Hamburg, xiii, xv, xvii. *See also Gesamtschule*
    Wiesi, in Hamburg; Gymnasium
    Weinberg, in Hamburg

foreign nationals in, 36n24
Leipzig versus, 201–17, 265–69, 305–6
migrants in, 91–92
students, on civil peace, 213
students, on current regime, 208–9
Harthörigkeit, 245–46, 250, 265–66, 268,
   271, 273, 320
Hartog, François, 317
Hatze, Mr, 48, 58, 149–50
Hauke (student), 93–94, 266
the *Hauptschule* (school), 14
Heide, Ms, 144–45, 151, 269–70
Heidi (student), 83–84, 127, 130, 153,
   252–54
Herrschaftsstrukturen, 12
Herzog, Mr, 49, 54, 60, 143, 284–85,
   296–97
historicization, 269–71
historiography, 4
history
   academic, rejections of, 240–41
   Alltagsgeschichte, xvi, 129
   cultural, 5
   emotion, in understanding of, 62
   family history and, 27, 100–101,
      129–30
   histories versus, xvi
   lessons of, 92–94, 102
   memory and, xvi, 1, 4
   opposing values in, 52–53
   politics of, xiii–xiv, 156–57
   reappropriation of, 4–7, 13
   rewriting, 185–86
   teaching, 39–40, 43, 51–52
   textbooks, 142
   uses of, 177–78
history classes, 117–18. *See also* teaching
   history of Nazism
   adolescent boys in, 136–38, 140, 144–46
   adolescent girls in, 136–38, 140, 144–46
   advanced, of Heide, 269–70
   Knopp documentaries in, 189
   pedagogic goals of, 51–52
   saturation in, 245–47, 250–51
   students bored with, 245–51, 254
   students "left behind" in, 224–25
   teachers' interpretation of past in, 178–79

Hitler, Adolf
   adolescent boys on, 146–47
   female teachers on, 147–48, 155
   films about, 147–48
   Johnny (student) on, 184–85
   male teachers on, 142–44
   student confusion about, 242–44
   student interest in, 82–83, 147–48
   Wolfgang (student) on, 183–84, 300
Hitler, an Overview (film), 147–48
Hitler's Women (film), 147–48
Hoggart, Richard, 30–32, 119, 177
Holocaust. *See* extermination policy; Jewish
   genocide; Nazism
Holocaust (television series), 1, 40
Horkheimer, Max, 71–72
household, 152–53
humanity, 131
human rights, 52, 54–55, 94–95

identification, with victims
   by adolescent girls, 129–30, 152
   Betroffenheit and, 65–70
   of genocide, 52, 65–70, 130
   process of, 65–67, 129
illegitimate uses, of Nazi past. *See* students,
   with illegitimate interpretations of Nazi
   past
images, 63, 83–84, 86–89, 158–60, 174n67
immigrants
   appropriations of Nazi past by, 103–4
   children, 78n30
   discrimination against, 103–4
   in Hamburg, xiii
   Marji (student), 103–13
   personal experiences of, 241–45
   students, 91–92
immigration policies, 196–201, 219
Inge, Ms, 149
introspection, reflection and, 59–60
Ivan (student), 290–92

Jeismann, Karl-Ernst, 102
Jewish genocide, 174n47. *See also*
   Betroffenheit, in teaching Jewish
   genocide
   Dohnanyi on, 71

388 • Index

Jewish genocide (*cont.*)
euphemisms and expressions for, 71–73
films for teaching, 62–67, 139, 147
identification with victims of, 52, 65–70, 130
images of, 63
incomprehension of, 73–74
learning to talk about, 125–26
as term, 79n68
victims of, 45–46, 66–69, 75
witnesses of, 63–64
Joey (student), 91–92, 241–43
Johannes (student), 94, 211, 255, 257
Johnny (student), 181–86, 191–93, 196–97, 290, 301–4
jokes, 279–84, 286–97, 304–6, 312, 314
Jürgen (student), 194–95

Kamm, Mr, 144
Kansteiner, Wulf, 189–90
Kant, Emmanuel, 48
Karl (student), 95, 286–87, 295–96
Karsten (student), 89, 234, 236, 286–87, 289–90, 295
Kevin (student), 87–89, 290–92, 294
Klein, Annika
on adolescent boys, 146–47
on images, of Holocaust, 63
on incomprehension, of genocide, 73–74
on independent thinking, 59
on stereotypes, 54
Werthe and, class of, 62–63, 85–90, 147
Klemperer, Victor, 130, 172n14, 199
Knoch, Habbo, 41
Knopp, Guido, 147, 189–92, 221n27
knowledge
as capital, 9–10
casual attitude toward, 118
in FDP, 117
historical, adolescents lacking, 2–3, 9
of Nazi past, 84, 118–20
politics and, 117
production of, 9
transmission of, 8, 10
Kolinsky, Eva, 9
Kolinsky, Martin, 9

kontroverse Didaktick, 59
Kordon, Klaus, 131

Lagroye, Jacques, 46–47
language, for genocide, 71–72
laughter, 290–91
Lavabre, Marie-Claire, 5, 103
learning, 43, 52–53, 118, 124–26
left-wing, xii–xiii, 18
legitimate and illegitimate culture, 177
legitimate discourse, on Nazi past
anti-school culture against, 224
catch up strategy, 97–102
in classrooms, 85–90
of female students and teachers, 218–19
militant strategy, 114–18
oppositional relation to, 180
reappropriations in, 81
as rejection of Nazism, 177
school norms in, 98–100, 181
second person voice and, 101–2, 105
self-evidence of, 82–84, 118–19
social status recovered through, 96–97, 106
students, teachers and, 91, 98–100, 223
uniformity of, in final year, 138–41
upward social mobility strategy, 103–13
legitimate knowledge, of Nazi past, 118–20
Lehingue, Patrick, 181
Leif (student), 134–35, 262
Leipzig, xiii, xv, xvii, 15
Betroffenheitspädagogik in, 45, 67–68
Communist regime, 46
Gymnasium Monnet in, 21–22, 44–45, 48–49, 203–7, 268
Hamburg versus, 201–17, 265–69, 305–6
NS taught in, 53, 75, 268
100th *Mittelschule* in, 22–23, 48, 239
students, 208–9, 211–13, 216–17
Leoni (student), 153–54, 156–57
Leonore (student), 130–31, 148
Lepoutre, David, 273, 280, 288–89, 293
lessons of history, 92–94, 102
liberalism, 115–17
Lieux de mémoire (Nora), xvi
lingua tertii imperii (LTI), 130
Die Linke, xii–xiv

Linksruck, 105–7, 109
lived experience, 4
LTI. *See lingua tertii imperii*
Lüdtke, Alf, 10–12, 40, 42, 143, 279–80, 283

Magdalena (student), 91, 250, 259–60
male language, transmission and, 141–47
manipulation, by dictators, 147–52
Mannheim, Karl, 36n29
Maren (student), 83, 131
Marji (student), 103–13, 122n47, 122n54
Markus (student), 240–41
Martin (student), 87–89, 290–92
Marxism, 11
"masculine" and "feminine" qualities, teachers on, 139–41
Mauger, Gérard, 224–25
Max (student), 127–28, 132
media, 1–3, 58, 151, 251–52, 320
Melanie (student), 290–91
memory, 309–10
    appropriations of history and, xv–xvii
    collective, 5, 7, 316
    as concept, xv–xvi
    construction, 5
    cultural, 5, 245–46
    in cultural history, 5
    duty of remembrance, 47–51, 73, 90–91, 93, 98, 101, 313–14
    history and, xvi, 1, 4
    of Nazi past, 6–7
    official, xvi, 5
    policies, 312–14
    politics of, 5
    social frameworks of, 316
Michael (student), 114–18, 128–29, 132, 211–12
migration, 13, 91–92, 241–45, 273
militant strategy, of legitimate discourse, 114–18
military defeat, 185–86
military history, adolescent boys on, 134–36
Mitläufer, 26, 37n36, 258
Moher (student), 226–30, 234–37, 239
Muslims, 55, 199–200

National Front, 181, 299
nationality, of parents of students, at Wiesi, 20
national pride, 203–7
National Socialism (NS). *See also* extermination policy
    on ARD, 2
    in German media, 1–3
    Hitler and, 143–44
    Steffen (student) on, 99–101
    teaching, 39–40, 44–45, 53, 75, 268
National Socialist party (NSDAP), 31, 144, 162, 182, 185
National Socialist Underground (NSU), xiii
Naute, Ms, 148
Nazi history, 52, 125. *See also* teaching history of Nazism
Nazi past. *See also* appropriation, of Nazi past; family history; legitimate discourse, on Nazi past; playful uses, of Nazi past; students, with illegitimate interpretations of Nazi past; teaching history of Nazism; transmission, of Nazi past
    adolescents on, xi–xiv, 25–26, 315–16
    on ARD, 2, 4
    Betroffenheit and, 75–76
    Bubis on, xi
    contextualized uses of, by adolescents, 3–4
    duty of remembrance, 47–48
    emotion, in teaching, 40
    family configurations in attitudes toward, 254–55
    FRG and, 180, 182–83, 195
    gender differences and, 13, 33, 126–36
    generational divide on, xi–xii, 2–3, 310
    Germanity and, 111
    in German media, 1–3
    goals of teaching, 46–47
    guilt and, 49, 95–96, 99–101
    historicization giving meaning to, 269–71
    Hitler and, 142
    human rights and, 94–95
    images of, 83–84, 158–60
    interview methods, for adolescents' views on, 25–27, 165–66
    lessons of, 92–94

Nazi past (*cont.*)
  memory of, 6–7
  moral lessons of, 92
  personal experiences of migration, giving
    meaning to, 241–45
  political uses of, 217–19, 310–11
  racism and, 51
  reappropriation of, 10–11, 13, 81, 176
  reinterpreting, 81
  in school context, 11
  social frameworks of political uses,
    217–19
  student attitudes toward, 8
  students on importance of, 83
  students with "substantial academic
    difficulties" on, 230–39
  transmission to adolescents, 2–3
  writing about, 85
Nazi past, relationship with
  adolescent boys, 138–39
  ambiguity in, 95–96, 119, 250
  choice and weight in, 103–4
  Marji (student) on, 111–13
  Richard (student) on, 247–50
Nazism, 25, 30–32. *See also* extermination
    policy; National Socialism; teaching
    history of Nazism; victims
  actors versus victims of, 125–26, 132–33,
    141, 190
  on Aryans, 111–12
  books about, 126–27, 131–32, 150–51
  emotion in rise of, 41
  films about, 54, 62–68, 132–34
  of grandparents, 258–66, 276n70
  historical context of, 269–71
  in history textbooks, 9
  media control in, 151
  Mitläufer and, 26, 37n36, 258
  perpetrators of, 129, 132, 141, 170–71,
    172n31
  propaganda, 190
  publications on, 2
  rejection of, 116–17
  remembering, 48
  risk of, 58
  in school context, 33
  television about, 128–29, 134, 251–52

neo-Nazis, 176, 179–80, 203, 290, 301–2
neo-Nazism, 120n1, 214
  in nineteenseventy1970s, 42
  activism against, 104–5, 111
  fear, danger of, 49–52
  racism and, 49, 51, 55
  symbolic effect of, 50
Neuengamme, 85–89
Neumeier, Ms, 48–49, 51, 160–62
never again, xiii–xiv, 47–51, 73, 90–91
Niethammer, Lutz, xvi, 24
Noiriel, Gérard, 4
Nolte, Ernst, 144
Nora, Pierre, xvi, 4
norms
  gender, 139–40
  at schools, 98–100, 180–81, 191, 321
Norte, Ms, 44–46, 147–48, 205–6
Nostalgie, 24
NS. *See* National Socialism
NSDAP. *See* National Socialist party
NSU. *See* National Socialist Underground

objects, 158–66
official memory, xvi, 5
Omeira (student), 230–31
Omer (student), 228–29, 233–34, 238, 243,
    294
100th *Mittelschule*, in Leipzig, 22–23, 48,
    239
oppositional appropriations, of Nazi past,
    201–2
oppositional relation, to school norms,
    180–81, 191, 321
others, 106–9, 112, 122n54, 178

Passeron, Jean-Claude, 9–10, 177
passive voice, in expressions for genocide,
    72–73
pedagogy, 32, 37n41, 40, 42–43, 51–52. *See
    also Betroffenheitspädagogik*
peer groups, adolescent, 279, 289, 297–300
Percheron, Annick, 152
perpetrators, of Nazism, 129, 132, 141,
    170–71, 172n31
Peter (student), 127, 158–60
photographs, 158–60, 174n67

Pingel, Falk, 43
PISA. *See* Program for International Student Assessment
Plato, Alexander von, xvi, 24
playful uses, of Nazi past, xiv, 33–34, 214–18, 278
  antisemitism and, 294–95
  by extreme right-wing students, 298–300
  jokes, 279–84, 286–97, 304–6, 312, 314
  laughter and, 290–91
  against loneliness, 301–4
  Nazischwein, Judensau and, 293–97
  political and peer-group positions, 297–300
  practices, strategies, tactics and, 281–84
  for saving face, in emotional situations, 290–92
  school space, teenage togetherness and, 285–92
  teachers on, 296–97
political activism, against neo-Nazism, 104–5, 111
political commitment, 54–57
political engagement, 54–55, 116
political system, faith in, 51–54
politico-economic system, 208–12
politics, 3, 172n22
  adolescent boys' interest in, 138
  democracy and, 115–16
  emotion in, 40, 42
  extremes in, 210–11
  families and, 246–47
  gender and, 166–67
  of history, xiii–xiv, 156–57
  knowledge and, 117
  of memory, 5
post-wall generation, 23–24
poverty, 148–49
presence of absence, 71–73
Program for International Student Assessment (PISA), 9
public policy, challenges to, 193–201

racism, 49, 51, 55–56, 149, 243
Realms of Memory Project (Nora), 4
the *Realschule* (school), 14

reappropriation
  by adolescents, 7–11
  as *Aneignung*, 10
  configurations and forms of, 304–6
  of history, sociology of, 4–7, 13
  of television programs, partial, 189–92
reappropriation, of Nazi past, 10–11, 13, 81, 176
Referendariat, 28
reflection, introspection and, 59–60
regimes of faith, 47–57
regimes of reason, 57–61
Reinhard, Ms, 77n17, 83, 145–46
religion, 198–99
René (student), 93, 96, 208–11, 259, 270–71, 297–98
reparations, 41, 76n4
representations, of the past, 4
repressive state, resistance to, 60–61
research practices, 165–69
resistance, 12, 60–61, 151
reunification, German, xiv, 24, 40, 44–45, 115, 207–8, 210, 318
Revel, Jacques, 177
Rhue, Morton, 150–51
Richard (student), 94–95, 247–50, 256, 260–65
Richter, Hans P., 127–28
Rohrsteg, Klara, 59, 63–64, 67, 73, 149, 167–69
Rommel, Erwin, 191–92
Rommelspacher, Birgit, 47
the Ruhr, xvi

Samira (student), 92
Sandy (student), 86–87, 90
saturation, Nazi past and, 2–3, 224, 245–47, 250–54, 309, 319–20
Saxony, xiii, 15, 193
Schindler's List (1993), 63–64, 139, 290–91
Schirrmacher, Frank, xi–xii
school-based uses, of Nazi past, 177
schools, xvii–xviii, 224. *See also* classrooms; students; teachers; *specific schools*
  Bourdieu on, 85
  citizenship and, 8
  coeducational, 124–25

schools (*cont.*)
  in constructions of likes and dislikes, 271–73
  family, gender and, 169–71
  of GDR, in 1950s and 1960s, 36nn26–27
  Nazi past in, 11
  Nazism, in context of, 33
  norms, 98–100, 180–81, 191, 321
  as social framework, for adolescents' reappropriations, 7–11
  space of, 285–92
  students experimenting in, 178
  transmission of knowledge in, 8
  transmission of Nazi past in, 178–79
Schulze, Mr, 28, 251
  on adolescent boys and girls, in history classes, 136–38, 140
  on affective pedagogic goals, 51–52
  on Auschwitz, 48
  on democratic values, 52–53
  on extreme right-wing student, 202–3
  on films, about Nazism, 54
  Die Geschwister Oppermann, shown by, 65–68
  on Leoni, 157
  students of, 83, 127, 130, 132
Schwan, Gesine, 47
Schwartz, Olivier, 27
second person voice, in discourse, 101–2, 105
seduction, by dictator, 147–50
self-evidence, of legitimate discourse, 82–84, 118–19
sexual stereotypes, 136–37, 145–46
shame, 95–96
siblings, in attitudes toward Nazi past, 254–55
Sider, Gerald, xvi
silence, in families, 165, 259
Simone, Ms, 39, 57
single-sex universities, 124
Smith, Gavin, xvi
Social Democratic Party (SPD), xiii, 246
social frameworks, 7–11, 217–19, 316
socially situated moral efficiency, 90–95
social mobility, legitimate discourse as strategy for, 103–13

social status, 96–97, 106
sociology, 4–7, 13–14, 124
socio-professional categories (SPC)
  of parents of students at 100th *Mittelschule*, 23
  of parents of students at Monnet, 21
  of parents of students at Weinberg, 16
  of parents of students at Wiesi, 19
SPD. *See* Social Democratic Party
Der Spiegel, 1–2, 128–29, 156
Steffen (student), 97–102, 106
Stein, Mr, 55–56, 142, 205, 228, 242
Stephan, Cora, 44
stereotypes, 54, 136–37, 145–46, 195–97
students, 7–8. *See also* adolescents; Hamburg; history classes; Leipzig; *specific students*
  Afghani, 50–51, 241–42, 281–82, 294
  anti-school culture of, 224
  on concentration camps, 86–89, 90, 138–39, 198
  Eigensinn of, 11
  experimentation in school, 178
  on extermination policy, 197–98
  extreme right-wing, xiv, 179–80, 202–3, 298–300, 312
  with family migratory background, 13
  gender differences, in use of past, 126–36
  on German history, 82
  "good students," 82–84, 91, 98, 104, 191
  on Hitler, 82–83, 147–48, 242–44
  images of Neuengamme by, 86–88
  immigrant, 91–92
  left behind in history classes, 224–25
  legitimate discourse, teachers and, 91, 98–100, 223
  on lessons of history, 92–94
  on moral requirements of teaching history of Nazism, 119
  Muslim, 55
  Nazi past knowledge, inexact, 84
  neo-Nazi, 176, 179–80, 203, 290, 301–2
  post-wall generation, 23–24
  reappropriations of Nazi past, 10–11
  on *Schindler's List*, 63–64
  school-based constructions of likes and dislikes, 271–73

with "substantial academic difficulties" on
    Nazi past, 230–39
tactics of, 279–84, 287
teachers and, xv, 10–11, 104
Turkish, 50–51
"weak" academically, interviewing,
    225–30
students, with illegitimate interpretations of
    Nazi past, 176, 179–80
antisemitism of, 195–97
as boys, 181
Domenico (student), 187–89, 195,
    197–98
on economic policy, unemployment and,
    193–96
on extermination policy, 197–98
family histories of, 184–89
"Great Germany" and, 181–89
on immigration policies, 196–201
Johnny (student), 181–86, 191–93,
    196–97
Jürgen (student), 194–95
public policy challenged by, 193–201
on television programs by Knopp, 189–91
Wolfgang (student), 183–84, 193,
    198–99

tactics, of students, 279–84, 287
Tajfel, Henri, 178
Täter, 129, 132, 141, 170–71, 172n13,
    172n31
teachers, 9, 296–97, 317–18. See also history
    classes; specific teachers
female, 147–52, 155, 218–19
gender differences and, 139–40
generational positions of, xv
at Gesamtschule Wiesi, in Hamburg,
    18–19, 60, 68, 239
"good students" and, 91, 98, 104, 191
interpretation of past, in history classes,
    178–79
legitimate discourse, students and, 91,
    98–100, 223
male language of, 141–47
on "masculine" and "feminine" qualities,
    139–41
on Nazism risk, 58

on playful uses of Nazi past, 296–97
socialization of, 208
strategies of, 280
students and, xv, 10–11, 104
at Wiesi, 18–19, 60, 68, 239
teaching, 61–62
extermination policy, 50, 52
NS, in FRG, 39–44
NS, in GDR, 44–45
NS, in Leipzig, 53, 75, 268
politicization of, 70
practices, gender and, 136–38, 152
teaching history of Nazism, 39, 40, 43, 218.
    See also Betroffenheit, in teaching Jewish
    genocide; legitimate discourse, on Nazi
    past
Betroffenheitspädagogik in, 125–26
faith in political system, 51–53
genocide, 61–70, 139
goals of, 46–47
Klein and Werthe, 62–63, 85–90, 147
manipulation and seduction by dictators
    for, 147–52
moral requirements of, 119
for political commitment, 54–57
regimes of faith in, 47–57
regimes of reason in, 57–61
saturation in, 250–51
for tolerance, 54
television programs
Holocaust, 1, 40
by Knopp, 147, 189–92, 221n27
about Nazism, 128–29, 134, 251–52
partial reappropriation of, 189–92
Thälmann, Ernst, 44
Third Reich, 130
Thomas (student) (far right), 194, 298–99
Thomas (teacher) (pseudonym), 162–67
Thorne, Barrie, 124
Tintin (Tisseron), 72
Tisseron, Serge, 72, 159
tolerance, 54
transmission, 8, 10, 53–54
transmission, of Nazi past, 2–3, 317
of family histories, 153–57, 168–69
history, 52, 125
male language and, 141–47

transmission (*cont.*)
  of objects, 158–65
  in schools, 178–79
Turkish students, 50–51

unemployment, 193–96
uniformity of discourse, in final year,
  138–41
Universal Declaration of Human Rights,
  54–55
the unsaid, the unspeakable and, 165–69
The Uses of Literacy (Hoggart), 177

values, 52–54, 224
victims, 41–42, 44. *See also* identification,
  with victims
  actors versus, 125–26, 132–33, 141,
    190
  empathy for, 125–26, 129, 131–32,
    139–40
  of genocide, identifying with, 65–70
  of Jewish genocide, 45–46, 66–69, 75,
    130
  of manipulation, German people as,
    58
virtuous emotion, 62–65

Walser, Martin, xi, 71, 254
war, adolescent boys' interest in, 134–36
The Wave (Rhue), 150–51
Weber, Florence, 152
Weimar Republic, 214–16, 268–70
Weinecke, Ms, 53, 59, 148–49, 205–6
Weise, Herbert, 20, 59, 146
Welzer, Harald, 102, 261, 265
Werthe, Karen, 290
  on Afghani and Turkish students, 50–51
  on family history, 154–55
  Klein and, history of Nazism class, 62–63,
    85–90, 147
  on racism, 51
  on students' interest in Hitler, 82–83
Wiesi. *See Gesamtschule* Wiesi, in Hamburg
Wilhelmshöhe, Groß von, 69–70
Wilkes, A. L., 178
Winter, Mr, 142–44
witnesses, of genocide, 63–64
Wolff, Mr, 45–46, 51, 56–57, 63, 67–68,
  143, 205, 268
Wolfgang (student), 183–84, 193, 198–99,
  298–300

xenophobia, 24, 196, 198–99, 243

www.ingramcontent.com/pod-product-compliance
Lightning Source LLC
Chambersburg PA
CBHW072141100526
44589CB00015B/2027